PROBLEMS AND CASES ON SECURED TRANSACTIONS

ASPEN PUBLISHERS

PROBLEMS AND CASES ON
SECURED TRANSACTIONS

James Brook

Professor of Law
New York Law School

Wolters Kluwer
Law & Business

AUSTIN   BOSTON   CHICAGO   NEW YORK   THE NETHERLANDS

Aspen Publishers
Attn: Permissions Department
76 Ninth Avenue, 7th Floor
New York, NY   10011-5201

To contact Customer Care, e-mail customer.care@aspenpublishers.com, call 1-800-234-1660, fax 1-800-901-9075, or mail correspondence to:

Aspen Publishers
Attn: Order Department
PO Box 990
Frederick, MD 21705

Printed in the United States of America.

1 2 3 4 5 6 7 8 9 0

ISBN 978-0-7355-7030-6

Library of Congress Cataloging-in-Publication Data

Brook, James, 1946-
  Problems and cases on secured transactions / James Brook. — 1st ed.
    p. cm.
  ISBN 978-0-7355-7030-6
  1. Security (Law) — United States — Problems, exercises, etc. 2. Security (Law) — United States — Cases. I. Title.

KF1050.B76 2008
346.7307'4 — dc22   2008023629

About Wolters Kluwer Law & Business

Wolters Kluwer Law & Business is a leading provider of research information and workflow solutions in key specialty areas. The strengths of the individual brands of Aspen Publishers, CCH, Kluwer Law International and Loislaw are aligned within Wolters Kluwer Law & Business to provide comprehensive, in-depth solutions and expert-authored content for the legal, professional and education markets.

CCH was founded in 1913 and has served more than four generations of business professionals and their clients. The CCH products in the Wolters Kluwer Law & Business group are highly regarded electronic and print resources for legal, securities, antitrust and trade regulation, government contracting, banking, pension, payroll, employment and labor, and healthcare reimbursement and compliance professionals.

Aspen Publishers is a leading information provider for attorneys, business professionals and law students. Written by preeminent authorities, Aspen products offer analytical and practical information in a range of specialty practice areas from securities law and intellectual property to mergers and acquisitions and pension/benefits. Aspen's trusted legal education resources provide professors and students with high-quality, up-to-date and effective resources for successful instruction and study in all areas of the law.

Kluwer Law International supplies the global business community with comprehensive English-language international legal information. Legal practitioners, corporate counsel and business executives around the world rely on the Kluwer Law International journals, loose-leafs, books and electronic products for authoritative information in many areas of international legal practice.

Loislaw is a premier provider of digitized legal content to small law firm practitioners of various specializations. Loislaw provides attorneys with the ability to quickly and efficiently find the necessary legal information they need, when and where they need it, by facilitating access to primary law as well as state-specific law, records, forms and treatises.

Wolters Kluwer Law & Business, a unit of Wolters Kluwer, is headquartered in New York and Riverwoods, Illinois. Wolters Kluwer is a leading multinational publisher and information services company.

In loving memory of my father

Gene Brook
(1921–2001)

to whom I owe so much.

SUMMARY OF CONTENTS

PART IV
PRIORITY ISSUES   207

PART V
SALES AND OTHER DISPOSITIONS OF COLLATERAL   285

PART VI
FURTHER ON THE SCOPE OF ARTICLE 9   341

PART VII
DEFAULT AND ENFORCEMENT   399

CONTENTS

CHAPTER 6
"VALUE" GIVEN AND THE DEBTOR'S "RIGHTS IN"
THE COLLATERAL   81

CHAPTER 7
INTRODUCTION TO THE PURCHASE-MONEY
SECURITY INTEREST   97

CHAPTER 8
FURTHER ISSUES REGARDING THE PMSI   113

PART VI

FURTHER ON THE SCOPE OF ARTICLE 9   341

PART VII
DEFAULT AND ENFORCEMENT
399

CHAPTER 31
DEFAULT
401

CHAPTER 32
REPOSSESSION
417

CHAPTER 33
THE FORECLOSURE SALE

CHAPTER 34
STRICT FORECLOSURE AND THE RIGHT
OF REDEMPTION

PREFACE

Welcome to the study of Secured Transactions. If you come to the subject with an open mind—and I have no reason to think that you do not—I believe you will find it a particularly *interesting* and *engaging* field of study. That statement might strike you as strange. Yes, you will have to wrestle with a complex and at some points frustrating statute—Article 9 of the Uniform Commercial Code. Yes, at times the matter at hand will seem fairly "technical" and call for a good deal of precise reading and application on your part. But beneath it all, remember, is the heartbeat of the subject, those human interactions which make this a statute worth studying and the details worth mastering. People enter into secured transactions because they have something to accomplish. If things go well they have much to gain. If, on the other hand, discord rears its ugly head, much can be at stake, and who got the "technicalities" right is anything but a dry academic concern.

You will meet many different actors along the way. We start out with the secured party and the debtor, but they are soon joined by all kinds of third parties—the searcher, the lien creditor, the bankruptcy trustee, other secured parties or claimants, sellers, buyers, and factors just to name the most obvious. By the final part of the book we even get to meet the professional repossession agent, the "repo man." As you work your way through this material, consider the goals and the concerns of each of these characters as they appear. The problems in this book are, I acknowledge, longer than those you may have dealt with in other casebooks. There is, I submit, some method to this seeming madness. As you work your way through any problem—at first on your own and then with your instructor—you might want to consider it something like the outline of a brief, but quite interesting, one-act play. As you read the problem, put yourself in the role of each of the actors. "What," you may reasonably ask yourself, "is my motivation? What am I feeling at this point?"

The organization of the book is fairly straightforward. Each chapter is structured in the same way. First comes an Introduction. In some instances this can be very brief, in others a bit more background is called for. Each chapter's Introduction is not, you should be aware, meant as a complete summing up of what you will be learning in the chapter. It is just enough to get you oriented and headed into the material.

Next in each chapter comes a section which I have labeled Preparation. The instructions here are as clear and concise as I could make them. Go to each of the sections of the Code and the Comments to which you are directed and give them a good read. You should not feel at this point that you must fully comprehend or appreciate every nuance of the Code material before you can move on. Try, however, to get enough of an understanding of what is in the sections and comments cited so that you will be able to refer back to this material in your statutory supplement as and when needed as you face the Problems and Cases. Think of the Preparation section as setting up a kind of tool kit which you will need to address the questions and conundrums that are to follow in the remainder of the chapter.

After you have completed the Preparation, you are ready to head into the Problems and Cases, which make up the final and longest part of the chapter. You will, I assume, first work through this material on your own. It will then be the script off of which you and your instructor will carry on a conversation during the class session. I do not claim any consistency, foolish or otherwise, as to the order in which I placed the problems and the cases. Each chapter seemed, after a great deal of work on my part I assure you, to dictate its own flow through the problems and cases. And, as you will see, I went with the flow.

I truly hope the flow works for you as well. And, yes, I really do believe you will find the subject interesting and engaging.

James Brook

June 2008

ACKNOWLEDGMENTS

I would like to thank Dean Richard Matasar and Associate Deans Steve Ellmann, Jethro Lieberman, and Carol Buckler of New York Law School, who have consistently shown their support for this project and all the other things I do around the school. I also wish to acknowledge the continuing contribution of my staff assistant, Silvy Singh, without whom my workdays would be considerably more difficult and certainly a lot less pleasant. Thanks as well to my faculty colleagues at New York Law School, members of our superb library staff, and to those students over the past few years with whom I first had a chance to work over and test out the materials that morphed into the substance of this book. The feedback that I have received from one and all, in ways subtle and not so subtle, has been of enormous help, even if I have not always said as much at the time.

Special thanks go to the special people of Aspen Publishers, and in particular to Eric Holt, Troy Froebe, John Devins, Carol McGeehan, Melody Davies, and Richard Mixter, without whom this book would not have come into being. Their consistent encouragement, gentle nudging when nudging was called for, and good-natured support make them a pleasure to work with and to know.

Finally, my thanks go out to my wife Isabelle, who has I know had to put up with a lot over the past years, at least some portion of which had to do with my working on this book. I owe her more than words can express.

A SPECIAL MESSAGE ON ARTICLE 1

In the study of Secured Transactions, as with any topic governed by the Uniform Commercial Code, it is often necessary to refer to the General Provisions, including a whole host of useful definitions, of the Code as set forth in Article 1. We are blessed to be living in interesting times, at least as far as Article 1 of the Uniform Commercial Code is concerned. As of the time when this first edition of the book was finalized, something like 32 states had adopted a recently Revised (2001) version of Article 1. The rest of the states were still stuck with the original (1960s) version.

If you have any question about the status of Article 1 in your state, or in any state for that matter, the go-to guy on the subject is Prof. Keith A. Rowley of UNLV's William S. Boyd School of Law and his web site dedicated to the continuing adventures of Revised Article 1: www.law.unlv.edu/faculty/rowley/ucc_updates.htm.

While there are some substantive differences between the two versions of Article 1, the main distinction between the two as far as you need be concerned is that they convey what is essentially the same information in sections which bear different numbers. Fortunately, it did not turn out to be difficult to prepare this book so that the "Preparation" instructions of each chapter give references to both of the versions, but in your studies you need only read and refer to one or the other.

In conjunction with your very first assignment, your instructor should make clear which version, original or revised, of Article 1 she or he expects you to be following. On that basis you should then look at and make reference to *either* the sections of the original version of Article 1 (cited as § 1-XXX) *or* those of the revised version (cited as § 1R-XXX). I assure you there is absolutely nothing to be gained from looking at both.

PROBLEMS AND CASES ON SECURED TRANSACTIONS

Introduction

A. THE UNSECURED CREDITOR

We start from the basic premise that at various times in our society, and for all
sorts of reasons both good and bad, one person will incur a legal obligation to
make payment to another. The person who has the obligation we call the
debtor. The person who is owed the money is the *creditor.* This situation may
have arisen in any of a variety of ways, many of which you will presumably
already have come across in your legal studies thus far. In Torts you examined
the possibility that one person may be liable to another for some wrongdoing
for which the law gives legal relief. Since it is the rare case where the court can
order that everything be put back as it was before the tort occurred — what
sense would it make for a court to order that the defendant unbreak the
plaintiff's two arms and two legs which were injured in a traffic accident
for which the defendant has been found responsible? — the result of a successful action in tort is usually a judgment that the defendant must pay the
plaintiff a specified amount of money. As the judge bangs down the gavel
upon pronouncement of the court's concluding judgment, the successful
plaintiff has, by virtue of his or her courtroom victory, become a *judgment
creditor* of the defendant, who now goes by the moniker of *judgment debtor.*
   In Contracts you would undoubtedly have seen a great number of cases
where the obligation of one party to pay the other was initially entered into
voluntarily. The creditor may have loaned some money to the debtor in
exchange for the debtor's promise to repay at some time in the future. Or
the creditor may have delivered some property or performed some service
for which the debtor has committed itself to pay in the future. If the creditor
has extended itself in this way in exchange for the debtor's promise of
payment in the future but has done no more to enhance the probability
of its being paid by the debtor when the time is right, we say that the
creditor, the party that is owed the money, is an *unsecured creditor.* The
debtor has taken on some measure of *unsecured debt.*

1

In this course we will focus our attention on one ingenious way that the party extending the credit can try to increase its chances of being paid by the debtor what it is owed and when it is due (if not before). The creditor will agree to lend money to, deliver property to, or perform services for the debtor in exchange for a promise that it be paid in the future on what we will end up terming *secured credit.* The creditor will, by making sure the transaction is carried out in a specified way, make sure that it can qualify as a *secured creditor* with special rights against some particular property — personal property or fixtures, for our purposes — owned by the debtor. If the debtor does not pay its debt when due, the secured creditor will have the right to enforce the *security interest,* about which we will have so much to say in what follows, against the debtor. The exact enforcement mechanisms to which the secured party will have recourse are the subject matter of the very last chapters of this book. All that comes before those chapters deals with, in effect, how the creditor makes certain that it will have these enforcement rights, good against the debtor and against other, third parties as well, if the need arises for them to be put into play as the creditor "goes against" the collateral.

It is important to emphasize from the outset, however, that while the situation of the unsecured creditor can often enough turn out to be a pretty sad one, in reality most unsecured debt is paid by the debtor to the creditor simply as a matter of course. Most debts are paid. Whether this is because debtors feel compelled to make good on their promises because of some deep underlying moral imperative which would not let them sleep at night were they to do otherwise, or because the debtor knows of the untoward legal consequences of not paying his or her bills, is not something on which we have direct evidence. Nor is it something that I would care to even speculate upon.

Before you start your studies of how a creditor can become a secured creditor and what advantage that brings, it is necessary to say a few words about the unsecured creditor and about how the unsecured creditor has to proceed in those situations — those rare but exceptionally troubling situations — when the debtor does not pay as and when it is committed to do so.

The unpaid unsecured or, as we sometimes say, "general" creditor will almost invariably first try some form of extra-legal (note, not illegal) means of collecting on a past-due debt. Often a simple friendly telephone call will be enough to stir the debtor into action. The action being, the creditor hopes, getting out his or her checkbook, writing out a check for what is due, and sending it off to the creditor by the next available post. Unfortunately, in some instances the creditor may have to get a little less friendly with each successive call or may have to resort to a dunning letter or two. The creditor may report the debtor's delinquency in payment to one or all of the credit rating agencies. A frustrated creditor who is not making any headway through such means may eventually decide the best course is to turn the unpaid debt over to a collection agency, whose employees will then take over the urging and prodding. Such collection agents are, as you might know, limited in what they can do by some very basic common law principles as well as by federal and state regulation detailing just how far they can go before they have crossed the line into prohibited territory. See, for example, the federal Fair Debt Collections Practices Act, 15 U.S.C. §§ 1692 et seq., first enacted in 1968 and as later amended.

The situation becomes even less pleasant — and in all likelihood even less promising — if the unsecured creditor has to resort to legal action in the attempt to get paid. If the unsecured creditor is owed money on, say, a contract theory, then it will have to retain a lawyer and sue for the amount due. The suit has to be carried through to the point where a judgment is ordered by a court. The creditor can then claim for itself the status of a judgment creditor, but a judgment on the books is most certainly not the equivalent of a certified check in the mail or cash in hand.

We can assume that in a majority of instances, once a judgment has been entered in favor of the creditor for a definite amount to be paid it by the debtor, the judgment will, in fact, be satisfied by the debtor's, given the fact of the court's final determination, coughing up the money. Still, that leaves a significant number of times when a judgment remains unsatisfied and at least initially only a momentary victory for the creditor, only one small step on the road to its eventually getting paid. Sometimes the debtor is just plain stubborn and refuses to pay even in the face of a court order. In other circumstances the debtor may by this time have simply disappeared. Even if the debtor is on the scene and actually willing to pay, it is just possible that he or she won't have the money to do so. The debtor may be ready and willing, but altogether unable, to pay even a portion of what he or she acknowledges to be due.

The question then reduces itself to how the creditor can get what we refer to as *satisfaction* of its judgment. What the creditor need do is first discover some valuable property in which the debtor has an interest. This could be real property or personal property. It could even be something like a steady stream of payments to which the debtor him or herself has a right — such as the debtor's wages or annuity payments. The goal then is to get that property in whatever form turned into a bundle of cash or its equivalent out of which the amount owed to the creditor — or at least some significant portion of this amount — can through appropriate legal means be diverted into the creditor's pocket. The legal process by which this may (and we do have to stress the word "may") be accomplished is referred to as *execution* against this specific property. Notice that the property of the debtor's against which the creditor will be attempting an execution will typically have no particular relationship to any transaction or event which gave rise to the debtor's obligation to the creditor. It is "just" some property of the debtor that the creditor believes it is worth pursuing on the underlying theory, if that is the word, that it can and should be used to pay off the creditor.

It is important to note that even if the creditor has settled on some property of the debtor's which it believes should be so used the creditor itself has no right to itself go and simply seize or encumber in any way the particular property. The unsecured creditor has no unilateral right to engage in anything like what we might be tempted to call "self-help" execution. I note this here to distinguish the situation we are now considering from what will see to be true — by the very last chapters of this volume — for a *secured creditor,* a party we are soon to meet. In Chapter 1, in fact.

The unsecured creditor, even if its claim has been reduced to a final judgment by a court of competent jurisdiction will usually have to come back to the legal system again for execution of that judgment to be played out. If the property which the creditor has put within its sights is in a state other than the one in which its initial judgment has been obtained, it might have to first have a court in this second state itself enter a judgment based on the initial one. The means by which this order is then carried out vary greatly, in actual practice and definitely in terminology, from state to state. To speak in only the most general terms, the creditor will have to obtain a *writ of execution* from a court in the correct state. If the property which is the subject of the writ is real property, the creditor may be able to file a notice of its judgment lien on the property in the land records where papers relating to that particular parcel of land are to be filed under the law of the state. If the property is personal property, then the creditor will have to take the writ of execution to the local sheriff (the word derives from the reeve of the shire, the Crown's chief executive officer in Merry Olde England) for execution. The sheriff may execute the writ by either *levying* on the property or, at least eventually, taking actual physical possession of it.

Note that some of a debtor's property — typically his or her homestead (at least up to some maximum amount), household goods, tools of the trade, and so on — will be exempt from execution under the laws of the state. If the sheriff does eventually gain power over or actual possession of some nonexempt property, then he or she, the sheriff, will auction it off at what is referred to as a *sheriff's sale.* For reasons that you can probably imagine, the price that goods go for at such sheriff's sales are not going to be on the high end. Whatever amount is taken in as proceeds from the sale of the property, after the sheriff deducts what he or she is due for services rendered, is then available for payment of the money owed to the judgment creditor. In the highly unlikely (make that exceptionally unlikely) instance in which the sheriff is still holding some proceeds after the judgment creditor has been fully paid off, any *surplus* would go to the debtor.

That is it in a nutshell. If all of this sounds difficult, time-consuming, and expensive, that is because it is. And, just to put this in perspective, the unsecured creditor may fare even worse if the debtor slips into bankruptcy.

B. BANKRUPTCY PROCESS

The state law of Secured Transactions, which we will be studying in this book, and the federal law of Bankruptcy are, as you will soon come to appreciate, inextricably linked both in theory and in practice. Yet they are almost invariably covered by distinct courses at any law school. I will leave it to your course in Bankruptcy and to whoever has prepared the class materials for that course selected by your Bankruptcy instructor, to get into the finer details of that system. The Bankruptcy course has more than enough material to cover, and it is simply impossible (and I have to think, therefor, unwise) to suggest that a course in Secured Transactions can substitute for or even cover some substantial measure of what you will have to learn elsewhere, in the Bankruptcy course.

That being said, it is also true that it is very hard to study the law of Secured Transactions without at least a bit of basic knowledge about the bankruptcy system. What follows is my attempt to lay out a very preliminary sketch of what you would ultimately study in a much more satisfactory survey of bankruptcy law in a full-blown (if that is the word) Bankruptcy course.

Bankruptcy is a process. Article I of the United States Constitution provides that among the enumerated powers of Congress is the power to establish "uniform Laws on the subject of Bankruptcies through the United States." Thus all bankruptcy law in the United States is necessarily federal law. At present the governing federal law is to be found in Title 11 of the United States Code, in what is commonly known as the Bankruptcy Code. The present version of the Code was originally enacted in 1978 and has been amended several times since then. One reason for the significant interplay between the Uniform Commercial Code, and in particular the UCC's Article 9 governing secured transactions, and the Bankruptcy Code is that, while by its very nature the Bankruptcy Code is federal law it often refers to (or defers to, depending on how you look at it) the "law of the state" with respect to one or another aspect of its application. And it is in the Uniform Commercial Code that such state law is so often to be found.

The Bankruptcy Code consists of several of what it refers to as "Chapters." Some of these chapters are of general applicability. The later chapters set out the process to be followed in a bankruptcy proceedings of different varieties. The first of the three principle chapters in this regard is Chapter 7, allowing for the liquidation of any debtor's estate and for his, her, or its coming out of the bankruptcy proceeding with most of its debts forgiven by law, thus giving the debtor the opportunity for what is generally referred to as a "fresh start," at least as to how his, her, or its financial future may unfold. The majority of bankruptcy cases are such Chapter 7 proceedings. You will sometimes hear of a Chapter 7 case being called a "straight bankruptcy." You should not take from this that cases proceeding under the other chapters are somehow "crooked" or improper. They are just different.

Under Chapter 11, a business organization is allowed to come up with some plan for reorganization of its financial situation which, once approved by the bankruptcy court, stands at least a fairly good chance of allowing it to continue on in business with a greater probability that it can make a go of it. Chapter 13 sets out a procedure under which an individual wage-earning debtor can formulate a new plan for the eventual repayment on a more "doable" schedule of the debts with which he or she had previously been all but overwhelmed.

Certain basic rules and terminology are consistent across all of the various types of bankruptcy, regardless of the chapter. The process begins when the debtor (in a *voluntary* situation) or the debtor's creditors (in an *involuntary* situation) files a *petition* with the bankruptcy court. The bankruptcy courts of the United States have been set up to deal with this area of law as a specialty, but they act under the supervision and direction of the various local United States District courts.

The exact moment at which the bankruptcy petition is filed becomes important for a number of reasons, the three principal ones being:

(1) Under § 541 (a) of the Bankruptcy Code, upon the commencement of a case at the filing of the petition a new legal entity, the bankruptcy *estate*, comes into being. This estate consists, with some exception or *exemptions* as they are known, of all legal or equitable interests that the debtor has in any property, "wherever located and by whomever held," as of the commencement of the case.

(2) In due course an individual will either be elected or appointed to serve as the *trustee* with respect to the particularly case. The trustee serves as the official "representative" of the estate and has the capacity to sue and to be sued as such (§ 323). Even though it may take a while for the actual trustee to be named, his or her powers under many of the other important sections of the Bankruptcy Code will relate back to the exact date of the filing of the petition.

(3) As soon as the bankruptcy petition is filed, an automatic stay is put into place under § 362. This stay enjoins, with only very limited exceptions, all creditors from taking the kind of remedial or protective measures which they would otherwise be entitled to take to collect on debts that arose prior to the filing of the petition. The effect of the automatic stay is not limited to those who have actual knowledge of the petition's being filed. It truly is automatic. The idea behind the automatic stay is, of course, that it freezes in place for a time everything and everybody who might otherwise be making mad dashes to the courthouse or mad lunges for just about anything of value they could plausible lay claim to. This allows for the orderly resolution of the bankruptcy case under the trustee's active participation and the bankruptcy court's patient guidance.

If any individual creditor wants to be released from its obligation to stay put under the automatic stay, that creditor will have to apply to the bankruptcy court for an order "terminating, annulling, modifying, or conditioning" the stay based on "cause, including the lack of adequate protection of [that creditor's] interest in some specified property now held by the estate. (§ 362(d)(1)).

Once the petition has been filed and the automatic stay has clanged into place, the trustee can get to work. Along with the petition the debtor will have filed two important listings, or *schedules*. The first will set forth all of the debtor's assets. The second is a rundown of all of the creditors to whom the debtor is indebted. The trustee will go over these listings to determine whether there are any issues lurking under the surface. The basic task of the trustee is then to collect all of the assets of the estate, sell them off, and distribute the proceeds of the distribution in an orderly and prescribed fashion. This is, of course, the case when the trustee is dealing with a straight bankruptcy. When the debtor is seeking a reorganization, the trustee's job is more to collect all the pertinent information, work with the various parties involved to try to formulate a plan for successful rehabilitation of the business, and, of course, all the while running the business day-to-day. Just to add one more kink to the system, in many Chapter 11 proceedings no trustee is ever appointed. Instead the current management of the business is allowed to stay in place, running its affairs as what is termed a *debtor in possession* (or "DIP") during the period in which a Chapter 11 *plan of reorganization*—if one can be hammered out given the divergent interests of the various key players—is arrived at.

In the course of carrying out his or her duties, the trustee may have to make any number of decisions, for example, as to what property is or is not exempt from being drawn into the estate, what interests in property of the estate claimed by others should be challenged, and so forth. As we will see in later chapters in this book—all in due time, I say—the trustee may want to challenge a party's argument that, in the language of the Bankruptcy Code, it has a *secured* claim rather than an *unsecured* one. The trustee may try to avoid a certain pre-petition transfer on the theory that it constitutes a *preference* or a *fraudulent transfer*, as these terms will later be explained. Having to make all of these decisions leads, naturally enough, to the trustee's either initiating or being drawn into litigation before the bankruptcy court. And that court, as has already been noted, will often be called upon to make determinations of what the "state law" is on one matter or another. This is why you will see so many cases in this book—even though it is a book on secured transactions and not bankruptcy law—that have been decided by a bankruptcy court and with the trustee often as a party.

Once the trustee has dealt with and resolved, with or without the aid of the court, all contested matters, it is time for distribution of what remains in the estate to the correct parties. Distribution is made according to a precise set of priorities, with payment of administrative expenses coming first, then certain claims entitled, for one reason or another, to special priority, then secured claims, and finally the claims of the all unsecured creditors. In making the distribution, the result need not be that all claimants be treated exactly the same, only that all claimants *in the same general category or class* be treated equally. For the purposes of your studies in secured transactions, two general observations are in order. First, those who are able to assert only unsecured claims, the so-called "general creditors," get only to share equally what is left in the pot after all the other priority claimants — including those with *secured* claims of the type we will study with such vigor — have been paid. Second, it is the rare bankruptcy case where the unsecured creditors end up with getting more than a few cents (a very few cents, really) on the dollar of what they had been owed by the debtor. There is no other way to say it. Unsecured creditors come out very poorly as the bankruptcy process grinds away relentlessly to its eventual conclusion.

That eventual conclusion of a bankruptcy case comes when, in a Chapter 7 case, the bankruptcy court discharges pretty much all of the debts of the debtor to the extent they exceed what the creditor has received in the distribution. If the debtor was a corporation or a partnership engaged in a business, that legal entity is then wound up and disappears into the sunset. In the situation of an individual debtor, the debtor does not disappear, but is given a "fresh start," allowing him or her to continue on trying to make a go of it — at least in the financial sense — unburdened by those debts which had, prior to the bankruptcy procedure, threatened to drown him or her in a sea of red ink. In a reorganization case, which is one under either Chapter 11 or 13, the case is resolved when a plan of reorganization is approved by the bankruptcy court. The debtor "exits" bankruptcy, now free to carry forward its financial affairs under what is thought to be a more realistic and manageable assemblage of burdens.

PART I

INTRODUCTION TO ARTICLE 9
AND
CLASSIFICATION OF COLLATERAL

CHAPTER
1

The Typical Secured Transaction

A. INTRODUCTION

1. *The Problem Presented*

The story of secured transactions takes place against a background problem which you have undoubtedly already confronted in your legal studies thus far: How does our society, and more specifically our legal system, deal with the simple fact that people can and do at times make promises which, when the time has come for performance, they are unable or unwilling to keep? In your initial Contacts course you will, I hope, have taken note that in probably the vast majority of situations a *promisor* will in fact make good on his or her promise to a given *promisee* simply as a matter of course. However many hotly contested cases you read and bitter disputes you encountered in Contracts, you were called upon to remember that these represented in some sense only the aberrant situations. Most promises are kept without the majesty of the law ever having to be invoked, or even considered. Why do people tend to keep their promises? There are all sorts of extralegal explanations. I don't think it unduly naive to suggest that most people most of the time genuinely want to do right by others. Even if a person is tempted to stray, the social consequences have to be considered. We all have to take into account what the effect would be to our reputation if we were to become known as someone who doesn't stand behind his or her word. This is true in all kinds of settings, but nowhere more so that in the world of business, where we might very well be expecting to deal with the same parties, or within the same commercial community, repeatedly over time.

In Contracts you then spent a good deal of time considering the question of what subset of promises will get legal enforcement should the promisor fail to fulfill the promise he, she, or it made. (I have to assume you remember "consideration" and all that.) Under certain circumstances a promise made will result in a legal obligation resting on the shoulders of the promisor. The parties who had first been denoted as promisor and promisee can then be redubbed with the equally awkward titles of the *obligor* and the *obligee*.

11

In the world of commercial law, and in secured transactions in particular, we generally refer to the two parties of interest as the *debtor* and the *creditor*. Partly this is just a matter of past history and of current convention. It also reflects, however, the fact that the only promises in which the commercial law shows interest are of the enforceable kind. (As you will see in a later chapter, the "consideration" requirement still comes into play, here under the rubric of the need for a showing of "value" having been given by the creditor to the debtor.) We tend to assume as well, although it is not strictly necessary, that the promise made by the debtor to the creditor is to pay a sum of money at some time in the future, either in one lump sum on a given date or in carefully specified periodic payments.

The question thus resolves itself for our purposes to what a creditor can do when a debtor doesn't make payment when and as due. Recollections of your Contracts course come in handy once again. The creditor may threaten suit against the delinquent debtor. Just the threat alone may be enough to end the matter. If not, then the creditor may actually have to bring suit. If all goes well, the creditor will end up with a judgment rendered by a court of law. The debtor is now under court order to make payment. The creditor stands now not simply as a contracting party believing him or herself to be owed a sum of money, but as a *judgment creditor*. There are, however, as you could not have failed to notice as your Contracts studies wore on, all kinds of practical hurdles that may stand in the way of the creditor's getting such a judgment. Certainly a creditor who is forced to actually bring suit and follow the process through to the very end, including perhaps one appeal or two, may end up feeling not so much victorious or vindicated as worn out and frustrated by the whole process. And then, of course, there are all those legal bills to pay.

Even once a creditor has received a final judgment in his or her favor, the story (and the frustrations) are not necessarily at an end. No doubt many debtors, once faced with a final judgment and with no further legal avenues to pursue, will dutifully make out a check for the full amount of the judgment entered and forward this payment to the creditor. There is no guarantee that this will happen, however, and the judgment creditor may find it necessary to engage the legal system once again, this time to gain its aid in *collecting* on the judgment previously entered. Collection on a judgment has its own set of difficulties. It may be difficult to gain jurisdiction, or for that matter even to find, the debtor by this point. Even if the debtor can be found and found willing in principle to pay all that is owed, he or she may simply not have the money to pay the judgment. All the legal process in the world can't extract payment from someone who is flat broke or close to it. Even more troubling, if the debtor has by this time entered into bankruptcy, the unsecured creditor, even one with a judgment having already been entered in its favor, is likely to come out being paid very little, only pennies on the dollar as the saying goes, by the time the bankruptcy process has run its course.

The preceding story, told in only the barest outline, is true only when the creditor is what we term an *unsecured creditor*. The unsecured creditor has the legal right to payment, but all too often as a practical matter finds this a difficult right to enforce. Which naturally enough leads to the following.

2. The Concept of Secured Credit

The basic idea behind secured credit — that the debtor put up something of value as *collateral* to back up the otherwise naked promise to pay — is as old as human history. It may in fact go back to prehistoric times, where by this we mean before the invention of writing. Stories are told of ancient tribes, clans, or call them what you will, finally putting an end to a period of hostility (most likely including a good old-fashioned barbaric battle or two) regarding something like the correct boundary between their lands by an oral accord to which each tribe agreed to be bound. The leaders of the two tribes shake hands, or whatever would be the prehistoric equivalent, on the deal. In addition, however, one other detail might make its way into the eventually terms of the truce. Suppose that Tribe A had the upper hand in the negotiations, having been on the whole victorious over Tribe B, which is now suing for a cessation in the hostilities. The final arrangement, besides laying out the agreed-to border between the two factions, would also provide for the eldest son, let us say, and heir apparent to leadership of Tribe B going to live among the people of Tribe A for a time. This individual would not be thought of or treated as a prisoner or a hostage. He might even be given the status of an honored guest among the people of Tribe A. At the same time, it would be perfectly clear to all concerned that his situation could change, and change dramatically, if his people, the good folks of Tribe B, were to violate the border set by the treaty or otherwise go back on their word. In this primitive, but I think you have to admit fairly sophisticated, way the chieftain of Tribe B would have put something of value to at least himself, into the hands of Tribe A as more than just a token — as something like human collateral — to secure his promise to abide by the treaty entered into. Agreements of this type apparently continued at least into the time of ancient Rome. As the increasingly far-flung Roman Empire made temporary peace treaties with the various Germanic and other outsider groups that came near to and threatened its borders, a truce might be concluded one term of which was that a valued member of the potentially hostile group would be relocated to Rome, or another prominent city of the Empire, to live among the Romans and, among other things, learn their ways. Of course what the "guest" often saw was that life within the Empire's dominions was distinctly more pleasant than life outside and would return to his own people with the kind of stories that made the outsiders all the more determined to get a piece of the action.

Well before the height of the Roman Empire, of course, emerging civilizations had evolved in many parts of the world to the point where a true money economy had developed. With money comes the possibility of lending, both for personal and commercial purposes. Those with extra money available would be able to lend some of it to those in need of some additional cash to further a particular goal to the benefit of both, at least if the price, in the form of interest, was right. One way that a savvy borrower could convince a potential lender to make the loan, or to make it on more favorable terms, was for the borrower to offer up some form of collateral which would be put into the possession of the lender until the debt was finally paid off. What would be offered up as collateral was typically smaller objects of inherent value — things like jewelry or treasured items of household property, made all the more valuable if they were made of precious metals or studded with valuable stones. The resulting arrangement was what would quickly come to be known, at least in the English speaking world, as a *pledge* or *pawn* of chattel — the word "chattel" being an older term for visible, tangible, moveable, personal property, what we would today more commonly refer to as "goods."

The distinct feature of the pledge of personal property, the first and most elemental of the "security devices" recognized by most legal systems was that the debtor's property had to be such that it could be put into the actual possession of the lender-creditor. Note this limited possible collateral in a number of significant ways. First, the collateral had to be relatively small and compact so that the creditor could take possession of it and store it safely with little difficulty. Second, the collateral had to be something for which there would be a ready market — that could be turned by the creditor into cash — should the debtor default on his loan. Finally, the collateral had to be property that the debtor could afford to part with for some significant period of time. It did no good for the debtor to pledge, say, the tools of his trade to another in order to get a loan. If he did so, how was he going to continue to ply that particular trade and generate income, just the income he would need to pay off his debt?

The pledge has a long history. There are references to it in the earliest legal codes of which we have knowledge thanks to the work of archaeologists and students of ancient history. It continued to be recognized as a valid and effective way of doing business through the middle ages and into the early modern period. As the common law legal system of England took shape, the pledge easily took its place among the forms of private agreements which the common law would recognize and enforce. At the same time, the English legal system was developing, defining, and then refining its treatment of the one other form of security device whose evolution had been proceeding along a parallel but distinct track, the *mortgage* of real property. As you are no doubt aware, the real estate mortgage remains an important security device down to the present day. It has remained, however, a matter unto itself, or rather a matter which falls within the purview of the law relating to ownership of and transactions concerning real property. As you will soon get to see, modern *commercial law,* as now set forth in the Uniform Commercial Code, carefully steers clear of real property and real property transactions. Such matters remain firmly under the heading of real property law—and the distinct courses covering real estate transactions which are to be found in another part of the law school curriculum.

3.   Necessity as the Mother of Invention

In his monumental treatise on Security Interests in Personal Property published in 1965, Professor Grant Gilmore, one of if not the singularly most important authority on the subject of the last century, made the following sweeping, but no doubt accurate, statement:

> Until early in the nineteenth century the only security devices which were known in our legal system were the mortgage of real property and the pledge of chattels. Security interests in personal property which remained in the borrower's possession during the loan period were unknown.

All this was to change, and change rapidly, in the following century. The explanation for what was to happen is no mystery. The nineteenth century was the era of the industrial revolution. As Gilmore writes:

> The unprecedentedly rapid expansion of industrial facilities created an equally unprecedented demand for credit. The financing institutions which were the source of credit naturally desired security for the loans which they were invited, even compelled to make. As industrialization progressed, personal rather than real property came to be the principal repository of wealth. The mortgage on Blackacre would no longer be enough to support the merchant's insatiable demand for credit and the banker's demand for security. Nor would the medieval institution of pledge suffice to take up the slack.

The industrial revolution of the nineteenth century had another profound effect. Where previously personal wealth had largely been represented by assets such as real property, the Blackacre to which Gilmore refers, and the kind of family heirlooms or valuable baubles which could be pledged, the prosperous new individuals whose fortunes were rising with the industrialization and expansion of the economy, those newly wealthy industrialists and merchants coming onto the scene, had plenty of assets but of a very different sort. Their wealth was to be found in valuable pools of assets which were themselves needed for the running of their businesses. As Gilmore notes, "personal rather than real property became the principal repository of wealth," by which he meant personal property such as industrial machinery, large stocks of raw materials or finished inventory, and even the accounts receivable that the new industrialists and merchants were piling up at such a remarkable pace.

Lenders were more than willing to come up with greater and greater levels of credit, if the loans could be secured in some fashion. Potential borrowers could take advantage of this credit to expand their operations every further. What they could not do, needless to say, was pledge their principal assets. For one thing, what creditor was in a position to actually take possession of the large and cumbersome stuff such as machinery, inventory, and the like which made up the great bulk of the prospective borrower's wealth? Beyond this, if this type of property were to somehow be put into the possession of the lender, how could the borrower continue to carry on his or her profitable enterprise? You can't sell widgets that you haven't made. And you can't make widgets if the machinery and raw materials you use to make them are tightly held in the hands of another.

What the situation called for, as commercially sophisticated parties soon recognized, was a means for a lender to be granted an effective *nonpossessory* security interest in the property of the borrower. Such parties, and presumably the lawyers to whom they went for assistance, were up to the task. During the latter part of the nineteenth century and the earlier part of the twentieth a whole series of new forms of security devices were introduced which sought to make possible a nonpossessory security interest in one or another type of industrial property. These devices went by a set of names only now beginning to fade into history — the chattel mortgage, factor's lien, conditional sales agreement, title retention agreement, just to name a few. Each new device had its own distinct form and was to play, at least according to its creators, by a distinct set of rules. As each new device arose, the courts and legislatures in each of the several states had to play a not-terribly-successful game of catch-up, attempting to recognize and regulate as necessary the workings of the new form of transaction. The result in any given state were, it was generally acknowledged, hit or miss at best. Add to this the fact that the same process was taking place separately in each of the states with no great uniformity of results, and what the commercial lawyer of the mid-twentieth century faced was what Gilmore described, in what I tend to think was if anything an understatement, as a body of law of "extraordinary complexity."

4. Enter the Uniform Commercial Code

In the 1940s, the National Conference of Commissioners on Uniform State Laws ("NCCUSL") and the American Law Institute (the "ALI") joined together in an ambitious project to prepare a comprehensive statutory scheme covering all the major areas of commercial law. The proposed product of the project, which was to be known as the Uniform Commercial Code (the "UCC" or the "Code"), was then to be presented to the legislatures of each of the several states. If the Code was then adopted by all of the states, the result would be a uniform body of law covering commercial law, identical (or at least nearly so) in all states, replacing the patchwork quilt of state-by-state common and statutory authority that had begun to make the practice of commercial law so difficult and troublesome, not just with respect to security devices but in other parts of the commercial law forest as well.

That part of the UCC which would deal with security interests in personal property was its Article 9. While the men and women charged with drafting the other articles of the Code often had prior uniform law, or a relatively settled and comprehensive body of common law uniform among the states, to act as a starting off point for their work, just the opposite was true in the area of secured transactions. The drafters of what was to become the official text of Article 9 as they got deeper and deeper into their work eventually came to the conclusion that, if what they produced was to be of real value to the national commercial community, they had to start from something like a clean slate. Article 9 was to be, it had to be if it was to be successful, the most innovative of all of the various articles of the Code. We can let the drafters tell it in their own words. Consider the following language excerpted from the Official Comment to the first section of that original Article 9 as it was first presented to the states in the 1960s:

> This Article sets out a comprehensive scheme for the regulation of security interests in personal property and fixtures. It supersedes prior legislation dealing with such devices as chattel mortgages, conditional sales, trust receipts, factors liens and assignments of accounts receivable.
>
> Pre-Code law recognized a wide variety of security devices, which came into use at various times to make possible different types of secured financing. Differences between one device and another persisted, in formal requisites, in the secured party's rights against the debtor and third parties, in the debtor's rights against the secured party, and in filing requirements, although many of these differences no longer served any useful function. . . . The recognition of so many separate security devices had the result that half a dozen filing systems covering chattel security devices might be maintained within a state, some on a county basis, others on a state-wide basis, each of which had to be separately checked to determine a debtor's status.
>
> Nevertheless, despite the great number of security devices there remained gaps in the structure. In many states, for example, a security interest could not be taken in inventory or a stock in trade although there was a real need for such financing. It was often baffling to try to maintain a technically valid security interest when financing a manufacturing process, where the collateral starts out as raw materials, becomes work in progress and ends as finished goods. Furthermore, it was by no means clear, even to specialists, how under pre-Code law a security interest might be taken in many kinds of intangible property — such as television or motion picture rights — which have come to be an important source of commercial collateral.
>
> The growing complexity of financing transactions forced legislatures to keep piling new statutory provisions on top of our inadequate and already sufficiently complicated nineteenth-century structure of security law. The results of this continuing development were increasing costs to both parties and increasing uncertainty as to their rights and the rights of third parties dealing with them.
>
> The aim of this Article is to provide a simple and unified structure within which the immense variety of present-day secured financing transactions can go forward with less costs and with greater certainty.
>
> The scheme of the Article is to make distinctions, where distinctions are necessary, along functional rather than formal lines. This has made possible a radical simplification in the formal requisites for creation of a security interest.
>
> A more rational filing system replaces the present system of different files for each security device which is subject to filing requirements. Thus not only is the information contained in the files made more accessible but the cost of procuring credit information, and, incidentally, of maintaining the files, is greatly reduced.
>
> The Article's flexibility and simplified formalities should make it possible for new forms of secured financing, as they develop, to fit comfortably under its provisions, thus avoiding the necessity, so apparent in recent years, of year by

year passing new statutes and tinkering with the old ones to allow legitimate business transactions to go forward.

The creation of an Article 9, as with all of the other articles, which would be acceptable to all of the states, and all of the various special interests that would be affected by the proposal if it were to become law, was a lengthy and exhaustive process. Eventually, after much drafting, redrafting, and redrafting a few more times, the process resulted in what was deemed to be the Official Text of 1966 (although you should be aware, for what it's worth, that the principal work on this text had been carried out and completed in large part by the late 1950s and is really more a product of that decade).

The Uniform Commercial Code, when finally released to the states for their serious consideration, was by any measure a huge success. By 1968 it had been enacted in all the states other than Louisiana, which because of its civil law tradition had trouble adopting a code so deeply rooted in common law antecedents. Even Louisiana did eventually adopt most of the articles of the Code, include the Article 9 of our particular interest.

Being the most innovative of the articles, Article 9 was the first to show signs of instances where the need for improvement was in order, and a revision of Article 9 was promulgated by NCCUSCL and the ALI in 1972. Another set of revisions, coordinating Article 9 with a revised version of Article 8 on Investment Securities, was sent to the states in 1977. Both of these revisions were eventually, if not necessarily immediately, adopted by all of the states.

5. The "New" Article 9

In the 1980s, NCCUSL and the ALI, the two groups responsible for the origination and now the continual upkeep of the UCC, began a series of projects which were to result in significant additions to or revisions of the various parts of the Code. Probably the most successful of these efforts was the drafting and promulgation of an entirely new version of Article 9 in 1998. For reasons that will become apparent as you study the subject, the revision of this article necessitated that all the jurisdictions adopt the new article to preserve uniformity and furthermore that it become effective in all the states as of the exact same date. The new version of Article 9 specified that no matter when it was officially enacted in any state it was to become effective in that state (as it was hoped in all others) on July 1, 2001. To the relief of all, and to the surprise of at least a few, the system worked with only a few relatively minor problems. By July 1, 2001 all of the states had adopted the revised Article 9, and all but four had adopted it effective as of that date. Those four states chose slightly later effective dates, but by the first day of 2002 the "new" Article 9 was the law in all jurisdictions.

The "new" or "revised" Article 9, the version which you will be studying in this book, was nothing like a set of minor revisions or mere tinkering with the product. While the basic notions underlying what must now be referred to as the "old" — or, in what seems to me a more gracious fashion, as the "former" — Article 9, were by and large retained, the new version does incorporate a number of truly significant differences from what had come before. The new version is also written in a very different style, if that's the word, from the former one. It is something like two and one-half times as long as its predecessor, contains a truly impressive number of new definitions and new sections, and is accompanied by a truly impressive supply of detailed and lengthy (often quite esoteric) commentary. The numbering system for the sections of the new Article 9 bears only occasional, and probably accidental, relationship to the numbering system of the prior version, which at least one generation of commercial lawyers and students in Secured Transactions had come to know almost by heart.

For those of you using this book, who are presumably confronting Article 9 of the UCC for the first time, what the former Article 9 *used* to say or what controversies *once* arose under that now superseded version will be for the most part of historical interest, if that. At the same time, there will be times when reading and understanding the current version of the article requires appreciation of what went before. This is certainly true when you are reading a case decided under that "old" version of Article 9, and it is only in the past few years that we are beginning to see the large number of cases in which the court is called upon to apply the newer version. In preparing this volume, I have tried to keep references to or cases decided under the former version of Article 9 to a minimum, but I do not claim to have been fully successful. Not that my simply ignoring the fact of the prerevision version of Article 9 altogether would have necessarily been a good thing, even if possible. Secured transactions is a subject, like so many others in your legal studies, for which at least some understanding of what came before is near to essential for a better appreciation of the law of the present day.

Now, however, it is on to the study of modern day secured transactions as governed by the current Article 9 of the Uniform Commercial Code. In this chapter we consider the basic scope of that article and are introduced to the principal players in the secured transaction enterprise.

B. PREPARATION

In preparation for discussion of the problems and the case in this chapter, read carefully the following parts of the Code:

- Section 9-109(a)(1) and Official Comment 2 to that section
- The first paragraph only of § 1-201(37) or all of § 1R-201(b)(35)
- The definitions in section 9-102(a)(12) (the first sentence only), (28)(A), (59)(i), (72)(A), and (73); also Comment 3b to § 9-102

C. PROBLEMS AND CASES

PROBLEMS

1.1 On July 1, Ed Owens visits the office of his friend Alexandra Fuller. Seeming a little embarrassed, he asks Alexandra, whom he knows to be fairly well off, for a loan of $20,000. He assures her that he will be able to pay the money back with 7% interest within a year. "You know I wouldn't normally ask for such a favor," he explains, "but I've been hit with some large medical bills all of a sudden, and I'm a little low on cash right now." When Alexandra shows some unwillingness to make such a hefty loan, Ed pulls out of his pocket an elegant gold pocket watch. He says, "As you can see, it bears the date 1842. I've been told I could sell it to a collector of antique watches at any time and get way more than the $20,000 for it, but I just can't get myself to do that. A distant ancestor of mine bought it originally before the Civil War, and it's been handed down from generation to generation in my family ever since. I have always planned on handing it down to my daughter Edie when the time comes. Here's the deal: If you make the loan to me, I'll let you have this watch with the understanding that you can hold onto it until I fully repay you." Alexandra agrees to make the loan to Ed, provided he does put the watch into her possession on those terms. Ed signs a paper she quickly draws up stating that he agrees to pay Alexandra $20,000 plus 7% interest no later than June 30 of the following year. He hands the watch over to Alexandra, who quickly puts it in a locked drawer of her desk. She then gives Ed a check for $20,000, which he promptly cashes.

(a) Is this transaction between Ed and Alexandra governed by Article 9? If so what is the obligation secured and what makes that obligation legally binding? What is the collateral? Who would be termed the debtor, the obligor, and the secured party with respect to the security interest created?

(b) Suppose that what Ed hands over to Alexandra in her office was not the watch itself but instead a writing signed by him and dated July 1 stating that he "hereby grants to Alexandra Fuller a security interest in one 1842 gold pocket watch, now owned by me, to secure my repayment of a loan being made by her to me on this date." Would this change any of your answers to the questions set out in part (a) above?

(c) Finally suppose that when Ed comes to Alexandra for the loan he does not himself own the watch, or anything else of comparable value, to give to her as collateral. He does, however, bring along his cousin and close friend John. It is John who owns and is now carrying with him a valuable antique watch. He states that in order to help his cousin out of his cash-flow problem, he, John, is willing to put the watch into Alexandra's possession until Ed pays off any loan Alexandra makes to him.

Alexandra takes the watch from John, has Ed sign the paper saying that he agrees to repay the loan and on what terms, and then gives the $20,000 check to Ed. Has an Article 9 security interest been created here? If not, why not? If so, how would you now answer all those questions from part (a)?

1.2 Winger and Bucks are next-door neighbors. One Friday, Winger borrows $300 in cash from Bucks, promising to pay him back on the following Monday. When Bucks isn't repaid on the Monday, he leaves several telephone messages on Winger's answering machine during the rest of the week, complaining that he has not been repaid. The following weekend, Winger appears at Bucks' front door. He says nothing about the money, but immediately says to Bucks, "I'm afraid that when I took that remote-control model plane I've been working on out for a test I lost control and it flew over the fence into your backyard. Could I come through and get it back?" Bucks tells Winger to wait at the front door. He then goes into his backyard and finds the model airplane, only slightly crumbled. He takes the plane and puts it into a storage cabinet on his rear porch. He then returns to the front door. There he tells Winger, "Yep, I've found it and it's safe and sound. And you can have it back as soon as you pay me that $300 you owe me." Winger protests that he is currently a little short of funds and that he doesn't see what one thing has to do with the other, but Bucks is adamant. "You get your toy back," he tells Winger, "when I get my money." In taking the position that he does, can Bucks be said to be acting legally (whether or not reasonably or as a neighbor should) because he has an Article 9 security interest in the model plane?

1.3 Sarah is the sole proprietor of a large retail store, Sarah's Sells-U-Stuff, which offers a wide range of audio, video, and computer equipment, as well as other more mundane household appliances, for sale. Ben comes into Sarah's store, looking to buy a new televison, the old one in his apartment just having broken down irretrievably. Ben quickly find just the model he wants, a large flat-screen style TV with powerful stereo sound, but is surprised to see how high the price of it is. Sarah assures him that this is actually a very good price, and if he doesn't have the money on hand to pay for it all at once she is more than willing to sell it to him on credit. Sarah pulls out a form headed "E-Z Pay Monthly Payment Plan Agreement." She quickly fills in a few blank spaces on the form, giving a description of the particular televison as the goods being sold, Ben's name and address as that of the buyer, and specifying twelve monthly payments which Ben will agree to make to Sarah. The monthly payment amount, Sarah explains to Ben, has been calculated based on the stated cash price of the item and a reasonable rate of interest. The form also states in bold letters that, "The parties hereto agree that title to any merchandise made the subject of this agreement will remain in the Seller until Buyer has made full and final payment of all amounts due hereunder." Ben signs this agreement, and the next day the new televison is delivered to his apartment where he quickly has it set up in his den. Has an Article 9 security interest been created by this transaction? If not, why not? If so, carefully describe who or what is each of the constituent parts of the secured transaction: the obligation, the obligor, the debtor, the secured party, and the collateral.

BROWN v. INDIANA NATIONAL BANK

Court of Appeals of Indiana, 1985
476 N.E.2d 888, 40 U.C.C. Rep. Serv. 1401

CONOVER, J.: [Andrew C.] Brown signed a contract in July, 1974 to play professional hockey for the Indianapolis Racers hockey franchise, then owned by IPS Management, Inc. Under the contract's terms, Brown was to play for 5 years, starting with the 1974-75 season. The contract also provided Brown could not be traded without his written consent. Finally, the contract provided for salary payments and an "interest factor". Both were to be paid over the first 5 years and the "interest factor" to be continued to be paid over the remaining 5 years. IPS Management shortly thereafter sold its hockey franchise to Indianapolis Racers, Ltd. (Racers, Ltd.).

Racers, Ltd. initially borrowed $500,000 from INB in late 1974. INB took a security interest in Racers, Ltd.'s assets, including all players' contracts. INB perfected this security interest by filing a financing statement in January, 1975. INB subsequently loaned Racers, Ltd. additional funds over the next two years, and took security interests in similar collateral.

By 1977, Racers, Ltd. was experiencing financial difficulties and had borrowed from INB nearly $1,000,000. In April, 1977, INB requested Racers, Ltd. to deliver to it copies of its players' contracts, one of which was Brown's. Racers, Ltd. complied. On June 3, 1977, INB called all previous Racers, Ltd. loans. INB notified Racers, Ltd. it (INB) would take possession of all Racers, Ltd. secured collateral which included Brown's player contract and would sell the same at a private sale to be held on or before June 13, 1977. INB, in June and July of 1977, made at least two salary payments to Brown after it took possession of his player contract.

Canadian businessman Nelson Skalbania (Skalbania) offered to buy various Racers, Ltd. assets. Skalbania formed the limited partnership Hockey World Ltd. (HW, Ltd.). He also formed a new organization, Indianapolis Racers, 1977 (Racers '77) and made it a general partner of HW, Ltd. In November, 1977, INB transferred nearly all of Racers, Ltd.'s assets to HW, Ltd. and in exchange received a 20% limited partnership interest in HW, Ltd. HW, Ltd., however, did *not* purchase Brown's player contract.

Unable to find a buyer, INB returned Brown's contract to the general partner of Racers, Ltd., in January, 1978 and reaffirmed its security interest therein. INB never received money from its 20% limited partnership status in HW, Ltd. INB lost an estimated 1.2 million dollars on Racers, Ltd. loans. Likewise, Brown was paid for the first three years of his player contract, up to the 1976-77 season. He has received no further payment.

Brown sued INB for fraud in its failure to notify him of (a) the security agreement it executed with Racers, Ltd. initially taking his player contract as collateral; (b) INB's possession of the player contract once Racers, Ltd. defaulted on its loans; and (c) INB's intention to sell Racers, Ltd. assets at a private sale. Brown also alleged a breach of INB's duty of good faith in regards to these transactions.

The case was tried initially before a jury. The trial court denied INB's motion for judgment on the evidence made at the end of Brown's case. However, INB renewed this motion at the close of all the evidence. The trial court granted the motion. Brown appeals.

Brown's amended complaint alleges INB had a duty to notify Brown of various events occurring after INB took a security interest in Racers, Ltd. assets. Had INB fulfilled its duty, Brown opines, he could have taken steps to minimize the loss he suffered by either suing Racers, Ltd. for breach of contract or declaring himself a free agent enabling him to accept a player contract elsewhere. We find INB owed Brown no duty to inform him of these events.

A. INB's Duty to Disclose Under Article 9

[The court first found that, while Article 9 does mandate disclosure of certain information to certain persons in a variety of situations — as you will see in the chapters to follow — none of these disclosure requirements were such as to give Brown the right to the disclosure he claimed he had been owed under the statute.]

B. Contractual Duty to Disclose

Brown suggests INB had a duty under his player contract to disclose certain events. He premises this contention on the claim the agreement between Racers, Ltd. and INB actually operated as an assignment rather than a security interest.

A security interest is "an interest in personal property or fixtures which secures payment for performance of an obligation." [Citing § 1-201(37), the precursor to § 1R-201(b)(35)]. An assignment is a transfer which confers a complete and present right in a subject matter to the assignee. *Title Guarantee and Surety Co. of Scranton, Pennsylvania v. State* (1915), 61 Ind. App. 268, 274, 109 N.E. 237, 239. In determining whether an assignment has been made, the question is one of intent. *L'il Red Barn, Inc. v. Red Barn System, Inc.* (N.D. Ind. 1970), 322 F. Supp. 98, 106. A written agreement assigning a subject matter must manifest the assignor's intent to transfer the subject matter clearly and unconditionally to the assignee. 6A C.J.S. *Assignments*, § 49 (1975). The assignee takes no greater rights than those possessed by the assignor. *University Casework Systems, Inc. v. Bahre* (1977), 172 Ind. App. 624, 636, 362 N.E.2d 155, 163.

The agreement between Racers, Ltd. and INB labeled "security agreement" provided in part:

> The Borrower grants to The Indiana National Bank ("Bank"), a security interest in the Borrower's accounts, contract rights, instruments, tangible intangibles [SIC] and general intangibles now owned and hereafter acquired together with all proceeds thereof, including but not limited to the following:
>
> (1) The Indianapolis Racer World Hockey Association franchise and all player contracts now existing or hereafter arising;
> (2) Proceeds of all gate receipts which may be due the Borrower as a result of all Indianapolis Racer games now existing or hereafter arising;
> (3) Proceeds derived from all radio and television rights and agreements connected with the broadcasting of Indianapolis Racer games, now existing or hereafter arising;
>
> in order to secure the payment and performance of all Liabilities of the Borrower in favor of the Bank.

It also described INB's possessory rights in the collateral in the event of default:

> *Upon the occurrence of any of the above events of default* and at any time thereafter (such default not having previously been cured) the Bank shall have, in addition to all other rights and remedies, the remedies of a secured party under the Uniform Commercial Code as adopted by the State of Indiana (regardless of whether the Code has been enacted in the jurisdiction where rights or remedies are asserted) including, without limitation, the right to take possession of the Collateral. (Emphasis supplied).

This language clearly did not unconditionally transfer ownership rights to INB. Instead, INB could exercise its right to possession only upon Racers, Ltd.'s default. This agreement clearly established a security interest and not an assignment of the specified collateral. Therefore it is governed by Article 9, as we have determined, INB owed no duties to Brown under it. Whatever the duties of disclosure imposed by Brown's player contract, they remained the exclusive responsibility of Racers, Ltd.

Brown not only failed to present sufficient evidence INB failed to discharge its duty to disclose; he also failed to establish INB initially owed such a duty to him. The trial court properly granted INB's motion for judgment on the evidence.

Affirmed.

QUESTIONS ON BROWN

As you might expect, the questions on this case for the moment ask only that you concentrate on the initial set-up of the security interest involved. Who was each of the obigor, the debtor, and the secured party? What was the obligation being secured? What was the collateral? Was Andrew Brown himself a party to the transaction?

PROBLEM

1.4 The manufacturing firm of Seneca Bolting and Welding Incorporated is in negotiation with a major bank, Gotham National, for a loan of ten million dollars. The company has agreed in principle to the basic terms of the loan, including the fact that it will put up as collateral the two acre site on which its manufacturing plant is located, land which it owns outright, as well as all of its industrial machinery. The deal is then turned over to the lawyers. The company's lawyer and the lead lawyer for the bank begin to exchange drafts of the document that the two parties are to sign on the closing of the loan. All sorts of terms, conditions, warranties, so on and so forth, are dickered over by the lawyers. One clause grants the bank interest in the land (meticulously described in an Exhibit A) and the machinery (listed in detail in an Exhibit B) as collateral securing the loan. The final clause of the contract document, which by now runs to thirty-two pages, reads as follows: "The parties hereto agree that their contract is to be governed solely by the terms of this agreement as interpreted under the common law of the State of New York. No other document, statute, treaty, or convention shall affect the rights or duties of the parties hereto." The presidents of the company and the bank come together at a closing and officially sign the final copy of this agreement, and in additional separately initial the final clause as they are told to do by the lawyers. What is the effect of this clause? Does Article 9 of the Uniform Commercial Code have any relevance to the legal relationship between the company and the bank?

CHAPTER
2

Types of Goods

A. INTRODUCTION

Even as they were creating a statutory scheme intended to recognize and regulate the use of a single unitary security device covering personal property of whatever kind, the drafters of the original Article 9 were perfectly aware that different kinds of personal property would have to be treated differently for one reason or another when serving as Article 9 collateral. They therefore drafted into the article itself a classification scheme under which all personal property which could be subject to an Article 9 security interest would be placed into one — and only one — class, or as they use the word "type," of collateral. Revisions of Article 9 over the years, and particularly the recent major revision, tweaked some of the definitions of types of collateral and indeed added a number of types to the general scheme, including some intended to delineate a very limited type of stuff dealt with by one or another highly specialized sphere of secured lending which we can and will not concern ourselves with in this, an introductory course on the subject.

It is essential for anyone studying Article 9 to understand and become comfortable using this classification scheme from the very outset. As you will quickly see, reading further into Article 9 requires it. Sections you will soon encounter state rules that may be applicable to all types of collateral, or to only some types, or to only one type, and failure to take this into account can easily lead one astray. Also, parties (and of course their lawyers) entering into an Article 9 secured transaction will often find that a document to be drafted, a form to be filled out, or a notice to be given is valid and works as intended only if it contains a proper "description" of the collateral. Those having to do the negotiation, drafting, and the like, will often take advantage of the statutory delineation of the types of collateral to make their job that much easier. At the same time, of course, if a party (or his, her, or its lawyer) treats collateral as one type when it is truly of another type, as a court will later find, the consequences can be dire.

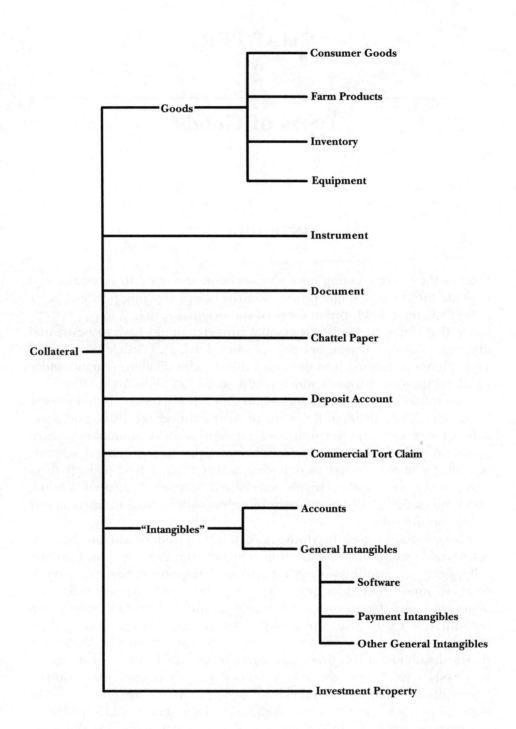

On the facing page you will find a diagram which I have put together in an attempt to set out the general classification scheme as we will study it, in this and the following two chapters. You shouldn't take from this diagram, or from the order in which we'll take up the various types of collateral, that any one type or form of collateral is higher in any imagined or real pecking order than any other. There is no hierarchy in the types of collateral. A given piece or collection of stuff that is meant to serve as collateral in any given transaction is what type it is, for better or worse and for richer or poorer, because of what it is (and, at least in some situations, because of who owns it or the use to which the owner is putting it.) Knowing what the types of collateral are, however, and how to identify and distinguish among them — that is an all-important part of the Article 9 enterprise and to practicing in this area of law.

In this chapter we will look at the four types of "goods." In Chapter 4, we'll look at the several types of what are collectively termed "investment property." In Chapter 3, we'll look at a variety of kinds of personal property that may serve as collateral other than types of goods or investment property — in other words everything in the middle of the diagram — each of which plays its role in modern commercial finance.

B. PREPARATION

In preparation, read carefully and be prepared to make use of:

- The definitions in section 9-102(a)(23), (33), (34), (35), (44), and (48)
- Official Comment 4a to §9-102.

C. PROBLEMS AND CASES

PROBLEM

2.1 The Fresno Furniture Company is in the business of making its own line of furniture that is sold in finer stores throughout the country. The company approaches a major commercial lender and suggests that it put up as collateral for a loan all of the pieces of furniture which are stored in the area of its plant where it keeps finished pieces.

(a) How would the lender have to classify this furniture as potential collateral to deal with this transaction properly?
(b) Suppose that Fresno sells a large selection of its furniture to a wholesale furniture distributor, Westcoast Home Products. What type of potential collateral is this furniture as property of Westcoast?

(c) Westcoast sells a portion of the Fresno Furniture it has on hand to a
    retailer, Fred's Furniture Boutique. How would you now classify this
    furniture as potential collateral which Fred might subject to a security
    interest in order to obtain a loan?
(d) Fred sells one of the sofas he has on hand, made by Fresno Furniture, to
    a customer, one Tanya. Tanya has the sofa delivered to her home where
    it is placed in her family's living room. What type of potential collateral
    is this sofa as owned by Tanya?
(e) What if Tanya, rather than placing the sofa in her living room were to
    put it in the waiting room of her dental office, which is in a set of rooms
    attached to her home? Would this change your characterization of the
    sofa as potential collateral?

NOTE

In this case, and the others that follow in this and the remaining chapters
of Part I, keep your focus on exactly what the collateral was, what type or
class of collateral it was being argued — by each of the parties — to be, and
how that issue was resolved. Try not to be overly distracted (even if it is all so
very interesting) by the particulars of *why* the correct classification of the
collateral at issue mattered. The problems of perfection, filing, etc. will all
be taken up soon enough, and you can then review these early cases with an
even greater appreciation of all that was going on and what was at stake.

IN RE ESTATE OF JOSEPH M. SILVER

Court of Appeals of Michigan, 2003
2003 Mich. App. LEXIS 1389, 50 U.C.C. Rep. Serv. 2d 1196

PER CURIAM: Respondents Kathleen Wilson and Mark S. Conti appeal as of
right from the probate court's order awarding four paintings to respondent.
The Joseph M. Silver Trust ("Silver Trust") in partial satisfaction of Mark S.
Conti's indebtedness to the Silver Trust. We reverse.

On September 10, 1996, Kathleen Wilson filed a financing statement with
the Secretary of State in connection with a security agreement entered into
with Conti that covered certain items, including equipment. Subsequently,
Conti entered into a series of security agreements with the Silver Trust from
May 26, 1998, through January 20, 1999. In these security agreements, Conti
granted the Silver Trust a security interest in eleven pieces of artwork. Subsequently, the Silver Trust perfected its security interest by taking possession
of the paintings. The probate court, finding that some of the artwork fell
under the category of "equipment" in Wilson's security agreement and
financing statement, determined that Wilson's filing with the Secretary of
State had properly perfected her security interest with respect to seven of
the eleven pieces of artwork and that, therefore, her claim for seven of the

pieces of artwork had priority over the claim of the Silver Trust. This finding is not in dispute on appeal. The probate court also determined that the remaining four paintings were consumer goods under the Uniform Commercial Code, and not equipment, rendering Wilson's security interest unperfected as to these particular works because neither the security agreement nor financing statement, nor any other evidence of Wilson's security interest, had been filed with the register of deeds. Accordingly, the probate court awarded these paintings to the Silver Trust.

Respondents Wilson and Conti first argue that the probate court erred in determining that the four paintings at issue in this case were consumer goods, requiring that Wilson file the security agreement and financing statement with the appropriate register of deeds in accordance with [Michigan's prerevision version of Article 9]. We agree.

During the time relevant to these proceedings, [the prerevision version of Article 9] provided in pertinent part that goods are:

> (1) "consumer goods" if they are used or bought for use primarily for personal, family or household purposes;
> (2) "equipment" if they are used or bought for use primarily in business (including farming or a profession) or by a debtor who is a nonprofit organization or a governmental subdivision or agency or if the goods are not included in the definitions of inventory, farm products or consumer goods. . . .

[The court notes that Article 9 of the Uniform Commercial Code had been substantially amended effective July 1, 2001. However, "the amendments do not affect an action . . . commenced before the effective date of the amendatory act." *Ford Credit Canada Leasing, Ltd. v. DePaul,* 247 Mich. App. 723, 727 n.3; 637 N.W.2d 831 (2001). This case, having commenced prior to the effective date of the amendatory act, was therefore to be decided under former Article 9].

Consistent with the statutory language, the determination whether goods are defined as "consumer goods" or "equipment" is dependent upon the primary use of the goods. Because the term "primarily" is not defined in the act, we consult the dictionary to aid in our construction of this term as used in the statute. *Random House Webster's College Dictionary* (2001) defines "primarily" as "essentially; chiefly." Applying this definition to the facts herein, we conclude the trial court erred by finding that Conti maintained the artwork at issue for his own "personal use." First, Conti testified that the paintings were initially purchased for use in his business. Second, the testimony established that the paintings had been displayed in model homes, condominiums, and in various offices of Conti's company, but never in Conti's home. Third, the testimony did not reflect that Conti ever displayed the paintings in his own personal office or that there was any personal, familial, or household use of the four paintings. Accordingly, we are compelled to conclude that the trial court clearly erred in finding that the four paintings at issue were used by Conti "primarily" for personal, family, or household purposes, and hold that the four paintings at issue in this case are appropriately classified, instead, as equipment.

Because we find that the paintings in dispute are equipment rather than consumer goods, we further conclude that Wilson's security interest was perfected in these four paintings by the filing of her financing statement with the Secretary of State. As such, her claim for these paintings also has priority over the claim of the Silver Trust.

Reversed and remanded for further proceedings consistent with this opinion.

QUESTION ON SILVER

If the timing of events had been such that the case had been decided under the current, revised version of Article 9, is there any reason to think that the result would have been different?

PROBLEMS

2.2 We return now to the manufacturing plant of Fresno Furniture Company. In considering whether or not to offer Fresno a secured loan, and on what terms, how should a potential lender characterize the following property in Fresno's possession:

(a) the large industrial table saws, lathes, and sanding machines which Fresno uses to make the furniture it sells,
(b) the piles of wood, mounds of stuffing material, and rolls of various fabrics that the company has in its store room, ready to be made into sofas, chairs, etc., as the need arises,
(c) the large quantities of nails, screws, sandpaper, and glue which the company uses in the fabrication of furniture,
(d) the partially completed pieces of furniture in various states of preparation now in the large and bustling workspace in Fresno's manufacturing facility, and
(e) the completed furniture, carefully wrapped and labeled, in the firm's end-product storage space?

2.3 Joshua Tillers is a farmer. And on his farm he grows raspberries, bushels and bushels of raspberries. If he were to apply for a secured loan from a local bank, how should the bank's attorney classify each of the following as potential collateral:

(a) the seed, fertilizer, and pesticides that Tillers has on hand before and during the growing season,
(b) the tractor which Tillers owns and uses on the farm,

(c) the supply of tractor fuel Tillers keeps in a storage tank on the farm,

(d) his raspberries as they are growing in the field, and

(e) the raspberries once harvested?

2.4 Farmer Tillers of the previous example regularly takes a portion of the raspberries he harvests and, rather than selling them to an agricultural distributor, himself produces home-made preserves. The preserves are then put into small jars labeled "Tillers' Tasty Raspberry Preserves," each jar with a holiday bow on it. Later in the year, when it is closer to the holiday season, Tillers is easily able to sell crates of these preserves to specialty food shops in the big city or at holiday crafts fairs. How would you classify these crates of preserves as they sit in the corner of his garage during the fall awaiting sale?

THE COOPERATIVE FINANCE ASSOCIATION, INC. v. B&J CATTLE CO.

Court of Appeals of Colorado, 1997
937 P.2d 915, 32 U.C.C. Rep. Serv. 2d 808

Roy, J.: Defendants, B&J Cattle Co. and its agent, Brett Bybee, (collectively B&J) appeal a summary judgment in favor of plaintiff, The Cooperative Finance Association, Inc., (Cooperative). We affirm.

Cooperative is the holder of a promissory note given by MRC-Sheaf Corporation (MRC), which was historically involved in the feeding and finishing of cattle. The promissory note is secured by, among other things, all of MRC's livestock "whether now owned or hereafter acquired by (MRC) and wherever located."

The security interest of Cooperative was evidenced by a security agreement and perfected by the filing of financing statements with the Colorado Secretary of State and the Morgan County Clerk and Recorder at different times by both Cooperative and its predecessor in interest. The promissory note matured and MRC defaulted.

Cooperative then commenced this action against MRC in replevin. The trial court appointed a receiver, designated collateral, and entered a temporary order to preserve the collateral.

MRC then purchased 203 holstein heifers from B&J for immediate resale to an identified buyer. MRC and B&J intended a cash sale with the purchase price to be wired immediately following, and from the proceeds of, the sale to MRC's buyer.

The heifers were delivered by B&J to a feedlot near Fort Morgan, Colorado, designated by MRC and owned by a third party. MRC acknowledged receipt upon delivery. MRC did not complete the sale to its buyer and did not wire payment to B&J as agreed. Subsequently, and at the insistence of B&J, MRC issued two checks to cover the purchase price but stopped payment on both. B&J immediately ordered the feedlot operator to maintain possession of the heifers for the benefit of B&J and against the interest of MRC. The time lapse between the delivery of the heifers and the dishonor of the checks for the purchase price was 13 days.

Cooperative, upon discovery of the heifers, amended its replevin claim to include the heifers and named B&J as a defendant. The trial court entered an order preserving the 203 heifers pending resolution of the case and the parties stipulated to their sale with the proceeds deposited in an interest bearing account. The litigation thence became a dispute over the proceeds from the sale of the heifers.

The parties filed cross-motions for summary judgment, each alleging there was no issue as to any material fact. The trial court found that Cooperative held a valid perfected security interest in all of MRC's livestock, which, by virtue of an after-acquired property clause . . . included the 203 heifers. The court also found B&J was a cash-seller with a right to reclaim pursuant to §2-507.

Relying on *Guy Martin Buick, Inc. v. Colorado Springs National Bank*, 184 Colo. 166, 519 P.2d 354 (1974), the trial court concluded Cooperative's perfected security interest had priority over B&J's right to reclaim the heifers, granted Cooperative's motion for summary judgment, and awarded it the proceeds from their sale.

[Among the several issues raised by B&J on appeal, and the only one which we need go into here, was whether the trial court had correctly characterized the heifers as collateral in the possession of MRC.]

We also reject B&J's contention that the trial court impermissibly resolved a disputed issue of fact in determining that the heifers were "inventory" as opposed to "farm products."

Classification of goods under [Article 9] is a question of fact and includes consideration of the purposes for which the debtor intended to use the goods. Thus, as an example, cattle used for recreational cattle drives can properly be classified as equipment. [Referring to *Morgan County Feeders, Inc. v. McCormick*, 836 P.2d 1051 (Colo. App. 1992).]

MRC had historically been in the business of "raising, fattening, (and) grazing" cattle, a farming operation, in both Iowa and Colorado. The trial court concluded, however, that MRC was not in that business at the time it purchased the 203 heifers from B&J and, therefore, such cattle were inventory. The trial court based its conclusion, in part, on the undisputed fact that MRC was no longer equipped and lacked the facilities to raise, fatten, or graze livestock. B&J here argues the trial court based its conclusion on inadmissible hearsay evidence. Cooperative submitted the deposition of B&J's agent who testified that he understood, based on the statements of MRC's agent, that there was an identified buyer for an immediate purchase of the heifers and B&J would be paid from the proceeds of the sale. B&J's agent further testified that: "We made an arrangement that the cattle would (not) go to another party until he (MRC's agent) got his money gathered up from his customer and paid B&J for the cattle and the checks were cleared before he got the cattle."

While the statements of MRC's agent through B&J's agent may be inadmissible hearsay for proving MRC's intent, they are clearly admissible as to B&J's knowledge and understanding of the transaction. The quoted testimony is, indeed, a statement of the contract as B&J, or its agent, understood it. B&J did not point to, nor do we find, evidence in the record to support any other intention on the part of MRC regarding its purchase of the heifers.

Therefore, the trial court did not impermissibly resolve any issue in classifying the heifers as inventory on the basis of inadmissible hearsay evidence.

Judgment affirmed.

QUESTION ON B&J CATTLE

Here you have a case where a decent sized herd of cattle was characterized as inventory in the possession of the particular debtor. And it cites to another case, *Morgan County Feeders*, in which some cattle (56 head to be exact) were found to be equipment. You should have no difficulty coming up with a fact pattern in which cattle, in whatever number, are farm products as held by the debtor. What about a situation where a heifer or two are consumer goods?

PROBLEM

2.5 Dumont Cashmore comes into Sarah's Sells-U-Stuff and asks to be waited on by Sarah personally as he has a big purchase to make. Sarah is more than happy to oblige. With her help Cashmore selects a particular top-of-the-line computer set-up. He tells her he wants to purchase a dozen of these machines along with the various add-on components that would be necessary to configure them into a highly reliable network. He also wants the computers to come loaded with a particular spreadsheet program and an accounting program, the names of which he reads off a slip of paper he has pulled from his pocket. On the paper he also has the address to which the purchase is to be delivered, which Sarah recognizes as that of one of the major downtown office buildings. Cashmore then asks if he can buy the entire lot under Sarah's E-Z Pay Monthly Payment Plan Agreement, under which he will pay the purchase price in monthly installments allowing all that is being purchased to serve as collateral to secure his obligation to her. Again, Sarah is more than happy to accommodate him. Together they fill out the necessary form. At one point the form calls for the customer to specify, by checking the appropriate box, the use to which the purchased merchandise will be put. Cashmore checks the box marked "Personal or family use." Sarah politely asks him if this is not a mistake. Shouldn't he have checked "Business or professional use" instead? She assures him that it makes no difference as far as the terms of the loan are concerned, but he is insistent that the form stay as he marked it. "I'm stating this stuff is for my personal use," he says, his voice rising, "and that should be good enough for you!" Sarah leaves the form as it is, and Cashmore signs it. Sarah later asks for your advice. Does she bear any risk in dealing with her security interest in the computer equipment sold to Cashmore as involving consumer goods as collateral?

KUBOTA CREDIT CORPORATION, USA v. TILLMAN

Court of Appeals of Tennessee, 2002
2002 Tenn. App. LEXIS 887, 49 U.C.C. Rep. Serv. 2d 926

FARMER, DAVID R., J.: The plaintiff creditor in this case filed suit to recover a tractor that was subject to a security agreement and was pawned to the defendant pawnbroker. The court below awarded summary judgment to the creditor. The pawnbroker appeals, claiming the creditor's security agreement was not properly perfected, and that the creditor therefore does not have a superior right to possession of the tractor. We find issues of material fact exist regarding whether the security agreement was perfected, whether the pledgor had authority to pawn the tractor, and whether the pawn transaction was entered into in good faith. We reverse summary judgment and remand.

In April of 1999, Wooten Tractor Co. and Deborah Hubbard (Ms. Hubbard) entered into two retail installment contracts and security agreements for Kubota tractors which were assigned to Kubota Credit Corporation ("Kubota"). The first transaction was for the purchase of a Kubota Model B7300HSD 16-hp tractor and a box blade. The second transaction occurred approximately two weeks later, and consisted of an exchange of the first tractor for a larger tractor, a Kubota Model L3010HST. The parties also completed a UCC-1 financing statement for $14,979.80 covering the larger tractor, which Wooten Tractor filed in the register's office of Tipton County. The documents name only Ms. Hubbard as the buyer/debtor, and list her address as 5235 Simmons Road, Drummonds, TN. The second tractor was picked up from Wooten Tractor by Ms. Hubbard's brother, Donald Long (Mr. Long), who brought it to his home. The tractor remained garaged at Mr. Long's home until June of 1999, when he pawned it to Bud Tillman, d/b/a Collateral Loan & Jewelry Co. (Bud Tillman and Collateral Loan & Jewelry Co. will be referred to collectively as Mr. Tillman). The pawn documents include an affidavit by Donald Long stating that he was the owner of the tractor and warranting the tractor against lawful claims and demands.

In April of 2001, Kubota filed a warrant [with] the Tipton County General Sessions court against Ms. Hubbard and Mr. Tillman, asserting a purchase money security interest and seeking to recover the tractor from Mr. Tillman.

The court awarded Kubota possession upon the filing of a bond, and Kubota recovered the tractor. Mr. Tillman appealed the general sessions' order to the circuit court, and counter-complained against Kubota, joining Ms. Hubbard, Donald Long, and Long's Construction as third-party defendants, for conversion in the amount of $13,500. Ms. Hubbard subsequently filed for bankruptcy. Kubota moved for summary judgment, arguing it had a purchase money security interest in the tractor and that the tractor was pawned by Donald Long individually and without authority. The court awarded summary judgment to Kubota. Mr. Tillman non-suited the third-party complaint against Ms. Hubbard, Donald Long and Long's Construction, and perfected an appeal to this Court.

ISSUES

Mr. Tillman submits the following issues for review by this Court:

(1) Whether a genuine issue of material fact exists regarding whether Deborah G. Hubbard gave Donald Long the authority to place the tractor which is the subject matter of this litigation with a pawnbroker, the appellant Bud Tillman, d/b/a Collateral Loan & Jewelry Company.
(2) Whether a genuine issue of material fact exists regarding whether Kubota Credit Corp's security interest was properly perfected, giving it priority over the interest of the appellant Bud Tillman, d/b/a Collateral Loan & Jewelry Company.

Kubota asserts that the dispositive issue is:

Whether Doug Tillman has shown that he has any right to possession of the tractor that is superior to Kubota Credit's claim for possession.

KUBOTA'S SECURITY INTEREST

Mr. Tillman submits that a genuine issue of fact exists regarding whether Kubota properly perfected its security agreement covering the tractor at dispute in this case. He contends that the tractor was neither farm equipment nor a consumer good, but equipment purchased for use by Long's Construction, a partnership of Ms. Hubbard, Donald Long, and their father, John Long. He asserts that Kubota's security agreement was accordingly not perfected [by a method which would have, under Tennessee's pre-revision Article 9, been necessary to perfect on nonfarm equipment].

Mr. Tillman argues that since the tractor was not a consumer good, Kubota does not have a perfected security agreement and has no superior interest in the tractor. He further argues that since Kubota's security interest was unperfected, the sale of the tractor to him by Donald Long [gave him full title to the tractor under Article 9, unencumbered by Kubota's security interest].

Kubota contends that the tractor was purchased by Ms. Hubbard as a consumer good, and that its purchase money security interest therefore was perfected without filing. In support of this assertion, Kubota submits an affidavit by Ms. Hubbard in which she states that she purchased the tractor for her own use and not for the benefit of Long Construction. Also included in the record is an affidavit of Steve Wooten, an owner and manager of Wooten Tractor. Mr. Wooten asserts that the tractor was sold for the personal use of Ms. Hubbard, and that Ms. Hubbard did not disclose any contemplated business uses for the tractor. Mr. Tillman notes, however, that the credit application completed by Ms. Hubbard does not state a contemplated use for the tractor, and that statements made by Ms. Hubbard in her deposition support the contention that the tractor was purchased, at least in part, for use by Long Construction.

In her deposition, Ms. Hubbard stated that she purchased the original, smaller tractor at the direction of her brother and partner, Donald Long, and that the down-payment was provided by her father, also a partner in Long's Construction. She stated that the exchange of this tractor for a larger one also was completed at Donald Long's direction, and that she did not know for what purpose the tractor was needed. When asked whether the tractor was intended for use in the construction business, Ms. Hubbard replied, "part of it." Ms. Hubbard also stated that Donald Long picked up the tractor from Wooten Tractor, and that it remained on his property from the time of purchase until it was pawned. She additionally stated that Donald Long previously had pawned several other pieces of large equipment to Mr. Tillman, apparently without incident.

Donald Long stated in his deposition that Long's Construction provided the down-payment for the tractor, and that the tractor was purchased for use by the construction partnership. He explained that the original, smaller tractor was exchanged for the larger model because the smaller tractor had nearly flipped over when used on a construction site. Donald Long further stated that Deborah Hubbard purchased the tractor in her name because the partnership lacked sufficient credit to finance it in its own name. He confirmed that he picked up the tractor from Wooten Tractor and that it remained at his home, which was also the location of the construction business. Donald Long further stated that the tractor was used for construction business purposes shortly after it was purchased.

The determinative factor for establishing the classification of goods is the purpose for which they are bought and used. *In re James Fritz Butler v. Murfreesboro Prod. Credit Ass'n,* 3 B.R. 182, 183 (Bankr. E.D. Tenn. March 5, 1980). When classifying goods in order to determine whether a security interest has been perfected, the court looks to the actual use of the goods, not to what use the goods could be put. *Id.* at 184. Upon review of this record, we find a genuine issue of material fact exists regarding whether the tractor is properly classified as a consumer good or equipment, and whether Kubota's security interest was perfected.

AUTHORITY OF DONALD LONG TO PAWN THE TRACTOR

[Kubota Credit made a couple of arguments which it claimed showed that Donald Long had no legal authority to pawn the tractor to Tillman. Tillman disputed both lines of argument, including the contention that he was not a "good faith purchaser" for the purposes of § 2-403 of the Code. The Court of Appeals concluded that each argument raised an issue of material fact that had to be decided at the trial level.]

CONCLUSION

This case raises an issue of material fact regarding the classification of the tractor which is the subject of this dispute. The determination of this issue is necessary to establish whether Kubota's security agreement was perfected. The evidence also raises issues of Donald Long's authority to pawn the tractor and whether Mr. Tillman was a good faith purchaser.

In light of the foregoing, we reverse summary judgment and remand for a trial on the merits.

CHAPTER
3

The "Intangibles" and "Quasi-Intangibles"

A. INTRODUCTION

This chapter deals with a number of other types of collateral — in fact all those that aren't either goods, of the last chapter, or investment property, to be dealt with in the following chapter.

The types of collateral we study here are sometimes grouped informally into the intangibles and the quasi-intangibles. These aren't official Article 9 categories, and you won't find either term defined anywhere in the Code. The ideas they are meant to convey may be useful to you, however, in sorting out all that we have before us. The *intangibles* are just as the word implies, valuable types of personal property that often serve as collateral but which take no material form. The *quasi-intangibles* do have a physical form, they occupy space, have to be present (and safely stored) somewhere, and can be lost or stolen. Their physical form, however, is not inherently valuable in itself. No one ever gained sustenance from eating a personal check, sheltered himself or herself under a warehouse receipt, or (I hope) kept warm by burning a pile of chattel paper. These quasi-intangibles are valuable because of what they represent. They embody in physical form legal rights, usually but not always the right to receive money or specific goods from some other party.

B. PREPARATION

In preparation for discussion of the problems and the one case in this chapter, read carefully the following parts of the Code:

- First, since you will need it in connection with some of the types of collateral dealt with in this chapter, and for just about every chapter

41

hereafter, see the definition of "record" in § 9-102(a)(69) and consult the first two paragraphs of Comment 9a to this section.
- Then review the definitions in § 9-102(a)(2), (11), (13), (29), (30), (42), (47), (61), (75), and (78) and Comments 5a through 5d.

If you have not previously studied the law of negotiable instruments, or feel you could use a quick review, see the following:

- Section 3-103(a)(8) and (12)
- Section 3-104(a), (b), (e), and (f)

If you have not previously encountered documents of title, look at:

- Section 1-201 (6), (15), and (45) or § 1R-201(b)(6), (16), and (42)
- Notice that unlike an instrument, which by definition will always be in negotiable form, a document may be in either negotiable or nonnegotiable form. See § 7-104.

C. PROBLEMS AND CASES

PROBLEMS

3.1 Louie owns and operates as a sole proprietorship a small jewelry store, Louie's of Litchfield, catering to only the most elite clientele. Leah Cashmore, a woman of fashion known to him, comes into his shop and picks out a emerald broach that she wishes to buy. Unfortunately, as she explains to Louie, she doesn't have her checkbook with her at the moment. She asks Louie if it would be possible for her to take the broach with her now, on her assurance that she would send him a check for its full price as soon as she gets back home. Louie agrees. Leah leaves the store with the broach. Louie, of course, has Leah's promise to pay him the price.

(a) How would you classify this promise as potential collateral among Louie's various types of personal property?
(b) Three days later, Louie receives a check from Leah for the amount due. How would you classify this check now in Louie's hands?
(c) By the end of the day, Louie has deposited the sizable check into a checking account he has with the National Bank of Hartford, which he opened many years ago to separate out the payments he receives and the checks he writes on behalf of his jewelry business from his own personal household account. How would you classify as potential collateral this checking account?

3.2 Knifty Knits Incorporated is a major manufacturer of sweaters and other knitwear with production facilities located in several parts of the country. It does not sell any part of what it makes directly to the public. Instead, it solicits orders from major retailers, mostly large department stores and fashion houses, whose buyers choose which of the various products in Knifty's seasonal catalogues to buy and in what amounts. The retailer then sends a purchase order to Knifty, which responds by directly delivering through its own fleet of trucks the chosen merchandise to the buyer, accompanied by an invoice informing the buyer of exactly how much is now due the manufacturer. As is customary in the industry, the invoice does not call for the buyer to make immediate payment, but that payment is due sixty days after the buyer receives delivery of the goods. Once Knifty has made delivery of a shipment of merchandise, how would you categorize the amount it is now owed by any particular buyer?

3.3 Carlos buys a new car from the "Spiffy New and Used Cars of Springfield" dealership. In exchange for the car he gives Spiffy each of the following.

(a) his used car as a trade-in;
(b) a check for the agreed-upon down payment amount;
(c) a signed piece of paper in which he, Carlos, promises to pay "to the order of Spiffy New and Used Cars of Springfield" certain amounts each month for the coming 48 months.

How would you categorize each of these items as potential collateral held by Spiffy?

3.4 Suppose, as is in fact extremely likely, that Spiffy also has Carlos of the previous problem sign a paper in which he grants to the dealership a security interest in the car being purchased to secure his, Carlos's, obligation to make the monthly payments called for in the paper described in (c) above. Suppose further that Spiffy then takes these two pieces of paper — the one from (c) and the one in which Carlos grants a security interest in his new car — and staples them together. How would you categorize these two pieces of paper *taken as a single unit?*

3.5 Ben comes into Sarah's Sell-U-Stuff store, looking to buy a new washer-dryer combination, the old one in his apartment just having broken down irretrievably. Ben quickly find just the model he wants, but is surprised to see how high the price of it is. Sarah assures him that this is actually a very good price, and if he doesn't have the money on hand to pay for it all at once she is more than willing to sell it to him on credit. Sarah pulls out a form headed "Retail Sales Installment Agreement." After Sarah has filled in the blank parts of the form with a description of the washer-dryer Ben is buying, Ben's full name as that of the "Buyer," and specification of the twelve monthly payments he has agreed to pay for the machine, Ben looks the form over. Its text includes language that "Buyer hereby agrees to make all payments as called for herein," and also that, "Buyer hereby grants to Sarah's Sells-U-Stuff a security interest is all merchandise being purchased by Buyer and made subject to this agreement to secure all of Buyer's obligations as set forth herein." Ben signs at the bottom of the form, which he then hands back to Sarah.

(a) How would you categorize this single piece of paper now in Sarah's possession?
(b) Would it make any difference to your answer if the form's text read instead, "The parties hereto agree that title to any merchandise made the subject of this agreement will remain in the Seller until Buyer has made full and final payment of all amounts due hereunder?"

3.6 At the end of the harvesting season, farmer Jessica Tillers has a lot of wheat on her hands. She takes large quantities of the wheat to Silas Silo's Grain Storage, a professional grain warehouse located near her farm. In return for the wheat stored she receives a negotiable warehouse receipt issued by Silas.

(a) How would you categorize this piece of paper, the warehouse receipt?
(b) In addition Tillers take a large quantity of wheat she hasn't stored with Silas directly to the local railyard where she delivers it to an authorized representative of Transcontinental Railways. The railway is to transport it to another part of the country where an agent of Tillers is to dispose of it in that market. Upon her delivery of the wheat, Tillers receives from the railway a bill of lading, acknowledging receipt of the wheat and setting forth the terms on which it will be shipped. Tillers leaves the railyard with no wheat, but with this paper in her possession. How would you categorize this paper?

3.7 Stella Startup fancies herself an entrepreneur at the very cutting edge of the information age. Using her own money she has acquired from its inventor the patent for a radically new type of computer chip. She has also paid an expert computer programmer handsomely to fashion a unique computer program which, she is confident, will along with the new chip allow her to produce a new type of "n-dimensional digital hyperwidget" which will be the "next big thing," becoming one of the major new products of the 21st century. Now all she needs is to actually fashion a prototype of the widget and then set up a manufacturing plant capable of turning them out in the thousands. She approaches several major lenders inquiring about the possibility of obtaining the kind of loan she will need. What she has to offer up as collateral are the patent and the program themselves. How should any potential lender categorize these items to insure it deals with them appropriately under Article 9?

LAKE REGION CREDIT UNION v. CRYSTAL PURE WATER, INC.

Supreme Court of North Dakota, 1993
502 N.W.2d 524, 21 U.C.C. Rep. Serv. 2d 774

LEVINE, J.: Franzella Gilliss appeals from a district court judgment foreclosing mortgages on real property, foreclosing security interests, and enforcing personal guaranties. We affirm.

Crystal Pure Water ("Crystal") is a closely held corporation which bottles spring water and distilled water. Crystal is owned by Russell Gilliss, Sr., Franzella Gilliss, Bruce Gilliss, and Renae Gilliss. The corporation's bottling plant is located on a .9 acre tract of land, referred to as the one-acre tract, in Eddy County. The wells and springs are located on a surrounding 50.63 acre tract, referred to as the fifty-acre tract. Since 1984, title to the one-acre tract has been held by the corporation. Russell and Franzella Gilliss resided on and held title to the fifty-acre tract.

The corporation and the Gillisses encountered financial difficulties, and in 1987 the First State Bank of New Rockford sued to foreclose a mortgage on the fifty-acre tract. A sheriff's sale was held on July 30, 1987.

The Gillisses contacted Lake Region Credit Union (hereafter "Credit Union") seeking to refinance their operation. The Credit Union agreed to loan $125,000 to Crystal to purchase the sheriff's certificate from First State Bank, pay off other outstanding debts and judgments, and pay insurance and taxes. The Credit Union took real estate mortgages against both tracts and received security interests in all of the corporation's personal property, including a water permit. The Gillisses each personally guarantied the corporate debt.

The parties agreed that, upon the refinancing, title to both tracts of land would be held by the corporation. The sheriff's certificate was purchased in the Credit Union's name, and it received a sheriff's deed when the period for redemption expired. The Credit Union then executed and tendered a quit claim deed of the fifty-acre tract to Crystal. The Gillisses apparently refused to accept the deed executed to the corporation, desiring to hold the fifty-acre tract individually.

The corporation defaulted on the loan, and the Credit Union brought this action to foreclose its mortgages and security interests, and to recover on the personal guaranties. Bruce and Renae Gilliss settled with the Credit Union before trial. The matter was tried to the court. Judgment was entered in favor of the Credit Union foreclosing its mortgages and security agreements, and against the Gillisses on their personal guaranties. The court also appointed a trustee to protect the property. Franzella Gilliss appealed.

Our review of many of the issues in this appeal has been hampered by Franzella's failure to provide a transcript of the proceedings. Many of her arguments are premised upon factual assertions that are contrary to the trial court's findings of fact. The appellant assumes the consequences and the risk for failure to file a complete transcript. If the record on appeal does not allow for a meaningful and intelligent review of alleged error, we will decline review of the issue. This rule applies with equal force when a party is acting pro se.

Franzella must suffer the consequences and the risks of her failure to file a transcript. We therefore decline to review those issues that are based upon factual assertions inconsistent with the trial court's findings of fact.

[Franzella first asserted that the trial court erred when it ordered a sheriff's sale of the fifty-acre tract, which she claimed as her homestead. The court found that this assertion failed, for a couple of reasons, and that the sale of the fifty-acre tract did not violate any asserted homestead rights of Franzella.]

Franzella asserts that the trial court erred in granting foreclosure of the Credit Union's security interest in "an absolute and perfected state water permit." Franzella has not cited any cases, authorities, or supportive reasoning for her assertion. Although her argument on this issue is somewhat confusing, we presume that she means to assert that a perfected water permit is not a property right subject to a security interest under the Uniform Commercial Code, as codified at Title 41, N.D.C.C.

[Article 9 of the U.C.C.], provides that a security interest may be created in personal property, including "general intangibles." [The court here quotes the prerevision version of Article 9:]

> "'General intangibles' means any personal property (including things in action) other than goods, accounts, chattel paper, documents, instruments, and money."

Although we have not found any case addressing whether a state water permit falls within the U.C.C. definition of general intangibles, other courts have held that similar permits and licenses issued by governmental authorities do constitute general intangibles subject to a security interest. See, e.g., *Freightliner Market Development Corp. v. Silver Wheel Freightlines, Inc.*, 823 F.2d 362, 369-370 (9th Cir. 1987) (transportation operating authorities issued to a motor carrier); *First Pennsylvania Bank, N.A. v. Wildwood Clam Co.*, 535 F. Supp. 266, 268-269 (E.D. Pa. 1982) (state clamming license); *In re Ridgely Communications, Inc.*, 139 Bankr. 374, 376-379 (Bankr. D. Md. 1992) (FCC radio broadcast licenses); *In re Cleveland Freight Lines, Inc.*, 14 Bankr. 777, 780 (Bankr. N.D. Ohio 1981) (state certificates of public convenience and necessity).

It is also generally held that, absent a specific prohibition in the state liquor laws, a liquor license or permit is a general intangible subject to a security interest under the U.C.C. See Annot., Security Interests in Liquor Licenses, 56 A.L.R.4th 1131 (1987), and cases cited therein. The provisions governing issuance, retention, and transferability of a state water permit are generally similar to those governing liquor licenses and other government-issued licenses and permits. See Chapter 61-04, N.D.C.C. There are specific criteria for issuance of a permit, procedures for revocation of a permit, and provisions for assignment or transfer of a permit. We find no specific prohibition in Chapter 61-04 against creation of a security interest in a water permit. We conclude that a water permit is a general intangible under [Article 9], and may be the subject of a valid security interest.

The Credit Union seeks sanctions against Franzella for her failure to comply with the provisions of Rule 30, N.D.R. App. P., regarding preparation of the appendix. The Credit Union asserts that Franzella included inappropriate materials in the appendix, including items not found in the record below, and that she failed to provide notice and an opportunity to designate parts of the record to be included in the appendix. The Credit Union was therefore required to prepare and file its own separate appendix.

The determination whether to administer sanctions for noncompliance with the Rules of Appellate Procedure rests wholly within the discretion of this court. In order to encourage respect for and compliance with the appellate rules, we have in the past assessed costs for failure to comply with the rules governing preparation of the appendix on appeal. We assess costs of $100 against Franzella for her failure to comply with our clearly stated rule, and to compensate the Credit Union for its costs in preparing a separate appendix.

The remaining issues raised by Franzella are either unreviewable because of the lack of a transcript, or are otherwise without merit. The judgment is affirmed.

PROBLEM

3.8 Ed Owens borrows $20,000 from his friend Alexandra Fuller in order to pay off some pressing medical bills. Ed promises to repay Alexandra at the rate of $1,000 a month for each of the next twenty months. In simple terms this is a loan. Another way of characterizing the transaction is that Alexandra has exchanged $20,000 in cash for Ed's promise to pay a stream of payments, twenty of them each of $1,000, at monthly intervals.

(a) For Article 9 purposes how would you categorize this new asset, this anticipated stream of payments, held by Alexandra?

(b) What if instead of just making this promise of periodic repayment, Ed had signed a paper stating that he promised to pay "to the order of Alexandra Fuller" the twenty payments, in the amount and at the times specified in the paper? How would you categorize this paper now in Alexandra's hands?

(c) What if the paper that Ed signed in addition stated that Ed was granting to Alexandra a security interest in "the old antique grandfather clock now standing in my hallway" to secure his repayment obligation? How would you now categorize the paper?

CHAPTER

4

Types of Investment Property

A. INTRODUCTION

In the colloquial sense of the word, people may "invest" in just about anything — art, wine, real estate, and on and on. In Article 9 terms, however, *investment property* is a very limited and precise term. See §9-102(a)(49). Aside from the "commodity contract" and "commodity account" — both of which are not Investment Securities under Article 8, and which must therefore be defined in Article 9 — the key definitions and concepts are all to be found in Article 8 of the Uniform Commercial Code.

I'd advise you not to worry at this point about dealings in commodity contracts or commoditiy accounts, but focus instead on the basics of the various types of *investment securities* as they are defined and dealt with in Article 8.

The key to distinguishing among the type of investment property — which is necessary not just for any further investigation into Article 8 which you may do in the future, but to your present understanding of how this type of personal property must be dealt with when it is functioning as Article 9 collateral — is to recognize that the different types of investment securities differ in the *form* in which they are held. In this chapter we will identify the basic forms of investment securities and get some initial understanding of the manner in which an investment security of any particular form is properly transferred from one owner to another party, either for purposes of sale or gift. This will help us later when we see how the various types of investment property are dealt with in Article 9 when the owner does not turn them over fully to another party, but does grant a security interest in them.

On the following page is a diagram which should be helpful. You'll notice that it starts off in effect at the lower right hand corner of the diagram on page 28, where the term "Investment Property" appears. We now have the need to, and the space for, breaking that one type of collateral into subtypes, and subsubtypes, in more detail.

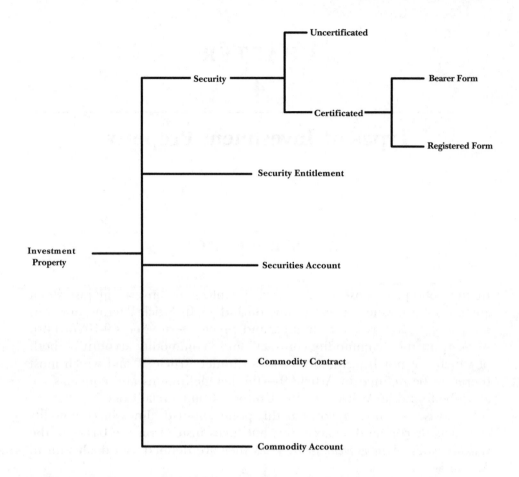

B.   PREPARATION

In preparation read carefully the following parts of the Code:

- Section 9-102(a)(49)
- Section 8-102(a)(15) and §8-201(a)
- Then back to further definitions in Section 8-102(a)(2), (3), (4), (7), (13), (14), (16), (17), and (18)
- Section 8-501(a) and (b)

While not essential reading for this chapter, if you have particular interest in the securities industry—how corporate shares and such are traded in what we might refer to as the "real" world—you will find it interesting and worth your time at this point to read at least Part I of the *Prefatory Note* at the very beginning of the current version of Article 8. Later, you may even want to come back and read Parts II and III. Unfortunately, not all statutory supplement volumes still include this *Note*, but you should be able to find it in another volume or online easily enough.

C. PROBLEMS AND CASES

PROBLEM

4.1   Stella Startup, the Silicon Valley entrepreneur, has acquired from its inventor the patent for a radically new type of computer chip. She has also paid an expert computer programmer handsomely to fashion a unique computer program which, she is confident, will along with the new chip allow her to produce a new type of "n-dimensional digital hyperwidget" which should make her a fortune. Before seeking further funding to take advantage of these assets, she decides to create a new corporation to produce a prototype and eventually manufacture and market the new widgets. She has an attorney form a corporation "Hyperwidgets, Inc." under the laws of the state of California. Stella formally transfers the patent rights and the rights to the specially created software to the corporation. In exchange she is to receive all of the 100 shares that are initially issued by the corporation. The lawyer prepares a stock certificate bearing the imprint Certificate #1 stating that Stella Startup is the owner of 100 shares of Hyperwidgets, Inc. This certificate is signed by the Treasurer and the Secretary of the corporation and the Secretary affixes the corporation's seal to it. The corporation's stock register is filled in to reflect the fact that Certificate #1 has been issued to Stella Startup in the amount of 100 shares. This certificate is handed over to Stella who places it in her safe-deposit box.

(a) Are the 100 shares of the corporation now owned by Stella her investment property, in the Article 9 sense of that phrase? If so, what type of investment property?
(b) Suppose that in addition the corporation had duly issued a Certificate #2 showing that 20 shares in the corporation had been issued to Stewart Startup, Stella's brother, who had initially loaned her some of the money which she used to acquire the patent. Does this change in any way your answers to part (a) above? And what about Stewart? Does he now have some investment property that might be of some value?
(c) Should either Stella or Steward later wish to transfer any of her or his shares to another person (and assuming such a transfer would not be in violation of any contractual agreement, state or federal law), how would she or he go about doing so? See the case that follows.

IN RE ESTATE OF WASHBURN

Court of Appeals of North Carolina, 2003
158 N.C. App. 457, 581 S.E.2d 148, 50 U.C.C. Rep. Serv. 2d 1190

BRYANT, J.: [Prior to her death, Vera Yarborough Washburn executed an Irrevocable Trust Agreement (the "Trust") appointing Jerry Scruggs and

John Cabiness as trustees. Accompanying the Trust agreement was an "Assignment of Assets to Trust" which provided that, along with other of her assets, all common stock she owned be put into the Trust. At the time of her death on October 23, 2000, Washburn was the record owner of 27,016 shares of a corporation named Branch Banking and Trust ("BB&T"). These shares were evidenced by two stock certificates:

    a. BB&T stock certificate No. BBT080224 . . . for 13,508 shares, and
    b. BB&T stock certificate No. BBT093753 . . . for 13,508 shares.

On the reverse side of certificate No. BBT080224 appeared her signature indicating a transfer on October 3, 1999 of the stock certificate to the trustees. The trustees had taken possession of this certificate prior to her death. At the time of her death, she was still in possession of certificate No. BBT093753, which had never been delivered to the trustees. When found in her residence after her death, the reverse side of this certificate "was blank, not completed for transfer, and not signed by" her. The trial court concluded that based on these facts the Trust property included the 13,508 shares represented by certificate No. BBT080224, but not those shares represented by certificate No. BBT093753. The shares represented by this second certificate were held to be assets of Washburn's estate. The trustees contested this latter holding.]

By definition, the creation of a trust must involve a conveyance of property, and before property can be said to be held in trust by the trustee, the trustee must have legal title. . . . Aside from the situation in which a settlor of a trust declares himself or herself trustee, separation of the legal and equitable interests must come about through a transfer of the trust property to the trustee. 90 C.J.S *Trusts* § 68, at 193-94 (2002) (footnotes omitted). Accordingly, "the owner must surrender control of the property which he or she has subjected to the alleged trust." 90 C.J.S. *Trusts* § 70, at 196. . . .

The trustees and the estate claim the trial court erred by failing to assign both stock certificate No. BBT080224 (Certificate 1) *and* stock certificate No. BBT093753 (Certificate 2) to them. The trustees, in support of their position, contend that the "Assignment of Assets" executed contemporaneously with the Trust was sufficient to transfer both stock certificates to the Trust. We disagree.

In order to determine the proper transfer of legal title to a security, we must look to Article 8 of the Uniform Commercial Code governing investment securities. Under Article 8, "a valid transfer of a certificated security requires both the indorsement and delivery of the certificate by its holder to the transferee." *Tuckett v. Guerrier*, 149 N.C. App. 405, 410, 561 S.E.2d 310, 313 (2002) (citing §§ 8-301 and 8-304 as enacted in North Carolina); *see* Russell M. Robinson, II, *Robinson on North Carolina Corporation Law* § 10.10, at 10-26 (7th ed. 2002) ("the title to a share certificate, and to the shares represented thereby, is normally transferred by the delivery of the certificate to the transferee, either duly endorsed or with a separate document containing a written assignment or a power of attorney to transfer the shares"). An "'indorsement' means a signature that alone or accompanied by other words is made on a security certificate in registered form or on a separate document for the purpose of assigning, transferring, or redeeming the security." § 8-102(a)(11). Delivery, in turn, "occurs when: (1) the (transferee) acquires possession of the security certificate; (or) (2) another person . . . acquires possession of the security certificate on behalf of the (transferee)." § 8-301(a)(1)-(2).

In this case, the parties do not contest that Washburn indorsed Certificate 1 by signing it and designating the "Vera Y. Washburn Trust Fund c/o Jerry R. Scruggs and John W. Cabiness, Trustees" as transferee in the allotted space on the certificate. The evidence is also clear that Certificate 1 was delivered to the trustees before Washburn's death. The estate nevertheless contends that because Washburn's signature was not guaranteed as required to transfer the stock on the corporate books, the transfer was not complete and could therefore not serve to create a trust in that stock. This argument is of no avail. "A registration of . . . a (stock) transfer on the stock transfer books of the corporation is not necessary to complete the transfer of title." *Robinson* § 10.10, at 10-26. It simply means that 'until the transfer is recorded on the stock transfer books, the corporation can treat the record holder as the true owner of the shares. *Id.*; *see also* § 8-306 (a guarantee merely warrants that the signature is genuine and that the person signing is the appropriate person to indorse the certificate and has the legal capacity to sign). Thus, in accordance with the statutory requirements for a valid transfer, the trustees acquired legal title of Certificate 1 when Washburn signed it over to the Trust and delivered it to the trustees. Certificate 2, on the other hand, which was not found until after Washburn's death, was neither indorsed nor delivered to the trustees. Under these circumstances, there was no transfer of legal title to Certificate 2 by Washburn to the trustees and the asset belongs to the estate. Therefore, the trial court did not err in distributing Certificate 1 to the Trust and Certificate 2 to the estate and dividing the respective dividends accordingly.

Affirmed.

PROBLEM

4.2 Alexandra Fuller tends to be conservative when it comes to her savings and investments. When she inherits a fairly large amunt of money from a distant relative, she decides to put it in a well-established mutual fund. After doing some research she decides on the Franklin Pierce Fund. She contacts the fund and arranges to purchase $50,000 worth of the fund's shares. She fills out the necessary forms and sends them, along with a certified check for $50,000, to the fund headquarters. She receives in return a letter from the fund manager stating that she is now the owner of 124.05 shares of the Franklin Pierce Fund, the number of shares having been calculated on the basis of the price of a share on the day her purchase was executed. She thereafter receives quarterly reports from the fund showing the value, as of the end of each financial quarter of her shares.

(a) Are these shares Alexandra's investment property? Of what type?
(b) Should Alexandra later want to redeem any of these shares, or transfer them to another person, how would she go about doing so? See the following case.

SECURITIES INVESTOR PROTECTION CORP. v. FIRST ENTERTAINMENT HOLDING CORP.

Court of Appeals of Colorado, 2001
36 P.3d 175, 45 U.C.C. Rep. Serv. 2d 610, 2001 Colo. J. C.A.R. 4412

DAVIDSON, J.: In this C.R.C.P. 69(g) proceeding, First Entertainment Holding Corp. (FEHC) appeals from the contempt order entered by the trial court pursuant to C.R.C.P. 107. We affirm.

[The case involved a series of stock options granted by the Board of FEHC to Abraham B. Goldberg, a director of the corporation. Things got confusing and contentious when the Board voted to "cancel" some of the options and Goldberg disputed the Board's right to cancel options previously issued to him.]

[Following commencement of this action by Securities Investor Protection Corp. ("SIPC"), the trial court ordered in September of 1999] FEHC to turn over "any and all evidence, wherever located, of the right of the Judgment Debtor to exercise an option or options to acquire up to 750,000 shares, or any other amount of the shares, of the common stock of FEHC, upon an exercise price of $0.21 per share or other exercise price."

FEHC's response stated, "There is no property of the judgment debtor which is subject to the Turnover Order." Also, FEHC asserted that it did not have in its possession or control the evidence requested, except for corporate minutes of the board meetings, which it attached to its response. Finally, FEHC stated, "While the Judgment Debtor may claim the right to certain shares of FEHC common stock and options to purchase shares of FEHC common stock, FEHC disputes this claim."

In October 1999, without informing SIPC or the court, FEHC canceled Goldberg's remaining options to purchase 400,000 shares at $.21 per share.

In January 2000, on SIPC's motion, the court issued a second order that acknowledged, inter alia, the existence of a dispute over certain shares, but nevertheless ordered FEHC to turn over any securities it held in Goldberg's name. The court also issued a contempt citation against FEHC pursuant to C.R.C.P. 69(g) and 107.

After the hearing, the court found FEHC in contempt for failing to comply with the court's orders. The court also ruled that FEHC could purge the contempt by filing a letter acknowledging the existence of Goldberg's uncertificated security interest in the form of an option to purchase 400,000 shares at $0.21 per share.

FEHC filed a letter purporting to comply with this order. In July 2000, however, the court ordered FEHC to resubmit the letter, so that it consisted solely of the first sentence of the previous letter, which read: "In accordance with your order on July 5, 2000, in the above-captioned case, this letter is to acknowledge that, as evidenced by the draft of the minutes of the Board of Directors of FEHC, which was provided to the Court on September 28, 1999 by FEHC, FEHC's records indicated that Goldberg was, on September 28, 1999, entitled to an uncertificated option to purchase up to 400,000 shares of FEHC restricted common stock at an exercise price of $[0].21 per share until March 11, 2002." The remainder of the letter, characterized by the court as argumentative, was ordered stricken. FEHC then brought this appeal of the contempt order.

[The Court first rejected SIPC's argument that the contempt order was not a final order as required under Colorado's Rules of Appellate Procedure and that therefore the appeal should be dismissed. It next considered whether the trial court had gone beyond its authority by proceeding as it had, given that the ownership of the options was a matter in dispute.]

[A]lthough we agree with FEHC that ordinarily, under C.R.C.P. 69, an ownership dispute effectively ends the trial court's ability to proceed, here, both disputed and undisputed securities were at issue. The court's January order did not decide any alleged dispute. Rather, based on the documents submitted by FEHC, the court properly acknowledged that ownership of some of the securities to be turned over appeared to be disputed, and ordered the remaining undisputed securities to be turned over immediately, pursuant to the September order.

FEHC also contends that the trial court erred in finding it in contempt of court. Again, we disagree.

The court may hold a party in contempt for disobeying a lawful order. C.R.C.P. 69(g), 107. We will overturn a finding of contempt only if the trial court abused its discretion. If the record supports the trial court's findings, they are binding on appeal.

Here, the court specifically ordered FEHC to turn over to the clerk of court any and all evidence of securities owned by Goldberg but in the control of FEHC. In response, FEHC attached corporate minutes that addressed, inter alia, the status of Goldberg's ownership of shares and options, some of which were disputed and some of which were not. The court then clarified that, although a dispute existed, any undisputed securities issued in Goldberg's name must be deposited with the clerk of court.

Although FEHC partially complied with the orders by submitting corporate minutes, FEHC was required to deposit with the court not merely evidence of the creation and existence of the undisputed options, but also was required to deliver to the clerk the uncertificated options themselves.

FEHC argues, however, that its submission of corporate minutes was adequate compliance. Specifically, FEHC argues, because the options were uncertificated, there was no certificate or paper that could be turned over, and the corporate minutes were the only evidence of these options. We disagree.

As a threshold matter, we note that, although FEHC is incorporated in Nevada, the Nevada Uniform Commercial Code, as pertinent here, is identical to the Colorado Uniform Commercial Code (UCC). Under the UCC, a security may be represented by a security certificate, see § 8-102(a)(16), or it may be uncertificated, meaning it is not represented by a certificate. See § 8-102(a)(18). A stock option is considered an uncertificated security. See § 8-102(a)(15).

Delivery of a certificated security is effected when another acquires possession of the certificate itself. See § 8-301(a). However, delivery of an uncertificated security occurs when the issuer registers the purchaser as the registered owner, see § 8-301(b)(1), or when a person other than a securities intermediary either becomes the registered owner of the uncertificated security on behalf of the purchaser or, having previously become the registered owner, acknowledges that it holds it for the purchaser. See § 4-8-301(b)(2) cmt. 3, C.R.S. 2000 (although use of the term "delivery" in conjunction with uncertificated securities seems solecistic, it is routinely used in the securities business).

Thus, whereas deposit of a certificated security with a clerk of court would be effected by delivery of the certificate, deposit of an uncertificated security, as here, requires not only evidence of the security's creation and existence, but also formal acknowledgment of its control by the clerk of court.

Indeed, SIPC's expert testified that, here, to deposit Goldberg's options with the court effectively, FEHC, as an issuer of securities, was required under the UCC to make an entry in its books showing the transfer of the options to SIPC or to the court, and submit to the clerk of court an acknowledgment that such a transfer had occurred. However, as of the date of the hearing, FEHC had made no such entry in its books, nor had it submitted such an acknowledgment. Moreover, the evidence at the hearing showed that FEHC was neither unaware that this was required nor unable to do so. Accordingly, the trial court's finding that FEHC was in contempt for failing to turn over property in its control belonging to Goldberg was legally correct and amply supported by the record.

The order is affirmed.

PROBLEMS

4.3 Lance Cashmore thinks of himself as a highly sophisticated and intelligent investor, very active on a regular basis in buying and selling stocks. He does his stock trading through an account (#13131313) he has with the brokerage firm of Hale & Hardy Associates. Does this account, taken as a single unit, qualify as a piece of investment property under Article 9? If so, what type? What term does Article 8 use to include a firm like Hale & Hardy with respect to the relationship it has entered into with Lance?

4.4 Several years have passed since the events of Problem 4.1. Stella Startup's plans for Hyperwidgets, Inc. have been proceeding apace. With the infusion of additional funds from a few private investors and specialized lenders, the technicians at the company has been able to fashion a working model of the 2-dimensional hyperwidget and are close to developing plans for a 3-dimensional model. The company has hired a number of highly paid consultants, adopted a very attractive new logo, and received a good deal of favorable press in the world of high-tech widgetry. It is time for the corporation to make an initial public offering of its shares to the public. After the public offering, Sarah and her initial private investors still own a majority of the common stock of the corporation, but there are also several million shares which can be and are held by, and actively traded by, members of the public at large. Lance Cashmore, of the previous problem, calls his personal broker at Hale & Hardy and tells her to buy one hundred shares of Hyperwidgets, Inc. to add to his account (#13131313) with the firm. By the end of the day, the broker calls Lance to tell him the purchase has been made as he had directed.

(a) Are these one hundred shares of Hyperwidgets, Inc.—Lance's hundred shares—his investment property under Article 9? If so, what form of investment property are they? What term does Article 8 use to identify Lance's position with respect to these shares?

(b) Should Lance later desire to sell these shares, what mechanism would he use to do so? See § 8-102(a)(8) and § 8-507(a).

PART II

CREATION OF THE ARTICLE 9
INTEREST — ATTACHMENT

CHAPTER

5

The Security Agreement

A. INTRODUCTION

Article 9 uses the word *attachment* to refer to those events which taken together give rise to an effective security interest granted to a specific secured party in some specific collateral owed by a specific debtor. If a security interest has attached to some collateral, then the secured party may enforce it against the debtor with respect to that collateral. Whether or not a security interest has attached, and if so what is the moment of attachment, are therefore critical questions that we have to be able to answer — or at least to see what the argument is about — with respect to any claimed security interest in particular property.

If the debtor is claiming a security interest that it turns out has never attached, or had not yet attached as of the moment when the secured party needs it to be effective, the secured party is left unsecured, at least with respect to that particular collateral.

Section 9-203(b) lays out three criteria, each of which must be met for attachment to have occurred. The debtor must have "rights in" the collateral, the secured party must have given "value" to the debtor, and there must be a valid *security agreement.*

While the fact of a proper security agreement is the last given in §9-203(b), we will be looking at it first. In this chapter we explore what makes for a valid security agreement under §9-203(b)(3). The following chapter will deal with the other two criteria for effective attachment.

B. PREPARATION

In preparation read carefully the following parts of the Code:

- Section 1-201(3), (39), and (46) or §1R-201(b)(3), (37), and (43)
- Section 9-102(a)(7), (69), and (73) as well as Comments 3b and 9 to this section

- Section 9-203(a) and (b) as well as Comments 2 and 3 to this section
- Section 9-108 and its Comments 2 and 3, and
- Section 9-204(a)

C. PROBLEMS AND CASES

PROBLEM

5.1   Ed Owens arranges to borrow $20,000 from his friend Alexandra Fuller. He orally promises to pay the money back with 7% interest within a year. He also hands over to her an antique pocket watch which has been in his family for generations saying, "You can hold onto this watch as collateral until I pay you back." Alexandra takes the watch and puts it in a locked drawer. She gives Ed a check for $20,000 which he quickly cashes.

(a) Has a security interest with Alexandra as the secured party now attached to the watch?
(b) Even if you conclude that a security interest has attached in this instance without any documentation, can you think of any practical reasons why you would suggest to Alexandra (were you present at the creation of this security interest) that she get something in writing from Ed?
(c) Suppose that, instead of holding onto the watch, Alexandra has said, "That's OK. There's no need for you to leave it here. Your word's good enough for me." How do you evaluate the situation now?

IN RE YANTZ

United States Bankruptcy Court for the District of Vermont, 2004
2004 Bankr. LEXIS 2279, 55 U.C.C. Rep. Serv. 2d 19

BROWN, J.: For the reasons set forth below, and based upon all papers filed in this matter and the evidentiary hearing held on July 8, 2004, the Debtor's objection to the secured claim of creditor Jane Osborne McKnight ("Attorney McKnight") is sustained and the claim of Attorney McKnight totaling $6,544.08 is allowed in full, as an unsecured claim.

BACKGROUND

The Court considers unique circumstances in this case. Attorney McKnight represented the Debtor in connection with a mortgage foreclosure action prior to his filing a chapter 13 case. Attorney McKnight filed a proof of claim in the chapter 13 case, asserting secured status [in the Debtor's 1999 Polaris snowmobile] for a portion of the claim. The Court confirmed the plan subject to a later determination of the status of Attorney McKnight's claim, and set an evidentiary hearing to ascertain whether the parties had entered into a secured transaction, whether a security interest had been created, and, ultimately, whether the claim could be allowed as a secured claim.

At the time of the evidentiary hearing, it was undisputed that Attorney McKnight had never presented to the Debtor for signature, and the Debtor had never executed and delivered to her, any document purporting to be a security agreement. The specific issue presented was whether the Debtor could be deemed to have granted Attorney McKnight a security interest in any of the Debtor's assets, to secure payment of the subject attorney's fees, notwithstanding the absence of an actual security agreement. Although the arguments evolved during the course of this contested matter, the issues ultimately presented for determination were as follows:

(1) whether a summary message regarding a telephone conversation constitutes a "writing" for purposes of the UCC;
(2) whether oral promises of a debtor that a debt will be paid upon the sale of certain property constitutes the granting of a security interest in that property; and
(3) whether a creditor can rely upon two separate writings, that are not contemporaneous and do not refer to one another, to demonstrate the existence of a security agreement, and, if so, whether the evidence demonstrates that there was a meeting of the minds that the parties intended these two documents to be construed together to create such a security agreement.

DISCUSSION

As the party alleging the security interest, Attorney McKnight had the burden to establish that an enforceable security agreement existed between the Debtor and herself. Attorney McKnight filed a proof of claim asserting that she holds a claim in the amount of $6,544.08 and that $2,500.00 of that claim is secured by a 1999 Polaris snowmobile. There is no question that the filing of the proof of claim constitutes *prima facie* evidence of the validity of the claim. The Debtor objected to the secured status of Attorney McKnight's claim, pointing to the lack of a security agreement. If the objecting party provides sufficient evidence questioning the validity of the claim, then the burden returns to the claimant to provide sufficient evidence to maintain and prove the claim. Consequently, Attorney McKnight had the burden of proof to establish the factors necessary to evidence an enforceable security interest, namely: (1) value has been given; (2) the debtor had rights in the collateral or power to transfer rights in the collateral to a secured party; and

(3) the debtor has authenticated a security agreement that provides a description of the collateral. § 9-203(b). Attorney McKnight also must establish whether there was a requisite meeting of the minds between the Debtor and herself at the time in order to use multiple documents together to establish the existence of a security agreement.

Attorney McKnight originally argued that snowmobiles were not governed by Article 9 of the UCC. In the alternative, she proposed that a security agreement under Vermont law did not require particular formality. Attorney McKnight further supported this proposition in her supplemental memorandum of law submitted following the evidentiary hearing. Moreover, Attorney McKnight proposed a broad definition for agreement as "a coming together of the minds." *Black's Law Dictionary* 62 (5th ed. 1979), and asserted that she could prove that this broad definition of agreement had been met between herself and the Debtor and thus that a security interest had been created. The parties each presented evidence at the July 8th hearing as to whether Attorney McKnight and the Debtor had a security agreement even though there is no document that is labeled as such and signed by the Debtor.

Under § 9-203(b)(3)(A), in order to establish a security interest, there must be an authenticated security agreement that provides a description of the collateral. Neither [the Article 1 definition of "security interest"] nor § 9-203(b)(3)(A) specifically requires a writing, but § 9-203(b)(3)(A) does require that the security agreement be authenticated. "Authenticated" means to sign or affix a symbol "with the present intent of the authenticating person to identify the person and adopt or accept a record." § 9-102(7)(A)(B). This implies that some sort of writing with a signature or symbol is required in order to enforce a security interest. In order to satisfy this requirement, Attorney McKnight offered into evidence a ratified retainer letter signed by the Debtor on October 26, 2003 (the "ratified retainer"). The Debtor signed the ratified retainer on June 24, 2003. It contained the language in the original retainer letter, which was not signed by the Debtor, but also had additional language specifically holding the Debtor liable for costs and fees incurred since the first retainer letter was signed on June 24, 2003. The ratified retainer does not satisfy the writing requirement for creation of a security interest in the snowmobile because it does not contain a description of the alleged collateral, or articulate the creation of—or the intent to create—a security interest. Moreover, the ratified retainer does not make reference to any collateral whatsoever. Although the ratified retainer may be sufficient to create an obligation by the Debtor to pay attorney's fees from June 24th forward, it does not, in and of itself, establish a security interest.

Under § 9-203(b), in order to establish an enforceable security interest, the authenticated security agreement must include a description of the collateral. To satisfy this requirement, Attorney McKnight relies solely upon the notes of her paralegal, Ms. Lockwood, that were taken in connection with a telephone conversation between Ms. Lockwood and the Debtor on December 16, 2003 from 3:58 P.M. to 4:05 P.M. (the "notes"). The notes, taken on a "While You Were Out" pad, include a description of the snowmobile by year and make. However, the notes do not include the signature of the Debtor and in fact, there is nothing in the notes that ties the description of the snowmobile to an offer of collateral to secure payment of the attorney's fees. Attorney McKnight argues that the notes constitute a separate writing which, taken together with the ratified retainer, constitute an authenticated security agreement that binds the Debtor. The Court has been presented no case law or statutory authority upon which it can rely to determine that notes from a telephone conversation taken down by a third party could be construed as a writing authenticated by the Debtor. Under [the definition in Article 1], a writing "includes printing, typewriting or any other intentional reduction to tangible form." While the notes from the telephone conversation may be construed as an "intentional reduction to tangible form," they were not placed into a tangible form by the Debtor or by Attorney McKnight, nor is it certain that they are a tangible form of the Debtor's thoughts. Since the author of the notes was a third party, Attorney McKnight's paralegal, at best, the notes would represent Ms. Lockwood's interpretation of the Debtor's thoughts. The notes do not establish that there was a meeting of the minds between Attorney McKnight and the Debtor with respect to the Debtor pledging any collateral to secure his payment of her legal fees, or constitute a description of the collateral for purposes of enforcing a security interest.

While the Court leaves open the question of whether some circumstances may compel a finding that separate documents maybe aggregated to create a security agreement in Vermont, there is no evidence that demonstrates the requisite meeting of the minds for such a finding between Attorney McKnight and the Debtor. During the Debtor's testimony, he was asked six times on direct and cross examination about whether he intended to give the snowmobile to Attorney McKnight as collateral and he answered in the negative each time. [The court quotes various portions of the record.]

Attorney McKnight offered the affidavit of Ms. Lockwood as evidence that during the December 16, 2003 conversation the Debtor in fact offered a security interest in the snowmobile to Attorney McKnight. The Court does not find that the affidavit establishes this fact. In Lockwood's recounting of the conversation, she said:

> He offered to bring his snowmobile to our parking lot. Said he does not owe a penny on it; that he bought it for $5,300.00. Debtor said to put a sale sign on it, and it would sell in a heartbeat for $3,500.00 and McKnight could keep the money.

The affidavit does not establish that the Debtor intended to give the snowmobile to Attorney McKnight as collateral for his obligation to pay the attorney's fees. In fact, the affidavit supports the Debtor's testimony that he wanted to sell the snowmobile from her parking lot but that he did not intend to give Attorney McKnight control of the snowmobile.

Attorney McKnight also presented a letter, written to the Debtor following the phone conversation with Ms. Lockwood, to demonstrate a meeting of the minds. She asserted that her letter operated as an acceptance of his "offer" to sell the snowmobile. The Court is not persuaded. Had she intended at that time to view the Debtor's offer as an offer of a security interest, she could have sent a writing with a description of the collateral for him to authenticate, in order to create a valid security agreement under § 9-203. As an attorney she would have known that such a document would be required to demonstrate creation of a security interest, and she probably had access to security agreement forms. Had she sent such a document to the Debtor, it would have demonstrated her understanding that the Debtor intended to offer collateral and her intent at that time to accept that offer and enter into a security agreement. However, she did not. Instead, she sent a letter expressing her appreciation for his offer to sell the Polaris and encouraging him to do so. The December 17th letter did not contain a demand for a security agreement nor any language to suggest that she viewed the Debtor's proposal regarding the Polaris snowmobile as an offer of collateral nor any language clearly accepting a security interest in the snowmobile. While the Court recognizes the fundamental unfairness of any 20-20 hindsight type analysis, where the creditor is an attorney and is arguing for a determination that a security interest exists notwithstanding the absence of virtually all of the formalities required to create a security interest, the Court must look at what opportunities the creditor had to establish those formalities and avoid the harsh result of a determination that no security interest exists.

CONCLUSION

After reviewing the evidence presented, this Court finds that Attorney McKnight failed to establish that an enforceable security interest existed between herself and the Debtor. Therefore, her claim must be determined to be unsecured.

The Debtor's objection to the secured claim of Creditor Jane Osborne McKnight is sustained, and the unsecured claim of Ms. McKnight is allowed in the amount of $6,544.08.

PROBLEMS

5.2 Returning now to the situation of Alexandra Fuller, Ed Owens, and Ed's antique watch. Assume now that the initial discussion between Alexandra and Ed, in which she agreed to loan him the money on his promise to put up the watch as collateral, had taken place over the telephone, as the two live at opposite ends of the country. Ed then sends Alexandra an e-mail in which he sets forth his promise to repay the loan on the agreed-to terms and further that he "grants to Alexandra a security interest" in the watch, which is described in detail as to its maker, the approximate year of its creation, and so on. After receiving this message, Alexandra reads it but does not print it out. She does store it on the hard drive of her computer in her "Miscellany" folder. Alexandra sends a check for $20,000 in the mail addressed to Ed. Ed receives the check and quickly cashes it.

(a) Has Alexandra's security interest attached to the watch?
(b) Would it make any difference to your answer if you were to find out that Ed's full name, as it appears for example on his driver's license and tax returns was Edwin Owens? He has signed the e-mail simply as "Ed."
(c) What if Ed hadn't signed the e-mail at all, but simply sent it directly to Alexandra from his e-mail address of "crazylegs789@hypocharacters. net?"

5.3   Friendly Finance is a very friendly lender indeed. It will lend to just about anyone if the loan is secured by the right collateral. Do you see any problem for this firm if it lends based on collateral described in the written security agreement as follows?

(a) "all pianos owned by the debtor"
(b) "all equipment"
(c) "all inventory, now held or hereafter acquired"
(d) "all consumer goods"
(e) "all of debtor's personal property"
(f) "one tractor, International Haybaler, serial #1234576" when the serial number of the debtor's sole tractor is actually #1234567

SHELBY COUNTY STATE BANK v. VAN DIEST SUPPLY COMPANY

United States Court of Appeals for the Seventh Circuit, 2002
303 F.3d 832, 48 U.C.C. Rep. Serv. 2d 790

DIANE P. WOOD, C.J.: Hennings Feed & Crop Care, Inc. (Hennings) filed a voluntary bankruptcy petition under Chapter 11 on August 23, 1999, after Van Diest Supply Co. (Van Diest), one of its creditors, filed a complaint against it in the Central District of Illinois. Shelby County State Bank (the Bank), another creditor of Hennings, brought this action in the bankruptcy proceeding against Van Diest and the Trustee for Hennings to assert the validity of the Bank's security interest in certain assets of Hennings. Van Diest was included as a defendant because the scope of Van Diest's security interest in Henning's assets affects the extent of the Bank's security interest. The Bank and Van Diest cross-moved for summary judgment, and the bankruptcy court granted the Bank's motion, finding that Van Diest's security interest was limited to the inventory it sold to Hennings (as opposed to the whole of Hennings's inventory). Van Diest appealed that order, and the district court reversed, finding that Van Diest's security interest extended to all of the inventory. Other claims that were at issue in those proceedings are not relevant to this appeal. The Bank now appeals. For the reasons set forth in this opinion, we reverse the decision of the district court and remand the case to the bankruptcy court.

Hennings, a corporation based in Iowa, was in the business of selling agricultural chemicals and products. As is customary, several of Hennings's suppliers extended credit to it from time to time to finance its business operations, and obtained liens or other security interests in Hennings's property and inventory to safeguard their advances.

The Bank is among Hennings's creditors. In December 1997, the Bank extended credit to Hennings for $500,000. In May 1998, the Bank increased this amount to a revolving line of credit of some $4,000,000. Hennings in return granted the Bank a security interest in certain of its assets, including inventory and general intangibles. Van Diest, also a creditor, entered into several security agreements with Hennings and its predecessor over the years to protect its financing of materials supplied to Hennings. These agreements were covered by the Uniform Commercial Code, which Iowa has adopted (including the revised Article 9).

A financing statement entered into by Hennings and Van Diest on November 2, 1981, provided for a blanket lien in "all inventory, notes and accounts receivable, machinery and equipment now owned or hereafter acquired, including all replacements, substitutions and additions thereto." On August 29, 1983, Hennings and Van Diest entered into a new security agreement (the Security Agreement), the language of which is at the core of this dispute. The Security Agreement was based on a preprinted standard "Business Security Agreement" form. In the field for the description of collateral, the parties entered the following language, drafted by Van Diest, describing the security interest as being in

> all inventory, including but not limited to agricultural chemicals, fertilizers, and fertilizer materials sold to Debtor by Van Diest Supply Co. whether now owned or hereafter acquired, including all replacements, substitutions and additions thereto, and the accounts, notes, and any other proceeds therefrom.

The Security Agreement contained a further preprinted clause providing

> as additional collateral all additions to and replacements of all such collateral and all accessories, accessions, parts and equipment now or hereafter affixed thereto or used in connection with and the proceeds from all such collateral (including negotiable or nonnegotiable warehouse receipts now or hereafter issued for storage of collateral).

The bankruptcy court found that the language of the Security Agreement was ambiguous and susceptible on its face to two interpretations: under one, the security interest extended to all of Hennings's inventory; under the other, it was limited to inventory sold to Hennings by Van Diest. Proceeding under Iowa law, that court applied several canons of contract interpretation to resolve the ambiguity. The upshot was that the court rejected the use of parol evidence and concluded that the Security Agreement extended only to inventory sold to Hennings by Van Diest.

The district court disagreed. It found that the bankruptcy court had created an ambiguity out of thin air and that the language of the Security Agreement supported only the view that the collateral included all inventory. It relied on the presence of the "after-acquired clause," which provides for future inventory to be deemed part of the collateral. Such a clause ensures that an entity having an interest in inventory retains the interest even when the original goods have been sold and replaced in the course of business, given the natural turnaround of inventory. *See, e.g., Larsen v. Warrington,* 348 N.W.2d 637, 639 (Iowa 1984). To reach this conclusion, the district court found that the qualifier phrase mentioning specific items found in the first paragraph quoted above, while it concededly modified the term "inventory," was mere surplusage. Accordingly, it found that the description of "collateral" must have extended to "all inventory," and reversed the bankruptcy court's findings.

As this case requires the interpretation of a contract, which is a question of law, we review the district court's decision *de novo.* The facts underlying the contract interpretation are not disputed in this case. In accordance with the Security Agreement's undisputed choice of law provision, we apply Iowa law.

In the process of divining the meaning of a contractual clause, a court must first establish whether the language in dispute supports more than one interpretation. The existence of such an ambiguity is a question of law, and under Iowa law, "the test for ambiguity is objective: whether the language is fairly susceptible to two interpretations." *DeJong v. Sioux Ctr., Iowa,* 168 F.3d 1115, 1119 (8th Cir. 1999). The description of the security interest in this case is a textbook example of ambiguous language: a term (all inventory) is followed by a qualifier (including all . . .) and then another (sold to Debtor by Van Diest). In the first edition of his book on statutory interpretation, Sutherland described the "doctrine of the last antecedent" as providing that "relative and qualifying phrases, grammatically and legally, where no contrary intention appears, refer solely to the last antecedent." J.G. Sutherland, Statutes and Statutory Construction § 267, at 349 (1st ed. 1891).

The Supreme Court recognized the existence of the "last antecedent" rule as early as 1799 in *Sims Lessee v. Irvine,* 3 U.S. (3 Dall.) 425, 444, 1 L. Ed. 665 n.a (1799). The Supreme Court of Iowa has also often endorsed resort to the doctrine in an attempt to resolve problems caused by ambiguously placed modifiers. The rule is now thought to extend generally to the placement of all modifiers next to the term to be modified. *See, e.g.,* Bryan A. Garner, *Guidelines for Drafting and Editing Court Rules,* 169 F.R.D. 176, 195 (1997) ("To avoid ambiguity, place a modifier next to the word or phrase it modifies.").

As a linguistic matter, therefore, the sentence is ambiguous. As both the Supreme Court and Iowa courts have recognized (and, indeed, as Sutherland himself pointed out) the rule is helpful in determining the existence of the ambiguity, but not in solving the puzzle when both readings are plausible. Unless one always followed a rigid formalistic approach, the rule would not cast light on which of the two interpretations should prevail. Instead, courts (including those in Iowa) turn to other canons of interpretation. Under Iowa law, those other canons should be used to resolve an ambiguity before parol evidence may be introduced. The rules in Iowa are the familiar ones used in contract interpretation in United States courts: the contract must be construed as a whole; the court requires a fair and reasonable construction; avoid illegality; the interpretation must account for surrounding circum-stances; and the parties' own practical construction is relevant. Iowa also applies the rule requiring the court to construe terms against the drafter of the instrument (still known to those fond of Latin phrases as the rule of *contra proferentem*); it favors specific terms over general terms; and it favors handwriting to typing and typing to printing.

Construing the contract before us as a whole leaves as many doubts as we had at the outset: nothing within it bears on the intended scope of the phrase "including but not limited to agricultural chemicals, fertilizers, and fertilizer materials sold to Debtor by Van Diest Supply Company." Van Diest could have acquired a security interest in everything that Hennings owned in inventory (as it had done, for instance, with the 1981 security agreement), or it could have limited its interest to the goods it supplied to Hennings. Without resort to other interpretive principles or to outside evidence, such as evidence of custom in the trade, it is impossible for a court to decide which reading the parties intended to adopt.

We do agree with the Bank's claim, however, that it would be bizarre as a commercial matter to claim a lien in everything, and then to describe in detail only a smaller part of that whole. This is not to say that there is no use for descriptive clauses of inclusion, so as to make clear the kind of entities that ought to be included. But if all goods of any kind are to be included, why mention only a few? A court required to give "reasonable and effective meaning to all terms," *AmerUs Bank v. Pinnacle Bank*, 51 F. Supp. 2d 994, 999 (S.D. Iowa 1999), must shy away from finding that a significant phrase (like the lengthy description of chemicals and fertilizers we have here) is nothing but surplusage.

Iowa law permits courts to consider the parties' conduct, such as the prior security agreements that Van Diest entered into with Hennings, as one way of resolving the ambiguity. Those earlier agreements at times provided for a blanket security with collateral in all inventory. This, too, is not terribly helpful here. On the one hand, the prior use of a general claim for all inventory demonstrates the availability in the trade of such a term and the willingness of Hennings, on occasion at least, to enter into such broad lien grants. On the other hand, it tends to show that the parties knew how to achieve such a result if they wanted to. There must be a reason why the historically used "all inventory," was modified in this case.

More useful is the parties' own practical construction of this particular agreement — a source that Iowa courts agree may be consulted without opening the door entirely to parol evidence. After the Security Agreement was executed, Van Diest sent to other lenders notices of its interest thereunder. In all the notices, it claimed a "purchase money security interest" only in the inventory it sold to Hennings. In a July 1993 letter to the Bank, for instance, Van Diest described its security interest as being in "all of Debtor's property (including without limitation all inventory of agricultural chemicals and additives thereto) purchased or otherwise acquired from the Secured Party. . . ." In the parenthetical, Van Diest then construed its own interest as being limited to the goods it sold to Hennings — not to the whole of Hennings's inventory, as it now claims.

As between the two parties to a contract, there is another doctrine that often resolves ambiguities: it is the rule requiring that ambiguous language must be construed against its drafter. Not only should the drafter be penalized by bearing the costs *ex post* of having cut corners *ex ante*, the penalty of interpretation against the drafter also aims to avoid overbearing behavior between contracting parties where the drafter, often the one in the better bargaining position, tries to pull a fast one over the party who can merely accept or reject the contract as a whole. Although this doctrine of *contra proferentem* is perhaps on the wane in some jurisdictions, it is alive and well in Iowa and in many interpretive contexts.

Unlike many jurisdictions that relegate the *contra proferentem* rule to the status of "tie-breaker," Iowa takes a strong view of the rule, holding that ambiguous language is to be "strictly construed against the drafter."

Here, the drafting party was Van Diest. It was Van Diest that was trying to obtain a security interest in certain property of Hennings, in order to protect its advances to the latter. At least if this were a case against Hennings, the use of the *contra proferentem* rule would provide a way out of the ambiguity in the key contractual language: construing it against Van Diest, the security interest extends only to the products Van Diest sold to Hennings, not to "all inventory." It is not such a case, however, and so we turn to the final consideration that persuades us that the Bank must prevail.

The most compelling reason to construe the language of this agreement against Van Diest is the fact that it was Van Diest that drafted the security agreement, and that the language of that agreement plays an important part for third-party creditors. Those creditors have no way of knowing what transpired between the parties; there is no parol evidence to which they may turn; and they have no way to resolve ambiguities internal to a contract. Here, we are not facing a garden-variety breach of contract action between the two contracting parties, both of whom were present during the negotiations. Instead, this case involves the effect of a contract between two parties (Hennings and Van Diest) on a third party (the Bank). The Bank, as we have already mentioned, is a stranger to the agreement, albeit one whose rights are affected by it. As the Bank could not have invested resources *ex ante* to avoid problems arising from ambiguous language, while Van Diest could have, it should be Van Diest who pays the price *ex post.*

A security agreement is a special kind of contract for which an important audience is third parties who need to know how much collateral has become encumbered. A potential creditor's decision whether to provide credit to Hennings (or anyone else), is contingent on the creditor's understanding of the extent of pre-existing security interests. An unclear statement of that extent should be avoided at all costs: if the creditor reads it reasonably, but too narrowly, when extending credit, it will be out of luck when the debtor defaults. If the potential creditor on the other hand takes a more conservative position and, fearful of the ambiguity, decides not to extend credit, the party seeking that credit is penalized in its access to capital by the shoddy work of its prior creditor — another result to be avoided.

By perfecting its security interest, Van Diest purported to give prospective creditors of Hennings notice of Van Diest's existing interest in Hennings's goods. A prospective creditor should have been able to look at Van Diest's filing and determine on that basis whether to extend credit to Hennings. Here, the Bank presumably did so, especially when it received Van Diest's letter in July 1993 telling it that the Van Diest security interest covered only goods bought from Van Diest. Whether this statement alone would have justified reliance on the Bank's part is debatable; but coupled with the language in the perfected Security Agreement that was susceptible to this interpretation, reliance was certainly reasonable.

The Supreme Court has also noted the special position that third parties occupy, given their limited ways of learning about the existence or the precise extent of a security interest. In *United States v. McDermott,* 507 U.S. 447, 123 L. Ed. 2d 128, 113 S. Ct. 1526 (1993), the Court expressed concern over the possibility that an after-acquired security interest clause might prevent the Government from asserting its interests. Like the Bank, the Government could not have protected itself by contracting with the parties or by analyzing the terms of the clause. The underlying rationale for the decision is equally applicable here: for the notice requirement to be a valid instrument of protection for potential creditors, that notice must be clearly expressed, and it must be such as is needed to inform the behavior of the potential creditor. "When two private lenders both exact from the same debtor security agreements with after-acquired-property clauses, the second lender knows, by reason of the earlier recording, that that category of property will be subject to another claim, and if the remaining security is inadequate he may avoid the difficulty by declining to extend credit." *Id. at 454.* When the earlier recording is ambiguous, the "second lender" does not know what collateral will be at its disposal.

In a broad sense, the problem of later creditors is similar to the problem of any third-party beneficiary. In the context of pension or welfare funds, which might be third-party beneficiaries to agreements between unions and multi-employer bargaining units, this court has held that the language of the collective bargaining agreement must stand on its own; it cannot be altered by oral agreements. Similarly, security agreements should be construed if at all possible without resort to external evidence, and they should be construed in a way that recognizes the important role they play for third-party creditors. Doing so here leads to the same result we have already reached: Van Diest's security interest extends only to the inventory it furnished. The limiting clause modifies the term "all inventory," and it is not surplusage.

For these reasons, we REVERSE the judgment of the district court and REMAND the case to the bankruptcy court for the entry of judgment in favor of the Bank.

PROBLEM

5.4   Essie Cashmore lives in a large mansion on an extensive estate in the ritziest suburb of Chicago. For many years now she has considered herself a patron of up-and-coming young artists and bought many of their earlier works, which she has proudly displayed throughout her mansion. In particular she owns six paintings done by the artist Graffito when he was still a young man. These paintings, which Essie acquired for very little when Graffito was still an unknown, are now worth conservatively at least $250,000 each and a couple quite a bit more than that. Essie finds herself temporarily in need of funds. She contacts Discreet Financial Services, a firm that is in the business of lending to high-end clients only. A manager from the firm comes to her estate. It is agreed that the firm will lend Essie $500,000 if the firm can take a security interest in a particular one of the Grafitto works, that which the manager appraises as the most valuable. A security agreement is to be drawn up. Unfortunately, each of Essie's six paintings by Graffito is titled simply "Untitled" and nothing more. Essie, as you can imagine, is not prepared to sign a security agreement describing the collateral as "all of the Debtor's artwork" or even "all of the Debtor's artwork created by the artist Graffito." The manager for DFS is not willing to grant the loan based on a security interest in "one of Debtor's artworks created by the artist Graffito," as you should be able to appreciate. Can you help them out? How might they go about describing in the written security agreement the one painting, and only that painting, which they have already agreed will be the collateral so there is no possibility of confusion later on? What further facts would you want to know?

IN RE SOUTHERN ILLINOIS RAIL CAR CO.

United States Bankruptcy Court for the Southern District of Illinois, 2002
301 Bankr. 305, 2002 Bankr. LEXIS 1433

GERALD D. FINES, J.: This matter having come before the Court on a Motion to Lift Stay and for Adequate Protection of Wells Fargo Equipment Finance Company and Debtor's Objection Motion to Lift Stay and for Adequate

Protection of Wells Fargo Equipment Finance Company; the Court, having heard arguments of counsel and being otherwise fully advised in the premises, makes the following findings of fact and conclusions of law pursuant to Rule 7052 of the Federal Rules of Bankruptcy Procedure.

[The matter was tried before the Bankruptcy Judge Fines on stipulated facts.]

A secured creditor only may receive relief from the automatic stay pursuant to § 362(d) of the United States Bankruptcy Code if that creditor's interest in property is not protected adequately or if the debtor does not have equity in such property and that property is not necessary to an effective reorganization. See: 11 U.S.C. § 362(d)(1) & (2). Wells Fargo asserts a security interest or lien in certain railcars (the "Equipment") and a railcar lease between Southern Illinois Railcar Co. (SIRC), as lessor, and OmniSource, LLC, as lessee (the "OmniSource Lease," with the Equipment the "Collateral"), and seeks to have the automatic stay lifted to permit it to foreclose upon the Collateral.

As a creditor seeking to lift the automatic stay, Wells Fargo has the burden of demonstrating the existence, the validity, and the perfection of its security interest in the Collateral. Whether Wells Fargo can meet this burden is dependent upon state law, because state law determines whether a valid security interest exists in any property. Article 9 of the Uniform Commercial Code (the "UCC"), governs the creation of security interests in personal property. Further, the application of the UCC in this matter should be governed by New York law, because Loan #3711 provides that it "shall in all respects be governed by and construed in accordance with the internal laws of the State of New York, including all matters of construction, validity and performance." However, because New York and Illinois adopted virtually identical versions of the revised UCC, case law from both states that interprets the UCC is persuasive and cited herein.

Section 9-203 of the UCC governs the enforceability of security interests. The relevant portion of that statute provides that a security interest only attaches to collateral so as to be enforceable against other parties if value has been given, if the debtor has rights in the collateral, and if the debtor has authenticated a security agreement describing the collateral. There are no disputes before the Court regarding whether Wells Fargo gave value for the Collateral, whether SIRC had rights in the Collateral, or whether SIRC executed writings regarding Loan #3711.

The UCC provides that a description of the property is adequate if it "reasonably identifies" the collateral. Moreover, collateral is reasonably identified as long as the "identity of the collateral is objectively determinable." Drawing from case law, this means that property is reasonably identified in a security agreement if a third party could determine what items of the debtor's collateral are subject to the creditor's security interest. Where a debtor owns numerous similar items of collateral that cannot be distinguished by a more general description, a description of collateral is insufficient without the correct serial numbers of collateral. See: *Bennett Funding,*

255 B.R. 616, 636-37 (applying the New York law to require a security agreement to include serial numbers of office equipment when the pledged items otherwise were indistinguishable from similar items owned by the debtor but not pledged to the creditor); accord *In re Keene Corp.*, 188 B.R. 881, 901 (Bankr. S.D.N.Y. 1995) (applying Illinois law to require a security agreement to have a detailed description of each Treasury note pledged when the debtor's account held numerous Treasury notes similar to the collateral at issue). A description of collateral in a security agreement is not adequate if the writing had unfilled blanks or omitted attachments that normally would provide the description of the collateral. See, e.g.: *In re Kevin W. Emerick Farms, Inc.*, 201 B.R. 790, 797-798 (Bankr. C.D. Ill. 1996) (applying Illinois law to find creditors' descriptions of collateral inadequate where one security agreement had blanks instead of the necessary description of the property and where the other security agreement described the collateral only in an attachment that was neither attached to or incorporated in the security agreement); *Rusch Factors, Inc. v. Passport Fashion Limited,* 67 Misc. 2d 3, 322 N.Y.S.2d 765, 768 (N.Y. Sup. Ct. 1971) aff'd, 38 A.D.2d 690, 327 N.Y.S.2d 536 (N.Y. App. Div. 1 Dept. 1971), appeal denied, 30 N.Y.2d 482 (1972) (applying New York law to find security agreement unenforceable because documents that would have described collateral and that purported to be incorporated in the agreement by reference were not attached to the agreement).

Under the cases cited above, Wells Fargo's security agreements fail to include an adequate description of its Equipment collateral. Loan #3711 purports to secure payment and performance with a lien in favor of the creditor on "Equipment as more fully described on Schedule A." However, no Schedule A is attached to the Loan and Security Agreement. This description is inadequate because it fails to identify which of the Debtor's thousands of railcars would be subject to Wells Fargo's lien such that any execution could occur. As a result, under case law interpreting the description requirement of the UCC, Wells Fargo did not obtain any enforceable security interest.

This Court must find that Wells Fargo failed to include an adequate description of the Equipment in its security agreement/s because of Well Fargo's failure to include descriptions of the Equipment in Loan #3711, and the ambiguities contained in the documents amending Loan #3711. As a result, Wells Fargo could not gain a security interest in the Equipment, and, thus, is not entitled to relief from the automatic stay on that collateral. Only Loan #3711, the Rental Rider, the July Rider, the Assignment Agreement, and the Substitution Agreement can be reviewed to determine the scope of Wells Fargo's collateral. The collateral's description cannot be construed based upon reference to the memoranda filed by the parties with the Surface Transportation Board ("STB"), the body with which secured creditors file memoranda to perfect liens regarding railcar and related collateral, for the purpose of perfecting Wells Fargo's purported security interest in the Collateral, by reference to later documents not prepared in conjunction with Loan #3711, or by reference to any other documents outside of the security agreements. Law interpreting the UCC clearly holds that parol evidence in the form of an additional loan document cannot be used to broaden the reach or cure defects in the collateral description in an otherwise clear security agreement.

As a result, Loan #3711, the Rental Rider, the July Rider, and the Assignment Agreement actually limit the scope of any purported security interest in favor of Wells Fargo to collateral described in those documents. It simply is not possible to identify the Equipment purportedly subject to a security interest in favor of Wells Fargo by reviewing those documents, because of the omission of any schedule of Equipment from Loan #3711, the ambiguities created by the documents that purport to modify and amend Loan #3711, and the inadmissibility of parol evidence to prove otherwise. Therefore, because Loan #3711 does not contain a description of the Equipment sufficient to permit a third party reasonably to identify the Equipment, there is no authenticated security agreement sufficient for a security interest to have attached to the Equipment. As a result, Wells Fargo does not have a valid security interest in the Equipment and its Motion for Relief from Stay should be denied as to that collateral.

BALDWIN v. CASTRO COUNTY FEEDERS I, LTD.

Supreme Court of South Dakota, 2004
2004 SD 43, 678 N.W.2d 796, 53 U.C.C. Rep. Serv. 2d 1

GILBERTSON, C.J.: A South Dakota circuit court determined Castro County Feeders I, Ltd. (Castro County) had an enforceable security interest in the proceeds of a sale of seventy-eight cattle owned by Ryan Baldwin (Baldwin). Baldwin sold the cattle through Livestock Sales in Wagner, South Dakota. On appeal, Baldwin argues the circuit court erred in finding that Castro County had a security interest in the cattle, and he also disputes the circuit court's conclusion that the proceeds of the sale were subject to arbitration. We affirm the judgment of the circuit court.

Both parties to this controversy reside in the State of Texas. Castro County runs a feedlot operation wherein it contracts to feed cattle placed in its lots as well as to provide the vitamins, minerals, and medicine necessary for the proper care of the cattle. Baldwin owns and operates a business specializing in the purchase and sale of cattle. As part of his business, Baldwin often placed his cattle with Castro County. Castro County would feed the livestock for a period of time and then release the cattle to Baldwin for transport and sale in Kansas. Generally, the sale proceeds were made payable to Baldwin and Castro County in order to reimburse it for the feed and related services provided to Baldwin's cattle.

Baldwin filed suit in circuit court seeking a Declaratory Judgment ordering Livestock Sales to release to him the proceeds of the sale. In response, Livestock Sales filed a motion to substitute parties and for removal of it as a defendant. Based upon stipulation of the parties, Livestock Sales was released from the action. Castro County was substituted as the only defendant in the action. Baldwin and Castro County stipulated to most of the facts in the case and agreed that only a question of law was before the court. After considering the facts, reviewing the relevant documents, and hearing argument of the parties, the circuit court found in favor of Castro County. The circuit court determined Castro County had a valid security interest in the cattle sold at Wagner. The circuit court also ruled the proceeds were subject to arbitration by the Texas Cattle Feeders Association as outlined by the Agreement executed by Baldwin and Castro County.

[Baldwin appealed the judgment of the circuit court and raised for review the issue of whether Castro County had a valid security interest in the proceeds of the sale of Baldwin's cattle.]

We review the circuit court's findings of fact under the clearly erroneous standard. The interpretation and application of South Dakota's statutes governing secured transactions require de novo review by this Court. Our construction of the state's commercial code is also guided by U.C.C. § 1-102 which provides in pertinent part:

(1) This title shall be liberally construed and applied to promote its underlying purposes and policies.
(2) Underlying purposes and policies of this title are
    (a) To simplify, clarify and modernize the law governing commercial transactions;
    (b) To permit the continued expansion of commercial practices through custom, usage and agreement of the parties;
    (c) To make uniform the law among the various jurisdictions[.]

The circuit court determined Castro County had a valid security interest in Baldwin's cattle sold in Wagner. South Dakota's codified version of Article 9 of the Uniform Commercial Code, governs secured transactions. Specifically, [§ 9-203(b)] lists three requirements that must be met before a security interest will be enforceable against a debtor. [The court then quotes from § 9-203(b).]

In this case, Castro County provided value in the form of feed and related services to the cattle in question. In fact, Castro County claims Baldwin owes it in excess of $94,000. Although Baldwin disagrees with this figure, he does not dispute that the owes Castro County some amount of money. Thus, the value-given requirement under subsection one is feedlots and clearly met. In addition, since Baldwin stipulated he owned the cattle placed in Castro County's feedlots and subsequently sold in South Dakota, the second requirement has been established.

The primary question Baldwin raises on appeal is whether the Agreement between himself and Castro County functions as a valid security agreement as required by § 9-203(b)(3)(A), set out above. First, Baldwin questions whether the Agreement was properly "authenticated." He points out the

Agreement twice refers to a "Rick Baldwin" as opposed to "Ryan Baldwin." A brief study of the document, however, shows "Ryan Baldwin" actually signed the document twice and scratched out the name "Rick" below the signature line. Furthermore, at trial Baldwin admitted he entered into the Agreement with Castro County and stipulated the document into evidence. Given these facts, we find Baldwin's argument that the Agreement was not authenticated to be without merit.

Second, Baldwin questions whether the Agreement provides a sufficient description of the collateral. [The court then quotes from §9-108.].

In particular, Baldwin argues the Agreement insufficiently described the collateral because it gave Castro County a security interest in all cattle "being specifically located in Lot(s) #_____ at Castro County Feeders, I, Ltd., Hart, Castro County, Texas." In other words, Baldwin believes the Agreement failed to sufficiently identify the cattle at issue in this case because it did not specify the feedlots in which his cattle were located. We disagree:

> The parties often adopt Code definitions to describe collateral in their security agreement. In many cases, a creditor argues that its interest in "inventory," "equipment," "general intangibles," "account," "proceeds," or such, includes the very property at issue and the debtor, bankruptcy trustee or other creditor(s) assert the contrary. Disputes of this nature should also be resolved by the Code's two-stage analysis: could the description plausibly be read to include the property claimed, and if so, did the parties so *intend?* In these cases, most courts resolve the problem solely as one of law.

4 White & Summers, *Uniform Commercial Code* § 31-3 (5th ed. 2002). To determine whether the description was sufficient, we must look to §9-108. Pursuant to subsection (a), the "test" for sufficiency is whether the description (specific or not) "reasonably identifies what is described." In the instant case, the description was "livestock." This is an example of an identification of collateral by category, which is specifically permitted under §9-108(b)(2). Comment 2 to §9-108 states:

> The purpose of requiring a description of collateral in a security agreement under Section 9-203 is evidentiary. The test of sufficiency of a description under this section, as under former Section 9-110, is that the description do the job assigned to it: make possible the identification of the collateral described. This section rejects any requirement that a description is insufficient unless it is exact and detailed (the so-called "serial number" test).

Moreover, "livestock" is included in the definition of "farm products". Therefore, even if the agreement had only provided for an interest in Baldwin's "farm products," the description would have been sufficient to include "livestock." In *Mushitz v. First Bank of South Dakota*, 457 N.W.2d 849, 853 (S.D. 1990) we held the description of "all farm machinery . . . and livestock owned by [debtor]" constituted a sufficient description of the collateral. We held that such descriptions reasonably identify what they describe.

Here, the Agreement did not attempt to give Castro County a security interest in all of Baldwin's property as prohibited by §9-108(c). Although the parties did not specify a particular lot or lots, the Agreement restricted the security interest to the cattle Baldwin delivered to Castro County's feedlot complex in the city of Hart, Texas. According to the Agreement, Baldwin also granted Castro County a security interest in the sale of these cattle. We believe this description was sufficient to make the collateral objectively determinable. A reasonable reading of the Agreement gave Castro County a security interest in only those cattle of Baldwin's to which it advanced feed and related services. It was not necessary for the agreement to list each individual head of livestock to which Castro County's security interest attached. Moreover, it was also reasonable for the Agreement to leave a specific lot number blank given the fact the cattle were not usually located in one of Castro County's lots when sold.

We believe the Agreement between Baldwin and Castro County constituted an authenticated security agreement that sufficiently described the collateral as those cattle to which Castro County provided feed and related services. Baldwin stipulated he owned the cattle placed at Castro County. Castro County provided value by advancing Baldwin's cattle feed and related services. Thus, the requirements for valid security interest as defined by §9-203 were met.

In this case, Baldwin delivered approximately 686 head of cattle to Castro County where they received feed and related care. By the terms of the Agreement, Castro County obtained a security interest in these cattle. Both parties agreed it was customary for Castro County to release Baldwin's cattle and then receive payment upon their sale in Kansas. When Castro County released the seventy-eight head of cattle at issue in this case, it retained a security interest in the proceeds of their sale. Here, the fact that Baldwin sold these cattle in South Dakota rather than Kansas did not change the nature of Castro County's security interest. We therefore affirm the judgment of the trial court on this issue.

QUESTION ON SOUTHERN ILLINOIS RAIL CAR AND BALDWIN

Do you believe these two cases to be inherently at odds with each other in their approaches to the problem at hand, or do you think there is a (legitimate and appropriate) way to reconcile them?

CHAPTER

6

"Value" Given and the Debtor's
"Rights In" the Collateral

A. INTRODUCTION

Attachment has been obtained by the secured party when, in addition to the existence of a security agreement as discussed in the previous chapter, the secured party has given value to the debtor and the debtor has rights in the collateral, unless the parties have expressly agreed to postpone the time of attachment to some later date.

The *value* requirement is usually not that difficult to deal with. Among other things, the secured party is presumably in a position to determine whether and when, if at all, it has given or is to give value to the debtor.

Whether the debtor has *rights in* the collateral — as that term is used in §9-203 but nowhere defined in Article 9 or anywhere else in the Uniform Commercial Code for that matter — can be a much trickier question. As you go through this material, you should be sure to give thought to what practical measures a potential lender will be able to and should take to minimize, even if it cannot entirely eliminate, the chances that it will later be proven wrong on whether the debtor ever had rights in or the right to grant a security interest in the all-important collateral.

B. PREPARATION

In preparation read carefully the following parts of the Code:

- Section 1-201(44) or §1R-204
- Section 9-203(b)
- Section 9-204(a) & (b) along with Comments 2 and 3 to this section

C.   PROBLEMS AND CASES

PROBLEMS

6.1   Gabriela opens a small restaurant, Gabriela's Place, using all of her savings to buy the initial furnishings for the place, its dining room and kitchen. After one particularly enthusiastic review in the city's major newspaper, the restaurant becomes one of the hottest spots in town. People are waiting on long lines to get a table and reservations are even harder to come by. Gabriela notes that there is a vacant retail space directly adjacent to hers, and she begins to consider expanding the size of her enterprise. To do so, however, she will need additional capital. She applies to the Springfield State Bank for a small business loan. After a thorough investigation of her finances and her current set-up, the bank loan officer determines that her loan request should be approved and on what terms. He explains these to Gabriela over the telephone and she says she is willing to borrow on the basis the loan manager has laid out. Gabriela comes into the bank. She signs a note made payable "to the order of Springfield State Bank" for $50,000, payable in specified monthly installments based on a stated rate of interest. She also signs a security agreement granting the bank a security interest in her "equipment, now held and hereafter acquired." The loan officer hands over to her a check for $50,000.

(a) As of this moment does the bank have a security interest which has attached to the tables, chairs, stoves, and so on now in her Place?

(b) Does it now have a security interest in the fresh fish, meat, and vegetables in her restaurant's refrigerator?

(c) While Gabriela is no doubt pleased to have the equivalent of $50,000 cash in hand as she walks out the door of the bank, can you think of any practical reason why this might not be the best way to have the loan money disbursed to her?

(d) What if instead, after Gabriela signs the note and the security agreement, the loan officer signs and gives to her a paper stating that the bank has granted her a "guaranteed line of credit" good for up to $50,000. She can call on this credit at any time when the need arises in conjunction with her expanding business. She can also pay down the amount of her outstanding obligation whenever she finds her business has sufficient extra cash on hand. Would this be a better way for her to take advantage of the credit the bank is willing to grant her?

(e) Assume that the situation is as laid out in part (d) above. Gabriela leaves the bank having been formally granted a line of credit, but she has yet to draw on the credit at all. She has yet to receive any cash or pay any bills with the available credit to which the bank has legally committed itself.

As of this moment does the bank have a security interest in all, or indeed in any, of Gabriela's present equipment?

6.2   While posing as just another interested customer at the jewelry counter of Sarah's Sells-U-Stuff, Theo takes advantage of a moment when the sales clerk is distracted to deftly take for himself a valuable star sapphire pendant of considerable value. He leaves the store without his theft being noticed. Theo then goes to Friendly Finance, a lender in a nearby town, where he arranges to borrow $14,000 from that firm putting up the pendant as collateral. He even gives the lender possession of the bauble to seal the deal. Has a security interest in favor of Friendly Finance attached to the star sapphire pendant in its possession?

NATIONAL PAWN BROKERS UNLIMITED v. OSTERMAN, INC.
Court of Appeals of Wisconsin, 1993
176 Wis. 2d 418, 500 N.W.2d 407, 21 U.C.C. Rep. Serv. 2d 1176

GARTZKE, P.J.: National Pawn Brokers and Hull Loan Systems ("pawn-brokers") appeal from a circuit court order returning jewelry to Oster-man, Inc. The jewelry was evidence in a trial on criminal charges against Donald Pippin. He had obtained it from Osterman, a retail jeweler in Madison, Wisconsin, by paying with a bad check and then pawned it to appellants in Minnesota. Both sides claim a security interest in the jewelry. We hold that the pawnbrokers' security interest are prior to Osterman's. We reverse.

[The one issue considered by the court which we look at here — there is more to come in later chapters — is whether Pippin had rights in the jewelry to which the pawnbrokers' security interests could attach, even though Osterman had reserved title to the jewelry and had prohibited its transfer until the purchase price was fully paid. The court concluded that Pippin did have such rights in the jewelry.]

The pertinent facts are undisputed. On November 24, 1990, Pippin purchased the jewelry from Osterman in Madison. The purchase price was $39,750.38. Pippin signed three documents in connection with the sale. The first was a credit application. It provides personal information regarding Pippin, including his Menomonie, Wisconsin, address and describes the jewelry. The second was a sales agreement. It describes the items sold, the purchase price, the amount paid by check and the balance payable under a "Super Charge" agreement. It provides,

> The balance due on this purchase is payable in installments under my credit plan contract and security agreement which is incorporated herein by reference. I agree that seller shall retain ownership of the items so purchased until entire balance is fully paid. . . .

The third was a "Super Charge Retail Charge Agreement," by which Pippin agreed that in consideration of the sale,

> A security interest in each item of goods purchased hereunder and the proceeds thereof shall remain with Seller until the unpaid balance directly relating to each such item of goods purchased is fully paid. Buyer will not dispose of the goods . . . or encumber them without written consent of Seller . . . until Buyer has fully paid for them.

Pippin paid Osterman $30,000 by check, and agreed to pay the balance in installments. The check was drawn on a closed account. On November 27, 1990, he pawned some of the jewelry to National in Bloomington, Minnesota, for a $6,995 loan and on November 30, 1990, he pawned the remaining items to Hull in Minneapolis for a $2,076.04 loan. He signed a promissory note and security agreement with Hull. No written security agreement with National is of record. On December 6, 1990, a criminal complaint issued in Dane County, Wisconsin, charging Pippin with violating sec. 943.24(2), Stats. (1989-90), issuing a check payable for more than $500, intending it not be paid. Having learned that Pippin had pawned the jewelry, the Madison police requested the Minnesota police to obtain a search warrant directed to the pawnbrokers' businesses. The Minnesota police did so, and on December 11, 1990, they seized the jewelry from the pawnbrokers and turned it over to the Madison police the next day. On December 13, 1990, the Madison police delivered the jewelry to Osterman but retook it the next day for use as evidence at the criminal trial. Pippin was convicted.

On December 26, 1990, the pawnbrokers petitioned the Dane County Circuit Court for Dane County, Wisconsin, for return of the jewelry. On February 12, 1991, Osterman also petitioned for its return. . . . On July 25, 1991, the pawnbrokers petitioned the Minnesota court which issued the search warrant for return of the jewelry to that court. On August 13, 1991, the Dane County Circuit Court entered the order before us on appeal, and on October 22, 1991, the Minnesota court denied the pawnbrokers' petition to it because they had chosen to litigate the matter in Wisconsin.

[The court first considered a jurisdictional challenge made by the pawnbrokers, but "declined to pursue the pawnbrokers' claim that this case belongs in Minnesota."]

A security interest is not enforceable against the debtor or third parties with respect to the collateral and does not attach unless the debtor signed a security agreement containing a description of the collateral or the collateral is in the possession of the secured party pursuant to agreement, value was given, and "the debtor has rights in the collateral."

Osterman asserts that the third requirement — the debtor has rights in the collateral — has not been met for the pawnbrokers' security interests to attach to the collateral. Osterman relies on the sales agreement which provides that Osterman retains ownership of the jewelry until the purchase price is fully paid, and on its security agreement which prohibits Pippin from disposing of the jewelry without Osterman's consent.

Article 9 of the Uniform Commercial Code does not define "rights in the collateral." Because Osterman's transaction with Pippin was a sale, Article 2 determines whether he had such rights. Osterman's sales agreement and security agreement do not affect Pippin's rights in the collateral. The debtor's "rights" in the collateral do not depend on whether the debtor has title to it. "Each provision of this Article with regard to . . . rights . . . applies irrespective of title to the goods. . . ." U.C.C. § 2-401.

Article 2 converts Osterman's retention of title into a security interest. "Any retention or reservation by the seller of the title (property) in goods shipped or delivered to the buyer is limited in effect to a reservation of a security interest." U.C.C. § 2-401(1). The attempted prohibition of sale in Osterman's security agreement is part of its security interest. A debtor may transfer its rights in collateral notwithstanding a provision in the security agreement prohibiting the transfer. [Citing the precursor to present § 9-401.]

Pippin had voidable title to the collateral because he procured it by a dishonored check. That was the rule at common law and is the rule under Article 2. "A person with voidable title has power to transfer a good title to a good faith purchaser for value. When goods have been delivered under a transaction of purchase the purchaser has such power even though . . . (b) the delivery was in exchange for a check which is later dishonored. . . ." U.C.C. § 2-403(1). Pippin therefore possessed the power to transfer title to a good faith purchaser for value.

Possessing the power under U.C.C. § 2-403(1) to transfer good title to a good faith purchaser for value, Pippin had the power and the right to transfer a security interest to a creditor, including an Article 9 secured party. *In re Samuels & Co.*, 526 F.2d 1238, 1243 (5th Cir. 1976) (en banc) (per curiam). Consequently, Pippin's rights in the collateral were sufficient to allow attachment of a security interest.

Because Pippin had a right in the jewelry purchased by a bad check from Osterman's, the pawnbrokers' security interests attached to the jewelry. . . . The interests of the pawnbrokers have priority over Osterman's interest. For that reason, the trial court erred when it ordered that possession of the collateral, the jewelry, be granted to Osterman's. On remand, the trial court shall enter judgment giving possession to the pawnbrokers.

Judgment reversed and remanded for further proceedings consistent with this opinion.

QUESTIONS ON NATIONAL PAWN BROKERS

What good reason can you see for the result in this case being different from what you concluded (I hope) in Problem 6.2? Would you call the reason you come up with a matter of practicality or of policy? In a situation like this, is there any need to distinguish between the two?

JERKE CONSTRUCTION, INC. v. HOME FEDERAL SAVINGS BANK

Supreme Court of South Dakota, 2005
2005 SD 19, 693 N.W.2d 59, 56 U.C.C. Rep. Serv. 2d 125

TICE, Circuit Judge: Home Federal Savings Bank, Inc. (Bank) appeals from an order entered against it in a declaratory judgment action initiated by Jerke Construction Corporation (Jerke). Jerke sought to establish its ownership of a bulldozer it had placed in the possession of Justin Peck (Peck), who in turn had offered the machine as collateral to Bank as security for a loan. Having concluded that no security interest attached to the machinery and that Jerke owned the bulldozer, the trial court ordered that Jerke was entitled to possession of the equipment. We affirm that order.

On December 4, 1995, Peck entered into a written agreement with Sweetman Corporation (Sweetman) to purchase a D-9 Caterpiller bulldozer (D-9) from Sweetman for $20,000. On December 12, 1995, Jerke provided a $6,000 check to Sweetman as a down payment on the D-9. On February 22, 1996, Jerke paid Diesel Machinery, Inc. $12,238.17 to fix the transmission on the D-9. On March 13, 1996, Jerke issued a check to Sweetman in the amount of $14,000 as the final payment on the D-9. Sweetman thereupon issued a bill of sale to Jerke for the D-9. In the spring of 1996, the D-9 was delivered to Peck. The D-9 remained in his possession from the time of the repair of the transmission until March 17, 1999, when Jerke physically took possession of the D-9.

Peck testified that the monies paid by Jerke were a loan to him in order that he might purchase the D-9. He further testified that it was agreed that he would reimburse Jerke by using the D-9 on Jerke jobs. This was referred to by Peck as a bartering agreement. Though Peck testified that he had completely reimbursed Jerke for the cost of the D-9, the records indicate that, at most, credit could be given by Jerke for somewhere between $14,000 and $18,000 for the work done by Peck. This was testified to by Peck.

Bank produced no evidence that Peck submitted billings or documents to Jerke indicating that his work with the D-9 was done to offset a financial obligation he owed to Jerke. The total amount paid out by Jerke for the D-9 and its repairs prior to delivery to Peck was $32,238.17. There was no written financing agreement in existence, nor was there any evidence presented as to what the terms of such an agreement might have been. No evidence at the trial established interest rates, methods of repayment, or a timeline for repayment of the alleged loan. No records suggested that Peck had an ownership interest in the D-9 other than the original purchase agreement between Peck and Sweetman.

Evidence clearly indicated that some work on behalf of Jerke was done with the D-9 under Peck's supervision. The value of that work was considerably less, however, than the $32,238.17 that the D-9 originally cost Jerke. While Peck testified that he had used the D-9 for non-Jerke projects during his three year possession, he provided no details regarding those projects.

Peck was aware that Jerke received a bill of sale from Sweetman upon the final $14,000 payment. There was no evidence that he sought to obtain a bill of sale from Jerke for himself. Peck never claimed any income tax benefit for depreciation on the D-9 nor did he give any other indication in tax documents that the D-9 was his. He was aware of the fact that Jerke was declaring the D-9 as its property and was depreciating the D-9 for income tax purposes.

On March 9, 1999, Peck obtained a $400,000 loan from Bank secured by his assets. His list of assets included the D-9. At the time of the agreement with Bank, the D-9 was on Peck's property. The only time the D-9 was observed by anyone connected with Bank was in December 1998. Bank never sought to obtain any evidence of ownership, such as a bill of sale, other than accepting the listing submitted by Peck at the time of the issuance of the loan. There was no evidence that Bank had any knowledge whatsoever of the original purchase of the D-9, nor of the use of the D-9 at any time. Bank did a UCC search of Peck's property which was referred to at some points as a title search. In the course of the UCC search, no liens against the D-9 were found that named Peck as the owner. The only evidence Bank had of the D-9's existence was the one observation in December 1998 and Peck's listing of it in his application for the loan obtained on March 9, 1999. On March 17, 1999, Jerke's employees serviced the D-9 on Peck's property and then proceeded to remove it to Jerke's property without Peck's permission.

Subsequent to a court trial, the court found, among other things, that Jerke had merely given Peck naked possession of the D-9, and that he did not possess sufficient rights in the collateral to which a security interest could attach. Further, the court found that, contrary to Bank's argument, Jerke was not estopped from challenging the validity of the security interest. On appeal, Bank argues that Peck owned the D-9 pursuant to the purchase agreement with Sweetman and a financing agreement with Jerke. Thus, it argues that Peck had sufficient rights in the collateral for a security interest to attach. Moreover, Bank argues that Jerke allowed Peck to appear to be the owner of the D-9 and should, therefore, be estopped from disputing the validity of the security interest.

ISSUE ONE: WHETHER PECK HAD RIGHTS IN THE COLLATERAL.

This case first requires us to examine the trial court's determination of whether Peck possessed rights in the collateral to which Bank could attach a security interest. We have previously noted that under § 9-203: "To claim a valid, perfected security interest in collateral, the security interest must attach to the collateral. A security interest attaches when (1) there is an agreement that it attach; (2) value has been given by the secured party; and (3) the debtor has rights in the collateral." *First Nat. Bank of Philip v. Temple*, 2002 SD 36, P 22, 642 N.W.2d 197, 204.

The phrase "rights in the collateral" describes the range of transferable interests that a debtor may possess in property. For example, such rights may be as comprehensive as full ownership of property with legal title or as limited as a license. "Essentially, the debtor normally can only convey something once it has something and that something may be less than the full bundle of rights that one may hold in such property." *Id.* Formal title is not required for a debtor to have rights in collateral. An equitable interest can suffice. On the other hand, mere naked possession does not create "rights in the collateral."

Against this background, this Court first addresses a key finding of fact, namely that Peck only had naked possession of the D-9. As already mentioned, naked possession cannot support a finding of rights in collateral. Hence, if the trial court's finding on this question is correct, its conclusion that no security interest could attach to the D-9 must be upheld.

The record supports the finding that Peck only had naked possession of the D-9. As between Jerke and Peck, Peck's conduct consistently established an intent not to claim direct ownership of the D-9. Though he maintained possession of it from the effective date of purchase until removal after the security agreement was entered into, he did nothing else to establish or indicate a belief that he was the owner of the D-9. He never sought to have Jerke provide him with a bill of sale or other indicia of ownership, he never sought to confirm a financing agreement of any kind with Jerke and he never claimed depreciation on the D-9 for income tax purposes. In addition, he never came close to paying the entire cost of the original acquisition of the D-9. Though he did on occasion use it for his personal interest, it appears to have been used more substantially for Jerke's benefit. Also, Peck never provided notice of any kind to Jerke of the set-off he claimed for the work he performed with the D-9 until a document for the purpose of this case was prepared in January 1999.

In addition to these facts, Bank failed to prove that Peck possessed a contractual right to the D-9. Despite the existence of the document identifying Sweetman and Peck as the parties to the agreement for Peck's purchase of the machine, Jerke subsequently wrote the check, received the bill of sale and claimed depreciation expenses on the equipment. This provided a prima facie showing that, notwithstanding the preliminary contractual document, Jerke became the owner of the D-9. Once that showing was made, the burden shifted to Bank to show that, by means of a financing agreement or otherwise, Peck possessed rights in the collateral. Bank failed to meet the burden of showing that Peck had rights in the collateral.

The evidence demonstrated that Peck abandoned the preliminary contract with Sweetman. Bank failed to prove the terms of any sort of financing agreement between Peck and Jerke, including the exact amount of money involved, the interest rate and the time and terms of repayment. Since the evidence regarding the alleged agreement was too vague to show that Peck possessed any contractual right in the D-9, that evidence was necessarily too vague to show that he had rights in the collateral to which a security interest could attach.

Based upon the foregoing, the trial court did not err in concluding that no security interest attached to the D-9 as Peck had only naked possession and nothing more.

ISSUE TWO: WHETHER JERKE SHOULD HAVE BEEN ESTOPPED FROM DISPUTING THE VALIDITY OF THE SECURITY INTEREST.

Bank also argues that Jerke should have been estopped from disputing the existence of a valid security interest in the D-9. Generally, if an owner of property effectively allows a debtor to appear as the owner of that property, and that appearance misleads a creditor, the owner may be estopped to deny the effectiveness of a security interest taken on the property by the creditor. As we have previously stated,

> If the owner of collateral allows another to appear as the owner or to dispose of the collateral, such that a third party is led into dealing with the apparent owner as though he were the actual owner, then the owner will be estopped from asserting that the apparent owner did not have rights in the collateral.

American Bank & Trust v. Shaull, 2004 SD 40 at P 16, 678 N.W.2d 779, 784, quoting *Pleasant View Farms, Inc. v. Ness,* 455 N.W.2d 602, 604 (SD 1990). In that regard, "control rather than ownership of collateral determines a debtor's rights to collateral."

Estoppel may not apply, however, if the allegedly misled creditor failed to make reasonable efforts to ascertain the ownership of the collateral. For example, in *First National Bank of Omaha v. Pleasant Hollow Farm,* 532 N.W.2d 60, 64 (SD 1995), the court determined that estoppel prevented a party from disputing a bank's security interest. The court noted in its decision that there was no showing that the bank "could have reasonably discovered" that a party other than the debtor possessed an interest in the property. *Id.* *See also Rohweder,* 765 F.2d at 113 (in general, the party asserting an estoppel must be without convenient access to knowledge contrary to the facts on which he relied).

The trial court determined in its conclusions of law that Jerke "did not allow Peck to appear as the owner of the (D-9) such as to mislead Home Federal." The court also found that the bank representative had witnessed the D-9 sitting idly on Peck's land, but that no evidence indicated that Bank had knowledge of Peck's operation of the D-9 on Jerke jobs. In addition, the court found that Bank's belief that Peck owned the D-9 was based primarily on Peck's word. Moreover, in the trial court's memorandum opinion, which was incorporated in the findings and conclusions, the court noted that "a more thorough investigation would have put Home Federal on notice of

Jerke's claim to the (D-9)." Consequently, the court concluded that estoppel was inapplicable. Though this is denominated as a conclusion regarding the appearance of ownership, it is more properly characterized as a finding of fact.

The record supports the finding that Jerke did not allow Peck to appear as the owner. Bank unconvincingly asserts, in effect, that it was misled by the conduct of Jerke in leaving the D-9 with Peck for three years. Bank failed, however, to show anything more than its observation of the D-9 on Peck's property three months before the loan was made, and that a UCC search discovered no liens on the machine. Under the circumstances of this case, the mere presence of the machinery on the property did not alone establish an estoppel.

The evidence supports the trial court's finding that Jerke did not cause Peck to appear as the owner of the D-9. Therefore, the court did not err in concluding that estoppel did not apply.

Affirmed.

QUESTION ON JERKE CONSTRUCTION

Had you been counseling the Bank at the time it made the loan to Peck, what would you have suggested it do differently, or in addition to what it apparently did do, to avoid the result of this case?

FIFTH THIRD BANK v. COMARK, INC.

Court of Appeals of Indiana, 2003
794 N.E.2d 433, 51 U.C.C. Rep. Serv. 2d 533

SHARPNACK, J.: Fifth Third Bank ("Fifth Third") appeals the trial court's grant of summary judgment to Comark, Inc., ("Comark"), denial of summary judgment to Fifth Third, and denial of Fifth Third's motion to correct error. Fifth Third raises two issues, which we restate as:

I. Whether the trial court erred by finding that Comark had a security interest in collateral owned by Vertica Solutions, LLC; and

II. Whether the trial court erred by finding that Fifth Third, as a creditor of Vertica Solutions, Inc., had no security interest in the collateral owned by Vertica Solutions, LLC.

We affirm.

The relevant facts designated by the parties follow. Vertica Solutions, LLC ("Vertica, LLC") was organized in October 1999. Christopher Heath is a principal and founding member of Vertica, LLC. Heath also incorporated Vertica Solutions, Inc., ("Vertica, Inc.") "as a vehicle to receive venture capital." Vertica, Inc., never operated as a business, held any assets, issued any stock, or held a meeting of board members or shareholders.

In July 2000, Vertica, LLC, purchased computer products from Comark for $2,800,000.00. Vertica, LLC, granted a security interest to Comark. The Comark security agreement identified the collateral as [all of the computer products purchased by Vertica, LLC from Comark].

In November 2000, Fifth Third loaned $250,000.00 to Vertica, Inc. In making the loan, Fifth Third met with Brian Joseph Locke and Tyrone Owens to discuss the business strategy of Vertica, Inc., visited the offices of Vertica, LLC, and reviewed computer equipment located in the offices. According to a website designated as simply "Vertica Solutions" without a corporate designation, Owens was the technology leader of "Vertica Solutions." Owens's business card identified him as the president and chief technology officer of "Vertica Solutions." Locke signed the promissory note and security agreement as CEO of Vertica, Inc. However, Locke was never a CEO, shareholder, or officer of Vertica, Inc., and Vertica, Inc., "never granted Locke the authority to enter into an agreement on behalf of" Vertica, Inc.

[Fifth Third apparently never entered into a security agreement with Vertica, LLC. It did, however, file an initial financial statement — the precise significance of which we'll see later — indicating it believed itself to have a security interest in all of the computer equipment owned by Vertica, Inc.]

After Vertica, Inc., defaulted on the loan, Fifth Third filed a complaint against Vertica, Inc., Locke, Owens, and Comark. Fifth Third obtained a default judgment against Vertica, Inc., entered into an agreed judgment with Locke, and obtained summary judgment against Owens. Comark filed a motion for summary judgment alleging, in part, that Fifth Third had a security interest in nonexistent collateral owned by Vertica, Inc., rather than collateral owned by Vertica, LLC, being held by Comark. Thus, Comark alleged that it was entitled to summary judgment on Fifth Third's claim to Vertica, LLC's collateral. . . . Fifth Third further alleged that it had a proper security interest in the collateral owned by Vertica, LLC.

The trial court entered findings of fact and conclusions thereon granting Comark's motion for summary judgment and denying Fifth Third's motion for summary judgment. [The trial court found that Comark had a valid security interest in the collateral at issue (computer products purchased by Vertica, LLC from Comark in July 2000 for $2,800,000) and had priority over any other claim against that collateral. It also ruled that First Third had no valid interest in this collateral.]

[The Court of Appeals first considered whether the trial court had been correct in determining that Comark had a security interest in all the computer collateral owned by Vertica, LLC giving it priority over any other party. It found the trial court to have been correct and that, consequently, the trial court had not erred by granting summary judgment to Comark.]

The next issue is whether the trial court erred by finding that Fifth Third, as a creditor of Vertica, Inc., had no security interest in the collateral owned by Vertica, LLC. The trial court found that, although Fifth Third filed a financing statement regarding its security interest in Vertica, Inc.'s "inventory, chattel paper, accounts, equipment, general intangibles, securities, investment properties and financial assets," Vertica, Inc., possessed no such assets. Further, the trial court found that:

> There is no designated evidence that the Bank had a security agreement or an UCC-1 Financing Statement relating to any property of Vertica, LLC. . . . Thus, this Court finds that Fifth Third does not have a security interest in the computer products purchased by Vertica, LLC, from Comark, Inc. in July 2000.

Fifth Third argues that Vertica, Inc., had rights to Vertica, LLC's Comark computer products. Under [§ 9-203], a security interest is not enforceable and does not attach unless the "debtor has rights in the collateral." Fifth Third points out that "rights in the collateral" does not necessarily mean "title" to the collateral. Fifth Third argues that Vertica, LLC, allowed Vertica, Inc., to appear as the owner of the Comark computer products. Specifically, Fifth Third argues that Vertica, LLC, permitted Owens "access to the Vertica, LLC, facility and equipment so that Fifth Third was led into dealing with the apparent owner, Vertica, Inc." Fifth Third argues that Vertica, LLC, did not "control the use of its name" and often "held itself out as" Vertica Solutions without a corporate designation. Thus, according to Fifth Third, Vertica, LLC, is "estopped from asserting that Fifth Third does not have rights in the Primary Collateral." Comark responds that Fifth Third designated no genuine issues of material fact to support its arguments.

Fifth Third relies upon *Pubs, Inc. of Champaign v. Bank of Ill. Champaign*, 618 F.2d 432 (7th Cir. 1980), and *In re Standard Foundry Prod., Inc.*, 206 B.R. 475 (N.D. Ill. 1997), reconsideration denied by 208 B.R. 164 (Bankr. N.D. Ill. 1997). In *Pubs*, Hein and Richardson, two directors, officers, and sole shareholders of a corporation, agreed to purchase restaurant equipment. Hein executed a promissory note and granted a security interest in restaurant equipment to the Bank. Hein and Richardson then sold the collateral to Pubs subject to the security interest. Richardson did not sign the promissory note until after the collateral was transferred. Pubs later filed for bankruptcy protection, and the trustee argued that a security interest did not attach because Richardson no longer had "rights in the collateral" when he signed the promissory note.

The Seventh Circuit held that "the requirement that there be 'rights in the collateral' illustrates the general principle that 'one cannot encumber another man's property in the absence of consent, estoppel or some other special rule.'" Estoppel was at issue in the case, and the Seventh Circuit noted that the doctrine of estoppel "is based upon the conduct of the true owner, whereby he has allowed another to appear as the owner, or as having full power of disposition over the property, so that an innocent person is led into dealing with such apparent owner." The court concluded that Pubs had notice of the security interest and was "chargeable with the knowledge of its officers and directors." Thus, "Pubs was estopped to deny the Bank's security interest and this estoppel gave Hein and Richardson 'rights in the collateral' within the meaning of §9-203 so the Bank's security interest attached to the collateral and was enforceable against Hein, Richardson, Pubs, and other parties, including the trustee."

In *Standard Foundry Products,* the company used certain equipment as collateral for a loan. However, the principals' son owned the equipment. The son was a former officer of the company. The son argued that he allowed his parents to use his equipment but did not authorize them to pledge the equipment as collateral. The Bank argued that the son was "estopped from denying that the assets were encumbered because he allowed the company to appear as the owner of the property and consented to the pledge of the disputed equipment to the Bank by the company as collateral for the loan."

The bankruptcy court noted that "rights in the collateral" has generally been recognized to include: (1) the debtor has possession and title to the goods; (2) the true owner consents to the debtor's use of the collateral as security; or (3) the true owner is estopped from denying the creation of the security interest. The court found that the son consented to the company's use and possession of the equipment, which created the appearance of ownership of the equipment in the company. Thus, the company had "rights in the collateral." However, in determining whether the son was estopped from asserting his ownership, the court found that the record was devoid of any evidence that the Bank was somehow misled by the son's silence into believing his items of equipment were actually owned by the company. Consequently, the court entered judgment for the son.

Here, no evidence was designated demonstrating that Vertica, LLC, "consented" to Vertica, Inc., encumbering its property. Further, no evidence was designated demonstrating that Vertica, Inc., was in possession of the equipment. As for estoppel, our supreme court has held that estoppel exists "if one party through his course of conduct knowingly misleads or induces another party to believe and act upon his conduct in good faith without knowledge of the facts." *Levin v. Levin,* 645 N.E.2d 601, 604 (Ind. 1994). No evidence was designated demonstrating that Vertica, LLC, knowingly misled or induced Fifth Third. In fact, no evidence was designated that Vertica, LLC, permitted Vertica, Inc., to appear as the owner of the computer products or that Vertica, LLC, had notice of the security interest established by Vertica, Inc. Rather, the designated evidence demonstrated that Locke, who signed the security agreement as CEO of Vertica, Inc., was never a CEO, shareholder, or officer of Vertica, Inc., and Vertica, Inc., "never granted Locke the authority to enter into an agreement on behalf of" Vertica, Inc.

Consequently, no evidence was designated demonstrating that Vertica, Inc., had "rights in the collateral" owned by Vertica, LLC. The trial court did not err by finding that, under the designated evidence, Fifth Third did not have a security interest in the computer products purchased by Vertica, LLC. Consequently, the trial court did not err by denying Fifth Third's motion for summary judgment because Fifth Third was not entitled to judgment as a matter of law.

For the foregoing reasons, we affirm the trial court's grant of Comark's motion for summary judgment and the trial court's denial of Fifth Third's motion for summary judgment.

Affirmed.

QUESTION ON FIFTH THIRD BANK

Had you been counseling Fifth Third Bank at the time it made the loan to Vertica Solutions, Inc., what would you have suggested it do differently, or in addition to what it apparently did do, to avoid the result of this case?

PROBLEMS

6.3 When Louie first opened his small jewelry boutique in 1992, Louie's of Litchfield, he was able to do so by obtaining a Small Business Line of Credit from First Bank of Connecticut. He granted the bank at the time a security interest in "all inventory now held or after-acquired" of his business. Over the years, Louie has proven a good customer of the bank. He regularly makes his monthly payments based on the rate of interest provided for in his loan agreement and the amount of credit he has outstanding at any given time. As a result, the Bank has steadily raised his guaranteed credit limit so that it now stands at $200,000, not all of which Louie is currently using. Bucky, a local farmer, comes into the store, and shows Louie a large broach which he has just received as his inheritance from a distance relative. It is obviously of significant value, but Bucky says that he has absolutely no use for it. He tells Louie that he has gotten it appraised by "a major jeweler in the big city" which offered him $8,000 for the piece. Louie says that he finds that a reasonable price and offers to buy it from him on the spot. Bucky agrees. He gives Louie the broach and Louie writes him a check for the price out of the Line of Credit he has with First Bank. Does First Bank's security interest attach to this particular piece of jewelry? As of when?

6.4 Leah Cashmore, a woman of fashion, finds herself temporarily in need of funds. She arranges for a representative of Discreet Financial Services to visit her home. She allows this representative to examine her small but highly selective collection of personal jewelry, which she keeps in a safe in her library. She arranges for a loan from DFS and grants to that firm a security interest in "all of my jewelry, now held or hereafter-acquired." About six months later, Leah is given a diamond bracelet, "just a small token really," by the members of her family on her sixtieth birthday. Does DFS's security interest attach to this bracelet? If so, when? If not, why not?

QUESTION ON § 9-204(b)

This provision was one of the few instances of what we might call consumer protection written into the original Article 9, and as you can see it has been retained in the Revised version. Why do you believe the drafters thought it worthy of inclusion? Is it potentially unfair to those, like DFS in the preceding problem, who are willing to lend to consumers based on their offering up some subset of their consumer property — probably all they have of significant value — as collateral?

CHAPTER

7

Introduction to the Purchase-Money
Security Interest

A. INTRODUCTION

Under pre-Code law, in the original version of Article 9, and now in the current version of that article, an individual security interest may be specially classified as being what is termed a *purchase-money security interest*. Note that for an interest to qualify as a PMSI, as it's often abbreviated, a creditor's interest must first and foremost be a security interest under Article 9. It must have attached just like any other security interest. It then must also meet the further criteria as set forth in §9-103.

We will not discuss in this chapter the importance of a security interest's being classified as that special type called a PMSI—*why* it matters is something that will come up in a number of later chapters. For the moment, it is sufficient if you accept as a given that whether a security interest is or is not a PMSI can be crucially important for a number of matters governed by Article 9 directly, as we will see, or for other issues that fall more properly withing the realm of bankruptcy law.

In this chapter, our object is only to be able to identify a PMSI when we run into one — or how to be sure we have created such an interest on behalf of a secured party when that is the intended result.

B. PREPARATION

In preparation read carefully the following parts of the Code:

- Section 9-103(a) & (b)(1) and Comment 3 to that section

C.   PROBLEMS AND CASES

PROBLEMS

7.1   Carlos enters into an agreement to buy a new car from the Spiffy New and Used Cars of Springfield dealership. He signs a note under which he will pay for the car through 48 monthly payments to Spiffy. The monthly payments are calculated by Spiffy based on the initial amount he is borrowing, $20,000, plus a given rate of interest and certain specified fees. Carlos also signs a paper under which he grants Spiffy a security interest in the very car he is purchasing, the security interest being given to secure Carlos's obligation to make his monthly payments to Spiffy. Is the security interest granted to Spiffy a purchase-money security interest?

7.2   Suppose that instead of financing his purchase through the dealership, Carlos decides to take out a car loan from his bank, First Federal of Springfield. He fills out a loan application stating that he wishes to borrow $20,000 from the bank which he will repay (including of course interest and fees) over 48 months. He states that his purpose in obtaining the loan is to purchase a certain automobile, which is described by make, model, and serial number, from Spiffy New and Used Cars. He also signs a security agreement which grants the Bank a security interest in the car — again well described — to secure his obligation to make his monthly payments to the Bank. He receives from the Bank a certified check made out "to the order of Carlos" for $20,000. Carlos immediately takes this check to Spiffy and indorses it over to the dealership. All other paperwork being complete, Spiffy gives him the keys to the car and a certificate of title showing that he is owner of the car. Carlos drives away in his new car.

(a) Under these facts is the Bank's security interest a purchase-money security interest?

(b) Now let's change the facts. Carlos takes the check given him by the bank and cashes it at a check-cashing establishment. He then heads directly to the local casino, which is a perfectly legal operation having been authorized by the state legislature to generate more money for education. Naturally (as he expects) Carlos quickly doubles his money. He then takes a limo to Spiffy's dealership where he gives Spiffy $20,000 of his winnings. Spiffy gives him the car, the title, and the keys, and Carlos drives off to spend the rest of his winnings in various ways. Does the Bank have a purchase-money security interest in the car under this scenario?

(c) Change the facts again: Now when Carlos goes to the casino he naturally (as we would expect) loses all of the $20,000 he got from the bank in short order. He takes a bus home. He realizes that in order to avoid any legal trouble or embarrassment he will still have to make the monthly payments he promised to the Bank, only now to pay off his gambling losses, not as car payments. Does the Bank have a purchase-money security interest here?

(d) The facts remain as in (c), except that when Carlos tells his mother about his shameful behavior she insists that, if for no other reason than to avoid embarrassment to the family in the small town of Springfield where news travels fast, she give him $20,000 from her savings. Carlos defers to his mother and takes the money. He immediately goes to the Spiffy dealership and hands the $20,000 over to Spiffy. Spiffy hands over the car, the title, and the keys to Carlos. Carlos drives the car off the dealer's lot. Does the Bank have a purchase-money security interest in the car?

(e) Finally, suppose you were counseling the loan officer at First Federal of Springfield. What practical means might you suggest she take as a matter of course in dealing with loans like those being offered to Carlos to avoid the kind of potential problems suggested by parts (b), (c), and (d) above?

7.3   Ben arranges to buy a new lawnmower from Sarah's Sells-U-Stuff to replace his current mower which has just broken down irretrievably. Sarah takes out a form headed "E-Z Pay Monthly Payment Plan Agreement." She quickly fills in a few blank spaces on the form, giving a description of the particular mower as the goods being sold, Ben's name and address as that of the buyer, and specifying six monthly payments which Ben will agree to make to Sarah. The form also states in that, "The parties hereto agree that title to any merchandise made the subject of this agreement will remain in the Seller until Buyer has made full and final payment of all amounts due hereunder." Ben signs this agreement and takes the new lawnmower away with him in the trunk of his car. Does Sarah have a purchase-money security interest in the mower?

7.4   Gabriela owns and operates a restaurant, Gabriela's Place. As part of her plan to redecorate the place, she contacts the firm of Restaurant Supplies Unlimited and orders from the firm's catalogue a large number of new brightly colored tablecloths and matching napkins. All this linen is delivered to her restaurant along with an invoice that calls for her to pay a given amount within 60 days of her receipt of the merchandise. Upon Gabriela's receipt of the new linens, does Restaurant Supplies have a purchase-money security interest in what it has just delivered to her restaurant securing her obligation to make the payment as stated in the invoice?

A BRIEF NOTE ON THE FOLLOWING TWO CASES

Whether or not a particular security interest qualifies as a purchase-money security interest is, of course, not merely of academic interest. As we will see in several chapters yet to come, it is a question on which a party's fortune may rise or fall. So it is in the two cases that follow, but I suggest that you focus in your reading of the cases not on *why* it mattered whether a given security interest was a purchase-money interest, but rather on *how* the court approached and decided the characterization issue. In other words, unless your instructor directs you differently, I suggest you not worry for the moment on that part of the cases which talk about "perfection," "filing," "priority" or the like. For the present it is sufficient to appreciate exactly what happened in each case, that one party was claiming a purchase-money interest, that another party was opposing (and not just to be persnickety) the characterization of that interest as a PMSI, and then concentrate on how the dispute was resolved.

NORTH PLATTE STATE BANK v. PRODUCTION CREDIT ASS'N

Supreme Court of Nebraska, 1972
189 Neb. 44, 200 N.W.2d 1, 10 U.C.C. Rep. Serv. 1336

WHITE, C.J.: This case deals with the priority of secured creditors, each having a perfected security interest in the same collateral. For convenience, the plaintiff-appellant, North Platte State Bank, is hereinafter referred to as Bank, and the defendant-appellee, Production Credit Association of North Platte, is hereinafter referred to as PCA.

[Starting in August 1967, Gerald S. Tucker received an "operating loan" from PCA, the loan being subject to annual renewal in the month of December. A contemporaneously executed security agreement granted PCA a security interest in "all livestock now owned or hereafter acquired by debtor, whether by purchase, natural increase or otherwise." PCA perfected its security interest by properly filing a financing statement which covered "all of the Debtor's livestock," and all subsequent transactions between PCA and Tucker.]

In October or November of 1968, Tucker approached D. M. Mann, hereinafter referred to as Seller, to purchase certain Angus heifers in the Seller's possession. Tucker agreed to purchase as many of the 100 head of cattle as tested pregnant, and the price was $225 per head. The Seller and Tucker agreed that Tucker *was to take delivery of the cattle before January 1, 1969*, but payment and transfer of a bill of sale were to take place after that date. Sometime in November and again in December of 1968, Tucker went to the Bank to discuss opening a line of credit but there was no discussion of a specific loan for any particular purpose.

On November 30, 1968, a trucking company hired by Tucker took 79 head of impregnated Angus heifers from the Seller's ranch and hauled them to the Tucker ranch. PCA had inspected the Tucker ranch earlier in November, and then in December 1968, PCA made a routine search of the security interest filing records in several counties pursuant to a loan renewal scheduled for December but not formally executed until

March 24, 1969. PCA did not see any Angus cattle on the Tucker ranch when it inspected in November, and the December search of the records revealed that only the PCA financing statement of August 1967 was on file.

On January 13, 1969, approximately *a month and a half after he took posses-sion of the cattle,* Tucker drew a check on the Bank for $17,775, the total purchase price for the 79 head of cattle. The Seller, payee of the check, mailed the check to the Bank for deposit. The check was returned for lack of funds, but upon the Seller's inquiry, the Bank acknowledged that a loan to Tucker had been discussed and that if Tucker would come in to complete the necessary papers, the loan would be granted and the check would be honored. Because of weather conditions, Tucker was unable to reach the Bank until January 30, 1969. A note advancing $20,000 to Tucker and a security agreement were executed that day and the next day the Bank honored the check presented by the Seller. Near this point in time, the bill of sale dated January 12, 1969, for the cattle was given to Tucker. On February 5, 1969, the Bank filed a financing statement, thus perfecting a security interest in the 79 head of cattle.

PCA became aware of the presence of the Angus cattle on the Tucker ranch sometime in February 1969. Tucker told PCA that the Angus cattle were purchased with the proceeds of a sale of several calves of another breed. Having checked the records in December 1968, and receiving this explanation for the presence of the Angus cattle, PCA saw to it that a loan renewal note was signed by Tucker and a security agreement including, specifically, the 79 Angus cattle, was executed on March 24, 1969.

In December 1969, unable to locate all of Tucker's cattle in which it had a security interest, PCA checked the filing records and found the Bank's financing statement of February 5, 1969. Late in December 1969, after Tucker defaulted on the PCA note of March 24, 1969, PCA took possession of all the cattle on Tucker's ranch, including the 79 head of Angus cattle. After the Bank claimed priority to the Angus heifers, PCA and the Bank agreed to sell the cattle and to hold the proceeds in escrow pending a determination as to the priority of their respective security interests.

The issue here is which of the secured creditors has priority to the pro-ceeds from the sale of the cattle. The district court held that the first cred-itor to file a financing statement, PCA, has priority. We affirm the judgment of the district court.

The primary purpose of Article 9 of the Uniform Commercial Code was to simplify and lend certainty to procedures for establishing security interests in goods. The heart of Article 9 is its notice filing system and the funda-mental rule therein is that when a conflict exists between security interests in the same collateral and the security interests were perfected by filing, the first in time to file a financing statement has priority. A special category called purchase money security interests was established to give those inter-ests qualifying a special priority. In this case, both security interests were perfected by filing so that unless [the special priority rule for a purchase-money security interest applies,] the first creditor, PCA, being the first to file, has priority. The second creditor, the Bank, claims that [the special priority rule for its purchase-money interest] does in fact apply and that, therefore, the second creditor has priority.

A purchase money security interest is defined in section 9-107 [the pre-revision version of current § 9-103]. It states:

A security interest is a "purchase money security interest" to the extent that it is

> (a) taken or retained by the seller of the collateral to secure all or part of its price; or
> (b) taken by a person who by making advances or incurring an obligation gives value to enable the debtor to acquire rights in or the use of collateral if such value is in fact so used.

Tucker and the Seller made an oral contract for sale sometime in November 1968. Later when the 79 pregnant cows were identified, they were finally delivered to Tucker on November 30, 1968. It is apparent, therefore, that the actual goods contracted for were delivered to the buyer under the previous contract for sale; that Tucker physically received them; and that they were therefore in his legal possession. The ordinary understanding of the term "possession" means that a person has possession when he has physical control of the property. The only further question to be determined here is whether the actual physical delivery of the cows and their acceptance by Tucker, the buyer, was affected by the fact that the payment of the price and the delivery of the bill of sale were postponed. It is true that delivery by a seller under a contract for sale can take place prior to the receipt of the goods by the buyer. Receipt is defined by section 2-103(1)(c), as taking physical possession. It is clear that the tender of delivery by the Seller took place here under section 2-503(1), and the buyer received and accepted the goods on arrival at his ranch. It is not argued and indeed, it could not be argued, that the postponement of payment and the later delivery of the bill of sale had any effect upon the time that Tucker received legal possession of the goods. The buyer had received the goods under the precise terms of the Code and this receipt was evidenced by his taking of the actual physical possession. It seems quite obvious that when the cows were delivered to Tucker under the contract for sale and were actually physically received by him, they were in his legal possession and we so hold.

We turn now to the question of whether Tucker on November 30, 1968, acquired more rights in the cows than their possession. It appears from the evidence in this case that Tucker acquired title to the cows as well on November 30, 1968. There is considerable colloquy about the understanding of the parties and particularly about the testimony of the Seller about what he relied upon in delivering the cows, and what he would have done had the cows not been paid for. What is important is that the Seller said Tucker's word was good enough for him. All of the indications of the oral testimony are that the Seller was relying on Tucker's willingness and ability to make payment of the price and that he was making a sale on open credit.

Whatever the parties may have thought, the provisions of the Uniform Commercial Code govern, and it is clear that title to the cows actually passed to Tucker when they reached his ranch and he received the actual physical possession of them. Section 2-401(2), says that unless otherwise *explicitly* agreed, title passes to the buyer at the time and place at which the seller completes his performance with reference to the physical delivery of the goods, despite any reservation of a security interest. There is no evidence that the sales agreement, either expressly or impliedly, contained an *explicit* provision or term reserving the title until payment had actually been accomplished. We therefore come to the conclusion that after November 30, 1968, once the cattle reached Tucker's ranch and came into his physical possession, under the completely oral transaction the Seller had no enforceable security interest in them and no other interest of any kind. Title and possession were merged in Tucker, it was an unsecured credit transaction, and no cause of action existed against Tucker except one for the agreed price of the cattle under the terms of the agreement.

What, then, was the nature of the Bank's security interest? We pause to observe that at the moment the cattle reached Tucker's ranch, PCA's perfected security interest immediately attached to the 79 cows. All of the conditions necessary had been met; there was a written security agreement with an after-acquired property clause containing a description sufficiently broad to include the cows, value had been given in the form of the original loan, and subsequent extensions of credit which had been renewed a number of times. As we have seen, Tucker had acquired both possession and title to the cows. At the time of delivery and possession of title to Tucker, on November 30, 1968, the financing statement of PCA was the only financing statement on file.

As we have pointed out, section 9-107(b), provides that a security interest cannot become a purchase money security interest unless it is taken by a person who by making advances or incurring an obligation gives value to enable the debtor *to acquire rights in or the use of collateral* if such value is in fact so used. Clearly, the Bank could not qualify as the seller of the 79 cows. Obviously, by advancing the $20,000 and taking the mortgage it did acquire a security interest in the cows. The distinction is vital to the disposition of this case. The money advanced by the Bank enabled Tucker to pay the price to Seller for the cows. But it was not used by Tucker to acquire any rights in the cows because he already had all the possible rights in the cows he could have with both possession and title.

[The court further held that even if the Bank's interest had been a purchase-money security interest, the Bank had failed to comply with the then applicable provision of Article 9 which would allow its purchase-money interest to take priority over the prior interest held by PCA. Therefore PCA's interest had priority for either of two reasons.]

The judgment of the district court is correct and is affirmed.

GENERAL ELECTRIC CAPITAL COMMERCIAL AUTOMOTIVE FINANCE, INC. v. SPARTAN MOTORS, LTD.

Supreme Court of New York, Appellate Division, 1998
246 A.D.2d 41, 675 N.Y.S.2d 626, 36 U.C.C. Rep. Serv. 2d 19

FRIEDMANN, J.: This appeal arises from a dispute between two automobile finance companies as to which had a superior security interest in two Mercedes-Benz cars—part of the inventory of the defendant Spartan Motors, Ltd. (hereinafter Spartan), a now-defunct car dealership. The issue presented is whether by advancing Spartan the funds to purchase the vehicles after Spartan itself had already paid for and received them, the defendant General Motors Acceptance Corporation (hereinafter GMAC) thereby acquired a purchase-money security interest in the merchandise that could defeat a previously perfected security interest in all of Spartan's inventory held by the plaintiff, General Electric Capital Commercial Automotive Finance, Inc. (hereinafter GECC). We conclude that under the circumstances presented here, GMAC has established that its postpurchase advance entitled it to a purchase-money security interest in the disputed collateral such that its lien enjoyed priority over GECC's prior "dragnet" lien.

FACTS

On September 28, 1983, a predecessor of GECC entered into an "Inventory Security Agreement" with Spartan in connection with its "floor plan" financing of the dealership's inventory. By assignment of that agreement, GECC acquired a blanket lien (otherwise known as a "dragnet" lien) on Spartan's inventory to secure a debt in excess of $1,000,000. "Inventory" was defined in the agreement as "[a]ll inventory, of whatever kind or nature, wherever located, now owned or hereafter acquired, and all returns, repossessions, exchanges, substitutions, replacements, attachments, parts, accessories and accessions thereto and thereof, and all other goods used or intended to be used in conjunction therewith, and all proceeds thereof (whether in the form of cash, instruments, chattel paper, general intangibles, accounts or otherwise)." This security agreement was duly filed in the office of the Dutchess County Clerk and with the New York State Secretary of State [as would have been required under the then-applicable version of Article 9].

On July 19, 1991, Spartan signed a new Wholesale Security Agreement with GMAC, in which the latter agreed to finance or "floor-plan" Spartan's inventory. According to its terms, Spartan covenanted, *inter alia*, as follows:

> In the course of our business, we acquire new and used cars, trucks and chassis ("Vehicles") from manufacturers or distributors. We desire you to finance the acquisition of such vehicles and *to pay the manufacturers or distributors therefor.*
>
> We agree upon demand to pay to GMAC *the amount it advances or is obligated to advance to the manufacturer or distributor* for each vehicle with interest at the rate per

annum designated by GMAC from time to time and then in force under the GMAC Wholesale Plan.

We also agree that to secure collectively the payment by us of *the amounts of all advances and obligations to advance made by GMAC to the manufacturer, distributor or other sellers,* and the interest due thereon, GMAC is hereby granted a security interest in the vehicles and the proceeds of sale thereof ("Collateral") as more fully described herein.

The collateral subject to this Wholesale Security Agreement is new vehicles held for sale or lease and used vehicles acquired from manufacturers or distributors and held for sale or lease. . . .

We understand that we may sell and lease the vehicles at retail in the ordinary course of business. We further agree that *as each vehicle is sold, or leased, we will faithfully and promptly remit to you the amount you advanced or have become obligated to advance on our behalf to the manufacturer, distributor or seller"* (emphasis supplied).

It is not disputed that GMAC's security agreement was duly filed. In addition, by certified letter dated July 17, 1991, GMAC officially notified GECC of its competing security interest in Spartan's inventory, as follows:

> This is to notify you that General Motors Acceptance Corporation holds or expects to acquire purchase money security interests in inventory collateral which will from time to time hereafter be delivered to Spartan Motors Ltd. of Poughkeepsie, New York, and in the proceeds thereof.
>
> Such inventory collateral consists, or will consist, of the types of collateral described in a financing statement, a true copy of which is annexed hereto and made a part hereof.

On May 7, 1992, Spartan paid $121,500 of its own money to European Auto Wholesalers, Ltd. to acquire a 1992 600 SEL Mercedes-Benz. Six days later, on May 13, 1992, GMAC reimbursed Spartan and the vehicle was placed on GMAC's floor plan.

On July 7, 1992, Spartan paid $120,000 of its own money to the same seller to acquire a second 1992 600 SEL Mercedes. Two days later, on July 9, 1992, GMAC reimbursed Spartan for that amount and placed the second vehicle on its floor plan. The two vehicles remained unsold in Spartan's showroom.

A few months later, on or about October 2, 1992, GECC commenced this action against Spartan, seeking $1,180,999.98, representing money then due to GECC under its agreement with Spartan. Claims were also made against the principals of Spartan, upon their guarantees, as well as against GMAC and Mercedes-Benz of North America, Inc. (hereinafter MBNA), to determine lien priority in the collateral.

After commencement of the litigation, Spartan filed a bankruptcy petition and ceased doing business. GECC, GMAC, and MBNA took possession of and liquidated their respective collateral pursuant to a prior agreement between the parties. Among the assets appropriated and sold by GMAC were the two Mercedes-Benz automobiles, which were auctioned for $194,500.

Since commencing this action, GECC has apparently settled its claims against all of the defendants except GMAC, which it has accused of converting the two Mercedes-Benz vehicles in violation of GECC's antecedent security interest.

The court granted GECC's motion for summary judgment, finding persuasive GECC's argument that a literal reading of GMAC's security agreement with Spartan, in conjunction with the wording of Uniform Commercial Code §9-107(b) [the precursor to current §9-103], required a holding that GMAC had a purchase-money secured interest *only* to the extent that it paid funds *directly* to "manufacturers, distributors and sellers" of Spartan's inventory *in advance* of the transfer of the merchandise to the car dealership. The court reasoned that because "[n]owhere in the contracts of adhesion signed by Spartan with GMAC is there an obligation by GMAC to *reimburse* Spartan for funds used to purchase automobiles" (emphasis supplied), GECC's previously perfected security interest in all of Spartan's inventory should prevail.

We now reverse and, upon searching the record, grant summary judgment to GMAC.

ANALYSIS

A perfected purchase-money security interest provides an exception to the general first-in-time, first-in-right rule of conflicting security interests. Thus, a perfected purchase-money security interest in inventory has priority over a conflicting prior security interest in the same inventory. However, as the Supreme Court, Dutchess County, observed, the purported purchase-money security interest must fit within the Uniform Commercial Code definition to qualify for the exception.

Uniform Commercial Code §9-107 defines a "purchase money security interest" as a security interest:

> (a) taken or retained by the seller of the collateral to secure all or part of its price; or
> (b) taken by a person who by making advances or incurring an obligation gives value to enable the debtor to acquire rights in or the use of collateral if such value is in fact so used.

The issue here is therefore whether GMAC's payment as reimbursement to Spartan *after* it had acquired the two Mercedes-Benz vehicles on two different occasions qualifies as an "advance" or "obligation" that enabled Spartan to purchase the cars, such that GMAC acquired a purchase-money security interest in the vehicles. The arguments *against* finding a purchase-money security interest under these circumstances are basically twofold: Firstly, of the few courts to construe Uniform Commercial Code §9-107(b), many have been reluctant to decide that a purchase-money security interest has been created where, as here, title to and possession of the merchandise have passed to the debtor *before* the loan is advanced. Secondly, the literal wording of the agreement between GMAC and Spartan appears to accord GMAC purchase-money secured status only when the finance company paid Spartan's "manufacturer, distributor or other seller" *directly*. As the Supreme Court noted, nothing in GMAC's contract with Spartan appears to contemplate any obligation on the part of the financier to "reimburse" the auto dealership for funds that the latter had already expended to purchase merchandise. These two interrelated arguments will be discussed *seriatim*.

(1) WHETHER AFTER-ADVANCED FUNDS MAY QUALIFY FOR PURCHASE-MONEY SECURITY STATUS UNDER UNIFORM COMMERCIAL CODE § 9-107(b)

Research indicates that there is no judicial authority in New York construing the application of UCC 9-107(b) to circumstances such as those presented here. Indeed, there has been little judicial discussion in any jurisdiction of the applicability of UCC 9-107(b) to a creditor's subsequent reimbursement of a debtor for an antecedent purchase of collateral. Accordingly, it is appropriate to examine the legislative history of UCC 9-107(b), to arrive, if possible, at the intent of the framers.

Professor Grant Gilmore, one of the original drafters of UCC article 9 has explained that UCC 9-107(b) was enacted at least in part to liberalize the rather rigid traditional rules, e.g., regarding the circumstances under which purchase-money secured status could be obtained by a creditor who enables a debtor to acquire new inventory (*see* Gilmore, *The Purchase Money Priority*, 76 Harv. L. Rev. 1333, 1373 (1963)).

For example, whereas under pre-Code law a person who advanced the purchase price on a buyer's behalf *directly to the seller* would be found to have a purchase-money interest in the items so acquired, no such security interest was guaranteed to the person advancing money *to a buyer* who then used the funds to pay for merchandise. Under UCC 9-107(b), however, if a financier can show both that his advance was made for the purpose of enabling the debtor to acquire the collateral and that it was in fact so used, he will be accorded purchase-money secured status.

Similarly, under pre-Code law the *sequence* of the transfers was dispositive. Indeed, as Professor Gilmore noted, even UCC 9-107(b), on its face, seems to assume "the sequence of loan first and acquisition second or . . . that the loan and acquisition take place simultaneously." Where, for example, "the buyer pays the price (or writes a check) on Monday and borrows that amount from the secured party on Tuesday," the secured party is faced with the obvious difficulty of satisfying both the " 'to enable' " and the " 'in fact so used' " prongs of the statute (Gilmore, *id.*, at 1374). However, under the Code, "in . . . the hypothetical [case] just put a court could reasonably find that the secured party had acquired a purchase money interest. If the loan transaction appears to be *closely allied* to the purchase transaction, that should suffice. The evident intent of paragraph (b) is to free the purchase money concept from artificial limitations; rigid adherence to particular formalities and sequences should not be required" (Gilmore, *id.*, at 1374 (emphasis supplied)).

If under UCC 9-107(b) neither the chronology of the financing nor the configuration of the cash flow is, without more, dispositive, how can we tell if a loan transaction is sufficiently "closely allied" to a purchase transaction to qualify for purchase-money status?

One factor that courts have considered is simple temporal proximity — that is, whether the value is given by the creditor "more or less contemporaneously with the debtor's acquisition of the property." However, it should be noted that early drafts of UCC 9-107 contained an additional subdivision (c), which envisioned a purchase-money interest to the extent of value advanced for the purpose of financing new acquisitions within 10 days of the debtor's receiving possession of the new goods, *even though the value was not in fact used to pay the price.* The subdivision was deleted, according to the sponsors, because it extended the purchase-money interest too far. It appears, then, that mere closeness in time is but another mechanical circumstance to be considered — a significant clue, but not one dispositive of the relationship between the transactions.

The authorities are agreed that the critical inquiry, as in all contract matters, is into the intention of the parties. "In determining whether a security interest exists, the intent of the parties controls, and that intent may best be determined by examining the language used and considering the conditions and circumstances confronting the parties when the contract was made" (*Baldwin v. Hays Asphalt Constr.,* 20 Kan. App. 2d 853, 857, 893 P.2d 275, 279). In assessing the relationship of the transactions, the test should be whether the availability of the loan was a factor in negotiating the sale, and/or whether the lender was committed at the time of the sale to advance the amount required to pay for the items purchased (*see Matter of Hooks,* 39 UCC Rep. Serv. 332, 341 (U.S. Bankr. Ct., M.D. Ga. 1984)).

Applying these principles to the matter before us: (1) The record establishes that GMAC's reimbursements to Spartan following its two Mercedes-Benz purchases were only six and two days apart, respectively. (2) GECC does not dispute GMAC's contention that a postpurchase reimbursement arrangement was common in the trade, as well as routine in Spartan's course of dealing with GMAC and its other financiers, depending upon the circumstances of the purchase. For example, GMAC employee Philip Canterino, who handled GMAC's account with Spartan, has averred without contradiction by GECC that although it was customary for GMAC to prepay a car manufacturer before it delivered new vehicles to Spartan's showroom, in a case of the sort at issue here — where the vehicles were difficult to obtain from the manufacturer but were readily available from a distributor — it was not uncommon for GMAC to reimburse Spartan after the cars had been delivered to Spartan's showroom, upon Spartan's presentation of proof of clear title. In the language of Uniform Commercial Code § 9-107(b): GMAC was committed to give value to enable the car dealership to acquire rights in the collateral. The value so extended was intended to and in fact did enable Spartan to acquire the two Mercedes-Benzes, as GECC does not seriously suggest that without GMAC's backing Spartan could have afforded to purchase the expensive vehicles. Accordingly, the literal requirements of Uniform Commercial Code § 9-107(b) are satisfied, notwithstanding the inverted purchase-loan chronology. Because GMAC's loans were "closely allied" with Spartan's inventory acquisitions, GMAC enjoys a purchase-money security interest in the contested merchandise.

Concededly, in making assessments of this sort, courts have considered an important factor to be whether or not title had passed to the borrower before the loan was issued. This is because, where the borrower already possesses all possible rights in the collateral, the value extended by the creditor looks more like a loan procured to satisfy a pre-existing debt than an advance "enabl[ing] the debtor to acquire rights in . . . the . . . collateral." However, it seems ill-advised to create an artificial rule premised upon this circumstance, as there will be cases where a purchase-money arrangement will not be established even though title has *not* passed, and other cases, like the one before us, where the passing of title is irrelevant to the creditor's demonstration that the value he extended was closely allied to the purchase of the collateral.

A classic case holding the opposite, *North Platte State Bank v. Production Credit Assn.* (189 Neb. 44, 200 N.W.2d 1), relied upon by GECC, is distinguishable for many reasons. There, the borrower took a loan from the plaintiff bank approximately one and one-half months after purchasing certain cattle, without informing the bank that the loan was intended for any particular purpose. The *North Platte* court noted that the debtor had merely borrowed money several weeks after acquiring title to and possession of a herd of cattle in order to discharge an antecedent debt. Although the "closely allied" test was not discussed by the *North Platte* court, which focused instead on the preloan passage to the debtor of all rights in the collateral, the case is in fact an illustration of a failure to meet that test's requirements. In contrast to the matter before us, there was no pretransaction meeting of the minds between debtor and creditor; the bank was not "obligated" to give value to enable the debtor to acquire rights in the collateral; and the purchase and loan transactions were not close in time, but were nearly two months apart. Put somewhat differently, in *North Platte* the availability of the loan was not a factor in the debtor's negotiation of the sale; and the plaintiff bank was not committed at the time of the sale to advance the amount required to pay for the items purchased.

In addition, the *North Platte* court's conclusion that the plaintiff had not acquired a purchase-money interest in the debtor's collateral was reinforced by the "even more fundamental" consideration that the plaintiff had neglected to [follow the procedure required by the Code to gain priority for a purchase money security interest]. Here, in contrast, it is not disputed that GMAC timely filed its purchase-money security interest in Spartan's inventory, and that in July 1991 it notified GECC of that interest [that is, followed the specified procedure as then required].

(2) WHETHER GMAC'S LIEN IS CIRCUMSCRIBED BY THE PRECISE LANGUAGE
OF ITS AGREEMENT WITH SPARTAN

It is well established that the terms of a written security agreement may be amplified by "other circumstances including course of dealing or usage of trade or course of performance" (UCC 1-201(3); see also UCC 1-205, 208 [which would be § 1R-201(b)(3) and § 1R-303 in Revised Article 1]). Here, GECC does not deny that, although the written terms of GMAC's contract with Spartan *appeared* to contemplate a single method of inventory financing (i.e., GMAC's payment to Spartan's sellers in advance of the purchase transaction), *in fact* it was not at all unusual for the parties to pursue the same end by somewhat different means (i.e., GMAC's posttransaction reimbursement to Spartan for its inventory purchases), as GMAC employee Canterino repeatedly explained.

Generally, the express terms of an agreement and a differing course of performance, course of dealing, and/or usage of trade "shall be construed whenever reasonable as consistent with each other." Only when a consistent construction would be "unreasonable" must express terms control over course of performance, and course of performance prevail over course of dealing and usage of trade. GMAC's election on some occasions to fund Spartan's floor planning by reimbursing the car dealership for its purchases can hardly be considered inconsistent with its decision on other occasions to accomplish the same goal by following the strict wording of the contract and prepaying the supplier directly. Rather, it is only reasonable to consider these two methods of financing to be entirely compatible with one another.

In any event, it is well established that a written contract may be *modified* by the parties' postagreement "course of performance." In this regard, GECC offered no rebuttal to the testimony and affidavit of GMAC's employee who had handled the financier's account with Spartan, to the effect that it was the custom in the trade, as well as in GMAC's course of dealing with Spartan and others, for the financier to reimburse the debtor following delivery of the merchandise to the debtor's showroom, and upon presentation by the debtor of proof of clear title.

There is no merit to GECC's suggestion that, because Spartan and GMAC had diverged in practice from the literal language of their contract, GECC lacked notice of the inventory covered by GMAC's security interest.

Under the UCC, the identification of a secured party's collateral is adequate if it is "reasonably" specific. Normally, the designation of the generic "type" of collateral covered by a security agreement will be found to be sufficient. Moreover, the purpose of judicial inquiry is solely to establish, first, whether the written description may reasonably be construed to include the disputed property, and secondly, whether the parties intended that the description include that property. Here, GMAC's security agreement and its timely notice to GECC adequately specified the precise nature of the vehicular inventory to which its lien attached, such that GECC should have been alerted to GMAC's claim to the two Mercedes-Benzes; and, as discussed above, it is clear that GMAC and Spartan intended these vehicles to be covered by their financing agreement.

GECC could only have been surprised to learn that the two Mercedes-Benzes were covered by GMAC's lien had it been tracking Spartan's inventory piece by piece, and tabulating when GMAC "advanced" payment to the seller directly, as opposed to when it "reimbursed" the car dealership after the fact. In addition to being factually implausible (indeed, GECC nowhere seriously contends that it had access to GMAC's checkbook, nor does it identify in what manner it relied to its detriment on when and how GMAC discharged its individual financing obligations to Spartan), the degree of "notice" specificity sought to be imposed by GECC is far in excess of the "reasonable identification" requirement of the UCC.

Conclusion

Accordingly, the Supreme Court erred when it found that, having financed the two vehicles at issue here by way of reimbursements—"the very opposite of an advance"—GMAC did not acquire a purchase-money security interest pursuant to Uniform Commercial Code 9-107(b). Rather, since GMAC has established—and GECC does not deny—that GMAC was "obligated" to give value to enable Spartan to acquire rights in the two Mercedes-Benzes, and the purchase and loan transactions were only days apart, it is clear that Spartan's purchase and GMAC's subsequent reimbursement were sufficiently "closely allied" to give GMAC a purchase-money security interest in the subject vehicles. Under these circumstances, we conclude, upon searching the record, that GMAC is entitled to retain the proceeds of the sale of the two contested vehicles and to summary judgment against GECC.

Therefore, upon reargument, the prior determination in the order entered July 10, 1996 is vacated, and the motion by GECC for summary judgment against GMAC is denied, and upon searching the record, summary judgment is granted to GMAC against GECC.

CHAPTER
8

Further Issues Regarding the PMSI

A. INTRODUCTION

Our introduction to the purchase-money security interest in the prior chapter focused on the principal characteristic that makes a PMSI stand out from all others. For a PMSI to exist there typically will be something like a direct one-to-one relationship, what Comment 3 to §9-103 chooses to refer to in classic legalese as a "close nexus," between the debtor's acquisition of the collateral and the secured party's provision to the debtor of credit with which it, the debtor, is able to make that acquisition. Most PMSI's you will encounter, either in this book or on the job, undoubtedly follow this model fairly closely. The lender — either a seller of goods extending credit to the buyer or a third party financial institution that lends to the debtor just enough to enable it to "acquire rights in or the use of the collateral" — is granted a security interest in the goods being purchased, and the goods themselves serve as the sole collateral to which the security interest attaches.

There will be instances, however, where things get more complex. What if, for example, a lender provides a debtor with a loan in an amount which is *greater* than the cost of the specific goods it is understood are to be acquired with the loan proceeds? The debtor then "in fact so uses" a portion of this loan to buy the goods and grants the lender a security interest in them. The remainder of the loan is taken by the debtor as cash, which it uses as it sees fit and as needed to pay for other goods or services. Does the fact that the loan is made by the lender to enable the acquisition of the collateral and other things as well mean that the security interest is no longer to be characterized, in whole or in part, as a purchase-money interest? And if we were to consider this transaction as creating, at least in part, a purchase-money interest, how do we determine in what way the purchase-money portion of the loan is to be distinguished from the non-purchase-money portion? Even if this last question does not seem that difficult to address when the loan is first granted, how does the picture change (other than just getting more blurry if not downright messy over time) as the debtor makes partial payments on the loan?

As you will see in this chapter, the definition of purchase money security interest in § 9-107 of the original version of Article 9, had little to say that was of any help in addressing these more difficult questions. Courts were left to their own devices is sorting out such situations. The results, to no great surprise, were not consistent or particularly easy to apply when the next case came along. The drafters of Revised Article 9 came to the rescue — or at least did what they could — to clarify the situation in their drafting of a much longer and more detailed § 9-103. How successful they were in clarifying the situation is a question you are certainly free to consider as you work through this material.

B.   PREPARATION

This is one chapter in which I suggest that you do *not* first look at the current provisions of Article 9. You should first read the two cases, each decided under the original version of that article, to appreciate the problem presented in each. You will then be asked to consider how the cases would be decided today under Revised Article 9. At that time you will want to read over carefully the following:

- Section 9-103(e) through (h) and Comments 7 and 8 to this section

C.   PROBLEMS AND CASES

FIRST NATIONAL BANK OF STEELEVILLE, N.A. v. ERB EQUIPMENT CO., INC.

Court of Appeals of Missouri, 1996
921 S.W.2d 57, 32 U.C.C. Rep. Serv. 2d 582

SMITH, Presiding Judge: Plaintiff, First National Bank of Steeleville, brought this action to recover the proceeds of sales of John Deere machinery by defendant, Erb Equipment Company. Erb had repossessed the machinery from AmEarth Corporation, a debtor of both plaintiff and defendant.

[The bank had loaned a total of over one-half million dollars to AmEarth, a mining and excavation company, repayment of the loans being secured by an interest in all of AmEarth's equipment of every kind and description, "whether now or hereafter owned, existing or acquired." AmEarth had then gone on to acquire from Erb a number of pieces of machinery, granting Erb a security interest in each piece to secure payment of its price beyond that which was covered by trade-in of older machines. Soon thereafter, AmEarth began experiencing financial difficulties. In an agreement dated Dec. 27,

1988, AmEarth and Erb consolidated the various debts owed to Erb under a new "global" financing plan. The effect of this plan was to bring together, in one security document covering five pieces of equipment, what the court characterized as "debt which was clearly purchase money debt, debt which was clearly not purchase money debt, and debt about which the parties are in disagreement as to its purchase money status."]

The [trial] court found that by the December 27 agreement Erb had transformed and extinguished any purchase money security status in the five items of AmEarth machinery. It further found that Illinois law applied as to the Bank's rights to the sales proceeds and found Erb to have become a purchaser rather than a secured creditor when it purchased the machinery for itself at the foreclosure sales. Therefore, because Erb took the machinery subject to the bank's prior security interest the court found Erb to be liable for conversion due to its retaining the machinery after the sales. The court granted Erb's motion for summary judgment on Bank's claim for prejudgment interest and punitive damages. Both parties appeal.

The key issue which must be resolved is which party had the superior lien as to the five items of machinery. That issue is determined in turn by whether Erb had a purchase-money lien on all or some of the items of machinery and that status is determined by the legal effect of the December 27 agreement between Erb and AmEarth.

The Uniform Commercial Code (UCC), which has been adopted in this state, provides the rules to be applied in determining the priority of conflicting security interests. The primary rule is that "Conflicting security interests rank according to priority in time of filing or perfection." [Citing the precursor section to current § 9-322(a)(1).] The Bank's blanket security instrument was prior in time of filing and perfection to Erb's December 27 agreement and if the first in time rule applies the Bank's lien is superior. There is an exception created for purchase money security interests. That exception is set out in [prerevision § 9-312(1) through (4)] depending on the nature of the item involved. The machinery involved here was operating equipment, not inventory. Therefore it is covered by [subsection (4)]. [Prerevision § 9-107] contains the definition of purchase money security interest:

A security interest is a "purchase money security interest" to the extent that it is

> (a) taken or retained by the seller of the collateral to secure all or part of its price; or
> (b) taken by a person who by making advances or incurring an obligation gives value to enable the debtor to acquire rights in or the use of collateral if such value is in fact so used.

The "to the extent" language has created problems for the courts in other jurisdictions. The effect of that language has not been addressed in this jurisdiction. The problem develops in at least two circumstances. The first is where refinancing occurs with a new security agreement to cover a pre-existing purchase money debt. The second is where a single security instrument covers debt, a portion of which arose as purchase money debt and a portion of which arose as non-purchase money debt. We are confronted with the latter and nothing contained herein is intended to express a position on refinancing. Two basic lines of authority have emerged referred to as the "transformation rule" and the "dual status rule."

Under the transformation rule unless the security covers only debt incurred in purchasing the collateral it is not a purchase money security. Any refinancing of the original purchase money debt or combining it with other debt transforms the debt to non-purchase money status. Some courts which utilize the transformation rule hold basically that in order to be considered a purchase money security interest the collateral must secure its purchase price and nothing else. Other courts have interpreted the refinancing as a novation, i.e., a new non-purchase-money loan is taken, and the prior purchase money debt is extinguished. Because the proceeds of the new loan are not used to acquire rights in the collateral, but rather to pay off the former loan, the new loan is not by definition purchase money. Courts that employ this second rationale find their support in comment 2 to §9-107 of the UCC, which prohibits including "antecedent debts" in the category of purchase money interests. The cases which have adopted the transformation rule do not discuss the "to the extent" language.

The dual status rule allows the security to be divided into that portion which encompasses purchase money debt and a different portion which represents non-purchase money debt. Priority in the purchase money portion of the security is given with the remainder of the security interest being subject to the time priority restrictions. The courts which have adopted the dual purpose rule premise their decisions largely on the "to the extent" language of §9-107 as evidencing that a single security may encompass both purchase money security and non-purchase money security. Many, if not most, of the cases dealing with the two rules are cases involving personal bankruptcies in which the issue concerned whether a refinancing destroyed the purchase money security status of the seller of a consumer item such as a TV set. In the absence of purchase money status the bankrupt debtor could retain the property under the exempt property rules. [An example of such a case follows.] We do not find those cases of much benefit in dealing with this case. In those cases the dispute was between the seller and bankrupt buyer and the exempt property rules are to be liberally construed for the benefit of the bankrupt. Here we deal with two secured creditors who did not deal with each other, but independently with a common debtor. Further there is no liberal construction rule present here.

We do not find it necessary to adopt either of the competing rules in this case. [Prerevision] Section 1-102(2) states that the UCC's underlying purposes are "(a) to simplify, clarify and modernize the law governing commercial transactions; (b) to permit the continued expansion of commercial practices through custom, usage and agreement of the parties; (c) to make uniform the law among the various jurisdictions." While lawyers and judges are wont to view statutes such as the UCC as existing for the resolution of litigation, we cannot lose sight of the fact that the major purpose and benefit of the UCC is to establish understandable rules for the conduct of commercial activities. Millions of transactions occur daily which are governed by the provisions of the UCC. An infinitesimal number ever reach litigation. The UCC provides the guidelines by which commercial activity occurs and the code is applied continually by non-lawyers in commercial activities. The UCC should be interpreted with that underlying practical fact in mind.

The requirements of the UCC concerning filing, notice and perfection all are intended to provide to those dealing with commercial activities knowledge of the status of the commodity with which they are dealing so that they may protect their interest and act in a commercially prudent manner. The status of a security interest should be determinable under the Code before another lender commits itself to providing additional funding to the debtor. In the case of a purchase money security interest a lending institution should be able to tell from the documentation whether a purchase money security interest is involved, the extent of that interest, how much of the payments which have been made have been applied to reduce the purchase money debt, and how much equity currently exists in the collateral covered by the purchase money security interest. As stated in *Southtrust Bank v. Borg-Warner Acceptance Corp.*, 760 F.2d 1240 (11th Cir. 1985), "Unless a lender contractually provides some method for determining the extent to which each item of collateral secures its purchase money, it effectively gives up its purchase money status." Loans can be made against the equity in merchandise covered by a purchase money security interest but only if the amount of that equity is clearly and easily determinable. Obviously, such equity can be readily ascertained if the security interest involved is the original purchase money security interest. Where the security interest covers not only the purchase money debt but additional debt having a lesser priority the equity in the collateral may not be readily apparent or easily determined.

Purchase money security interests are an exception to the usual "first in priority rule," and receive that status to encourage suppliers to furnish necessary commodities, equipment, machinery, etc. to businesses which may have borrowed from another source and have blanket security liens on all their property including after-acquired property. The purchase money exception protects borrowers from being tied to a single lender and reduces the potential unfairness created by monopolization of credit. But the treatment of purchase money security interests is an exception and as an exception the interest claiming that status must clearly appear to meet the requirements imposed.

We are not prepared to say that under no circumstances can purchase money debt and non-purchase money debt be combined in a single security interest document. We do conclude, however, that the "to the extent" language was intended to require that the instrument creating the purchase money security interest clearly delineate the respective debts involved, which item of collateral secures its purchase money, and the amount of the payments which are to be applied against each purchase money portion of the instrument. In the absence of such delineation the instrument does not meet the requirements of the "extent" to which it is purchase money security. With such delineation it becomes possible for other lenders, including lenders with blanket security interests, to advance money in reliance on the equity in the collateral.

The security agreement of December 27, 1988, does not meet the criteria we find necessary to qualify it as a purchase money security interest. The agreement sets forth the amount of each item making up the total amount of the indebtedness. It then credits trade-ins against the indebtedness total. The agreement does not provide any delineation of how payments are to be applied or against which indebtedness any portion of any payment is to be applied. A lender examining the document would have no way of knowing whether the collateral had any equity value over and above the purchase money lien and if it did what that equity value would be. The trial court correctly determined that Erb did not have a purchase money security interest in the collateral and that Bank's preexisting blanket security interest was superior.

[The court affirmed the lower court on this issue. It then went on to reverse on a distinct issue relating to the damages that had been awarded below.]

QUESTION ON FIRST NATIONAL BANK OF STEELEVILLE

If the same situation were to come before a court today, and because of the timing of events was to be decided under § 9-103 of the Revised Article 9, do you think the outcome should be any different from what the court decided here? If so, how? If not, why not?

IN THE MATTER OF HILLARD

United States Bankruptcy Court for the Northern District of Alabama, 1996
198 Bankr. 620, 32 U.C.C. Rep. Serv. 2d 1182

CADELL, B.J.: This matter is before the Court on the motion of the debtors seeking to avoid the lien of American General Finance ("American") to the extent that such lien impairs their exemption in household goods pursuant to 11 U.S.C. § 522(f)(2) of the United States Bankruptcy Code (the "Code").

The facts of the case are essentially undisputed. On September 5, 1995, American financed the debtors' purchase of certain household goods from Holderfields' Furniture, taking a purchase money security interest against the household goods in the amount of $2,525.84. The terms of the retail installment contract included a one year payment period with monthly payments of $231.56 at 17.99% interest.

On January 30, 1996, the debtors refinanced the loan by executing a Note and Security Agreement with American in the amount of $2,057.11. American included a provision in the accompanying Disclosure Statement, pursuant to which American purported to retain "a secured purchase money interest" in the household goods initially financed by American on September 5, 1995. In addition to satisfying the original loan, American advanced $25.71 to pay the debtors' Single Decreasing Credit Life Insurance premium, and included a $15.00 UCC-1 recording fee to the financed amount. The new note also increased the interest rate from 17.99% to 22.36%, extended the payment period from one year to eighteen (18) months, and decreased the monthly payments from $252.00 to $141.00.

On February 23, 1996, the debtors filed a voluntary petition under Chapter 7 of Title 11 of the Bankruptcy Code. Then on the 18th day of April 1996, the debtors filed the present motion to avoid lien, and assert in support thereof that American lost its purchase money security interest in the household goods upon refinancing the same. American contends that the resulting lien is a purchase money security interest not subject to avoidance under Section 522(f) of the Bankruptcy Code which provides in pertinent part as follows:

(f)(1) Notwithstanding any waiver of exemptions, but subject to paragraph (3), the debtor may avoid the fixing of a lien on an interest of the debtor in property to the extent that such lien impairs an exemption to which the debtor would have been entitled under subsection (b) of this section, if such lien is

. . .

(B) a nonpossessory, nonpurchase-money security interest in any
(i) household furnishings, household goods, wearing apparel, appliances, books, animals, crops, musical instruments, or jewelry that are held primarily for the personal, family, or household use of the debtor or a dependent of the debtor[.]

The definition of purchase money security interest in not contained in the Bankruptcy Code. Accordingly, the Court must consider relevant state law to determine whether American lost its purchase money security interest in the debtors' household goods upon refinancing the previously purchased items. Alabama enacted the standard Uniform Commercial Code definition of purchase money security interest under which:

[a] security interest is a "purchase money security interest" to the extent that it is:
(a) Taken by the seller of the collateral to secure all or part of its price; or
(b) Taken by a person who by making advances or incurring an obligation gives value to enable the debtor to acquire rights in or the use of collateral if such value is in fact so used.

In *Snap-On Tools, Inc. v. Freeman (In re Freeman)*, 956 F.2d 252 (11th Cir. 1992), the Court of Appeals for the Eleventh Circuit interpreted section 7-9-107 as follows:

> A security interest in collateral is "purchase money" to the extent that the item secures a debt for the money required to make the purchase. If an item of collateral secures some other type of debt, e.g., antecedent debt, it is not purchase money. *In re Fickey*, 23 Bankr. 586, 588 (Bankr. E.D. Tenn. 1982). A purchase money security interest cannot exceed the price of what is purchased in the transaction wherein the security interest is created. *In re Manuel*, 507 F.2d 990, 993 (5th Cir. 1975).

The underlying purpose of the purchase money security interest is the protection of consumer, as well as commercial, purchasers. *Southtrust Bank of Ala. Nat'l Ass'n v. Borg-Warner Acceptance Corp.*, 760 F.2d 1240 (11th Cir. 1985) (determining that a commercial creditor lost its purchase money security interest upon exercising future advance and after-acquired property clauses contained in the creditors security agreement).

"There is a split of authority among the circuits concerning whether a purchase money security interest is extinguished when the original purchase money loan is refinanced through renewal or consolidation with another obligation." *In re Short*, 170 Bankr. 128, 132 (Bankr. S.D. Ill. 1994). The first line of cases follow the transformation rule pursuant to which a "purchase money security interest used to secure the purchase price of goods sold in a particular transaction is 'transformed' into a non-purchase money security interest when antecedent or after-acquired debt is consolidated with the new purchase under one contract." *In re Freeman*, 124 Bankr. 840. Because the resulting lien no longer qualifies as purchase money, the lien can be avoided pursuant to Section 522(f) of the Bankruptcy Code. *In re Short*, 170 Bankr. at 132-33.

Jurisdictions following the "dual status rule" criticize the transformation rule as being unnecessarily restrictive, and ignoring the commercial reality of the credit transactions. *In re Freeman*, 124 Bankr. at 843; *Lee v. Davis/McGraw, Inc. (In re Lee)*, 169 Bankr. 790, 793 (Bankr. S.D. Ga. 1994). The dual status rule is premised upon the phrase "to the extent" found in Section 9-107 of the UCC. Court's that apply this rule hold "that a lien may be partially purchase-money and partially nonpurchase-money and that the purchase money aspect of a lien is not automatically destroyed by refinancing or consolidation with other debt." *In re Short*, 170 Bankr. at 132. Under this approach, American's security interest in the debtors' household goods would be purchase money to the extent that it secures the original purchase price of the goods.

However, the Eleventh Circuit declined the defendant's invitation to adopt the dual status rule in the case of *In re Southtrust Bank*, 760 F.2d at 1243. For the court, Judge Tuttle responded:

> "Without some guideline, legislative or contractual, the court should not be required to distill from a mass of transactions the extent to which a security

interest is purchase money." (quoting *In re Coomer,* 8 Bankr. 351, 355 (Bankr. E.D. Tenn. 1980)). Unless the lender contractually provides some method for determining the extent to which each item of collateral secures its purchase money, it effectively gives up its purchase money status.

Then, in the case of *In re Freeman,* 956 F.2d 252 (11th Cir. 1992), the Eleventh Circuit implicitly adopted the transformation rule. Thus, the outcome of this case shall be controlled by the transformation rule. *In re Lee,* 169 Bankr. at 793 (recognizing that stare decisis requires courts in the Eleventh Circuit to follow *In re Freeman*). However, the Court recognizes that the present case is somewhat distinguishable from the facts presented *In re Freeman.*

At issue in *In re Freeman* was whether a creditor lost its purchase money security interest where the creditor consolidated the debtor's purchase of tools on a revolving credit account. The security agreement included a first-in/first-out payment schedule, but failed to include a provision for the allocation of payments between sales tax, interest, and the purchase price of the tools. The Eleventh Circuit held that the creditor's security interest did not survive the debt consolidation because the payment allocation method contained in the security agreement was "inadequate to determine which tools had been paid for and which secured their own purchase price." For the court, Judge Godbold explained as follows:

> Lender[s] must provide some method "for determining the extent to which each item of collateral secures its purchase money." Southtrust Bank of Alabama, Nat. Asso. v. Borg-Warner Acceptance Corp., 760 F.2d 1240, 1243 (11th Cir. 1985). . . . Because the method for allocating the payments made by Freeman is inadequate to determine which tools have been paid for and which secure their own purchase price, [the creditor's] security interest does not survive the consolidation of debts.

In the present case, American refinanced the debtors' original purchase by extending the payment terms and lowering the monthly payments due under the terms of the new note. The debtors argue that new consideration was also given because American increased the interest rate and added approximately $35.00 to the amount financed under the new note. In the case of *In re Hatfield,* 117 Bankr. 387, 389 (Bankr. C.D. Ill. 1990), the court held that the purchase money character of a creditor's security interest survived a simple refinancing where "the only changes involved in the refinanced note were an extended payment period and a small reduction in the amount of the monthly payments." The Illinois Bankruptcy Court rejected the dual status and transformation rules, and instead adopted a case by case analysis under which the court considered the degree by which the original obligation changed upon being refinanced. Applying this analysis, the court believed that it was significant that no additional funds were advanced, and that the interest rate remained the same under the refinanced note.

In the present case, it is uncontroverted that American possessed a purchase money security interest in the debtors' household goods when the goods were originally financed on September 5, 1995. Although, the present case does not involve the traditional consolidation of debt found in *In re Freeman*, the Court believes that American converted its purchase money security interest into a nonpurchase money security interest upon refinancing the original loan. In addition to extending the payment terms and reducing the monthly payments, American increased the interest rate, and increased the loan amount by $35.00.

After consideration of the evidence, the Court finds, and it is a ORDERED, ADJUDGED AND DECREED that the debtor's motion to avoid the lien of American be and hereby is GRANTED, and the non-purchase money security interest of American in the debtors' household furnishings is hereby avoided to the extent that such lien impairs the debtors' exemptions.

QUESTION ON HILLARD

If the same situation were to come before the same court today, to be decided under § 9-103 of the Revised Article 9, do you think the outcome should be any different from what the court decided here? If so, how? If not, why not?

PART III

PROTECTION OF THE ARTICLE 9
INTEREST — PERFECTION

CHAPTER
9

Introduction to Perfection, Perfection by Filing, and Where to File

A. INTRODUCTION

1. The Nature of "Perfection"

Once a security interest has attached to some collateral, this assures the secured party of certain specified rights against the debtor with respect to the collateral. The exact nature of those rights — what the secured party may do to enforce its interest against a defaulting debtor — will be explored in plenty of detail in the final chapters of this book.

As a practical matter, the secured party can't be, or at least should not be, satisfied with only those rights that attachment brings with it. The secured party will be just as interested, if not more so, in whatever rights it can gain against *third parties*, parties other than the debtor, with whom it may later be in contention over the right to claim the value of the collateral. These third parties can be of a variety of sorts — other secured parties, lien creditors of the debtor, people who buy or otherwise take possession of the collateral from the debtor, and of course the all-important bankruptcy trustee. The details on how the secured party fares in conflict with all these other potential combatants is dealt with in the next part of the book, under the general heading of "Priorities." For the moment you will just have to take it on faith that a secured party is unlikely to do very well in any priority contest if it hasn't successfully perfected its interest initially and kept its perfection effective over time.

If it's worth taking a security interest, that is, meeting the criteria for attachment, it is worth perfecting. Or at least if a secured party decides not to perfect it is making a business decision involving a degree of risk of which it should be aware and to which it should have given some serious consideration.

The fundamental idea behind Article 9's requirements for perfection is that what is sometimes referred to as the "perfection step" or what I may refer to as the means or method of perfection — that is, whatever the

125

secured party has to do to attain perfection of its interest — should be an effective way of giving *notice* to third parties that the secured party may be claiming a security interest in the collateral involved. If third parties are to be affected by a perfected security interest created by the debtor and the secured party in a two-person transaction, it is only fair and reasonable that those third parties have a means of checking on personal property owned by the debtor to see if it is potentially encumbered by a security interest claimed by another. That is where the concept of effective notice comes in.

So as you study the various means of perfection you should always be thinking of these not just from the perspective of the secured party but also from the perspective of a third party, someone who is often referred to somewhat dramatically but also appropriately as "the searcher." Given the various ways a security interest may be perfected, what will a diligent searcher — fully schooled in the rules of Article 9 of course — do to protect its own interests?

2. *The Means of Perfection*

Article 9 allows for perfection by four different methods. Not all are available for all types of collateral, so you will have to pay attention to what means of perfection are available in any given circumstance. You will also come across instances when more than one method of perfection may be available, and again you should note these. It is not unusual or in any way inappropriate to perfect by *more than one* method. There's no rule that the secured party has to pick one and only one perfection step.

The four means or methods of perfection provided for under Article 9 are:

- Filing,
- Possession of the Collateral by the Secured Party,
- "Control," which is a special means of perfection carefully defined and available for only certain types of collateral, and
- Automatic Perfection, that is, perfection upon attachment without the need for the secured party to do any more. When automatic perfection is available, the secured party need take no additional "perfection step" to attain perfection of its interest.

3. *Perfection by Filing*

We start our discussion of perfection with perfection by filing. This is not because filing is the "best" or "most perfect" way to perfect, but it is in some sense the default mechanism of perfection. By this I mean that if the secured party can't point to a distinct rule in Article 9 which allows it to perfect by one of the other three means it had better file. Filing thus also serves as a kind of exemplar of what perfection is all about and how it is meant to protect third parties. When we get to the other means of perfection we will naturally have to ask whether each of the other means gives notice to a diligent searcher "equivalent to a filing" in some way, and if so how. If there isn't equivalent notice given, we will have to question what policy might justify this variation from what is in effect meant to be the norm.

Before we get into the details — of which there will be a slew — we should just quickly say what we mean by perfection by filing. This means of perfection requires the delivery to the appropriate government filing office of a record called an initial financing statement, along with the appropriate filing fee of course. This initial financing statement should then be accepted by the filing office and the information it contains put on the official records of that filing office. That information is then public information, and any searcher, if he or she knows where to look and what to look for, should be able to find it in an appropriate search.

4. Where to File

To get an appreciation of the filing system — the very heart and soul of the whole Article 9 enterprise — we have to consider *where* an initial filing should be made, *what* that filing should consist of, *how* that filing is actually carried out, and furthermore when and in what form any *additional* filings may be necessary to maintain continued and uninterrupted perfection by filing.

I start us out with the question of where to file for a couple of reasons. First, at least since the introduction of the Revised Article 9, effective as of July 1, 2001 in almost every state, the question of where to file has been made dramatically simpler than had been true under the prerevision version. Beginning on July 1, 2006 all filing and searching — with only some minor exceptions which can I think be safely put to the side, no matter how much I or your professor may be tempted to get into little kinks in the present system or how things used to be in the "old days" before the revision — will be done where the current Article now specifies. Starting with what turns out to be perhaps the simplest part of the process doesn't seem such a bad idea. (As of this writing, I can note, I am not aware of any cases which have had even to consider any controversy of whether a filing under Revised Article 9 was done in the correct place. The same could certainly never have been said about life under the prerevision version of the article, when whether or not a filing had been made in the correct place was one of the most often litigated issues.)

The second reason for beginning with the question of where to file is that in the following chapters I will suggest, or your professor may insist, that you pick one state whose requirements for filing, search procedure, fee schedule, and so on, you can explore on your own — in the books or online — to get a better appreciation of how it is "actually done" in "real life." It will make sense for you to pick a state in which you should anticipate you will be doing a large part of your filing should you go into this line of work. So where to file again seems a logical place to start.

Note that the question of where to file breaks down to two separate questions: First of all, in what state should I file? Secondly, with what office in that state should I file? Fortunately for us, both of these questions have been made radically simpler with the revision of Article 9. There I go, tempted to talk about the "old days," and how difficult these questions used to be. But I will resist the temptation and get on with business.

B. PREPARATION

As an introduction to the whole notion of perfection and in preparation for discussion of the issue of where to file, read carefully the following parts of the Code:

- Start with § 9-308 (a)-(c) and Comment 2 to this section
- Then to § 9-310(a) and its Comment 2
- For a definition of "financing statement," see § 9-102(a)(39)
- Section 9-301(1) and the first paragraph of its Comment 4
- Section 9-302
- Section 9-307(a)-(e)
- Section 9-501(a) and its Comment 2
- You will also need the definition of "organization" in § 1-201(28) or § 1R-201(b)(25) as well as that of "registered organization" in § 9-102(a)(70)

C. PROBLEMS AND CASES

PROBLEMS

9.1 Essie Cashmore lives (some would say as a recluse) in a large mansion on an extensive estate in Welloff, Illinois, probably the ritziest suburb of Chicago. For many years now she has considered herself a patron of up-and-coming young artists and bought many of their earlier works, which she has proudly displayed throughout her mansion. In order to build up her collection even more, she negotiates a loan from Discreet Financial Services, granting that lender a security interest a several of her most valuable acquisitions, a listing of which is carefully set out in the security agreement. Discreet Financial Services operates as a corporation, organized under the laws of Delaware, with its sole office in Palm Springs, California. Where should DFS file to perfect its security interest in Essie's artwork?

9.2   Jonathan Stringer pays a visit to the mansion of his friend Essie Cashmore, of the previous problem, while on a visit to the Chicago area from his home in Phoenix. While there he sees in the corner what appears to be a fine old cello just sitting around collecting dust. Essie tells him that she bought the instrument many years ago, when she was thinking of taking up playing the cello, but that she'd quickly given up because of "all those notes." Stringer, who is a collector of rare and valuable string instruments says he would love to buy the old cello from her. Essie obviously has a good idea of its worth, and the two are quickly able to come to an agreement about the price. Essie says she is perfectly willing to let Stringer take the instrument with him if he will just write her our a check for the amount then and there. Stringer, of course, knows that he should first check to see whether the instrument may possibly be the subject of a potential security interest claimed by some other party. In what filing system or systems should he search to be sure he isn't later surprised by finding out that he's bought a cello encumbered by someone else's security interest?

9.3   Lance Cashmore is a jet-setting (some would say shiftless playboy) younger member of the Cashmore clan. Or at least one of them. At his penthouse apartment in downtown Chicago, Lance meets with a representative of Discreet Financial Services. He arranges for a loan from that firm, granting it a security interest is his large collection of expensive watches. How should DFS go about determining where to file to perfect this interest? Based on what additional information it reliably obtains, where do you suggest it file?

9.4   Gabriela is able to obtain a $50,000 line of credit to open up her restaurant, Gabriela's Place, in the heart of Manhattan's Greenwich Village from the Large Apple Bank, putting up all of the restaurant's equipment as collateral. Gabriela herself lives in Hoboken, New Jersey. Large Apple Bank is organized under the laws of New York and has its chief executive office in Manhattan.

(a) Where should the bank file to perfect its interest?
(b) Suppose instead that the restaurant Gabriela's Place is initially started up by Gabriela and her friend Raoul operating under a simple partnership agreement written for them by a local attorney. Raoul lives in Bennington, Vermont. All other facts remain the same. Where should the bank file to perfect its interest?
(c) Finally, suppose that when the partnership of Garbriela and Raoul come to Large Apple Bank their initial Greenwich Village Restaurant has been doing so well that they have opened up other locations of Gabriela's Place, one in Hamden, Connecticut and one in Hoboken, New Jersey. The bank agrees to loan to them taking as collateral all the equipment in all the locations. Where should it file on which collateral?

9.5   Knifty Knits Incorporated is a major manufacturer of sweaters and other knitwear with production facilities located in Oregon, Nevada, Alabama, and Maine. Knifty, which is a corporation organized under the laws of Delaware, has its main corporate headquarters in the Knifty Knits Building, a glass high-rise tower in the center of Los Angeles. Knifty enters into an agreement to borrow a large sum of money from American Flag Bank and Trust. As part of the loan agreement it grants a security interest in "all accounts, now held or hereafter acquired" to the lender.

(a) Where should the lender file to perfect this interest?
(b) What would your answer be if the collateral were instead "all equipment, now held or hereafter acquired" of the corporation?

9.6   Do-All Limited is a corporation organized under the laws of the Canadian province of Ontario. While it does have a small office in Toronto, its main headquarters are in New York City. American Flag Bank and Trust agrees to lend to Do-All, taking as collateral "all equipment, now held or hereafter acquired" owned by the company.

(a) Where should the lender file to perfect this interest?
(b) Suppose instead that Do-All's main headquarters is in Toronto. It does, however, have several operating facilities in cities in New England and New York state. The bank is taking as collateral "all equipment, now held or hereafter acquired" and located in one of those United States locations. Where should the bank file under these circumstances?
(c) Would your answer to part (b) above be the same if instead Do-All Limited was organized under the laws of Ukraine and had its main headquarters in Kiev? What if it was a Ukrainian corporation but its headquarters building was located in New York City?

CHAPTER
10

The Initial Financing Statement

A. INTRODUCTION

To perfect by filing it is necessary to file with the correct filing office an *initial financing statement* that is "sufficient" under § 9-502(a). Note that this subsection actually gives the criteria of sufficiency for a "financing statement," which by definition consists of an initial financing statement *together with* any later filing or filings relating to it. Any filer would, of course, want its initial financing statement to fit the bill from the start. Otherwise, what is the point? (We will later deal with subsequent filings that might be necessary or desirable to keep the entire packet, the full financing statement, in good shape.)

The initial financing statement has traditionally and still is referred to as the UCC1 form. For an idea of what this form usually looks like, see the suggested (I would say highly suggested) format which actually appears in the statute in § 9-521(a). Note, by the way, that this is labeled both at the top and at the bottom as the "UCC Financing Statement" when it really is the format for the *initial* financing statement as that term is now used in revised Article 9.

On the form you'll see a number of boxes to fill in with which we won't deal with in this chapter (the debtor's mailing address, for example). You will see the importance of these other bits of information in the next chapter.

In this chapter we will deal with the three most crucial pieces of information which § 9-502(a) absolutely requires for a financing statement to be sufficient to its task:

- the name of the debtor,
- the name of the secured party, and
- an indication of the collateral.

Some people have taken to referring to these as "the three holies" of the financing statement. Each must be given, and given correctly, for the financing statement to be sufficient. While under § 9-506 "minor errors"

might not render the filing insufficient — and hence of no value whatsoever in perfecting the security interest — you may be struck by how infre-
quently this "saving" section can be expected as a practical matter to help
the filer who makes a mistake, even what may strike you or me as a genuinely trivial one, in how he or she fills out the UCC1.

B.   PREPARATION

In preparation, read carefully the following parts of the Code:

- Section 9-502(a) and Comment 2 to that section
- Section 9-503 and its Comment 2
- Section 9-504 and its Comment 2
- Section 9-506 and its Comment 2
- Section 9-521(a) and its Comment 2

I suggest (and your professor may do more than just suggest) that you also
pick one filing jurisdiction, one of the states or the District of Columbia,
and learn a bit more about the exact mechanics of filing in that jurisdiction. Yes, the states and D.C. have all adopted the *uniform* statute that is
Article 9, but things like the day-to-day mechanics of running the filing
system, filing fees, and (most unfortunately of all) the "standard search
logic, if any" that the various state offices have promulgated by regulation
can be crucially different in detail.

Your pick of a specific jurisdiction may be based on the place where your
school is located, where you think you might eventually go into practice,
where you think you'll be doing a lot of filing (based on what you learned in
the last chapter), or just on whim. Or to keep everyone in the class working
on the same page, your professor may pick a state to work with. In this and
the following chapters, I'll refer to your choice (or that of your professor) as
"your state."

For this chapter you will want to hit the books — or more likely go
online — to find whatever regulations, printable forms, or other information such as "guides for the perplexed filer" the relevant state government
office has made available to the public. If you can't think of any particular
state of interest, you may want to join me and my students at the New York
Secretary of State's site www.dos.state.ny.us/corp/ucc.html. (I admit I particularly like this site because when you click on Frequently Asked Questions
you get the strangely fascinating "What is a UCC?")

You will probably find a lot more on your state's site than you need for
the moment (or maybe ever). For this chapter it will help if you can find
and print out a full-size version of the UCC1, including any instructions
which the state may have placed on the back. If nothing else this full-size
version should be easier to read that the cramped form you'll find in your

statute book. You should also look for anything that gives a rendition of the "standard search logic" used by that office. (You can safely ignore any information about how to search filings made before July 1, 2001, the effective date of the revised Article 9 and the start date for the new filing system. You are interested in how the state files and then provides searches for filings made under the new system only.)

One other thing you might want to check out at this point is whether your state's system allows for searches on line of the new filing system. If so, are these searches conducted using the "standard search logic" which the filing office itself uses or some other search mechanism? The importance of this last question will soon become apparent.

C.   PROBLEMS AND CASES

IN RE FV STEEL AND WIRE COMPANY

United States Bankruptcy Court for the Eastern District of Wisconsin, 2004
310 Bankr. 390, 2004 Bankr. LEXIS 748

SUSAN V. KELLY, B.J.: PSC Metals, Inc. ("PSC") filed Motions in these chapter 11 cases for relief from stay and/or for adequate protection and to compel payment of administrative expenses arising out a Scrap Supply and Consignment Agreement, as modified by an Account Reconciliation Agreement (collectively the "Agreement"), between PSC and one of the Debtors. The Debtors objected to the Motions on a number of grounds, and the parties engaged in negotiations to attempt to resolve their disputes.

A major issue between the parties was the validity of a Uniform Commercial Code (UCC) financing statement filed on May 10, 2001 by PSC against "Keystone Steel & Wire Co." At a hearing on March 29, 2004, counsel for PSC represented that the facts concerning the effectiveness of the financing statement were not in dispute, although the parties were categorically opposed on the legal issue. Counsel suggested that if the court determined this single issue on a summary judgment type basis, it would "save a lot of time [and] a lot of money," and facilitate resolution or determination of the remaining disputes in an expeditious manner. The Debtors and Unsecured Creditors Committee agreed, and a briefing schedule was established. The sole issue is whether the financing statement which was filed in the Debtor's trade name, rather than its corporate name, is effective against the Debtor, as debtor in possession. [As the court notes, Section 544 of the Bankruptcy Code gives the trustee the power to avoid unperfected security interests. In Chapter 11 cases without a trustee, this "strong arm power" may be exercised by the character known as the "debtor in possession."]

Article 9 of the UCC governs the creation and perfection of security interests in personal property. Article 9 was completely overhauled in

2001, and Revised Article 9 became effective for transactions entered into after July 1, 2001. Sections 9-702 and 9-703 of Revised Article 9 provide Savings Clauses for pre-existing perfected security interests. For the most part, those transactions continue to be evaluated under old Article 9. In this case, the Agreement is dated January 31, 2001, prior to the effective date of Revised Article 9. The Agreement states that it is governed by Illinois law. Accordingly, the validity of the financing statement is determined under the Illinois UCC as it existed prior to the effective date of Revised Article 9.

[The court then reviews the provisions of old Article 9 applicable to the issue at hand. Those provisions stated first of all and not surprisingly that the financing statement give the name of the debtor. Further it was stated that a financing statement is sufficient if it contains the "corporate name," whether or not it "adds trade names" of the debtor. There was also a section which stated that a financing statement containing only minor errors would still be effective if the errors did not render the filing "seriously misleading," although old Article 9 — unlike the present version — contained no further delineation of or test for what would make a filing "seriously misleading."]

PSC filed its financing statement against "Keystone Steel & Wire Co.," a trade name used by the Debtor. PSC does not dispute that the Debtor's correct legal name is "Keystone Consolidated Industries, Inc.," but argues that the filing is not seriously misleading. In support of its argument, PSC relies heavily on *In re Paramount Int'l, Inc.*, 154 B.R. 712 (Bankr. N.D. Ill. 1993). In that case, at the time of the original loan, the debtor's name was "Paramount Attractions, Inc." Two months after the creditor filed its financing statement under that name, the debtor changed its legal name to "Paramount International, Inc." The debtor continued to use "Paramount Attractions, Inc." as a trade name, and the creditor never amended its financing statement to reflect the true corporate name. When the debtor filed bankruptcy, it sought to use the avoidance powers of §544(a) of the Bankruptcy Code to defeat the creditor's security interest. The "ultimate question" for the bankruptcy court was whether the filed financing statement was seriously misleading. Recognizing divergent views, the court in *Paramount* ruled for the creditor. PSC points out the similarities between *Paramount* and the instant case, including that the first names of the debtor's legal names and corporate names are the same, and that a search under the term "Paramount" as a search under the term "Keystone" revealed a significant number of filings, including the erroneous financing statements.

Although many of the facts here are similar to those in *Paramount*, several key facts are different. [While the court notes certain factual differences, the main point to be noted here is that, as the court itself later points out, the *Paramount* case was soon called "dead wrong," by a leading treatise. Barkley Clark and Barbara Clark, The Law of Secured Transactions Under the Uniform Commercial Code P 2.09[1][b](2003). I think it fair to say that most, if not all, other commentators thought the same. Certainly those involved with the drafting of Revised Article 9 did.]

Finally, *Paramount* preceded the adoption of Revised Article 9 by many years, while PSC's financing statement was filed within 60 days of the new statute's effective date. It is undisputed that under Revised Article 9, PSC's financing statement would be insufficient as a matter of law. Section 9-503(a) now requires the financing statement to contain the name of a corporate debtor "indicated on the public record of the debtor's jurisdiction of organization," and §9-503(c) expressly states: "A financing statement that provides only the debtor's trade name does not sufficiently provide the name of the debtor."

The comment to §9-503 states:

> Together with subsections (b) and (c), subsection (a) reflects the view prevailing under former article 9 that the actual individual or organizational name of the debtor on a financing statement is both necessary and sufficient, whether or not the financing statement provides trade or other names of the debtor and, if the debtor has a name, whether or not the financing statement provides the names of the partners, members, or associates who comprise the debtor.

Moreover, a statutory definition of "seriously misleading" was adopted in §9-506(c) of Revised Article 9, which states:

> If a search of the records of the filing office under the debtor's correct name, using the filing office's standard search logic, if any, would disclose a financing statement that fails sufficiently to provide the name of the debtor in accordance with Section 9-503(a), the name provided does not make the financing statement seriously misleading.

A multitude of seminars and articles heralded the advent of Revised Article 9. [Citations to a slew of articles by a number of the leading Article 9 authorities omitted.]

One of the mantras espoused by the experts was the necessity of using the debtor's correct legal name, not a trade name or nickname. For example, Steven O. Weise, the ABA advisor to the Revised Article 9 Drafting Committee said this about the debtor's name:

> Revised Article 9 continues the requirement that the financing statement include the debtor's name. *Article 9 also continues to disapprove of the use of a fictitious name.* Revised Article 9 contains a statutory rule to determine when a mistake the debtor's name is so incorrect as to make the financing statement ineffective. The financing statement is effective if a computer search run under the debtor's correct name turns up the financing statement with the incorrect name. If it does not, then the financing statement is ineffective as a matter of law. The court has no discretion to determine that the incorrect name is "close enough." As a result, the secured party is dependent on the kind of computer search logic used by a particular state's filing office. *The simple solution is to get the debtor's name right.*

Steven O. Weise, *An Overview of Revised Article 9,* in The New Article 9 Uniform Commercial Code 7 (Corinne Cooper ed., 2d. ed. 2000) (citations omitted; emphasis supplied).

In this heady atmosphere of the adoption of Revised Article 9, PSC and the Debtor entered into the Agreement and PSC filed its financing statement. PSC knew the Debtor's correct legal name, as evidenced by the Scrap Supply and Consignment Agreement itself. Given the impending adoption of Revised Article 9, with the publicity about the importance of using the debtor's correct legal name, and PSC's knowledge of the true corporate name, PSC ignored the correct legal name and filed under the trade name at its own peril.

In *First Nat'l Bank of Lacon v. Strong,* 278 Ill. App. 3d 762, 663 N.E.2d 432, 215 Ill. Dec. 421 (Ill. App. Ct. 1996), the Illinois Appellate Court construed a financing statement filed under old Article 9 against the debtor's trade name "Strong Oil Co." when the correct legal name was "E. Strong Oil Company." Relying on a substantial body of authority, the court held that the financing statement was seriously misleading because a search of the financing statement records under the correct corporate name would not have revealed the financing statement. "To hold otherwise would frustrate the underlying purpose of the Code's filing requirements. A rule that would burden a searcher with guessing at misspellings and various configurations of a legal name would not provide creditors with the certainty that is essential in commercial transactions." The *Strong* decision places the burden where it belongs, on the creditor with the erroneous filing. PSC would have the searchers required to inquire under the trade name, when neither the old nor Revised Article 9 countenances that requirement.

Strong and the numerous courts in its camp place a heavy burden on those filing erroneous financing statements. PSC has not met that burden in this case, and PSC's financing statement was "seriously misleading," under [the governing prerevision provision of Article 9]. For the foregoing reasons, it is therefore,

ORDERED: that the financing statement filed by PSC Metals, Inc. against Keystone Steel & Wire Co. on May 10, 2001, is determined to be seriously misleading and ineffective to perfect a security interest in the collateral described in that financing statement.

PROBLEMS

10.1   Knifty Knits and Knacks, Incorporated is a major manufacturer of sweaters and other knitwear with production facilities located in several parts of the country, selling directly to major retailers. Universal Bank for Commerce ("UBC") agrees to loan it a large amount of money based on its grant of a security interest in "all equipment, inventory, and accounts, now held or hereafter acquired."

(a) Assuming that Knifty Knits has been incorporated in your state, where on the standard UCC1 form should its name be filled in. How should the name be rendered?

(b) Suppose that the lawyer filing the UCC1 renders its name as "Nifty Knits and Knacks, Incorporated." Will this be a sufficient filing?

(c) What if the name is filled in as "Knifty Knits and Knacks Corporation"?

(d) What about "Knifty Knits & Knacks, Incorporated"?

(e) What if Box 1a is filled in with "Knifty Knits and Knacks, Incorporated, a corporation duly organized under the laws of this state"?

10.2   Gabriela Dominiquez and Raoul Riviera enter into a common law partnership under which they operate a restaurant, Gabriela's Place, in New York City. They are able to obtain a $50,000 line of credit from the Large Apple Bank, granting the bank a security interest in all their equipment.

(a) When the bank files an initial financing statement to perfect this interest, how should it render the debtor name or names on the UCC1?

(b) If the bank gave "Gabriela's Place" as the name of a debtor, would this necessarily make the filing insufficient?

(c) As it turns out, Gabriela is, in addition to being a restaurant owner, a member of the bar. When the bank enters her name in the boxes making up 1b on the standard UCC1 form, it places "Esq." in the box reserved for a suffix to an individual name. Does this render the filing incorrect, at least as to her as a debtor?

IN RE KINDERKNECHT

United States Bankruptcy Appellate Panel for the Tenth Circuit, 2004
308 Bankr. 71, 52 Collier Bankr. Cas. 2d 46, 53 U.C.C. Rep. Serv. 2d 167

THURMAN, B.J.: The Chapter 7 trustee timely appeals a final Judgment of the United States Bankruptcy Court for the District of Kansas in favor of Deere and Company and Deere Credit Services, Inc. (collectively, "Deere"), refusing to avoid Deere's interests in the debtor's property pursuant to 11 U.S.C. § 544(a)(1). The parties have consented to this Court's jurisdiction because they have not elected to have this appeal heard by the United States District Court for the District of Kansas. Upon review of the entire record, including the Brief of Amicus Curiae Ron Thornburgh, Secretary of State of Kansas (Secretary of State) and Deere's response thereto, we REVERSE the bankruptcy court's Judgment.

I. BACKGROUND

It is undisputed that the debtor's legal name is "Terrance Joseph Kinderknecht." In addition, it is undisputed that the debtor is informally known as "Terry."

The debtor granted Deere security interests in two farm implements. Deere promptly filed financing statements in the appropriate place, listing the debtor as "Terry J. Kinderknecht."

Subsequently, the debtor filed a Chapter 7 petition. His petition, while signed by "Terry Kinderknecht," is filed under his legal name, "Terrance J. Kinderknecht."

The trustee in the debtor's Chapter 7 case commenced an adversary proceeding against Deere, seeking to avoid its interests in the debtor's farm implements pursuant to 11 U.S.C. § 544(a)(1). According to the trustee, Deere's interests in the property were avoidable because they were not perfected under the Kansas Uniform Commercial Code inasmuch as its financing statements, listing the debtor by his nickname as opposed to his legal name, were "seriously misleading" and ineffective. Deere argued that providing the debtor's commonly used nickname in its financing statements was sufficient, and that its interests in the debtor's property were perfected under Kansas law. Cross motions for summary judgment were filed.

The bankruptcy court entered Judgment in favor of Deere, holding that Deere's interests in the debtor's property were not avoidable by the trustee under § 544(a)(1). In its Memorandum Opinion, the bankruptcy court concluded that Deere's financing statements were sufficient to perfect its interests in the debtor's property even though Deere listed the debtor in its financing statements by the debtor's nickname.

The trustee timely appealed the bankruptcy court's Judgment to this Court. After the trustee's appeal was submitted, the Court granted the Secretary of State leave to appear and file a Brief as Amicus Curiae. Under Kansas law, the Secretary of State is charged with maintaining the data base used to track the filing of financing statements in Kansas, and with promulgating "standard search logic" for conducting searches of that data base. Like the trustee, the Secretary of State advocates reversal of the bankruptcy court's Judgment.

II. Discussion

The issue in this case is whether the bankruptcy court erred in concluding that Deere's interests in the debtor's property were perfected as of the petition date so as to make them immune from avoidance under 11 U.S.C. § 544(a)(1). We must determine, therefore, whether the bankruptcy court erred in holding that Deere's financing statements, listing the debtor by his nickname, were sufficient to perfect its interests in the debtor's property. We review this legal issue *de novo*, and therefore, give "no form of appellate deference" to the bankruptcy court's conclusions. For the reasons stated below, we conclude that the bankruptcy court erred in holding that Deere's financing statements were sufficient and served to perfect its interests in the debtor's property. For a financing statement to be sufficient under Kansas law, the secured creditor must list an individual debtor by his or her legal name, not a nickname.

It is undisputed in this case that whether Deere's interests were perfected on the debtor's petition date depends on Kansas law. It is also undisputed that the applicable law is stated in Article 9 of the Kansas Uniform Commercial Code, as revised and adopted by the Kansas Legislature in 2000. The relevant portions of Revised Article 9, as adopted in Kansas, are as follows. [The court then cites and quotes from all the relevant sections of Article 9 and the comments thereto.]

Although § 9-503 specifically sets parameters for listing a debtor's name in a financing statement when the debtor is an entity, it does not provide any detail as to the name that must be provided for an individual debtor — it simply states that the "name of the debtor" should be used. This could be construed, as it was by the bankruptcy court, as allowing a debtor to be listed in a financing statement by his or her commonly-used nickname. But, we do not agree with that interpretation because the purpose of § 9-503, as well as a reading of that section as a whole, leads us to conclude that an individual debtor's legal name must be used in the financing statement to make it sufficient under § 9-502(a)(1).

As discussed above, § 9-503 is new, and it was enacted to clarify the sufficiency of a debtor's name in financing statements. The intent to clarify when a debtor's name is sufficient shows a desire to foreclose fact-intensive tests, such as those that existed under the former Article 9 of the UCC, inquiring into whether a person conducting a search would discover a filing under any given name. Requiring a financing statement to provide a debtor's legal name is a clear cut test that is in accord with that intent.

Furthermore, § 9-503, read as a whole, indicates that a legal name should be used for an individual debtor. In the case of debtor-entities, § 9-503(a) states that legal names must be used to render them sufficient under § 9-502(a). Trade names or other names may be listed, but it is insufficient to list a debtor by such names alone. A different standard should not apply to individual debtors. The more specific provisions applicable to entities, together with the importance of naming the debtor in the financing statement to facilitate the notice filing system and increase commercial certainty, indicates that an individual debtor must be listed on a financing statement by his or her legal name, not by a nickname.

Our conclusion that a legal name is necessary to sufficiently provide the name of an individual debtor within the meaning of § 9-503(a) is also supported by four practical considerations. First, mandating the debtor's legal name sets a clear test so as simplify the drafting of financing statements. Second, setting a clear test simplifies the parameters of UCC searches. Persons searching UCC filings will know that they need the debtor's legal name to conduct a search, they will not be penalized if they do not know that a debtor has a nickname, and they will not have to guess any number of nicknames that could exist to conduct a search. Third, requiring the debtor's legal name will avoid litigation as to the commonality or appropriateness of a debtor's nickname, and as to whether a reasonable searcher would have or should have known to use the name. Finally, obtaining a debtor's legal name is not difficult or burdensome for the creditor taking a secured interest in a debtor's property. Indeed, knowing the individual's legal name will assure the accuracy of any search that that creditor conducts prior to taking its secured interest in property.

Additionally, we note that although use of the Official Forms is not mandated, the language in the Financing Statement Form set forth in § 9-521 expressly states that the preparer should include the "DEBTOR'S EXACT FULL LEGAL NAME." This Form, which is meant to "reduce error," indicates to us an intent to increase certainty in the filing of financing statements by requiring a debtor's legal name. Our holding in this case will foster that intent.

By using the debtor's nickname in its financing statements, Deere failed to provide the name of the debtor within the meaning of § 9-503(a), and its financing statements are not sufficient under § 9-502(a). Because the financing statements do not "sufficiently . . . provide the name of the debtor" under § 9-503(a), they are "seriously misleading" as a matter of law pursuant to § 9-506(b). Furthermore, the undisputed facts in this case show that § 9-506(c) does not apply in this case. That section saves a financing statement from being "seriously misleading" if a search of UCC filings "under the debtor's correct name, using the filing office's standard search logic, . . . would disclose a financing statement that fails sufficiently to provide the name of the debtor" in accordance with § 9-503(a). Included in the record before us are the results of a UCC search conducted by Deere's counsel in Kansas's official and unofficial UCC search systems. Under both systems, she found no matches for the debtor's legal name "Terrance," but numerous matches for his nickname "Terry" and the initial "T." Thus, a search of the debtor's "correct name" did not disclose a financing statement, and therefore, § 9-506(c) does not apply. The result of Deere's UCC searches underscores the need for a clear-cut method of searching a debtor's name in UCC filings. The logical starting point for a person searching records would be to use the debtor's legal name. When a UCC search of the debtor's legal name does not provide any matches, parties in interest should be able to presume that the debtor's property is not encumbered, and they should not be charged with guessing what to do next if the legal name search does not result in any matches. Deere's financing statements, being seriously misleading, do not perfect its interest in the debtor's property and, therefore, the bankruptcy court erred in refusing to avoid its interests as against the trustee as a hypothetical lien creditor under 11 U.S.C. § 544(a)(1).

III. Conclusion

For the reasons stated herein, the bankruptcy court's Judgment is REVERSED.

QUESTIONS ON KINDERKNECHT

So it is clear, at least in the 10th Circuit and I would think anywhere else, that giving an individual debtor's nickname on a financing statement is generally not sufficient. Only the debtor's "legal name" will do. Does this eliminate any problems or guesswork for the secured party? Where and how does the diligent secured party find out the exact "legal name" of an individual debtor? There's the rub. As many have commented both before and after this decision, in the United States individuals do not necessarily have a single and distinct "legal name" any more than we have an individual citizenship or resident's number. Simply consider what you usually give as your "legal name" when asked. Is it the exact same string of alphanumeric characters as appears on your birth certificate? On you Social Security card? On your driver's license, perhaps first issued long ago? Do you or any of your acquaintances use one name for, say, business purposes and another for personal? Many people, usually women but not necessarily, of even *my* generation have opted for this compromise upon marriage. And, note, this is all perfectly legal. We don't want to get into a full discussion of the law of names and naming, but the general rule in the United States is that you can legally use any name you choose as long as it hasn't been adopted in an attempt to defraud. Given all this, what do you suggest the careful and risk-averse filer do when filing on an individual debtor?

PANKRATZ IMPLEMENT CO. v. CITIZENS NATIONAL BANK

Supreme Court of Kansas, 2006
281 Kan. 209, 130 P.3d 57, 59 U.C.C. Rep. Serv. 2d 53

Davis, J.: Pankratz Implement Co. (Pankratz) attempted to perfect its security interest in equipment sold to Rodger House. In filing with the Secretary of State, Pankratz spelled the debtor's name as *Roger* House. Citizens National Bank (CNB) later attempted to secure the same property using the debtor's correct name, Rodger House. Rodger House filed for bankruptcy; Pankratz obtained relief from the bankruptcy stay order and filed suit against CNB in order to realize its security interest. The district court determined in accordance with recently enacted amendments to Article 9 of the Kansas Uniform Commercial Code (UCC) effective July 1, 2001, that Pankratz was entitled to summary judgment because use of the debtor's incorrect name was a minor error and not seriously misleading. The Court of Appeals reversed, concluding that the use of the debtor's incorrect name was seriously misleading. We granted Pankratz' petition for review and affirm the Court of Appeals.

FACTS

The facts in this case are uncontroverted. On March 18, 1998, Rodger House purchased a Steiger Bearcat tractor from Pankratz. House signed a note and security agreement in favor of Pankratz using his correct name, Rodger House. Pankratz listed the debtor's name in the agreement as "Roger House" instead of "Rodger House." Pankratz, in turn, assigned its interest in the note and the collateral to Deere and Company (Deere). Deere then filed a financing statement with the Kansas Secretary of State on March 23, 1998, using the same misspelled name, Roger House.

On April 8, 1999, House executed a note and security agreement in favor of Citizens National Bank (CNB), from which House obtained a loan. House pledged as collateral, among other things, all equipment "that I now own and that I may own in the future." On March 4, 1999, CNB filed a financing statement with the Kansas Secretary of State using the correct name of the debtor, Rodger House.

On June 10, 2002, House filed a petition for bankruptcy under Chapter 7 in the United States Bankruptcy Court for the District of Kansas. On July 1, 2002, Deere reassigned the House note and security interest to Pankratz. Pankratz obtained relief from the automatic stay pursuant to 11 U.S.C. § 362 (2000) and filed suit in the district court against CNB seeking a declaratory judgment concerning its purchase money security interest.

DISCUSSION AND ANALYSIS

The sole question presented for resolution on undisputed facts is one of law to be determined under recently enacted amendments to Article 9 of the UCC. Because our answer depends upon the interpretation of the amendments to the UCC, our standard of review is de novo. *Heckert*, 278 Kan. at 225. Although the general issue in this case has been litigated previously in Kansas courts, no Kansas court has addressed the issue since the Revised Article 9 became effective on July 1, 2001. Thus, the case presents an issue of first impression.

[The court then set out the text of §§ 9-503 and 9-506.] [T]he undisputed facts in this case establish that a search under the debtor's correct name *using the filing office's standard search logic* did not disclose Pankratz' financing statement with the debtor's misspelled name. The express provisions of K.S.A. 2003 Supp. 84-9-506(b) provide that "except as otherwise provided in subsection (c), a financing statement that fails sufficiently to provide the name of the debtor in accordance with K.S.A. 2003 Supp. 84-9-503(a) and amendments thereto, is seriously misleading." Thus, Pankratz' financing statement using the misspelled name of the debtor, while prior in time, was seriously misleading, causing the Court of Appeals to direct that judgment be entered for CNB.

Our analysis involves a construction of the provisions of both statutes, *in pari materia*, and leads us to the conclusion that Pankratz' filed financing statement was seriously misleading, confirming the Court of Appeals decision. We could end our discussion and conclude that the expressed provisions of the law support the decision of the Court of Appeals. However, Pankratz advances several arguments in support of its position that the misspelled name of the debtor is only a minor error not seriously misleading. Pankratz asserts that the name requirements are not sufficiently defined especially for individuals under the new amendments and that a careful reading of subsection (c) does not support the bright-line rule adopted by the Court of Appeals, *viz.*, that failing to meet the requirements of subsection (c) makes the financing statement seriously misleading. The object of Pankratz' arguments is to place upon the party claiming a superior lien the responsibility to conduct a diligent search of past records filed with the Secretary of State to determine whether a prior lien exists. If the name requirements of the debtor are not fixed and certain, the use of a nickname or a misspelled name on the financing statement filed with the Secretary of State may require just such a search on the part of the party claiming a superior lien.

On the other hand, if the legislature intended by its amended version of the UCC set forth above to fix and make certain the name of the debtor requirement, such a change shifts the responsibility of the one filing with the Secretary of State to follow the name requirement with the effect being that the party searching for prior liens on the same property may rely on the name used on the financing statement eliminating the need to conduct diligent searches. We believe that the language used by the legislature and the intent behind the adoption of the most recent amendments had the effect of shifting the responsibility of getting the name on the financing statement right to the filing party, thereby enabling the searching party to rely upon that name and eliminating the need for multiple searches using variations of the debtor's name. This would have the effect of providing more certainty in the commercial world and reducing litigation as was required prior to the amendments to determine whether an adequate search was made.

[The court then goes on to discuss at length the *Kinderknecht* litigation, quoting at length with approval from the 10th Circuit's opinion, concluding that "the decision and reasoning of the 10th Circuit is sound and accurately reflects the legislative intent behind the new amendments to the UCC."]

The few other jurisdictions that have had an opportunity to construe the amendments have also been in accord with the *Kinderknecht*/Court of Appeals reasoning. See *In re FV Steel and Wire Co.*, 310 Bankr. 390, 394 (Bankr. E.D. Wis. 2004) (holding that a "rule that would burden a searcher with guessing at misspellings and various configurations of a legal name" would decrease the certainty desirable in commercial transactions and that the burden of filing under the correct name is properly on the filer); *In re Asheboro Precision Plastics, Inc.*, 2005 Bankr. Lexis 1091, *25, 2005 WL 1287743, *8 (Bankr. M.D.N.C. 2005) (unpublished opinion) ("Under Revised Article 9 and the underlying policy of simplifying financing statement searches" a financing statement is seriously misleading where a search under the correct name using standard search logic does not turn up the statement).

Finally, in determining legislative intent, the *amicus* brief filed by the Secretary of State proves instructive. The brief reinforces the notion, implied very strongly by the above discussion, that the intent of the filing requirements of Revised Article 9 is to shift the burden of filing correctly onto the filers and to allow searchers to rely on one search under the correct legal name of the debtor. Several experts who played a role in drafting and implementing the Revised Article 9 share this interpretation of the filing requirements of Revised Article 9.

Darrell W. Pierce, chair of the Article 9 Filing Project and member of the Article 9 Study Committee for the Permanent Editorial Board for the UCC, wrote that "case law that has served to protect filers at the expense of searchers by giving effect to filings not readily retrievable by a search will be overturned by Revised Article 9 . . . and, in doing so, obviates the need for complicated search logic and multiple name searches." Pierce, *Revised Article 9 of the Uniform Commercial Code: Filing System Improvements and Their Rationale*, 31 UCC L.J. 16, 17 (1998).

Harry Sigman sat on the Revised Article 9 Drafting Committee, and wrote that Article 9

> "does not provide an absolute requirement of perfection. At the same time, it does not burden searchers with the obligation to dream up every potential error and name variation and perform searches under all possibilities. Revised Article 9 allows a searcher to rely on a single search conducted under the correct name of the debtor and penalizes filers only for errors that result in the nondisclosure of the financing statement in a search under the correct name." Sigman, *The Filing System Under Revised Article 9*, 73 Am. Bankr. L.J. 61, 73 (1999).

The *amicus* brief references several other experts, including Steven O. Weise, the ABA Advisor to the Article 9 Drafting Committee, and Carl Ernst, publisher of *The UCC Revised Article 9 Alert* (Ernst Publishing Co. LLC, March 2002). These comments run along similar lines as those mentioned above.

The Kansas Court of Appeals in its decision, the express provisions of the revised amendments read *in pari materia*, and the Official UCC Comments are all in accord that the primary purpose of the revision of the name requirement is to lessen the amount of fact-intensive, case-by-case determinations that plagued earlier versions of the UCC, and to simplify the filing system as a whole. The object of the revisions was to shift the responsibility to the filer by requiring the not too heavy burden of using the legal name of the debtor, thereby relieving the searcher from conducting numerous searches using every conceivable name variation of the debtor. The effect of the revision is to provide more certainty in the commercial world and reduce litigation to determine whether an adequate search was done. The cases cited by Pankratz in support of its position mostly were decided prior to the adoption of the revisions. The more recent cases decided after the revisions of UCC Article 9 are in accord with the Court of Appeals' decision in this case.

Finally, the practical public policy considerations outlined by the 10th Circuit Bankruptcy Appellate Panel in *Kinderknecht,* and the opinions of several of the drafters of the Revised Article 9, while merely persuasive authority, support the decision of the Court of Appeals in this case. We conclude that such authority, as well as the express provisions of *K.S.A. 2003 Supp. 84-9-503* and *K.S.A. 2003 Supp. 84-9-506* construed *in pari materia,* demonstrate that Pankratz' filed financing statement was "seriously misleading."

Affirmed.

PROBLEM

10.3 Friendly Finance is a very friendly lender indeed. It will lend to just about anyone if it can get the right collateral. Assuming in each case that the firm has a valid security agreement describing the collateral sufficiently, do you see any problem for Friendly Finance if it indicates the collateral in the *initial financing statement* as follows?

(a) "all pianos owned by the debtor"
(b) "all equipment"
(c) "all inventory, now held or hereafter acquired"
(d) "all inventory,"
(e) "all of debtor's assets"
(f) "one tractor, International Haybaler, serial #1234576," when the serial number of the debtor's sole tractor is actually #1234567

IN RE PICKLE LOGGING, INC.

United States Bankruptcy Court for the Middle District of Georgia, 2002
286 Bankr. 181, 49 Collier Bankr. Cas. 2d 1103, 49 U.C.C. Rep. Serv. 2d 971

JOHN T. LANEY, III, B.J.: On October 10, 2002, the court held a hearing on the Motion of Deere Credit, Inc. to Reconsider Order on Motion for Adequate Protection and to Reconsider Order on Motion to Determine Secured Status, both orders dated September 3, 2002. At the conclusion of the hearing, the court took the matter under advisement. After considering the evidence presented at the hearing on August 16, 2002 and the continued hearing on August 21, 2002 hearing, the parties' briefs and oral arguments, as well as applicable statutory and case law, the court makes the following findings of fact and conclusions of law.

FACTS

Pickle Logging, Inc. ("Debtor") is an Americus, Georgia based company doing business in the tree logging industry. In an effort to cure an arrearage to Deere Credit, Inc. ("Movant"), Debtor refinanced eight pieces of equipment. The refinancing was done with Movant.

On April 18, 2002, Debtor filed for Chapter 11 bankruptcy protection. Prior to the bankruptcy filing, in addition to the refinancing mentioned above, Debtor had put the same eight pieces of equipment, as well as other assets, up as collateral in transactions with other creditors. Because there were multiple security interests in the eight pieces of equipment, Debtor filed motions to determine the secured status of a number of different creditors. After consent orders resolved much of the conflict between secured creditors as to priority and extent of security interests, the final issue remained as to the value of the eight pieces of equipment. The values assigned to each piece of equipment would determine the amount due to the secured creditors for adequate protection.

At a hearing held on August 16, 2002 and the continued hearing on August 21, 2002 to determine the value of the eight pieces of equipment, the present issue was raised: whether Movant had a perfected security interest in one specific piece of equipment, a 548G skidder serial number DW548GX568154 ("548G skidder"), which had been mislabeled in both the financing statement and the security agreement as a 648G skidder, serial number DW648GX568154. After hearing testimony from expert witnesses that a 548G skidder is substantially different in appearance, performance, and price from a 648G skidder, the court held that Movant did not have a perfected security interest in the 548G skidder because of the mislabeling. Therefore, Movant was an unsecured creditor as to the 548G skidder. The court did not assign a value to the 548G skidder for adequate protection payments. Movant has asked the court to reconsider its September 3, 2002 orders regarding adequate protection payments and the secured status of Movant as to the 548G skidder.

Movant contends that the mislabeling is not seriously misleading because it is off by only one digit. Movant urges that a person of ordinary business prudence would be put on notice to inquire further about the 548G skidder despite the mislabeling. Therefore, Movant has a perfected security interest in the 548G skidder and would not be subordinate to Debtor.

Debtor argues first that the 548G skidder owned by Debtor is not listed in the security agreement or the financing statement, therefore Movant does not have a security interest in the 548G skidder. Furthermore, Debtor argues that a person of ordinary business prudence would know that a 548G skidder differs substantially from a 648G skidder. Debtor contends that the mislabeling is seriously misleading because of the difference in the two models. Debtor argues that there is nothing patently erroneous about the serial number listed on the security agreement or the financing statement to put a person of ordinary business prudence on notice to inquire further. Finally, Debtor contends that, in order for a secured party to have a security interest in a piece of collateral, the security agreement must include a valid description of the collateral. Under contract law, Movant might have the right to reform the contract. However, because of the Chapter 11 bankruptcy proceeding, this remedy is not available to Movant. Even with reformation, Debtor, with the status of a lien creditor, would have higher priority than Movant would receive with a reformed security agreement.

Conclusions of Law

Under the Bankruptcy Code ("Code"), a debtor-in-possession has the same rights and powers as a trustee. Additionally, under the "strong arm" provision of 11 U.S.C. §544(a)(1), a debtor-in-possession acquires the status of a hypothetical lien creditor, deemed to be perfected as of the filing date of the bankruptcy petition.

Under Georgia law, the definition of a lien creditor includes a trustee in bankruptcy. See §9-102(a)(53)(C). Since a debtor-in-possession acquires the same rights and powers as a trustee, a debtor-in-possession has the status of a lien creditor under Georgia law as well. Further, under Georgia law, a party with an unperfected security interest is subordinate to a lien creditor. See §9-317(a)(2)(B). The question is whether Movant's security interest in the 548G skidder is perfected despite the mislabeling on the security agreement and the financing statement.

Pursuant to §9-203(b)(3)(A), a security interest in collateral is not enforceable against the debtor or third parties unless the debtor has signed, executed, or otherwise adopted a security agreement that contains a description of the collateral. §9-203(b)(3)(A); see also §9-102(a)(7). The description of the collateral in the security agreement and the financing statement, if required, must comport with §9-108(a). The description of collateral is sufficient if it reasonably identifies what is described. See §9-108(a). "The question of the sufficiency of [a] description of [collateral] in a [recorded document] is one of law. ...." *Bank of Cumming v. Chapman*, 245 Ga. 261, 264 S.E.2d 201 (1980), quoting *First National Bank of Fitzgerald v. Spicer*, 10 Ga. App. 503(1), 73 S.E. 753 (1911).

Any number of things could be used to describe collateral and satisfy §9-108(a). A physical description of the collateral, including or excluding a serial number, could be used so long as it "reasonably identifies what is described." The description merely needs to raise a red flag to a third party indicating that more investigation may be necessary to determine whether or not an item is subject to a security agreement. A party does not lose its secured status just because the description includes an inaccurate serial number. See *Yancey Brothers Company v. Dehco, Inc.*, 108 Ga. App. 875, 877, 134 S.E.2d 828, 830 (1964). However, if the serial number is inaccurate, there must be additional information that provides a "key" to the collateral's identity.

Here, the description in the security agreement and the financing statement are identical. Both documents list a 648G skidder with the serial number DW648GX568154. There is nothing obviously wrong with the model number or the serial number. 648G is a model number for one type of skidder sold by Movant. The serial number listed for the disputed skidder is in accordance with other serial numbers issued by Movant. The insurance value listed on the security agreement for the disputed skidder is only $10,000 less than the 648G skidder, serial number DW648GX564990 ("648G-4990 skidder"). With the $35,000 difference in insurance values between the 648G-4990 skidder and the 648G skidder, serial number DW648GX573931 ("648G-3931 skidder"), a $10,000 difference in insurance values would not raise a red flag.

According to testimony at the August 16, 2002 hearing, Debtor owned more than one of Movant's skidders, including at least two 548G skidders and at least two 648G skidders. There is nothing in either the financing statement or the security agreement that raises a red flag to a third party. A potential purchaser of the 548G skidder in dispute here could easily assume that the skidder is not covered by either the security agreement or the financing statement.

If just the model number was incorrect or if just the serial number was incorrect, the result may be different. It is apparent from the other items listed on the security agreement and the financing statement that the model number is reflected in the serial number. If the model number was not repeated in the serial number, then it would be apparent that something was wrong with one of the two numbers. At a minimum it should raise a red flag to a person of ordinary business prudence that further investigation is necessary. However, with both of the numbers reflecting a 648G skidder, there is nothing to indicate that there was a mistake.

Therefore, the court's order dated September 3, 2002 will not be changed. The 548G skidder is misdescribed in both the security agreement and the financing statement. The rights of Debtor, as a hypothetical lien creditor, are superior to the rights of Movant.

An order in accordance with this Memorandum Opinion will be entered.

QUESTIONS ON PICKLE LOGGING

Do you think the court in this case was unmindful of or not sufficiently sensitive to the overriding goals of the Article 9 filing system or the language in Comment 2 to § 9-108 that, "This section rejects any requirement that a description is insufficient unless it is exact and detailed (the so-called 'serial number' test)"? Given the result do you want to rethink your answer to Problem 10.3(f)?

PROBLEMS

10.4   Suppose that Friendly Finance lends to a particular debtor under a security agreement, agreed to by the debtor of course, which describes the collateral as "all musical instruments, now owned or hereafter acquired by the debtor." Friendly Finance files an initial financing statement which describes the collateral as "all pianos, now held or hereafter acquired." Does Friendly Finance have a security interest in the debtor's several valuable tubas and trombones? On what collateral, if any, does it have a perfected security interest?

10.5   Friendly Finance lends to another musically inclined debtor under a security agreement, again agreed to by this debtor, which describes the collateral as "all pianos, now owned or hereafter acquired by the debtor." Friendly Finance files an initial financing statement which describes the collateral as "all musical instruments, of whatever type, now held or hereafter acquired." In what collateral, if any, does the finance company have a security interest? In what collateral, if any, does it have a perfected security interest?

10.6   Discreet Financial Services ("DFS") makes a large loan to Acme Incorporated, a corporation organized under the laws of Delaware. It files an initial financing statement with the appropriate office in Delaware in which the collateral is indicated to be, "Certain equipment now owned by debtor, as more fully listed in detail in Exhibit A to the Security Agreement entered into on September 1, 2005 by the debtor and secured party named herein."

(a) When Acme files a bankruptcy petition in 2007, a representative of DFS immediately sends a copy of what he claims to the Security Agreement, along with its Exhibit A, to the bankruptcy trustee, demanding that the trustee acknowledge that DFS has a perfected security interest in all the equipment listed in the exhibit. If you were the trustee, would you accede to this demand? Do you believe a court would or should eventually find that DFS was perfected on the listed equipment?
(b) How would you deal with this question if instead the collateral has been indicated in the UCC1 as "Such collateral as is set forth in the Security Agreement entered into on September 1, 2005" by the named debtor and secured party?
(c) Suppose DFS had filed a UCC1, using the standard form as shown in § 9-521(a), and filled in Box 4 with only, "Such collateral as the debtor and secured party named herein have agreed. Call 1-800-555-6712 for details." Has DFS perfected in this situation?

10.7   Friendly Finance Company files a UCC1 in the proper place relative to a security interest it has taken in a particular debtor's accounts. In filling out the form it gets the debtor's name perfectly correct and indicates the collateral in a perfectly satisfactory manner. Unfortunately, the person responsible for the filing renders the secured party's name, in Box 3a, as "Friendly Financing Associates," although he does give the firm's mailing address correctly in Box 3c. This form is accepted by the filing office with no problem. Is Friendly Finance Company's security interest perfected by this filing?

CHAPTER

11

The Process of Filing

A. INTRODUCTION

We assume in this chapter that in representing the secured party we have decided in which state or states to file an initial financing statement. We have also prepared that statement in written form or have collected the information we will need to file electronically where the state so permits.

So now how do we actually get the filing done? What can go wrong in the filing process, or to put it more positively, what should we do to ensure that nothing does go wrong and the filing is effective? What then is the result of such a filing?

B. PREPARATION

In preparation for discussion of the problems and the single case in this chapter, read carefully the following parts of the Code:

- Reread § 9-308(a), especially its final sentence
- Section 9-502(d) and Comment 3 to this section
- Section 9-509(a) & (b) and Comments 2 through 4 to this section
- Section 9-510(a)
- Section 9-516 and its Comments 2, 3, and 9
- Section 9-517
- Section 9-518(a) and (c)
- Section 9-520(a) through (c) and its Comment 2
- Section 9-525(a)

You will also want to return to whatever source—in printed form or online—you have been using to check out the details of filing in your state, at least to answer the first problem presented.

C. PROBLEMS AND CASES

PROBLEMS

11.1 Spend some time looking over the rules and regulations of the office in your state where Article 9 filings are to be made. Among other matters you should be able to determine:

(a) If your state allows hand delivery of Article 9 filings, where would you have to show up to make the delivery? What are the hours of operation during which such filings will be accepted?
(b) If your state allow for delivery by mail, to what address should the mailing be sent?
(c) If your state allows for electronic delivery of Article 9 filings, how is such filing done?
(d) What fee must be tendered along with an initial financing statement in order to get the filing office to accept the filing? In what form must the tender of the fee be made, when the filing is delivered by hand, sent by mail, or if possible made electronically?

11.2 The debtor, Makes-U-More, Incorporated, a manufacturing corporation organized under the laws of Texas, authorizes the secured party, Lone Star Bank, to file an initial financing statement covering all of its inventory with the Texas Secretary of State's office. The bank's attorney prepares an initial financing statement giving the debtor's name as "Makes-You-More, Incorporated." This initial financing statement along with the necessary filing fee is delivered in a proper manner to the Secretary of State's office. As it happens this office also keeps track, in a separate filing system, of all corporations organized under the laws of the state of Texas.

(a) Would the filing office have the discretion to reject this filing, sending it back to the bank with a note that, "We have no record of a Texas corporation of the name indicated as debtor"?
(b) What if the filing office did accept the filing? Would it have been wrong to do so? What would be the legal effect of the filing?
(c) What if instead the initial financing statement had been prepared correctly by the bank's attorney, that is, bearing the correct legal name of "Makes-U-More, Incorporated," and the filing office had accepted the filing, but it had then indexed the filing under the incorrect name? What is the legal status of the bank's filing in this situation?

11.3 The debtor continues to be Makes-U-More, Incorporated and the secured party is the Lone Star Bank. The initial financial statement prepared by the bank's attorney gives the debtor's correct name but fails to indicate in any way the jurisdiction under which the debtor corporation was organized.

(a) *Must* the filing office accept this filing, assuming of course the correct fee has also been tendered?
(b) *May* the filing office accept this filing?
(c) If the filing office does accept the filing, what is its legal effect?

11.4   Finally, at least with respect to these parties, assume that the initial financing statement prepared by the bank's attorney fails to give the bank's name correctly (it fills in "Loan Star" instead of "Lone Star") as that of the secured party, although it does give the correct address for the bank. The filing office accepts the filing fee and accepts this filing. What is its legal effect?

UNITED STATES OF AMERICA v. ORREGO

United States District Court for the Eastern District of New York, 2004
2004 U.S. Dist. LEXIS 12252, 54 U.C.C. Rep. Serv. 2d 145

JOHNSON, Senior District Judge: On January 5, 2004, Plaintiff, the United States of America ("the Government"), brought suit against Defendant, federal inmate Adalberto Orrego, a/k/a "Adalberto Orrego Buritica," pursuant to 28 U.S.C. § 2201-02 (Declaratory Judgment Act), 18 U.S.C. § 1341 (fraud injunction statute), N.Y.U.C.C. § § 9-625 and 9-509 (N.Y.U.C.C. statutes), and 31 U.S.C. § § 3729 et seq. (False Claims Act). The Government also sought preliminary and permanent injunctive relief against Defendant. The Government's Complaint alleged that Defendant recorded false and invalid Uniform Commercial Code ("UCC") "liens" against the real and personal property of United States District Court Judge Edward R. Korman ("Chief Judge Korman"), Assistant United States Attorney Tracy Dayton ("AUSA Dayton"), and Mr. Michael A. Zenk ("Mr. Zenk"), Warden of the Metropolitan Detention Center, Brooklyn ("MDC"). The Government also brought suit against the Secretary of the State for the State of New York ("Secretary of State") to obtain an order directing it to effectuate a termination of the liens filed or recorded, or caused to be filed or recorded, by Defendant. The Government and the Secretary of State have since entered into a stipulation settling the matter.

On February 4, 2004, this Court granted the Government's motion for a temporary restraining order. On February 13, 2004, this Court granted the Government's motion for a preliminary injunction and found that Defendant Orrego violated the temporary restraining order, but reserved on what sanction should be imposed. On February 23, 2004, the Court held that a contempt sanction of $5,000 was appropriate, in order to coerce Defendant's compliance with the Court's orders. The Government now moves for summary judgment against Defendant, and Defendant does not oppose the motion. For the reasons stated herein, the Government's motion is GRANTED, and the Government is awarded a judgment of $5,500.

Fraud Injunction Statute (18 U.S.C. § 1341)

The Government requests permanent injunctive relief under the fraud injunction statute. The statute provides that the Attorney General may commence a civil action in any Federal court when a person is "violating or about to violate this chapter [including 18 U.S.C. § 1341, which prohibits mail fraud]." A person violates the mail fraud statute if he devises "any scheme or artifice to defraud or for obtaining money or property by means of false or fraudulent pretenses, . . . [and] places in any post office . . . any matter or thing whatever to be sent or delivered by the Postal Service." Thus, to establish a violation, Plaintiff must show: "(1) a scheme to defraud (2) furthered by use of the mails (3) for the purpose of obtaining money or property."

In this case, Defendant devised and executed a scheme to defraud for the purpose of obtaining money or property through the filing of false liens with the Secretary of State. These false liens contained false claims of payments due to Defendant by Chief Judge Korman, AUSA Dayton, and Mr. Zenk, all of whom were listed as Defendant's debtors. Defendant claimed that he had "copyrighted" his name and that these individuals had used his name in fulfillment of their official duties, without first obtaining permission to do so. Defendant's scheme to file liens against these government officials was therefore a fraudulent one.

Defendant also testified that he intended to obtain money from this scheme. ("My intention was to assure my fees for the unauthorized use of my property.") ("Q. By submitting this invoice to AUSA Dayton you intended for her to submit payment of six million dollars to you, is that correct? A. Yes.") He clearly contemplated harm to Chief Judge Korman, AUSA Dayton, and Mr. Zenk through the mere filing of the liens, with or without payment. ("Q. And you knew by listing Warden Zenk on Ex. B and AUSA Dayton on C and E that you would be damaging their credit rating? A. Yes.")

[The court also found that the defendant indisputably used the mails to further his scheme to defraud and further that the ongoing scheme — Oreggo has also testified that he intended to continue filing such liens against government employees that use his name in the course of their official duties — justified the grant of injunctive relief.]

New York Uniform Commercial Code (N.Y.U.C.C. § § 9-625 and 9-509)

Under New York law, a debtor is entitled to $500 in statutory damages from a person who files a record that the person is not entitled to file under N.Y.U.C.C. § 9-509(a). See N.Y.U.C.C. § 9-625(e)(3). Pursuant to § 9-509(a), a person may file an initial financing statement only if: (1) the debtor authorizes the filing by (a) authenticating or (b) being bound to a security agreement or (c) acquiring collateral, or (2) the person holds an agricultural lien and the collateral at issue is only that related to the agricultural lien. Here, none of the listed debtors acquired collateral and Defendant does not have an agricultural lien. Therefore, the only way that Defendant could have been authorized to file a lien under the New York statute would have been if the purported debtors authorized the filing by authenticating or being bound to a security agreement.

Although Defendant purported to file a security agreement, Chief Judge Korman, AUSA Dayton, and Mr. Zenk could not have authenticated it before Defendant filed the initial financing statements against them, since Defendant did not send any copies of the lien-related documents to Chief Judge Korman and AUSA Dayton until March 12, 2003, and has not yet sent anything to Mr. Zenk.

Defendant asserts that by using his name in official documents, the alleged debtors authorized him to file the lien. However, Defendant cannot bind these individuals simply by asserting, within the security agreement, that their use of his name will cause them to be bound. Additionally, no basis in law exists for Defendant's alleged copyright of his own name. Accordingly, this Court imposes statutory damages in the amount of $500 in accordance with N.Y.U.C.C. § 9-625(e)(3).

FALSE CLAIMS ACT (31 U.S.C. §§ 3729 ET SEQ.)

Under the False Claims Act any person who "knowingly presents, or causes to be presented, to an officer or employee of the United States Government . . . a false or fraudulent claim for payment or approval . . . is liable to the United States Government for a civil penalty of not less than $5,000 and not more than $10,000, plus 3 times the amount of damages which the Government sustains because of the act of that person. . . ." The term "knowingly" means that a person "has actual knowledge of the information; acts in deliberate ignorance of the truth or falsity of the information; or acts in reckless disregard of the truth or falsity of the information. . . . No proof of specific intent to defraud is required." The term "claim" includes: "any request or demand, whether under a contract or otherwise, for money or property which is made to a contractor, grantee, or other recipient if the United States Government provides any portion of the money or property which is requested or demanded, or if the Government will reimburse such contractor, grantee, or other recipient for any portion of the money or property which is requested or demanded."

The Court finds that Defendant's liens and lien notices are "claims" within the context of the False Claims Act. Defendant submitted an invoice in the amount of six million dollars to AUSA Dayton for the use of Defendant's name in the Complaint, Indictment, and Plea Agreement. This invoice was a false claim that violated the False Claims Act. With regard to the scienter requirement, it is indisputable that Defendant submitted a false invoice to AUSA Dayton with no basis in law or fact and that he did so intentionally or with willful blindness or reckless disregard for the truth.

Having determined that Defendant knowingly made a false claim, the Court finds that Defendant violated the False Claims Act and that there is no genuine issue of material fact for trial. As for damages, the Court finds that Defendant, an inmate with limited resources, is liable to the government in the amount of $5,000.00. The Court does not award the Government treble damages because the Government has not made a showing of damages.

CONCLUSION

For the foregoing reasons, the Court grants the Government's motion for summary judgment. In addition, the Court orders the following:

(a) All liens filed by Defendant against all present and former federal employees are declared null, void, and of no legal effect;
(b) Defendant is permanently enjoined from filing any lien or taking any steps to file any liens in any jurisdiction relating to any present or former federal employees, without first obtaining leave of this Court;
(c) Any and all filings in contravention to the permanent injunction are void ab initio, absent a court order to the contrary;
(d) Defendant must pay a civil penalty of $5,000 under the False Claims Act;
(e) Defendant must pay $500 in statutory damages under the New York Uniform Commercial Code;
(f) Defendant shall pay the United States' costs in this action in an amount to be determined; and
(g) Defendant's inmate account shall be attached for payments of the aforementioned civil penalty, statutory damages, attorney's fees, and costs, until he has completely satisfied all such payments.

QUESTIONS ON ORREGO

First of all, what error at the New York Secretary of State's office allowed these "bogus" initial financing statements to get on its publicly available records in the first place?

Secondly, what was the legal effect of the filings made by Orrego?

More generally, consider the practical implications: This opinion is actually about twice as long as it appears in this edited version. As the court pointed out in one footnote, the United States sued on behalf of Chief Judge Korman, AUSA Dayton, and Mr. Zenk, "all of whom were subject to these false liens for actions in their official capacity." Orrego represented himself in the action, presumably having time on his hands. Had Orrego made similar filings against another, private individual how much do you expect it might have cost her or him in legal fees to get an order such as the United States got on behalf of its representatives in this case? How likely is it that she or he would get her or his costs reimbursed by Orrego in conformity with the judge's order? If a private individual came to you and told you that she was having problems with such harassing "bogus" filings, what would you advise? Would you suggest she just ignore the situation?

PROBLEMS

11.5 Gabriela opens a small restaurant, Gabriela's Place. The restaurant begins to do very well, and she begins to consider expanding the size of her enterprise. To do so, however, she will need additional capital. In July of 2006, she applies to the Springfield State Bank for a small business loan, filling in a formal loan application, and later delivers to the bank a variety of documents requested by the loan officer so that he may give her application "full consideration." After a thorough investigation of her finances and her current set-up, the bank loan officer determines that her loan request be granted and on what terms. He explains these to Gabriella over the telephone, and she says she is willing to borrow on the basis the loan manager has laid out. On September 1, Gabriela comes into the bank. She signs a security agreement granting the bank a security interest in her "equipment, now held and hereafter acquired." The loan officer then signs and gives to her a paper stating that the bank has granted her a "guaranteed line of credit" good for up to $50,000. She can call on this credit at any time when the need arises in conjunction with her expanding business. The paper also sets forth her obligation to make monthly payments to the bank, based on the amount of credit outstanding as of any given month and a stated rate of interest. On September 10, the loan officer sends an initial financing statement, complete in all respects, to the filing office (which you may assume is the correct place for filing on this interest). The initial financing statement is received by the filing office on September 13, and is accepted by it on that date.

(a) As of what date is the bank's security interest attached to the collateral?
(b) As of what date is the bank's initial financing statement effective?
(c) As of what date is the bank's security interest in the collateral perfected?

11.6 Suppose instead that when Gabriela initially makes her application for the loan, the bank asks not only for various financial documents about her and her business, but also that she sign a paper authorizing it, the bank, to file in the proper place an initial financing statement covering the collateral she is offering up. She does so sign, and the bank files this initial financing statement in the proper place on July 8, 2006. This filing is received and accepted by the filing office on July 11. Once again the loan officer decides to approve her loan, and on September 1 she comes into the bank to finalize the deal. She signs the security agreement prepared by the loan officer. He signs and gives her the paper stating the bank's commitment to a $50,000 line of credit she can call on at any time.

(a) As of what date is the bank's security interest attached to the collateral?
(b) As of what date is the bank's initial financing statement effective?
(c) As of what date is the bank's security interest in the collateral perfected?

CHAPTER

12

Later Filings and Changes
in the Situation

A. INTRODUCTION

In this chapter we will assume that a sufficient initial financing statement has been filed in the proper place by the secured party, which had been authorized to make that filing. Is that the end of the story? Not necessarily. We deal first with the fact that the initial financing statement is not perpetually effective. It may need to be continued by the filing of a *continuation statement* if its role in perfecting a security interest is to last beyond a finite period set by the statute.

We must also consider the possibility that the filing is no longer necessary to perfect an interest, the obligation of the debtor having been paid off. The debtor will want a to clear up the public record by the filing of a *termination statement* relating to the initial financing statement.

While we tend to speak of the continuation statement and termination statement as distinct kinds of filings, note that each is just a particular instance of what Article 9 refers to as an *amendment* to the financing statement. To see what form an amendment (at least one in written form) will usually take, see §9-521(b) and the format reproduced in that section. Note in particular the place for the filer to check the particular box or boxes that apply to his or her situation in parts 2 through 8 of that form.

In all that follows, remember that the *financing statement* is defined for Article 9 purposes as "a record or records composed of an initial financing statement [that which was the topic of the last few chapters] and any filed record relating to the initial financing statement [of the type we'll explore in this chapter]." It is the filing office's responsibility to keep this accumulation of filings in good order and available to anyone searching the records. The question of what to make of all this information retrieved in response to a request—what exactly the legal effect of the accumulated filings is—stands as the responsibility of the searcher.

The later material in this chapter deals with a related problem, or really a set of problems, about which the secured party must be concerned. During the course of the secured transaction, the debtor may take some action which requires the secured party to refile in a fairly short period of time — either by amending the existing financing statement or even perhaps by having to file a new initial financing statement in a different jurisdiction — if it is to prevent any lost of or damage to its perfected status. Consider, for example, the following:

Relocation of the Debtor: The location of the debtor is, as we know, the key to with which state the financing statement is to be filed. See § 9-316(a)(2). If the debtor relocates to another jurisdiction the secured party is given four months to refile in the new jurisdiction.

Change in Location of the Collateral: Under the prior version in effect until the middle of 2001, a change in location of the collateral, even sometimes a move only to another part of the state, could have made necessary a refiling by the secured party. This is no longer true under the revised version of Article 9. Still, I'm sure you can imagine the purely practical reasons why the secured party may want to insist that the debtor agree either not to relocate the collateral without the secured party's permission, or at least to give timely notice when it intends to do so.

Change in Name of the Debtor: See § 9-507(c). If the change of name has the effect of rendering the financing statement "seriously misleading," then at least with respect to some later acquired collateral, the secured party had better file an amendment to the financing statement giving the correct name within four months of the change in name.

Transfer of the Collateral to a Person Who Thereby Become a Debtor: In many instances when the original debtor transfers all or a part of the collateral to another person that person will not be a debtor under Article 9, since he, she or it will have taken the collateral free-and-clear of the secured party's interest — as we'll see in a later chapter. This is not always true, however. If the transferee takes the collateral still *subject to* the secured party's interest then the transferee fits within the definition of "debtor" given in § 9-102(a)(28)(A). If the transferee in such a situation is located within the same state as the transferor, no new filing is required. See § 9-507(a). Under § 9-316(a)(3), however, if the transferee is located in another state, the secured party is given one year to make a new filing in that state under the transferee's name.

Given the significance of actions such as this on the debtor's part, you would expect a well-drafted security agreement to contains the debtor's promise either not to take any such action, to do so only under carefully prescribed circumstances, or perhaps to do so only after giving adequate notice of the contemplated action to the secured party. We can even assume that in most instances the debtor will make good on its obligations set forth in the security agreement. Still, would you think the secured party could feel totally at ease knowing that the debtor has bound itself to such provisions in the security agreement? Even the most well-intentioned and honest debtor may occasionally forget or fail to properly follow through on all of the duties it has committed itself to by signing the security agreement with all its fine print and clause after clause. The secured party will be well-advised to set up its own procedures to monitor the situation so that the type of behavior on the debtor's part which will call for a refiling does not pass undiscovered. You will want to consider as you go through the later problems how the secured party will have to protect itself against an unpleasant surprise.

At the same time, as you will see, because the workings of Article 9 do give the secured party some time, either four months or a year depending on the situation, to file in a new jurisdiction and preserve its *continuous* perfection, this will of course put some risk on those searching in this new jurisdiction for filings under the debtor's name during this period. What will the diligent searcher have to do — what questions might it have to ask or information pursue — to minimize the possibility that *it* will be caught by surprise by a later, but to some degree retroactive, filing?

B.   PREPARATION

In preparation for the initial material in this chapter through Problem 12.4, on the amendment process, take a preliminary look at the following:

- Section 9-509(d)
- Section 9-510(c)
- Section 9-512, and Comments 2 and 3 to this section
- Section 9-513, and its Comments 2 and 3
- Section 9-515(a), (c), (d), and (e)
- Section 9-521(b)
- Section 9-522
- Section 9-625(b) and (e)(4)

In preparation for the later problems, dealing with changes in the situation which may necessitate a new filing by the secured party, look to:

- Section 9-316(a) and (b), and Comments 2 and 3 to this section
- Section 9-507 and all comments to this section

C. PROBLEMS AND CASES

PROBLEM

12.1 In 2006 Gabriela was able to arrange for a $50,000 line of credit from the Springfield State Bank, which she has since used as a source of working capital to most efficiently run and carefully expand her business, a successful restaurant. To obtain the loan she granted to the bank a security interest in "all her equipment now held or hereafter acquired." As part of her initial application for this loan she had authorized the bank to file an initial financing statement on the proposed collateral prior to its award of the loan. The bank filed an initial financing statement in the proper place on July 8, 2006. This filing was received and accepted by the filing office on July 11. After the loan officer decided to approve her loan she came into the bank on September 1 to finalize the deal. She left the bank on that day with the bank's commitment to the $50,000 line of credit on which she must make regular monthly payments, based on the amount of the credit she has actually called upon and on a stated rate of interest. The line of credit is not written to have any end date or fixed term.

(a) Does the filing made by the bank in July 2006 perfect its interest in Gabriela's equipment? If so, does it perfect this interest indefinitely?
(b) Suppose that the bank files a proper continuation statement on May 13, 2011. What is the effect of its having made this filing?
(c) Suppose instead that the bank's continuation statement was not filed until July 15, 2011. What is its effect?
(d) Suppose that it filed its continuation statement on January 5, 2011. What is the situation then?
(e) Finally, what if it filed not a continuation statement but an entirely new initial financing statement on May 13, 2011?

BARNES v. TURNER

Supreme Court of Georgia, 2004
278 Ga. 788, 606 S.E.2d 849

FLETCHER, Chief Justice: The issue in this legal malpractice case is what duty attorney David Turner, Jr. owed his client, William Barnes, Jr., with respect to maintaining Barnes's security interest that lapsed. The Court of Appeals held that Turner's only duty was to inform Barnes that his security interest required renewal in five years. Because under that view the statute of limitations expired before Barnes filed his malpractice action, the Court of Appeals affirmed the trial court's decision to grant Turner's motion to dismiss. We conclude, however, that if Turner failed to inform Barnes of the renewal requirement, Turner undertook a duty to renew the security interest himself. The statute of limitations has not expired for an alleged breach of that duty, and therefore we reverse.

On October 1, 1996, Barnes sold his company, William Barnes' Quality Auto Parts, Inc., to James and Rhonda Lipp for $220,000. The Lipps paid $40,000 at the closing and executed a ten-year promissory note in favor of Barnes for the $180,000 balance. The note was secured by a blanket lien on the Lipps's assets. On October 30, 1996, Turner perfected Barnes's security interest by filing UCC financing statements. Viewing the facts in the light most favorable to Barnes (as the non-moving party), Turner did not, however, inform Barnes that under OCGA § 11-9-515, financing statements are only effective for five years, although their renewal for another five years is expressly provided for in that statute. The renewal is effected by filing continuation statements no earlier than six months before the end of the initial period. No renewal statements were filed, and on October 30, 2001, the original statements lapsed.

Unknown to Barnes, the Lipps had pledged the same collateral to F&M Bank and Trust Company and to Mid-State Automotive Distributors on December 28, 1998 and January 29, 2001, respectively. Both of these companies filed UCC financing statements, which put them in a senior position to Barnes when his financing statements lapsed. Barnes is still owed more than $142,792.09 under the promissory note, and James Lipp is now in Chapter 7 bankruptcy.

Barnes sued Turner for malpractice on October 18, 2002. The trial court granted Turner's motion to dismiss. Finding that the only possible incident of malpractice was Turner's failure to inform Barnes of the renewal requirement in October 1996, the Court of Appeals held that the four-year statute of limitations had run and affirmed the trial court. We granted Barnes's petition for certiorari.

Barnes contends that the Court of Appeals erred in simply looking to Turner's actions in October 1996 as constituting the malpractice. If Turner had renewed the financing statements in 2001, Barnes argues, there would have been no lapse in his security interest and thus no malpractice. Barnes contends that Turner's duty was to safeguard his security interest, which Turner could have satisfied by *either* informing Barnes of the renewal requirement or renewing the financing statements in 2001. Under this view, Turner breached his duty in 2001, when he failed to do both, and thus the statute of limitations on Barnes's action has not expired. For the following reasons, we agree.

A motion to dismiss should only be granted if "the allegations of the complaint, when construed in the light most favorable to the plaintiff with all doubts resolved in the plaintiff's favor, disclose with certainty that the plaintiff would not be entitled to relief under any state of provable facts." Accordingly, the grant of Turner's motion to dismiss was only proper if Barnes's duty ended in 1996.

Turner contends that he was not retained to file renewal statements. While Georgia's appellate courts have not previously addressed this issue, decisions from other states make clear that an attorney in Turner's position must at least file original UCC financing statements, even absent specific direction from the client. We agree. An attorney has the duty to act with ordinary care, skill, and diligence in representing his client. In sale of business transactions where the purchase price is to be paid over time and collateralized, it is paramount that the seller's attorney prepare and file UCC financing statements to perfect his client's security interest. See *Practical Offset, Inc. v. Davis*, 404 N.E.2d 516, 520 (Ill. App. 1980). The failure to file a UCC financing statement has even been held to constitute legal malpractice as a matter of law. See *Lory v. Parsoff*, 296 A.D.2d 535, (N.Y. App. Div. 2002); Deb-Jo Constr. v. Westphal, 210 A.D.2d 951 (N.Y. App. Div. 1994). We further hold, for the reasons given below, that if the financing statements require renewal before full payment is made to the seller, then the attorney has some duty regarding this renewal. Otherwise the unpaid portion of the purchase price becomes unsecured and the seller did not receive the protection he bargained for.

Safeguarding a security interest is not some unexpected duty imposed upon the unwitting lawyer; it goes to the very heart of why Turner was retained: to sell Barnes's business in exchange for payment. We do not, as the dissent contends, demand that the lawyer "ascertain the full extent of the client's 'objectives' "; only that the lawyer take reasonable, legal steps to fulfill the client's *main, known* objective — to be paid for the business he sold.

The dissent views only the sale of the business as important since this is what happens at the closing; but why does a client sell his business if not to receive payment? When the dissent argues that Turner's duty was simply to "close" the transaction, it fails to recognize that closing this particular transaction meant taking the reasonable steps that competent attorneys would take to legally secure their clients' right to receive payment for the businesses they have sold. Where payment is to be made in less than five years, Georgia law does not require renewal of the initial financing statements and thus the lawyer's duty is only to file the initial statements. But where payment is to take longer than five years, the lawyer — being trusted by his client to know how to safeguard his security interest under Georgia law — has some duty regarding renewal of the financing statements. The question is the nature of that duty.

Under the dissent's view, a client has to specifically ask his lawyer to renew the financing statements for this to be among the lawyer's duties. But how can the client be expected to know of this legal requirement? He hires the lawyer because the lawyer knows the law. The client cannot be expected to explicitly ask the lawyer to engage in every task necessary to fulfill the client's objectives.

The Court of Appeals held that a failure to inform by Turner was the sole possible grounds for malpractice. But this is too narrow a definition of Turner's duty. The duty was not necessarily to inform Barnes of the renewal requirement; often transactional attorneys do no such thing and simply renew the financing statements themselves. These attorneys have not breached a duty. Turner's duty was to safeguard Barnes's security interest. There were two means of doing so: by informing Barnes of the renewal requirement, or by renewing the financing statements himself in 2001. Either one would have been sufficient to comply with Turner's duty, and any breach of that duty occurred only upon Turner's failure to do both.

Further, if Turner's only duty arose in 1996, then Barnes had to bring suit before the financing statements could even be renewed to comply with the four-year statute of limitations. Barnes contends that any such action would have been dismissed as unripe because he was still a secured party at the time. He is correct. The dissent's view deprives Barnes and any clients in his position of any remedy for malpractice. The dissent's view precludes Barnes from ever maintaining a malpractice suit against Turner, who failed to take a simple, necessary action that will likely leave Barnes without his business and without over 78% of the purchase price he is still owed for that business.

The dissent's hyberbole about the effect of this opinion mischaracterizes our holding, which is based on a unique set of facts: a collateralized, pay-ment-over-time arrangement in exchange for a sale of business where the payment period exceeds the five-year life span afforded to initial financing statements under OCGA § 11-9-515. The lawyer, being retained to protect his client's interests in connection with the sale of his business, is the only party who knows the legal requirements for maintaining the effectiveness of the security interest. He can either share this knowledge with his client — a very simple step — or renew the financing statements before they expire — an equally simple step. The dissent's concern over the expansion of attorney duties is unwarranted.

In light of the foregoing considerations, we reverse the Court of Appeals's decision that affirmed the trial court's grant of Turner's motion to dismiss. Barnes's malpractice action was filed within four years of the failure to renew the financing statements in 2001, and thus may proceed.

Judgment reversed. All the Justices concur, except Benham, Thompson and Hines, JJ., who dissent.

PROBLEMS

12.2   Essie Cashmore lives in a large mansion on an extensive estate in the ritziest suburb of Chicago. For many years now she has considered herself a patron of up-and-coming young artists and bought many of their earlier works, which she has proudly displayed throughout her man-sion. In particular she owns a number of paintings done by the artist Graffito when he was still a young man. In 2007, she arranges for a loan from Discreet Financial Services, a firm that is in the business of lending to high-end clients only. As part of the loan agreement, DFS is granted a security interest in two particular paintings in Essie's collection ("Untitled #1" and "Untitled #2"). These two paintings are carefully described in the security agreement and this same description is carried over to the initial financing statement which DFS files with the Secretary of State of Illinois prior to finalizing the loan. In 2009, Essie contacts DFS. She has been asked to make a donation of Untitled #1 to the Chicago Museum of Fine Arts, but she knows she cannot do this without DFS agreeing to release it security interest in that particular painting. The loan manager who deals with her account says that his firm would be willing to do this only if she were to substitute some additional collateral worth no less than this painting, as her outstanding loan balance has not dropped dramatically from what it was at the origination of the loan. She says she is willing to put up another one of her works by Graffitto ("Unitled #3), in substitution. An appraiser of contemporary art employed by DFS comes to Essie's home to view this work and concludes that it is worth at least as much as Untitled #1. What further investigation and follow-up paperwork will DFS have to do to accommodate Essie's request that the one painting be substituted for the other one as collateral for her loan? What filing will it need to make?

12.3   Suppose further than in 2011, Essie is able to fully pay off all of the amount she has borrowed from DFS based on her putting up the paintings as collateral.

(a) Is DFS obligated to file a termination statement with the Secretary of State of Illinois reflecting this fact?
(b) Would you answer to this question be any different if all of the various paintings which Essie had put up as collateral to secure the loan from DFS had never been kept at her home, but had instead hung on the walls of a business office she maintains in downtown Chicago?

12.4   You work in the commercial loan department of Longhorn Bank, one of the largest commercial lenders in the Dallas-Fort Worth area. You are approached by the President of Makes-U-More, Incorporated, a relatively new manufacturing corporation organized under the laws of Texas. She tells you that she would like to explore the possibility of her company taking out a sizable loan from your bank, the purpose of which would be to expand the enterprise, and which she suggests be secured by an interest the corporation would grant in "all inventory and equipment," now held or hereafter acquired. As part of your preliminary investigation, you have a search of all Article 9 filings made with the Texas Secretary of State in which the debtor's name is given as the organization "Makes-U-More, Incorporated." The search reveals an initial financing statement filed in 2007 on the corporation, giving the name of Lone Star State Bank, another major lender in the area, as that of the secured party, and indicating the collateral as "all inventory and equipment." The search also shows that a termination statement relating to this initial financing statement was filed in 2009, in fact just a few weeks before your initial meeting with the President of the corporation, and was duly accepted by the Secretary of State's office. When you ask her about this, she tells you, "No need to worry yourself about that. We did some business with Lone Star for a while, but as you can see that's all over with now." Does that fully put you mind to rest and assure you that you will be able to take a security interest in the corporation's inventory and equipment that will be the only such interest that company has outstanding?

NOTE

As you work through Problems 12.5 through 12.8, you should be looking for not only the "correct answers," to each, but thinking through what the implications are of those answers for parties who use and rely upon the Article 9 filing system. What pitfalls do you see for the unwary?

From the point of view of the secured party, what provisions might you want to include in the security agreement entered into with the debtor to help flag potential problems? Beyond that, what might you do to "monitor" independently—in addition to checking your mail and phone messages regularly in case the debtor has written or called to tell you when certain changes have taken or are soon to take place—to keep things in order and to protect your interest?

Then think about it from the point of view of the "searcher." What questions should you ask of a party which has proposed putting up some particularly collateral or selling you some personal property to avoid getting caught in a "tricky" situation? Beyond asking questions, what more might you want to do to minimize the chance of an unpleasant surprise somewhere down the road?

PROBLEMS

12.5 Louie Glitz operates a small jewelry boutique, Louie's of Litchfield, as a sole proprietor. In 2006 he is able to obtain a Small Business Line of Credit from First Bank of Connecticut, granting the bank a security interest in "all inventory, now held or after-acquired" of his business. At the time of his initially obtaining this loan, Louie lived in a house in Litchfield, walking distance from his store. In 2009, Louie decides to relocate his store to the town of Milbrook, New York, naturally enough changing the name of the store to "Louie's of Milbrook."

(a) Assuming that the bank made a filing correct in all respects at the time its arrangement with Louie was initiated in 2006, does it have to make any new or further filings in 2009 because of the store's relocation and change in name to continue its perfection on Louie's inventory?
(b) What if instead of moving his store in 2009, he had left the store where it was but had rather moved himself and his family to a new home in Milbrook, New York?

12.6 Suppose that Louie Glitz of the previous problem doesn't move either his store or his residence during 2009. Things do change for him dramatically, however, when he meets a charming local artist, Kendra Knot, and they decide to marry. When Louie is talking one day with the loan officer who is in charge of his account at First Bank of Connecticut, he just can't resist telling her of his good news. In the course of the ensuing conversation, the loan officer asks Louie if either he or his bride-to-be expect to change his or her name once they are married. "Well," says Louie, "frankly, we haven't quite worked that out. We've sorta been thinking of using Glitz-Knot, or perhaps Knot-Glitz, which Kendra seems to prefer, in social settings and the like. But I guess I'll still be using my own real name in the business." Based on this conversation, the loan officer wonders whether there is any need to consider any change or addition to the filings which the bank has made in connection with its loan to Louie. What do you advise?

12.7 The Fresno Furniture Corporation is in the business of making its own line of furniture that is sold in finer store throughout the country. The corporation was initially organized under the laws of the state of California many years ago. Since the early 1990's, the bank has operated with help of a large loan from a major commercial lender, The Commerce Group, which has been given an interest in "all equipment, now held or after-acquired" of Fresno. The Commerce Group initially made a proper filing to perfect its interest and has filed continuation statements as needed. In 2008, under the advice of its lawyers, Fresno Furniture reincorporates under the laws of Delaware. Other than that, nothing changes in the manner or place of the furniture company's operations. Does The Commerce Group need to take any action in light of this reincorporation to protect its security interest?

12.8 Essie Cashmore has granted a security interest in several pieces of artwork owned by her to Discrete Financial Services. The particular pieces are all listed carefully in the security agreement and the UCC1 initially filed by DFS with the Secretary of State of Illinois. The lender filed in that state since it was clear that Essie's principal residence was in Welloff, Illinois, a ritzy suburb of Chicago. Essie, forgetting exactly which of her paintings have been so encumbered, sells one of them which is in fact among those in which DFS has an interest, to her next-door neighbor, Lionel Doughboy. (As you will later learn, this sale, even if in violation of Essie's agreement with DFS, will be effective to transfer title in the painting to Lionel, but he will end up having title to the painting *subject to* DFS's security interest.)

(a) Does DFS have to refile in order to protect its perfected status?
(b) Would your answer be any different if Lionel the buyer was not a next-door neighbor of Essie's, but was in fact a friend of hers whose principal residence was in California?

CHAPTER
13

Perfection by Possession

A. INTRODUCTION

While we started by considering perfection by filing, this is not the only mechanism recognized by Article 9 for perfecting a security interest. In this chapter we consider the possibility of perfection by the *secured party's taking possession* of the collateral.

The use of possession to give fuller protection to a security interest has a long history. It still is often referred to by the term which has been used for centuries, the "pledge." You will also hear it referred to as a "pawning" of goods or an "hypothecation" of some kind of paper or papers that make up the collateral.

In going through this material you should be considering what exactly counts as "possession" for the purposes of perfection under the current law. Beyond this, what justification is there for allowing a security interest to be perfected—and hence effective against third parties in many situations—even though the secured party has not filed a notification in the public records of its interest in the property? How can a third party protect him, her or itself against being surprised to find its position potentially affected to its detriment by a security interest perfected in this way?

B. PREPARATION

In preparation, read carefully the following parts of the Code:

* Section 9-310(b)(6)
* Section 9-313(a), (c), and (d) along with that section's Comments 2 through 4

169

C.   PROBLEMS AND CASES

PROBLEM

13.1   Ed Owens arranges to borrow $20,000 from his friend Alexandra Fuller. He orally promises to pay the money back with 7% interest within a year. He also hands over to her an antique pocket watch which has been in his family for generations saying, "You can hold onto this watch as collateral until I pay you back." Alexandra takes the watch and puts it in a locked drawer of her desk. She gives Ed a check for $20,000 which he quickly cashes.

(a) Does Alexandra has a perfected security interest in the watch?
(b) What if Alexandra soon comes to the conclusion that the watch is just cluttering up her drawer and that in fact she is uncomfortable with having such a valuable object where it is, as she frequently forgets to lock he drawer, which otherwise just holds office supplies. She takes the watch to the nearby office of a friend, Arnold Armstrong, who she knows to have a safe in his office. She asks him if she can store the watch in his safe, and Arnold agrees. The watch is put into his safe, which he then closes with a reassuring thud. Arnold tells Alexandra she can have the watch back anytime she wants, although she may have to give him some forewarning of when that will be since he doesn't come in to his office every day, having semi-retired. Do you think Alexandra has jeopardized the perfected status of her interest?
(c) What if instead Alexandra, wanting to get the watch out of her drawer, had contacted Ed Owens directly. He suggests that his cousin Gary would be a good person to hold onto the watch on her behalf. Gary comes to Alexandra's office where he gives Alexandra a paper signed by him that reads, "I, Gary Owens, agree that I am acting as agent of Alexandra Fuller in holding on her behalf one antique watch pledged to her by Ed Owens." Gary leaves with the watch. How would you characterize Alexandra's interest now?
(d) Finally, suppose the situation is as we originally saw it. Ed pledges the watch to Alexandra and she puts in into a locked drawer. A few months later Ed returns to her office and asks if he can "have the watch back for just a couple of days." He is going to visit an uncle of his, and this particular uncle always asks to see the old family heirloom and assure himself that Ed is taking good care of it. Alexandra agrees provided that Ed leave something else of comparable value with her during the time the watch will be away. Ed takes off a diamond pinkie ring and hands it to Alexandra. She gives him the watch and puts the ring safely in the drawer. A couple of days later, Ed comes back to the office, gives Alexandra back the watch and picks up his ring. Has this interlude lead to any change in Alexandra's position with respect to the watch?

NATIONAL PAWN BROKERS UNLIMITED v. OSTERMAN, INC.

Court of Appeals of Wisconsin, 1993
176 Wis. 2d 418, 500 N.W.2d 407, 21 U.C.C. Rep. Serv. 2d 1176

GARTZKE, P.J.: [As you may recall, we looked at this case earlier, in Chapter 6. A unscrupulous fellow named Pippin had purchased some jewelry from Osterman in Madison, Wisconsin for a total price of $39,750.38. Pippin gave Osterman a check for $30,000 and agreed to pay the remainder of the price in installments. Pippin also granted Osterman a security interest in the jewelry itself securing his payment obligations. The $30,000 check turned out to be no good, having been drawn on a closed account. By the time Osterman became aware of this, Pippin had already pawned the jewelry to a couple of pawnbrokers in Minnesota. The jewelry was recovered from the pawnbrokers and turned over to the Madison police for use as evidence in the criminal case against Pippin. Pippin was convicted. The jewelry remained in the hands of the Madison police. The pawnbrokers petitioned the court for return to them of the jewelry. Osterman also petitioned the court for return of the jewelry to him. The court was thus called upon to decide whether both Osterman and the pawnbrokers had any right to the jewelry and, if both did, who had priority. In the first part of the opinion, as we saw, the court concluded that Pippin did have the right to create a security interest in the jewelry in favor of the pawnbrokers, even though Osterman had reserved title to the jewelry and had prohibited its transfer until the purchase price was fully paid. The pawnbrokers then argued that their interests had been perfected at the time they first came into possession of the property — prior to when Osterman filed an initial financing statement perfecting his claim. Osterman argued that the pawnbrokers' perfection by possession was lost when the jewelry was taken away from them and handed over to the police. The pawnbrokers argued otherwise. The court took up this issue.]

"A security interest in . . . goods . . . may be perfected by the secured party's taking possession of the collateral. . . . A security interest is perfected by possession from the time possession is taken without a relation back and continues only so long as possession is retained, unless otherwise specified in this Article. . . ." U.C.C. § 9-305 [the precursor of present § 9-313]. The parties cite no Minnesota case that discusses whether a security interest perfected by possession remains perfected when police seize the collateral pursuant to a search warrant.

Although it authorizes perfection by the secured party's taking possession of the collateral, the Code does not define "possession." Without a definition, "possession" is protean and ambiguous.

> Throughout the law "possession" is a notoriously slippery concept; age-old property law recognizes and distinguishes among constructive possession, physical possession, actual possession, mere custody, and a host of other similar notions. . . . In the course of the hundreds of decisions which have dealt with its meaning, the word "possession" has taken on a wonderfully plastic form and has

accommodated itself to the needs of the real property law, the law of consignment, insurance, and the criminal law. The drafters of the UCC were aware of this history, and they wisely declined the futile task of defining possession in the Code. . . . We are left, therefore, with several hundred years of cases and with the policy of Article Nine to help us define the word possession.

2 White & Summers, Uniform Commercial Code, sec. 24-12, at 350-51 (3rd ed. 1988).

We therefore analyze "possession" in [Article 9], in light of the reason why a security interest may be perfected by possession of the collateral.

In his discussion of perfection by possession, Professor Gilmore states:

> The requirement that a secured party take possession of his collateral — or at least effectively remove it from his debtor's possession and control — in order to perfect his interest dates from the beginning of legal history. . . . The basic idea is that the secured creditor must do something to give effective public notice of his interest; if he leaves the property in the debtor's possession and under his apparent control, the debtor will be given a false credit and will be enabled to sell the property to innocent purchasers or to induce other innocent persons to lend money to him on the strength of his apparently unencumbered assets.

1 G. Gilmore, Security Interests in Personal Property, sec. 14.1, at 438 (1965) (footnote omitted).

White and Summers comment that "possession (particularly by one known to be in the lending business) is a perfectly sound indication of a security interest." White & Summers, sec. 24-12, at 347-48. They add that

> the pledge, like automatic perfection of security interests in consumer goods, facilitates secured financing in small-sum transactions. Pawnbrokers make numerous small loans. Requiring a financing statement for each such transaction might seriously curtail the availability of informal loans or significantly increase the cost of such credit to those least able to bear increased costs.

Id. at 348.

The notice function of possession by the secured creditor persuades us that police seizure does not interrupt that possession under U.C.C. § 9-305. Third parties know the police make no claim to own the property they seized pursuant to a warrant. For that reason, we are satisfied that seizure from the pawnbrokers did not interrupt their possession for purposes of [Article 9].

The discussion by White and Summers of a bankruptcy case, *In re Republic Engine and Manufacturing Co.*, 3 U.C.C. Rep. Serv. 655 (Bankr. N.D. Ohio 1966), convinces us that this should be the law.

In *Republic Engine,* after the sheriff levied on the debtor's equipment, a creditor (who was also the debtor's landlord) locked the doors of the building in which the equipment was located. When the debtor filed bankruptcy, the creditor surrendered possession of the equipment to the sheriff. White and Summers reject the bankruptcy court's holding in *Republic Engine* that the creditor's "surrender of possession to the sheriff subsequent to the lockout dissolved any perfection which he might have had during the time the goods were locked up on the premises. . . . Secured creditors should be encouraged to cooperate with law enforcement officers. Moreover, possession by the sheriff will deter further reliance on the collateral by third parties." White & Summers, sec. 24-12, at 352-53.

Far from cooperating with the Minnesota police, the pawnbrokers refused to surrender the collateral, and that resulted in the warrant and seizure. But depriving the pawnbrokers' security interests of perfection merely because the police seize the collateral under a warrant will hardly encourage future cooperation by creditors with the police.

Because possession is not interrupted when law enforcement officers levy on the collateral, possession should be deemed continuous even if the police seize it.

Because Pippin had a right in the jewelry purchased by a bad check from Osterman's, the pawnbrokers' security interests attached to the jewelry, they perfected their security interests by possession, and that possession was not interrupted, for purposes of [Article 9], when Osterman perfected its security interest. The interests of the pawnbrokers have priority over Osterman's interest. For that reason, the trial court erred when it ordered that possession of the collateral, the jewelry, be granted to Osterman's. On remand, the trial court shall enter judgment giving possession to the pawnbrokers.

PROBLEM

13.2   The debtor, Makes-U-More, Incorporated, a large manufacturing corporation which sells the various stuff made in its Texas manufacturing facility to numerous large retailers around the country, enters into an agreement in which it grants Big Boots Bank of Dallas a security interest in "all its accounts, now held or hereafter acquired." Is the Bank going to be able to perfect on this interest by taking possession of any or everything relating to the accounts?

IN RE EQUITABLE FINANCIAL MANAGEMENT, INC.

United States Bankruptcy Court for the Western District of Pennsylvania, 1994
164 Bankr. 53, 1994 Bankr. LEXIS 188

BERNARD MARKOVITZ, B.J.: The chapter 7 trustee seeks pursuant to 11 U.S.C. §544(a)(1) to avoid the security interest of defendant Colonial Pacific Leasing Company (hereinafter "CPL") in two equipment leases. According to the chapter 7 trustee, CPL's security interest may be avoided pursuant to this court's holding in *In re Funding Systems Asset Management Corporation*, 111 Bankr. 500 (Bankr. W.D. Pa. 1990), because debtor possessed "duplicate originals" of the chattel paper evidencing CPL's security interest. CPL asserts that its security interest cannot be avoided because the documents debtor possessed do not constitute "duplicate originals" of the chattel paper CPL possesses. According to CPL, all chattel paper pertaining to the leases in question remained in its exclusive possession at all relevant times. Judgment will be entered in favor of CPL and against the chapter 7 trustee for reasons set forth below.

Debtor was engaged in the business of leasing equipment to end-user lessees. It first would lease equipment to a lessee and then would obtain necessary financing from a third party in order to purchase the equipment. CPL was such a third party.

Debtor and the end-user lessee would execute a lease agreement to which was attached an equipment schedule describing the equipment subject to the lease. Among other things, the lease agreement itself set forth the names and addresses of the lessor and of the end-user lessee and specified the terms of the lease. It also included a certificate of delivery and acceptance which the end-user lessee dated and executed. The lease agreement also was dated and executed in ink by the debtor as lessor and by the end-user lessee.

The equipment schedule attached to the lease agreement and incorporated therein set forth: the name of the lessor; the name of the end-user lessee; the location of the equipment; the date of the lease; the lease number; and the quantity and description of the leased equipment. The equipment schedule was dated and executed in ink by the end-user lessee. Debtor did not execute this document.

Debtor entered into two (2) lease agreements in 1990 that are at issue in this case. Eachles & Associates, Inc. of Phoenix, Arizona was the end-user lessee in the first lease. Coors/RMS of Washington, Pennsylvania, was the end-user lessee in the second lease. Although debtor certified to CPL that it had delivered all documents relating to the lease transactions, in fact unbeknownst to CPL debtor retained certain documents relating to previously aborted but related transactions.

The version of the Eachles lease agreement CPL possessed had been executed in ink by debtor as lessor and in ink by Eachles as lessee. The execution date of the lease agreement, the lease commitment date, the rental commencement date, and date of the certificate of delivery and acceptance executed in ink by Eachles was March 14, 1990.

The version of the Eachles lease agreement debtor possessed differed in material respects from CPL's version. Debtor's version had been executed in ink only by Eachles. Debtor had not executed it. There was no lease commitment date and no rental commencement date. Although the execution date of the lease agreement itself was March 14, 1990, the certificate of delivery and acceptance executed in ink by Eachles was dated March 13, 1990.

The version of the Eachles equipment schedule CPL possessed had been executed in ink by Eachles and made reference to the lease agreement dated March 14, 1990.

The version of the Eachles equipment schedule debtor possessed was a photocopy of the document CPL possessed. It had not, however, been executed in ink by Eachles.

[The court then goes through a similar analysis of all of the various papers relating to the second, the Coors/RMS lease agreement CPL.]

Subsequent to the execution of the above lease agreements, debtor obtained financing from CPL in order to purchase the equipment subject to the leases. In return for the financing provided by CPL, debtor granted CPL a security interest in the leases and in the equipment. Debtor also assigned the leases themselves to CPL. The assignment contained a provision wherein debtor warranted that the lease was genuine and enforceable and was the only lease agreement with respect to the equipment. CPL agreed to pay debtor a specified up-front lump-sum amount in return for debtor's interest in all future payments due under the leases.

Upon its receipt of the lump sum payments from CPL, debtor delivered to CPL chattel paper pertaining to the two lease transactions. The chattel paper delivered to CPL included: original executed lease agreements; original executed equipment schedules; original executed assignments; and other miscellaneous original documents pertaining to the lease transactions. On March 15, 1991, debtor filed a voluntary chapter 11 petition. The case was converted to a chapter 7 proceeding on May 16, 1991. The chapter 7 trustee was appointed the next day. On May 12, 1993, the chapter 7 trustee commenced the above adversary action against CPL.

Trial was held on the trustee's complaint on January 13, 1994, at which time both sides were given an opportunity to present any evidence they deemed appropriate. The chapter 7 trustee in this case qualifies under Pennsylvania law as a lien creditor as of the date on which the chapter 11 petition was filed — i.e., as of March 15, 1991. If CPL's security interest in the above leases was unperfected as of the date in which debtor filed its voluntary chapter 11 petition, its interest is subordinate to the rights of the chapter 7 trustee as hypothetical lien creditor and may be avoided by the trustee pursuant to 11 U.S.C. §544(a)(1).

According to Pennsylvania law: "[a] security interest in . . . chattel paper may be perfected by the secured party's taking possession of the collateral. . . . A security interest is perfected by possession from the time possession is taken without relation back and continues only so long as possession is retained. . . ." 13 Pa. C.S.A. §9305 [the precursor section to current §9-313].

As has been noted, debtor had delivered to CPL fully executed original lease agreements and fully executed original equipment schedules for the Eachles and Coors/RMS leases. Without CPL's knowledge or consent, however, debtor possessed certain documents pertaining to the leases. What it possessed and how they differed from what CPL possessed has been detailed and will not be reiterated here.

The issue presented is whether or not CPL's security interest was fully perfected as of March 15, 1991 by virtue of its possession of the above chattel paper which debtor had delivered to it. According to the chapter 7 trustee, CPL's security was unperfected because the documents which debtor retained also constitute original chattel paper. CPL insists that its security interest in the above leases was perfected when the chapter 11 petition was filed. According to CPL, it had exclusive control and possession at all relevant times of all original chattel paper pertaining to the leases.

A secured party fails to perfect by possession its security interest in a lease when it fails to exercise absolute dominion and control over all chattel paper pertaining thereto. Accordingly, CPL's security interest in the above leases is unperfected by possession only if an entity other than CPL had control and possession of chattel paper pertaining thereto. In order for the above documents possessed by debtor to defeat CPL's claim to perfection by possession, the documents must constitute "chattel paper," which is defined in pertinent part as follows: [the court then quotes the prerevision definition of "chattel paper," which is essential the same as the current definition of "tangible chattel paper"].

The chapter 7 trustee's contention that CPL's security interest in the above leases was unperfected because debtor had retained possession of chattel paper pertaining thereto is without merit. As the above-quoted language . . . makes abundantly clear, "chattel paper" in a given instance may consist of more than one "writing." Both the lease agreements and the equipment schedules referred to therein and appended thereto must be taken into consideration when determining whether debtor had retained possession of any "chattel paper" pertaining to the leases in question. The lease agreements make reference to and incorporate the equipment schedules. Without the equipment schedules, the lease agreements are incomplete.

Careful examination of the documents retained by debtor compels the conclusion that they "evidence" neither a "monetary obligation" nor a "lease of specific goods." As has been noted, the lease agreements in debtor's possession had been executed only by the end-user lessees. Debtor had not executed them at all. The places where debtor was to affix its signature were blank in the lease agreements debtor possessed. Absent debtor's signature, these documents do not "evidence" any obligation, monetary or otherwise, and do not constitute valid and legally enforceable leases of any kind.

The lease agreements debtor possessed were merely preliminary versions and were not completed documents having any legal effect. A representative of debtor who was familiar with the Eachles and Coors/RMS leases testified, without contradiction or impeachment, that debtor did not intend for the lease agreements upon which the trustee relies to be legally binding.

The matter does not end there. The equipment schedules which were incorporated by reference into the lease agreements in debtor's possession are similarly deficient. The equipment schedules debtor possessed were only photocopies of the originals CPL possessed. As such, they have no more binding legal effect than would a photocopy of, say, a ten dollar bill. No reasonably prudent purchaser of chattel paper would have accepted the photocopied equipment schedules as original equipment schedules constituting a portion of the lease agreements.

The trustee's assertion that debtor, had it so elected, could have affixed its signature in ink to the lease agreements it possessed is to no avail. The documents debtor possessed would not thereby have become "chattel paper," as previously defined. Debtor still would not have been able to sell such "doctored" documents in the ordinary course of business to a *bona fide* purchaser because of other critical discrepancies.

As has been noted, both the lease agreement and the equipment schedule referred to and incorporated therein must be considered when determining whether debtor possessed any chattel paper in this case. The date of the Coors/RMS lease agreement debtor possessed is April 12, 1990. The lease date referred to in the equipment schedule is June 8, 1990. Even if debtor had so affixed its signature to its version of the lease agreement, the documents it possessed pertaining to the Coors/RMS transaction still would not evidence a monetary obligation and a lease of specific goods. Any attempt to sell such "doctored" documents in the ordinary course of business to a reasonably prudent *bona fide* purchaser of chattel paper would have been thwarted by this discrepancy.

The same can be said for the documents debtor possessed pertaining to Eachles, although for a different reason. The discrepancy is internal to debtor's version of the Eachles lease agreement. The date of execution of the lease agreement debtor possessed is at variance with the execution date of the certificate of delivery and acceptance contained therein. The former date is March 14, 1990 while the latter date is March 13, 1990. A reasonably prudent *bona fide* purchaser in the ordinary course of business of chattel paper would notice this discrepancy and would recognize that the Eachles documents debtor possessed did not constitute a finalized agreement evidencing a monetary obligation and a lease of specific goods.

An appropriate order shall be issued.

PROBLEM

13.3   Upon his retirement, Dean Whiplash of Downtown Urban Law School ("DULS") makes arrangement with the librarian of the school for his considerable collection of antiquarian law books, many of them quite rare and valuable, to be moved from the office he is vacating to the library's rare book room. It is agreed that this collection is being loaned to the school for an indefinite period of time, pending a later determination of how it will be disposed of upon his death. Two years into his retirement, Whiplash decides that he could use some additional cash to take the extended round-the-world tour he has always dreamt of. He contacts Discrete

Financial Services and arranges for a loan which is to be secured by the book collection now housed in the DULS library. The lender does all that is necessary to obtain a properly attached interest in the books. A representative of the lender then sends a notification to the DULS librarian stating that her firm, Discrete Financial Services, has obtained and now rightfully claims a security interest in these books.

(a) Does Discrete Financial Services now have a perfected security interest in the books?
(b) Would your answer be any different if the notification sent to the librarian had been signed by Whiplash as well?

NOTE ON THE DUTIES OF A SECURED PARTY HAVING POSSESSION

Section 9-207(a) imposes on the secured party the obligation to use "reasonable care in the custody and preservation" of any collateral in its possession. Subsection (b) of this section states some additional rules which apply when the secured party has possession of the collateral. You should read these two subsections now, along with Comment 2 to § 9-207, which will guide you through the following problems.

PROBLEMS

13.4   The situation is that of Problem 13.1, except that when Ed hands Alexandra the watch she merely places it upon the top of her desk, not in a locked drawer. When Alexandra returns to her office the next day she discovers that several valuable items which had been in her office have gone missing overnight. Apparently when she left the day before she forgot to lock the door to her office and some unidentified person must have slipped in during the night and made off with her things. Among the items missing is Ed's watch.

(a) Is Alexandra responsible to Ed for the value of the lost watch?
(b) What if instead Alexandra had, as we had originally hypothesized, put the watch in a locked drawer as soon as it was given to her. When she left at the end of the day she carefully locked her office door behind her. Unfortunately, over the next several days a particularly severe hurricane comes through the area. The attendant high winds and floods do great damage to the downtown area where Alexandra's office is located. When she is finally able to make it back to her office, she finds that the desk in which the watch had been locked is nowhere to be found. It has apparently floated away in the flooding and is, as far as she can tell, gone forever. Alexandra's insurance covers the loss of the desk, but not of any valuables which were in it at the time of the loss. Under these circumstances would she be liable to Ed for the value of the lost watch?

13.5   Abe borrows $100,000 from Fidelity National Bank, putting up as collateral 200 shares of stock he owns in Tip-Top Pharmaceuticals, a major corporation whose stock is publicly traded on the over-the-counter market. At the time this loan is arranged, the stock has been trading steadily on that exchange in the range of $100 to $120 dollars for the past several years. Abe's shares are represented by a certificate issued by the corporation and bearing his name as that of the registered owner. Abe gives this share certificate indorsed in blank to the bank, which puts the certificate in a locked file cabinet along with the other documentation relating to the loan to Abe. Within a couple of months, there is a report seriously questioning the safety of one of Tip-Top's principal products. The value of its shares immediately drops to $80, and several stock analysts predict that it will drop even further. Within a couple of months the shares are trading for $40. Abe in informed by the bank that he will have to put up additional collateral to secure his loan.

(a) Abe argues that the bank's failure to notice the dropping value of the shares it held as collateral and to sell them when it could have gotten $80 a share is a failure on the bank's part to use reasonable care in the preservation of the value of the collateral. Do you believe this argument will succeed?

(b) Would it make any difference to your determination if Abe were to show that he had left an urgent message for his loan manager at the bank telling her, at the time the shares were worth $80 each that, "You should sell off that Tip-Top stock quickly and put what you get for them into some other investment that isn't going to lose value." The loan officer never responded to this message.

CHAPTER
14

Automatic Perfection — The PMSI in Consumer Goods

A. INTRODUCTION

So far we have covered two means which the secured party may use in the appropriate situations to perfect its interest, filing and taking of possession of the collateral. In this and the next chapter we consider what is conventionally referred to as *automatic perfection*. By this we mean perfection that requires *no* additional action or required behavior by the secured party. The security interest becomes perfected — either as in the situation we'll consider in this chapter permanently, or as in some other situations to be discussed in the next chapter for at least some defined period of time — when the security interest attaches to the collateral as long as attachment continues.

This chapter deals with one particularly important instance of automatic perfection — that is the automatic perfection provided for the purchase-money security interest taken in consumer goods, other than those limited instances of consumer goods (most typically automobiles) which are covered by state certificate of title laws.

You really should have little trouble working through the problems of this chapter — provided you are comfortable with recognizing "consumer goods" for what they are (see Chapter 2 for review if needed) and with knowing a "purchase-money" security interest when you are confronted with one (Chapters 7 and 8).

B. PREPARATION

In preparation for discussion of the problems in this chapter, read carefully the following parts of the Code:

* Section 9-309(1) and Comment 3 to this section
* Section 9-310(b)(2)

181

C. PROBLEMS AND CASES

PROBLEMS

14.1   Fred of Fred's Furniture Boutique, sells a living room suite he has on display in his showroom to a customer, one Tanya. Tanya does not have the cash to pay for the furniture right away, but signs a note agreeing to pay Fred for the furniture through monthly payments over the next year. She also signs a security agreement granting Fred a security interest in the furniture she is then buying from him, which she agrees will serve as collateral assuring her payments called for in the note. Tanya has the sofa delivered to her home where it is placed in her family's living room.

(a) Does Fred have to file an initial financial statement or take any other action to perfect upon the security interest Tanya has granted him?
(b) What if instead Fred tells Tanya that he is not in a position to sell to her on credit. Tanya goes to a local branch of Friendly Finance where she arranges for a loan, to be repaid over the course of the next year, the purpose of which she states is "to purchase furniture for personal use from Fred's Furniture Boutique." Tanya signs both a note and a security agreement, listing the living room suite as described in more detail as the collateral. Tanya is given a check for the purchase price of the furniture made out by Friendly Finance "to the order Fred's Furniture Boutique." She takes this check directly to the furniture store where she hands it over to Fred personally. Later in the week the furniture is delivered to Tanya's home where she places it in her living room. Does Friendly Finance have to file in order to perfect its security interest in the living room suite?

14.2   Ben arranges to buy a new lawnmower from Sarah's Sells-U-Stuff to replace his current mower which has just broken down irretrievably. Sarah takes out a form headed "E-Z Pay Monthly Payment Plan Agreement." She quickly fills in a few blank spaces on the form, giving a description of the particular mower as the goods being sold, Ben's name and address as that of the buyer, and specifying six monthly payments which Ben will agree to make to Selma. The form also states in that, "The parties hereto agree that title to any merchandise made the subject of this agreement will remain in the Seller until Buyer has made full and final payment of all amounts due hereunder." Ben signs this agreement and takes the new lawnmower away with him in the trunk of his car. Does Sarah have to file an initial financing statement to perfect on this interest?

CONSIDERING THE RULE OF § 9-309(1)

Automatic perfection of a purchase-money security interest in consumer goods has a fairly long history. It was to be found in prerevision

Article 9, and as far as I know there was no serious consideration given to changing the situation in the revision. What reason or reasons might there be that the Article 9 drafters thought it appropriate to allow for automatic perfection in an instance such as this? What protection, in any, is there for a third party who might become interested in either buying or itself taking a security interest in the collateral — the new furniture in Tanya's living room in the prior problem and Ben's new lawnmower here — while it is still subject to the seller's or the enabling lender's interest?

PROBLEMS

14.3 Dumont Cashmore comes into Sarah's Sells-U-Stuff and asks to be waited on by Sarah personally as he has a big purchase to make. Sarah is more than happy to oblige. With her help Cashmore selects a particular top-of-the-line computer set-up. He tells her he wants to purchase a dozen of these machines along with the various add-on components that would be necessary to configure them into a highly reliable network. He also wants the computers to come loaded with a particular spread-sheet program and an accounting program, the names of which he reads off a slip of paper he has pulled from his pocket. On the paper he also has the address to which the purchase is to be delivered, which Sarah recognizes as that of one of the major downtown office buildings. Cashmore then asks if he can buy the entire lot under Sarah's E-Z Pay Monthly Payment Plan Agreement, under which he will pay the purchase price in monthly installments allowing all that is being purchased to serve as collateral to secure his obligation to her. Again, Sarah is more than happy to accommodate him. Together they fill out the necessary form. At one point the form calls for the customer to specify, by checking the appropriate box, the use to which the purchased merchandise will be put. Cashmore checks the box marked "Personal or family use." Sarah politely asks him if this is not a mistake. Shouldn't he have checked "Business or professional use" instead? She assures him that it makes no difference as far as the terms of the loan are concerned, but he is insistent that the form stay as he marked it. "I'm stating this stuff is for my personal use," he says, his voice rising, "and that should be good enough for you!" Sarah leaves the form as it is, and Cashmore signs it. The various computer equipment is to be delivered to the address given by the beginning of the following month.

(a) Sarah later asks for your advice. Does she have to file a financing statement covering this collateral to perfect her interest?
(b) Is Sarah *barred* from filing an initial financing statement using the information she has been given by Cashmore?
(c) What, finally, do you advise?

14.4   Essie Cashmore lives in a large mansion on an extensive estate located in the ritziest suburb of Chicago. For many years now she has considered herself a patron of up-and-coming young artists and bought many of their earlier works, which she has proudly displayed throughout her mansion. In order to build up her collection even more, she negotiates a loan from Discreet Financial Services, granting that lender a security interest a several of her most valuable acquisitions, a listing of which is carefully set out in the security agreement. Need DFS file or take some other action to perfect its security interest in these works of art?

14.5   Gabriela owns and operates a restaurant, Gabriela's Place. As part of her plan to upgrade the place, she visits the showroom of Oven Boys of Brooklyn, Inc., and orders from the firm's catalogue a particularly large and expensive oven suitable for use in a busy restaurant. The oven will have to be specially ordered by Oven Boys from its manufacturer and is to be delivered to and installed in Gabriela's Place within six weeks of her order. Gabriela signs a note payable "to the order of Oven Boys of Brooklyn, Inc." which commits her to make specified monthly payments beginning at the start of the following month and for 23 months thereafter. She also signs a security agreement granting the supplier a security interest in the particular stove, securing her obligation to pay on the note. Does Oven Boys of Brooklyn need to file an initial financing statement covering the oven to perfect its interest?

CHAPTER
15

Perfection on and Through Instruments and Documents

A. INTRODUCTION

In this chapter we consider some special rules that come into play when the collateral being dealt with consists of either instruments or documents as those types of collateral are defined for Article 9 purposes. While it is, of course, possible for the collateral to be a single instrument (typically a note as defined in Article 3) or document of title, it is often true that the lender will be basing its loan on a collection, a large pool as we might say, of similar items which are created in the regular and, all would hope, steady course of the debtor's business.

Under § 9-312(a), it is possible for the secured party to perfect upon such collateral by means of a proper filing. As a practical matter, however, the lender will usually want to perfect by taking actual possession of each piece of paper — each note or each document of title as it is created and becomes property in which the debtor has "rights" for the purposes of attachment. The reason for this is that notes and negotiable documents have the special property of negotiability. You should recall that all notes, as a form of instrument under Article 3, are necessarily negotiable, as the definitions we looked at earlier make clear. Documents, on the other hand, such as bills of lading and warehouse receipts, may be issued in either negotiable or nonnegotiable form.

As the Comments to § 9-312 you will be looking at suggest, because such distinct kinds of "quasi-intangible" collateral do come in a physical form but also are negotiable, it is possible under well established principles of commercial law as more fully explicated in other parts of the Code — Article 3 with respect to instruments or Article 7 with respect to documents — that an instrument or a negotiable document may under given circumstances find its way into the possession of some innocent third party who will be able to legitimately claim not only ownership of the paper, but ownership *unburdened* by any security interest asserted by the secured party even if that interest had earlier been perfected by filing. The lender's insistence that it take physical possession of the instrument or negotiable document is, understandably enough, meant to reduce the chances of this unfortunate event, unfortunate for the secured party, ever coming about. (Note here that a slightly revised Article 7 was promulgated in 2003 by the keepers of the Uniform Commercial Code. One purpose of this revision, which has been adopted in a number of but not all states, was to provide for the possibility of an *electronic* document of title. This explains why portions of Article 9 had to be slightly rewritten to substitute the term "tangible document of title" for what was previously simply the traditional document of title, all such documents having been quite decidedly tangible, that is, all-paper-all-the-time, up until just the past few years.)

The general practice of lenders requiring that they get actual possession of each piece of collateral has been recognized to create its own set of problems. It takes some time—even if that time has grown shorter with the introduction of speedier means of delivery such as the overnight, if more costly, delivery of parcels—for the collateral to make its way into the hands of the lender. Also, if the debtor needs to deal in some way with any one instrument or with the goods covered by a negotiable document of title, it will not be free to do so until it can get back into its possession the instrument or document involved, at least for some limited period of time. It is concerns such as these that motivate the special rules we will be exploring in this chapter.

B. PREPARATION

In preparation for discussion of the problems in this chapter, read carefully the following parts of the Code:

- Section 9-312(a), (c), (d), (e), (f), and (h), and Comments 2, 3 (second paragraph only), 7, 8, and 9 to this section
- The definition of "new value" in § 9-102(a)(57) along with Comment 21 to this section
- Sections 9-330(d) and 9-331(a)

C. PROBLEMS AND CASES

PROBLEMS

15.1 Costumes Unlimited, Limited is a company that manufactures a variety of Halloween-type costumes. It runs its manufacturing plant throughout the year, making different costumes during each month.

Since the company does not itself have sufficient storage space to keep all that it manufactures on its premises until just before the Halloween marketing season, when it will sell off virtually all of its annual production to a few large distributors in a matter of weeks, it regularly stores the costumes it makes during the year in Watson's Warehouse, a large and well-regarded warehouse in Columbus, Ohio. At the end of each month of production Costumes packs up into crates the costumes it has made that month and delivers then to Watson's, which issues the manufacturer a negotiable warehouse receipt covering the delivered goods. In order to finance its operations over the course of the year, Costumes enters into a loan agreement with the State Bank of Columbus. As part of the agreement, the company grants to the bank a security interest in "all documents of title it now holds or will later procure covering any or all of the goods it produces." Under the agreement, the company is required to turn over any such documents to the bank within ten days of its having acquired the document. In November it makes a large quantity of superhero costumes, delivers these to the warehouse and receives in return a negotiable warehouse receipt covering "72 crates said to contain costumes manufactured by the bailee." It immediately turns this document over to the bank. In December it does the same with skeleton costumes, in January devil outfits, and so on through the year. Upon the receipt and review of each document by the bank, the line of credit which is available to Costumes increases by a previously agreed-to amount based on the number of crates the company has newly delivered to the warehouse. The bank never makes any filing with respect to this security agreement.

(a) Does the bank have a perfected security interest in the *warehouse receipts* it regularly receives from the costume company? If so, by what means has this perfection been obtained?

(b) Does the bank have a perfected security interest in the *manufactured costumes* represented by the warehouse receipts issued to the costume company? If so, by what means was perfection on the costumes themselves obtained?

(c) Would your answers to the two prior parts of this problem be the same if Watson's Warehouse issued instead nonnegotiable warehouse receipts to the costume company when it received delivery of any month's production?

15.2   The situation is that of the prior problem, with the warehouse issuing negotiable warehouse receipts upon Costumes Unlimited's delivery to it of crates of costumes and the manufacturer's quickly sending these documents on to the bank. In April of 2009, the management of the costume company becomes concerned that the small imitation pitchforks which it had included in all of the devil costumes manufactured in January, and now in storage at Watson's warehouse, were finished off with three sharp points each. They worry that this might be considered a unsafe condition that would either make these particular costumes difficult to sell or, even worse, subject the company itself to possible liability if someone were to get hurt because of this arguably dangerous condition. The president of the company contacts its loan officer at the bank. He explains the company's concerns and requests that he be sent back the warehouse receipt issued by the warehouse at the end of January, which would cover the devil costumes in question. The loan officer agrees and on April 5 has this single warehouse receipt delivered via an over-night delivery service to the Costumes Unlimited headquarters. An officer of the company takes this receipt to the warehouse and there surrenders it to the person in charge in exchange for the crates of costumes represented by this particular warehouse receipt. These crates are taken back to Costume's manufacturing plant where the company has a number of its workers repackage each devil costumer — after securely fastening three blunt spongy tips onto each of the miniature pitchforks and affixing a prominent warning label on each of them. The costumes are then returned to the crates in which they had originally been stored. These crates are taken back to Watson's where they are put into the possession of the warehouse. The warehouse returns the warehouse receipt to the company's representative. This receipt is delivered back to the loan officer at the State Bank of Columbus by April 16.

(a) Has the status of the bank's security interest in the devil costumes been affected in any way by this sequence of events?

(b) How would you analyze the situation if the warehouse receipt had not been delivered back to the bank until April 30? What if it never made its way back to the bank?

(c) As a practical matter, what considerations would you hope the loan officer had taken into account, or what additional precautions might she have undertaken, before releasing the single warehouse receipt back into the possession of the debtor, even for the limited stated purposes and for promised short period of time?

15.3 Dr. Tina Nolens, an ophthalmologist, opens up a clinic equipped to perform the newest form of laser eye surgery intended to correct for poor vision without the need for glasses. The clinic is located in her hometown of Traverse City, Michigan, in the north of that state's lower peninsula. She realizes from the start that since the amount she will have to charge for the procedure ($8,000 per eye) is high she would do well to institute — and widely advertise — a "See Better Now, Pay Later" plan, under which she is willing to extend credit to patients so that they can pay for the work done over a two-year period. When a patient qualifies for the plan, he or she can have the procedure done immediately, as long as he or she signs a note made payable "to the order of Dr. Tina Nolens" allowing for payment in twenty-four monthly installments. Her practice flourishes. She quickly accumulates a large number of such notes as she performs more and more procedures, but her cash on hand is never that great as the small periodic payments on the notes seem to her only to be trickling into her bank account. She is anxious to have the money to buy herself a large house in the area and perhaps to make other investments. Nolens realizes that she can use the notes themselves as collateral to obtain a loan for herself. After making inquiries of various commercial lenders, she decides that she will get the best terms overall if she borrows from the Woodward Bank of Detroit. She enters into a series of telephone, fax, and e-mail communications with a loan officer at the bank. Among the documents she sends to the bank is a listing of the notes she will initially put up as collateral, how much is now owed on each, whether payment on any note is now overdue, and so on. The loan officer uses a formula taking all these factors into account, as well as the interest his bank charges on such a loan, to compute how much the bank is willing to lend Nolens based on this collateral. He also explains to the doctor how this number will be adjusted at the end of each month based on how the value of each note put up as collateral will decrease in value as its maker makes monthly payments, but also taking into account any new notes that have been added to the collateral pool. On one day late in December of 2008, Dr. Nolens travels to the bank's headquarters in Detroit, where she and the loan officer first meet in person and do everything necessary to close the loan deal. Nolens signs a security agreement which the loan officer has written up in connection with the loan. The collateral is described as "certain notes made payable to Dr. Tina Nolens, as listed in Exhibit A attached hereto, and as that Exhibit may from time to time be amended upon agreement of the parties." Exhibit A is a written listing which the doctor had previously prepared of all the notes she is offering up as the initial collateral. Nolens has brought each of these notes with her on her trip to the big city. She hands them over to the loan officer, who examines each one and checks to be sure that it is properly identified on Exhibit A. When he is through, he assures her that he will immediately authorize a release of funds, to be wired to the personal checking account she has with Traverse City Trust, equal to the amount agreed to as the initial loan proceeds. "When you get home," he assures Nolens, "you'll find the money in your account." True enough, when the doctor checks her Traverse City Trust account balance later in the day it includes the significant sum she has now borrowed from the Woodward Bank. The Woodward bank makes no filing with respect to the security interest it claims in the notes. Does the bank have a valid and perfected security interest in each of the notes listed on Exhibit A and now in its possession?

15.4   We continue with the story of the previous problem. At the end of a particularly busy month of January 2009, Dr. Nolens collects all of the new notes that she has received from clients for work done during that month. She makes a listing of these notes, heading it "Addendum to Exhibit A." On February 1, she faxes this listing to the loan officer at the Woodward Bank. The next day, she receives a telephone call from the loan officer telling her that if all of the notes listed are added to those held by his bank, he can authorize an increase in the amount of her loan from his bank. She says,

"Great, I will send them to you right away." On the basis of this assurance, the loan officer authorizes that an additional amount be wired immediately to the doctor's personal account at Traverse City Trust. The amount shows up in her account by the end of the day. On February 4, Dr. Nolens arranges for these new notes to be sent to the Woodward Bank. That bank receives this package on February 6, and the loan officer assures himself that all the notes listed on the Addendum he had received as a fax are indeed as indicated on that listing.

(a) Does Woodward Bank's security interest extend to these new notes? If so is that interest perfected? As of what date?
(b) Would your answer to this last question change if the doctor had dawdled in sending on the notes so that they didn't arrive at the Detroit bank until March 3? What if they were never sent to the bank?

15.5   One final problem based on the financing arrangement which Dr. Nolens of Traverse City has entered into with the Woodward Bank of Detroit: Wally Peepers is one of the first clients to take advantage of the new service, and the chance to pay for the procedure over time, offered by Dr. Nolens. In early January 2009, he has the laser surgery done on his left eye. Later that month he has his right eye fixed. Each time he pays by signing a note payable to Dr. Nolens in twenty-four monthly installments. The two notes signed by Peepers are among those sent to the Woodward Bank at the beginning of February 2009. For the next few months, Peepers makes his monthly payments to Nolens as called for in the notes. Then, in late August of 2009, Peepers makes a call to Nolens. It seems that Peepers has just found out he is going to be getting a "small inheritance" due to the recent death of a distant relative. He has decided that one of the first things he will do with this money coming his way is "pay off all that I owe you for my new eyes." Nolens does a quick calculation and agrees with Peepers that if he comes into her office with a cashier's check for a given amount during the first week of September, he will then fully pay what is still due on the two notes he has given her. Peepers points out that, naturally, he will expect to receive the notes themselves, marked "Paid in Full" in return for the cashier's check. Nolens makes a call to the loan officer at the bank. She explains the situation and asks that the two notes, which she carefully describes by date, name of the maker, and number, be sent to her as soon as possible. The loan officer agrees and sends her the notes, which she receives on August 30.

(a) On September 3, Nolens gets a call from Peepers. He explains that his expected inheritance has turned out to be much smaller than he had expected and that he has decided not to pay off what he owes to Nolens all at once. He will instead just continue to make his monthly payments. Nolens tells his that this is not a problem. She then sends the two notes back to the bank, which receives them on September 8. Has the status of the bank with respect to these two notes been affected in any way by what has transpired?

(b) Suppose instead that Peepers does come into Nolens's office on September 3 with a cashier's check in the proper amount. Nolens writes "Paid in Full" across each of the notes and hands them over to Peepers, who leaves with the notes in hand. It is now, of course, impossible for Nolens to return these notes to the bank. Does this mean that she is necessarily going to be in trouble with her lender? How do you expect the rest of this story should play out so that both Nolens and the Woodward bank are left satisfied with the results and can continue with a mutually beneficial and strong working relationship?

CHAPTER

16

Perfection by Control

A. INTRODUCTION

A final method of perfecting a security interest, the taking of *control* over the collateral, was introduced into the Article 9 game only in 1994 along with a revision that year of Article 8. That article, as you know, deals with investment securities, which we see in Article 9 as collateral classified as investment property. "Control" — carefully defined as to each kind of investment security — was set out as a means of perfecting on that type of collateral.

The concept of perfection on this type of collateral by control was deemed to be such a productive idea that it was taken up by the drafters of the Revised Article 9. The possibility of perfection by control was, in fact, extended to some other types of collateral.

The first thing to note is that perfection by control is *not* generally available with respect to all, or even most, types of collateral. Article 9 reserves the possibility of perfection by control to those instances when the collateral is investment property, deposit accounts, letter-of-credit rights, electronic chattel paper, or electronic documents. For our purposes it will be sufficient if we consider taking control when the collateral is either investment property or a deposit account.

Second, you should be aware that just because it is possible to perfect by control in these instances, it does not necessarily follow that perfection can't be obtained by one of the other methods we've already looked at. The secured party may file on investment property, for example. It will turn out, however, as we will later see (in Chapter 20) that perfecting by control, when possible, will have some distinct advantages over other means of perfection.

Finally, notice that when a deposit account is concerned, control is the *only* method of perfection available under Article 9.

B. PREPARATION

In preparation for discussion of the problems in this chapter, read carefully the following parts of the Code:

- Section 9-312(b)(1), and Comments 4 and 5 to this section
- The final sentence of §9-313(a)
- Section 9-314(a) and Comment 2 to this section
- Section 9-104(a) and its Official Comments
- Section 9-106(a) and (c), which leads you to
- Section 8-106 and Comment 1 to this section

C. PROBLEMS AND CASES

PROBLEMS

16.1   When Stella Startup, the hyperwidget entrepreneur, first organized the corporation Hyperwidgets, Inc., she received 100 shares in the corporation. The only other person to gain shares in the new corporation was Stella's brother Stewart, who received 20 shares. Stewart was given a stock Certificate #2, duly issued by the corporation, evidencing that these 20 shares were held in his name. The corporation is doing well, and it is apparent that these 20 shares are of substantial value. Stewart enters into an agreement to borrow $100,000 from The Venture Loans Group, his intention being to start up his own business making organic animal foods and treats. As part of this loan agreement, Stewart grants the lender a security interest in his 20 shares of Hyperwidgets.

(a) Could Venture Loans perfect on this interest by filing a UCC1 in the correct place and indicating the collateral with sufficient clarity? If so, would this be considered perfection by control?
(b) Suppose instead that Stewart simply handed over his Certificate #2 to Venture Loans, which kept the certificate in its possession. Would its interest be perfected? If so, could it now claim perfection by control?
(c) What exactly *would* Venture Loans have to do for it to be able legitimately to claim perfection by control over Stewart's 20 shares in Hyperwidgets?

16.2   Alicia Kent has a securities account with the brokerage firm of Hale and Hardy. Among the securities she long has had credited to the account are 5,000 shares of Interpersonal Communications Incorporated ("ICI"), a large, publicly held company whose shares are regularly traded on the New York Stock Exchange. These shares are currently trading in the $9 to $10 range, and are thought to be a relatively stable investment vehicle.

In order to meet some unexpected medical bills, Alicia arranges to borrow $20,000 from her local bank, The National Bank of Royalton. It is agreed she will put up "her ICI shares" as collateral for this loan.

(a) To facilitate this transaction, the bank opens up a securities account with Hale and Hardy. Alicia then orders Hale and Hardy to transfer the 5,000 shares of ICI held in her account into the account newly opened by the bank. The bank has, of course, agreed to transfer these shares back into Alicia's account upon her repayment of everything due under the loan. Has the bank perfected its security interest in these shares by gaining control over them?

(b) Suppose instead that Alicia and a representative of the bank had simply written up a document in which Alicia agreed that the bank was authorized upon any default on her part with respect to the loan agreement to send Hale and Hardy an entitlement order on its own initiative directing the brokerage to sell these ICI shares and deliver the proceeds of the sale to it, the bank. Alicia signs this contract, as does a representative of the bank. Would this be sufficient to give the bank control over these ICI shares in Alicia's account? If not, what more would be required?

16.3   Lance Cashmore thinks of himself as a highly sophisticated and intelligent investor, very active on a regular basis in buying and selling stocks. He does his stock trading through an account (#13131313) he has with the brokerage firm of Shakes and Rattles. As part of his relationship with this brokerage and to maximize his opportunities for "playing the market," he has entered into an agreement under which he may borrow up to a specified percentage of the total value of the securities in his account at any given time directly from the brokerage firm. (That is, he has arranged to trade, as it is said, "on margin" to greater leverage his investing opportunities.) The brokerage firm takes a security interest in all the securities in his account to secure whatever he may owe the firm under this arrangement. What more, if anything, must the firm of Shakes and Rattles do to perfect its interest by gaining control over its collateral?

16.4   Suppose that Lance Cashmore of the previous problem wants to borrow money from the Venture Loans Group in order to start up a business of his own. Among the collateral he offers up to that lender is his entire securities account at Shakes and Rattles.

(a) What action or actions might the Venture Loans Group take to perfect on Lance's securities account by taking control of it?

(b) Would it necessarily defeat Venture's claim of perfection by control if any agreement it enters into with Lance and with the brokerage firm allows for Lance continuing to give the brokerage orders with respect to securities that are to be added to or sold from his account?

16.5   Knifty Knits Incorporated, the major manufacturer of sweaters and other knitwear, enters into an agreement to borrow a large sum of money from Large Lenders of America, a major commercial lending firm. As part of the loan agreement, Knifty grants a security interest in "all accounts, now held or hereafter acquired" to the lender. The security agreement entered into by the two parties also provides that Knifty will open a new bank account with The California Bank for Industry and furthermore that Knifty will, immediately upon receipt, deposit all checks that it receives from those who buy from it on credit into this bank account and this account only. Large Lenders perfects its security interest covering all of Knifty's accounts by filing a sufficient initial financing statement in the proper place, indicating the collateral to be "all accounts, now held or hereafter acquired."

(a) If Large Lenders wants also to perfect on the bank account into which Knifty has agreed to make the specified deposits, may it do so by simply adding a careful description of the particular bank account to the UCC1 it files?

(b) If your answer to the above question is no, what must Large Lenders do to perfect on the bank account?

CHAPTER
17

Goods Covered by Certificates of Title

A. INTRODUCTION

As we have earlier seen, one of the principal problems with which lenders have to cope when the debtor offers up some particular personal property as collateral is that there is generally no sure-fire way for the lender to determine whether the debtor does in fact truly own, or as we said in Chapter 6 have "rights in," the collateral. That is because the legal system under which we operate does not have for personal property anything equivalent to the complex and detailed recording statutes which feature so prominently when "title" to real property is the matter in question. For most personal property it is simply not possible for the owner, even if he or she really very much wishes to do so, to record or gain certification in any accepted way of his or her possession through a system established and kept secure by governmental or other trusted authority.

The one major exception to this state of affairs is the system of certificate-of-title statutes which have been adopted by each of the states with respect to ownership of motor vehicles. Under such statutes a person's ownership of a automobile — or other "motor vehicle" that comes within the definition of that term as set out in the specific statute being relied upon — is made official by that person's being issued by the state a paper certificate testifying to his or her ownership of the vehicle. Some states reserve this certification process for motor vehicles only. In others, similar statutory treatment has been extended to other big-ticket items, most often mobile homes, boats, and farm tractors. Another feature of such certificate-of-title statutes, and one that we understandably are especially interested in, is that they typical provide that any lien or security interest in the subject property is to be noted directly on the certificate, the piece of paper which is then retained by the owner him- or herself.

197

A major problem remains, however, as the certificate-of-title statutes of the states vary in crucial details to a significant extent. The resultant arrangement is something of a patchwork affair of inconsistent, and sometimes imprecise or simply unclear, state statutes in which there are noticeable openings between the patches. It is apparently not terribly difficult for scam artists who know where those holes are and how to work their way through them to obtain a certificate for a vehicle which is not rightfully theirs or to obtain a "clean" title — a certificate which has been cleaned of any notation which it should rightfully carry indicating the rights of a lien holder or secured party — even though the lien has not been lifted or the security interest terminated. In an effort to deal with this situation, the National Conference of Commissioners on Uniform State Laws promulgated in 2005 a Uniform Certificate of Title Act. A Prefatory Note to that Uniform Act includes the following:

> This Uniform Certificate of Title Act (Act) is intended to respond to several principal, though by no means exclusive, factors affecting transfers of interests in motor vehicles: Diversity of state treatment; the increasing use of electronic records, including efforts to reduce and prevent title and other vehicle fraud, and contracting; evolving commercial practices and current legal issues; and the impact of revised Article 9 of the Uniform Commercial Code.
>
> Each year, on the order of 70 million motor vehicles are titled in the United States. While there is almost universal consistency in some industry standards, for example Vehicle Identification Number (VIN) usage, these vehicles are titled by the states under some sixteen different types of systems, virtually none of which is entirely compatible with the others for purposes of information exchange and title interchange. The states also vary in designation of the officials who administer titles and transfers, and collect state taxes, and there are variations in the definitional scope of titling statutes. As with other states' files the move from paper to electronic records is not uniform either within or among the states.
>
> . . . .
>
> In addition, as business conditions and practices have evolved, state certificate of title laws that are nonuniform and sometimes outmoded have become inadequate to deal with current and emerging issues. The need for a consistent informational structure and uniform rules dealing with common title problems has become increasingly apparent.

Unfortunately, as of this writing no state has adopted this Uniform Act, and there is no clear indication of when if ever wide-spread adoption of this or some other measure intended to create a more uniform and reliable system will come to pass. We are left, at least for the moment, with a clearly far-from-ideal situation. You will have to keep this in mind as you consider in this chapter the extent to which Article 9 defers to and depends on the certificate-of-title laws of the several states.

B.   PREPARATION

In preparation for discussion of the material in this chapter, read carefully the following parts of the Code:

- The definition of "certificate of title" in § 9-102(a)(10)
- Section 9-303
- Section 9-311, and Comments 3 and 4 to this section

If you are concentrating in your studies on the law of a particular state, you might also want to look at that state's enacted version of § 9-311(b)(2) to see what types of personal property other than motor vehicles, if any, may be covered by a certificate-of-title law in that state.

C.   PROBLEMS AND CASES

PROBLEMS

17.1   First City National Bank makes a small business loan to Flora the florist. As part of the loan agreement, the bank is granted a security interest by Flora of "all of my equipment, now held or hereafter acquired." The bank files an initial financial statement, indicating its collateral as "all equipment," under the correct name and in the proper place. One piece of Flora's equipment is a van which she uses to make deliveries. Does the bank's security interest cover this delivery van? Has the bank perfected its interest as to the van?

17.2   Joshua Tillers is a farmer. He owns a tractor. Under the law of the state in which Joshua resides and where he does his farming, a certificate-of-title law covers farm tractors. At the time he acquired the tractor he obtained from the state a certificate indicating his ownership. Later, when he is in need of some ready cash, Tillers drives the tractor to Paula's Pawn Shop. He borrows some money and signs a paper granting Paula a security interest in the tractor. He then drives the tractor around to the back of Paula's establishment where it is locked up in a lot along with other pieces of farm machinery and other larger outdoor items which Paula has taken in pawn. Tillers takes a bus back to his farm, still holding the certificate of title covering the tractor in the back pocket of his overalls. Later Tillers is forced to declare bankruptcy. Does Paula have a security interest in the tractor which will stand up against the bankruptcy trustee's efforts to avoid the interest? Would your answer be any different if Paula were to have asked for and received the certificate of title covering the tractor at the time of her loan?

17.3 Irving's Autos of Irvine, California, a dealership selling new and used cars, sells a new car to a customer, Matteo, who purchases the car for his personal use. Matteo's purchase of the car is made possible by a loan made to him by the dealership. Among the documents signed by Matteo at the time of his purchase is a Security Agreement in which he grants to the dealership a security interest in the new car, securing his obligation to make monthly payments to pay off the loan. The dealership, through an oversight on the part of one of its employees, never goes through the steps necessary to get notice of its interest placed on the certificate of title which Matteo obtains covering the new car. If a question of perfection ever arises, can the dealership successfully claim perfection based on its having taken a purchase-money security interest in consumer goods? Revisit § 9-309(1).

IN RE LORTZ

United States Bankruptcy Court for the Central District of Illinois, 2006
344 Bankr. 579, 60 U.C.C. Rep. Serv. 2d 90

THOMAS L. PERKINS, Chief Bankruptcy Judge: The issue is whether a creditor that mistakenly releases its lien on a certificate of title to a motor vehicle and returns the title to the owner causes its security interest to become unperfected so as to be avoidable by a Trustee in bankruptcy.

The parties have stipulated to the facts as follows. On July 14, 2005, Charles W. Lortz, the Debtor (Debtor), obtained financing from Ford Motor Credit Company (FMCC) to purchase a 2005 Ford Ranger. The amount financed of $16,657.89 was payable over five years with interest at 15.25% in equal installments of $400.90 per month. The first payment was due August 28, 2005. FMCC perfected its security interest in the vehicle by having its lien noted on the certificate of title.

Between August 25, 2005, and November 14, 2005, FMCC's records show that it posted twelve payments on the loan sufficient to pay it off in full. Its records also show that each of the twelve payments was returned for insufficient funds within days of receipt. FMCC concedes that it mistakenly failed to reverse the credits on the account when the payments were returned. As a result of its error, FMCC'S records reflected that the account had been paid in full as of November 14, 2005, despite the fact that no collectible funds had ever been received. After posting the November 14 payment, FMCC automatically generated a paid in full letter, executed the lien release on the title and mailed the letter and the title to the Debtor. Apparently realizing its mistake soon thereafter, FMCC repossessed the vehicle on November 22, 2005. In its brief, FMCC states that when it realized that the title was released in error, it took action to secure the collateral. FMCC does not allege that it attempted to repossess or replevy the certificate of title.

On December 2, 2005, the Debtor filed a Chapter 7 petition. The Trustee contends that FMCC's lien is vulnerable to avoidance in the exercise of his strong arm powers under Section 544(a) of the Bankruptcy Code. FMCC contends that its lien, having been released by mistake, remains valid. Characterizing the lien release as a "clerical error," FMCC points to its prompt repossession of the vehicle, which occurred prior to the filing of the bankruptcy petition, as evidence of an intent not to release its security interest. Accordingly, the Court must determine whether, under Illinois law, the judicial lien granted to the Trustee pursuant to Section 544(a)(1) has priority over the lien of FMCC, which was released on the certificate of title by mistake.

Under Illinois law, the interest of a judicial lien creditor takes priority over an unperfected security interest. Accordingly, a bankruptcy Trustee prevails over the holder of a security interest in a vehicle who fails to perfect its security interest in accordance with the statute.

Although the pledge of a vehicle to secure a debt is an Article 9 security interest, the Illinois Vehicle Code provides the exclusive means for perfecting and giving notice of security interests in motor vehicles. 625 ILCS 5/3-207. A security interest in a vehicle is perfected "by the delivery to the Secretary of State of the existing certificate of title, if any, an application for a certificate of title containing the name and address of the lienholder and the required fee." 625 ILCS 5/3-202(b). It is then the responsibility of the Secretary of State's office to issue the certificate of title with the secured party's lien properly noted thereon. It is not disputed that FMCC had, for a time, a perfected security interest in the Debtor's 2005 Ford Ranger as a result of filing its application with the Secretary of State and the Secretary of State's issuance of a certificate of title showing FMCC as the lienholder. Rather, the issue is whether FMCC'S execution of the release on the certificate of title and return of the title to the Debtor rendered it unperfected as of the petition date when the Trustee's rights accrued.

Initially, it is worth emphasizing the distinction between a security interest and perfection of that interest. It is entirely possible for a creditor to hold a valid security interest that is not perfected. A signed security agreement stands by itself and governs the creditor's rights in collateral with respect to the Debtor. A security agreement is enforceable against a Debtor even if the security interest is not perfected. Perfection is only significant, indeed critical, with respect to the creditor's rights vis-a-vis third parties. On the other hand, perfection may not be achieved or maintained without a valid security interest granted by the Debtor. If a security agreement is invalid or is terminated, a lien noted on a title is worthless.

With that background, the Court accepts FMCC's argument that the mistaken release of lien did not discharge the Debtor's liability for the unpaid loan balance or terminate FMCC's security interest in the vehicle. The issue before the Court, however, turns on the question of perfection alone. Lack of perfection relates only to the issue of priority over other creditors' interests in the collateral and does not, by itself, terminate or impair the secured party's rights as against the Debtor. The Illinois Vehicle Code addresses perfection and release but not in a comprehensive fashion. Perfection is defined as follows:

> A security interest is perfected by the delivery to the Secretary of State of the existing certificate of title, if any, an application for a certificate of title containing the name and address of the lienholder and the required fee. The security interest is perfected as of the time of its creation if the delivery to the Secretary of State is completed within 21 days after the creation of the security interest or receipt by the new lienholder of the existing certificate of title from a prior lienholder or licensed dealer, otherwise as of the time of the delivery.

625 ILCS 5/3-202(b). Notably, perfection is not defined as occurring when the secured party's lien is noted on the certificate of title. Instead, perfection occurs at that earlier point when the Secretary of State receives the necessary documents to enable it to identify and note the lienholder on the title. Thus, the possibility exists that a lien may be perfected even though it is not noted on the title where, for example, the Secretary of State's office, having received the application and title, hasn't gotten around to completing the notation yet or fails to do so in error.

The case at bar, however, involves not a lien that was never noted on the title but one that was properly noted and then subsequently released. The release was effected by an FMCC employee executing the portion of the certificate of title specifically designated for the purpose of a lienholder to release its lien by execution or signature. The Vehicle Code authorizes the Secretary of State to prescribe a form of certificate of title that includes the naming of a lienholder and the assignment or release of the security interest of a lienholder. It further provides that a certificate of title issued by the Secretary of State is *prima facie* evidence of the facts appearing on it. The purpose of this provision is to provide the public with a readily available means of identifying the owners and lienholders of the vehicle and parties dealing with the vehicle are entitled to rely upon the information that appears on the face of the certificate of title.

Although the Vehicle Code does not expressly define the effect of execution of the lien release portion on a certificate of title, it is not disputed that such execution is the accepted method by which liens are released and by which public notice is given of the release of motor vehicle liens. Section 3-205 describes the process by which a creditor releases a security interest as consisting of two steps: (1) executing a release, and (2) mailing or delivering the release and the certificate of title to the next lienholder or, if none, the owner. 625 ILCS 5/3-205. Although Section 3-205 requires a creditor to release its security interest within 21 days after payment of the secured loan, it is clear that this section does not make full payment a prerequisite to a valid release. There is no question that a secured party has the power to release the security interest or only the lien before full payment of the secured debt.

Of greater significance is Section 3-207, which provides that the stated method for perfecting and "giving notice of security interests" in motor vehicles is exclusive of any recording or filing requirement. 625 ILCS 5/3-207. The method referred to for giving notice of security interests is the notation of the lien on the original certificate of title. The importance of the original title for the purpose of giving notice of liens is obvious when one considers that it is the title that is the necessary document both to transfer ownership of a motor vehicle and to perfect a security interest in a motor vehicle. A lien that is noted on the title, by the very fact of its presence there, gives conclusive notice so that any subsequent transferee or lender necessarily acquires their interest subject to the lien. Just as well, a lien that is released on the title is notice of its termination which may be relied upon by a transferee or lender so that they take free and clear of the released lien. An unperfected security interest in a titled vehicle is not valid against subsequent transferees or lienholders. 625 ILCS 5/3-202(a). Using the original certificate of title as the exclusive method of giving such notice allows transactions concerning motor vehicles to be conducted easily and with certainty.

The Court also accepts FMCC's representation that it did not intend to release its security interest for anything less than full payment of the loan, which is simply another way of saying that the lien was released by mistake. As with all perfection laws, however, which focus on third party perceptions and clarity and certainty of notice, the intent of the secured party is not relevant to questions of perfection and errors can be fatal.

It is also critical, here, that FMCC returned possession of the original certificate of title to the Debtor. Had FMCC executed the lien release but then caught the error before mailing the title to the Debtor, its perfected status may well have been preserved. By giving up possession of the title, however, FMCC in effect placed it back into the stream of commerce where it became open to reliance by third party purchasers and lien creditors with no notice that the lien had been released in error.

FMCC also contends that even though its lien was released on the title, the records of the Secretary of State continued to reflect FMCC's lien. Unlike the laws of other states, however, the Illinois Vehicle Code does not require the lienholder to submit the title to the Secretary of State in order for a release of lien to be effective. While it may be viewed as unfair to deprive a secured creditor of its lien because of an honest mistake, Illinois law places a "strong emphasis" on the need to obtain and maintain perfection in accordance with the statutory method; the consequent gain in certainty and regularity outweighs any such perceived unfairness.

This Court concludes that the effect of a release of lien, as to third parties, is not dependent upon full payment or the intent of the secured party, questions of fact that are not reflected on the certificate of title and that are "outside the record," so to speak. Because the certificate of title is the exclusive method of perfecting and giving notice of a lien, what appears on the face of the certificate of title must be determinative where third party interests are involved. The Court holds that by returning the original certificate of title, with its lien released, to the Debtor, FMCC became so far unperfected that a judicial lien creditor would gain a priority interest in the vehicle under Illinois law. Therefore, FMCC's lien is avoidable by the Trustee.

PROBLEM

17.4   Big Bank of California makes a loan to Irving's Autos of Irvine. It takes as collateral all of the dealership's "inventory, now held of hereafter acquired." Big Bank files an initial financing statement in the proper place, giving the debtor's name and other information required on the UCC1 form correctly and indicating the collateral as "all inventory." Has Big Bank properly perfected on the autos in Irving's inventory?

UNION PLANTERS BANK, N.A. v. PENINSULA BANK
Court of Appeal of Florida, 2005
897 So. 2d 499, 56 U.C.C. Rep. Serv. 2d 356

ROTHENBERG, Judge: InterAmerican Car Rental, Inc. (InterAmerican), a car rental company, defaulted on its loans in 2002. Several of its creditors attempted to recover money owed to them. Two of its creditors, Ocean Bank and Peninsula Bank, noted their liens on vehicle certificates of title, and also filed sworn statements of lien as required by Chapter 319, Florida Statutes (2002). Union Planters Bank (Union Planters) failed to note its liens on the certificates of title but did file UCC-1's and filed them prior to those filed by Ocean Bank and Peninsula Bank. Union Planters claims that based upon section 679.3111, Florida Statutes (2002), it properly perfected its security interest in InterAmerican's vehicles by filing its UCC-1's and since its UCC-1's were filed prior to those filed by Ocean Bank and Peninsula Bank, Union Planters argues that its interest takes priority.

In support of this claim, Union Planters claims that since InterAmerican sold approximately 4,000 vehicles per year, earning 60-70% of its revenue in this manner, that it was "in the business of selling used cars," and thus section 679.3111 provides for an exception to the requirement in section 319.27, Florida Statutes (2002), that liens be noted on the vehicles' certificates of title. Chapter 319 provides that:

> (1) Each lien . . . on a motor vehicle . . . shall be noted on the face of the Florida certificate of title. . . .
> (2) No lien . . . shall be enforceable in any of the courts of this state . . . unless . . . such lien has been noted upon the certificate of title of the motor vehicle. . . .

[N]o title, lien, or other interest in [a motor] vehicle . . . shall be valid unless evidenced in accordance with this chapter [319].

Chapter 319 provides one exception to this rule when a debtor is a *licensed dealer* selling motor vehicle "floor plan stock." § 319.27(1), Fla. Stat. (2002). As stated earlier, InterAmerican is *not* a licensed dealer. Therefore, the lone exception to the notation requirements provided for in Chapter 319 is inapplicable to the facts herein.

Union Planters, however, claims an exemption to the title notation statute in Chapter 319 pursuant to section 679.3111(4), Florida Statutes (2002), which provides that perfection in motor vehicles is obtained by filing a UCC financing statement where the motor vehicles are: "inventory held for sale or lease by a person . . . in business of selling goods of that kind. . . ."

Union Planters argues that InterAmerican's rental fleet was "inventory held for sale" and because InterAmerican sold approximately 4,000 vehicles per year, earning 60-70% of its revenue in this manner, that it was "in the business" of selling used cars.

The official comment to this UCC provision notes that the "fact that the debtor eventually sells the goods does not, of itself, mean that the debtor is 'in the business of selling goods of that kind.'" See U.C.C. § 9-3111 cmt. 4. After a review of the evidence and case law, the trial court concluded that InterAmerican was *not* in the business of selling cars. We agree.

It is not disputed that InterAmerican is in the business of renting motor vehicles and only sold its used vehicles after nine to ten months when they had lost their usefulness to its rental business. All of its vehicles were sold through wholesale auctions or by selling them directly to wholesalers and dealers. None of these vehicles were ever sold directly to individuals, nor were they advertised for sale or displayed in any manner to the public for sale. It is also undisputed that InterAmerican was *not* a licensed dealer, as it never held a dealer's license. It has always held itself out exclusively as a short-term rental car company.

Additionally, section 320.27(1)(c), Florida Statutes (2002), exempts certain vehicle sales from its definition of "dealer" sales:

The term "motor vehicle dealer" does not include persons not engaged in the purchase or sale of motor vehicles as a business who are disposing of vehicles acquired for their own use or for use in their business. . . .

§ 320.27(1)(c)(5), Fla. Stat. (2002). As InterAmerican is merely "disposing" of the vehicles it acquired for its use in its car rental business, InterAmerican's conduct clearly falls within the exception articulated in section 320.27(1)(c)(5), Florida Statutes (2002).

To conclude otherwise would require tortured logic and lead to an absurd result. Inter-American sells gasoline and automobile insurance to those who rent their vehicles, and yet no one would argue that it is in the insurance or gasoline sales business. It is axiomatic that in order to operate a car rental company, one by necessity must constantly phase out (sell) its older inventory and restock its fleet with new or newer vehicles. The disposal of these vehicles at wholesale auction or by selling them directly to wholesalers or dealers for that purpose clearly was not intended to fall within the definition of what constitutes a "motor vehicle dealer." We therefore affirm the trial court's order granting final summary judgment in favor of defendants Ocean Bank and Peninsula Bank, and denying Union Planters' cross-motion for summary judgment.

Affirmed.

PART IV

PRIORITY ISSUES

CHAPTER

18

Introduction to Priority and the Basic Rules of Priority

A. INTRODUCTION

1. Matters of Priority

We begin with the exceptionally important language of § 9-201(a), "Except as otherwise provided," in the Code, "a security agreement is effective according to its terms between the parties, against purchasers of the collateral, and against creditors." Note also that the word "purchaser" covers a wide range of characters under § 1-201(32) & (33) (or the equivalent § 1R-201(b)(29) & (30)). If some party other than the debtor itself claims an interest in the collateral — an interest that may have arisen in any number of ways — the secured party will often want to asserts its interest, its valid attached security interest, against that third party. The secured party will assert and hope to be able to prove that its interest takes precedence over the interest held by the third party. It will be claiming the *priority* of its interest over that of the other claimant. The rules for determining which party's claim in any particular item or items of collateral has priority are, as you can imagine, extremely important to the whole Article 9 enterprise. When things get dicey — that is, when the debtor's economic condition has already begun to deteriorate or is threatening to do so — is just the moment when the secured party may need to call upon the rights it has obtained with respect to the collateral by taking a security interest in it. But what if others also claim an interest in this same property? Coming in second in a priority dispute at such a moment can leave a secured party in a pretty sorry state, with its security interest in the collateral (even if perfectly attached and perfected upon) being worth not much of anything.

As you will have picked up by now, how a secured party fares in the priority game often depends on whether it has effectively perfected its interest, and if so how and when. That is why we spent so much time on the means of perfection in the prior material. Recall the following language from Comment 2 to § 9-308: "A perfected security interest may still be or become subordinate to other interests. . . . However, in general, after perfection the secured party is protected against creditors and transferees of the debtor and, in particular, against any representative of creditors in insolvency proceedings instituted by or against the debtor." In this and the following chapters of this part we see how Article 9 makes good on this generalized promise — and also when and why things may not work out for the secured party as well in a particular instance as they do "in general." When will the secured party fail to gain the priority over others it presumably has been counting on? What could it have done in advance to minimize this possibility?

2.   The Secured Party vs. the Lien Creditor

The first type of priority dispute we consider is that where the two contenders are the secured party and someone with the status of a *lien creditor* as that term is defined in § 9-102(a)(52). As you will see, § 9-317(a) provides the basic rule we'll need for dealing with this situation.

3.   The Secured Party vs. the Trustee in Bankruptcy

When a bankruptcy petition is filed, either voluntarily by the debtor or involuntarily by a creditor or creditors of the debtor forcing it into bankruptcy, the bankruptcy case has begun. Soon an individual with the title of the *trustee in bankruptcy* will be named. (In some situations, as you would discover in the course on bankruptcy law, the debtor itself can take on the role, acting as what is termed a "debtor in possession," but for our purposes we need not worry about this.) While it may take some time for the trustee in bankruptcy to be named, he or she will gain significant powers arising *as of the date the bankruptcy petition was filed.* From the Article 9 perspective, it would be enough to point out that the trustee in bankruptcy is deemed a lien creditor under § 9-102(a)(52)(A) "from the date of the filing of the petition." The rules of § 9-317 apply to the trustee as they would to any lien creditor.

The federal law of bankruptcy goes beyond this, giving the trustee in bankruptcy considerable powers beyond simply the right to invoke Article 9 as just another lien creditor. Consider, for example, the following tantalizing excerpt from the Federal Bankruptcy Code:

§ 544. Trustee as lien creditor and as successor to certain creditors and purchasers.

(a) The trustee shall have, as of the commencement of the case, and without regard to any knowledge of the trustee or of any creditor, the rights and powers of, or may avoid any transfer of property of the debtor or any obligation incurred by the debtor that is voidable by —

(1) a creditor that extends credit to the debtor at the time of the commencement of the case, and that obtains, at such time and with respect to

such credit, a judicial lien on all property on which a creditor on a simple contract could have obtained such a judicial lien, whether or not such a creditor exists;

(2) a creditor that extends credit to the debtor at the time of the commencement of the case, and obtains, at such time and with respect to such credit, an execution against the debtor that is returned unsatisfied at such time, whether or not such a creditor exists; or

(3) a bona fide purchaser of real property, other than fixtures, from the debtor, against whom applicable law permits such transfer to be perfected, that obtains the status of a bona fide purchaser and has perfected such transfer at the time of the commencement of the case, whether or not such a purchaser exists.

This is the so-called "strong-arm clause" of the Bankruptcy Code. We can leave to your course in bankruptcy a detailed analysis and explanation of §544(a). For present purposes it is sufficient to recognize and fully appreciate how it applies to the study of secured transactions. Under the definitions of the Bankruptcy Code, any security interest granted by the debtor would be considered a "transfer of property [the subject collateral] of the debtor." The collateral is now part of what is referred to as the bankruptcy *estate*. The trustee will want to establish, if he or she can, that the collateral is not only part of the estate but that it is *unencumbered* by any liens or security interests which would lessen or totally wipe out any value it could contribute towards paying off at least some portion of what is owed to the debtor's unsecured creditors.

When the secured party makes a claim against the bankruptcy estate (what would be termed a "secured claim" in bankruptcy lingo), the trustee will investigate. If the trustee believes that there is some reason that the security interest being asserted by the secured party would be "subordinate" to the trustee's interest under §9-317(a)(2), then the trustee will make that argument. Beyond this, the trustee can invoke the strong arm clause of the Bankruptcy Code quoted above to "avoid" the security interest entirely. If the trustee is successful with his or her arguments, then the security interest is totally avoided. It is rendered null and void as the bankruptcy process works its way through to a conclusion. To be sure, the secured party's *claim* to be paid whatever it is owed on the outstanding obligation of the debtor is not avoided, but it has become merely an *unsecured claim* being made against the estate in bankruptcy. It is lumped in with all those other unsecured claims which will likely be paid off at a rate of only some pennies to the dollar by the end of the day.

4. Secured Party vs. Secured Party

Whether the secured party's interest is being asserted in a bankruptcy context or otherwise, it may have to contend with a security interest claimed by another party in the same collateral. The general rules governing such priority contests (we'll see other more particularized rules in subsequent chapters) are set out in §9-322(a) and will be explored in the later problems in this chapter.

5. *Where Are the Cases?*

It might surprise you to see that in a chapter as important as this one I have not included any cases. You certainly should not take from this that matters of priority are not regularly and vigorously litigated. Any such litigation, however, will usually focus not on exactly how the basic rules of priority work. Once you get the hang of them, and especially given the loving care with which they are set out in the Revised Article 9, there will rarely be any ambiguity about what exactly the rule of priority is in the vast majority of cases. Most litigation, if litigation there be, will therefor come down to a controversy about some aspect of Article 9 which we have already covered. Did the party claiming a security interest in some specific property ever attach on that property? Did it attempt to perfect? If so, was its perfection effective and, if so, as of when? Was this particular property among the covered collateral? That kind of thing.

From which follows two things: First of all, everything that you learned in the preceding chapters finally pays off. In a sense all that came before, as interesting as it may have been for its own sake, was really in large part "merely" preparation for entering into consideration of priority questions.

Secondly, I will from time to time in this chapter refer you back to a case considered in an earlier chapter. You need not prepare to revisit that case as if from scratch, but you should reconsider it now with an added understanding of exactly why the parties were contesting the particular point or points that were there at issue. Much more than bragging rights were at stake, as you now will be more able to appreciate.

B. PREPARATION

In preparation for discussion of the problems in this chapter, read carefully the following parts of the Code:

*   Section 9-317(a), and Comments 2 and 3 to this section
*   The definition of "lien creditor" in § 9-102(a)(52)
*   Section 9-322(a) and its Comments 2 through 5
*   Comment 3 to § 9-323

C. PROBLEMS AND CASES

PROBLEMS

18.1 Lance Cashmore has as his principal residence a luxurious penthouse apartment in downtown Chicago. Finding himself temporarily short of funds, Lance meets with a representative of Discreet Financial Services. He arranges for a loan from that firm, granting it a security interest in his large collection of expensive antique and contemporary watches. DFS writes up a security agreement which provides as a description of the collateral a detailed listing of each watch in the collection. Lance signs this security agreement on June 15, 2008 and in return is given a check for $110,000. DFS files an initial financing statement proper in all respects and indicating the watch collection as the collateral covered with the Secretary of State of Illinois on the following day. In 2009, Buddy Best, a long-time business associate of Lance's, files suit against Lance claiming damages arising from a breach of contract by Lance on a real estate deal the two had entered into some time earlier and which has since gone sour. Buddy is awarded a judgment for $80,000. Lance resists paying this judgment, saying among other things that, "Even if I really owed it to you, I just don't have that kind of cash right now." Frustrated by his failure to get what is due him, and knowing that Lance still has in his possession his collection of expensive watches, Buddy does what is necessary under Illinois law to have the sheriff levy on the watches in order that his judgment lien be satisfied out of the proceeds of a sale of the watches.

(a) When the watch collection is eventually sold off by the sheriff, which party should be paid first out of the proceeds, DFS or Buddy?
(b) What would be your answer to this question if for some reason DFS had never filed an initial financing statement with respect to its security interest?

18.2   This problem begins as does the previous one. In 2008, Lance Cashmore grants a security interest in his valuable watch collection to Discreet Financial Services in order to obtain a loan of $110,000. DFS immediately files an initial financing statement, proper in all respects and in the correct place. In 2009, however, and without Buddy Best having anything to do with it, Lance is forced to declare bankruptcy by his accumulated debts. In due course a trustee in bankruptcy is named in connection with this bankruptcy proceeding.

(a) As a matter of Article 9 law, who will have priority in the watches, DFS or the bankruptcy trustee?
(b) Will the trustee in bankruptcy be able to avoid, as a matter of bankruptcy law, the security interest claimed by DFS in the particular property in the bankruptcy estate, that is, Lance's watch collection?
(c) How would your answers to parts (a) and (b) above be affected if it were to turn out that DFS had never filed an initial financing statement with respect to the security interest it obtained in 2008 in all those watches? What if it had filed a UCC1, but the trustee could prove that its filing was ineffective to perfect the interest, for instance because it had been filed in the wrong place or with the debtor's name rendered in a seriously

misleading way? If the trustee in bankruptcy were successful in making such an argument, where would that leave DFS?

REVISITING SOME EARLIER CASES

Analysis of the previous problem and the statutory material it invokes, should give you an even greater appreciation of how crucial is the concept of perfection under Article 9, which we labored over in the previous chapters. We have now seen particular instances which support that language in Comment 2 to § 9-308, to which I return us once again, that, "[I]n general, after perfection the secured party is protected against creditors and transferees of the debtor and, in particular, against any representative of creditors [the archetype of which is the trustee in bankruptcy under federal law] in insolvency proceedings instituted by or against the debtor. See, e.g., Section 9-317."

Review the *Kinderknecht* and *Pankrantz* cases in Chapter 10. You should be able to appreciate why and how the trustee in each case argued as he or she did that John Deere's security interest could be "avoided" by him or her, the trustee, once a bankruptcy petition had been filed.

See also the *Pickle Logging* case of Chapter 10, noting, as that decision explains, that under bankruptcy law a so-called "debtor in possession" has the same power as would a trustee to invoke § 544(a) of the Bankruptcy Code. How did the debtor in possession argue for avoidance of John Deere's security interest in that case?

Finally, revisit *Equitable Financial Management, Inc.* in Chapter 13.

PROBLEMS

18.3   In 2009, Danby Enterprises, Inc., borrows $100,000 from the First Bank of Springfield, granting that bank a security interest in all of its "accounts, now held or hereafter acquired." Through a foul-up at First Bank, no initial financial statement is filed with respect to this transaction. In 2011, Danby borrows $80,000 from Second State Bank of Shelbyville, granting this bank a security interest in "all accounts, now held or hereafter acquired." Second State Bank quickly files an initial financial statement, correct in all respects and in the proper place, covering Danby's accounts. As of the end of 2011, which lender has priority in Danby's accounts? Is there anything you can think of that the loser in this priority contest can now do to reverse the result?

18.4   Gabriela opens a small restaurant, Gabriela's Place. The restaurant is soon doing very well, and she begins to consider expanding the size of her enterprise. To do so, however, she will need additional capital. In July of 2009, she applies to the Springfield State Bank for a small business loan. As part of her application, the bank asks not only for various financial documents about her and her business, but also that she sign a paper authorizing it, the bank, to file in the proper place an initial financing statement covering the collateral she is offering up. She does so sign, and the bank files this initial financing statement in the proper place which is received and accepted by the filing office on July 11. After a thorough investigation of her finances and her current set-up, the bank loan officer determines that her loan request should be granted and on what terms. He explains these over the telephone to Gabriela, who says she is willing to borrow on the basis the loan manager has laid out. On September 11, Gabriela comes into the bank. She signs a note made payable "to the order of Springfield State Bank" for $80,000, payable in specified monthly installments based on a stated rate of interest. She also signs a security agreement granting the bank a security interest in her "equipment, now held and hereafter acquired." The loan officer turns over to her a check for $80,000. As it happens, during August Gabriela had been visited by a representative of InstaCredit, a firm new to town which is aggressively seeking out businesses which may want to borrow from it on its "friendly expedited basis." This person looks about Gabriela's business and quickly offers to lend her $50,000 on what the restauranteur deems to be very favorable terms. By the end of the week, Gabriela has her loan from InstraCredit. She has also signed a note promising to repay this loan and a security agreement by which she grants to InstaCredit a security interest in "all equipment, including that after-acquired." InstaCredit files a financing statement on her equipment, proper in all respects and in the correct filing office, on August 23, 2009.

(a) As of September 15, 2009, does Springfield State Bank have a security interest in Gabriela's equipment? Is this interest perfected?
(b) As of September 15, 2009, does InstaCredit have a security interest in Gabriela's equipment? Is this interest perfected?
(c) If you conclude that each has a security interest, whose interest has priority? Is there anything you can think of that the loser in this priority contest can now do to reverse the result? What might it have done earlier to avoid this result?

18.5   Ed Owens arranges to borrow $20,000 from his friend Alexandra Fuller. He orally promises to pay the money back with 7% interest within a year. He also hands over to her an antique pocket watch which has been in his family for generations saying, "You can hold onto this watch as collateral until I pay you back." Alexandra takes the watch and puts it in a locked drawer. She gives Ed a check for $20,000 which he quickly cashes. A few months later, Ed goes to visit another friend, Bucky Adams, and asks Bucky for a loan of $30,000, "to tide him over some temporary cash-flow problems." When Bucky shows some reluctance to lend his friend such a large sum, Ed responds, "Tell you what. You know that gold watch that has been in my family for years, the one with all the jewels? I've got it locked up in my safety deposit box right now, and I know I could sell it to get the money I need, but I just can't bear the thought of doing so. How about I grant you a security interest in the watch as collateral assuring you will be repaid?" Bucky agrees to lend to Ed on that basis, having vivid memories of his friend's gold and jewel-encrusted watch and knowing how much it means to Ed. Being a lawyer, Bucky knows just what to do. He prepares a security agreement which he has Ed sign under which Ed grants to him a security interest in the watch as carefully described. He also files an initial financing statement covering the watch proper in all respects and with the correct filing office. When all this is done, he gives Ed a check for $30,000, which Ed quickly cashes.

(a) Does each of Alexandra and Bucky have a valid enforceable security interest in Ed's watch? Whose interest has priority?
(b) Suppose instead that just before Ed goes to see Bucky to ask for the loan he returns to Alexandra's office and asks if he can "have the watch back for just a couple of days." He explains that he is going to visit an uncle of his, and this particular uncle always asks to see the old family heirloom and assure himself that Ed is taking good care of it. Alexandra agrees, provided that Ed leave something else of comparable value with her during the time the watch will be away. Ed takes off a diamond pinkie ring and hands it to Alexandra. She gives him the watch and puts the ring safely in her drawer. A couple of days later, after Ed has his meeting with Bucky, Ed comes back to Alexandra's office, gives her back the watch and picks up his ring. How, if at all, does this change your analysis of the situation?

REVISITING AN EARLIER CASE

Look again at the part of the *National Pawn Brokers Unlimited* case reproduced in Chapter 13. You should now be able fully to appreciate why Osterman was making the argument — even if it eventually turned out to be unsuccessful — that the pawnbroker's "possession" of the jewelry had been interrupted when the law enforcement officials took it for use as evidence in the criminal trial against Pippin.

PROBLEM

18.6 In order to finance the expansion of its manufacturing plant, The Fresno Furniture Company, borrows $400,000 in 2003 from Commerce Bank of California, the loan to be repaid through monthly payments (including, of course, interest as set out in the agreement) over four years. In order to secure this loan, Fresno Furniture grants to the bank a security interest in "all equipment, now held or hereafter acquired." The bank files an initial financing statement, proper in all respects and with the correct filing office, in 2003. In late 2006, when Fresno has only about $80,000 left to pay on this loan, it negotiates a loan from another bank, Pacific Coast Bank, for $240,000, granting Pacific Coast an interest in its equipment which that bank quickly and correctly perfects upon by filing. In 2007, when Fresno makes it final payment to Commerce Bank, no termination statement is filed. Rather, Fresno enters into another loan agreement with Commerce, this time to borrow $475,000 to be paid back over the next four years and again granting Commerce a security interest in its equipment. Commerce gets from Fresno a new note, representing its obligation to repay this new loan, and a new security agreement. Commerce does not, however, make any new filing to reflect the 2007 transaction. It does, however, file a proper continuation statement during the proper period in 2008. In 2009, Fresno files for bankruptcy. At the time of the bankruptcy, Fresno owes Commerce Bank approximately $350,000 and owes Pacific Coast Bank approximately $200,000. The bankruptcy trustee is able to sell off all of Fresno's equipment for $400,000.

(a) How will Commerce Bank argue the proceeds from the sale of the equipment should be distributed as between it and Pacific Coast?
(b) How will Pacific Coast argue the proceeds should be distributed?
(c) Whose argument will succeed?
(d) What general lesson has been learned by the loser in this particular priority contest?

CHAPTER

19

Special Priority for the PMSI

A. INTRODUCTION

The general rules governing priority as we saw them in the prior chapter are, as you might expect, subject to a number of exceptions. This chapter explores the special rules of priority which come into play when a secured party can establish that it has taken not just any old security interest but a purchase-money security interest. As you will discover, the holder of a PMSI may be granted a certain grace period—now 20 days—in which to perfect its interest by filing. (You should be aware that prior to the 2001 revision of Article 9 this grace period was given in the Official Version of Article 9 as 10 days, although many states had lengthened it by nonuniform amendment, often to 20 days, well before 2001.)

You will also discover that a purchase-money interest can often "skip to the head of the line," gaining priority over another interest which would, under the general rules of the previous chapter, have had priority under the first-to-file-or-perfect rule. How and when a PMSI can attain this special priority status will occupy us through most of this chapter.

The question remains, of course, as to *why* a PMSI should get such favored treatment. One answer is that is has long been this way. But what reason or reasons, beyond wanting to follow historical precedent, would justify the preferential treatment given to the holder of the PMSI? Do these rules operate as an unfair burden on other parties, in particular the holder of a non-PMSI who may lose an expected priority because of them? Or can this other non-PMSI holder, if he or she knows fully how these rules operate, prevent being hurt or unfairly surprised by their operation? You should be considering all of these questions as you work through this chapter.

B.   PREPARATION

In preparation for discussion of the problems and the case in this chapter, read carefully the following parts of the Code:

- Section 9-317(e) and Comment 8 to this section
- Section 9-324(a), (b), (c), and (g), and Comments 2 through 4 and 13 to this section

If the financing of livestock is something in which you have or believe that you will later have a particular interest, you may also wish to glance over subsections (d) and (e) of §9-324. Notice how these provisions are mostly parallel to, but differ in at least one important respect from, subsections (b) and (c).

C.   PROBLEMS AND CASES

PROBLEM

19.1   Lydia, a certified public accountant, is concerned that she has lately lost a number of clients to other accounting firms and concludes that this may be because the technology she uses in office has become too old to handle the demands of an up-to-date accountancy practice. One Saturday, March 9, she pays a visit to Chip's Computer Heaven, a large local store that sells (not surprisingly) computer equipment and accessories. There she sees how much faster and more versatile the most recent models of computers, printers, and the like are, compared to the set-up she currently is using. Chip waits on her personally. He quickly help her "put together" an entirely new computer system, with all the bells and whistles which he insists are absolutely necessary to meet her particular needs. Lydia realizes that she really would like to buy all this new stuff, but that its total cost is more than she can afford at the moment. Chip assures her this is no problem since she can purchase the whole deal from him on credit, which he is more that willing to provide. Lydia decides to take him up on his offer. He quickly pulls out and fills in a form of retail sales installment agreement under which she agrees to purchase the equipment, which Chip lists on the form. Under the agreement, Lydia will pay for her purchase in monthly installments over the next year. She also grants to Chip a security interest in all of the items being sold under the agreement to secure her obligation to make the agreed-upon payments. "Just sign right here," Chip tells her, "and the stuff will be delivered to your office first thing Monday morning. I'll even come over and set it all up." Lydia signs. True to his word, Chip personally delivers the equipment and installs Lydia's new computer system on Monday, March 11. On March 22, Chip files an initial financing statement, proper in all respects and with the correct filing office, covering the equipment he has sold to Lydia. As it turns out, on March 17, Lydia has been forced to confront the fact that her business is doing even more poorly than she had thought, and that even all this new technology isn't going to help her out of her problems. She files a petition in bankruptcy on March 18.

(a) Will the trustee in bankruptcy be able to avoid Chip's security interest in all the new computer equipment he sold to her?
(b) Suppose that in addition it were to turn out that Lydia had originally set up her own practice and has been operating for several years with the benefit of a small business line of credit from a local bank, Old Glory Bank. As part of her arrangement with this bank, she granted it a security interest in "all equipment, inventory, and accounts, now held or hereafter acquired" by her. The bank had perfected on this interest by filing, and it has kept its filing correct and continuously effective. Does the bank's interest attach to the new computer equipment delivered to her office by Chip on Monday, March 11? When, if at all, does this interest become perfected?
(c) Which creditor—as between Chip and Old Glory Bank—has priority in all the computer stuff delivered to Lydia's office on March 11?

QUESTIONS ON § 9-317(e) AND § 9-324(a)

What reasons might there be, other than that it has "always been done this way," for allowing the PMSI interest the grace period for filing? Does it serve a legitimate business function, or is it just another rule we have to be prepared to apply and learn to live with?

Again, what reason or reasons might there be for allowing the PMSI to gain a special priority such as it may under § 9-324(a)? If this possibility were not available, what would be the consequences for a borrower who has once put up as collateral all of its equipment, say, including all that is after-acquired, to some general lender? Is the ability of the PMSI holder to gain priority over this general lender, even though he, she, or it comes into the picture much later in time, "unfair" to the general lender who has previously taken a blanket interest in "all equipment, now held or hereafter acquired?"

BRODIE HOTEL SUPPLY, INC. v. UNITED STATES

United States Court of Appeals for the Ninth Circuit, 1970
431 F.2d 1316, 8 U.C.C. Rep. Serv. 113

HAMLEY, Circuit Judge: Brodie Hotel Supply, Inc. (Brodie), brought this action against the United States to determine which of the parties had priority, under their respective chattel mortgages, to the proceeds of the sale of certain restaurant equipment. The facts were stipulated and the property was sold and proceeds impounded by agreement. The district court granted summary judgment for Brodie and the United States appeals.

In 1959, Brodie sold the restaurant equipment to Standard Management Company, Inc., for use in a restaurant at Anchorage, Alaska. Standard Management went bankrupt. Brodie repossessed the equipment but left it in the restaurant. With the consent of Brodie, James Lyon took possession of the restaurant and began operating it on June 1, 1964. Throughout the summer of 1964, Brodie and Lyon negotiated over the price and terms under which Lyon was to purchase the equipment.

On November 2, 1964, Lyon borrowed seventeen thousand dollars from the National Bank of Alaska and, as security for the loan, which was evidence by a promissory note, executed a chattel mortgage covering the restaurant equipment. This equipment consisted of 159 separate types of items, including a refrigerator, a dishwasher, an ice cream cabinet, spoons, forks, cups, ladles, pots, pans, and assorted glassware and chinaware. The bank assigned its mortgage to the Small Business Administration (SBA), represented in this action by the United States. On November 4, 1964, the bank filed a financing statement, showing the SBA as assignee.

On November 12, Brodie delivered to Lyon a bill of sale covering the equipment. On the same day Lyon executed a chattel mortgage on the equipment, naming Brodie as mortgagee. This mortgage was given to secure the unpaid purchase price of the equipment. Brodie filed a financing statement on November 23, 1964.

Alaska has adopted the Uniform Commercial Code (Code). Under section 9-312(5)(a) [the precuser to present §9-322(a)(1)] of the Code, the general rule of priority, if both interests are perfected by filing, is that the secured party who first files a financing statement (in this case SBA as assignee of the bank) prevails, regardless of when his security interest attached. However, there is a special exception for purchase-money security interests in collateral other than inventory. Brodie had such an interest. Under this exception, the purchase-money security interest prevails over conflicting interests in non-inventory collateral if "the purchase money security interest is perfected (*i.e.*, here it was perfected by filing a financing statement) at the time the debtor receives possession of the collateral or within 10 days after the debtor receives possession." [Citing the precursor to present §9-324(a). Note that the grace period given for filing on a PMSI, now 20 days, had been 10 days under the prerevision version of Article 9.]

On the basis of these stipulated facts, Brodie moved for summary judgment. Brodie contended that although Lyon received possession of the restaurant equipment on June 1, 1964, over five months before Brodie's financing statement was filed, Lyon did not become a "debtor," and the equipment did not become "collateral" until November 12,

1964, when Lyon received the bill of sale and executed Brodie's chattel mortgage. Accordingly, Brodie contended, it was not until November 12, that "the debtor (Lyon) receive(d) possession of the collateral" within the meaning of the statute referred to above. As already indicated, Brodie's financing statement was filed within ten days of that date. The district court agreed with this analysis in granting summary judgment for Brodie.

If, in [the applicable statutory section], the term "debtor" is given the meaning ascribed to it in [the then-applicable definition in Article 9], Brodie was entitled to priority. It was not until November 12, 1964, that Lyon purchased the equipment and became obligated to pay the purchase price. Until that obligation came into being, Lyon was not Brodie's debtor with power to mortgage the restaurant equipment as collateral for the unpaid purchase price.

But the United States argues that in the context of this case the priority statute, is ambiguous as to whether "debtor" is used in the sense defined in [Article 9], or whether it is used merely to identify an individual in possession, who ultimately becomes indebted to the purchase-money mortgagee. In contending that this "ambiguity" should be resolved in favor of the latter construction, the United States refers to the history and underlying purposes and policies of the Code, the assertedly different language of the prior Uniform Conditional Sales Act, and the fact that, under [Article 9] a financing statement may be filed before a security agreement is made or a security interest otherwise attaches, notwithstanding the fact that this section refers to "debtor," "secured party," and "security interest."

We are not persuaded that either recourse to the history or consideration of the underlying purposes of the Code supports the Government's position. In our view, the term "debtor" as it is used in this particular priority statute, means "the person who owes payment or other performance of the obligation secured" [The prerevision Article 9 definition]. Although Lyon might have been liable for the reasonable rental of the equipment or for its return to Brodie, he did not owe performance of an "obligation secured" by the collateral in question until November 12, 1964, and therefore was not a "debtor" for purposes of [Article 9]. Brodie's filing was therefore within the ten-day period and Brodie has priority over the conflicting security interest held by SBA.

The Government has urged us to look at the policy and the purposes of the Code to resolve what it considers to be the ambiguous meaning of "debtor." The Code has granted a specially favored position to the holder of a purchase-money security interest in non-inventory collateral. The holder of such an interest need not follow the notice procedures which are prescribed for the holders of purchase-money interests in inventory. Such a holder is also given a special priority position. His interest, perfected second, but within the ten-day grace period, will prevail over any previously perfected security interest. This priority exists even though the framers of the Code knew that the holder of the conflicting security interest would be relying on the possession of the collateral and upon the absence of a prior filing. Similarly, the holder of a purchase-money security interest in non-inventory collateral will have priority over a previously perfected security interest which includes the collateral by virtue of an after-acquired property clause. Such a holder therefore is not required to search the files to determine the existence of such a conflicting interest in order to be sure of his priority.

The protection which the Code confers upon a purchase-money interest in non-inventory collateral is not unduly extended by a decision giving priority to Brodie's interest. Although it is true that Brodie could have filed a financing statement as soon as Lyon went into possession and thus protected itself, it is also true that the bank, SBA's assignor, could have protected itself by inquiring into Lyon's interest in the equipment before accepting his chattel mortgage. Due to the favored status given by the Code to the holder of a purchase-money interest in non-inventory collateral, we are not convinced that the trial court erred in refusing to impose this burden on Brodie.

Affirmed.

QUESTIONS ON BRODIE

As you can see, the *Brodie* case is an early one, decided when Article 9 was young. (The court is still referring to a "chattel mortgage," when what it means, of course, is an Article 9 security interest.) What exactly was the issue the court had to decide? What was its determination? Over the ensuing years the result in *Brodie* has been often questioned and not always followed by other courts. From what you can tell, what is the position of the drafters of the 2001 Revision of Article 9 on the issue in *Brodie?*

PROBLEMS

19.2 Return now to the basic facts of Problem 19.1. Suppose that when Chip comes to deliver and install the computer system on March 11, he quickly discovers that one of the key components is malfunctioning, the "wireless hyperdigit interactive exchange port," without which the "integrated system" he had designed for Lydia can't get up and running. With Lydia's permission, he neatly repackages all of the components and places them in a storage closet in her office. He promises to get a working replacement for the crucial component as soon as possible. On March 15, he does return with the new part and is able to fully install the system. Chip files his initial financing statement covering the equipment on April 2. As before, Lydia files a petition in bankruptcy on March 18.

(a) What argument can the trustee in bankruptcy make in an attempt to avoid Chip's security interest?
(b) What argument can Chip make in response?
(c) Which argument do you think should win?

19.3 Louie Glitz operates a small jewelry boutique, Louie's of Litchfield, as a sole proprietor. In 2006 he is able to obtain a substantial business line of credit from First Bank of Connecticut, granting the bank a security interest in "all inventory, now held or after-acquired" of his business. The bank files an initial financing statement, correct in all respects and in the right filing office, in connection with its loan to Louie, indicating the collateral to be "all inventory, now held or after-acquired." In 2007, Opal, the representative of Opaline, Inc., a new line of one-of-a-kind high-end pieces of jewelry, pays a visit to Louie's place of business. She tries to convince him that he should purchase a representative collection of jewelry from her business. "Display them properly," she tells Louie, "and they're sure to sell like hot-cakes. We're working on placing them in only the better jewelry stores around the country, and will soon go national with a truly impressive ad campaign." Louie says that it has been his policy, which has worked fairly well so far, to stock only jewelry from a limited number of established, well-known makers. Opal says that her company is particularly interested in placing its line of wares in just such stores as his and in order to convince him to buy from the line the firm is willing to deliver them to Louie's store on credit, and is so eager to have him as a customer that it will not ask for any interest on the credit extended for the first 90 days after items have been delivered to his store. Opaline will, however, want to be granted a security interest in any of its jewelry which is delivered to Louie to secure his eventual payment for the goods. Louie finds these terms too good to pass up, and agrees to the idea. Will it be possible for Opaline to deliver its products to Louie while retaining a security interest in them which will have priority over any interest that will be asserted by First Bank of Connecticut? If so, what must it do to accomplish this result?

REVISITING SOME EARLIER CASES

Look back at the two cases that concluded Chapter 7, *North Platte State Bank* and *General Electric Capital*. You should now be able to more easily appreciate why in each case one party was arguing—unsuccessfully in the former case, successfully in the latter—that the security interest it held could properly be characterized as a *purchase-money* security interest.

What reason might there be for the additional and what would appear to be more stringent requirements for a PMSI taken in inventory to gain special priority than what was true when the collateral was other than inventory? It may be hard for you to fully appreciate at this point, but it will help for you to know — as you will see in material to follow — that those who lend on inventory in general, that is, where the collateral is something like "all inventory now held or hereafter acquired," will usually take special precautions to monitor what goods exactly are in the inventory which makes up their collateral and how the value of the inventory should be appraised. This monitoring may even be done on a piece-by-piece basis. So, for example, in a situation such as in Problem 19.3, the First Bank of Connecticut may regularly check the inventory in Louie's store to see how its collateral is holding up, what jewelry is there and available for sale and how valuable each, at least of the major pieces, appears to be. Comment 4 to § 9-324 should help you think through this question.

PROBLEM

19.4   After graduating from college where he jointly majored in philosophy and cultural studies, Andre Auteur naturally enough decides to become an independent film maker. He visits the sales room of Emoticon Enterprises, a dealer in cameras, lighting, and the like — all the equipment needed for film production — where he makes a list of what he will need, at a minimum, to start working on his first film. The package will cost him $45,000. He is told that Emoticon will sell the equipment to him partially on credit, but that he will have to come up with at least one-third of the price in cash. Andre goes to his father, Otto Auteur, who is a lawyer with a successful practice in criminal law. Happy that his son has settled on something to do with his life, Otto agrees to lend Andre the $15,000 he will need, but insists that, "we make it a real legal loan." He writes a check for $15,000 payable jointly to the order of Andre and Emoticon Enterprises. He has his son sign a promise to repay the money within two years and also a security agreement, which he quickly writes up, under which Andre grants to Otto a security interest in all the equipment Andre is to acquire from Emoticon. After Andre leaves with the check, Otto quickly files a financing statement relating to the security interest he has been granted. Andre takes the check directly to Emoticon and hands it over to that firm. They then ask him to sign a note for $30,000 payable to them in monthly installments over the next 36 months and also a security agreement in which he grants Emoticon a security agreement in all that he is purchasing from Emoticon to secure his obligation to make his payments to that firm. Emoticon quickly files on this interest. When his first film, which he dashes off in only a few months, is not the financial success which he, naturally enough, assumed it would be, Andre finds he can no longer keep up with his monthly payments to Emoticon. That firm threatens to repossess all the collateral, which they estimate now has a value as used equipment of approximately $25,000. When he hears what is to happen, Otto says, "Well, at least I'll get my money back." Will he? In other words, does either Emoticon or Otto have priority over the other in the equipment that was sold to Andre less that a year ago?

CHAPTER

20

Priority in Investment Property
and Deposit Accounts

A. INTRODUCTION

As we saw in Chapter 16, the various kinds of investment property and deposit accounts are different from most other types of collateral in one significant way—they are collateral on which it is possible to perfect by taking "control" over the collateral. (Perfection by control is also possible under §9-314(a) when the collateral is letter-of-credit rights, electronic chattel paper, or electronic documents, but we are not dealing directly with these types of collateral, which we would expect to confront only in a fairly specialized practice.)

The rules for priority in investment property and deposit accounts are distinct in that they have to take into consideration the possibility of perfection by control. As you will see, perfection by this method turns out to be a particularly powerful means of perfection. Once the possibility of perfection by control came into the picture—as it initially did with the introduction of perfection by control over investment property in 1994—a new element was added to the priority puzzle. To be more specific, the rules then focus not so much as has been true up to this point on the *timing* of certain events, but rather on consideration of what *method* of perfection any given secured party has used to perfect its interest.

In dealing with priority of interests in deposit accounts, we will not try to go into the more advanced rules. These come into play, and only make sense, when the deposit account is one into which what we will later term "proceeds" acquired on the disposition of the collateral by the debtor are deposited—and will naturally have to wait until we deal with proceeds at a later point.

B. PREPARATION

In preparation for discussion of the problems in this chapter, read carefully the following parts of the Code:

- Review §9-312(a) and (b)(1)
- Section 9-328 (1), (3), and (5), dealing with investment property, along with Comment 2 and the first paragraph to Comment 3 to this section
- Section 9-327(1), dealing with deposit accounts, and Comment 2 to this section

C. PROBLEMS AND CASES

PROBLEMS

20.1 Stella Startup owns 100 shares of Hyperwidgets, Incorporated, a newly formed corporation. These shares are evidenced by a certificate, Certificate #1, issued by the corporation to her, a certificate which she keeps in her safe deposit box. She also has a number of shares in a mutual fund, the Franklin Pierce Fund, which shares are not evidenced by any share certificate. In addition she has a securities account (#007-2145) with the brokerage firm of Hale and Hardy, which contains various amounts of shares in a number of publicly held companies, as is evidenced by her monthly statements from the brokerage. In 2008, Stella borrow some money from The Venture Loans Group. She grants that firm a security interest in, among other things, her investments in Hyperwidgets, The Franklin Pierce Fund, and "those investments held through a securities account with Hale and Hardy." Venture Loans files an initial financing statement indicating all the collateral properly with the correct filing office, but takes no other action with respect to this collateral. In 2010, Stella declares bankruptcy. Will Venture Loans' security interest in the different types of investment property owned by Stella be subject to avoidance by the bankruptcy trustee?

20.2 Suppose that the situation starts out as in the previous problem. Stella grants a security interest in her various forms of investment property to The Venture Group in 2008, and Venture perfects by filing. In 2009, Stella borrows additional funds from Adventurous Financial. She grants that firm a security interest in her shares in Hyperwidgets, Incorporated, and delivers to that firm the Certificate #1, which she had been holding in her safe deposit box. She does not indorse the certificate in any way. Adventurous Financial makes no filing with respect to the security interest it has been granted. As of the end of 2009, which firm's interest — that of Venture Group or Adventurous Financial — has priority in the 100 shares of Hyperwidget, Incorporated?

20.3   Now suppose that in 2008, Stella also borrows from Midtown Savings Bank, granting that firm a security interest in her shares in The Franklin Pierce Fund. Midtown Savings does what is necessary to obtain control over these shares. As of the end of 2008, which lender's interest — that of Venture Group or Midtown Savings — has priority over this part of Stella's investment portfolio?

20.4   Stella's need for cash just doesn't let up. In 2009 she borrows from Downtown Federal Bank a significant amount, granting that bank an interest in "her investment account #007-2145 maintained with the brokerage firm of Hale and Hardy and all financial assets contained therein." Downtown Federal does what is necessary to obtain control over Stella's securities account.

(a) As of the end of 2009, which lender's interest — that of Venture Group or Downtown Federal — has priority over this part of Stella's investment portfolio?

(b) As it turns out, Stella's account agreement with Hale and Hardy allows her to buy investments to be made part of the account on margin. That is, Hale and Hardy agrees to lend to her a portion of the purchase price of investments that she wants to add her securities account. As part of this margin-loan arrangement, Stella agrees that Hale and Hardy will have a security interest in all of the assets credited to her account to secure her payment of any amount which she may end up owing to the brokerage firm at any time. Given this additional information, how would you rank the priorities of interests claimed by the three lenders — Venture Group, Downtown Federal, and Hale and Hardy — in Stella's securities account?

20.5   As you may recall from Chapter 16, when Stella Startup first organized Hyperwidgets, Incorporated, the only other person to gain shares in the new corporation was Stella's brother Stewart, who received 20 shares. Stewart was given a stock Certificate #2, duly issued by the corporation, evidencing that these 20 shares were held in his name. The corporation is doing well, and it is apparent that these 20 shares are of substantial value. Stewart enters into an agreement to borrow $170,000 from The Venture Loans Group, his intention being to start up his own business making organic animal foods and treats. As part of this loan agreement, Stewart grants the lender a security interest in his 20 shares of Hyperwidgets. He also grants the lender a security interest in a personal savings account he has with Buchanan Bank and Trust, a local bank. At the time he grants this interest, this account has approximately $80,000 in it.

(a) What would you counsel Venture Loans to do in order to perfect its interest in Stewart's shares of Hyperwidgets, Incorporated?

(b) What would you counsel it do to perfect its interest in Stewart's savings account?

CHAPTER

21

Fixtures

A. INTRODUCTION

1. As Goods Become "Fixtures"

At the very outset of your study of Secured Transactions you were introduced to the fundamental principle, as set out in §9-109(1)(a), that Article 9 of the Uniform Commercial Code applies to any transaction, "regardless of form, that creates a security interest in personal property *or fixtures* by contract." You may have been curious at the time about what exactly was meant by the word "fixtures" and why a distinct reference to them was required in the most elemental scope provision of Article 9. And if fixtures are not personal property, which they must not be if the foregoing quotation is to make any sense, what precisely are they? You will have also noticed in several sections of that article which we have already subjected to scrutiny interesting references to "goods that are or are to become fixtures." Up until this point, these materials, and most likely your professor, have asked that you hold your curiosity at bay until the moment is right. It is now time to consider fixtures. What makes some stuff, which we might initially be correct in characterizing as goods under the Article 9 definition of that term, metamorphose into that which we must treat as fixtures? And what does all this have to do with security interests governed by Article 9, the subject of this course as you are no doubt aware?

We begin by looking at §9-102(a)(41): Fixtures, we are told, "mean goods that have become so related to particular real property that an interest in them arises under real property law." Article 9 in effect declines to give us a more precise definition or test for what is or is not a fixture. It leaves that determination to the real property law of the relevant jurisdiction — that state in which is located the "particular real property" to which some goods may or may not have been "so related" as to become fixtures. Fixtures are basically a property, a real property, concept. The question of what is or is not a fixture with respect to some given parcel of real property is one that comes up in the law of real property in a great variety of situations, not just the problems with which we will be concerned in this chapter, looking at it from the Article 9 secured transactions point of view. The courts of the several states have had to wrestle with the question of what exactly makes for a "fixture," as a matter of real property law, for a long time and they continue to do so to this day. It will not surprise you to learn that, while different tests have been devised by the courts to address this issue, there is no consensus on exactly what the test is or should be, nor are the cases necessarily uniform in how the question is eventually resolved.

2. Goods Brought onto Land

It is not our purpose here to delve into the deeper mysteries or complexities of the law of fixtures, much less into the frustration that any such study might very likely lead to. It is necessary, however, for you to get at least a first-level understanding of what kind of stuff is or may likely be a fixture. Note first of all the fairly obvious proposition that any goods, having as they do a physical tangible presence, must be situated *somewhere.* That is, they must be located on some specific and identifiable piece of real property. What then is the relationship between those goods and the real property on which they reside? We are given some help, I believe, by a passage in Comment 3 to § 9-334:

> [T]his section recognizes three categories of goods: (1) those that retain their chattel character entirely and are not part of any real property; (2) ordinary building materials that have become an integral part of the real property and cannot retain their chattel character for purposes of finance; and (3) an intermediate class that has become real property for certain purposes, but as to which chattel financing may be preserved.

Notice that the authors of the comment early on let us in on the fact that they are using the older term "chattel" instead of the statutory term "goods." This should not be a problem for us, but it does highlight that the tugging in two directions that is exerted on even the simplest fixture — on one hand by the notion of and law relating to personal property, and on the other by the world of real property and real estate transactions — is nothing new. The concept of fixtures as living partly in one world and partly in the other has been around and spawning "interesting issues" for a long time.

Let us apply the language of the comment quoted above by taking a quick tour through, let us say, a single-family residence set on a quiet street in your typical all-American neighborhood. Inside we find a lot of furniture, artworks hanging on the walls, knick-knacks on the shelves, and so on. It should be clear that all of these things are goods of the first category set out in the commentators' scheme of things. Even if they were purchased by the proud homeowners with this specific space in mind, they remain separate from the real property. They were and will always remain "chattel" in nature. They have been brought onto the land and into the house. There they now reside. They may, however, be removed from the house with only the effort of taking them in hand (or several hands if they are heftier pieces, granted) and taking them off the property.

Suppose that we were to learn that the homeowners had recently gone to a design store where they purchased a quantity of wallpaper. They then brought that wallpaper back to the house and, after it sat around in their storage closet for a number of months, they had eventually gotten around to their do-it-yourself project of applying it to the walls. It looks very nice. Rolls of wallpaper are, we know, when held by a wallpaper manufacturer or a home-improvement center, just one example of goods. These particular rolls held on to their chattel quality even as they sat in that storage closet waiting for the homeowners to go forward with their plans. If nothing else, the homeowners could have had second thoughts about wallpapering the rooms and returned these rolls, sold them to someone else as a sale of goods, or just discarded them in the trash. Once the wallpaper was applied to their home's walls with wallpaper paste, however, they became *part of* the home itself. They represent, as I think you have already guessed, the second category of goods set out in the comment. Wallpaper would be considered just one example of "ordinary building materials that [once hung out to dry on the walls] have become an integral part of the real property and cannot retain their chattel character for purposes of finance." Or for any other purposes for that matter.

Finally let us take note of the large and ornate marble water fountain which dominates the home's backyard. It may have originally been created as a one-of-a-kind piece by an experienced sculptor, or it may have been fabricated in a factory that makes garden "accessories" of just this kind. It may have previously graced another location, been uprooted from that spot and thence transported to its present location or it may have given shipped directly from the factory where it was made to this address. Whatever may be the case, we can see that it is *at present* firmly attached to a concrete base that has been prepared in the backyard of this particular house. It has also been connected to the home's water supply by some underground piping, joints, and spigots. I think it fair to conclude, by whatever test that may be applied as we will consider later, that this fountain is now a fixture making it in effect "part of" the real property. It arrived at the location as simply goods. It has, however, at some point "become so related to [this] particular real property" that any interest in the real property is an interest with the fountain part of the entire real estate package. At the same time, note, that should the homeowners tire of it, they would presumably be able to sever it from their land with little damage overall and convey it, then as goods, to another in what would be a strictly personal property transaction — a sale of goods. Whatever else is true of the fountain, as long as it remains affixed to this particular property it is of the "intermediate class of goods" referred to in the above-quoted comment.

3. The Test(s) for What Constitutes a Fixture

There is no sense in pretending that there is any single, well-established test for when goods brought onto land are so affixed as to make it into the class of fixtures. Remember, this will be a question of the real property law of the jurisdiction, and the courts of the various jurisdictions have proposed or adopted different tests, at different times, and in different circumstances. Many opinions start from the premise that the question is to be addressed by considering three factors, which I will here try to summarize:

(1) How securely the goods have been affixed to the real property. That is, if they could be removed by the mere loosening of a few bolts with a hand tool, they are more likely not to be characterized as fixtures. If it would take considerable labor to remove them, and if the result would be a large gapping hole in the real property, even if their removal would not necessarily jeopardize the structural integrity of the real property, the more likely we are dealing with fixtures.

(2) How closely the distinct uses to which the goods are to be put parallels the uses to which the real estate is to be put. The installation of an electrical generator in a building meant to house such generators, switches, and so forth, is more likely to be a fixture than is a set of shelves attached to the walls for the purpose of holding all the manuals that came with the machinery.

(3) The intention of the party bring the goods upon the land and affixing them to it. Does it appear that this party "intended to make a permanent accession to the freehold," as our friends in real property law might say? If so, the more likely it was at the time of its initial introduction to the property, and will henceforth remain, a fixture.

A number of courts state that this last factor, the intention of the person first affixing the goods to the land, is the most important. But this is definitely not an opinion universally held. Many courts appear to be taking each factor into account and appear to be carefully weighing each in the balance. Then again, some opinions simply make reference to these three factors and then focus on the one which, under the particular circumstances of the case, seems to be the most relevant or most helpful in reaching a decision.

A number of authorities in the field have concluded that when all is said and done perhaps the most that can be said about how to know a fixture when we see one is that an ordinary reasonable observer taking a tour of the property looking at the thing situated where it is and affixed as it is would consider the thing "belonging to" or "a part of" the real property. That is, a reasonable person considering acquisition of the property would in effect assume that should she or he buy the real estate the fixtures would by their very nature "come with" the real estate unless a specific agreement to the contrary was made in favor of the seller. And any potential lender who anticipates taking a real property mortgage covering the real estate to secure the loan would, in making its independent appraisal of the land's worth, take into account the extent to which the fixtures add (or subtract) from its value.

Just to add one additional layer of difficulty to the matter, you should be aware that some jurisdictions have adopted unique rules governing distinct type of fixtures, particularly where commercial rental property is involved. For instance, some courts will term "trade fixtures" all personal property necessary to a commercial tenant's business, even if the property is not attached to the leased premises in any manner. For Article 9 purposes, it would seem, such trade fixtures are not fixtures at all but properly classed as goods, and more specifically equipment, of the lessee. Another wrinkle is the so-called "integrated" or "assembled industrial plant" doctrine, according to which all personal property associated with a going business, whether or not affixed to the building in which the business is being carried out are to be considered fixtures with respect to that real property. This doctrine has in the past been generally identified only with Pennsylvania, but a recent Connecticut decision suggests, while not formally adopting the doctrine for that state, that it represented a "modern trend" in the case law elsewhere as well. See *ATC Partnership v. Town of Windham*, 268 Conn. 463, 845 A.2d 389 (2004).

No one has ever said that it will necessarily be easy to sort out what is and what is not a fixture, and I am certainly not about to make that assertion here. The first two cases of this chapter, *Pella Plastics* and *In the Matter of Bennett*, will give you at least some further sense of how individual courts work out the issue. Beyond that we will leave the problem to further investigation in your advanced studies of real estate transactions. Do note, however, as you read through the material set out in the Preparation section below, that the commentators to Article 9 at a couple of points remind the faithful reader that when in doubt a secured party need not risk all on making the correct characterization — fixture or not? — of its collateral. When in doubt, the secured party is advised in effect, to treat it as both. A little extra filing, as we have seen in several previous situations, can prevent future problems and present headaches.

4. Taking Interest in Fixtures

As the comment we have been looking at concludes, it is in the nature of fixtures that they have become just another part of some identifiable piece of real property "for certain purposes," it is also true that "chattel financing may be preserved" in them. In other words, an Article 9 security interest may be taken in goods which are fixtures. Such an interest may also be taken in goods which are to become fixtures, in which case the personal property security interest may continue even when the goods are so affixed to real property as to become fixtures and under the law of real property a part of the real property itself.

What makes things particularly interesting when the collateral consists of fixtures is that those parties who have an interest in the real property, an interest created and governed by the real property law of the jurisdiction in which the real property is located, may *also* claim an interest in the fixtures under the law of real property. The two simplest examples, and the only ones with which we will concern ourselves, are a purchaser of the real property and a lender which takes a mortgage in the property. A deed which memorializes and when recorded properly results in the transfer of some real property from one owner to another will typically include some language to the effect that the transferee is being granted ownership in the property "including all improvements, appurtenances, structures, and fixtures now part thereof." A typical real estate mortgage will include similar language, but extended even further to include such things "now present or hereafter affixed to said property or any replacements thereof." There seems to be no question that such language—and even that much less verbose but which all those familiar with how real estate transactions are fashioned would know attempts to accomplish the same thing—is effective in favor of the transferee or the mortgagee.

We are thus faced with a situation in which issues of priority reach a new level of complexity. A secured parties under Article 9 may have a valid interest in a particular fixture, but that secured party's interest may come into conflict not only with liens on the fixture or other Article 9 interests in it, but also with those who claim an interest through the real property system in the real property to which the fixture is affixed.

5. Perfecting on and Priority in Fixtures

As that Comment to §9-334 quoted earlier states, what makes fixtures— that third "intermediate" class of goods to which it refers—particularly noteworthy from our perspective is that while the goods have become part of the reality "for certain purposes," it is still possible to preserve "chattel financing" in them. If, as this translates into our present usage, an Article 9 security interest may be taken in goods which are fixtures or which are to become fixtures, it is natural enough to ask how perfection of such interests is to be carried out and maintained. As it turns out, an Article 9 secured party may perfect on fixtures in either of two ways. It may perfect just as it would on any other goods, filing a regular initial financing statement in the location of the debtor indicating the collateral to be whatever it is. As it turns out, perfection by this means will be adequate if all the secured party is concerned with is the possibility of a later priority contest with another Article 9 secured party or a lien creditor, including of course that uniquely important party and formidable opponent, the bank-ruptcy trustee should he or she later come into the picture.

Perfection on a fixture by the regularly method does not, as you will see in the problems of this chapter, give the Article 9 secured party the protection he or she may want, however, against others who can legitimately claim an interest in the same stuff through his or her interest, either as owner of or as one holding a mortgage on, the real estate to which the fixture in question is affixed and of which it has become a part. For that added protection of its interest the secured party will have had to file a valid *fixture filing* covering the collateral. The problems will help you appreciate what it takes for a filing to be a proper fixture filing—both what information the filing must contain and where it must be filed to be effective. With the concept of a fixture filing firmly in place, the later problems of this chapter will lead you through at least some of the more fundamental priority conflicts which arise under the circumstances, and how § 9-334 attempts to sort them out.

B.   PREPARATION

Begin by reading once again the definition of "fixtures" in § 9-102(a)(41). On the "fixture filing" and what it must contain look to:

- The definition of that term in § 9-102(a)(40)
- Section 9-502(a) and (b), as well as Comments 5 and 6 to that section
- Take another look at the standard form found in § 9-521(a)

On the question of where to file a fixture filing, see:

- Section 9-301(3)(A) and Comment 5b to that section
- Section 9-501(a)(1)(B) and Comment 4

On priority in fixtures, read:

- Section 9-334 through subsection (e) and Comments 2 through 9 to that section
- Note the definitions of "encumbrancer" and "mortgage" in § 9-102(a)(32) and (55)

C.   PROBLEMS AND CASES

PELLA PLASTICS, INC. v. ENGINEERED PLASTIC COMPONENTS, INC.

Court of Appeals of Iowa, 2005
2005 Iowa App. LEXIS 301

MAHAN, P.J.: Engineered Plastic Components, Inc. (EPC) appeals from a district court judgment in favor of Pella Plastics, Inc. in the amount of $144,489. We affirm.

On November 6, 2002, Pella Plastics entered into a contract that provided for the sale of its plastic manufacturing equipment to EPC. The parties' written agreement set forth in detail the assets EPC was to acquire. Specifically, the agreement included the following assets:

> Machinery and Equipment: Other Tangible Assets. All of Pella Plastics' (sic) fixtures, machinery, equipment, support equipment, tools, supplies, parts, furniture, stores, computer hardware and software (to the extent assignable by Pella Plastics), and other similar miscellaneous tangible assets, including, but not limited to, injection molding and auxiliary equipment as listed on Schedule B ("Equipment").

The purchase agreement expressly excluded all of Pella Plastics's "other assets and properties which are known as its real estate. . . ." The term "real estate" was defined in the agreement as "an identified parcel or tract of land, including improvements, if any."

Pursuant to the purchase agreement, EPC was allotted nine months from the date of closing to remove the acquired assets from the Pella manufacturing facility. Accordingly, on January 15, 2003, the parties executed a rent-free lease of the premises for the nine-month period. In September of 2003 EPC requested an extension of the lease. This request prompted Pella Plastics to conduct an inspection of the premises. During the inspection, Pella Plastics discovered EPC was removing electrical components from the property, including breakers, switch gear, and transformers. Pella Plastics believed these items were not included in the sale of its assets to EPC because the items were properly characterized as real property. Following the completion of the inspection, Pella Plastics provided EPC with written notice demanding replacement of the removed items within ten days. EPC failed to comply with the conditions set forth in the written notice.

Consequently, on October 2, 2003, Pella Plastics filed an action asserting breach of contract and conversion claims against EPC. Pella Plastics maintained they retained title to the electrical components because real property was specifically excluded from the agreement with EPC. EPC asserted the removed fixtures were expressly included in the parties' purchase agreement. On February 9, 2004, the district court entered judgment in favor of Pella Plastics on the breach of contract/conversion claims. The district court concluded the removed items were not included in the assets sold to EPC because they were fixtures and had become part of the real estate. The court awarded Pella Plastics $144,489 in damages. EPC filed a motion to enlarge or amend findings and conclusions asserting the assets for which Pella Plastics received judgment were included in the asset purchase agreement because the items were either fixtures or trade fixtures. The district court denied the relief requested in EPC's motion on March 2, 2004. EPC appeals.

The district court determined the electrical components were wrongfully removed by EPC. The court found the removed items were fixtures and excluded from the terms of the contract as real property. On appeal, EPC asserts the district court erred because the components were expressly included in the contract.

We must first address whether there was substantial evidence to support the district court's conclusion that the electrical components constituted fixtures. "A fixture is, by definition, real property because it is incorporated in or attached to the realty." 35A Am. Jur. 2d *Fixtures* §3, at 840 (2001). Personal property becomes a fixture when

> (1) it is actually annexed to the realty, or to something appurtenant thereto;
> (2) it is put to the same use as the realty with which it is connected;
> (3) the party making the annexation intends to make permanent accession to the freehold.

Young v. Iowa Dep't of Transp., 490 N.W.2d 554, 556 (Iowa 1992). In determining whether personal property has become a fixture, the paramount factor is the intention of the party annexing the personalty to the realty. The evidence presented at trial established the electrical components at issue were annexed to the real estate and essential to its dedicated use as a functioning manufacturing facility. Mr. Jim Lockwood, the maintenance manager at Pella Plastics, testified that various buildings were deprived of the power necessary to run essential operations due to EPC's removal of the electrical components. Additionally, Mr. Lockwood's testimony established the components were designed and placed in such a manner so as to permit flexibility and alternate usage of the facility, indicating Pella Plastics's intent to make a permanent accession. Thus, we conclude substantial evidence supported the district court's conclusion the removed electrical components were fixtures. *See, e.g., K & L Distribs., Inc. v. Kelly Elec., Inc.*, 908 P.2d 429, 432 (Alaska 1995) (finding industrial lighting and circuit breakers were fixtures because the components were essential to the building's function as a processing facility); *230 Park Ave. Assocs. v. Penn Cent. Corp.*, 178 A.D.2d 185, 577 N.Y.S.2d 46, 47 (App. Div. 1991) (determining transformers that were an integral part of a facility's electrical system were fixtures).

Next, we must determine whether the district court correctly interpreted the parties' agreement. In its ruling on EPC's motion to enlarge or amend, the district court determined the contract contained an ambiguity and therefore considered extrinsic evidence in order to ascertain the intention of the parties. After weighing the evidence, the district court concluded the parties did not intend to include the electrical components at issue in the purchase agreement. EPC asserts the district court's interpretation was in error because the express language of the contract evidenced the parties' intent to include fixtures in the sale.

In interpreting a contract, we give effect to the language of the entire contract in accordance with its commonly accepted and ordinary meaning. The object of a court in interpreting an agreement is to ascertain the meaning and intention of the parties as expressed in the language used. The parties' intent is determined by the language in the contract, unless it is ambiguous. An ambiguity exists when a genuine uncertainty exists over two or more meanings of the terms of the contract. The test for ambiguity is an objective one: "Is the language fairly susceptible to two interpretations?" If the language of a contract is found to be ambiguous, extrinsic evidence is admissible as an aid to interpretation of the contract.

Applying these principles to the case before us, we are convinced, as was the district court, that an ambiguity exists within the parties' purchase agreement. The purchase agreement expressly includes the term "fixtures." However, in a separate section, the contract specifically excludes real estate, which is defined as a parcel or tract of land, including improvements. A fixture, by virtue of its definition, is an improvement to real property that no longer retains its identity as personalty and becomes part of the realty. 35A Am. Jur. 2d *Fixtures* § 2, at 840. Thus, the contract both includes and excludes fixtures from the assets acquired by EPC. Because the contract is susceptible to two reasonable interpretations, an ambiguity exists and the district court was correct in ascertaining the parties' intent by consideration of extrinsic evidence.

Consequently, we must next consider whether the district court's conclusion that the parties did not intend to include the electrical components in the sale of assets was supported by substantial evidence. We conclude that it was. As the district court noted in its order, there are several factors that indicate the parties did not intend to include the electrical components as part of the sale. First, the components were recent additions to the facility and were designed to allow for flexibility and alternate uses of the facility. Secondly, these components were essential to the building's function. Without them, the building lacked adequate power to perform essential functions. Additionally, goods and assets were primarily the subject of the acquisition, not realty. This fact is evidenced by EPC's letter of intent, which specifically excluded real property from the basic transaction.

Our conclusion is further bolstered by the doctrine of *ejusdem generis*. This well-established rule of contract construction provides that when a contract contains both general and specific provisions on a particular issue, the specific provisions are controlling. Here, the parties' agreement generally included fixtures, machinery, equipment, support equipment, tools, supplies, parts, furniture, stores, computer hardware and software, and other similar miscellaneous tangible assets. These general terms were followed by an exhaustive list of the equipment EPC was acquiring in the sale. This comprehensive listing was over one-inch thick, but failed to list any of the electrical power distribution equipment involved in this appeal. Pursuant to the rules of contract construction, these specific terms of the contract are controlling. For these reasons, we conclude substantial evidence supported the district court's interpretation of the contract. Accordingly, we affirm the decision of the district court.

NOTE ON PELLA PLASTICS

As is probably apparent to the reader, this case has been included for more than one reason. First of all, of course, it is a typical example of how a court will consider and decide the question of what is and what is not a fixture. Beyond that, however, it serves as yet one more example of a lesson you were presumably presented with again and again in studying Contracts 101: Think of how much fuss and bother could have been avoided if the parties had given the problem a little attention at the time the written agreement was entered into, and then addressed it with some clear and unambiguous drafting.

PROBLEMS

21.1 Lucille Longhours, an associate in a large Manhattan law firm, lives in an apartment she rents only a few blocks from her office. In 2007, Lucille inherits from a distant relative a small but charming summer cottage situated in Candlewood Lakes, a quiet, artistic community tucked away in the green woods of Connecticut. When the deceased relative's estate is eventually settled, Lucille ends up with title to the property, unencumbered by any mortgage or other lien, in her name. She eventually gets to take a weekend off from her work to go up to the cottage. As soon as she enters the building she comes to the realization that three large windows facing the lake are, when all the grime is scrubbed from them, actually vivid works in colored glass. A neighbor with long roots in the community tells her that these must be works of a previous owner, Piffany, whose name Lucille immediately recognizes as a noted maker of art glass of the early twentieth century whose works are exceptionally valuable. Lucille is able to arrange a loan of $100,000 from Discreet Financial Services ("DFS"), granting that firm a security interest in the three windows as they stand in the cottage. Before handing the money over to Lucille, DFS, which has of course gotten its own appraisal of the windows and made sure that Lucille had adequately insured the entire cottage including the valuable windows, files a standard UCC1 with the Secretary of State of New York under the correct name and sufficiently indicating the collateral in which it has been granted an interest. Lucille uses the money from the loan to make a down payment on a small but serviceable condominium apartment in Manhattan. In 2010, Lucille suffers a series of financial setbacks and is forced to declare bankruptcy.

(a) The trustee in bankruptcy dealing with Lucille's case will, of course, be able to count among her assets the cottage in the woods. Will the trustee be able to avoid DFS's security interest in the three art glass windows?

(b) Suppose instead that in 2010 Lucille's fortunes are altogether different. She has in fact been made a junior partner in her firm. Realizing that she now will have virtually no chance to get to her Connecticut cottage at any time in the foreseeable future, she decides to sell it. She sells the cottage to one Larry Lazyboy, a law school classmate of hers who has just received tenure as a law school professor and figures he will have plenty of time to spend in the bucolic retreat. When Larry buys the cottage is his title encumbered by DFS's interest in the windows?

(c) Finally suppose that, while the situation is as above in part (b) — that is, Lucille's financial prospects are on the rise — that she decides that rather than sell the cottage she will take out a real estate mortgage on that property, using the cash generated to buy an even bigger condo in Manhattan fitting her station in life. She enters into a mortgage agreement with Nutmeg Bank. That banks loans her money and files a conventional real estate mortgage on her Candlewood Lakes property in the conventional way. Is Nutmeg Bank's interest in the property subject to the interest which DFS took in 2007 in the Piffany-glass windows?

21.2   Considering your assessment of DFS's position in the latter parts of the previous problem, what action do you believe it could have and should have taken in 2007 to further protect its position? What form should it have filed at the time the loan was initiated? Where should it have filed?

21.3   Springfield Natural is a company that bottles and distributes its own brand of bottled water out of a bottling plant in Springfield, Vermont. Since it first set up operation in 1990, the land on which this plant is located has been subject to a standard commercial real estate mortgage held by Alpha Bank. In 2008, Springfield is in need of some additional operating funds. It borrows from Middleborough Bank granting that bank an interest in an exceptionally large water pump which Springfield had first brought into the plant building (which had previously served as a roller-skating rink) and bolted securely to a specially prepared substructure when it first set up operations in 1990. In 2010, the company is approached by another bank, Beta Bank, which offers to refinance its real estate mortgage at a lower rate of interest. Springfield agrees to the refinancing, as a result of which the money owed to Alpha Bank is paid off and that bank executes a release of its mortgage on the land. This release is filed by Beta Bank. That bank follows this filing with a filing of its own real estate mortgage covering the land.

(a) As of the completion of this refinancing of the real estate mortgage, which lender, Middleborough or Beta, has a superior interest in the large water pump situated in, and firmly attached to, Springfield's bottling facility?

(b) Would your answer be any different if the refinancing had taken instead the form of Alpha Bank assigning its original mortgage, executed and recorded in 1990, to Beta? The instrument of assignment would, of course, be filed in the real estate records, but in 2010.

21.4   One of Springfield Natural's main competitors in the bottled water market is Ukrainian Springs, which operates out of a bottling plant in Waterville, Maine. Its plant has been subject to a conventional commercial real estate mortgage, held by Delta Bank, since 1992. The land is not subject to any other encumbrances nor are any of the fixtures to be found in the plant. In 2009, the manager of the plant is told that its principal high volume water pump, with which it draws water from the municipal water supply to put in its bottles, is on its last legs and threatens to break down at any time. A replacement is needed as soon as possible. The manager contacts Piping and Pumping of Portland ("PPP") which fortunately happens to have on hand a replacement pump that will do nicely. The pump is, however, expensive. PPP offers to finance its sale of the pump to Ukrainian Springs taking a specified payment from the borrower each month over a period of four years. The manager immediately goes to the offices of PPP, where she hands over a check to cover the down payment on the pump. She also signs an agreement under which her firm purchases the new pump, at the same time granting PPP a security interest in the pump to secured her firm's payment of the remainder of the purchase price. As soon as the down payment check clears, employees of PPP come to Ukrainian Springs's plant where they dismantle and discard the old water pump and install the new one in its place. The installation takes place on September 6, 2009. PPP files a fixture filing covering the new water pump, correct in all respects and in the proper office, two days later. As of October 2009, which lender, Delta Bank or PPP, has priority of interest in the new water pump now pumping away in the Ukrainian Springs bottling plant?

IN THE MATTER OF BENNETT

United States Bankruptcy Court for the District of Nebraska, 2002
2002 Bankr. LEXIS 1793

TIMOTHY J. MAHONEY, Chief Judge: By stipulation of the parties, this adversary proceeding was submitted to the court on affidavit evidence and oral and written argument. The dispute between Gothenburg State Bank ("the Bank") and GreenPoint Credit is limited to the validity, extent, and priority of liens held by each on the debtors' manufactured home.

The Bank claims a superior perfected security interest in the home by virtue of a real estate deed of trust which includes all fixtures attached to the real estate. GreenPoint asserts that it holds a perfected purchase money security interest in the home as a result of the notation of its lien on the home's certificate of title.

The home at issue is a 1998 Schult Lakewood manufactured home, 28' by 61', purchased new by the debtors in October 1997 from a dealer in North Platte, Nebraska. The house came with air conditioning, as well as a range, refrigerator, and dishwasher. The price of the house was $86,500; the debtors paid ten percent as a down-payment and financed the remaining

$77,850 over thirty years at eight percent interest. The Bank advanced $22,450 to the debtors to purchase and install the home. The County Clerk of Lincoln County, Nebraska, issued a certificate of title for the home on October 31, 1997, on which the lien of GreenPoint's predecessor in interest was noted.

Allowing the home to become part of any real estate without the seller's consent is an event of default under the installment sales contract; however, the debtors informed the home's seller, at the time of purchase, of their intention to permanently affix the house to their real property as their primary and permanent residence. The purchase contract identified the planned location of the house.

The home was transported in two sections to the debtors' ranch in rural Gothenburg, Nebraska. There, the two sections were bolted together and the house was placed over and attached to a poured concrete basement and foundation. It was attached to water lines, underground electrical and telephone lines, and a complete plumbing system, including septic tank. The roof, hinged for transport, was raised and fixed. Shingles, cedar siding, and interior drywall were installed. A deck was later added along two sides of the house.

The Bank's appraiser describes the home as "United Builders' Code ("UBC") approved," which the appraiser states is typically of higher quality than a mobile home. The appraiser also stated that a UBC home is more likely than a mobile home to be permanently installed, in part because a UBC home lacks a steel frame to which wheels and a tongue could be attached to tow it.

The debtors and the Bank's appraiser indicate that to be moved from its location, the house would either have to be split in half, unfastened from the foundation, and placed on a trailer, or it would have to have steel beams placed underneath it to support it as it is removed from the foundation. Moving it would decrease its value to approximately $44,000.

The Bank and its predecessor in interest have loaned money to the debtors since the mid-1990s, as represented by a number of promissory notes. Those notes are secured by liens on debtors' real estate and crops, livestock, equipment, vehicles, and other assets. The Bank's security interest in real estate is represented by two deeds of trust with future advance clauses, one recorded in March 1997 and the other recorded in August 2000. Neither deed of trust was taken as part of the home purchase transaction in October 1997, although as noted above, the Bank did advance a total of $22,450 in connection with the purchase and installation of the house pursuant to the future advances clause of the 1997 deed of trust. The Bank asserts that it considered the house a fixture on the property at the time it took the second deed of trust, and relied on the absence of other liens of record at the time it extended additional credit to the debtors.

[Following a careful review of the motor vehicle registration statutes of Nebraska, the court concludes that] a home such as this is defined as a mobile home under [those statutes]. As such, it may be issued a motor vehicle certificate of title. Security interests in a mobile home are to be noted on that title.

Under Nebraska U.C.C. law as it existed at the time this home was purchased, and until July 2001, the characterization of mobile or manufactured homes moved to a building site was unclear. Buyers, sellers, and lenders were left to wonder whether such homes were personal property or real property for the purpose of perfecting a security interest in them.

With the revisions of U.C.C. Article 9, effective July 1, 2001, the Unicameral clarified the status of security interests in manufactured homes. Under this recently enacted statute, if the holder of a purchase-money security interest in a manufactured home as defined in Neb. U.C.C. § 9-102(53) perfects the security interest by noting it on the certificate of title, that security interest has priority over a conflicting interest of an encumbrancer or owner of the real property on which the home is placed. Neb. U.C.C. § 9-334(e)(4). This statute became effective July 1, 2001, as to transactions occurring after that date.

Therefore, if Article 9 in its current form were to apply to the present case, it appears that GreenPoint's lien is properly noted on the certificate of title and would take priority as a fixture filing over competing security interests in the real estate. The Official Comment to § 9-334, at paragraph 10, states that under the new rule regarding priority of security interests in manufactured homes, "a security interest in a manufactured home that becomes a fixture has priority over a conflicting interest of an encumbrancer or owner of the real property if the security interest is perfected under a certificate of title statute. . . ."

However, this case must be decided under the "pre-revision" version of Article 9. The transactions at issue here — the purchase of the manufactured home and the perfection of a security interest therein, and the filing of the Bank's deeds of trust — occurred in 1997 and 2000. This bankruptcy case was filed April 19, 2001. All of those events occurred prior to the operative date of the Article 9 revisions. The law is clear that statutes covering substantive matters in effect at the time of the transaction govern the transaction, not later enacted statutes.

The priority of liens on the debtors' property depends on whether the home became a fixture and therefore subject to the real estate rules regarding lien perfection, or remained personal property and subject to the perfection requirements of the motor vehicles certification statute.

"Fixtures" are goods that have become so related to particular real property that an interest in them arises under real property law. Neb. U.C.C. § 9-102(41).

Three factors are considered when determining whether an item has become a fixture: (1) actual annexation to the realty, or something appurtenant thereto; (2) appropriation to the use or purpose of that part of the realty with which it is connected; (3) the intention of the party making the annexation to make the article a permanent accession to the freehold. *Metropolitan Life Ins. Co. v. Reeves*, 223 Neb. 299, 389 N.W.2d 295, 296-97 (Neb. 1986) (quoting *Bank of Valley v. United States National Bank of Omaha,* 215 Neb. 912, 341 N.W.2d 592, 594-95 (Neb. 1983)).

The third prong of the test, focusing on the party's intent, is generally given the most weight. *Reeves,* 389 N.W.2d at 297; *Bank of Valley,* 341 N.W.2d at 595.

The Bank's evidence as to the debtors' intent is convincing. They informed the seller of their intent to make the unit their permanent home. The debtors make clear that they intended, before they ever purchased this home, to make it their permanent residence on their land in rural Lincoln County. They dug a basement, poured a foundation, installed a complete plumbing system, ran underground electrical lines, and established an underground telephone line connection to the main line two miles away.

In addition, after moving the home to the site and making it fit for habitation, the debtors constructed a wooden deck on two sides of the house, poured a sidewalk, installed concrete steps, and fenced in the house yard.

The Bank's appraiser opines that the house was placed on the real estate in such a manner that it would become a permanent improvement on the property. Moreover, Mr. Roberts notes that the home is UBC-approved, and such a home "is typically of higher quality than a HUD home, and in my experience is normally installed to become a permanent addition to the real estate."

It is abundantly clear from the evidence that this house cannot simply be hitched to a truck and moved. Moving this house would necessitate detaching it from its foundation and utility lines and disassembling it. I find as a fact that the house is a permanent accession to the real estate.

GreenPoint has provided affidavit evidence from two of its employees and the manufactured-home dealer noting that at the time the house was sold to the debtors, at the time the debtors signed the retail installment contract, and at the time GreenPoint's predecessor perfected its security interest on the certificate of title, the housing unit was personal property and not in any way affixed to real property. GreenPoint asserts that it should not be penalized for relying on its perfected security interest instead of constantly monitoring the fixture status of its collateral.

GreenPoint's argument, however, flies in the face of reality. It is unreasonable to think this home could have or should have remained personal property. There is no evidence before the court that this house could have been used as a home in a manner other than the way the debtors are using it, in other words, by attaching it to the real estate.

Moreover, because of the nature of this type of home, in that it is sold in two halves and put together on-site and therefore is not "mobile" as that term is generally used, GreenPoint or its predecessor in interest should have known that the home was likely to be "affixed" to real estate, and therefore could have taken steps to make a fixture filing or obtain a subordination agreement from the Bank in order to protect its interest.

GreenPoint may have a breach of contract claim against the debtors because they attached the house to real estate without the financing company's permission, but the triggering of an event of default under the contract does not give rise to or affect GreenPoint's lien priority status.

IT IS ORDERED Gothenburg State Bank holds a perfected lien in the debtors' home, which has become a fixture permanently attached to the real estate, and such lien takes priority over that of GreenPoint Credit.

NOTE ON TRAILERS, MOBILE HOMES, AND MANUFACTURED HOMES

As the court points out in the decision in *Bennett,* prior to the most recent revision of Article 9 the characterization of trailers, mobile homes, and the like was "unclear." That is undoubtedly an understatement. The particular home at issue in *Bennett* was, given its nature and all the circumstances, not that difficult to characterize as a fixture under just about whatever test you were to use. Not all situations are as relatively easy as this one to determine. As the court also points out, the drafters of the 2001 Revision to Article 9 did what they could to help by their addition of the provision now found in § 9-334(e)(4). Now would be a good time to look at Comment 10 to § 9-334. You should be aware, however, that not every structure of this sort, initially wheeled to but then dropped on the land, will qualify as a "manufactured home" as that term is defined in § 9-102(a)(53). Nor do all states have certificate-of-title statutes covering any or all structures of this sort. We can expect cases to continue to surface in which § 9-334(e)(4), for one reason or another, does not apply and the court will have to muddle through the issues presented, using precedents decided under the law prior to 2001 if any helpful precedents do exist, as they have done in the past.

PROBLEM

21.5 We return to the situation set out in Problem 21.4. In 2011, PPP takes note of the fact that it has not received the promised monthly payment from Ukrainian Springs for the past four months.

(a) As we will see in a later chapter, a secured party may (under § 9-609), upon the default of the debtor, repossess its collateral. Does PPP have the right to get its workers into the bottling plant, disassemble the pump it has sold to Ukrainian Springs, and haul it away. Look at § 9-604(b) through (c).

(b) Suppose instead that by the time PPP decides to take action Ukrainian Springs has already declared bankruptcy. The pump provider is now barred from repossessing the pump because of the automatic stay which was triggered by the filing of the petition in bankruptcy under § 362 of the Bankruptcy Code. The bankruptcy trustee is quickly able to sell the entire bottling plant, including all "fixtures now attached thereto" to another bottler which thinks it can make a go of the business by running the plant as before only with a new sleeker designed bottle for its "New Wave Water" and a totally different marketing strategy than that which Ukrainian Springs had been operating, and floundering, under. The price which the buyer is willing to pay for the plant is higher than it could have paid for an empty commercial building of the same size in the same area. It is willing to pay a premium because the building comes fully equipped with all it will need to run a bottling operation — including the new and efficient PPP pump installed in the building in 2009 and already attached to the municipal water supply. The bankruptcy trustee announces her intention to deliver the full amount received from the sale of the plant to Delta Bank, which holds as you recall a real estate mortgage covering the building including any fixtures which were initially or later became "part of" the real estate. Can you think of an argument for PPP that it should receive some portion of the money received by the bankruptcy estate upon the sale of the bottling plant? Do you think this argument will succeed? Read the case that follows and the Note which follows that.

TUSTIAN v. SCHRIEVER

Supreme Court of Utah, 2001
2001 UT 84, 34 P.3d 755, 45 U.C.C. Rep. Serv. 2d 921

Durrant, Justice:

BACKGROUND

Pinnacle Financial Services, Inc., sold mobile and manufactured homes in Weber County, Utah, under the name Outlook Homes, Inc. In April 1996, Deere agreed to finance Pinnacle's acquisition of manufactured homes. Under the agreement, Deere received a purchase money security interest in Pinnacle's inventory and proceeds. On April 15, 1996, Deere filed a UCC-1 financing statement evidencing its security interest with the Utah Division of Corporations and Commercial Code ("Division of Corporations").

In October 1996, Deere advanced funds to Pinnacle under the security agreement so Pinnacle could purchase a manufactured home. Pinnacle moved the manufactured home to a one-acre lot it owned in Tremonton, Box Elder County, Utah (the "Tremonton property"). At approximately the same time, Pinnacle executed a trust deed for the Tremonton property in favor of Sodberry Ltd. (the "Sodberry trust") as security for a $35,000 loan.

In October 1997, Pinnacle defaulted on its security agreement with Deere in the approximate amount of $42,000. Pinnacle also defaulted on its obligations under the Sodberry trust. After recording a notice of default in November 1997, the Sodberry trustee began taking steps to sell the Tremonton property.

In January 1998, Schriever won a civil judgment against Pinnacle in the amount of $71,168. In March 1998, acting under a writ of execution Schriever had obtained the previous day, the Box Elder County Sheriff attached the Tremonton property.

On April 1, 1998, Schriever bought the Tremonton property for $70,000 at a trust deed foreclosure sale administered by the Sodberry trustee. After paying the sale expenses and Pinnacle's loan balance, the trustee deposited $25,155.56 in excess proceeds with the clerk of the First District Court of Box Elder County. The trustee also submitted a letter listing [Deere and Schriever] among those who might claim an interest in the proceeds. [There was at least one other potential claimant as well, but I have edited him out as he lost at the trial level and did not appeal.] The district court ruled that it would consider the parties' pleadings as cross-motions for summary judgment. . . .

[T]he district court ruled that Deere has first priority in the excess proceeds of the trust sale [over Schriever] and granted Deere's cross-motion for summary judgment.

ANALYSIS

In granting summary judgment in favor of Deere, the district court relied on two alternative lines of reasoning to conclude that Deere had priority in the excess proceeds of the trustee's sale. One alternative was premised on the manufactured home remaining chattel; the other was premised on the home becoming a fixture. Although Deere advanced arguments in favor of both alternatives in its appellate brief, at oral argument before this court, Deere expressly waived the alternative premised on the manufactured home remaining chattel.

Specifically, during oral argument, Deere's counsel stated the following:

> The one disputed fact is whether or not the mobile home, the modular home, was affixed to the property. But for purposes of this proceeding, we are more than willing, we're happy, to stipulate that it was affixed, sure. We will give [Schriever] that, because it doesn't matter. The reason that it doesn't matter is because resolution of this case hinges, really, completely on Utah Code Annotated 70A-3-313. This provision deals with fixtures, and who wins priority disputes regarding fixtures.

Schriever does not contest Deere's characterization of the manufactured home as a fixture; indeed, Schriever argues in favor of this characterization in her brief. Accordingly, we accept Deere's waiver of its right to claim priority based on statutes other than those governing fixtures. Thus, for purposes of this appeal, we will consider the manufactured home a fixture on the Tremonton property, and reject as waived the district court's alternative reasoning premised on the home not becoming a fixture

In reviewing the remaining alternative — that Deere has priority in the excess proceeds of the trustee's sale of the Tremonton property despite the manufactured home becoming a fixture — we address three main questions:

1. Did Deere's filing of a UCC-1 financing statement with the Division of Corporations perfect (i.e., give constructive notice of) its security interest in the manufactured home against a subsequent judgment lienor on the real estate on which the home was a fixture?
2. Given that the trustee sold not only the manufactured home, but all of the Tremonton property, to what extent did Deere obtain a security interest in the rest of the Tremonton property (e.g., land) when the manufactured home became a fixture on the property?
3. Does Article 9 of the Uniform Commercial Code permit the holder of a perfected security interest in a fixture to claim a perfected security interest in the proceeds of a sale of the fixture and underlying land?

We address each question in turn.

A. PRIORITY IN THE MANUFACTURED HOME

A fixture straddles the line between personal and real property. 35 Am. Jur. 2d *Fixtures* § 1 (1967). Originally a good or chattel, a fixture has become so related to real property that it has become part of the realty. *See* Utah Code Ann. § 70A-9-313(1)(a) (1997) (repealed 2001) (defining fixtures). Since a fixture is part of the real property, encumbrances on the real property encompass its fixtures. Moreover, absent an agreement to the contrary, a sale of real property generally includes its fixtures. Yet a fixture also retains enough of a separate identity that the law may continue to recognize some of its chattel character. For example, the U.C.C. prescribes conditions under which perfected security interests in goods that have become fixtures have priority over conflicting real estate interests. *See* Utah Code Ann. § 70A-9-313 (1997). [Note that the court, here and throughout, cites to and applied the prerevision version of Article 9.]

[Following a review of Article 9's general treatment of fixtures, the court concludes on the first issue it has set out as before it as follows.] Under the U.C.C., a real estate interest arising from a purchase materially differs from an interest arising from a judgment lien. In particular, the U.C.C. does not require that a judgment lienor receive constructive notice via a fixture filing for a fixture financer to retain priority. Instead,

> [a] perfected security interest in fixtures has priority over the conflicting interest of an encumbrancer . . . of the real estate where . . . the conflicting interest is a lien on the real estate obtained . . . after the security interest was perfected by *any method* permitted by [U.C.C.] Article [9].

Utah Code Ann. § 70A-9-313(4)(d)(emphasis added). In elaborating on the permissible methods of perfection against judgment lienors, the Official Code Comments state that a fixture security interest if perfected first should prevail (against a judgment lienor) even though not filed or recorded in real estate records, because generally a judgment creditor is not a reliance creditor who would have searched records. Thus, even a prior filing in the chattel records protects the priority of a fixture security interest against a subsequent judgment lien. U.C.C. §9-313 cmt. 4(c). Deere filed "in the chattel records" when it filed a UCC-1 with the Division of Corporations. This filing came before Schriever's judgment lien attached. Accordingly, we agree with the district court that Deere's security interest in the home had priority over Schriever's interest in the home arising from her judgment lien on the Tremonton property.

B. PRIORITY IN THE REAL ESTATE

This ruling does not inevitably lead to the conclusion that Deere has priority in the excess proceeds of the trustee's sale. Since the sale included all of the Tremonton realty (land, home, etc.), the resulting proceeds were attributable not only to the manufactured home, but to the land and anything else forming a part of the realty. Neither the district court nor Deere has explained how Deere's priority interest in the manufactured home permits Deere to claim indiscriminately first priority in the excess proceeds. The court's conclusion that Deere has priority in the proceeds, coming as it does in the absence of an agreement apportioning the proceeds between the home and the rest of the realty, implicitly assumes Deere obtained a priority interest in the realty as a whole when the home became a fixture.

Section 70A-9-313 does not, however, purport to give a person with a perfected security interest in a fixture an interest in the rest of the realty. In *FGB Realty Advisors v. Bennett,* 44 Conn. Supp. 156, 672 A.2d 545, 547-49 (Conn. Super. Ct. 1995), for example, the court held that under U.C.C. section 9-313, a perfected security interest in an in-ground swimming pool had priority over a mortgage on the real estate only as to this one fixture, not as to the realty as a whole. *See also Capitol Fed. Sav. & Loan Assoc. v. Hoger,* 19 Kan. App. 2d 1052, 880 P.2d 281, 283-84 (Kan. Ct. App. 1994) (holding that under Kansas U.C.C. section 9-313, although fixture filing gave chattel financer priority interest in furnace and air conditioner that became fixtures, financer's interest did not extend beyond fixtures to rest of realty). Thus, Deere had an interest with respect to one fixture, the manufactured home. Only the trust beneficiary and Schriever, through her judgment lien, had an interest in the realty as a whole.

C. PRIORITY IN THE PROCEEDS

We next turn to the question of whether, despite our conclusion that Deere had a security interest only in the home, Deere could nonetheless claim priority over Schriever in the excess proceeds of the entire trust property. In concluding that Deere had priority over Schriever in the proceeds, the district court relied on section 70A-9-306. However, this section does not apply to a disposition (e.g., sale) of the Tremonton property and affixed manufactured home due to their status as real property. *See* Utah Code Ann.

§ 70A-9-104(j) (excluding real estate transactions from Chapter 9, except as provided for fixtures in section 70A-9-313). In contrast to the approach of the district court, other courts have focused on section 70A-9-313 when considering whether an interest in a fixture continues in the proceeds. *See, e.g., Maplewood Bank v. Sears,* 265 N.J. Super. 25, 625 A.2d 537, 539-40 (N.J. Super. Ct. App. Div. 1994) (relying on section 70A-9-313, not section 70A-9-306, in determining whether fixture financer could claim priority interest in proceeds of sale of real estate that included fixtures).

Section 70A-9-313 provides one express remedy for cases where a fixture financer has priority over all real estate interests in the fixture: removal of the fixture. *See* Utah Code Ann. § 70A-9-313(8). The U.C.C. does not address "whether [a] secured party may do something else in lieu of removal, such as . . . make a claim against the proceeds of a real estate foreclosure sale." William D. Hawkland et al., *Uniform Commercial Code Series* § 9-313:7 (2000).

Courts appear unanimous in interpreting this omission as preventing a fixture financer from sharing in the proceeds of a sale of real estate. *See Maplewood,* 625 A.2d at 539-40 (holding that under U.C.C. section 9-313, a fixture financer with priority interest in kitchen fixtures, having foregone right of removal, could not claim priority over mortgage lender in proceeds of sale of real estate); *Hoger,* 880 P.2d at 288-89; *see also FGB Realty Advisors,* 672 A.2d at 548 (noting that, upon default, removal provides the only remedy to fixture financer despite impracticality of removing in-ground swimming pool (dicta)); *cf.* Hawkland § 9-313:7 (arguing that, given difficulties in estimating fixture's contribution to real estate sale proceeds, fixture financer with right to remove fixture should not have right to await foreclosure sale and claim proceeds, unless removal would breach peace).

Unlike the situation in cases like *Maplewood,* Deere may not have had the option of removing the home before the trustee's sale. Specifically, Deere's failure to comply with section 70A-9-313's fixture filing requirements likely rendered its interest in the home subordinate to that of the Sodberry trust beneficiary. *See* Utah Code Ann. § 70A-9-313(4), (5) (requiring fixture filing to retain priority against most types of real estate interests, unless certain conditions are met (e.g., holder of real estate interest disclaims interest in fixtures)); *cf.* 35 Am. Jur. 2d *Fixtures* § 51 (1967) (noting that mortgage covers subsequently-annexed fixtures even though the mortgage instrument did not refer to fixtures (citing cases)). If Deere's interest was inferior to that of the trust beneficiary, Deere could not have claimed a statutory right to remove the home. *See* Utah Code Ann. § 70A-9-313(8) (conditioning right of removal on fixture financer having interest superior to all other real estate interests). But we need not decide whether the existence of the trust precluded removal, for Deere's right to claim an interest in the proceeds does not turn on whether Deere could remove the home, as discussed below.

Construing section 70A-9-313, we see no evidence that the legislature intended that, when removal is unavailable, a fixture financer have an interest in the proceeds of the sale of the real estate. First, section 70A-9-313 makes no mention of any remedy other than removal. Moreover, the drafters of section 9-313 intended to provide only a limited set of exceptions to the general rule that, in a priority dispute, real estate interests trump interests in chattel that have become fixtures. *See* U.C.C. §9-313 cmt. 1 (stating that "chattel interests [are] subordinate to real estate interests except as protected by the priorities" in section 9-313). The absence of express authorization, together with the default rule favoring real estate interests, makes it unlikely the legislature intended to grant a fixture financer a priority interest in proceeds of a sale of real estate. *Cf. Olson v. Salt Lake City Sch. Dist.*, 724 P.2d 960, 966 (Utah 1986) (relying on canon of construction under which the enumeration of specific items in a statute indicates the legislature's intent to exclude other items. Second, when the legislature intended to grant an interest in proceeds in other contexts, it did so expressly. *See* Utah Code Ann. §70A-9-306 (permitting security interest to continue in proceeds); *cf. Maplewood Bank*, 625 A.2d at 540 (declining to construe U.C.C. section 9-313 as permitting fixture financer's interest to continue in proceeds because this "would be legislating" and noting that, in the one state (Louisiana) that allows this remedy, the legislature expressly authorized it by adding nonuniform language to U.C.C. §9-313(8)).

Accordingly, we conclude the district court erred in granting Deere a priority interest in the proceeds of the trust sale.

We reverse the district court's grant of summary judgment in favor of Deere. On remand, the district court should exclude Deere from those eligible to claim an interest in the proceeds. We offer no opinion as to whether Deere's security interest in the home remained effective after the trustee's sale, as this issue is not before the court.

CONCLUSION

Although Deere had priority in the manufactured home against Schriever's judgment lien, the version of the U.C.C. governing this case did not provide Deere the right to claim priority in proceeds derived from the sale of the realty to which the home was affixed. Accordingly, we reverse the order of the district court awarding Deere priority in the excess proceeds and remand for disposition of the excess proceeds in a manner consistent with this opinion.

NOTE ON TUSTIAN

This was decided, as you saw, under the prerevision version of Article 9 and followed closely a well-known, if not particularly highly regarded, case from the New Jersey Superior Court, *Maplewood Bank v. Sears*. In a footnote to the *Tustian* decision, Justice Durrant added for the Utah Supreme Court,

"We recognize that the recently revised U.C.C. may dictate a different result in future cases. *See* Utah Code Ann. § 70A-9a-604(2) (Supp. 2001); U.C.C. § 9-604 cmt. 3 (stating that the new section 9-604 "serves to overrule cases holding that a secured party's only remedy after default is the removal of the fixtures")." You may want to check on Comment 3 to the current § 9-604 at this time.

NOTE ON ACCESSIONS AND COMMINGLED GOODS

Related to the concept of fixtures is that of goods which become *accessions* to other goods. Fixtures, as we have now seen often enough, are goods that become part of a particular parcel of real estate. Accession, as that term is defined in § 9-102(a)(1), "means goods which are physically united *with other goods* in such a manner that the identity of the original goods is not lost." The emphasis is clearly my own, but you see how it distinguishes accessions from all those fixtures we have been worrying about in this chapter up to this point. You should now look over § 9-335 which sets out the rules regarding security interests in accessions. It is only fair to note that the possibility of goods becoming accessions to other goods apparently creates nowhere near the number of problems or controversies than does the notion of fixtures, at least if we are to judge by the number of reported cases (hardly any when it comes to accessions) on the two topics. For completeness's sake, however, Problem 21.6 below will give you an opportunity to work through a situation which requires use of the § 9-335 principles relating to accessions.

A third and final related notion is that of *commingled goods*. The necessary definition appears in his instance not in § 9-102, but in § 9-336(a): "In this section, 'commingled goods' means goods united with other goods in such a manner that their identity is lost in a product or mass." The question of whether a security interest in goods which are later commingled with others, and thus lose their distinct identity, can survive in the resulting commingled mass and if so to what degree—a question which appears to just about never arise in practice, perhaps because lenders are careful to avoid situations under which they would ever have to deal with the truly messy situation it engenders—is dealt with in the remainder of § 9-336 and in Problem 21.7.

———————

PROBLEMS

21.6 Carolyn Carnie owns a number of carnival rides which are small enough that she can move them from place to place by jacking them up on wheels attached to their undersides and towing them with an ordinary tow truck. During the summer she sets up her moving carnival in the parking lot of a local mall, operates "Carnie's Carnival" on that spot for one week, and then moves on to another community and another mall for the next week. For several years she has operated with the help of a loan from County State Bank, in connection with which she has granted that bank a security interest in all of her equipment. The bank, you may assume, has properly perfected its interest. One of the most popular rides at Carnie's Carnival is a carousel. One day in July of 2009, during the height of Carnie's season, the motor which keeps the carousel turning dies. Carnie quickly determines that there is no way it can be repaired. She arranges to buy a new motor from Eagle Equipment, which is able to bring the motor to the site where the carnival is at the time located and install the new motor in the carousel by the next day. Carnie agrees to pay Eagle Equipment for the new motor on a monthly basis over the next two years. One of the papers she signs in connection with her purchase of the new motor grants Eagle a security interest in the motor to secure her full payment for the item. As of January 2011, which creditor — County State Bank or Eagle Equipment — has priority of interest in the new motor now installed in, and functioning smoothly, in Carnie's carousel? What additional information do you need to answer this question?

21.7 Marvin runs a business, which he calls Specialty Foods, as its sole proprietor. Marvin likes ketchup. He also likes peanut butter. He especially likes to eat them mixed together and suspects that others will like the combination as well if they just try it. Marvin obtains $300 worth of ketchup from the Redstuff Company. Because of this and other purchases he has made from Redstuff, he owes that company $400. Marvin has granted Redstuff a security interest in the ketchup to secured the full debt, and Redstuff has correctly perfected on its interest. Marvin also buys $500 worth of peanut butter from Goobers Unlimited, granting that firm a security interest in the peanut butter to secure a total debt of $700 which he owes that company. Goobers perfects on this interest. Marvin then mixes up the ketchup and the peanut butter into a large quantity of what he calls "Tomato-Nut Swirl."

(a) Assuming first that the resulting quantity of Tomato-Nut Swirl is easily sold by Marvin to a specialty food store chain for $1,000, what interest does each of the suppliers — Redstuff and Goobers — have in this amount when it is received by Marvin as proceeds of the product he sells?

(b) Assume instead that Tomato-Nut Swirl is not the hit that Marvin had anticipated it would be. He is finally able to get rid of all of the stuff by selling it for $600 to a company which distributes foods to school cafeterias. What interest does each supplier now have in the $600 Marvin obtains for the stuff?

A LOOK AHEAD TO FARMERS COOPERATIVE ELEVATOR

In Chapter 25 you will get a chance to read the case of *Farmers Cooperative Elevator Co. v. Union State Bank.* As you will see there, a seller of livestock feed which had been fed to the debtor's hogs made the argument that the fattened hogs were what will be there discussed as "proceeds" of the feed. The Supreme Court of Iowa found that the "ingestion and biological transformation of feed" totally used up the feed leaving nothing for the seller of the feed to claim as its collateral. In a separate part of the opinion, we are told the seller tried a second ingenious argument. It claimed that the feed and the hogs had, as the hogs gobbled up the feed putting on weight in the process, become *commingled* goods in which it, the feed seller, could claim a continuing interest. How would you guess this argument went down with the court?

CHAPTER

22

Claims Arising Under Article 2

A. INTRODUCTION

Article 2 of the Uniform Commercial Code is, as you are no doubt aware, that part of the Code which governs sales of goods. As such it deserves, and typically gets, a course all its own, the course on Sales. (Or, as is sometimes now true, a pretty hefty workout in the introductory Contracts course or an upper-level survey course on Commercial Transactions.) There are, however, two specific aspects of Article 2 which bring it into direct contact, if not necessarily contention, with the topic of Secured Transactions and the workings of Article 9. We look at these two points of intersection of Articles 2 and 9 in this chapter.

First of all, we will look at the security interest which arises under Article 2 in favor of a buyer who has prepaid all of part of the purchase price of some goods which, upon delivery, are discovered to be defective and which the buyer chooses to reject (or in some cases take the slightly different Article 2 route of a "revocation of acceptance," an Article 2 distinction which need not concern us here). In such a situation, the rejecting buyer is generally "under a duty after rejection to hold [the rejected goods] with reasonable care at the seller's disposition for a time sufficient to remove them" under Section 2-602(2)(b). This is all well and good, but suppose that the seller, acknowledging the problem with the goods and the buyer's rejection, immediately comes to the buyer's location, picks up the faulty goods, and takes them away. Can you see the difficulty this may pose for the seller, who, remember, has prepaid all or part of their price? To deal with this problem, Article 2, in § 2-711(3) creates a security interest, as defined in the very first line of § 1-201(37) or § 1R-201(b)(35), in favor of the seller. This security interest is, of course, not an Article 9 security interest of the type we have been spending so much time on. It has been created not "by contact," as is required by § 9-109(a)(1), but by the operation of a statute, Article 2 of the Uniform Commercial Code. As you will see, however, in Problem 22.1, Article 9 does recognize and govern a security interest arising in this fashion.

The security interest arising under §2-711(3) has never been seen as a reason for much discussion or dispute by commentators or brought forth any significant amount of litigation. The same cannot be said of the second instance in which a right created under Article collides (and I choose my word carefully here) with the entire Article 9 structure for governing secured transactions. Under 2-702(2) a seller who delivers goods on credit to a buyer whom, it is later discovered, was insolvent at the time of its receipt of the goods may be able to claim what is referred to as a *right of reclamation* with respect to the goods. Simply put, if the seller can successful invoke such a right it should be able to get the goods back. The trouble arises because, if the buyer is truly insolvent, there may be others, most notably the trustee in bankruptcy or those who have lent to the now insolvent seller, claiming a valid security interest in the goods. To make things that much more interesting, portions of Article 2, while not as straightforward as §2-702, can be read to give a similar reclamation right to an unpaid cash seller. This last statement may strike you as strange. How can a seller who receives cash in exchange for the goods ever find itself "unpaid" at the end of the day? The answer lies in recognizing that Article 2 considers a sale where the buyer tenders a check in exchange for the goods as a cash sale, not a sale on credit. But checks have been known to bounce, have they not? The result is in effect an unpaid cash seller.

The consequences of a seller's right of reclamation arising under Article 2, and the interplay between this right and the general workings of Article 9, have given rise to a great deal of both commentary and litigation. In fact the cases never seem to end. The two remaining problems in this chapter and the case that follows will, I hope, get you up-to-date, at least as of this writing, on this most vexing situation.

B.   PREPARATION

On the security interest created under Article 2 for the buyer who has rightfully rejected or justifiably revoked its acceptance of goods on which all or partial payment of the price has already been made, see:

- Section 2-711(3) and Comment 2 to this section
- Section 9-109(a)(5)
- Section 9-110 and its Comments 2 through 4
- Section 9-309(6)

On the right of reclamation to which a seller may be entitled under Article 2, see:

- Section 2-702(2) and (3) and Comment 2 to this section on the credit seller

- Section 2-507 and its Comment 3 on the unpaid cash seller
- The UCC's definition of "insolvent" is found in § 1-201(23) or § 1R-201(b)(23)

Read also the following from the Bankruptcy Code:

§ 546. Limitations on avoiding powers.

. . . .

(c)(1) . . . subject to the prior rights of a holder of a security interest in such goods or the proceeds thereof, the rights and powers of the trustee under sections 544(a), 545, 547, and 549 are subject to the right of a seller of goods that has sold goods to the debtor, in the ordinary course of such seller's business, to reclaim such goods if the debtor has received such goods while insolvent, within 45 days before the date of the commencement of a case under this title, but such seller may not reclaim such goods unless such seller demands in writing reclamation of such goods

(A) not later than 45 days after the date of receipt of such goods by the debtor; or

(B) not later than 20 days after the date of commencement of the case, if the 45-day period expires after the commencement of the case.

C. PROBLEMS AND CASES

PROBLEMS

22.1 The Fresno Furniture Company orders a large quantity of high-quality upholstery fabric from the firm of Top-Notch Textiles, which is located in Stockton, California. Because the fabric is to be specifically produced to meet the specifications of Fresno's order, the contract between the parties calls for Fresno to pay half of the full purchase price of $380,000 up front, that is, upon the signing of the contract in January. Fresno makes this payment, and Top-Notch gets to work making the fabric. On Monday, March 15, a truck operated by Top-Notch arrives at Fresno's plant and a large number of rolls of fabric, the exact number called for in the agreement, are unloaded from the truck into Fresno's supply warehouse. The next day when some workers at the furniture manufacturer's plant begin to examine the fabric they quickly discover that none of it meets the most basic specification of the contract — the fabric is uniformly narrower than the width called for in the contract. They quickly inform the company's President. She telephones the President of Top-Notch on Tuesday and explains the situation making clear that she has no choice but to reject the delivery in its entirety. The President of Top-Notch says, "Well, if it really is all too narrow, I can't contest your right to reject. Why don't I send a truck down to your place tomorrow to take the stuff off your hands? Once it gets back to my place, I'll get my accounting department working on a refund of the $190,000 you've paid. It might take a month or so knowing how those guys work, but you'll get your money back, I promise." You are consulted by the President of the furniture company. She needs to make a decision, and she needs to do so in a hurry. Do you see any difficulty with her going along with this suggestion and allowing the textile firm to take the nonconforming fabric back into its possession on Wednesday? If so, what different arrangement might she want to propose to the President of Top-Notch?

22.2 Top-Notch Textiles places an order for a large, industrial-size amount of woolen yarn from Yuba City Yarn, a distributor from which it has regularly obtained supplies in the past. As in the past, Yuba City delivers the yarn in a timely manner along with an invoice that calls upon the seller to pay the purchase price (here $57,634) within sixty days of its receipt of the shipment. Top-Notch receives the shipment on Monday, March 22. On March 24, the President of Yuba City becomes aware through a reliable trade journal that Top-Notch has not been paying its debts to other suppliers as they have become due since the beginning of the month. The President of Yuba City sends an over-night letter to Top-Notch demanding that the textile manufacturer not make any use of the yarn it received on Monday and furthermore that his firm was "invoking its rights to reclaim these goods and demanding prompt return of them."

(a) Is Top-Notch obligated to comply with this demand?
(b) Suppose that instead of sending the yarn to Top-Notch allowing it sixty days to make payment, Yuba City had delivered the goods directly to the buyer in exchange for a check from Top-Notch for the full purchase price of $57,634. By March 26 the President of Yuba City is informed by that company's bank that this check has been returned unpaid with the explanation that Top-Notch did not have sufficient funds in its account to cover the check? Can Yuba City assert the right to reclaim the shipment under this set of facts?
(c) Finally, suppose that Top-Notch had filed a petition in bankruptcy on March 22. Will the trustee in bankruptcy (or the management of Top-Notch acting as a "debtor in possession" as the firm tries to work out a plan or reorganization) have to allow Yuba City to reclaim this shipment of yarn or does the bankruptcy cut off the seller's reclamation rights?

22.3 We now add one additional wrinkle, and one more important party, to the situation presented in the prior problem. Assume that for several years Top-Notch has operated its business with the benefit of a loan from Golden State Bank. As part of the loan agreement, Top-Notch granted to the bank a security interest in "all of borrower's inventory, now held or hereafter acquired." The bank had properly perfected this interest by a filing in the correct office indicating the collateral to be "all inventory, now held or hereafter acquired," and has carefully kept up its perfection by the diligent filing of continuation statements as necessary. Can the bank claim its interest extends to the shipment of yarn received by Top-Notch from Yuba City on March 22? You should be able to see why the bank would be concerned, as its debtor seems to be in financial difficulty, whether or not it eventually goes into bankruptcy, if this valuable stuff is sent back to the seller in light of the seller's reclamation right and its demand for return. What argument can you make for the bank in light of its interest either that the yarn should not be returned to Yuba City or that, even if it is, the yarn remains subject to a security interest held by the bank? Do you think this argument should succeed? Will it? See the following case.

IN RE TUCKER

United States Bankruptcy Court for the District of Arizona, 2005
329 Bankr. 291, 59 U.C.C. Rep. Serv. 2d 1131

RANDOLPH J. HAINES, United States Bankruptcy Judge: This case presents the issue of whether a reclaiming seller has priority over an unperfected secured creditor. The Court concludes that it does, because an unperfected secured creditor does not qualify as an "other good faith purchaser."

PROCEDURAL BACKGROUND

This matter is before the Court on cross-motions for summary judgment filed by Par Wholesale Auto, Inc. ("Par") and DAVCO Enterprises dba DAVCO Motors & DAVCO Leasing, and C.T. Cook (collectively "DAVCO"). The issue is the ownership of three vehicles sold by Par to Harvest Car Company, which was a dba of the Debtor Edward Tucker (hereafter referred to as "Tucker" or "Harvest"). On June 23, 2005, the Court ruled in favor of Par and against DAVCO as to ownership of the three vehicles, indicating that a subsequent opinion would more fully explain the Court's analysis and rationale. This is that opinion.

UNDISPUTED MATERIAL FACTS

The parties are not in total agreement on all the facts, but there are sufficient undisputed material facts upon which the Court is able to enter summary judgment. These are: Tucker inspected vehicles at Par's place of business in Texas and purchased the three vehicles from Par in April 2001. Tucker delivered a check for one of the vehicles and promised to pay the balance for all of the vehicles. The vehicles were transported from Texas to Arizona and delivered to Tucker at Harvest Car Company.

Tucker and DAVCO had a financing agreement whereby DAVCO or C.T. Cook provided floor financing to Tucker to allow Tucker to purchase vehicles and hold them for resale. Per the financing agreement and business dealings between DAVCO and Tucker, Tucker would sign the certificates of title and deliver them to DAVCO. DAVCO would then hold these "open" titles until Tucker sold the vehicles. At least for the vehicles at issue here, DAVCO did not immediately record its alleged interest in the vehicles with the Arizona Motor Vehicle Division, or otherwise indicate the transfer with any other vehicle titling agency, including the Texas Department of Transportation. Nor did DAVCO file a U.C.C.-1 financing statement to perfect its security interest pursuant to Article 9 of the Uniform Commercial Code ("U.C.C."). At all times until DAVCO obtained new titles in Arizona, DAVCO held Texas certificates of title that had been endorsed by the previous owners.

When the check tendered by Tucker to Par to pay for at least one of the vehicles failed to clear Tucker's bank, Par timely made demand for replacement funds or for return of all of the vehicles. Unable to make good on the purchase price, Tucker agreed to return the vehicles, and they were returned to Par on May 24, 2001. At the time the vehicles were returned to Par, DAVCO did not hold registered title to the vehicles and DAVCO's interest was not reflected in the records of either the Arizona Motor Vehicle Division or the Texas Department of Transportation.

Par applied for new certificates of title in Texas, and they were issued to Par in May 2001. DAVCO applied for and obtained certificates in Arizona in June 2001. Also in June 2001 DAVCO terminated the financing agreement with Harvest Car Company and Tucker, and demanded return of the vehicles.

At no time did DAVCO ever have possession of the vehicles. The vehicles were held on Tucker's car lot until they were returned to Par in May 2001. DAVCO merely held the Texas certificates of title that had been executed by the previous owners, which DAVCO calls "open" titles. DAVCO held these open titles to secure payment for the monies advanced to Tucker and Harvest Car Company. The executed certificates of title show the transfer from Par to Tucker, but regarding the transfers from Tucker to DAVCO, on at least one of the certificates of title, C.T. Cook signed for both Tucker and DAVCO.

DAVCO's Ownership Claim Fails Due to Lack of Possession

The first issue is DAVCO's claim to be the owner of the vehicles, rather than merely a secured lender, at the time they were returned to Par. Arizona Revised Statutes (hereinafter "A.R.S.") §44-1061(A) requires a seller of goods to immediately transfer the goods, followed by the buyer's actual and continued possession, in order for the sale to be valid as against claims of the seller's creditors. [This statute, it turns out, pre-dates Arizona's statehood and, in the words of the court goes "all the way back to the inception of fraudulent conveyance law more than 400 years ago." After a lengthy discussion of the statute's application in the instant case, the court concludes:] Because A.R.S. § 44-1061 invalidates DAVCO's claim of ownership, its interest must be limited to that of a secured creditor. And because it never perfected either by filing a UCC financing statement, nor reflected its lien on the certificates of title before Par executed its reclamation, it must be regarded as an unperfected secured creditor at the time of the events in question.

SELLERS' RIGHTS OF RECLAMATION VS. SECURED CREDITORS

Pursuant to A.R.S. § 47-2702 (U.C.C. § 2-702), a seller has a right to reclaim goods when the seller discovers that the buyer has received goods on credit while insolvent. The demand for reclamation must occur within ten days of the buyer's receipt of the goods sold. Under Arizona law, there is no requirement that the demand for reclamation must be in writing, so an oral demand will suffice. A seller's reclamation rights are subordinate to the rights of subsequent buyers in the ordinary course, other good faith purchasers, or lien creditors. A.R.S. § 47-2702(C).

In the present case, Par sold one of the vehicles in exchange for a check tendered by Tucker and was therefore a cash seller on that vehicle. A check is a negotiable instrument and the seller who accepts a check for payment is a cash seller because the transaction is considered a cash sale under the U.C.C. The other two vehicles were sold on credit in exchange for two bank drafts, and Par was a credit seller for those two vehicles. But the U.C.C., as adopted by Arizona, abolished the common law distinction between cash and credit sellers, and both now have reclamation rights. The cash buyer who issues a check for payment receives conditional title as against the seller, and the buyer's right to retain or dispose of the goods is conditional upon his making the payment due. The rights of a cash seller are also bound by the insolvency requirement and ten-day limitation period for reclamation.

As previously stated, Tucker issued a check for one of the vehicles, and intended to pay the balance of the purchase price for the remaining vehicles under two bank drafts. When the check was dishonored and returned to Par, Par immediately contacted Tucker to demand replacement funds or return of the vehicles. Tucker was unable to provide replacement funds and offered to return the vehicles to Par. Based on Tucker's inability to pay his debts in the ordinary course of business or pay the debts as they come due, Tucker was insolvent for purposes of the reclamation statute. Par also made the demand for reclamation within ten days of delivery, as required by the statute. Tucker purchased the vehicles on April 21, 2001 and upon notification of dishonor of the check tendered by Tucker, Par made the demand for return of the vehicles on April 28, 2001. Par met all of the requirements under the Arizona statute for the reclamation of the vehicles, and Par retook possession of the vehicles in May 2001.

Par's reclamation rights are subject only to the rights of a buyer in the ordinary course, other good faith purchaser, or a lien creditor. A.R.S.

§ 47-2702(C). DAVCO's security interest in the vehicles will defeat Par's reclamation rights only if it renders DAVCO a buyer in the ordinary course, an other good faith purchaser, or a lien creditor. [The court then determines that DAVCO could not be considered either a "lien creditor" under § 9-102(A)(52) since that term does not include a consensual secured lender. Nor was it a "buyer in the ordinary course" of the vehicles as that term is defined in § 1-201(9) or § 1R-201(b)(9).]

Having found that DAVCO is neither a lien creditor nor a buyer in the ordinary course, the court must also consider whether DAVCO would fall under the "other good faith purchaser" exception to Par's right to reclaim the goods. The Ninth Circuit's seminal 1979 holding in *Los Angeles Paper Bag Co. v. James Talcott, Inc.*, 604 F.2d 38, 39 (9th Cir. 1979), established that a secured creditor has the status of a good faith purchaser under A.R.S. § 47-2403. The U.C.C. definition of "purchaser" is broad enough to include an Article 9 (Secured Transactions) secured party. The issue that *Talcott* did not resolve, however, is whether all secured creditors qualify for "other good faith purchaser" status, or only perfected secured creditors. The creditor in *Talcott* was in fact perfected, so the Ninth Circuit had no occasion there to determine whether its conclusion would also apply to unperfected secured creditors.

A long line of cases suggests that perfection is required to qualify for the good faith purchaser priority over reclaiming sellers, but in each case the creditor was in fact perfected so reliance on such status in those cases was, at best, dictum. This Court has found only one reported case that considers the relative rights of an unperfected creditor and a reclaiming seller, *Guy Martin Buick, Inc. v. Colo. Springs Nat'l Bank*, 184 Colo. 166, 519 P.2d 354 (1974) (en banc). The Colorado Supreme Court there held that because a seller's reclamation right was not listed in U.C.C. § 9-301 (now § 9-317) as having priority over an unperfected security interest, the unperfected security interest must have priority over the seller's reclamation right. And although the reclaiming seller argued that it should be regarded as holding a perfected security interest upon retaking possession (and by § 9-301's cross reference to § 9-312 (now § 9-322), the first to perfect has priority), the court rejected this argument by concluding that a reclamation right is not a species of a security interest.

Guy Martin was decided in 1974, and its analysis is not applicable in the Ninth Circuit after the *Talcott* decision in 1979. *Talcott* makes clear that priority is not determined by whether the reclamation rights are recognized in then § 9-301, but rather by whether the secured creditor qualifies as an "other good faith purchaser." Moreover, *Talcott* relied on two other decisions, the Arizona Supreme Court's decision in *Gen. Elec. Credit Corp. v. Tidwell Indus., Inc.*, 115 Ariz. 362, 565 P.2d 868 (1977), and the Fifth Circuit's decision in *Stowers v. Mahon (In re Samuels & Co.)*, 526 F.2d 1238 (5th Cir. 1976). Both of those cases equated the reclamation right to an unperfected security interest. Therefore to the extent that *Talcott* implicitly adopts the reasoning of *GECC* and *Samuels*, the reclaiming seller in *Guy Martin* would have prevailed because he perfected by obtaining possession before the unperfected secured creditor perfected.

To prevail under *Talcott, GECC* and *Samuels,* the secured creditor must qualify as a "good faith purchaser." As *Samuels* correctly notes, a secured creditor expressly satisfies the U.C.C.'s definition of purchaser. To qualify as a "good faith" purchaser, the secured creditor must observe "reasonable commercial standards of fair dealing in the trade." This Court concludes that an inventory financer such as DAVCO fails to observe reasonable commercial standards of fair dealing when it fails to file a financing statement so that credit sellers can become aware of the risk to their reclamation rights and protect themselves by perfecting an inventory purchase money security interest, which requires notification to the conflicting inventory financer. An inventory financer who had an opportunity to perfect and failed to do so therefore fails to qualify as an "other good faith purchaser," and therefore is subordinate to the rights of a reclaiming seller.

Based on all of the foregoing, the Court finds and concludes that Par had a right to reclaim the three vehicles; Par timely and properly exercised its rights of reclamation; and DAVCO does not possess an interest in the vehicles that is superior to Par's reclamation rights under A.R.S. § 47-2702.

CONCLUSION

For these reasons, the Court finds and concludes that Par's interest in the three vehicles is superior to DAVCO's and that DAVCO does not have any legal basis to defeat Par's superior interest. Accordingly, the Court finds that Par is entitled to summary judgment as against DAVCO.

*NOTE OF THE SELLER'S RIGHT OF RECLAMATION
UNDER THE BANKRUPTCY CODE*

In a footnote to the opinion in the *Tucker* case, Judge Haines adds the following:

> The Bankruptcy Code also recognizes the seller's right of reclamation. 11 U.S.C. § 546(c). The Bankruptcy Abuse Prevention and Consumer Protection Act ("BAPCPA") (2005) has amended that provision, effective for cases filed after October 17, 2005. The amended § 546(c) extends the time for making the reclamation demand [under the bankruptcy code section] to 45 days (or 20 days after the commencement of the bankruptcy case). Prior to this amendment, the provision had been understood as "recognizing, in part, the validity of section 2-702 of the U.C.C." H. Rep. No. 595, 95th Cong., 1st Sess. 371-72 (1977); S. Rep. No. 989, 95th Cong., 2d Sess. 86-87 (1978). But since the U.C.C. still requires a demand within 10 days, perhaps the amended § 546(c) creates its own reclamation right, rather than merely validating the right that exists under the U.C.C. This impression is supported by the fact that the amendment also strikes the reference to "any statutory or common law" right to reclaim, and instead simply states that the trustee's powers are subject to "the right of a seller" to reclaim. If the amended

§ 546(c) creates its own reclamation right, then the analysis made here by applying the U.C.C. provisions and definitions may not apply in a bankruptcy case filed after BAPCPA's effective date, and the issue may instead be whether the amended Bankruptcy Code provision — "subject to the prior rights of a holder of a security interest in such goods or the proceeds thereof" — applies equally to an unperfected security interest as to a perfected security interest. On the other hand, it may be a mistake to assume that the amended § 546(c) was intended to provide an entirely new and self-contained body of reclamation law, because it fails to recognize the rights of buyers in the ordinary course, other good faith purchasers and lien creditors, who were always protected under the U.C.C. Perhaps the intent was to incorporate and expand on the U.C.C. reclamation rights, rather than to supplant them entirely, in which case some U.C.C. analysis may continue to be relevant in interpreting and applying the new § 546(c).

As you can see, the *Tucker* court was able to resolve the case before it without use, or further analysis, of this recent revision to Bankruptcy Code § 546(c). Prior to the 2005 revisions in the Bankruptcy Code the courts generally held that this section created no independent right of reclamation for the seller in such a situation, but that any right of the seller under this Bankruptcy Code section was predicated on its having reclamation rights under state law, that is, under the Uniform Commercial Code. As the prior passage indicates, whether this is still true following the 2005 revision in the Bankrupcy Code is, to say the least, unclear. For further discussion, but no resolution, of this issue, see *In re Incredible Auto Sales LLC,* 2007 Bankr. LEXIS 1024, 62 U.C.C.2d 357 (D. Mont. 2007).

CHAPTER

23

Special Issues in Bankruptcy

A. INTRODUCTION

1. The Bankruptcy Trustee's Avoidance Powers

Bankruptcy law uses the term "debtor" to refer to that person — either an individual, partnership, or corporation — who has either on his, her, or its own initiative "voluntarily" filed a bankruptcy petition or against whom creditors have initiated the procedure via an "involuntary" filing. After a filing has triggered the commencement of a bankruptcy proceeding, an individual will be named to serve as trustee for the particular case. The trustee is to take charge of and serve as "the representative of the estate" of the debtor under § 323(a) of the Bankruptcy Code. Under § 322(b), the trustee has the capacity to sue (and to be sued) in this representative capacity. The "estate" which the trustee is to administer consists, under § 541, of essentially all property which the debtor had an interest in as of the filing of the bankruptcy petition. So first among the duties of the trustee is to round up and gain control over all of the property which is rightfully part of the estate. The more property which can be brought into the estate and the greater its value, the more there will be for the trustee to ultimately apply to the various claims which will be made against the estate.

In dealing with and making disbursements from the estate, the trustee will have to deal distinctly with what under bankruptcy terminology are referred to as secured and unsecured "claims." As a general matter — and of course all of this would be dealt with in far greater detail and nuance in the Bankruptcy course — secured claims are to be given priority over unsecured ones as the bankruptcy process works its way to its conclusion, whether this is to be the eventual liquidation or a reorganization of the debtor's affairs. It will not surprise you that the assertion by a creditor of what we have been referring to since the first page of this book as an Article 9 security *interest* in some specified personal property of the debtor will be considered a secured *claim* as far as bankruptcy law is concerned — that is, of course, *if* the interest was perfected as of the time of the filing of the bankruptcy petition.

As we saw in Chapter 18, §544(a), the so-called "strong-arm clause," of the Bankruptcy Code working in tandem with §9-317(a)(2) of our old friend the Uniform Commercial Code gives the trustee the power to *avoid* any security interest which was not properly perfected at the time of the commencement of the bankruptcy case. The trustee can and will challenge any secured claim grounded on a supposedly perfected Article 9 security interest if there is some argument either that the security interest was never properly perfected (including, of course, the possibility that it never even attached) or that the perfection had lapsed prior to the filing of the bankruptcy petition. If the trustee's challenge is successful, the claim is not entirely disallowed. It is, however, dealt with as an unsecured claim and not a secured claim. And this can make all the difference between the creditor being paid all, or at least a goodly part, of what it is owed by the debtor (if the claim is secured) or what is usually only pennies on the dollar (on an unsecured claim).

The above is all by way of review. In this chapter we look at two different aspects of the trustee's power. Recall that the trustee is responsible for bringing into the estate as much as possible of the debtor's property. Under either of the two concepts — preferential transfers and fraudulent conveyances — the trustee will attempt to avoid as a matter of law transfer of property by the debtor prior to the commencement of the bankruptcy case. If the trustee is successful in avoiding on either ground such a prepetition transfer, the property involved must be returned to the bankruptcy estate, putting that much more into the pot from which rightful claimants are to be paid what is owed them by the debtor to the extent that this is possible and according to the rules by which the trustee is to dispose of what is available in the estate.

2. *Preferential Transfers*

Under §547 of the Bankruptcy Code, the trustee is given the power to challenge certain transfers the debtor has made of an interest in any of its property prior to the filing of the bankruptcy petition on the grounds that the transfer constituted a "preference" or a "preferential transfer" of the property. If a given transfer is determined to be a preference under §547, that the trustee has the power to void the transfer and recapture the property preferentially transferred, or if necessary the monetary equivalent if the exact property is no longer available, from the transferee and add it back into the estate. Section 547 is a long and convoluted big of statutory prose, and you will have to rely on your Bankruptcy course for a full-fledged treatment of the law relating to preferential transfers. Our purpose here is only to introduce the concept in its broadest detail and to see how it quickly interacts — indeed, in many instances in crucially dependent upon — the state law of secured transactions as set out in Article 9.

But first a look at §547. That section, abridged as much as possible given our limited agenda but with due respect for its importance, is set out below.

Don't feel obliged to try to master it on a single reading. I'll provide some, I hope, helpful comments following.

§ 547. Preferences

(a) In this section —

(1) "inventory" [is defined basically as it is in Article 9];

(2) "new value" means money or money's worth in goods, services, or new credit, or release by a transferee of property previously transferred to such transferee in a transaction that is neither void nor voidable by the debtor or the trustee under any applicable law, including proceeds of such property, but does not include an obligation substituted for an existing obligation; . . .

(b) Except as provided in subsections (c) and (i) of this section, the trustee may avoid any transfer of an interest of the debtor in property —

(1) to or for the benefit of a creditor;

(2) for or on account of an antecedent debt owed by the debtor before such transfer was made;

(3) made while the debtor was insolvent;

(4) made —

(A) on or within 90 days before the date of the filing of the petition; or

(B) between ninety days and one year before the date of the filing of the petition, if such creditor at the time of such transfer was an insider; and

(5) that enables such creditor to receive more than such creditor would receive if —

(A) the case were a case under chapter 7 of this title;

(B) the transfer had not been made; and

(C) such creditor received payment of such debt to the extent provided by the provisions of this title.

(c) The trustee may not avoid under this section a transfer —

(1) to the extent that such transfer was —

(A) intended by the debtor and the creditor to or for whose benefit such transfer was made to be a contemporaneous exchange for new value given to the debtor; and

(B) in fact a substantially contemporaneous exchange;

(2) to the extent that such transfer was in payment of a debt incurred by the debtor in the ordinary course of business or financial affairs of the debtor and the transferee, and such transfer was —

(A) made in the ordinary course of business or financial affairs of the debtor and the transferee; or

(B) made according to ordinary business terms;

(3) that creates a security interest in property acquired by the debtor —

(A) to the extent such security interest secures new value that was

(i) given at or after the signing of a security agreement that contains a description of such property as collateral;

(ii) given by or on behalf of the secured party under such agreement;

(iii) given to enable the debtor to acquire such property; and

(iv) in fact used by the debtor to acquire such property; and

(B) that is perfected on or before 30 days after the debtor receives possession of such property;

(4) to or for the benefit of a creditor, to the extent that, after such transfer, such creditor gave new value to or for the benefit of the debtor —

(A) not secured by an otherwise unavoidable security interest; and

(B) on account of which new value the debtor did not make an otherwise unavoidable transfer to or for the benefit of such creditor;

(5) that creates a perfected security interest in inventory or a receivable or the proceeds of either, except to the extent that the aggregate of all such transfers to the transferee caused a reduction, as of the date of the filing of the petition and to the prejudice of other creditors holding unsecured claims, of any amount by which the debt secured by such security interest exceeded the value of all security interests for such debt on the later of—

(A) (i) with respect to a transfer to which subsection (b)(4)(A) of this section applies, 90 days before the date of the filing of the petition; or

(ii) with respect to a transfer to which subsection (b)(4)(B) of this section applies, one year before the date of the filing of the petition; or

(B) the date on which new value was first given under the security agreement creating such security interest;

(d) . . .

(e) (1) For the purposes of this section . . . a transfer of a fixture or property other than real property is perfected when a creditor on a simple contract cannot acquire a judicial lien that is superior to the interest of the transferee.

(2) For the purposes of this section, except as provided in paragraph (3) of this subsection, a transfer is made—

(A) at the time such transfer takes effect between the transferor and the transferee, if such transfer is perfected at, or within 30 days after, such time, except as provided in subsection (c)(3)(B);

(B) at the time such transfer is perfected, if such transfer is perfected after such 30 days; or

(C) immediately before the date of the filing of the petition, if such transfer is not perfected at the later of—

(i) the commencement of the case; or

(ii) 30 days after such transfer takes effect between the transferor and the transferee.

(3) For the purposes of this section, a transfer is not made until the debtor has acquired rights in the property transferred.

(f) For the purposes of this section, the debtor is presumed to have been insolvent on and during the 90 days immediately preceding the date of the filing of the petition.

Subsection (a) sets out some preliminary definitions. So far, so good. The core of the section is, as you no doubt noted, then to be found in subsection (b). This provides a listing of the five criteria each of which must be shown to be true by the trustee if a prepetition transfer of an *interest* in the debtor's property—which may certainly include an Article 9 security interest of the type we are concerned with in this volume—is to be characterized as a preference. The five criteria are:

(1) The transfer had to be "to or for the benefit of a creditor" of the debtor,
(2) The transfer had to be made "for or on account of an antecedent debt," that is, a debt owed by the debtor prior to the time the transfer was made,
(3) The transfer had to be made at the time the debtor was insolvent. The Bankruptcy Code's § 101(32) has a definition of "insolvent" which says that a debtor is insolvent when the amount of its debts exceeds a fair valuation of its assets. As a practical matter, however, the important provision is § 547's subsection (f). For the purpose of the preference

section, "the debtor is presumed to have been insolvent on and during the 90 days prior to the date of the filing of the petition." This presumption is rarely challenged. Certainly not with any success.

(4) The transfer was made within 90 days prior to the filing of the petition, or if the transfer was to an "insider" within one year before that date. An "insider" is defined in § 101(31) as you might expect. It includes relatives of an individual debtor, partners of a partnership, and officers, directors, or other persons "in control" of a corporation.

(5) The transfer can be shown to have resulted in the creditor-transferee coming out better overall than it would have had the transfer not been made and it had received only what it would have under a straight Chapter 7 liquidation of the estate.

The simplest example of a preferential transfer that may be avoided by the trustee does not involve any Article 9 interest, or any Article 9 law at all, but it serves well to illustrate the concept of a preference and is a good place to start. Suppose that a debtor, Dexter Manufacturing, owes each of two creditors, Alpha Dogs Corporation and Beta Versions Unlimited, $10,000 on unsecured trade credit. Dexter, having assets worth in total only $12,000, pays Alpha off fully just a week before it files a petition in bankruptcy. Alpha, being fully paid off, need make no claim in the bankruptcy. Beta, still owed $10,000, will receive only one-fifth of that amount when it receives $2,000 (all that is left in the bankrupt's estate) through the bankruptcy procedure. You should be able to see that the $10,000 payment to Alpha would be considered a preferential transfer and the trustee should be able to recover that amount from Alpha for the estate. The trustee would then distribute $6,000 to each of Alpha and Beta, to pay off each of the creditors — who had up until one week before the petition's filing been similarly situated — as much of the debtor's debts as the amount in the estate makes possible. Had the $10,000 payment to Alpha not been avoided, that creditor would have ended up with full payment of what it was owed and Beta would have received only $2,000.

The hypothetical of the previous paragraph leaves one question unanswered: Why might Dexter Manufacturing, the debtor, have paid Alpha off fully just before declaring bankruptcy? While hypothetical characters don't necessarily need to have reasons for what they do, this turns out to be a question worth considering. One reason the debtor, Dexter in our hypo, might have made the prepetition transfer to Alpha of practically all of its assets and all that it owed Alpha, leaving Beta to bear the adverse consequences of this decision, is that Dexter simply liked Alpha better than it liked Beta. Or perhaps the management of Dexter had some indirect reason or reasons for being more protective of the interests of Alpha than it did of Beta. Friendship is a noble sentiment, as we would all agree, but general bankruptcy policy frowns on the debtor, knowing that it is or may be facing an imminent bankruptcy, favoring one of its creditors over a similarly situated creditor. A principle goal of the bankruptcy process is said to be that all claimants of the same class or status should be treated alike.

Another possible reason why Dexter may have made the $10,000 to Alpha is that this one of its two unsecured creditors was being far more aggressive in demanding payment from Dexter. (Remember, its full name is Alpha Dogs Corporation, which could just be a coincidence, but maybe not.) Alpha may have even been threatening suit to get it's money, a possibility which would surely push Dexter over the line from being "close to" filing for bankruptcy into a position where it would have no choice but to do so. Alpha's assertive behavior would have deprived Dexter of any chance to turn its fortunes around and avoid having to declare bankruptcy, making it through a tough period but coming out of it successfully. Were it not for the rules which allow for avoidance of a preferential transfer, a debtor's creditors, believing the debtor to be sliding towards bankruptcy, would too easily end up pressuring the debtor for payment to such an extent that the possibility of a bankruptcy could become an inevitability — to the benefit of no one. As an oft-quoted portion of the legislative history of the Bankruptcy Code explains:

> The purpose of the preference section is two-fold. First, by permitting the trustee to avoid prebankruptcy transfers that occur within a short period before bankruptcy, creditors are discouraged from racing to the courthouse to dismember the debtor during his slide into bankruptcy. The protection thus afforded the debtor often enables him to work his way out of a difficult financial situation through cooperation with all of his creditors. Second, and more important, the preference provisions facilitate the prime bankruptcy policy of equality of distribution among creditors of the debtor. Any creditor that received a greater payment than others of his class is required to disgorge so that all may share equally. H.R. Rep. No. 595, 95th Cong., 1st Sess. 177-78, *reprinted in* 1978 U.S. Code Cong. & Admin. News 5787, 5963, 6138.

The first problems in this chapter will explore further when a transfer is, or may be, a preferential transfer subject to avoidance under § 547(b), and particularly in those situation where an Article 9 security interest is part of the picture. We will further want to explore some of those five situations set out in § 547(c) in which what would otherwise be characterized as a preferential transfer under subsection (b) may *not* be avoided by the trustee, some significant and interesting exceptions to the general rule.

3. Fraudulent Transfers

The law regarding which transfers by a debtor of interests in its property are to be considered fraudulent transfers, and what relief is available to creditors of the debtor affected to their detriment by transfers which are determined to fit the description, has a long history, going back to the Statute of 13 Elizabeth in 1570. Today most states have a statute dealing with what are termed either "fraudulent transfers" or "fraudulent conveyances." Most of these state statutes are based on the Uniform Fraudulent Transfers Act (UFTA), promulgated by the National Conference of Commissioners on Uniform State Laws in 1984 to modernize and replace the Uniform

Fraudulent Conveyances Act (UFCA) of 1918. For our purposes it probably easiest to look to the substantial similar provision as found in §548 of the Bankruptcy Code. That section—again severely abridged—reads as follows.

§ 548. Fraudulent transfers and obligations

(a) (1) The trustee may avoid any transfer . . . of an interest of the debtor in property, or any obligation . . . incurred by the debtor, that was made or incurred on or within 2 years before the date of the filing of the petition, if the debtor voluntarily or involuntarily—

(A) made such transfer or incurred such obligation with actual intent to hinder, delay, or defraud any entity to which the debtor was or became, on or after the date that such transfer was made or such obligation was incurred, indebted; or

(B) (i) received less than a reasonably equivalent value in exchange for such transfer or obligation; and

(ii) (I) was insolvent on the date that such transfer was made or such obligation was incurred, or became insolvent as a result of such transfer or obligation; (II) was engaged in business or a transaction, or was about to engage in business or a transaction, for which any property remaining with the debtor was an unreasonably small capital; (III) intended to incur, or believed that the debtor would incur, debts that would be beyond the debtor's ability to pay as such debts matured; or (IV) made such transfer to or for the benefit of an insider, or incurred such obligation to or for the benefit of an insider, under an employment contract and not in the ordinary course of business.

. . . .

(d) (1)For the purposes of this section, a transfer is made when such transfer is so perfected that a bona fide purchaser from the debtor against whom applicable law permits such transfer to be perfected cannot acquire an interest in the property transferred that is superior to the interest in such property of the transferee, but if such transfer is not so perfected before the commencement of the case, such transfer is made immediately before the date of the filing of the petition.

(2) In this section—

(A) "value" means property, or satisfaction or securing of a present or antecedent debt of the debtor, but does not include an unperformed promise to furnish support to the debtor or to a relative of the debtor; . . .

The operative part of this provision is, as you could see, subsection (a)(1). The trustee is given the power to avoid the transfer of any interest in the debtors property where the transfer was made within two years prior to the filing of the bankruptcy petition in either of two situations. This section covers—as do the similar state statutes addressing fraudulent transfers or conveyances—two distinct situations: both actual fraud (in (a)(1)(A)) and what has come to be referred to as "constructive fraud" (in (a)(1)(B)).

A transfer is "actually" fraudulent under (a)(1)(A) when it can be shown to have been made with the debtor's subjective intention of hindering, delaying, or defrauding any of the debtor's present or potential future creditors. A simple example of this, not involving any security interest at all but sufficient for our present purpose, is where the debtor, concerned about the possibility that she will be sued in connection with a business deal that has gone decidedly sour, transfers title in her residence and title to her expensive automobile to, let us say, her brother by way of gift. She gets nothing in return, but the debtor continues to live in the home and make use of the car just as she had in the past.

The trustee will be able to show that a transfer is avoidable under the "constructive fraud" provision of (a)(1)(B) without having to prove anything about the debtor's subjective intent. Under this theory, and this part of §548, in order to avoid a transfer by the debtor of an interest in his or property within two years prior to the filing of the bankruptcy petition the trustee will have to show that the debtor received "less than a reasonably equivalent value" in exchange for what he transferred to another *and* that at the time of the transfer the debtor was, or had good reason to expect he would soon be, in financial difficulty of some sort. That's what the four possibilities of (a)(1)(B)(ii) are all about. An example of this variety of fraudulent transfer would be if the debtor within two years prior to filing a bankruptcy petition and when he was clearly "insolvent" as that term is defined in the Bankruptcy Code had sold his residence or his luxury automobile to his sister at a price well below what could be shown to be the fair market value of either the home or the auto at the time of the sale. In Problem 23.7 below we will look at a situation where the granting of a security interest in property may (or may not) be found to be a fraudulent transfer subject to the trustee's avoidance powers.

Finally, it should be noted that a trustee who is unable to take advantage of §548 to avoid a transfer, perhaps because the time of the transfer was indisputably 25 months prior to the filing of the bankruptcy petition, may be able under §544(b) of the Code to step into the shoes of an actual creditor of the debtor and avoid the transfer by invoking the applicable state statute on fraudulent transfers, many of which provide for a longer "look-back" period than the two years of §548. For our purposes it is certainly sufficient to look only at the Bankruptcy Code provision, that is, §548.

B. PREPARATION

If you have read the introductory section carefully, and if you are primed to refer back to those sections of the Bankruptcy Code quoted therein as the need arises, then you are prepared to deal with the problems and the single case which follow.

PROBLEMS

23.1 In early 2008, Dexter Corporation borrows $50,000 from Gamma Rays Bank, granting that bank a security interest in all of its previously unencumbered equipment. The equipment at the time has a value of roughly $80,000. Dexter makes a payment on this loan to Gamma Rays on February 1, 2009 of $15,000. On March 15 of 2009, Dexter files a petition in bankruptcy. The value of Dexter's equipment is still, as of the date of bankruptcy worth about what it was in 2008.

(a) Will the trustee in bankruptcy be able to avoid Dexter's February 2009 payment to the bank of $15,000?
(b) Change one fact: Assume that at the time of the initial borrowing by Dexter, and at the time of the bankruptcy filing, the equipment had a value of roughly $30,000. Would this change your analysis of whether Dexter's payment on the loan had been an avoidable preference?

23.2   As of the beginning of 2009, Dreben Manufacturing Corporation borrows $40,000 from Delta Landing Lenders on short-term unsecured credit. By early August of that year, Delta is demanding repayment, but Dreben does not have the cash available to pay off Dreben. To ease the nerves of that lender, and to gain some more time to repay the loan, Dreben grants Delta a security interest in its otherwise unencumbered inventory. Delta immediately prefects this interest. On October 1, 2009 is forced by this and all of its other debts to file a petition in bankruptcy. Will the bankruptcy trustee be able to avoid Dreben's grant of the security interest in August as a preference?

23.3   On April 12, 2009, Dreadmore Industries borrows $25,000 from Pi Chart Bank of Athens, Georgia. At the time of this borrowing Dreadmore grants the bank a security interest in some particular well-specified pieces of its equipment having a value of approximately $35,000, and the bank immediately perfects this interest. On May 7, Dreadmore files a petition in bankruptcy. Can the trustee avoid Dreadmore's grant of the security interest as a preference?

23.4   In 2007, the Delmore Corporation borrows $100,000 from Upsilon Creek Bank. In order to obtain this loan it grants to the lender a security interest in all of its equipment. The bank does not initially perfect on the interest. On March 30, 2009, just one month before the Delmore Corporation goes into bankruptcy, Upsilon Creek finally does file an initial financing statement, proper in all respects and with the correct filing office, to perfect its security interest in the equipment. Will the trustee in bankruptcy be able to avoid Upsilon Creek's security interest as a preference?

23.5   The Dumbel Corporation owns and operates three fitness clubs. The management of Dumbel believes that to boost the sagging enrollment in the clubs it needs some newer equipment. It decides that it should add two new Exerflex Excruciator machines to the exercise floor of each of its clubs. The Exerflex company is willing to sell it the six machines for a total of $60,000. Dumbel goes to the firm of Rho and Psi Associates ("RPA"), a company that specializes in making loans to small business borrowers.

On January 10, 2009 RPA loans Dumbel $60,000 in the form of a check made out to the order of Exerflex. At the same time it has Dumbel sign a note, promising to repay the loan and a security agreement under which RPA is granted a security interest in the six Exerflex machines which Dumbel is to buy with the check. Dumbel does take the check to the Exerflex offices and gives it to the appropriate person at that company. Within a few days the six machines are delivered to the fitness clubs. RPA files an initial financing statement, proper in all respects and with the correct filing office, on January 15. Two days later, on January 17, the management of Dumbel Corporation comes to the conclusion that nothing is going to rescue its failing business, and the company files a petition in bankruptcy.

(a) Will the trustee in bankruptcy be able to avoid RPA's security interest as a preference? Consult § 547(c)(3).
(b) Would your answer to the above question be any different if RPA had not gotten around to filing its initial financing statement until January 20?

NOTE ON THE AUTOMATIC STAY

You might have been worried, for RPA's sake, in part (b) of the preceding problem when you read that it had filed an initial financing statement on a date *after* the petition in bankruptcy had been filed. Wouldn't this be a violation of the all-important automatic stay which goes into effect immediately upon the filing of a bankruptcy petition? Indeed this would seem to be a problem for RPA given the broad scope of the automatic stay as initially set forth in § 362(a).

§ 362. Automatic stay
    (a) Except as provided in subsection (b) of this section, a petition filed under section 301, 302, or 303 of this title . . . operates as a stay, applicable to all entities, of —
        (1) the commencement or continuation, including the issuance or employment of process, of a judicial, administrative, or other action or proceeding against the debtor that was or could have been commenced before the commencement of the case under this title, or to recover a claim against the debtor that arose before the commencement of the case under this title;
        (2) the enforcement, against the debtor or against property of the estate, of a judgment obtained before the commencement of the case under this title;
        (3) any act to obtain possession of property of the estate or of property from the estate or to exercise control over property of the estate;
        (4) any act to create, perfect, or enforce any lien against property of the estate;
        (5) any act to create, perfect, or enforce against property of the debtor any lien to the extent that such lien secures a claim that arose before the commencement of the case under this title;
        (6) any act to collect, assess, or recover a claim against the debtor that arose before the commencement of the case under this title;

(7) the setoff of any debt owing to the debtor that arose before the commencement of the case under this title against any claim against the debtor;
and

(8) the commencement or continuation of a proceeding before the United
States Tax Court concerning a corporate debtor's tax liability for a taxable
period the bankruptcy court may determine or concerning the tax liability of
a debtor who is an individual for a taxable period ending before the date of
the order for relief under this title.

Subsection 362(a)(4) in particular gives us pause. Fortunately, again for
RPA in Problem 23.5(b), the automatic stay section includes a number of
exceptions including the following:

(b) The filing of a petition . . . does not operate as a stay—

. . . .

(3) under subsection (a) of this section, of any act to perfect, or to maintain or continue the perfection of, an interest in property to the extent that
the trustee's rights and powers are subject to such perfection under section
546(b) of this title or to the extent that such act is accomplished within the
period provided under section 547(e)(2)(A) of this title.

Checking with §546(b) of the Bankruptcy Code we find the following.

(b) (1) The rights and powers of a trustee under sections 544, 545, and 549 of
this title are subject to any generally applicable law that (A) permits perfection
of an interest in property to be effective against an entity that acquires rights in
such property before the date of perfection. . . .

As we recall, §9-317(e) of the Uniform Commercial Code, which we considered in Chapter 19, is just such a "generally applicable law." It provides
that if a purchase-money security interest is perfected by filing within
20 days of the debtor's receiving delivery of the collateral that PMSI will
have priority over "over the rights of a buyer, lessee, or lien creditor which
arise between the time the security interest attaches and the time of the
filing." And the bankruptcy trustee is, of course, a lien creditor whose rights
arise as of the filing of the petition. All of which leads us to the conclusion
that RPA's filing of an initial financing statement after—but not too long
after—the petition in bankruptcy was filed was *not* in violation of the automatic stay.

PROBLEM

23.6   For many years Mega Bank of Iota, Louisiana has had a properly
perfected security interest in all of the inventory, including that after
acquired, of Dynamic Kitchens Corporation, a company which sells larger
pieces of restaurant equipment, such as stoves and refrigeration units, in the
Baton Rouge area. This interest secures Dynamic's obligation to make payments under a revolving line of credit which it has with the bank. On
December 30, 2010, Dynamic files a petition in bankruptcy. It is determined

that as of that date Dynamics owed the bank $456,000, and that the equipment — much of which had come into the firm's possession during the 90 days prior to December 30 — it had in stock had a total value of $300,000. It is also determined that on October 1, 2010 the firm had owed the bank $400,000 and the value of its inventory had been $500,000.

(a) The trustee in bankruptcy argues that he should be able to avoid any security interest that the bank may be claiming in those pieces of the inventory which came into Dynamics possession during the 90 days prior to Dec. 30 arguing that the bank's security interest in these items all arose during that preference period under the language of §547(e)(3)? While the trustee's argument may seem initially convincing, and troubling for the bank, look to §547(c)(5).

(b) What if instead it were determined that on Oct. 1, while Dynamic had owed the bank $456,000, the value of its inventory had then been only $200,000?

IN THE MATTER OF CLARK PIPE & SUPPLY CO., INC.

United States Court of Appeals for the Fifth Circuit, 1990
893 F.2d 693

E. GRADY JOLLY, Circuit Judge: [One of the issues the court was called upon to decide in this case was whether a lender, Associates Commercial Corporation ("Associates") had received a preference under the so-called "improvement in position" test of §547(c)(3).] In order to determine whether Associates improved its position during the ninety-day preference period, we must apply the test we adopted in *Matter of Missionary Baptist Foundation of America, Inc.*, 796 F.2d 752, 760 (5th Cir. 1986) (*Missionary Baptist II*):

> The "two-point net improvement" test of Section 547(c)(5) requires . . . a computation of (1) the loan balance outstanding ninety days prior to the bankruptcy; (2) the value of the [collateral] on that day; (3) the loan balance outstanding on the day the bankruptcy petition was filed; and (4) the value of the [collateral] on that day.

By comparing the loan balance minus the value of Associates' collateral on February 5 with the loan balance minus the value of Associates' collateral on May 7, it can be determined whether Associates improved its position during the ninety-day period. The loan balances on February 5 and May 7 are not at issue here. The dispute concerns the value to be assigned the collateral.

Associates argues that in valuing the inventory, the bankruptcy court should have employed the going-concern method of valuation rather than the liquidation method. Associates contends that because the bankruptcy court employed the wrong valuation method, it found a pre-ference where there was none. Moreover, Associates contends that even if the liquidation method is appropriate here, the bankruptcy court impro-perly viewed the value of inventory from the debtor's perspective rather than the creditor's perspective, and subtracted out operating costs of Clark bearing no relation to the liquidation of inventory. Finally, Associates argues that because the bankruptcy court failed to give reasons for its choice of valuation method, and the district court merely affirmed the bankruptcy court without discussing the valuation question, we must reverse and remand.

We consider first whether the record is sufficiently complete to permit review in the absence of precisely articulated reasons for the actions of the bankruptcy court. In *Missionary Baptist II* we remanded, finding the record unreviewable because, in applying section 547(c)(5), the bankruptcy judge had not given specific reasons for his choice of valuation method. Viewing this record as a whole, however, we conclude that it is adequate for purposes of review. In its Conclusions of Law, the bankruptcy court rejected Associ-ates' argument that going-concern value should be used in determining the value of the collateral and explicitly accepted the expert testimony offered by the trustee that liquidation value should be used. That expert testimony contained reasons in support of its conclusion. Thus, we conclude that the bankruptcy court adopted the reasoning of the trustee's expert, and there-fore we cannot say that the case must be remanded before we can properly review it on appeal.

Having concluded that the record is reviewable, we must examine the record to determine whether the bankruptcy court adopted the appropriate method of valuing the collateral. The Code does not prescribe any particular method of valuing collateral, but instead leaves valuation ques-tions to judges on a case-by-case basis. *See* H.R. Rep. No. 595, 95th Cong., 1st Sess. 216, 356 (1977), *reprinted in* 1978 U.S. Code Cong. & Ad. News 5787, 5963, 6176, 6312. Valuation is a mixed question of law and fact, the factual premises being subject to review on a "clearly erroneous" standard, and the legal conclusions being subject to *de novo* review.

The bankruptcy court adopted the view of the trustee's expert that Clark was in the process of liquidation throughout the ninety-day period from February 5 to May 7. This finding of fact was not clearly erroneous. Thus, for purposes of determining whether Associates improved its position at the expense of other creditors during that period, we conclude that the liquida-tion method of valuing the collateral was proper at both ends of the pre-ference period.

Associates maintains that even if the liquidation method is appropriate in this case, the bankruptcy court improperly valued inventory from the per-spective of the debtor (Clark), rather than the creditor (Associates). More-over, Associates contends that in valuing the inventory, the bankruptcy court erroneously deducted all of Clark's corporate expenses, including general overhead.

We agree with Associates that the bankruptcy court erroneously valued inventory from the perspective of the debtor rather than the creditor. The "ultimate goal" of the improvement in position test is to "determine whether the *secured creditor* is in a better position than it would have been had bankruptcy been declared ninety days earlier." Cohen, Value Judgments: Accounts Receivable Financing and Voidable Preferences Under the New Bankruptcy Code, 66 Minn. L. Rev. 639, 663-64 (1982) (emphasis added); H.R. Rep. No. 595, 95th Cong., 1st Sess. 216, 374 (1977), *reprinted in* 1978 U.S. Code Cong. & Ad. News 6176, 6330 ("A creditor . . . is subject to preference attack to the extent he improves his position during the 90-day period before bankruptcy."); *see also Missionary Baptist II,* 796 F.2d at 761. Cases that have addressed the valuation of inventory in the "improvement in position" test have repeatedly focused on value in the hands of the creditor. The bankruptcy court's adoption of a debtor perspective, by valuing inventory based upon a realization percentage to the debtor, contravenes the time-honored creditor focus of section 547(c)(5) and undermines the purposes of that provision. Thus, the courts below erred in valuing inventory from the perspective of Clark, rather than Associates. The appropriate measure of collateral value here is the net amount that could be received by Associates if, and when, it could have seized and sold the inventory.

Because we have determined that the courts below erroneously focused on the value of inventory in the hands of Clark, Associates' contention that the bankruptcy court erroneously deducted expenses of Clark unrelated to the cost of liquidation is largely rendered moot. However, we emphasize that, on remand, only costs related to a seizure and sale by Associates should be deducted in determining the value of inventory in the hands of Associates. Furthermore, in valuing inventory (or receivables) the court should consider the specific economic realities surrounding a transfer. In this connection we note that, even if the bankruptcy court's decision to value the inventory from the vantage point of the debtor had been correct, its choice of a value of 60% below cost is subject to serious question in the light of consistent record testimony to the effect that (i) the pipe market was stable during the ninety-day period, (ii) the fair market value of pipe was approximately 100% of cost, (iii) Clark actually liquidated inventory during the ninety-day period at 93-123% of cost and (v) pipe vendors were willing to give credit for returned pipe at or near 100% of cost. *See In re Ebbler Furniture and Appliances, Inc.,* 804 F.2d 87 (7th Cir. 1986), for a useful discussion of the valuation of collateral under the improvement in position test.

The parties stipulated at trial that, in the event we determined that the value of inventory from the perspective of Associates was relevant, the case should be remanded for the presentation of evidence on that point. We therefore remand for further proceedings regarding the value of inventory from the perspective of Associates.

———————

PROBLEM

23.7   In March of 2009, Dash Cashmore is approached by a friend of his, Buddy Best, who says he needs a favor. Buddy is trying to obtain a loan from Terminal Bank of Omega, Oklahoma, in connection with a business opportunity he has in that state. The loan is to be repayable in five years and Buddy is fully confident that he will easily be able to repay the loan when due, but the bank is insisting that it get some collateral to secured the loan. Buddy knows that Dash has a collection of expensive pinkie rings, both antique and contemporary, and he asks if Dash would be willing to put up this collection as collateral to secure Buddy's repayment obligation. "It's just a formality." Buddy assures Dash. "I'm not going to have any problem repaying the loan, but the bank has these rules, you know. If you are willing to do it, I'll even give you one new ring to add to your collection." Dash signs a paper under which he grants to the bank a security interest in all rings owned by him whether now owned or after acquired. The bank, after receiving this paper properly files to perfect this interest. In March of 2009, Dash receives a package containing a new ring, worth about $2,700, along with a thank-you note from Buddy. In late 2010, Dash files a petition in bankruptcy.

(a) Will the trustee be able to avoid Dash's grant of a security interest in his ring collection as a preference?
(b) Will the trustee be able to avoid this grant of a security interest as a fraudulent transfer under §548? What additional information would you need to properly answer this question?

PART V

SALES AND OTHER DISPOSITIONS
OF COLLATERAL

CHAPTER

24

Does the Interest Survive the Disposition?

A. INTRODUCTION

In this part of the materials we look at what happens if the debtor sells or otherwise disposes of all or a portion of the collateral which has been made subject to the secured party's security interest. Note that under §9-401(b) even if the debtor were to bind itself under the security agreement (as will often be the case) not to transfer the collateral to anyone else during the life of the security agreement, the transfer, while a violation of the debtor's commitment, "does not prevent the transfer from taking effect." The transfer, whether it be a sale, a gift, or whatever, will be effective. The important question to be dealt with in this chapter is whether the transferee ends up holding the property in question *free from* or still *subject to* the secured party's interest.

The default rule, as you can see in §9-201(a) and §9-315(a)(1), is that a transfer by the debtor *does not* render the security interest any less enforceable against the transferee than it would be against the original debtor. As a general rule, the property transferred "comes with" the burden of the security interest still attached. Neither the law nor practice in this area has ever come up (fortunately, in my opinion) with any term like "unattachment" or "disattachment" of a security interest. We speak instead of whether the transferee may take the property "free from" or "no longer subject to" the security interest.

One way in which the transferee may be able to get the property free from the security interest is suggested by the concluding language of §9-315(a)(1). The secured party may have "*authorized* the disposition *free of the security interest*." It is very important to appreciate that what is needed here is not just the authorization of the security party that the debtor may dispose of the collateral, but that the authorization clearly be for a disposition "free of" the secured party's interest.

How is such an express authorization obtained? In some instances, the security agreement as initially worked out by the debtor and the secured party will specify in advance those circumstance — usually, as you can imagine, those fairly restricted and carefully defined circumstances — under which the debtor is authorized to dispose of the collateral, or some part of it, free and clear of the secured party's interest. One typical example of this is that if the secured party has taken a security interest in all of the debtor's inventory the security agreement might contain a provision under which the secured party agrees in advance to the debtor's sale of a piece of its inventory to someone who fits very the character of what we will see defined in the Code as a "buyer in ordinary course of business."

In other instances the secured party's authorization to a disposition free of its interest will have to be obtained for a particular transfer at a later date, at the time of the planned disposition. The debtor, the intended transferee, or often both will come to the secured party with a proposition. If the terms are right, the secured party will agree to let go of its security interest in the property involved, and the paperwork can be completed to allow the transferee to take free-and-clear of the interest.

Other than having the clear agreement of the secured party that the disposition can take place free of its interest, the transferee may be able to take free if the situations fits within one of the statutory rules to be found in Article 9 which provide for such a disposition as a matter of law. Note that § 9-201 begins with the phrase, "Except as otherwise provided" in the Code. Section 9-315 is introduced by, "Except as otherwise provided in this article and in Section 2-403(2)." I suggest, unless your professor instructs you otherwise, not to worry about § 2-403(2) at the moment. We will have enough to deal with in this chapter considering the statutory rules in Article 9 which allow for dispositions free of established security interests.

The rules we will look at come in two places. Which rule the transferee may — and we have to stress that *may* — be able to take advantage of will depend on whether the security interest being asserted against him, her, or it, was perfected at the time of the disposition. The rule applicable to dispositions when the security interest had not been perfected is found in § 9-317(b). The two rules to which the transferee may look for aid when the security interest had been properly perfected are found in § 9-320(a) and (b).

B.   PREPARATION

In preparation for discussion of the problems and the cases in this chapter, read carefully the following parts of the Code:

- Section 9-201(a) and Comment 2 to this section
- Section 9-315(a)(1) and its Comment 2
- Section 9-317(b) and its Comment 6
- For the Code definition of "knowledge," see § 1-201(25) or § 1R-202(b)

- Section 9-320(a) through (c) and Comments 2 through 6 to this section
- The definition of "buyer in ordinary course of business" in § 1-201(9) or § 1R-201(a)(9)

C.   PROBLEMS AND CASES

PROBLEMS

24.1   Over the years Essie Cashmore has accumulated a significant collection of expensive artworks. In 2006 she arranges for a sizable loan from Discreet Financial Services, putting up her various pieces of art as collateral. The security agreement carefully lists each piece in his description of the collateral. Unfortunately, due to a slip-up by the person handling the loan for DFS, that firm never files an initial financing statement relating to its security interest. In 2008, in a moment of exuberance, Essie commits herself to donating to the Chicago Museum of Art one of her most important pieces of art, "Dog and Pony," a painting by an important early American artist. The painting is carefully transferred to the Museum, where it is hung in a position of prominence along with a small placard describing the work and noting that it was a gift to the museum from Essie. As the painting hangs in the museum is it still subject to the security interest granted to DFS by Essie?

24.2   Suppose that in 2008 Essie also sells one of her paintings, this time "Peach and Pear" by a 19th century French artist, to her neighbor, Nettie Nouveau, who has just begun to take an interest in fine art and very much wants this particular painting to start out her collection. Essie drives a hard bargain, and gets a considerable sum for the work. After the deal is concluded, does Nettie own the painting free of or subject to the security interest claimed by DFS?

(a) Assume first that, as in the previous problem, DFS had simply failed to file any initial financing statement at all in connection with its interest?
(b) What if instead DFS had filed an initial financing statement, but that the statement had given the debtor's name as Essie Cashmora?

SNOW MACHINES, INC. v. SOUTH SLOPE
DEVELOPMENT CORPORATION

Supreme Court of New York, Appellate Division, 2002
300 A.D.2d 906, 754 N.Y.S.2d 383, 50 U.C.C. Rep. Serv. 2d 613

KANE, J.: Appeal from an order of the Supreme Court (Rumsey, J.), entered March 28, 2002 in Cortland County, which granted plaintiff's motion for an order of seizure.

In October 1999, plaintiff sold three snow-making machines to Song Mountain Resort, LLC with payments due in installments. Plaintiff was to retain title to the machines as collateral until the contract was paid in full. Song Mountain defaulted on the payments, with an outstanding balance due of $51,360. In June 2001, plaintiff commenced a replevin action against Song Mountain and obtained an order of seizure from Supreme Court, permitting plaintiff to recover the machines. While attempting unsuccessfully to execute that order, plaintiff learned that Song Mountain had transferred possession of the machines to defendant, together with other real and personal property comprising the Song Mountain ski area.

Defendant had entered into a contract of sale with Tully Recreation, LLC, owner of Song Mountain, to purchase the ski resort. Although the contract was dated September 11, 2000, the sale actually closed in May 2001. In the interim, defendant and Tully entered into a master lease agreement which provided that defendant could "manage, operate and control" Song Mountain from October 1, 2000 to March 31, 2001, during which time defendant was to obtain financing. The lease agreement further provided that defendant would pay Tully monthly rent, a portion of which would apply to the purchase price if the parties closed on the sale. As additional rent, defendant was also required to pay taxes and insurance premiums on Song Mountain. By letter dated December 8, 2000, plaintiff's president informed defendant's representative of plaintiff's interest in the three snow-making machines. On May 21, 2001, the parties closed on the sale, and the snow-making machines and other personal property, as well as the realty, were transferred to defendant.

Plaintiff commenced this action against defendant seeking the return of the snow-making machines and/or full payment on the balance due. By order to show cause, plaintiff sought a prejudgment order of seizure and a temporary restraining order against defendant. Supreme Court granted the motion, prompting this appeal. Since plaintiff satisfied its burden of establishing the probability of its success on the merits in the underlying action, we find that Supreme Court properly granted plaintiff's motion for the prejudgment order of seizure.

Defendant first argues that Supreme Court improperly concluded that defendant was not a bona fide purchaser for value because defendant had notice of plaintiff's security interest before the collateral was delivered to defendant and before defendant gave value. Pursuant to UCC 9-317(b), one who purchases property in which another holds a security interest takes title free and clear of that interest, "if the buyer gives value and receives delivery of the collateral without knowledge of the security interest . . . before it is perfected." We concur with Supreme Court's finding that defendant gave value and took delivery not in September 2000 as defendant argues, but in May 2001 at the closing. Although the contract of sale permitted defendant to enter Song Mountain "for the purpose of preparing for the upcoming ski season," the contract specified that "Possession of the Premises shall be provided to Buyer at Closing," which clearly contemplated that possession under the contract of sale would remain with the seller. Alternatively, defendant contends that it received delivery under UCC 9-317(b) when it gained the ability "to manage, operate and control" Song Mountain pursuant to the parties' lease agreement. However, as Supreme Court properly noted, when defendant took possession of the property in September 2000, it did not do so pursuant to the contract of sale but, rather, pursuant to the lease agreement and, thus, defendant was a lessee, not a buyer.

Nor do we subscribe to defendant's reasoning that since rent payments were applied to the ultimate purchase price and insurance premiums had to be maintained, the lease payments were, in effect, installment payments of the purchase price. Clearly, the parties manifested no intention for the lease agreement to operate as a purchase agreement. Significantly, the lease agreement did not give defendant title rights to any of the items of personal property located on the premises or to the premises itself; all title remained in the seller, Tully, until it was transferred at the closing in May 2001. Thus, although UCC 1-201(14) provides that "delivery" refers to a voluntary transfer of possession, Supreme Court properly concluded that to benefit under UCC 9-317(b), such transfer of possession must "be clearly referable to the ultimate purchase" and not, as here, to a grant of temporary possession under a lease agreement.

Next, we reject defendant's argument that it paid value by making a down payment on the property on September 11, 2000 pursuant to the parties' purchase agreement, and made several installment payments, based on the parties' lease agreement, between October 2000 and December 2000 prior to learning of plaintiff's security interest. Defendant's reliance on UCC 1-201(44) [of prerevision Article 1, now in § 1R-204], which provides that value is given "(c) by accepting delivery pursuant to a pre-existing contract for purchase; or (d) generally, in return for any consideration sufficient to support a simple contract," is misplaced. Here, defendant had not accepted delivery pursuant to the contract before it learned of plaintiff's security interest. Further, the down payment made by defendant was not applied to the contract price, but was to be refunded to defendant when the full contract price was paid. The taxes and insurance premiums that defendant paid to Song Mountain prior to closing were not applied to the actual purchase price but, rather, were denominated "additional rent" under the lease.

Contrary to defendant's argument, plaintiff was not required to perfect its security interest in order to give it effect. Indisputedly, plaintiff's security interest was not perfected at any time prior to May 2001, but a security interest may be enforceable even in the absence of perfection (see UCC 9-203(a)). Despite defendant's contention that it believed plaintiff's interest either did not exist or that the matter had been resolved, and that plaintiff did not file to perfect its interest, defendant had actual knowledge of plaintiff's interest based on the December 2000 letter that it received from plaintiff's representative. Defendant, having become aware of plaintiff's prior interest in the machines, had a responsibility to ensure that the interest no longer existed at the time of closing in May 2001 or bear the risk of purchasing the property without doing so. Significantly, the seller's obligation under the contract to deliver the property free of encumbrances was an obligation effective at closing of title and not on delivery of the property under the lease. With respect to the snow-making machines, defendant, at closing, had the option of paying plaintiff's claim and deducting the sum from the purchase price as well as other remedies.

ORDERED that the order is affirmed, without costs.

PROBLEM

24.3 Sarah is the major shareholder and President of a corporation, Stuff, Incorporated. This corporation operates a chain of stores under the name "Sarah's Sells-U-Stuff," each of which offers a wide range of audio, video, and computer equipment, as well as other more mundane household appliances, for sale. For several years the corporation has operated with the benefit of a loan from Fortress America Bank, which has taken and properly perfected on an interest in all of the corporation's "inventory, now held or hereafter acquired." Ben comes into one of the corporation's stores, looking to buy a new DVD player, the old one in his apartment just having broken down irretrievably. He quickly finds a model he wants and buys it, paying for his purchase with a credit card. He takes the DVD player home and plugs it into his elaborate home entertainment system.

(a) Does the DVD player now in Ben's home remain subject to a security interest held by Fortress America Bank?

(b) Would your answer to the question be changed if it were to turn out that Ben, who just happens to be a paralegal in the law firm which does all the legal work for Stuff, Incorporated, was aware that the corporation had put up all of its inventory as collateral in connection with a financing arranged with Fortress America Bank?

INTERNATIONAL HARVESTER CO. v. GLENDENNING

Court of Civil Appeals of Texas, 1974
505 S.W.2d 320, 87 A.L.R.3d 1, 14 U.C.C. Rep. Serv. 837

CLAUDE WILLIAMS, C.J.: This appeal is from a take nothing judgment in a suit to recover damages for wrongful conversion of three tractors.

International Harvester Company and International Harvester Credit Corporation (both hereinafter referred to as International) brought this action against Don Glendenning in which it was alleged that International was the holder of a duly perfected security interest in three new International Harvester tractors; that such security agreements had been executed in favor of International by Jack L. Barnes, doing business as Barnes Equipment Company, an International Harvester dealer; that Barnes and

Glendenning had entered into a fraudulent conspiracy wherein Glendenning had wrongfully purchased the three tractors from Barnes; that Glendenning was not a buyer in the ordinary course of business; that he did not act in a commercially reasonable manner and did not act honestly, therefore taking the tractors subject to International's security interest. It was further alleged that Barnes and Glendenning had wrongfully conspired to convert the ownership of the tractors and to deprive International, by fraud and deceit, of its ownership of the tractors by virtue of their security interest therein in that (1) Glendenning acquiesced in falsifying a retail order form so that it was made to indicate receipt of $16,000 in cash and the trade-in of two used tractors allegedly worth a total of $8,700, while in fact both Glendenning and Barnes knew that Glendenning had only paid the sum of $16,000 in cash, a sum far below the market value of the tractors; (2) that Glendenning, in the furtherance of the conspiracy and unlawful conversion, represented to a representative of International that he, Glendenning, had, in fact, traded certain used tractors to Barnes, which was untrue; and (3) Glendenning removed the new tractors in which International had a security interest to the State of Louisiana where he sold the same and converted the proceeds to his own use and benefit. International sought damages in the sum of $24,049.99 which was alleged to be the reasonable value of the tractors on the date of conversion.

Glendenning answered by a general denial and with the special defense to the effect that he purchased the tractors in the ordinary course of business and that such purchase was made in good faith and without any knowledge of any security interest held by International. The only issue before the court was whether Glendenning was a buyer of the tractors in the ordinary course of business as that term is defined in the Texas Business and Commerce Code.

The court submitted the case to the jury on one special issue: Do you find from a preponderance of the evidence that on the time and occasion in question, the defendant, Don Glendenning, was a buyer in the ordinary course of business?

In connection with this issue the court instructed the jury that the term "buyer in ordinary course of business" means "a person who in good faith and without knowledge that the sale to him is in violation of the ownership rights or security interest of the third party in the goods buys in the ordinary course from a person in the business of selling goods of that kind."

The court instructed the jury that by the term "good faith" means "honesty in fact in the conduct or transaction concerned." [The trial court was, of course, quoting from the prerevision version of Article 1.] The jury answered the special issue "Yes."

Prior to the submission of the issue to the jury International had timely filed its motion for an instructed verdict in which it contended that there was no evidence of probative force to justify the submission of any issue to the jury and that it should recover, as prayed for. Subsequent to the receipt of the jury verdict International filed its motion for judgment *non obstante veredicto* in which it contended that there was no evidence of probative force to support the affirmative answer of the jury to the sole special issue submitted and that such answer should be disregarded and judgment rendered for the amount pleaded. These motions were overruled and judgment was rendered that International take nothing.

In twenty-five points of error, appellants primarily seek a reversal and rendition of this judgment. However, we have concluded that the main thrust of appellants' contentions is contained in points 1, 4, 6, 7, 10, 11, and 12 in which it is asserted that there is no evidence of probative force to support the answer of the jury to the sole special issue submitted and that the motion for judgment *non obstante veredicto* should have been sustained because the evidence conclusively establishes, as a matter of law, that Glendenning was not a purchaser in the ordinary course of business as defined by the court. We sustain these points and reverse and render the judgment.

The applicable law is found in Texas Business and Commerce Code Annotated (Vernon 1968). Section 9.307 of the code [the precursor to current §9-320(a)] entitled "Protection of Buyers of Goods" provides that "(a) a buyer in ordinary course of business . . . takes free of a security interest created by his seller even though the security interest is perfected and even though the buyer knows of its existence."

Section 1.201(9) of the code, [defines a buyer in ordinary course of business as]: "[A] person who in good faith and without knowledge that the sale to him is in violation of the ownership rights or security interest of a third party in the goods buys in ordinary course from a person in the business of selling goods of that kind but does not include a pawnbroker."

Section 1.201(19) of the code defines "good faith" as being: ". . . honesty in fact in the conduct or transaction concerned."

With these rules in mind we turn to a resolution of the law question presented, that is, whether there is any evidence of probative force to sustain the answer of the jury to the special issue submitted. Our determination of the question is governed by the well established rule that we must consider only the evidence which supports the jury verdict, rejecting all evidence and inferences to the contrary. Our supreme court in *Associates Discount Corporation v. Rattan Chevrolet, Inc.*, 462 S.W.2d 546 (Tex. 1970), stated that the question of whether a sale is in the ordinary course of business is a mixed question of law and fact and that such question cannot be resolved without viewing all of the circumstances surrounding the sale. We have examined the record in the light of these rules. The material testimony presented to the court and jury may be summarized, as follows:

At the time of the trial of this case appellee Glendenning was a farmer in Collin County. He described himself as being not only a farmer but a trader. He said that he frequently traded tractors and other farm equipment as well as anything else from which he could make a profit. He has had almost twenty years' experience in the business of buying and selling farm tractors. In the early 1950's he owned an International Harvester dealership in Frisco, Collin County, Texas. From 1956 to 1960 he was a salesman for

International Harvester. After leaving International he began trading farm equipment of his own, using some of the implements on his own farm and holding others strictly for resale. For many years he had been familiar with International Harvester's custom of "floor-planning" tractors and other farm equipment. By this plan International would supply tractors and other equipment to the dealers who, in turn, would give International a note and security agreement to protect International in its investment. When a dealer sold a piece of equipment from the floor he would pay International the amount due. He also testified that he knew that when used tractors were taken as trade-ins by International Harvester dealers such used tractors were also mortgaged or covered by the security agreement to International. He admitted that International Harvester always kept close tabs to see what was wrong with the used tractors and that International always wanted to know what its dealers traded for in connection with new equipment sales. Glendenning acknowledged that any false information contained on a retail order form would provide incorrect information concerning the transaction to International Harvester, or any other lender.

Glendenning said that he had known Jack L. Barnes, an International Harvester dealer, for two or three years and during that time he had bought several tractors from him. In the early part of July 1971 Barnes, and Joe Willard, another friend, came to his home in Collin County and talked to him about buying some tractors. He said that Barnes had eight tractors to sell but that he was only interested in buying three of the machines. Barnes described the tractors and told Glendenning that he wanted $18,500 for the three. Glendenning declined that offer but told Barnes that he would give $16,000 cash for the three. Barnes accepted the offer.

At the time of this transaction Glendenning knew that the three tractors were reasonably worth $22,500. Willard went to Vernon, Texas, and got the tractors and delivered them to Mr. Glendenning's home. Glendenning asked Willard to bring him a bill of sale when he returned with the tractors. Willard received from Barnes an instrument entitled "Retail Order Form" dated July 5, 1971, which recited that Glendenning had purchased from Barnes three tractors for the total price of $24,700 with a cash payment of $16,000 leaving a balance of $8,700. The instrument recited that Glendenning had traded in four tractors with values totaling $8,700 so that the total consideration of $24,700 was shown to have been paid.

Glendenning said that the next day Barnes came to his home to get payment for the tractors. At that time Glendenning requested a "bill of sale" and he watched Barnes fill in another retail order form similar to the one that he had obtained from Willard the day before. This order form stated that Glendenning had traded in four tractors worth $8,700 in addition to payment of $16,000 in cash making a total purchase price of $24,700. After Barnes had completed filling out this form and signed the same Glendenning said that he put his signature on the instrument also. He then gave Barnes $16,000.

Concerning the contents of the retail order form Glendenning said that at the time Barnes filled in the blanks indicating that Glendenning was trading in four tractors he knew that he was not trading anything and that he did not question Barnes about the trade-in information contained in the form. He admitted that he did not ask Barnes whether the tractors which he purchased were free and clear nor did he call International to determine whether or not such company had a mortgage on the tractors. Glendenning admitted that he knew that the information contained in the printed form concerning trade-ins and total consideration for the sale of the three new tractors was false; that he knew of this falsification when he signed the order form; and that he also knew that such falsification would mislead any creditors relying on the document such as a dealer, a manufacturer or a bank lending money with the equipment as collateral. He admitted that at the time of the transaction in question Barnes was probably "trying to come out even" or that he did it to make his books balance. Glendenning admitted that he was suspicious of the manner in which Barnes prepared the order form and confessed that his actions amounted to dishonesty. He said that to his knowledge he had never before signed an order form with false trade-ins. He admitted that such action was "unusual."

A few days after the transaction a Mr. McKinney, collection manager for International Harvester Company, and a representative of International Harvester Credit Corporation, telephoned Glendenning concerning the transaction in question. In that conversation Glendenning told McKinney that he had traded four tractors to Barnes in addition to paying $16,000 cash for the three new International tractors. Glendenning testified that he knew that he had lied to Mr. McKinney concerning the trade-ins and that such oral misrepresentation or lie was dishonest.

After receiving the tractors Glendenning removed them to a barn near Alexandria, Louisiana, although it was his usual practice to place equipment on his own premises or at another dealer's place of business. He subsequently sold the three tractors in Louisiana.

As a part of his direct examination Glendenning testified that he considered the deal to be a purchase of three tractors for $16,000; that he had no side agreement with Barnes; that he thought he was making a good deal; and that he was acting in good faith.

At the very beginning of this trial appellee Glendenning confessed the validity of appellants' cause of action against him based upon fraud, conspiracy and conversion, but sought to evade legal liability by assuming, the burden of going forward and establishing his sole defense that he was a buyer in ordinary course of business within the meaning of § 9-307(a). This assumption carried with it the additional burden of establishing by competent evidence that Glendenning acted in good faith and without knowledge that the sale to him was in violation of the ownership rights or security interest of a third party. Good faith, as the court correctly charged the jury, means honesty in fact in the conduct or transaction concerned. In an effort to establish this affirmative defense and thereby evade liability, appellee Glendenning testified on direct examination with the broad conclusory statement that he had acted in good faith. However, this subjective and conclusory statement was immediately annihilated by factual evidence falling from the lips of Glendenning himself.

Appellee Glendenning's own testimony immediately removes him from the category of an innocent Collin County farmer who seeks to purchase one or more tractors in the ordinary course of business. By his own testimony he has had many years of experience as a tractor dealer, a salesman and one of the most active traders of farm equipment in Collin County. Based upon this experience he is knowledgeable in the very nature of business done by International by "floor-planning" its equipment. With all of this knowledge and information in his possession he purchased the equipment for considerably less than its value, made no investigation of International's security interest, acquiesced in the falsification of the retail order form showing nonexistent trade-ins, and misrepresented the particulars of the transaction to International's representative by stating that there were, in fact, trade-ins. He confesses that his actions were dishonest.

Thus it is evident to us that Glendenning's own testimony, which is the only material testimony offered, is entirely devoid of honesty in fact and completely negates his contention that he was a buyer in the ordinary course of business within the meaning of the Texas Business & Commerce Code.

The complete picture revealed by all of the material testimony in this case reveals a definite pattern of lies, deceit, dishonesty and bad faith. We find no competent evidence in this record to support the jury's answer to the special issue submitted and therefore the same should have been set aside and disregarded by the trial court.

We find it unnecessary to pass upon the remaining points presented in appellants' brief. The judgment of the trial court is reversed and judgment is here rendered that International Harvester Company and International Harvester Credit Corporation do have and recover of and from Don Glendenning the sum of $24,049.99 together with interest thereon at the rate of 6 per cent from date of this judgment until paid.

Reversed and rendered.

QUESTION ON INTERNATIONAL HARVESTER

This case was, as you saw, decided at a time when the definition of "good faith" applicable to the situation was still the total subjective standard requiring only "honesty in fact." Do you see any reason to think the case would come out differently today under the current Article 9 definition of good faith or the definition as now found in most states' version of Revised Article 1?

PROBLEMS

24.4 We return to the situation of Problem 23.3, with Sarah, her corporation, and her chain of appliance stores. One day Sarah is visited in the office she keeps in one of the stores by one Allen Advert, who is the owner of a local advertizing agency that has recently done a considerable amount of work for Sarah's company. Advert has come to see Sarah about a bill for his services which he sent her some time ago, but which has not been paid. Sarah explains that at the moment she is suffering a bit of a "cash-flow problem," but that she expects she'll have no problem paying Advert's bill after the upcoming holiday season, when her sales can be expected to pick up considerably. Advert does not seem terribly satisfied by this reply. Sarah then says, "Tell you what. Instead of paying you in cash, why don't you take it in some of the stuff I have right here in the store?" Taking Advert out to the sales floor, she points to one elaborate wide-screen TV which is marked as having a sale price some $200 greater than the amount she acknowledges Advert is owed for his work and which he has billed her for. "How about you take one of those in payment?" she suggests to Advert. After some thought, Advert agrees to the deal. By the end of the week, the wide-screen TV has been delivered to and set up in the den of Advert's home. Recalling that Fortress America bank has a perfected security interest in all of the Stuff Incorporated's inventory, is that bank's interest still attached to the TV in Advert's den?

24.5 Arnie's Bagel Bakery maintains an operating loan from First Bank of Brooklyn under an agreement in which it has granted to the bank a security interest in all of its equipment. The bank has properly filed on its interest and kept its filing effective. In the process of remodeling, Arnie sells one particularly large oven unit to Gabriela, who is to use it in her restaurant, Gabriela's Place.

(a) Does Gabriela take the oven free from the security interest held by First Bank of Brooklyn?

(b) What if, in order to buy the oven, Gabriela had obtained a loan from Staten Island Federal Bank and had granted that bank a valid purchase-money interest in the oven? Which bank's interest has priority? To work this one out, look back at §9-322(a)(1) and §9-324(a). Also consider §9-325.

24.6 Suppose that in the prior problem Arnie's Bagel Bakery had sold the used oven not to Gabriela but to Heatum's Cooking Equipment, a firm which buys and sells used professional-grade kitchen appliances of the type used in restaurants and others in the food-preparation industry. Heatum's then resells this oven to Gabriela. Under this set of facts, does Gabriela take the oven free from the security interest held by First Bank of Brooklyn?

24.7 Melody Davies, who works in the book publishing business, enjoys playing the piano in her spare time. She arranges to buy a particularly good grand piano from The Music Emporium, a store in her area that sells a wide variety of musical instruments. The price of the piano is $18,000. Melody pays $2,000 as a down payment and enters into a retail sales installment agreement drawn up by the store under which she agrees to pay the remainder of the price, along with specified interest charges, in 36 monthly payments over the next three years. Under this agreement, she also agrees that the store will retain a security interest in the piano until her final payment is made. The piano is delivered to her house in 2008. The store makes no filing with respect to this transaction. Only a few months after her purchase, Melody finds herself burdened by other unanticipated expenses. She decides that it simply is not reasonable for her to keep the piano (and, of course, the monthly payments) under the circumstances. She quickly arranges to sell the piano to a friend, Eric, who will take it for his own personal use. Eric pays $17,500 to Melody for the piano and arranges to have it picked up and delivered to his house.

(a) Is the piano now residing in Eric's home subject to any security interest that could be claimed by The Music Emporium?
(b) Would you answer to this question be any different if The Music Emporium had filed an initial financing statement, proper in all respects and with the correct filing office, when it sold the piano to Melody on credit?
(c) How would you analyze the situation if The Music Emporium had not filed anything when it sold to Melody, as we initially hypothesized, but the reason Eric was buying the piano was to use in his business of giving piano lessons?

24.8 Farmer Jebediah Tillers, who resides in northern South Dakota, owns a large patch of land in southern North Dakota on which he regularly plants wheat. For as many years as he can remember Tillers has, as did his father before him, contracted to sell his entire annual harvest of wheat at a price per bushel (negotiated just prior to that year's harvest) to Heartland Commodities, Incorporated, a major purchaser of grain crops in the area. Can Heartland rest easy that the wheat it purchases from Tillers will not be subject to any security interest Tillers may have previously granted to a lender in the crop because it, Heartland, would qualify as a buyer in ordinary course of business? If not, what precautions should Heartland take to be sure that the wheat that it buys from Tillers will be free of any such interest? See the following case.

FIN AG, INC. v. HUFNAGLE, INC.

Supreme Court of Minnesota, 2006
720 N.W.2d 579, 60 U.C.C. Rep. Serv. 2d 629

HANSON, Justice: This case concerns the impact of grain "fronting" on the respective rights of buyers of farm products and those who hold a security interest in those products. The security interest holder, respondent Fin Ag, Inc., brought suit against the buyer, appellant Kent Meschke Poultry Farms, Inc. (Meschke), for conversion of corn grown by the debtors, Larry and Ronda Buck, doing business as Buck Farms (Buck). The corn had been sold to Meschke in the names of third persons not involved with the debt to Fin Ag. The district court granted summary judgment to Fin Ag, holding that, under 7 U.S.C. § 1631 (2000) — enacted as part of the federal Food Security Act of 1985 (FSA) — the registration of Fin Ag's security interest in Buck's name put Meschke on notice of the interest and that the appearance of third persons as the sellers did not protect Meschke from the security interest created by Buck. The court of appeals affirmed, holding that Buck had constructive possession of the corn and Meschke had constructive knowledge of the security interest against Buck's corn. Meschke sought further review, arguing that section 1631 requires actual, not constructive, possession or knowledge and that a buyer from a disclosed seller takes title free of a security interest that is in the name of an undisclosed owner. We affirm.

A. THE STATUTORY FRAMEWORK

To develop a proper framework for the analysis of this case, we must consider the interaction between the state and federal statutes that address the conflict between the rights of buyers of farm products and the rights of those who hold a security interest in those farm products. Because the Minnesota statutes governing security interests in farm products have been revised from time to time, it is helpful to first consider what that interaction was when Congress first enacted 7 U.S.C. § 1631 in response to perceived shortcomings in the Uniform Commercial Code (UCC).

Prior to 1985, the UCC generally reflected a policy that favored the rights of the holders of security interests, presumably to promote the availability of credit on reasonable terms. Thus, UCC section 9-201 [the Court here and throughout, unless otherwise noted, is citing Article 9 prior to its most recent revision] recognized that "a security agreement is effective according to its terms between the parties, against purchasers of the collateral and against creditors." U.C.C. § 9-201 (1972). And the general rule embodied in UCC section 9-306 was that a security interest in goods continues despite the sale of those goods by the debtor. U.C.C. § 9-306 (1972). That general rule was subject to an exception under UCC section 9-307, where a "buyer in the ordinary course of business" could take the goods free of some security interests, but only those that were "created by his seller." U.C.C. § 9-307 (1972). But that exception did not apply to buyers of "farm products." Thus, the UCC protected buyers in the ordinary course of business only from security interests created by the buyer's seller; and buyers of farm products were excluded from even this narrow protection.

[The Court adds in a footnote: Although the Commissioners on Uniform State Laws modified Article 9 in 2000, the only relevant change to section 9-307(1) was to renumber it as section 9-320(a). Prior to the passage of the FSA, Minnesota followed the recommended uniform provisions by adopting the general rule that security interests continue in the goods after they are sold, providing an exception for buyers in the ordinary course, and excluding buyers of farm products from that exception. *See* Minn. Stat. §§ 336.9-306, 336.9-307 (1984). In 2001, Minnesota renumbered the buyer in the ordinary course of business exception to be Minn. Stat. § 336.9-320(a) (2004), following the 2000 changes to the UCC.]

The practical effect of the exclusion of farm products from UCC section 9-307 was that buyers of farm products became guarantors of their seller's debt. As a result, more than a third of the states amended UCC section 9-307 in various ways, generally attempting to reduce the bias in favor of lenders by providing mechanisms that would assist buyers in protecting their interests. Charles W. Wolfe, *Section 1324 of the Food Security Act of 1985: Congress Preempts the "Farm Products Exception" of Section 9-307(1) of the Uniform Commercial Code,* 55 UMKC L. Rev. 454, 461-64 (1987). The various state amendments were not consistent with one another and diluted the uniformity goals of the UCC. Wolfe, *supra,* at 455, 461-64.

Congress became concerned with the impact of the UCC on buyers of farm products and with the inconsistent amendments to UCC section 9-307 by many states. Often, buyers of farm products did not know of a security interest or have any practical way to discover it and thus were required to pay twice for the product — once to the seller and a second time to the security holder if the seller defaulted on the debt. *See* 7 U.S.C. § 1631(a). To address this situation, Congress in 1985 enacted 7 U.S.C. § 1631 (titled "Protection for purchasers of farm products"). Where it applies, section 1631 preempts all conflicting state laws. *See* 7 U.S.C. § 1631(d) (prefacing the statutory rule by stating "notwithstanding any other provision of Federal, State, or local law").

The title and congressional findings of section 1631 suggest that it was intended to protect buyers of farm products from having to make "double payment for the products, once at the time of purchase, and again when the seller fails to repay the lender." 7 U.S.C. § 1631(a)(2). But the protection actually provided by section 1631 was not as sweeping as the statement of intent might suggest. As explained below, section 1631 did not provide that the buyer would take free of all security interests, but instead only established a notice system that provided a mechanism for buyers to protect themselves from some, but not all, security interests.

Section 1631 established, contrary to the UCC, that a buyer of farm products in the ordinary course of business takes free of security interests created by the seller. Section 1631(d) provides:

> Except as provided in subsection (e) of this section and notwithstanding any other provision of Federal, State, or local law, a buyer who in the ordinary course of business buys a farm product from a seller engaged in farming operations *shall take free of a security interest created by the seller,* even though the security interest is perfected; and the buyer knows of the existence of such interest.

7 U.S.C. § 1631(d) (emphasis added). Notably, section 1631(d) adopted the same narrow scope of protection as provided in section 9-307 [and now, in revised section 9-320] of the UCC—it only provides protection against a security interest "created by the seller." Therefore, this language provides no protection for a buyer of farm products from any valid security interest that was created by someone other than the immediate seller.

The federal statute does provide exceptions to section 1631(d). Under these exceptions a buyer of farm products takes subject to a security interest created by the seller when notice has been given by one of three specified notice procedures. Two of the notice procedures apply where states have established central filing systems to provide notice to registered farm product buyers.

Minnesota created such a central filing system in 1992. Under Minnesota's system, a lender is authorized to register the security interest with the Secretary of State by filing an "effective financing statement." The Secretary of State compiles a list of debtors whose farm products are subject to security interests and makes this list available to registered farm products dealers and to others on request. Minn. Stat. § 336A.08 (2004). Before purchasing farm products, a buyer is expected to check the list. Cf. 7 U.S.C. § 1631(e)(2, 3).

To summarize, under 7 U.S.C. § 1631 a buyer of farm products in the ordinary course of business (1) takes free of security interests created by the seller, unless notice of the seller-created security interest has been given by one of three specific notice procedures, which include the Minnesota central filing system provided under chapter 336A; but (2) takes subject to security interests created by someone other than the seller.

B.   THE SUMMARY JUDGMENT RECORD

With this legal framework in mind, we turn to the undisputed facts in this record. In 1999, Fin Ag made an operating loan of $249,995 to Buck. As collateral for this loan, Buck granted Fin Ag a security interest in Buck's corn crops for 1999. Fin Ag filed UCC financing statements in Hubbard and Wadena Counties (where the crops were grown), but not in Itasca County (where the Bucks resided). Fin Ag also filed an "effective financing statement" with the Minnesota Secretary of State, which caused the security interest to be listed in Minnesota's central filing system.

Meschke purchased several loads of corn that were produced by Buck. Because Meschke is a registered farm products dealer, he received an electronic copy of Minnesota's listing from the central filing system of sellers whose grain is subject to security interests. Meschke learned from the central filing system that Buck's corn was subject to a security interest held by Fin Ag. When Meschke bought corn directly from Buck, he generally included Fin Ag's name on the check. But twice Meschke bought corn directly from Buck without making the check payable to both Buck and Fin Ag; the amount of these sales was $7,129.24. Meschke does not dispute Fin Ag's claims with regard to these two payments.

Meschke was also offered corn by persons who claimed that the sellers were, variously, Mark Tooker, Mickey Buck, Paul Zuk, and Ryan Buck (collectively the Tookers). [The Court notes: Mark Tooker and Paul Zuk were employees of the Bucks. The parties agree that Mickey and Ryan Buck were Ronda and Larry Buck's minor children.] The Tookers were not listed in the central filing as having corn that was subject to any security interest. Meschke made payment for this corn solely in the names of the Tookers. Meschke bought corn from the Tookers on seven separate occasions and paid a total of $38,443.85. Each of the checks to the Tookers was subsequently deposited into Buck's bank account but was not applied to Buck's debt to Fin Ag.

When Buck failed to repay the Fin Ag loan, Fin Ag sued Meschke for conversion of Fin Ag's collateral in the corn that was involved in the Tooker sales and the two Buck sales. Fin Ag moved for summary judgment against Meschke. Meschke opposed the motion, arguing that he was entitled to take the corn free of Fin Ag's security interest under 7 U.S.C. § 1631 because he did not receive notice of Fin Ag's security interest when he checked the central filing system for the names of the Tookers. The district court granted summary judgment in favor of Fin Ag, awarding damages for the seven Tooker sales and two Buck sales in the amount of $45,573.09, plus costs and interest. The court of appeals affirmed, and we granted Meschke's petition for review.

I

The record submitted in connection with Fin Ag's motion for summary judgment does not fully explain the circumstance under which the Tookers became involved with the sales to Meschke. Conceivably, the Tookers could have been involved in any one of three capacities: (1) as agents selling on behalf of Buck as an undisclosed principal; (2) as "commission merchants" or "selling agents," defined terms under 7 U.S.C. § 1631(c)(3, 8) (2000); or (3) as owners of the corn, selling on their own behalf. Although there may be genuine issues of fact concerning which of those three capacities applies to the sales to Meschke, Fin Ag argues that those issues of fact are not material, and do not preclude summary judgment, because Meschke would take the corn subject to Fin Ag's security interest under each of these alternative capacities.

Fin Ag's argument requires us to consider how section 1631 works in the situation of "fronting" sales. The parties describe "fronting" as being where a seller of farm products that are subject to a security interest has a third party sell them under the third party's name. Here, Meschke bought the corn from the Tookers and, when Meschke checked the central filing system, he found no security interests listed in the Tookers' names. As a result, both Meschke and Fin Ag can be viewed as innocent parties in the sense that they each did everything they were required or expected to do under the FSA.

Meschke advances several policy-based arguments that emphasize how difficult it is for a buyer of farm products to discover a security interest in a fronting situation. We recognize that difficulty, but we are constrained to apply the plain language of the statutes, as enacted by Congress and the Minnesota Legislature, and to follow where they lead. The difficulty with those statutes, as highlighted earlier, is that the protection for the buyer is narrowly limited by the clause "created by the seller."

The presence of this limitation in UCC section 9-307 has received much criticism, both from the courts and scholars. Yet, all efforts to eliminate or amend this clause have failed since the UCC was rewritten in 1957. *See* Richard H. Nowka, *Section 9-302(a) of Reviewed Article 9 and The Buyer in the Ordinary Course of Pre-Encumbered Goods: Something Old and Something New*, 38 Brandeis L.J. 9, 23-24 (1999-2000). And, as noted, Congress essentially incorporated this clause in section 1631 when it attempted to correct some of the other shortcomings, from the perspective of buyers, of UCC section 9-307.

Neither Congress nor the Commissioners on Uniform State Laws have enunciated a policy reason for this clause. But the Official Comment to section 9-320, when revised and renumbered in 2000, makes it clear that the "created by the buyer's seller" clause is a serious limitation on the rights of buyers in the ordinary course of business, citing this example:

> Manufacturer, who is in the business of manufacturing appliances, owns manufacturing equipment subject to the perfected security interest in favor of Lender. Manufacturer sells the equipment to Dealer, who is in the business of buying and selling used equipment. Buyer buys the equipment from Dealer. Even if Buyer qualifies as a buyer in the ordinary course of business, Buyer does not take free of Lender's security interest under subsection (a) [of section 9-320], because Dealer did not create the security interest; Manufacturer did.

U.C.C. § 9-320, official cmt. 3 (2000).

The inclusion of the "created by the seller" clause in section 1631 means that the statute does not provide protection for buyers in a fronting situation where the security interest from which protection is sought was not created by the fronting parties. Under the facts of this case, no matter what factual assumptions we make, there are none under which Meschke could take the corn free of Fin Ag's security interest. This is because if we view Buck as the seller, we must conclude that Meschke's rights are subject to Fin Ag's security interest under section 1631 because Fin Ag filed an "effective financing statement" that put Meschke on notice of Fin Ag's security interest in Buck's products. And, if we view the Tookers as the sellers, we must conclude that Meschke's rights are subject to Fin Ag's security interest, under either section 1631 or Minnesota's UCC, because both statutes only protect a buyer from a security interest created by the seller and not from a security interest created by an undisclosed owner, which continues in the product despite the sale.

II

We first analyze the transactions under 7 U.S.C. § 1631. As noted, the rule under section 1631 is that a qualified buyer takes free of a security interest "created by the seller." 7 U.S.C. § 1631(d). Thus, the first question is who was Meschke's "seller." Section 1631 does not define "seller." Under our facts, Meschke's "seller" could be either Buck (as the undisclosed principal of the sale) or the Tookers (as those who were identified as the sellers when the transactions occurred). But we need not resolve that ambiguity because neither alternative would allow Meschke to take the corn free of Fin Ag's security interest under section 1631.

The court of appeals treated Buck as the seller, concluding that Buck had constructive possession of the corn and Meschke had constructive knowledge of Fin Ag's security interest in Buck's corn. We doubt that constructive notice or constructive knowledge are viable concepts under section 1631, but we need not reach that issue. If we consider the application of section 1631 under each alternative — with either Buck as the seller or the Tookers as the sellers — we come to the same conclusion.

If we view Buck as the seller, assuming that the Tookers sold the corn as agents for Buck as an undisclosed principal, the exception in section 1631(e) for a security interest as to which notice has been given would apply because Meschke received notice of Fin Ag's interest against Buck, and Meschke did not secure a waiver of the interest from Fin Ag. See 7 U.S.C. § 1631(e)(3). Accordingly, Meschke's interest in the corn would be subject to Fin Ag's security interest.

If we treat the Tookers as the sellers, assuming that the Tookers sold the corn on their own behalf, we need to consider whether they sold the corn as a "commission merchant" or as "selling agents," as defined by section 1631, or as owners, having taken title to the corn (by purchase or gift).

If the Tookers sold the corn as "commission merchants" or as "selling agents," section 1631 provides that such a merchant or agent is subject to the security interest created by the seller if the "commission merchant or selling agent has failed to register with the Secretary of State" and the "secured party has filed an effective financing statement that covers the farm products being sold" in a state that has a central filing system. 7 U.S.C. § 1631(g)(2)(C) [In a footnote: A "commission merchant" is defined as "any person engaged in the business of receiving any farm product for sale or commission, or for or on behalf of another person." 7 U.S.C. § 1631(c)(3) (2002). A "selling agent" is defined as "any person, other than a commission merchant, who is engaged in the business of negotiating the sale and purchase of any farm product on behalf of a person engaged in farming operations." 7 U.S.C. § 1631(c)(8) (2002). The Tookers could qualify as one or the other, depending on the terms under which they made the sale for Buck, if they were in the business of making/receiving products for sale, or of making such a sale.] There is no evidence that the Tookers registered as commission merchants or as selling agents.

If the Tookers took title to the corn and sold to Meschke on their own behalf, they would have taken title subject to Fin Ag's security interest because Fin Ag filed an effective financing statement with the Secretary of State and there is no evidence that the Tookers registered with the Secretary of State. And if the Tookers took title to the grain subject to Fin Ag's security interest, their sale to Meschke would only be free of any security interest created by the Tookers, and would be subject to Fin Ag's security interest because it was created by Buck.

Thus, if the transaction is governed by section 1631 and we consider all of the factual scenarios possible on this record, we must conclude that Meschke took the corn subject to Fin Ag's security interest.

The only other possible analysis that could be made is to assume that the transfer of possession by Buck to the Tookers transformed the corn from a "farm product," covered by section 1631, to "inventory," not covered by section 1631. Because that analysis is not made under section 1631, we will discuss it under the analysis of the UCC below. [The court concludes the result would be no different as the applicable UCC provision includes the "created by the seller" criterion just as does the FSA.]

Affirmed.

NOTE ON THE FOOD SECURITY ACT OF 1985

Under current § 9-320(a), as under its predecessor section in the earlier versions of Article 9, the rule that someone who qualifies as a buyer in the ordinary course takes free of any security interest created by the seller even if knowing of the existence of that interest does not apply when the buyer is a "person buying farm products from a person engaged in farming operations." The standard explanation for what is often dubbed this "farm products exception" is, as the court in the *Fin Ag* case notes, that it furthers the goal of making credit on reasonable terms more available to farmers than would otherwise be the case. Why is this? The distinction is often made between the typical sale to a buyer in the ordinary course — by a manufacturer, a distributor, or retailer out of its inventory — where each sale is usual of only one small part of the designated collateral, "all inventory, now held or hereafter acquired" and the typical sale by a farmer of his or her entire crop at one time and in one large transaction. In a sale out of inventory, the secured party may lose its interest in the one item or the small subset of the collateral that is being sold, but it retains an interest in all the inventory that is left, and in fact its interest will, it is assumed, soon attach to more inventory as it is subsequently acquired by the debtor. This is in some sense what makes possible the financing arrangement known as the floating lien in inventory and justifies the rules found in Article 9 which facilitate such an arrangement. Under this arrangement it is also contemplated that the lender will get paid in regular payments throughout the year, either in monthly installments or, in some instances, in individual payments that the debtor is obligated to make as each individual piece of inventory is sold off.

Lending to a farmer on the basis of his or her crops in thought to subject the lender to a different level of risk. The lender who takes an interest in a farmer's crop will usually expect to be paid off in one large lump sum out of the one even larger lump sum payment the farmer gets for selling off its entire crop to a buyer of agricultural commodities at the end of the growing season. Because of this, the typical security agreement entered into in this situation will require the farmer at the very least to notify the lender when this one big pay-off is to be made. The security agreement may also provide that the farmer agrees not to sell off his or her product without the express written consent of the lender, or even that any check issued by the buyer of the crop be made payable to the lender or to the farmer and the lender together as joint payees. These provisions are meant to minimize the possibility that the farmer, even if he or she has expressly agreed not to do so, will sell off the entire crop and not use the proceeds of the sale first and foremost to pay off what is owed the lender. But what if the farmer doesn't do as agreed but uses the money he or she has gotten for the crop to pay off other debts, or (in what we have to assume is a rare occurrence, but one which the lender still has to be concerned about) simply gives up farming altogether and absconds with the funds? Were the buyer to get the "normal" buyer in the ordinary course protection, the lender would have nowhere to turn to recoup its losses. And so we find the law lessens the lender's having to take on the risk of such an outcome by providing that the buyer, even the buyer in ordinary course, normally takes the farm products it is buying from a farmer *subject to* the lender's security interest. If the farmer doesn't pay the lender what is owed, the lender can go against the crop itself, now in the hands of the buyer.

The upshot is that the buyer of farm products can take what it purchases *free from* the lender's security interest only if the lender expressly authorizes the disposition "free of the security interest" as provided for in §9-315(a)(1). This in turn makes it particularly important that anyone who regularly buys farm products from farmers have an effective means of knowing with respect to any farmer and any particular crop that may be up for sale if that crop is encumbered by a security interest and, if so, who the secured party is and how the sale of the crop is to be carried out in a manner which will get the agreement of the lender that the disposition is free from its interest.

As the court in the *Fin Ag* case sets out, over time several states adopted non-uniform amendments to their versions of the UCC or other statutes meant to deal with this problem — the problem as seen now from the point of view of those who regularly purchase farm crops in large quantities. The results were inconsistent and confusing. In light of this, Congress in 1985 enacted 7 U.S.C. § 1631, or what is known as the Farm Security Act. The full text of the act should be available in whatever statutory supplement volume you are using in connection with your course. Where it applies, section 1631 preempts all conflicting state laws. The core provision of the act is § 1631(d):

> Except as provided in subsection (e) of this section and notwithstanding any other provision of Federal, State, or local law, a buyer who in the ordinary course of business buys a farm product from a seller engaged in farming operations shall take free of a security interest created by the seller, even though the security interest is perfected; and the buyer knows of the existence of such interest.

As you might expect, what then becomes all-important is what exception or exceptions are provided for in § 1631(e). The key to the three exceptions provided for in subsection (e) is the concept that the potential buyer should have already been given or have readily available access to reliable notice, by one means or another, of the lender's interest in the particular crop, as carefully described in the notice. The buyer will then have the opportunity to know what it will have to do to in connection with its purchase to obtain an effective waiver of the lender's interest in the given farm products upon their disposition.

Subsection (e) provides for three different ways in which the buyer may avoid being excluded from the general rule of (d) which would allow it to take the products purchased free of any interest created by its seller. Under (e)(1), the secured party will have sent out to any potential purchaser of the crop in which it has an interest a notice of that interest. How does the lender determine to whom to send such a notice? It may have acquired from the farmer the farmer's own listing of those to whom it might eventually sell his or her crop. Under the terms of the security agreement, the farmer will then be committed to sell only to a party on that listing, or to give the lender advance notice if it intends to sell to someone not on the original listing. The knowledgeable buyer can, of course, further add to those to whom it sends its notice other known large-scale purchasers of the type of farm product in question who operate in the area. The notice that the lender sends to each of these potential purchasers will set out in detail a description of the crop, its security interest in the crop, and furthermore information on "any payment obligations imposed on the buyer by the secured party as conditions for waiver or release of the security interest." The buyer of the crop will then know what to do to purchase the crop free of the secured party's interest. Under subsection (e)(1), only if the buyer has received such a notice within one year prior to its purchase and then "failed to perform the payment obligation" as set out in the notice, will its purchase be excepted from the general rule of subsection (d) and will the crops it purchases remain subject to the secured party's interest.

Subsections (e)(2) and (e)(3) set out the other two methods by which a purchaser of farm products may take free of any security interest created by its seller. Both of these subsections come into play only when a state has elected to create a "central filing system" for crops being grown or raised within the state, the specifics of which are laid out in (c)(2) of § 1631. It is important to note that the type of financing statements or notices which are filed with the Secretary of State under such a system is not the UCC1 initial financing statement with which we have become so familiar. The necessary filing for purposes of the FSA requires a good deal more detail on the exact crop covered by the filing. It may even be filed in a different state than is the UCC1 which will be filed by the secured party to perfect its interest under Article 9. If the state has established such a filing system for crops — as something close to 20 states have done to this point — then a potential buyer of such crops can get the notice it needs to avoid buying the crops subject to any security interest in one of two ways. The buyer may register its desire to receive on a regular basis a listing of all those notices which have been filed with the state and entered into its central filing system. See subsections (c)(2)(D) and (E). Or a potential purchaser who has not so registered may inquire of the central filing office whether any notice has been filed with respect to a particular crop, and the filing office is to respond with an oral confirmation within 24 hours, followed up by a written confirmation under (c)(2)(F).

Under subsection (e)(2), if a purchaser has failed to register with the central office or make an appropriate inquiry and purchases a crop upon which an effective notice has been filed by the secured party, its purchase will be subject to the secured party's interest. If the purchaser has received the notice, under either the (c)(2)(E) or (F) route, it will have the information necessary about what it must do to obtain an effective waiver or release of the secured party's interest upon its purchase "by performing any payment obligation [typically making out the check in the proper manner] or otherwise." If the purchaser has notice of the interest but fails to meet the criterion set out in the notice for completing a purchase not subject to the interest, then it, of course, gets the goods, but subject to the interest.

CHAPTER
25

What Are Proceeds?

A. INTRODUCTION

In the prior chapter we dealt with the important rule of §9-315(a)(1). In general—although we saw that there were a number of exceptions not to be ignored—a security interest in collateral continues "notwithstanding sale, lease, license, exchange, or other disposition thereof."

Now take a look at the second part of that subsection, §9-315(a)(2): Except as otherwise provided—and here the exceptions won't be that many—"a security interest attaches to any identifiable *proceeds* of collateral." Notice that this is true whether or not the security interest continues in the original collateral. Speaking in broad terms, if the collateral is disposed of by the debtor in such a way that the transferee takes free of the security interest, the secured party will have obtained in its place a security interest in the proceeds presumably generated by that disposition. If the transferee takes the original collateral subject to the secured party's security interest, then the secured party will continue to have an interest in the original collateral and *in addition* will have a newly created interest in any proceeds.

In this chapter we will explore what rightly constitute the proceeds of any particular collateral. When are proceeds generated? Of what do they consist? Note particularly that the term collateral is defined in §9-102(a)(12)(A) to include "proceeds to which a security interest attaches." Thus, if the initial proceeds of any collateral are disposed of, or otherwise themselves generate proceeds, this second generation of proceeds should itself be understood to be proceeds of the original collateral as well. As we sometimes say, and not just as a play on words, remember that, "proceeds of proceeds are proceeds."

In the following chapters we will look at the rules regarding attachment of the security interest to proceeds, perfection on proceeds, and priority in proceeds when more than one party claims an interest in them. For the moment, we are only concerned with the more limited problem of how to recognize proceeds when and as we confront them.

B. PREPARATION

In preparation for discussion of the topic covered by this chapter, read carefully the following parts of the Code:

- The definition of "proceeds" in §9-102(a)(64)
- The distinction between "cash proceeds" and "noncash proceeds" in §9-102(a)(9) and (58)
- Comment 13 (of which you can skip part (b)) to §9-102

C. PROBLEMS AND CASES

PROBLEMS

25.1   Spiffy's New and Used Cars of Springfield is a major automobile dealership. For many years it has operated under a financing arrangement entered into with Grand Bank of Toledo, under which the bank has been granted a security interest in all of Spiffy's "inventory, now held or hereafter acquired." Carlos comes and buys a new car from Spiffy. To pay for the car, Carlos conveys to Spiffy:

(a) his used car as a trade-in,
(b) a check for the agreed-upon down payment amount,
(c) a signed piece of paper in which he, Carlos, promises to pay "to the order of Spiffy's New and Used Cars of Springfield" certain amounts each month for the coming 48 months.

Would any or all of these items be considered proceeds of the individual auto which Spiffy has sold to Carlos? If so, would each be considered cash or noncash proceeds?

25.2   Suppose that Spiffy quickly deposits the check he has received from Carlos in a checking account he has specially set up with Capital National Bank under the name of "Spiffy's New and Used Cars of Springfield" and which he uses only for the conduct of his, Spiffy's, auto business.

(a) Would it be correct to say that this account now contains proceeds from the sale of the new auto to Spiffy?
(b) What if instead Spiffy deposits this check into a personal account he keeps with Hometown Bank, an account in which he also keeps money he receives from other sources and from which he pays his household bills? Has Grand Bank lost its interest in the value represented by this check as proceeds of collateral in which it had an interest?

25.3   A month after he buys the car, Carlos sends to Spiffy a check for the amount he has committed himself to pay in each of the next 48 months. Is *this* check rightly considered proceeds of the car initially sold to Carlos?

25.4   Assume that as part of his purchase agreement entered into with Spiffy, Carlos has agreed to get and maintain adequate insurance to cover any loss in value of the car which may occur through accident or theft. A year after Carlos's purchase, his car is stolen and nowhere to be found. He reports the lost to the insurance company from whom he'd obtained his insurance, and that firm agrees to evaluate his claim. Is the amount he will be paid by the insurance company rightfully considered proceeds of the car itself?

25.5   When his sister Stella wanted to form a new corporation, Hyperwidgets, Incorporated, Stewart agreed to invest some cash in the enterprise. As was agreed, Stella got 100 shares when the corporation was initially organized and Stewart got 20. These 20 shares are evidenced by a stock certificate (Certificate #2), which was issued to him by the corporation and which he keeps in a drawer in his desk. A couple of years later, in 2007, Stewart borrows some money from The Providence Bank, granting that bank a security interest in his twenty shares of Hyperwidgets stock. In 2009, Hyperwidgets, Incorporated declares a cash dividend amounting to $10,000 for each share held. Stewart receives a check from the corporation for $200,000. Providence Bank claims that this money must be considered proceeds of the Hyperwidgets shares which it took as collateral. Stewart points out that this money came to him without his having disposed of his 20 shares of stock. Providence, he argues, still has its security interest in those shares and they have no right to "any more collateral" because of the dividend. Who do you think should win this argument?

FARMERS COOPERATIVE ELEVATOR CO. v UNION STATE BANK

Supreme Court of Iowa, 1987
409 N.W.2d 178, 4 U.C.C. Rep. Serv. 2d 1

LARSON, J: Rodger Cockrum operated a farm and hog confinement operation in Madison County, Iowa. For several years financing for a substantial portion of the operation came from Union State Bank of Winterset (Union State). In February 1981, Union State loaned Cockrum a large sum of money and took a security agreement covering

> all equipment and fixtures, including but not limited to sheds and storage facilities, used or acquired for use in farming operations, whether now or hereafter existing or acquired; all farm products including but not limited to, *livestock, and supplies used or produced in farming operations whether now or hereafter existing or acquired.* . . . (Emphasis added.)

In December 1983 and January 1984, Cockrum entered into several purchase money security agreements with Farmers Cooperative Elevator Company (CO-OP) for livestock feed. For each transaction, CO-OP filed a financing statement with the Secretary of State, which stated:

> This is a purchase money security interest which covers Collateral described as all feed sold to Debtors by Secured Party and all of Debtors' feeder hogs now owned or hereafter acquired including . . . additions, replacements, and substitutions of such livestock, including all issues presently or hereafter conceived and born, the products thereof, and the proceeds of any of the described Collateral.

Cockrum defaulted on his obligations to both Union State and the CO-OP. CO-OP commenced an action against Cockrum seeking possession of collateral.

Union State filed a statement of indebtedness and requested that its security interests be established as a first security lien on Cockrum's hog inventory and any sale proceeds therefrom. CO-OP responded by filing an amendment to its petition, joining Union State as a defendant and alleging that its right to the hogs is superior to Union State's.

On CO-OP's motion to adjudicate law points, the district court ruled that Union State's security interest in the hogs was prior and superior to the CO-OP's. CO-OP has appealed from that decision.

We first address CO-OP's argument that its interest in the livestock and proceeds therefrom is superior to Union State's under section 554.9312(4) [the predecessor to current §9-324(a)]. That section provides:

> A purchase money security interest in collateral other than inventory has priority over a conflicting security interest in the same collateral or its proceeds if the purchase money security interest is perfected at the time the debtor receives possession of the collateral or within twenty days thereafter.

Union State concedes that CO-OP held a purchase money security interest in the feed. The question, however, is whether such a priority interest continues in livestock which consume the feed.

In essence, one who takes a purchase money security interest under section 554.9107(a) [precursor to current §9-103] is the equivalent of the old conventional vendor—a seller who has, in effect, made a loan by selling goods on credit. See J. White & R. Summers, Uniform Commercial Code § 25-5, at 1043 (2d ed. 1980). Put more simply, a purchase money security interest "is a secured loan for the price of new collateral." Henderson, Coordination of the Uniform Commercial Code with Other State and Federal Law in the Farm Financing Context, 14 Idaho L. Rev. 363, 375 (1978). In this case, CO-OP took the purchase money security interests to secure the price of the feed, not the hogs. Consequently, by definition, CO-OP does not have a purchase money security interest in the hogs.

CO-OP, nevertheless, argues that their priority interest in the feed continues to be superior in the hogs pursuant to section 554.9203(3) because the hogs are "proceeds" of the feed. That section provides, "unless otherwise agreed a security agreement gives the secured party the rights to proceeds provided by section 554.9306." Subsection 1 of section 554.9306 [of prerevision Article 9] defines proceeds to include "whatever is received upon the sale, exchange, collection or other disposition of collateral or proceeds."

CO-OP contends that the "other disposition of collateral" language in section 554.9306 includes ingestion and the biological processes involved when livestock consume feed, and as a result, fattened livestock are proceeds of the feed they consume. Such an argument was rejected in a case on all four hooves, so to speak. In *First National Bank of Brush v. Bostron*, 39 Colo. App. 107, 564 P.2d 964, 966 (Colo. App. 1977), the court emphasized that "[the livestock producer] received nothing when he disposed of the collateral by feeding it to the . . . cattle . . . the collateral was consumed, and there are no traceable proceeds to which the security interest may be said to have attached."

We agree with the result reached by the Colorado court. Ingestion and biological transformation of feed is not a type of "other disposition" within the contemplation of section 554.9306. For UCC purposes, the hogs are not proceeds of the feed.

AFFIRMED.

QUESTION ON FARMERS COOPERATIVE ELEVATOR

Given its date, this case was necessarily decided under the prerevision version of Article 9. The definition of "proceeds" in revised Article 9, according to Comment 13 to §9-102, "expands the definition beyond that contained in former Section 9-306 and resolves ambiguities in the former section." Were the case to come up today, do you think the Co-op would be any more likely to succeed with its argument that the hogs which were fattened up by eating the feed it had sold to Cockrum were, in whole or in part, "proceeds" of that feed? For a recent case in which the Supreme Court of Arkansas followed this case's lead in holding that crops were not to be considered proceeds of the seeds from which those crops were grown, see *Searcy Farm Supply, LLC v. Merchants & Planters Bank*, 2007 Ark. LEXIS 285, 62 U.C.C. Rep. Serv. 2d 737.

CHAPTER
26

Attachment, Perfection, and Priority in Proceeds

A. INTRODUCTION

As we saw in the last chapter, proceeds cannot be thought of as just some incidental remnants of a secured transaction or as a subject of merely tangential interest. Proceeds, however they come into the hands of the debtor and whatever their form, *are* collateral, and collateral in which the careful secured party has to take the keenest interest. This being so, we have to ask the same questions about proceeds collateral as we have been asking all along about the original collateral with which the parties were initially concerned: Does the secured party's interest in proceeds attach? Is this interest perfected or need more be done to gain perfection? When more than one party can legitimately claim an interest in some specific proceeds, what are the rules of priority that will be applied to the dispute?

The question of attachment is seldom a difficult one. Section 9-315(a)(2) states that with rare exception a secured party's security interest in any collateral automatically attaches to any "identifiable proceeds" of collateral. One difficulty which we will have to consider is that which the secured party may face is proving that certain property — especially when that property arguably constitutes *cash* proceeds of collateral in which it has an interest — is, in fact, *identifiable* proceeds. Cash proceeds can easily become commingled with other cash belonging to the debtor and the knotty matter of whose money is whose can be difficult to sort out.

As to perfection, you will see that perfection in proceeds is automatic, at least for a short time. In some instances, however, the secured party will have to take additional steps to continue its perfection in the proceeds beyond that time. Furthermore, priority in collateral usually — but with some notable exceptions to be explored in the next chapter — translates into priority in the proceeds of that collateral.

What the debtor is supposed to do with proceeds when they come into its possession is not something that is apparent from a reading of Article 9 itself. It all depends on what the debtor will have presumably committed

317

itself to do, or what it promised not to do, in the security agreement. In some transactions, the debtor will have bound itself to hold on to the collateral for the length of the agreement. Any disposition by the debtor will then necessarily be a breach of the agreement. The secured party's interest in the collateral may or may not, as we have seen in Chapter 24, continue in the original collateral. As a practical matter, however, the secured party's best chance of coming out satisfactorily will be for it to assert its interest in the identifiable proceeds of the disposition, even if such a disposition was never contemplated—and in fact distinctly ruled out—by the security agreement.

In other situations, it will be part of the very nature of the financing that the debtor will be anticipated to sell off the collateral in whole or in part. This is necessarily true if the collateral is inventory, for example. (Consider what the consequences would be—for both the debtor and the secured party—if the debtor were to put up its inventory as collateral and at the same time commit itself never to part with any of it.) The security agreement will not bar the debtor from disposing of the original collateral, far from it. What the security interest may specify in some detail, however, is under what circumstances such a disposition is permitted and furthermore what the debtor is to do with the proceeds from any authorized disposition to stay in compliance with the security agreement and stay "in trust," as we sometimes say, with the secured party.

B. PREPARATION

In preparation for discussion of the topics covered by this chapter, read carefully the following parts of the Code:

- Section 9-203(f)
- Section 9-315(a)(2), (b) through (e) and Comments 3 through 7 to this section
- Section 9-322(b)(1) and Comment 6 to this section
- Reread §9-324(a), looking now to the language regarding proceeds
- Section 9-332 and its Comment 2 through Example 1

C. PROBLEMS AND CASES

REVISITING AN EARLIER CASE

Look back at the *International Harvester* case of Chapter 24, noting what measures the secured party apparently used as a matter of course to keep close tabs on the proceeds which it could anticipate the debtor, Barnes, would be receiving any time he disposed of an individual item from his inventory.

PROBLEMS

26.1 Louie has for many years operated his small jewelry boutique, with the help of a Small Business Line of Credit from First Bank of Connecticut. In connection with his first obtaining this loan he granted the bank a security interest in "all inventory now held or after-acquired" of his business. The bank perfected on its interest by filing an initial financing statement — proper in all respects and with the correct filing office — indicating the collateral covered as "all inventory" of Louie as the named debtor. The bank has properly continued this filing as necessary as the years have gone by. In February of 2008, Angie Splatters, an artist who has her studio and a small gallery of her works near to Louie's store, spots a particularly attractive necklace in his shop that she would like to get for her mother as a Mother's Day gift. When told the price of the item, $700, Angie tells Louie that she just doesn't have that kind of money available at the moment, but she makes the following offer. "You know that one painting in my gallery that you were admiring the other day? I'll trade it for the necklace." Louie, who had indeed liked the painting (titled "Connecticut Morning") very much and noted it was marked for sale at $1,000, decides to take Angie up on her offer. After closing up his business for the day, he takes the necklace over to Angie's gallery and picks up the painting in question. The next day he proudly hangs it in a prominent place on the wall of his store.

(a) Does First Bank's security interest attach to the new painting now hanging on the wall of Louie's business?
(b) Is the bank's interest in the painting perfected? Does the bank have to take any special action after the arrival of the painting to assure its perfection in that item does not lapse?

26.2 A few months following the events of the prior problem, a tourist traveling through Litchfield drops into Louie's store and quickly picks out a number of pieces of jewelry she would like to buy. Louie totals up the price of these pieces, which come to $2,070. The tourist says, "That will be no problem," and quickly produces this amount in cash, which she hands over to Louie. After the buyer leaves with her purchases, Louie decides to take the cash directly to the local bank, Beauty of Litchfield Trust ("BLT"), in which he has his checking account (#200789) so that he can deposit this cash as soon as possible. On the way he passes Angie Splatters' gallery and notices a painting in the window which immediately falls in love with. He goes into the gallery and offers to buy the painting ("Vermont at Dusk") for $800. Angie agrees to the sale. While Angie is wrapping up the painting, Louie complete his trip to BLT where he deposits $1,270 in cash. He then returns to Angie's gallery where he exchanges $800 in cash for the painting. He then goes home. The next day he hangs this second painting on the wall of his business.

(a) Does First Bank's security interest attach to this second new painting now hanging on the wall of Louie's business?

(b) Is the bank's interest in the second painting perfected? Does the bank have to take any special action after the arrival of this painting to assure its perfection in that item does not lapse?

(c) Would it be correct to conclude that First Bank now has a perfected security interest in all or part of account #200789? Does First Bank have to do anything more to perfect its interest in this amount?

VAN DIEST SUPPLY CO. v. SHELBY COUNTY STATE BANK

United States Court of Appeals for the Seventh Circuit, 2005
425 F.3d 437, 59 U.C.C. Rep. Serv. 2d 1089

WILLIAMS, Circuit Judge. Van Diest Supply Co. and Shelby County State Bank ("Shelby") both assert a security interest in proceeds of accounts resulting from inventory Van Diest sold to Hennings Feed and Crop Care ("Hennings"). This case arose after Hennings filed for bankruptcy and was unable to pay for certain inventory it had purchased from Van Diest. Pursuant to a loan agreement with Hennings, Shelby had received the proceeds of many Hennings accounts receivable. Van Diest claimed a first, perfected purchase money security interest in proceeds of inventory it sold to Hennings and sued Shelby for conversion, seeking to recover the proceeds of inventory it sold to Hennings. The district court, in granting Shelby's motion for summary judgment, ruled that Van Diest had not presented evidence sufficient to carry its burden of identifying the proceeds. We agree and so affirm the decision of the district court.

I. BACKGROUND

At issue here are the proceeds of certain inventory that Van Diest Supply Co. sold to Hennings Feed and Crop Care. Hennings was a retail dealer in agricultural products, including chemicals, fertilizer, and limestone who purchased inventory from multiple suppliers, including Van Diest. In 1983, Van Diest and Hennings executed an agreement that granted Van Diest a purchase money security interest in inventory supplied by Van Diest, and the proceeds from such inventory. We concluded in an earlier case that the security interest did not extend to all Hennings inventory; instead, it was limited to inventory Van Diest supplied to Hennings. *Shelby County State Bank v. Van Diest Supply Co.*, 303 F.3d 832, 840 (7th Cir. 2002). [You may recall reading this earlier decision in Chapter 5, as an example of how an ambiguously worded security agreement had to be interpreted by the court.

And how the court ruled against Van Diest's claim that it had a security interest in *all* of the inventory, not just that supplied by it.]

Although Hennings had multiple suppliers, it did not (1) segregate inventory by supplier, (2) track inventory by supplier, or (3) know on any given day how much inventory it had on hand from any supplier. On May 16, 1998, Hennings and Shelby signed a "Draw Note-Fixed Rate" agreement that allowed Hennings to draw up to $4 million at a time, and Shelby made advances to Hennings under the Note in exchange for Hennings's accounts receivable. Shelby then collected the receivables. Shelby purchased Hennings's receivables from May 1998 until either December 14, 1998 or January 7, 1999 and received payments totaling over $2 million.

In late March or early April 1999, Van Diest received a financial statement from Hennings dated September 30, 1998. Based on the financial statement, Van Diest's credit manager believed Hennings was insolvent. Van Diest had already shipped additional product to Hennings, and payment was not due until June 11, 1999. Hennings was still current on its obligations, and Van Diest did not take any steps to enforce its rights under its security agreement with Hennings.

April 1999 also marked the first time that Hennings conducted a physical inventory. At the time, Hennings's computer records listed an inventory of approximately $7 million, but a check of the physical inventory revealed a missing $2.5 million in inventory.

Hennings first defaulted on a payment to Van Diest on June 11, 1999 and that day, Van Diest sent a demand letter to Hennings requesting payment in full. Van Diest did not learn of Shelby's factoring arrangement with Hennings until July 1, 1999. Hennings filed for bankruptcy the next month, on August 23, 1999. Van Diest then demanded payment of the funds paid to Shelby from the accounts factored under the Note, and Shelby refused to pay Van Diest.

Van Diest filed suit against Shelby, alleging that Shelby converted its property. The district court granted summary judgment in favor of Shelby, and Van Diest now appeals.

II. ANALYSIS

Van Diest sued Shelby under a theory of conversion, [arguing that a certain "identifiable" portion of money paid to Shelby was in fact proceeds to which it, Van Diest had a right], a dispute governed by state law. It is clear in Illinois that commingling does not necessarily make proceeds unidentifiable. First, § 9-205 [the precursor to present § 9-205] specifically provides that "a security interest is not invalid . . . by reason of liberty in the debtor to use, commingle, or dispose of all or part of the collateral . . . or to use, commingle, or dispose of proceeds." In addition, § 9-306(2) states that a security interest "continues in any identifiable proceeds." Finally, the Illinois Supreme Court recognized in *C.O. Funk & Sons, Inc. v. Sullivan*

Equip., Inc., 89 Ill. 2d 27, 431 N.E.2d 370, 372, 59 Ill. Dec. 85 (Ill. 1982) that a security interest could continue in a commingled account if the proceeds were identifiable. *See also Brown & Williamson Tobacco Corp. v. First Nat'l Bank,* 504 F.2d 998, 1001-02 (7th Cir. 1974). Therefore, so long as the proceeds were identifiable, Van Diest's security interest in the proceeds of the sale of the inventory it supplied to Hennings continued.

The Code does not define the term "identifiable." It does, however, direct that its provisions should be supplemented by "principles of law and equity." § 1-103 [or its equivalent § 1R-103(b) in Revised Article 1]. Like many other courts, the Illinois Supreme Court has construed this provision to allow a party to identify proceeds using a tracing theory known in the law of trusts as the "lowest intermediate balance rule."

In this case, the district court concluded that Van Diest did not present evidence sufficient to allow it to identify its proceeds. Therefore, it concluded that Van Diest had not presented evidence that it had an ownership interest in the proceeds Shelby received from the sale of Hennings's inventory, an immediate right to possession of those proceeds, or that Shelby assumed wrongful control over those proceeds. Because Van Diest had not presented sufficient evidence on elements for which it had the burden at trial, the district court granted Shelby's motion for summary judgment.

On appeal, Van Diest contends the district court erred when it found it could not trace its proceeds. Unfortunately, Hennings's commingling of the inventory it purchased from multiple suppliers makes this case difficult. Hennings purchased the same product from more than one supplier, but it did not segregate the inventory it received by supplier. In addition, although Hennings maintained records of the products it sold, these records did not track the company that had supplied Hennings with the product sold.

Funk is the only Illinois Supreme Court case to consider whether proceeds of collateral were sufficiently identified to subject them to a security interest. In that case, the court placed the burden of identification on the party seeking to identify the proceeds, stating, "Since Funk is claiming a prior security interest in property which is otherwise identified as collateral belonging to the bank under its after-acquired property clause, the burden of identifying the proceeds is properly upon Funk." The court then found that Funk failed to identify the proceeds, stating:

> Funk argues that it established a *prima facie* case by showing that secured property was sold, that the proceeds were deposited into an account, and that other items of inventory were purchased from that account, and that upon such showing the burden should shift to another to segregate the wrongfully commingled funds. Were we concerned here with the rights of Funk against Sullivan this argument would have considerable merit. The bank, however, was neither responsible for Funk's position nor for the commingling and is at least as innocent as Funk. We find no principles in law or equity which dictate that the innocent third party must suffer the consequences of Funk's predicament. Section 9-306 says that the security interest attaches to

identified proceeds. . . . Funk failed to offer the proof required to identify the claimed proceeds and is not now entitled a second opportunity to do so.

Funk makes clear that Van Diest has the burden of identifying the proceeds from the sale of the inventory it supplied. Van Diest has admitted that it "cannot at this time state the amount of its pro rata share in the mass of inventory." It contends, however, that the amount of its pro rata share is an issue of fact for trial or relevant only to damages. We disagree that tracing of Van Diest's proceeds is only a means to calculate damages and is not relevant to liability, as *Funk* clearly states that a security interest continues only in "identifiable proceeds." When it recently considered the same argument, the Eighth Circuit explained, "tracing . . . is not a measure of damages. It is the primary means of demonstrating the plaintiff's rights, and therefore the defendant's liability, in cases involving commingled accounts. . . . Without equitable tracing, [the plaintiff] cannot make out a claim for conversion because it cannot establish that the funds allegedly converted were identifiable proceeds in which it had a security interest." *General Elec. Capital Corp. v. Union Planters Bank, N.A.*, 409 F.3d 1049, 1059 (8th Cir. 2005).

We also disagree with Van Diest that it has presented sufficient evidence to survive summary judgment and that only an issue of fact as to the amount of its pro rata share remains. To carry its burden of identifying proceeds, Van Diest has chosen to employ a pro rata tracing method that it contends was used in *In re San Juan Packers, Inc.*, 696 F.2d 707 (9th Cir. 1983), and *GE Bus. Lighting Group v. Halmar Distribs., Inc. (In re Halmar Distribs., Inc.)*, 232 B.R. 18 (Bankr. D. Mass. 1999). Although Illinois courts have not considered whether proration is an appropriate means of tracing where more than one creditor has a security interest in commingled proceeds, *cf. Funk*, 431 N.E.2d at 372-73 (recognizing lowest intermediate balance rule as an appropriate method of tracing), other courts have recognized that proration can be used to trace commingled proceeds. *See Halmar*, 232 B.R. at 26; *Gen. Motors Acceptance Corp. v. Norstar Bank, N.A.*, 141 Misc. 2d 349, 532 N.Y.S.2d 685 (N.Y. Sup. Ct. 1988); *Bombardier Capital, Inc. v. Key Bank of Maine*, 639 A.2d 1065 (Me. 1994). Shelby agrees that, as a general matter, the pro rata method of tracing is an acceptable methodology for tracing collateral. It contends, however, that the method is not appropriate here.

The court in *Halmar* described the proration method of tracing proceeds as an approach where "a court may consider identifiable proceeds as a pro rata share of the commingled account, the share being determined by the percentage of collateral owned by the secured creditor before the proceeds were commingled." In this case, as a result of the Note agreement between Hennings and Shelby, Hennings's customers either paid Shelby directly or wrote checks to Hennings which Hennings delivered to Shelby. Van Diest maintains it can demonstrate that each payment resulted from the sale of its collateral by showing the proportion of Hennings's inventory on the date of each transaction attributable to inventory Van Diest had supplied to Hennings. As the district court explained, Van Diest's approach posited that if, "for example, on October 1, 1997, Van Diest had supplied Hennings with 10% of its inventory in Product A, then Van Diest would have had a security interest in 10% of the total inventory in Product A on that day, and 10% of the proceeds from the sale of Product A on that day."

The problem with the methodology Van Diest has employed is that it requires it to present evidence at some point in time of the percentage of Hennings inventory supplied by Van Diest. Van Diest, however, has presented no such evidence. To the contrary, Van Diest acknowledges that "It was not possible to know the total amount of any particular product that was on hand on any particular day. No records exist that show the various percentages of products supplied by different suppliers as of any particular day."

If there was evidence of the proportion of Hennings inventory attributable to Van Diest, then to show the proportion of sale attributable to Van Diest product on any given day, Van Diest could present evidence of increases and decreases in Hennings's inventory over time as Hennings purchased more inventory from suppliers and sold inventory to customers. Without an initial percentage, however, Van Diest's methodology fails.

In an effort to present the necessary evidence, Van Diest submitted the affidavit of Douglas Main, a paralegal, numerous records, and reports Main produced from these records. Main selected October 1, 1997 as the starting point for determining Van Diest's interest in inventory it supplied to Hennings. He then created reports, including a report summarizing Hennings's purchases by product during the period from October 1, 1997 through December 9, 1998. This report detailed the total dollars of all purchases, the total dollar of purchases from Van Diest, and the resulting percentage of Van Diest's purchases to the total of all purchases. For each product detailed, Main then multiplied this percentage against every account for which an invoice appeared on Shelby's records, regardless of when the account was generated or whether the account had been paid by check from an account debtor or by Hennings from its general deposit account. Main concluded that Shelby received $5,095,034.15 from the sale of Hennings's inventory and that 18.66%, or $950,477.55, was the proportionate share subject to Van Diest's security interest.

Main stated that in arriving at his conclusions, he made several assumptions. These assumptions included that the data he received concerning Hennings's purchases of inventory was accurate and that "Van Diest's shares of the beginning product inventories were in the same proportion to its shares of those same products which it supplied during the period of 10/1/97 through 12/9/98." The district court concluded that neither assumption had support in the record.

Van Diest contends that the district court's determination that the records were unreliable constituted a factual or credibility determination not proper at the summary judgment stage. It is undisputed, however, that on any given day in 1998 or 1999, Hennings did not know how much inventory it had in its warehouse from any supplier. Moreover, Hennings did not check its records against a physical inventory until April 1999.

It is also undisputed that the physical inventory count revealed that the computer records used by Main, which listed inventory of $7 million, overstated the actual inventory by $2.5 million.

Significantly, even if Hennings's records accurately recorded the inventory as of October 1, 1997, Van Diest has not presented any evidence of the amount of that inventory that was subject to its security interest. Main assumed that Van Diest's proportion of Hennings's inventory on that date was the same as the proportion in which it supplied Hennings thereafter, but there is nothing in the record to support that assumption. Van Diest cannot overcome a motion for summary judgment with speculation. Because the starting balances of each product necessarily affect later percentages, speculation as to the starting proportions means that all future percentages Main calculated were also merely speculative. Showing the amount of product supplied to Hennings after October 1, 1997 is not sufficient when there is no evidence of the starting proportion.

Although the court in *Halmar* found a creditor had identified proceeds using the pro rata method, *Halmar* does not help Van Diest. In *Halmar*, the parties agreed on the quantity of inventory before commingling and agreed on the proportion of starting inventory subject to the secured creditor's claim. From there, the secured creditor presented evidence of the total product shipped to a company and calculated the percentage attributable to it. *Id.* Unlike the plaintiff in *Halmar*, however, Van Diest has presented no evidence of the percentage of inventory it supplied before the goods were commingled.

In short, Van Diest had the burden of identifying its proceeds, and it has not presented evidence to show that it could do so under the only methodology it presented. Of course, this is a difficult result for Van Diest, as Hennings, one of its long-time customers, failed to pay it for inventory it had ordered. Noticeably absent from this case, of course, is Hennings. Hennings's inability to pay its debts means that there are insufficient funds to pay both Van Diest and Shelby. Under Illinois law, however, the burden fell to Van Diest to identify its proceeds. *See Funk*, 89 Ill. 2d at 33 ("We find no principles in law or equity which dictate that the innocent third party must suffer the consequences of Funk's predicament. . . . Funk failed to offer the proof required to identify the claimed proceeds and is not now entitled a second opportunity to do so.") Because Van Diest did not present evidence that it could do so, we are compelled to affirm.

III. Conclusion

For the foregoing reasons, the decision of the district court is AFFIRMED.

QUESTION ON VAN DIEST

This case was decided, as you could see, applying the prerevision version of Article 9. Do you find anything in the present version that suggests whether the court's approach to the facts presented would have or should have been any different had the revised version been applicable?

PROBLEM

26.3 In 2006, Lance Cashmore borrows $70,000 from Discreet Financial Services ("DFS") to be repaid at the end of four years, granting that firm a security interest is his large collection of expensive vintage and "classic" watches. DFS files a initial financing statement covering the watches in the correct filing office. In 2008, Lance finds that he his bills are piling up and that he has only $600 in the personal checking account he has with High-flier's Bank. He sells his entire watch collection for $100,000 to one Ernesto, a dealer in fine watches who sells watches out of a fashionable shop in Milan. Lance takes the check he receives from Ernesto and deposits it in the Highflier's checking account temporarily raising the amount in this account from $600 to $100,600. For the next year, Lance writes checks out of this account to pay off the bills that have been accumulating — what he has due to his landlord, various credit card companies, the stable where he boards his polo ponies, and so on — and new bills as they come in. By early 2010, the amount in his checking account is down to $1,000. In a last-ditch effort to avoid financial ruin, Lance sells all of his prized polo ponies in late January, netting a total of $120,000, which he deposits in his checking account. It soon becomes clear to Lance, however, that even with this new infusion of funds he is in no position to pay off all of what he already owes to a whole host of creditors, including but by no means limited to DFS. When Lance declares bankruptcy in June of 2010, his checking account in Highflier's contains a total of $82,000. DFS becomes aware of the bankruptcy, and also that there is no way it can find, much less gain possession of, all the watches once owned by Lance. DFS wants to claim that it has a perfected security interest in all of the money now in Lance's checking account? Will this claim be successful? If DFS has a valid interest in only a portion of these funds, how much at most will that claim be good for? Consider the excerpt below.

METROPOLITAN NATIONAL BANK v. LA SHER OIL COMPANY

Court of Appeals of Arkansas, 2003
81 Ark. App. 269, 101 S.W.3d 252, 51 U.C.C. Rep. Serv. 2d 213

[I]t is established law that a secured creditor has the burden to trace and identify the funds as the proceeds from secured collateral. When proceeds of a sale of collateral are placed in the debtor's bank account the proceeds remain identifiable, and a security interest in the funds continues even if the funds are commingled with other funds. The rules employed to distinguish the identifiable proceeds from other funds are liberally construed in the creditor's favor by use of the "intermediate-balance rule." Most courts that have considered the question have adopted this test. This rule provides a presumption that proceeds of the sale of collateral remain in the account as long as the account balance equals or exceeds the amount of the proceeds. The funds are "identified" based on the assumption that the debtor spends his own money out of the account before he spends the funds encumbered by the security interest. If the account balance drops below the amount of the proceeds, the security interest in the funds on deposit abates accordingly. This lower balance is not increased if non-proceeds funds are later deposited into the account. The rule is analogous to the presumption which arises when a trustee commingles trust funds with his own. If a presumption such as the lowest intermediate balance rule were not used, no funds placed in an account with funds from other sources could be "identified."

The rule, which operates on a common-sense view that dollars are fungible and cannot practically be earmarked in an account, provides a presumption that proceeds remain in the account as long as the account balance is equal to or greater than the amount of the proceeds deposited. The proceeds are "identified" by presuming that they remain in the account even if other funds are paid out of the account.

PROBLEMS

26.4 Returning to the unhappy story of Lance Cashmore as set out in Problem 26.3, suppose that it could be shows with certainty that in February 2010, Lance had written a check for $5,000 to make a contribution to add to the endowment of one of his favorite charities, The Lite Opera of Chicago. Will DFS be able to successfully claim a perfected interest in $5,000 of the Opera's endowment fund?

26.5 The Fresno Furniture Company has its main manufacturing facility, naturally enough, in Fresno, California. In 2008, in connection with its obtaining a loan, it grants a security interest in "all equipment, now held or hereafter acquired" to the First Fresno Bank. The bank perfects on its interest by a filing that is correct in every respect. In June of 2009, the management of the company becomes aware that it is in need of an additional forklift to use in moving around the large stacks of lumber and other raw materials it maintains in the storage yard located adjacent to its plant. The company purchases a Hoister Model #235 forklift directly from its manufacturer, the Hoister Corporation, which sells the piece to the company on credit, agreeing to take payment over three years and retaining a purchase-money security interest in the piece. Hoister files an initial financing statement covering the one particular forklift with the proper filing office on the very day that it delivers the piece to Fresno Furniture. Two months later, someone breaks into the furniture company's facilities over the weekend and makes off with this forklift. In spite of an intensive search by the Fresno Police, the identity of the thief is never discovered, nor is the forklift found. Within a couple of months, Fresno Furniture gets a check for the full replacement value of the item from its insurance company. A manager takes this check to Ernie's Equipment Emporium, a local dealer in tractor's and the like, and negotiates this check over to Ernie in exchange for the one new forklift which Ernie has readily available at his place of business, a Superlift 5000 made by the Hefter International Incorporated. The Superlift 5000 is delivered to Fresno Furniture and immediately put to use in its storage yard.

(a) As of the end of 2009, has First Fresno Bank's security interest attached to the Superlift 5000? If this interest perfected?
(b) As of the end of 2009, does Hoister Corporation have a security interest in the Hefter Superlift 5000? If this interest perfected?
(c) If you conclude that both the bank and the Hoister Corporation have an interest in the new forklift, which party's interest would have priority?

CHAPTER
27

Chattel Paper and Account Financing

A. INTRODUCTION

This chapter deals with some special issues that arise when a debtor operating as a retailer or distributor acquires all or a good part of its inventory on credit. This can be done in a couple of ways. The debtor may take delivery of the goods it is to sell from the manufacturer directly or from a supplier agreeing that the goods it receives are subject to a PMSI retained by the seller. Or the debtor may finance its acquisition of collateral with a loan from a lending institution which then is granted a security interest in the debtor's inventory including that after-acquired.

In either situation the inventory financer, as the secured party in such a relationship is often referred to, has to expect that items will regularly be sold by the debtor out of its inventory and that the inventory financer's security interest in the items sold will be cut off by the sale — that is, if the debtor is selling as it should, to people who qualify as buyers in the ordinary course of its business. The inventory financer does not merely expect that this will happen with some frequency, it must necessarily *hope* that this is the case. If none of the debtor's inventory is selling this is certainly not a sign of that the debtor's business is doing well. And if the debtor isn't doing well, it stands to reason that it will not be generating the cash that it will need to make the payment or payments its has committed itself to make to the financer. If all things are running smoothly, the financer's concern that its security interest in the collateral is well protected is really of secondary importance. What matters most to a the inventory financer, like any creditor, is that its debtor pays as and when payment is due.

Still, as we have been exploring in earlier chapters in this part, the inventory financer will have to be concerned that when any item of inventory is sold off to a buyer in the ordinary course that the proceeds of this sale are used by the debtor in the appropriate manner. If the debtor is in the kind of business where most of its sales are for cash, it will be expected that the cash that the debtor accumulates will be used, at least in part, to make payments as called for to the inventory financer. We dealt with some of the concerns that an inventory financer will have with being able to sufficiently "identify" — and then get its hands on, if things start to go awry — any cash proceeds in which it has a security interest because they were generated by the sale of inventory in which it held a security interest.

In this chapter we consider what happens when the debtor's business involves selling either larger big-ticket items or large quantities of stuff, no matter the size of any single piece, in a commercial context. If the debtor usually sells in this manner, then the proceeds which the sale will generate may be cash proceeds, but they often are not. The debtor itself will sell to its customers under some type of credit arrangement, and the proceeds resulting from the sale will typically be in the form of either accounts or pieces of chattel paper. The inventory financer will then have to be concerned about how these accounts or chattel paper will be transformed either in a single step or in a series of steps into the kind of thing that amount to payment to it, the inventory financer, of what it is expecting in return for the credit it has extended to the debtor.

There are any number of variations on what may be contemplated and set down we hope unambiguously in the underlying security agreement between the inventory financer and the retailer-debtor in such situations. In some instances, the debtor (typically a retailer dealing in individual sales of big-ticket items such as cars, tractors, boats, or the like) will be expect to inform the financer of each individual sale and to account in some fashion for the proceeds of that sale. This may include, for example, turning over to the financer the chattel paper generated by the individual sale or perhaps instead the debtor's quickly paying down its outstanding debt by a specified amount. In other cases, the debtor will be expected to itself collect the monies coming in to it as payment on the accounts or chattel paper and use this cash to make its regularly monthly payments to the lender as called for in the loan agreement.

Another variation on this theme is that the debtor will itself turn its accumulated accounts or stack of chattel paper into a present lump of cash by either selling them off in exchange for cash or using them as collateral to obtain a loan from some third party. Such third parties who are in the business of either buying or lending on accounts or chattel paper generated by business parties as a result of their sales are often referred to as "factors" or the decidedly more clunky term "accounts receivable financers." There is no inherent conflict between the interests of the inventory financer and the accounts receivable financer in such a situation. The inventory financer may even welcome the introduction of the accounts receivable financer into the picture. The accounts receivable financer makes possible the debtor's conversion of outstanding accounts or chattel paper into easy-to-handle cold hard cash — and that cash can be used by the debtor to pay the inventory financer in the most simple of fashions. The check will be in the mail.

Unfortunately, however, things do not always run as smoothly as they are supposed to, and this type of arrangement can afford the duplicitous, or the desperate, debtor, to takes liberties when it is not supposed to, resulting in the kind of priority battle we have become used to by this point. One reason for giving some special attention to this kind of problem is that, as you will discover, deals involving chattel paper are "facilitated" by some special rules unique to this type of collateral. The prospect that the accounts receivable financer will benefit from what is often referred to as "special chattel paper treatment" has a long and venerated, at least by some, history. As a matter of fact, when the recent revision of Article 9 was being drafted a number of commentators offered their suggestions that this "special treatment" for those in the business of purchasing chattel paper either be done away with or in some way cut back. These suggestions were, I am sure, taken seriously by the revision drafters, but they ended up carrying forward the traditional treatment with only minor clarifications.

Two further points before you head into the materials: First, you will note that in the present version of Article 9 there will be references to a party who takes possession *or control* of chattel paper. This is because revised Article 9 contemplates the possibility that there may arise some day a type of collateral it calls "electronic chattel paper." See §9-102(a)(31). When that day arrives, the best way to perfect on electronic chattel paper will be to take "control" of it, as set forth in §9-105. Taking control of electronic chattel paper is expected to be the information age equivalent of the tried-and-true centuries-old tradition of a buyer or lender taking *possession* of what we now have to more carefully describe as "*tangible* chattel paper" as defined in §9-102(a)(78). For our purposes in what follows, I will stick with tradition, that is, tangible chattel paper—the kind of paper that is actual paper and that you can get your hands around.

Also, I should point out that, as you will consider in more detail in Chapter 29, the outright sale of accounts or chattel paper will itself be a transaction governed by Article 9. See §9-109(a)(3). What is more important for the present is that you note that either the buyer of accounts or chattel paper or a lender who takes a security interest in such things will be considered a "purchaser" of them. See §1-201(32) & (33) or §1R-201(b)(29) & (30). "Purchase" is defined very broadly in the Uniform Commercial Code, and you will need to keep this in mind for what follows.

B. PREPARATION

In preparation for discussion of the topics covered by this chapter, read carefully:

- Section 9-330(a), (b), and (f) and Comments 2 through 6 to this section
- Permanent Editorial Board Commentary No. 8, which should be available in the selected statutes volume you are using in your course (if not, head to the web).

- The definitions of "account debtor" and new value" in §9-102(a)(3) and (57)
- Section 9-406(a)

C. PROBLEMS AND CASES

PROBLEMS

27.1 Knifty Knits Incorporated is a major manufacturer of sweaters and other knitwear which sells its products directly to major retailers, mostly large department stores and fashion houses, whose buyers choose which of the various products in Knifty's seasonal catalogues to buy and in what amounts. Each individual buyers sends its purchase order to Knifty, which then arranges for delivery of the chosen merchandise, accompanied by an invoice informing the buyer of exactly how much is now due the manufacturer. As is customary in the industry, the invoice does not call for the buyer to make immediate payment, but states that payment is due 60 days after the buyer receives delivery of the goods. Knifty Knits approaches Lone Star Bank of Texas with a proposal under which it would put up the accounts which are generated in this fashion as collateral in connection with its obtaining a line of credit from the bank. The loan officer at the bank has a search done of the Article 9 filings in the state of the company's incorporation (using of course the company's exact legal name) and finds only one financing statement of record. It is a financing statement filed by a California-based bank which indicates that it covers "all inventory and accounts, now held or hereafter acquired" of Knifty Knits.

(a) That being the case, could Lone Star loan to the company assured that any interest it took and properly perfected on its accounts would have priority should any dispute arise?
(b) Would your answer be any different if the financing statement filed by the California bank indicated the collateral as only "all inventory" of the company?

27.2 Foster's Farm Equipment is an authorized dealer for the full line of International Combine and Haybaler products, which include tractors, haybalers, and the like. Under its general floor plan agreement with that company ("ICH"), Foster regularly receives delivery of a representative selection of currently available ICH products, which it is then able to arrange around a demonstration lot adjacent to its sales office for display to prospective buyers. ICH reserves a security interest in each of the pieces of farm equipment it delivers to Foster and has properly perfected by filing its interest in "all inventory, now held or hereafter acquired" by Foster. The dealer is perfectly happy to sell to customers who can demonstrate sufficient creditworthiness. Foster asks such customers to make a modest down payment. In addition they sign both a note, under which the buyer promises to make a series of monthly payments, and a security agreement, under which the buyer grants to Foster a security interest in the item he or she is purchasing which secures his or obligation to make payments as called for in the note. Under the agreement between Foster and ICH, the dealer is to notify the manufacturer whenever any individual piece of equipment is sold and account for the proceeds. In particular it is to forward to ICH the note and accompanying security agreement both signed by the buyer. ICH then notifies the buyer that it is to make his or her monthly payments on the note directly to ICH rather than to Foster. Is the buyer obligated to do so?

27.3 The situation is as in the previous problem. One week in early 2010 is a particularly good one for Foster as he makes a number of credit sales of expensive items. Unfortunately for him, however, Foster also finds himself in desperate financial straits and in need of a quick infusion of cash if he is to avoid being dispossessed from the location on which he runs his business. Rather than forward the notes and accompanying security agreements to ICH as he is obligated to do, he takes them to the offices of Ready Factors Associates (RFA), a firm which is in the business of both making loans on the basis of chattel paper collateral or buying chattel paper outright. Foster receives a loan of $74,000 from RFA by granting that firm a security interest in the pieces of chattel paper he has brought with him. RFA takes possession of the chattel paper.

(a) Does ICH have a security interest in these pieces of chattel paper now in RFA's possession?
(b) If you conclude that ICH does have a security interest in these particular pieces of chattel paper, which party's security interest — that of ICH or RFA — has priority?
(c) Would your analysis of either of the two previous parts of this question be any different if Foster had, instead of borrowing from RFA using the chattel paper as collateral, sold the chattel paper outright to that firm for a set price?

AETNA FINANCE CO. v. HENDRICKSON

Court of Appeals of Indiana, 1988
526 N.E.2d 1222, 6 U.C.C. Rep. Serv. 2d 1610

HOFFMAN, J.: Aetna Finance Company, d/b/a Thorp Credit, Inc. of Indiana (Thorp) is appealing a negative judgment rendered in favor of Sperry New Holland, a division of the Sperry Corporation (Sperry). The trial court reached its decision after a trial without a jury and the court determined that Sperry's security interest in certain equipment had priority over Thorp's security interest in the same equipment. Although the case was decided on stipulated facts, a fairly complete factual recitation is necessary to understand the issues presented.

This appeal stems from the activities of John Ream, who was the principle owner of Martinsville Equipment Company, Inc. (MEC). MEC was a farm machinery dealership located in Morgan County, Indiana. In 1977 MEC became a dealer of Sperry farm machinery, as evidenced by a document titled, "Dealer Security Agreement." This agreement essentially created a standard floor planning arrangement whereby Sperry financed MEC's inventory of Sperry-manufactured equipment and retained a security interest in each item and in any proceeds. MEC, in turn, was obligated to remit the proceeds to Sperry after each sale. The agreement also gave Sperry the right to inspect MEC's premises, inventory, and financial records.

In September 1979, MEC was having financial difficulties. John Ream induced an employee, Kevin Hendrickson, to sign a sales contract for a Sperry combine and other farm equipment with a total contract price of more than $45,000.00. Hendrickson agreed to sign, although he was not a farmer, because John Ream told him that he, Ream, would make all the payments, and that the deal would be a good way to establish a credit rating. The sales contract granted MEC a security interest in the equipment, and immediately after signing, MEC assigned its security interest to Thorp for a cash payment of $45,000.00. Thorp, in turn, took all applicable steps to perfect its interest. Despite the sales contract, it is undisputed that Hendrickson never took possession of the equipment, and the equipment was never removed from MEC's unsold inventory list. Moreover, in violation of the Dealer Security Agreement, MEC did not send the money received from Thorp to Sperry, instead the money was retained and used as working capital.

Thereafter, in November 1979, MEC sold part of the equipment involved in the Hendrickson contract to a David Ream, who was John Ream's son. The record indicates that the son was unaware of his father's machinations, and took possession of, and legitimately used, the equipment on his own farm. The sale to the son also involved a sales contract which, this time, MEC assigned to Sperry as payment for pre-existing debt. The son made payments in accord with the terms of his sales contract until he defaulted in February 1981. At this time Sperry repossessed and resold the equipment. It is undisputed that Sperry acted without knowledge of Thorp's involvement.

Also, in April 1980, before repossessing the son's equipment, Sperry terminated its dealership relationship with MEC. Incident to this action Sperry repossessed and resold MEC's inventory including some equipment involved in the Hendrickson contract.

Additionally, Thorp received Hendrickson's 1980, 1981, and 1982 contract payments. In reality, the money Hendrickson used for the more than $12,000.00 annual payments came directly from John Ream, but when the final, 1983 payment came due Ream was unable to provide the funds and consequently Hendrickson defaulted. The default caused Thorp to attempt to repossess the equipment which Sperry had previously resold. Ultimately, the scheme unraveled and Thorp filed the present action in June 1983.

The trial court, in written findings, awarded Thorp a judgment against Hendrickson and Ream jointly for the unpaid loan balance, and the court assessed punitive damages solely against John Ream. As previously indicated, the court found that as between Thorp and Sperry, Sperry had the superior claim to the equipment and to the proceeds of the resale. It is only this adverse finding that Thorp is appealing. . . .

Resolution of this case rests on the application and applicability of Ind. Code § 26-1-9-308 (1982 ed.). [This was the precursor section to present § 9-330.] Research reveals no Indiana appellate level cases applying this section of the Secured Transactions Chapter of Indiana's Uniform Commercial Code. Nonetheless issues strikingly similar to those of the case at bar have been addressed by courts in other jurisdictions, and while not controlling here, these cases do provide persuasive authority.

As effective for the time period relevant here, U.C.C. § 9-308 reads:

> A purchaser of chattel paper or a non-negotiable instrument who gives new value and takes possession of it in the ordinary course of his business and without knowledge that the specific paper or instrument is subject to a security interest has priority over a security interest which is perfected under section 9-304 (permissive filing and temporary perfection). A purchaser of chattel paper who gives new value and takes possession of it in the ordinary course of his business has priority over a security interest in chattel paper which is claimed merely as proceeds of inventory subject to a security interest (section 9-306), even though he knows that the specific paper is subject to the security interest.

The focus in this case must narrow to the second part of this section [that is, the equivalent to present § 9-330(a)], since Sperry's security interest arises solely from its position as inventory financer and its consequential claim to proceeds.

This second section, which establishes the priorities between the retail financer and the inventory financer, is unusual because it plainly grants priority to a party, the retail financer, whose interest arose last, and who acted with knowledge of the prior security interest. Clearly then, from a policy perspective, this section places the retail financer in a favored position. In this case, Thorp acted as a retail financer, and in order for it to claim the protection of U.C.C. § 9-308 Thorp must show that it was 1) a purchaser; 2) of chattel paper; 3) which gave new value; and that 4) it took possession of the chattel paper; 5) in the ordinary course of its business.

On review of the facts, it appears that there is virtually no question that Thorp fulfilled most of the requirements of § 9-308. It is undisputed that Thorp was in the business of buying sales contracts, and it clearly gave new value and took possession of the contract after it made the purchase. The only remaining question regarding Thorp's eligibility for U.C.C. § 9-308 protection is whether the sales contract was, in fact, chattel paper. "Chattel paper" is defined at U.C.C. § 9-105(1)(b) and the term means, "a writing or writings which evidence both a monetary obligation and a security interest in or a lease of specific goods."

From this definition, it is obvious that Thorp at least intended to purchase chattel paper. Since the Hendrickson contract unquestionably evidences a monetary obligation, the question to be decided here becomes, whether the Hendrickson contract also evidences a valid security interest. . . . [A] security interest is not valid until the interest attaches and the prerequisites to attachment are there must be an agreement, value must be given, and the debtor must acquire rights in the collateral. Here, the sales contract represents Hendrickson's agreement to become indebted, and the $45,000.00 payment clearly represents value given. Accordingly the central issue again reduces to whether Hendrickson acquired sufficient rights in the property for Thorp's security interest to attach.

This question is actually the core question underlying this appeal. Sperry contends, and the trial court held, that the fraudulent nature of the transaction between Hendrickson and MEC invalidated the sale and resulted in Hendrickson acquiring no rights in the collateral. Conversely, Thorp argues that, regardless of any underlying fraud, the security interest attached, and the elements of § 9-308 were fulfilled; thus establishing its priority.

There are no Indiana cases discussing what degree of rights a debtor must have in the collateral before a security interest can attach; however, cases from other jurisdictions are illustrative. Initially, it is useful to recognize that requiring the debtor to have rights in the collateral is simply an application of the general principle that one cannot encumber another's property without consent. . . . A growing number of cases hold that the debtor's signing of a sales contract for the purchase of goods, by itself, represents sufficient rights to permit attachment of a security interest in the goods.

While the logic of these cases is well grounded in the policies supporting the Uniform Commercial Code, in the present case, it is unnecessary to hold that a sales contract alone creates sufficient rights for [the section governing attachment] to operate, because here there is significantly more evidence.

Not only did Hendrickson sign a sales contract but there is also a record of three years and over $36,000.00 in payments on the sales contract. Extensive payments on a sales contract is unquestionably stronger evidence that a debtor has rights in the collateral than simply a sales contract alone. It is immaterial that the money for Hendrickson's installment payments came from a third party, because as between the creditor, Thorp, and the debtor, Hendrickson, the source of the payments is irrelevant to the sales contract. Thus, in this case, the sales agreement, coupled with the substantial contract payments is ample evidence that Hendrickson had sufficient rights in the farm machinery for Thorp's security interest to attach.

Since Hendrickson had rights in the collateral and since it is undisputed that Hendrickson agreed to the sales contract and that Thorp gave value, it follows that Thorp's security interest attached and, accordingly, Thorp's security interest is valid Since Thorp's security interest is valid and since the contract also evidences a monetary obligation, then the Hendrickson contract is chattel paper. Since Thorp purchased chattel paper, it must be concluded that Thorp fulfilled the requirements of U.C.C. § 9-308 by purchasing chattel paper for new value and taking possession of the chattel paper in the ordinary course of its business. The conclusion that Thorp satisfied the elements of U.C.C. § 9-308 leads inexhorably to the conclusion that the trial court erred and that Thorp's security interest is superior to Sperry's interest.

The trial court, in reaching its decision, recognized the foregoing facts and acknowledged U.C.C. § 9-308. Nonetheless, the court held that the fraud involved in the transaction essentially suspended the operation of U.C.C. § 9-308. [The court then discusses how the trial court came to this conclusion, and finds the trial court to have been in error in its determination.] The foregoing analysis, concluding that the fraudulent nature of Hendrickson's transaction with MEC does not affect Thorp's rights under U.C.C. § 9-308, is also supported by several cases from other jurisdictions. [The court first discusses *Borg Warner Acceptance Corp. v. C.I.T. Corp.* (1984), Tex. App., 679 S.W.2d 140.] Another case that involves extremely similar facts is *American State Bank v. Avco Financial Services* (1977), 71 Cal. App. 3d 774, 139 Cal. Rptr. 658. While this case is not citeable authority, *see* 141 Cal. Rptr. 447, 570 P.2d 463, it still contains persuasive analysis and a valuable presentation of the underlying policies.

The California case again resolved a priority conflict between an inventory financer and a retail financer holding chattel paper produced by a sham sale. The California appeals court applied U.C.C. § 9-308 and decided that the retail financer held the superior security interest. In reaching its decision the court reasoned:

> In other words, the effective functioning of the mercantile community in this area requires that those institutions financing retail purchases by means of the purchase of chattel paper be entitled to rely on the represented validity of that paper unless they have such knowledge as to preclude their being bona fide purchasers. The same reasons for placing the risk on the flooring lender, if the dealer absconds with the funds received from the bank that it was bound to pay to the flooring lender, should apply to the set of facts before us where the sales were dummied up from the start. Parenthetically, in the reasoning which underlies it, this result parallels the well-established rule in the negotiable instruments field that a drawee who has paid a bill of exchange or check on which the drawer's or maker's signature has been forged cannot recover the payment from a holder in good faith for value and without fault. Beyond that, it may be too elementary to observe, but, once this step has been taken to recognize that chattel paper, although irregular in its inception, can become valid and enforceable in the hands of a bona fide purchaser (just as can a forged bill of exchange), it necessarily follows that the right to possession of the tangible property subject to the chattel paper is dictated by the terms thereof.
>
> In summary then, once a dealer has launched even irregular chattel paper in the mercantile stream and into the hands of a bona fide purchaser, chattel paper which covers tangible property which once was collateral of the dealer's financing party, the chattel paper becomes the collateral and the rights in that chattel paper control and represent the power to dispose of the tangible property upon default of the obligation stated in the chattel paper. This is the expectation under which the mercantile community operates, and the law should reflect it.

One additional case supporting the retail financer's priority should be noted. *Aetna Finance Corp. v. Massey Ferguson, Inc.*, (S.D. Ind. 1985), 626 F. Supp. 482, also stemmed from the activities of John Ream and his Martins-ville Equipment Company. The primary factual difference between the present case and the federal court case is that, in the earlier case, the court did not specifically find that the underlying sale was fraudulent, despite the fact that the equipment was never delivered. Nonetheless, Massey Ferguson's primary argument for the superiority of its inventory financer's security interest was that the equipment purchaser did not acquire any interest in the equipment.

Judge Steckler analyzed the situation and found the issue of actual delivery to be irrelevant. Instead the court applied U.C.C. §9-308 and held Thorp's retail financer's interest to be superior. Thus, it is clear that the operation of U.C.C. §9-308 is the same, regardless of fraud in the underlying transaction and that the present case is in harmony with this federal court case and the many cases like it.

Since Thorp has established its eligibility for the protection of U.C.C. §9-308 and since Sperry has failed to divert the operation of the Code, this case is reversed.

PROBLEM

27.4 Sarah owns and operates a store, "Sarah's Sells-U-Stuff," which offers to the buying public a wide range of audio, video, and computer equipment, as well as other more mundane household appliances. Many of the sales she makes of more expensive items are financed by the buyer's signing a form of Retail Sales Installment Agreement she has prepared under which the buyer promises to pay for the item being purchased in a 24 monthly payments. The agreement also provides that Sarah as seller reserves a security interest in the item being sold to secure the buyer's payment obligation. In 2009, Sarah enters into a loan agreement with the Lone Star Bank under which the bank grants her a line of credit. The amount of credit made available to her is agreed to be 45% of the price she paid for her current inventory plus 80% of the value of any of the Retail Sales Installment Agreements she holds not in default more than 30 days — this amount to be recalculated at monthly intervals. In connection with this loan, Sarah grants to the bank a security interest in "all of her inventory and chattel paper, now held or hereafter acquired," and the bank perfects this interest by filing a sufficient initial financing statement in the proper location, the filing indicating the collateral as "all inventory and chattel paper, now held or hereafter acquired." The security agreement signed by Sarah under which this interest is granted to the bank requires that she clearly mark any Retail Sales Installment Agreement entered into by any of her customers with a legend stating that the Agreement is subject to a security interest held by the bank and that "any attempted assignment of this agreement to another party will be in violation of the rights of Lone Star Bank." During the rest of 2009 and for most of 2010, Sarah marks all of the agreements as required. When her store's December 2010 sales prove disappointing, Sarah finds herself in need of some ready cash to pay various bills — for advertising and the like — that have been piling up. She takes a number of the Retail Sales Agreement forms which have not yet been marked with the required legend and puts them in her briefcase. She then takes these papers to the offices of Ready Factors Associates (RFA), a firm which is in the business of both making loans on the basis of chattel paper collateral or buying chattel paper outright. She sells the papers she has brought with her to RFA in exchange for a check for $95,000, which she deposits into a checking account from which she then pays her other creditors a total of close to $94,000 on her outstanding debts. When the Lone Star Bank eventually becomes aware of what has happened, it demands that RFA turn over to it the papers it has purchased. When RFA refuses to turn the papers over to the bank, it threatens to sue RFA for them. Do you expect the bank's suit to be successful?

PART VI

FURTHER ON THE SCOPE
OF ARTICLE 9

CHAPTER
28

Leases of Goods and Article 9

A. INTRODUCTION

As any commercial lawyer could tell you, the world is full of transactions billed as "leases" of goods — that is, the document is titled a Lease, the parties are denoted as the lessor and the lessee, reference is made to periodic rental payments, and so forth — which are in reality not what they would have you believe. Why would two reasonable intelligent parties, and their presumably intelligent and knowledgeable lawyers, create what appears at first glance to be a lease of goods when it is in reality, when judged by the *substance* of what the transactions is to accomplish and not just by the *form* it has been rendered in, a sale of goods with title to the goods passing at the inception of the "lease period" from one party to another along with the party parting with the goods reserving a security interest in them for some specified period during which the price of the goods is paid in a series of specified payments over time? Don't they know — doesn't everybody know? — that under the Uniform Commercial Code a transaction is characterized by what it accomplishes in substance, not by its form? In the first chapter we immediately became acquainted with the most fundamental of rules, that Article 9 of the Code — the Secured Transactions article — governs any transaction, *"regardless of its form*, that creates a security interest in personal property or fixtures by contract." And goods are most definitely a type of personal property. No doubt about that.

The question of why parties would do such a thing has many answers, or sometimes no good answer at all. At various times the parties may be planning on showing the transaction on their books as a lease, which under accounting rules shows up on the balance sheet in a different way than does a purchase of goods on secured credit. Or one party or the other may be hoping to take advantage of a more favorable tax treatment if the transaction is accepted by the taxing authorities, which play by their own set of rules and not the Uniform Commercial Code, as a lease of goods for tax purposes. Apparently, in some instances the only reason that one can get out of the parties as to why they have structured their deal as a "lease" when it is in fact no such thing is that they have "always done it that way" or "we are involved in the ever-growing and exciting world of equipment leasing, that's why." Such is life.

In our present universe, that of commercial transactions including the ever-present possibility of a bankruptcy, we need not worry about whether the ruse is successful when the question is how the transaction is to be treated for accounting or tax purposes. As the Uniform Commercial Code and the Bankruptcy Code would have it, if it isn't a "true lease" — an awkward phrase (something like the "true facts") that has arisen to characterize a "lease" of goods which is *really* a lease and not a present sale coupled with a security interest, in substance and not just in form — then Article 2A of the UCC governs and the bankruptcy system will deal with it as they would any other lease. If the transaction documented to appear as a lease is in fact *not* a true lease, then Article 2 will govern the sales aspect of the transaction and Article 9 will govern the secured transaction which the parties have entered into.

There have been, and I'm afraid we will have to assume there will always be, a steady — in fact, I think I can fairly call it an unrelenting — stream of cases in which the court is called upon to make the call of whether a transaction purporting to be a lease of goods is or is not what it purports to be. Prior to 1987, the courts where all over the place on how they approached the task of correctly characterizing the transactions with which they were confronted. When Article 2A was introduced into the UCC in 1987, the drafters of that article also added some language — which they stuck at the end of §1-201(37), the general definition of "security interest," apparently for lack of any better place to put it — intended to help the courts find a more consistent and principled way to make the determination. This same language, touched up only a bit, was given its own section, §1R-203, in the 2003 version of Article 1.

The situation thus resolves itself to this:

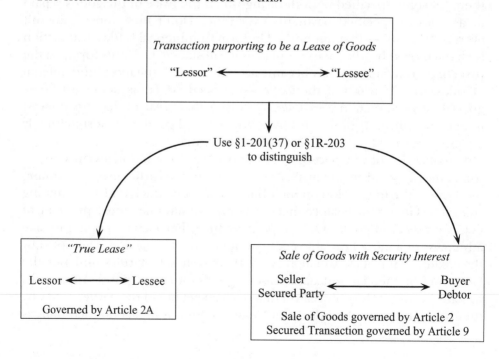

How to run any transaction whose character is disputed through the black box mechanism of § 1-201(37) or § 1R-203 is what this chapter is all about. You will, I believe, find a lot of help in the *Grubbs* case that forms the centerpiece of the chapter.

One further point before heading into the materials. You may naturally enough be interested in why it matters—for our purposes, allowing the accounting professionals and the taxing agencies to deal with it as they may—how the transaction is characterized? What practical difference does it make? For one thing, you should be aware that there is no requirement anywhere that public notice be given, that is, a UCC1 be filed, on a true lease. That is one big difference right there. The cases in that steady stream I mentioned earlier almost invariably come up in the bankruptcy context. If the trustee can show that a secured transaction and not a lease was involved, then the failure of the "lessor" to file, or its filing of an insufficient financing statement, would be fatal to its cause. Beyond that, the secured transaction and the true lease are treated very differently in a bankruptcy proceeding. If the transaction was in fact a sale with a security interest then the goods in dispute will be part of the bankruptcy estate and the "lessor" will be making a secured claim in an attempt to get paid the rest of what it is owed for the goods out of the estate. And its success in this quest will, of course, depend in good part on whether its security interest was properly perfected at the time the bankruptcy petition was filed. If the lease is a true lease, then the goods involved are never part of the bankruptcy estate. The lease agreement is, however, an executory contract to which the debtor was a party at the time of the bankruptcy filing. Under various provisions of the Bankruptcy Code, for example § 365, the trustee is given a fixed period of time during which he or she may choose to either reject or assume the benefits and burdens under the lease. The details of the process by which the trustee makes the determination whether to "assume or reject any executory contract or unexpired lease of the debtor," as § 365(a) would have it, and the consequence of doing one as opposed to the other, are complex and better left to your course in bankruptcy law. The bankruptcy courts, however, must first look to the law of the state, that is, the Uniform Commercial Code, to determine whether an "unexpired lease" exits at all.

B. PREPARATION

For this chapter you should look at:

- Section 2-106(1) for the Code's definition of a "sale"
- Section 2A-103(1)(j) for the definition of "lease" and Official Comment j to that section

- Section 1-201(37)(starting at it's second paragraph) or § 1R-203, and in either case the commentary that goes with the section you are using
- Section 9-505 and its Comment 2

C. PROBLEMS AND CASES

PROBLEM

28.1   Harriet "Happy" Moments works as a professional photographer, taking pictures of weddings and other momentous family occasions. She enters into an agreement with Darkroom Supplies under which she will lease a new sophisticated photo enlargement and printing apparatus (the "All Smiles XL") from the supply house for a period of four years. She agrees to make monthly payments of $500 for a period of 48 months. At the end of the 48 months she is to return the unit in good condition "normal wear and tear excepted" to Darkroom Supplies. When she is at the Darkroom Supplies store she notices that she would instead be able to buy a used four- or five-year-old All Smiles XL for approximately $15,000, but decides to go with the leasing plan instead.

(a) Is the agreement between Happy and Darkroom Supplies a true lease or something else?
(b) Suppose instead she enters into a lease agreement under which she will get a new All Smiles XL for 48 monthly payments of $800, which agreement also gives her the option to buy the unit at the end of four years for $1. How would you characterize this transaction as of its inception?
(c) Finally, suppose that she enters into a lease agreement calling for 60 monthly payments of $600, but which makes no mention one way or the other about whether she will have any option to buy it at the end of this "lease term." How would you characterize the transaction which she has entered with Darkroom Supplies?

IN RE GRUBBS CONSTRUCTION COMPANY

United States Bankruptcy Court for the Middle District of Florida, 2005
319 Bankr. 698, 55 U.C.C. Rep. Serv. 2d 501

Michael G. Williamson, United States Bankruptcy Judge: The issue before the Court is whether the equipment leases between the Debtor, Grubbs Construction, Inc. ("Grubbs"), and Banc One Leasing Corporation ("Banc One") are to be characterized as true leases or as secured transactions. This issue has been the subject of many court decisions, the common thread of which has been to conduct a fact-intensive analysis to determine the "economic realities" of the transactions. Applying that test to the leases between Grubbs and Banc One, the Court finds that under the facts of this case, it is clear that the economic realities of the lease transactions between the parties compel a finding that they must be interpreted and enforced as security agreements subject to Article 9 of the Uniform Commercial Code.

FINDINGS OF FACTS

[In November of 1998, Grubbs and Banc One entered into a Master Lease Agreement containing the general provisions governing individual agreements under which Grubbs financed the purchase of certain equipment from third-party vendors. The part of this decision reproduced here concerns four such transactions occurring from November 1998 through September 1999. The Master Lease Agreement did not contain the actual financial terms or identify the individual items of equipment ("Equipment"). Rather, it simply described the general terms of the parties' relationship. The terms of the specific equipment lease transactions are incorporated by reference in individual schedules ("Lease Schedules") executed as part of each of the later equipment purchase transactions. Under the terms of the Master Lease Agreement, Grubbs was to be unconditionally liable for all rental payments, without regard to whether the equipment was faulty. It also bore the risk of loss of the equipment. The Master Lease Agreement also contained a "Tax Benefits Indemnity" provision under which Banc One's entitlement to certain "Tax Benefits" is guaranteed by the bank.]

Under the terms of the Master Lease Agreement, it initially appears that at the end of the terms of the individual Leases, Grubbs can elect to either return the Equipment or purchase the Equipment by paying an amount equal to the fair market value of the Equipment. However, the terms of the Master Lease Agreement are superseded by the specific Lease Schedules relating to each Equipment purchase. Four of the five Lease Schedules contain "Early Buyout Option Addendums" ("Early Buyout Options" or "EBOs") and "Renew-or-Purchase Addendums" ("Renew-or-Purchase Addendums"). [What follows is the court's consideration only of these four Lease Schedules.]

With respect to the four EBO Leases, Grubbs is provided three alternatives at the end of the Lease terms. [Using Lease No. 93096 as an example, the the court then ran the numbers, giving a detailed analysis of what the consequences of each alternative — both of two early buy-out provisions versus the decision not to take an early buy-out — would be for Grubbs. It concluded as follows.]

As set forth above, Grubbs has three alternatives under the EBO Leases. Again using Lease No. 93096 as an example, under Alternative #1, it can pay a total of $637,687.32 over 66 months and own the Equipment at that time; under Alternative #2, it can pay a total of $648,733.44 over 72 months and own the Equipment at that time (assuming that Banc One does not take the position that fair market value exceeds the defined Minimum Value under the Lease, in which case the price to acquire ownership would increase); or, under Alternative #3, it can pay a total of $659,020.32, and not own the Equipment (but instead have an option to purchase the Equipment based on its fair market value to be determined at that time or return the Equipment and incur substantial additional costs to refurbish aged Equipment).

It was clear from the Debtor's perspective, as credibly testified by the Debtor's chief financial officer who considered various financing sources and negotiated the lease terms with Banc One, that from the inception Grubbs did not have any other choice from an economic perspective other than purchasing the Equipment under the Early Buyout Option Addendum.

Indeed, if one analyzes all of the terms and conditions of the Leases between Grubbs and Banc One, it is clear that sensible economics dictate that the Equipment be purchased under the Early Buyout Option. That is, the only economically sensible course for Grubbs, absent default, was to exercise the Early Buyout Option as testified to by Grubbs' chief financial officer. It was the clear intent of Grubbs, based on the economics of the Leases at their inception, to exercise the Early Buyout Options as they became available.

Indeed, the advantages to Grubbs are obvious. Grubbs has the right to obtain ownership at the lowest finance charge. While it appears likely that Banc One would accept the Minimum Value percentage in deriving the purchase price under the second alternative, the overall cost to the Debtor will still be more than the EBO price. The worst alternative for the Debtor is the third one under which the Debtor must still pay a fair market value which, even if greatly diminished because of the age of the Equipment, would be in addition to $659,020.32 in payments — by far the greatest cost for the Equipment. The additional obligation under the third alternative of refurbishing the Equipment at substantial expense was also financially disadvantageous. Clearly, the cost of performing under the EBO (Alternative #1) is less than performing under Alternative #2 or Alternative #3.

It is also clear that under all three alternatives, Banc One will receive back its principal plus interest and lease-related charges. In fact, as discussed above, one of the factors considered by the Debtor's chief financial officer when he surveyed alternative financing sources in 1998 was a consideration of internal interest rates effectively charged by the various lenders under the EBO alternative. For Banc One, this rate ranges from 5.52 percent to 7.15 percent. It does not appear from the evidence that Banc One ever had an expectation of actually receiving the Equipment back at the end of the Lease terms to be leased again to other lessees.

[The Court also concluded that the EBO Leases were structured to insure a return of full principal and interest to Banc One either in the event of a default, casualty loss, as well as] under each of the non-default alternatives available to the Debtor. It is also clear that under none of the options available to Grubbs was it within the reasonable expectations of the parties that (at the end of the Lease terms) the Equipment would be returned to Banc One. As discussed above, absent default, a financially healthy Grubbs would choose the option most beneficial to it by exercising the Early Buyout Option.

CONCLUSIONS OF LAW

CHARACTERIZATION OF THE LEASES UNDER U.C.C. SECTION 1-201(37)

As long ago as 1972, White and Summers, in the first edition of their often-cited Horn Book on the Uniform Commercial Code, noted that the "lease v. security interest" issue is one of the "most frequently litigated issues under the entire Uniform Commercial Code." White & Summers, *Uniform Commercial Code* § 22-3, at 760 (West 1972 edition). This theme continues in the most recent version of their treatise where they descriptively recite, "A fecund source of disputes . . . is the question whether a particular document labeled a lease' is a true lease — and is outside of Article 9 and under Article 2A — or whether it is a security agreement that creates a security interest under the terms of section 1-201(37)." White & Summers, *Uniform Commercial Code* § 30-3 at 11 (West 2002 edition) ("White & Summers 2002 ed.")

Indeed, the issue of whether a financing transaction denominated as a "lease" is a true lease or a disguised security agreement is one of the most vexatious and oft-litigated issues under the Uniform Commercial Code.

From a review of the litigated cases dealing with this issue, it is clear that the distinction between "true lease" and "security agreement" takes on added importance in cases, such as this one, involving a trustee or debtor-in-possession arguing that the "lease" is truly a security agreement and the financing company arguing that the transaction truly is a lease and not a transaction subject to Article 9 of the Uniform Commercial Code.

In this regard, White and Summers comment, "Why do secured creditors persist in claiming to be lessors? There are many reasons." White & Summers 2002 ed., § 30-3c.1., at 30. In fact, in the bankruptcy arena, the reasons are obvious. The treatment afforded to "true" lessors of personal property is far superior to the treatment given to holders of secured claims. For example, under Bankruptcy Code Section 365, leases are typically assumed or rejected at some point during a bankruptcy case. If the lease is assumed, then any defaults must be cured and adequate assurance of future performance under the lease provided. Importantly, during the time period commencing 60 days after the filing, the trustee or debtor-in-possession must make the contractual payments called for under the lease. Any contractual payments that are missed are typically accorded administrative priority status under section 503 of the Bankruptcy Code.

Rather than a lease's being cured of defaults on assumption (as required for a true lease), under a financing agreement, the secured claim is subject to being reduced to the value of collateral under section 506 and the payment terms restructured under the "cram down" provisions of section 1129(b). In addition, the interest of a true lessor is not subject to the trustee's "strong arm" powers, which operate to avoid for the benefit of the estate unperfected security interests. That is, in a "worst case" from the lender's perspective, if there is a problem in the loan documentation, such as a failure to file a financing statement or problems with the collateral description or proper name of the debtor, the lien may be subject to avoidance under section 544. Even if the lessor has filed a financing statement, if the transaction is construed to be a secured transaction not subject to avoidance under section 544, the treatment of a lessor is still superior to that of a holder of a secured claim. For example, in a chapter 11 case when the debtor-in-possession continues to use the collateral, the holder of the secured claim is only entitled to adequate protection fashioned to compensate for the decline in value of the collateral. If the value of the collateral is less than the amount of the claim, no post-petition interest accrues on the claim. Based on the advantageous treatment to be accorded to lessors of personal property—as opposed to secured lenders of the same property—there is an obvious financial incentive for equipment financers to structure their financing arrangements as leases, as opposed to security agreements. The tension in the cases dealing with this issue is the finance companies' attempt to draft an agreement in the form of a true lease versus the need to interpret such agreements based on their economic substance as opposed to their form.

Many of the cases that have dealt with this issue have done so under the prior definition contained in U.C.C. 1-201(37). The original version of U.C.C. 1-201(37) was substantially rewritten in conjunction with the promulgation of Article 2A in 1987 dealing with personal property leases. Some courts are of the view that the amendment was not intended to change the substantive law. A more precise statement of the effect of the change, however, is that revised U.C.C. 1-201(37) [or, note, now § 1R-203] adopts an analysis based on the "economic realities." White & Summers 2002 ed., § 30-3c at 23. Accordingly, the cases arising under the prior version of U.C.C. 1-201(37) and applying the "economic realities" test ("Economic Realities Test") are still instructive in interpreting the current version of U.C.C. 1-201(37).

The Bankruptcy Code's definition of security agreement set forth in section 101(50) is entirely consistent with the approach taken in defining a security agreement under both the new and old versions of U.C.C. 1-201(37). According to the legislative history, "Whether a lease 'is a true or bona fide lease or, in the alternative, a financing lease' or a lease intended as security, depends upon the circumstances of each case. The distinction between a true lease and a financing transaction is based upon the economic substance of the transaction and not, for example, upon the locus of the title, the form of the transaction or the fact that the transaction is denominated as a 'lease.'"

Some leases are obviously true leases and need very little analysis. The most obvious example of a lease that is unquestionably not a disguised financing arrangement is a typical short-term car rental agreement. No one ever questions such transactions. The rental charges compensate the car rental company for the loss of value over the term of the rental through the actual depreciation due to aging, wear, and obsolescence as well as providing for overhead and a profit margin. There is no question that someone who rents a car is acquiring no equity in the vehicle. At the end of the rental period, the car is returned and the car rental company rents it to another customer.

The drafting of leases has evolved over the years, and the simple older cases of $1 options or plain language making clear the lack of any residual interest on the part of the lessor do not necessitate the analysis required in more artfully drafted leases—where a court must dig below carefully crafted language to determine the actual economic realities of a transaction. As aptly stated by the court in *State ex rel. Celebrezze v. Tele-Communications, Inc.*, 601 N.E.2d 234 (Ohio 1990) at 239: "The cumulative learning and skill of those who practice in these fields have resulted in agreements of great sophistication and detail, sometimes written for the express purpose of obscuring the character of the agreement. While a document may be denominated a 'lease,' and refer to the parties as 'lessor' and 'lessee,' it may nevertheless be written to accomplish a purpose unrelated to bailment or rental. Consequently, courts and commentators have been required to formulate modes of analyses to uncover the precise nature of the agreement."

[The court then quotes § 1-201(37) in relevant part.] As can be seen, the process of determining whether a "lease" is a true lease as opposed to a security agreement starts with the basic proposition: "Whether a transaction creates a lease or security interest is determined by the facts of each case. . . ." In determining whether a lease is a true lease, the form or title chosen by the parties is not determinative.

Section 1-201(37) (para. 2) then goes on to simplify the process by providing a bright line test, which if the conditions are met, establishes that the agreement is *per se* always a security agreement. Under this test, a transaction creates a security interest if the consideration the lessee is to pay the lessor for the right to possession and use of the goods is an obligation for the term of the lease, not subject to termination by the lessee, and: (1) the original term of the lease is equal to or greater than the remaining economic life of the goods; (2) the lessee is bound to renew the lease for the remaining economic life of the goods or is bound to become the owner of the goods; (3) the lessee has an option to renew the lease for the remaining economic life of the goods for no additional consideration or nominal additional consideration upon compliance with the lease agreement; or (4) the lessee has an option to become the owner of the goods for no additional consideration or nominal additional consideration upon compliance with the lease agreement.

Importantly, the four instances in which a lease will always be determined to be a security agreement all relate to the residual value to the lessor of the personal property at the end of the lease term. In this regard, in all four of the instances covered by U.C.C. 1-201(37) (para. 2), the personal property either no longer has any economic value at the end of the lease term when the lessor obtains possession of the property or the lessee has the right to obtain ownership of the property for no additional consideration or nominal additional consideration. Thus, all four of the enumerated instances contemplate that at the end of the lease, the lessor will be paid in full the amounts advanced to purchase the personal property and will thereafter have no anticipation of any remaining investment return from the leased property having received full payment of the financed purchase price.

The inquiry does not end there, however. Once the court finds that the leases are not security interests *per se*, it is necessary to examine all the facts to determine whether the economic realities of a particular transaction nevertheless create a security interest. That is, if it is determined that "the transaction is not a disguised security agreement per se, [we] must then look at the specific facts of the case to determine whether the economics of the transaction suggest such a result." *In re Pillowtex, Inc.*, 349 F.3d 711 (3d Cir. 2003) at 717. Accordingly, failure to meet one of these conditions means only that the document is not conclusively a security agreement:

> The pinball has safely rolled past four holes each marked security agreement. Evasion of these four holes does not earn one enough points to become a lessee. Finding economic life beyond the lease term and seeing no nominal consideration option, what should a court do? The court must then answer whether the lessor retained a reversionary interest. If there is a meaningful reversionary interest — either an up-side right or a down-side risk — the parties have signed a lease, not a security agreement. If there is no reversionary interest, the parties have signed a security interest, not a lease.

In re Sankey, 307 B.R. 674 (Bankr. D. Alaska 2004) at 680 (citing White & Summers 2002 ed., § 30-3c.1., at 30).

The central feature of a true lease is the reservation of an economically meaningful interest to the lessor at the end of the lease term. Ordinarily, this means two things: (1) at the outset of the lease the parties expect the goods to retain some significant residual value at the end of the lease term; and (2) the lessor retains some entrepreneurial stake (either the possibility of gain or the risk of loss) in the value of the goods at the end of the lease term. Accordingly, even when it is determined that the bright-line test has not been satisfied, an examination of all the facts and circumstances of the case must still be made to determine whether the agreement in question is a true lease or disguised security agreement.

Thus, U.C.C. 1-201(37) shifts the focus from "the intent of the parties" to the "economic realities" of a given transaction in determining whether the transaction is a true lease or a disguised security arrangement. The Economic Realities Test as set forth in White & Summers, 1980 ed.,

§ 22-3 at 881, states that: "If at the end of the term [of the lease], the only economically sensible course for the lessee is to exercise the option to purchase the property, then the agreement is a security agreement."

The Economic Realities Test requires an analysis of all terms and conditions of a purported lease transaction to determine whether the lessee has no sensible alternative other than to exercise the purchase option. *See, e.g., In re Lykes Bros. Steamship Co., Inc.*, 196 B.R. 574 (Bankr. M.D. Fla. 1996) at 581-82 (finding that debtor had no sensible alternative other than to pay $44 million to purchase leased equipment as opposed to paying $91 million in rent for an additional five years and, therefore, the purchase option was nominal); *In re Cook*, 52 B.R. 558, 563 (Bankr. D.N.D. 1985) (cost of removal of "leased" irrigation equipment "really leaves [the lessee] with no choice at the end of the lease term" other than to exercise the purchase option); *Sight & Sound of Ohio*, 36 B.R. at 889-90 ("The only really plausible alternative available to [the] lessee at the end of the ... lease agreement would be to purchase refrigerator outright ... [for] the option price of $69.75 [rather than continuing to rent refrigerator at $717.60 per year]."); *In re Berge*, 32 B.R. 370, 372-73 (Bankr. W.D. Wis. 1983) (noting that "if the fair market value of the property contemplated at the end of the lease term was less than the cost of reassembly and transport of the equipment to the lessor ... the exercise of the option would be virtually compelled 'or the only sensible course,' and the consideration [required to exercise the option] ipso facto nominal"); and Richard L. Barnes, *Distinguishing Sales and Leases: A Primer on the Scope and Purpose of* UCC Article 2A, 25 U. Mem. L. Rev. 873, 885 (1995) ("The option price is nominal if the sensible lessee would in effect have no choice [other than to exercise the purchase option] and, in making the only sensible choice, would cut off the lessor's reversionary interest. Where a person is left with no real economic choice, the price of taking the action must be nominal.").

The Economic Realities Test has also been variously referred to as the "sensible person test." Put another way, it is the "No Lessee in its Right Mind Test."

The "sensible person" test provides that "where the terms of the lease and option to purchase are such the only sensible course for the lessee at the end of the lease term is to exercise the option and become the owner of the goods, the lease was intended to create a security interest." *In re Triplex Marine Maintenance, Inc.*, 258 B.R. 659 (Bankr. E.D. Tex. 2000) at 671. "Articulated in a less genteel manner, if only a fool would fail to exercise the purchase option, the option is generally considered nominal and the transaction characterized as a 'disguised security agreement.'" *In re Howell*, 161 B.R. 285 (Bankr. N.D. Fla. 1993) at 289. "No matter how the option amount is expressed, if the only sensible course of action is to exercise the option, then it is one intended for security." *Id.* (citing Barnes, 25 U. Mem. L. Rev. at 885 and cases cited therein).

The Economic Realities Test focuses on all the facts and circumstances surrounding the transaction as anticipated by the parties at contract inception, rather than at the time the option arises. One of the factors considered both in the context of the Economic Realities Test and the application of U.C.C. 1-201(37)(a)(4) ("the lessee has the option to become the owner for ... nominal consideration ...") is whether the option price is nominal. If the price is nominal, the agreement is a security agreement. Importantly, U.C.C. 1-201(37)(c)(1) states that "additional consideration is nominal if it is less than the lessee's reasonably predictable cost of performing under the lease agreement if the option is not exercised."

In *Lykes*, 196 B.R. at 582, Judge Paskay was presented with a complex set of facts and an option price "one must concede at first blush was facially not nominal at all, in that in order to exercise the option, Lykes was required to pay Blue Water the greater of the fair market value of the vessels or $44.4 million dollars. If this provision is viewed in a vacuum and any other surrounding provisions are disregarded, one might conclude that this is a true lease with an option to purchase." However, looking at the economic realities of the entire transaction, Judge Paskay observed that if Lykes did not exercise the option, it would have a remaining obligation to make charter payments for an additional five years which would total $91 million. Under such circumstances, as a matter of common sense and sound economics, it would have made no sense for Lykes to pay $91 million in rent for the five years following the year 2002, when it could purchase the vessels in the year 2002 for the greater of their fair market value or $11.1 million each.

Some courts have taken the simplistic view that a fair market value option — no matter what the underlying economics of the transaction — precludes a finding that the agreement is a security agreement. To the contrary, there is substantial authority that if the "economic realities" dictate otherwise, the inclusion of a fair market value option (and even the total absence of any option at all) does not require a finding that the agreement is a true lease. "However, such a mechanical application of that subsection without recognition of the existing economic realities of the transaction belies the very standard that § 1.201(37) seeks to impose." *Triplex*, 258 B.R. at 671. Even with such a purchase option standard, "the 'lease' will still be deemed one intended as security if the facts otherwise expose economic realities tending to confirm that a secured transfer of ownership is afoot." *In re Fashion Optical*, 653 F.2d 1385 (10th Cir. 1981) at 1389. Thus, whether viewed in the context of the bright-line factor articulated in § 1.201(37)(B)(iv) or under an application of the general rule to examine all of the surrounding economic circumstances of the transaction, a transaction will be considered to be a security agreement notwithstanding of the inclusion of a fair market value option if the economic realities otherwise indicate.

Perhaps the most revealing provisions of the "lease agreement" are those relating to "termination" and "return of vehicle." Often such provisions in a termination formula recognize the equity of the "lessee" in the equipment because the lessee is required to bear the loss or receive the gain from its wholesale disposition. In this regard, an equity in the "Lessee" is one of the distinctive characteristics of a lease intended for security. As stated in the case of *In re Royer's Bakery, Inc.*, 1 UCC Rep. Serv. 342 (E.D. Pa. 1963): "Whenever it can be found that a lease agreement concerning personal property contains provisions the effect of which are to create in the lessee an equity or pecuniary interest in the leased property the parties are deemed as a matter of law to have intended the lease as security within the meaning of Sections 9-102 and 1-201(37) of the Uniform Commercial Code."

Accordingly, the default and remedies provision of the Banc One Leases in this case also provide further insight as to whether the Lease was intended as security. The Leases provide that in the event of default by the lessee, the lessor may repossess the Equipment and resell the Equipment. This provision further provides that in the event Lessor takes possession of the Equipment, Banc One must give Grubbs credit for any sums received by Lessor from the sale or rental of the Equipment after deduction of the expenses of sale or rental and Lessor's residual interest in the Equipment. This provision recognizes the creation of an equity or pecuniary interest in the lessee. Upon the recognition of such an interest, the parties are deemed as a matter of law to have intended the lease as security. For instance, if the lessee is entitled to any surplus of proceeds after the lessor claims liquidated damages under the agreement, then the agreement recognizes an "equity" in the lessee.

On the other hand, the Leases provide that in the event that there is a deficiency after a repossession and sale, the lessor may recover the deficiency from the lessee. This provision also recognizes the creation of an equity or pecuniary interest in the lessee. Upon the recognition of such an interest the parties are deemed as a matter of law to have intended the lease as security. Indeed, this latter factor—whether the lessee acquires an ownership interest or equity in the property—has been described as "the pivotal issue in characterizing a lease purchase agreement." *In re Airlift International, Inc.*, 70 B.R. 935 (Bankr. S.D. Fla. 1987) at 939.

Finally, as noted above, a provision requiring return of the leased property at the end of the term does not negate the possibility of the agreement being a security agreement. That is, even when a lease does not contain a purchase option, the lease "will still be deemed one intended as security if the facts otherwise expose economic realities tending to confirm that a secured transfer of ownership is afoot." *Tulsa Port Warehouse Co., Inc. v. General Motors Acceptance Corp.*, 4 B.R. 801 (N.D. Okla. 1980) at 811. There are also cases where the option to purchase was considered not dispositive or of secondary importance because other evidence showed that the "lessee" was acquiring an equity interest in the property.

In addition, the totality of the other rights and responsibilities of the parties to the transaction are still relevant in considering the economic realities of the transaction. The Court concludes that the facts of this case clearly establish (and are without material dispute) that the transactions between Grubbs and Banc One are security agreements governed by

U.C.C. Article 9. The facts that support this conclusion are described above. . . .

In summary, it is clear that given the Court's factual findings concerning the economic realities of these transactions, the proper characterization of the Leases is as security agreements under U.C.C. 1-201 (37) and not as true leases.

PERFECTION OF BANC ONE'S SECURITY INTEREST

Grubbs and its primary secured creditor, SouthTrust Bank, contend that Banc One failed to perfect its security interest and that, therefore, Banc One's claims are unsecured. Indeed, having found that the Leases are security agreements, any lien rights that Banc One has may be subject to avoidance under the "strong arm" powers which operate to avoid for the benefit of the estate unperfected security interests. 11 U.S.C. § 544(a). That is, a failure to file a proper financing statement makes any lien subject to avoidance under section 544. [The court determines that Banc One had properly perfected its security interest by filing of a proper UCC-1.]

CONCLUSION

For the foregoing reasons, the Court concludes that the lease transactions between Grubbs and Banc One are in the nature of security agreements and not true leases. The facts are substantially without dispute and clearly establish a relationship under which it was never contemplated that Banc One would retain a meaningful reversionary interest in the Equipment. Rather, the only sensible course, absent default, was for Grubbs to exercise the Early Buyout Option under the EBO Leases. Similarly, in the event of default, the Leases provided to Banc One remedies that were the same as those that typically appear in security agreements.

PROBLEM

28.3 Slater Shingling is a company that does roofing work on larger commercial buildings. After obtaining the contract to do the roofing for a new building being completed, the Cashmore Casino and Resort, it enters into what is termed a "rental purchase" agreement with the firm of Insta-Buildings Incorporated under which a storage unit of a particular size will be delivered to the building site so that it may be used by Slater to store its equipment and supplies at the site during the course of the job. The agreement calls for Slater to make 36 monthly payments to Insta-Buildings of $131.06 each, although it can terminate the agreement at any time by giving two weeks notice that it no longer needs the structure and allowing Insta-Buildings to come and take it away. The agreement also provides that Insta-Buildings retains title to the portable structure until Slater makes all 36 payments. If Slater does continue making payments for all 36 months Slater would "acquire title to the structure for no additional consideration." Slater files for bankruptcy protection about two months into the casino project, while the storage unit is still at the construction site and being used by it. How do you believe a bankruptcy court would characterize this transaction? Two other facts may be helpful in making the call:

(1) It will be stipulated that the useful economic life of a storage unit such as the one that is the subject of this agreement is at least 12 to 14 years, and

(2) Slater Roofing has entered into similar agreements with Insta-Buildings many times in the past as the need has arisen in connection with various projects. It has usually completed the projects and called Insta-Buildings telling it to pick up the storage unit it has provided within three to five months of the storage unit's first being delivered to the construction site.

CHAPTER

29

Other Transactions Governed
by Article 9

A. INTRODUCTION

In the previous chapter we discovered that Article 9 does *not* apply to a transaction that is a true lease of goods. It *does* apply, however, to any transaction which is denoted by those who enter into it as a lease of goods but which is in reality a present sale of goods with the seller retaining a PMSI in the goods sold. That follows directly from the prime directive of §9-109(a)(1) that Article 9 applies to "any transaction, *regardless of its form*, that creates a security interest in personal property or fixtures by contract."

In this chapter we explore a number of other transactions to which Article 9 applies by virtue of other parts of §9-109(a). To be more specific, the following material deals with agricultural liens, sales of receivables, and at least some subset of consignments.

B. PREPARATION

The principal Code provisions for this chapter are:

- Section 9-109(a)(2), (3), and (4) and Official Comments 3 through 6 to that section
- Section 9-103(d) and Comment 6 to that section
- Sections 9-318 and 9-319 with the Comments to each

You'll also want to review, or in other cases read for the first time, the following sections, which provide much-needed clarification of terminology:

- The second sentence of §1-201(37) or of §1R-201(b)(35)
- The definitions in section 9-102(a)(3), (5), (12), (19), (20), (21), (28), (72), and (73)

C. PROBLEMS AND CASES

PROBLEM

29.1 Joshua Tillers is a farmer. At the beginning of the growing season, he receives large quantities of seed, fertilizers, and pesticides from the firm of Bumpers Seed and Supply for which he agrees to pay within thirty days of the harvest of his crop in late summer. As it happens, the state in which Tiller's farm is located has a statute that provides in part that, "Any person who shall make advances in provisions, supplies and other articles for agricultural purposes shall have a lien in such agricultural inputs and any crops grown from or through the use of such inputs."

(a) Is either the transaction under which Bumper's sells supplies to Tillers or the lien arising by virtue of the state statute governed by Article 9 by virtue of § 9-109(a)(1)?
(b) What about § 9-109(a)(2)?
(c) Under the nomenclature of the Uniform Commercial Code, which, if any of the following statements would be correct and not cause embarrassment if said in the company of a group of knowledgeable commercial lawyers?
  (i)   "Under the statute, Tillers's crop has become collateral subject to a security interest taken by Bumpers."
  (ii) "Bumpers is a secured party for Article 9 purposes."
  (iii) "Tillers is a debtor for Article 9 purposes."

ON THE AGRICULTURAL LIEN

As you have discovered, while an agricultural lien does not create a security interest on behalf of the supplier, the transaction and the lien *are* governed by Article 9 and its myriad of provisions. We then, naturally enough, have certain questions to ask, which should be answered by a careful reading of the article. For instance, can we rightly speak of the "attachment" of an agricultural lien? No, under § 9-203(a) that term is reserved for use when a security interest is involved. We will have to make do with saying that an agricultural lien "becomes effective" as and when the statute under which it arises specifies. Note that we can say that an agricultural lien may be (and therefore in all practicality should be) perfected under § 9-308(b) when it is effective and "the requirements for perfection in Section 9-310 have been satisfied."

Speaking of § 9-310, we notice that under its subsection (a) a filing will be required to perfect an agricultural lien. Where would the supplier have to perfect? Look to § 9-302. The filing must be done not in the state in which the debtor is located, as we know is generally true for Article 9 security interests, but in the state when the farm products are located. Which pretty much means where the farmland is. I assume you can spot a trap for the unwary here.

What about priority? How does the holder of an agricultural lien hold up against other parties who might also be claiming an interest governed by Article 9 in the same collateral? We note first of all that in § 9-317(a) and § 9-322(a), the two principle priority provisions, that an agricultural lien is to be treated just as a security interest is. Note, however, that § 9-322(a) is expressly made subject to other provisions in that section, and subsection (g) states, "A perfected agricultural lien on collateral has priority over a conflicting security interest in or agricultural lien on the same collateral if the statute creating the agricultural lien so provides." See also Comment 12 to § 9-322.

PROBLEMS

29.2   Downhill Equipment manufacturers a full line of skiing products. It sells these in large quantities to sporting goods stores and ski shops prior to the skiing season. As is customary in the trade, Downhill sells on unsecured trade credit, under which the buyer agrees to make full payment for that which has ordered and which has been delivered to it 120 days after the goods have been delivered. As the ski season begins, Downhill finds that has a lot of outstanding accounts. It also finds that it will be needing cash to tide it over the next months, so that it can continue to pay the mortgage on the plant from which it operates, its employees' wages, and so on. The Treasurer of Downhill explores two possibilities: Under the first it could take out a loan from First Bank of Vermont, putting up its accounts as collateral. The bank has calculated that it would give a loan of X dollars based on the listing of accounts with which it has been furnished by Downhill. A second possibility is that it sell the accounts outright to a company called Fir Lined Factors ("FLF"). Based on the same listing of accounts, the manager of FLF has told the Treasurer of Downhill that his firm would pay Y dollars to buy the accounts. The Treasurer has come to you for advice. In determining which plan she should pursue, is there any reason not to go with whichever — the bank which would loan or the factor which would buy — has offered the greater amount of cash, that is, simply by looking at whether X or Y is a higher figure? What other differences are there between the two contemplated transactions?

29.3   Assume that the Treasurer decides to go with the option of selling the accounts to FLF, and this transaction is completed. Do you, as someone very knowledgeable in the precise language of Article 9, find anything to fault in the following bold, if seemingly dry, statement? "Downhill and FLF have entered into a transaction governed by Article 9. Downhill is the debtor. FLF is the secured party having obtained a security interest in the accounts, which serve as the collateral."

29.4   In addition to having an authorized representative sign a well-crafted document evidencing the purchase and sale of the accounts (which could be correctly characterized as a "security agreement," right?), what action or actions would you advise the manager of the factoring firm to take to fully protect its interest in the accounts?

ON THE SALE OF RECEIVABLES

Section 9-109(a)(3) states that Article 9 applies to "a sale of accounts, chattel paper, payment intangibles, or promissory notes." The reason such sale transactions are included in the scope of Article 9 is set out in the first paragraph of Comment 4 to § 9-109. There are any number of variations on the theme of how receivables can be and are dealt with as collateral, either subject to a security interest of the § 9-109(a)(1) variety or having been sold outright, that it makes dealing with such things a lot easier for experienced commercial parties if they can be confident that however they structure their transaction it will be governed by Article 9.

This means, of course, that those experienced commercial parties must be careful to play by the Article 9 rules in every detail whether that article applied to the transaction into which they have entered by virtue of either § 9-102(a)(1) or § 9-102(a)(3) or "one or the other, it doesn't matter which." The interest of the buyer must attach according to the rules for attachment. The interest must be perfected if it is to have the kind of priority the lender or seller will want it to have in tangling with other parties who might be claiming an interest in the same collateral. Note that at least for accounts, this means that perfection will have to be obtained through a filing, as there is nothing tangible there and perfection by possession is simply not possible. Perfection on chattel paper may be accomplished by either filing or the taking of possession under § 9-313. As laid out in Comments 4 and 5 to § 9-109, and for underlying reasons that I believe to be beyond the scope of the introductory course in Secured Transactions, the purchase of a payment intangible or a promissory note is "treated differently," at least in some respects, from the purchase an account or chattel paper. Perfection, for example, is automatic under § 9-309(3) or (4) upon attachment. Parties who purchase promissory notes will necessarily be more concerned with the rules for negotiation of such instruments found in Article 3 than with any potential problem arising under Article 9.

PROBLEMS

29.5   Suppose that Downhill Equipment does sell a large number of its accounts to FLF. The factoring firm makes no filing with respect to the transaction. When the funds that Downhill has received from this sale is running low and its bills still need to be paid, Downhill goes to a local bank, Pine Tree National, and arranges for a loan under which the bank will get a security interest in these same accounts — as listed in an Exhibit which is made part of the written security agreement signed by an authorized party on behalf of Downhill. The bank then files an initial financing statement in the correct place and under Downhill's correct name, indicating the collateral to be "Certain Accounts as listed in Exhibit A attached hereto." Exhibit A is indeed attached and made part of Pine Tree's filing. Which of the parties whose cash has been shoring up Downhill — FLF or Pine Tree National — will have priority in this set of accounts and in any proceeds generated by them, that is, the amounts that are eventually paid by Downhill's customers as they become due?

29.6 For this problem take Pine Tree out of the picture and return to the simpler situation of Problems 29.3 and 29.4. Add to those facts the unhappy news that due to a severe downturn in the popularity of downhill skiing, Downhill Equipment is forced to declare bankruptcy. The trustee in bankruptcy insists that the accounts sold by that company to FLF be transferred back to her as they are part of the bankruptcy estate which she is to administer. Will she be successful in sweeping these accounts back and into the estate? Recall that Bankruptcy Code § 541 states that, with some exceptions not relevant here, the estate is comprised of "all legal or equitable interests of the debtor in property as of the commencement of the case." For the opinion of the drafters of Revised Article 9 on this point, see Comment 5 to § 9-109. If you just can't get enough of this stuff, you could also look at Permanent Editorial Board Commentary No. 14.

29.7 Louie Glitz operates a small jewelry boutique, Louie's of Litchfield, as a sole proprietor. In 2010, Goldie, the representative of Golden Baubles, Inc., a new line of one-of-a-kind high-end pieces of jewelry, pays a visit to Louie's place of business. She tries to convince him that he should purchase jewelry from her business to add to his inventory. Louie says he is not interested in doing this, as he has no idea how well such high priced items will sell to his regular clientele. Louie does enter into an agreement with Goldie under which Golden Baubles will deliver to his shop a representative selection of its line of jewelry, with prices on each piece being set by the company. If any piece sells, Louie will pay over to the company 85% of what he gets for the item. If the Golden Baubles's jewelry ends up not selling as well as that company estimates it will, either that company or Louie can decide that he will no longer attempt to sell their products, and all jewelry not sold will be returned to Golden Baubles.

(a) What term does Article 9 use to describe this type of transaction?
(b) Is this transaction governed by Article 9? If so, does the standard Article 9 set of terms — security interest, debtor, secured party, and collateral — apply? How?

(c) If the arrangement between Louie and Golden Baubles is a consignment governed by Article 9, what action or actions would you advise Golden Baubles take to protect itself to the extent possible again any creditors of Louie's or the possibility that Louie may declare himself bankrupt?

ON THOSE CONSIGNMENTS GOVERNED BY ARTICLE 9

Once it is determined that a transaction results in a consignment which falls within the scope of Article 9, the course to follow is remarkably clear. The consignment is treated as a PMSI which the consignor has reserved in the goods consigned, which are considered to be goods held by the consignee as inventory. The consignor is therefore well advised to perfect on the goods and also to follow the procedure laid out in §9-324(b) for gaining the advantage of the special priority rule which applies to the PMSI in inventory.

One further point. In the previous chapter we dealt with the question of when a transaction purporting to be a "lease" by the parties entering into it is in reality not a lease at all but rather a present sale of goods with the supposed "lessor" really the seller of goods which retains an Article 9 security interest in them. The supposed lessor is, therefore, obliged to follow all the rules required of a secured party under Article 9 or suffer the consequences. In determining what type of transaction a given transaction "is," the Uniform Commercial Code follows the rule of substance over form. The same type of characterization problem can arise when a transaction is set up as a "consignment," but is really not meant to work the way a true consignment does. In some trades, it is not unusual for inventory to be delivered to a retailer or distributor under an agreement which is written up as a consignment but under which the parties have no expectation that the "consignor" will bear the risk that the goods do not sell and be willing to take them back if they do not. What is — for reasons arising not out of the Uniform Commercial Code, but having to do with other considerations, or for no good reason other than that "this is the way it is always done" — a transaction which is in economic reality a present sale with a PMSI reserved is written up as a consignment of goods. It will not surprise you to learn that in such an instance if an issue arises this so-called "disguised consignment" will be treated by the courts as what it is in fact, a sale with a PMSI attached.

There remains one final consideration: What if a consignment, a true consignment, of goods is made but it does not fall within the definition of that term as set out in §9-102(a)(20)? See the problem below and the case following.

PROBLEM

29.8 We return to the jewelry store run by Louie Glitz. One day Nettie Nouveau, a woman from the town who he has always thought to be quite well-off comes to him and a in muted voice explains to him that she is "temporarily a little strapped for funds." She takes out of her handbag a necklace studded with diamonds and emeralds and asks whether Louie would be interested in buying the item. He replies that he would not, but that he would be willing to put it on display in his shop and try to sell it for her. If he does sell it he would hand the money he receives over to her, minus only a 10% commission. They agree that if it doesn't sell within six months the necklace will be returned to her. Is the agreement Nettie and Louie have entered into a consignment to which Article 9 applies? If not, what exactly is the legal framework which will govern their rights, and also any rights to the necklace that either may want to assert against third parties?

IN RE MORGANSEN'S LTD.

United States District Court for the Eastern District of New York, 2005
59 U.C.C. Rep. Serv. 2d 1121

Spatt, District Judge: This appeal arises from the October 14, 2003 Memorandum of Decision and Order by United States Bankruptcy Judge Stan Bernstein which granted the application of the Chapter 7 Trustee of Morgansen's Ltd. to hold an auction sale.

I. Background

The following facts are taken from the parties' submissions on this motion and the bankruptcy record on appeal. They are undisputed except where noted.

On February 11, 2001, the Appellant, Gail S. Goss ("Goss" or the "Appellant") as Executrix of the Estate of Esther A. O'Keeffe (the "Estate"), entered into written agreement with Morgansen's Ltd. ("Morgansen's" or the "Appellee" or the "Debtor") for the sale of personal property entitled "CONSIGNMENT AGREEMENT BETWEEN MORGANSEN'S LTD. ("MORGANSEN'S"). . . ." (the "Agreement") (emphasis in original).

The Agreement stipulated that Morgansen's would sell the Appellant's property for the benefit of the Estate with a 10% commission of the gross proceeds as compensation for its services. Under the Agreement, Goss set the minimum reserve price and could withdraw any item on 30 days' notice without charge. There is no evidence that Goss filed any UCC financing statements with respect to the consigned goods.

During various evidentiary hearings and status conferences, a representative of the Debtor testified that it was engaged in the business of selling various expensive items such as jewelry, art, collectibles, and furniture in a shop in South Hampton, New York. Morgansen's acquired their goods by direct purchase from liquidating estates in the area and by consignment. Approximately 70% of their items were obtained by consignment. These items were sold to retail customers, other dealers, and interior decorators. The Debtor also conducted auction sales of its inventory. The Debtor's representative further testified that its core base of customers were interior decorators who would, in turn, resell the items to their clients. All of the goods obtained by direct purchase and by consignment were commingled in the shop and were displayed in cases. During the summer, the shop was open five to seven days a week. During the remainder of the year, the shop was open only two or three days a week.

On February 20, 2003, Morgansen's filed a voluntary petition with the United States Bankruptcy Court for the Eastern District of New York for relief pursuant to Chapter 11 of the Bankruptcy Code. On August 26, 2003, the Bankruptcy Court converted the petition into a Chapter 7 case. Also, on that same date, the court appointed Neil H. Ackerman, Esq. as the trustee (the "Trustee"). The Appellant contends that she never received notice of the bankruptcy filing or the conversion.

Subsequently, the Trustee conducted a lien search, and found no liens of record. He subsequently instructed David Maltz & Co., an auctioneer, to secure the Debtor's premises and arrange for an auction sale, for which the Trustee would seek approval from the Bankruptcy Court. The Trustee also instructed the auctioneer to place a notice on Morgansen's door stating that the Debtor was in bankruptcy, and setting forth the auctioneer's phone number to be called if there were any questions. The auctioneer received calls from numerous people who had previously consigned goods to the Debtor. The Trustee's review of the list of creditors and schedules that had been filed by the Debtor indicated that there were many individuals who had not been listed by the Debtor at the time of the bankruptcy filing.

On September 17, 2003, the Trustee filed an application with the Bankruptcy Court to hold a hearing on a twelve day expedited notice with regard to a proposed auction sale (the "Notice"). On September 19, 2003, the Bankruptcy Court granted this request and scheduled a hearing for October 1, 2003. The Notice also stated that objections to the auction were to be filed by September 30, 2003. The counsel for the Trustee served the Notice on all persons known at that time to be creditors, consignors, or who were otherwise believed to have an interest in the case, including Goss. Prior to the hearing, several consignors, including Goss, filed written objections to the auction sale. In addition, in a letter to the Trustee dated September 19, 2004, William F. Bates, Esq. ("Bates"), as counsel for Goss, stated that several large items were still in the possession of Morgansen's and that "[n]one of this property belongs to Morgansen's Ltd. None of it should be sold at auction." According to this letter, the estimated value of the "large items of personal property" that were in the possession of Morgansen's was approximately $35,000.

During the October 1, 2003 hearing, at which Appellant's counsel was present, the Bankruptcy Court heard arguments and factual presentations from the Trustee and the named auctioneer, David R. Maltz ("Maltz"). They proposed to have the auction on the premises of the Debtor, as opposed to the Maltz warehouse, because it would be prohibitively costly to relocate the goods from South Hampton to the auctioneer's warehouse in Plainview, New York. In addition, there was a great risk that in the process there would be substantial breakage of fragile goods. They also proposed to conduct the auction as soon as possible given the probable onset of adverse weather conditions and their concern that buyers might not remain in the resort town of South Hampton during the winter months. Furthermore, the Trustee stressed that monthly costs for rent, utilities, and insurance were accruing and that he had no assurance that those costs would not materially increase. Everyone present at the hearing had the opportunity to cross-examine Maltz.

At this hearing, the Bankruptcy Court also heard arguments from the various consignors. The Appellant's counsel presented numerous arguments to the Bankruptcy Court but did not call any witnesses or present any evidence in support of his contention. The Bankruptcy Court granted the objectors additional time to brief the issues and permitted them to file memoranda by October 13, 2003. The Court also granted a continuance of the hearing until October 14, 2003. Goss did not file additional objections.

Also at the October 1, 2003 hearing, the Trustee advised the Court and all present, that a creditors' meeting pursuant to 11 U.S.C. § 341 would be held on October 9, 2003. It was announced that all consignors and other interested persons could attend this meeting and examine the Debtor's principal at length with regard to the relevant issues. The Appellant did not attend the October 9, 2003 meeting. Nor did she conduct any discovery, or attempt to contact or subpoena any witnesses. The Appellant did not testify or produce any witnesses to testify before the Bankruptcy Court.

On October 14, 2003, the consignors and the Trustee reconvened before the Bankruptcy Court. Felicia Branescu, the Debtor's principal, appeared at this hearing but Goss did not request to examine her.

On October 14, 2003, the Bankruptcy Court overruled all of the objections brought by the interested parties and granted the Trustee's motion to hold the auction sale. In a written decision issued that same day, Judge Bernstein stated the relevant law as follows:

> The law of consignments is governed by Uniform Commercial Code (UCC), especially sections UCC 9-102(a)(20) and next UCC 2-326, as amended by the State of New York, effective July 1, 2002 [2001?]. The standard approach is first to go to section 9-102(a)(20), and if the transaction does not fit under this section, then go next to section 2-326; if the transaction does not fit under section 2-326, then the transaction falls entirely outside the Uniform Commercial Code, and the Court must then fall back on the common law of bailments and other traditional practices.

Corrected Mem. and Order dated 10/14/03

In applying this analysis, Judge Bernstein first determined that the consignors did not carry their burden of establishing that the protections afforded by Section [Article?] 9 of the New York Uniform Commercial

Code (the "UCC") applied. The Bankruptcy Court then conducted an analysis pursuant to section 2-326 of the UCC. In so doing, Judge Bernstein determined that because the goods in question were delivered to Morgansen's on a "sale or return basis," they are "subject to the buyer's creditors while in the buyer's possession." Accordingly, Judge Bernstein found that "the law is painfully clear — anybody who delivers goods with a "right of return" to a merchant who sells them under its own name is at risk that the merchant may file for bankruptcy relief, and the trustee will liquidate the goods for the benefit of the creditors." Thus, the court granted the Trustees motion to hold an auction sale and overruled any objections to the sale. The Court notes that the Appellant did not file a formal request to stay the auction sale with either the Bankruptcy Court or this Court.

Thereafter, an auction sale was held in accordance with the Bankruptcy Court's decision. It is not clear from the papers the exact date of the auction. The auction sale raised $88,554.40 in revenue.

On October 27, 2003, Goss appealed from the Bankruptcy Court's Decision authorizing the auction sale. On appeal, the Appellant raises the following issues:

1. Whether the Appellant was denied due process when she did not receive adequate notice of Morgansen's bankruptcy, the conversion of Morgansen's case from Chapter 11 to Chapter 7, or of the auction sale?
2. Whether the Bankruptcy Court erred in concluding that the transaction at issue was governed by the New York Uniform Commercial Code and that Appellant's personal property was subject to the rights of creditors?

II. Discussion

[On the first issue, the Court found that, under the circumstances of the case, the Appellant's due process rights were not violated. It then moved on to the second issue raised by the Appellant.]

The Appellant argues that the Bankruptcy Court erred in applying the New York UCC because the transaction at issue falls outside its scope. Rather, the Appellant argues that the Bankruptcy Court should have applied common law agency principles.

At the outset, the Court enunciates the policy underlying the law of consignments:

> The basis for this hostility to consignment arrangements from the bankruptcy courts is fairly obvious. Regardless of the legal theory of the consignment, in practical operation it looks like a sales transaction in which the unpaid seller retains a secret lien in his goods. *From a creditor's point of view, the consigned goods appear to be part of the regular inventory of the consignee which, therefore, ought to be subject to their claims.* What is more, unlike a pre-code chattel mortgage, there is no public filing or other notoriety respecting the consignment to warn the creditors that the consignor may have rights in the goods which are superior to theirs.

In re Truck Accessories Distributing, Inc., 238 B.R. 444, 448 (Bankr. E.D. Ark. 1999) (emphasis added) (internal quotations and citations omitted).

Section 541 of the Bankruptcy Code broadly states that a bankruptcy estate is created by the commencement of a case under 11 U.S.C. §§ 301, 302, or 303. Pursuant to Section 541(a)(1), all interests of the debtor in personal property as of the commencement of the case becomes property of the estate. Also, "items in the possession of the debtor may become property of the estate only to the extent of the debtor's property interest in those items." 5 *Collier on Bankruptcy*, § 541.06[1-a] (15th Ed. rev. 1999).

To determine whether the items in question, which were undeniably in the possession of the Debtor at the time of the bankruptcy filing, are part of the bankruptcy estate, the Bankruptcy Court correctly looked first to Article 9 and then to Article 2 of the UCC. Prior to July 1, 2001, UCC distinguished between a "true" consignment and a consignment intended as a security interest. A "true" consignment sale, was addressed in UCC § 2-326. Prior to the 2001 amendment, this section essentially stated that "while goods are in the possession of the consignee, they will be subject to the claims of the possessing party's creditors unless the consignor complies with an applicable sign-posting statute, the possessing party is known by his or her creditors to be dealing in the goods of others, or the consignor complies with the filing provisions of Article 9." On the other hand, consignment intended as a security interest were covered by Article 9 which governed secured transactions. Thus, in order to protect the security interest in the consigned goods, the consignor would have to prefect his or her security interest by filing the requisite financing statement

On July 1, 2001, Section 2-326 was amended so that transactions involving consignments would generally be covered by Article 9. However, as set forth below, certain consignments, such as the one at issue in this case, that are not consignments under § 9-102(a)(20) may be covered by UCC Article 2. *See* UCC § 2-326, Official Comment P4 (stating that "*[C]ertain* true consignment transactions were dealt with in former Sections 2-326(3) and 9-114. These provisions have been deleted and have been replaced by new provisions in Article 9.") (emphasis added).

Article 9, Section 102(a)(20) of the UCC defines "consignment" as follows [reproducing that definition.]

The Bankruptcy Court found that the transaction at issue did not satisfy this definition. First, the Bankruptcy Court found "[u]nder (A)(i), the debtor is indisputably a merchant who deals in goods delivered to it for the purpose of sale, and the debtor operates under a trade name other than the names of the 'consignors.'" As to the second element, namely, whether the merchant is an auctioneer, Judge Bernstein held that although, "the consignors who opposed the auction represented that the debtor was, in fact, an auctioneer by virtue of its holding several auctions a year, especially during the summer months, at its least premises in the Hamptons," Morgansen's "did not exclusively act as an auctioneer" because the it sold its own goods and some of the consigned goods in "non-auction" transactions.

The Court notes that although Morgansen's operated under the name "Morgansen's, Ltd., Auctioneers & Appraisers," and its website, business cards, telephone book listing, and other advertising materials, which all indicate in one way or another that Morgansen's is in the auction business, as pointed out by the Bankruptcy Court, the exact proportion of Morgansen's business that is actually dedicated to auctions is not clear. In any event, with regard to the third element, the Bankruptcy Court found that "none of the objecting consignors put on any proof that the debtor was not generally known by its creditors to be substantially engaged in selling the goods of others." (internal quotation omitted). Thus, the Bankruptcy Court concluded that the transaction at issue was not a consignment under Article 9. The Court agrees. Significantly, Goss does not object to the Bankruptcy Courts conclusion that her transaction is not covered by Article 9.

Although Article 9 does not apply, the court must next analyze this transaction under Article 2. This section is construed broadly and states "[u]nless the context otherwise requires, this Article applies to transaction in goods. . . ." UCC § 2-102.

Section 2-326 states as follows [quoting that section]. Pursuant to this section, when delivered goods may be returned by the buyer and the goods are delivered primarily for use the transaction is a "sale on approval." On the other hand, if the goods are delivered primarily for resale, the transaction is a "sale or return." According to the Official Comment to this section, goods that are "sale on approval" are subject to the claims of the buyer's creditors only at acceptance, while goods that are "sale or return" are subject to claims of creditors while in the buyer's possession. UCC §§ 2-326(1) and 2-326(2) (McKinney 1991).

The Bankruptcy Court concluded that this section applied to the transaction at issue. In particular, with respect to this section, the Bankruptcy Court found that Morgansen's was authorized to sell the Appellant's item by private sales, and/or by auction, and its only written obligation was to pay to Goss the net proceeds of the sale, less its commission. As such, the Bankruptcy Court found that "[u]nder UCC Section 2-326 as amended, goods which are consigned for sale, are property of the bankruptcy estate of the 'consignee,' and subject to the claims of the creditors of the entity doing the sale (Morgansen's)."

The Appellant claims that the Bankruptcy Court erred in applying this section of the UCC. Rather, the Appellant argues that "Article 2 only applies to the sale of goods," and that this transaction created a mere agency relationship.

At the outset, the Official Comment to the revised UCC § 2-326 indicates that certain consignments are covered by Article 2. Turning to the language of Section 2-326, the record reveals that the Appellant delivered the property to the buyer, Morgansen's, with the intent and understanding that Morgansen's would sell the items, either by private sales or auction. Morgansen's had complete discretion to sell the consigned goods at any time, place, or manner it saw fit. In addition, pursuant to the agreement,

Goss could not demand that the goods be immediately returned, but rather could only do so on 30 days, notice. Pursuant to the policy governing this statute, Morgansen's was under no obligation to reveal to a customer or creditor whether the goods were on consignment or owned by Morgansen's. Although the Appellant asserts that "it is unreasonable to conclude that creditors or anyone else dealing with Morgansen's would not know that Morgansen's is not the owner of the substantial portion of the goods in its possession and that these goods are not available to creditors," the record does not support this contention. *See, e.g., In re Wicaco Machine Co., Inc.,* 770 F.2d 1074 (3d Cir. 1985) (evidence that one-fifth of the creditors had knowledge that the debtor engaged in the sale of other people goods was not sufficient to demonstrate that the debtor dealt in the sale of other people's goods even though the one fifth represented 63% of the value of the claims against the Debtor.).

Upon close review of this matter, the Court finds that there is one important issue with respect to the application of section 2-326 upon which the Bankruptcy Court failed to elaborate, namely the fact that this section refers to goods that are delivered to a *buyer.* According to Section 1-103 of the UCC, which is applicable here, a "buyer" is a "person who buys or contracts to buy goods." With respect to classifying a transaction as a "sale or return," "[a]lthough a buyer retains the right to return goods, a completed sale is generally deemed to have taken place and title passes to the buyer." *Paramount Pictures Corp. v. Carol Pub. Group, Inc.,* 25 F. Supp. 2d 372, 375 (S.D.N.Y. 1998) (internal quotations and citations omitted). Although the Bankruptcy Court characterized Morgansen's as a "'buyer' for resale," there is no evidence that title passed from Goss to Morgansen's with respect to any of the consigned items.

Thus, with respect to Section 2-326, the Court requires clarification of the term "buyer for resale" as used by the Bankruptcy Court to define Morgansen's. Accordingly, this issue will be remanded to the Bankruptcy Court to address this concern and any other related matter that might arise.

II. CONCLUSION

Based on the foregoing, it is hereby

ORDERED, that the Order of United States Bankruptcy Judge Stan Bernstein dated October 14, 2003, is affirmed in part and remanded in part; and it is further

ORDERED, that this matter is respectfully remanded to the Bankruptcy Court for further proceedings in accordance with this Order; and it is further

ORDERED, that the Clerk of the Court is directed to close this case.

SO ORDERED.

CHAPTER
30

Interests Not Covered by Article 9

A. INTRODUCTION

1. Certain Interests Not Covered

Subsection 9-109(1), on which we have been relying for our understanding of the general scope of Article 9, does begin with the important language that the article applies to transactions, which it then goes on to enumerate, "except as otherwise provided in subsections (c) and (d)." We now turn to a consideration of those exceptions — not all of them, but at least the most significant. Even before that, however, we take a quick look via the first problem that follows at subsection (b), which does not so much narrow the scope of Article 9 as clarify its treatment of a situation which might otherwise be open to some question. After that first problem, it is on to some particularly interesting — and in many situations critical — instances which fall within the exceptions of (c) or (d).

2. When Federal Law Preempts

Subsection 9-109(c)(1) provides that Article 9, as state statutory law, does not apply to the extent that "a statute, regulation, or treaty of the United States preempts" the article. Since the original introduction of Article 9 in the 1960s, this exemption has been known to pertain without question to a number of types of property for which the federal government keeps its own official listing of ownership *and* where that listing also allows for the recording of any security interest in the property which is subject to, and the ownership of which is presumably recorded with, a federal agency under the relevant federal law. For example, the Federal Aviation Act calls for the Federal Aviation Administration to set up a central filing system to record any conveyance of or interest taken in any "civil aircraft of the United States" as well as certain engines, propellers, and stores of spare parts maintained by and for air carriers. So if a lender takes a security interest in such stuff it must perfect on that interest by making a proper filing *with the FAA*. Filing a UCC1 in the regular matter will not perfect the interest. In a similar fashion, the Surface Transportation Board — an agency created in 1996 upon the abolition of the Interstate Commerce Commission — has as part of its mission recordation of all liens taken in railroad equipment, such as railcars and the like. This federal scheme for keeping track of security interests in railroad equipment effectively preempts Article 9.

In recent years, the question of what federal statues may preempt Article 9 has moved into a particularly significant — and potentially troubling — arena. Many forms of what is today referred to as *intellectual property* is either created or recorded under one federal statute or another. This has lead to a good deal of discussion and litigation about where the proper place is to file notice of a security interest taken in a copyright, a trademark, a patent, and so on. We enter into these fascinating, if murky, waters with Problem 30.2.

3.   The Federal Tax Lien Act

Federal Tax law is, well, a law unto itself. Commercial lenders have a special concern because the Internal Revenue Service has the power, when a taxpayer fails to pay as the IRS expects, to assess what is due and to put a federal tax lien for this amount on all of the taxpayer's property. You will not be surprised to find out that under the Internal Revenue Code such federal tax liens may have priority over liens or security interests held in the taxpayer's property arising under other law, say for instance, Article 9 of the Uniform Commercial Code. In fact, under certain circumstances the federal tax lien make have precedence even over an interest that was properly filed upon *prior* to the tax lien's being attached to the property. This makes up the third topic of this chapter.

4.   Miscellaneous Other Liens or Interests

Finally, as you can see by just taking a glance at § 9-109(d), there is a whole laundry list of other interests which for one reason or another have been written out of the Article 9 sphere of influence. Any one of the 13 exceptions listed in subsection (d) would, I am sure, make for interesting reading. I have decided to focus on just a couple of these cases, those set out in (d)(1) and (d)(2), to round out the material in this chapter. I trust that will be enough, even for the most inquisitive.

B.   PREPARATION

In preparation for discussion of the topics covered by this chapter, read carefully the following parts of the Code:

- Section 9-109(b), (c), and (d)(1) & (2)

When time comes for discussion of the Federal Tax Lien statute, I will reproduce a few choice words from the Internal Revenue Code at that time.

C.   PROBLEMS AND CASES

PROBLEMS

30.1   Homer buys a house with the help of a substantial sum of money borrowed from The First State Bank of Springfield. In connection with this loan he signs a note under which he promises to pay the bank a series of monthly payments over the next 30 years. He also signs an agreement under which the obligation to pay on the note is secured by an interest in the property itself.

(a) Is this transaction — and in particularly Homer's grant of a security interest in the home to the bank — a transaction governed by Article 9?
(b) Suppose the bank were to put up the note it has received from Homer as collateral for a loan it, the bank, is granted by another lender? Does Article 9 apply to *this* transaction?
(c) What if The First State Bank of Springfield sells this note to some other financial institution? Is this an Article 9 transaction?

30.2   The firm of Hyperwidgets, Inc. has recently received a patent for a device which will allow it to power the digital hyperwidgets that it manufactures on ethanol. It enters into an agreement with the Silicon Valley State Bank under which it will borrow a substantial sum of money, using this new patent as collateral in connection with the loan. A representative of the bank comes to you for advice. In dealing with this loan should the bank perfect on the security interest it will obtain in the patent by a filing in the state of incorporation of Hyperwidgets, Inc. or by a filing with the United States Patent and Trademark Office? If the answer seems simple to you, give a careful read of the case that follows.

IN RE CYBERNETIC SERVICES, INC.

United States Court of Appeals for the Ninth Circuit, 2001
252 F.3d 1039, 44 U.C.C. Rep. Serv. 2d 639

Susan P. Graber, Circuit Judge: As is often true in the field of intellectual property, we must apply an antiquated statute in a modern context. The question that we decide today is whether 35 U.S.C. § 261 of the Patent Act, or Article 9 of the Uniform Commercial Code (UCC), as adopted in California, requires the holder of a security interest in a patent to record that interest with the federal Patent and Trademark Office (PTO) in order to perfect the interest as against a subsequent lien creditor. We answer "no"; neither the Patent Act nor Article 9 so requires. We therefore affirm the decision of the Bankruptcy Appellate Panel (BAP).

Factual and Procedural Background

The parties stipulated to the relevant facts: Matsco, Inc., and Matsco Financial Corporation (Petitioners) have a security interest in a patent developed by Cybernetic Services, Inc. (Debtor). The patent is for a data recorder that is designed to capture data from a video signal regardless of the horizontal line in which the data is located. Petitioners' security interest in the patent was "properly prepared, executed by the Debtor and timely filed with the Secretary of State of the State of California," in accordance with the California Commercial Code. Petitioners did not record their interest with the PTO.

After Petitioners had recorded their security interest with the State of California, certain creditors filed an involuntary Chapter 7 petition against Debtor, and an order of relief was granted. The primary asset of Debtor's estate is the patent. Petitioners then filed a motion for relief from the automatic stay so that they could foreclose on their interest in the patent. The bankruptcy Trustee opposed the motion, arguing that Petitioners had failed to perfect their interest because they did not record it with the PTO.

The bankruptcy court ruled that Petitioners had properly perfected their security interest in the patent by following the provisions of Article 9. Furthermore, the court reasoned, because Petitioners had perfected their security interest before the filing of the bankruptcy petition, Petitioners had priority over the Trustee's claim in the patent and deserved relief from the stay. Accordingly, the bankruptcy court granted Petitioners' motion. The BAP affirmed. Petitioners then filed this timely appeal.

Discussion

Article 9 of the UCC, as adopted in California, governs the method for perfecting a security interest in personal property. Article 9 applies to "general intangibles," a term that includes intellectual property. The parties do not dispute that Petitioners complied with Article 9's general filing requirements and, in the case of most types of property, would have priority over a subsequent lien creditor. The narrower question in this case is whether Petitioners' actions were sufficient to perfect their interest when the "general intangible" to which the lien attached is a patent. The parties also do not dispute that, if Petitioners were required to file notice of their security interest in the patent with the PTO, then the Trustee, as a hypothetical lien creditor under 11 U.S.C. §544(a)(1), has a superior right to the patent.

The Trustee makes two arguments. First, the Trustee contends that the Patent Act preempts Article 9's filing requirements. Second, the Trustee argues that Article 9 itself provides that a security interest in a patent can be perfected only by filing it with the PTO. We discuss each argument in turn.

A.   PREEMPTION

1. The Analytical Framework

The Supremacy Clause, U.S. Const., Art. IV, cl. 2, invalidates state laws that "interfere with, or are contrary to," federal law. [Citations here, and in much of what is to follow, omitted.] Congress may preempt state law in several different ways. Congress may do so expressly (express preemption). Even in the absence of express preemptive text, Congress' intent to preempt an entire field of state law may be inferred "where the scheme of federal regulation is sufficiently comprehensive to make reasonable the inference that Congress 'left no room' for supplementary state regulation" (field preemption). State law also is preempted "when compliance with both state and federal law is impossible," or if the operation of state law "stands as an obstacle to the accomplishment and execution of the full purposes and objectives of Congress" (conflict preemption). In all cases, "congressional intent to preempt state law must be clear and manifest."

The Patent Act does not contain preemptive text, so express preemption is not an issue here. Concerning field and conflict preemption, the Supreme Court has adopted a "pragmatic" approach to deciding whether the Patent Act preempts a particular state law. Congress, in the Patent Act, "has balanced innovation incentives against promoting free competition, and state laws upsetting that balance are preempted." "State regulation of intellectual property must yield *to the extent that it clashes* with the balance struck by Congress" in the Patent Act. Using this form of analysis, the Supreme Court has held, on numerous occasions, that the Patent Act preempts a state law that grants patent-like protection to a product. Those cases do not control, however, because we are confronted not with a state law that grants patent-like protection to a product but, rather, with a state commercial law that provides a method for perfecting a security interest in a federally protected patent.

That distinction is key because the Supreme Court has instructed clearly that the Patent Act does not preempt every state commercial law that touches on intellectual property. For example, in *Aronson v. Quick Point Pencil Co.*, 440 U.S. 257, 262, 59 L. Ed. 2d 296, 99 S. Ct. 1096 (1979), the Supreme Court observed that commercial agreements "traditionally are the domain of state law. State law is not displaced merely because the contract relates to intellectual property which may or may not be patentable; the states are free to regulate the use of such intellectual property in any manner not inconsistent with federal law."

It is within this framework that we evaluate the Trustee's claim. The Trustee argues that the recording provision found in 35 U.S.C. § 261 requires that the holder of a security interest in a patent record that interest with the PTO in order to perfect as to a subsequent lien creditor. Section 261 provides:

> *Ownership; assignment*
> Subject to the provisions of this title, patents shall have the attributes of personal property.
>   Applications for patent, patents, or any interest therein, shall be assignable in law by an instrument in writing. The applicant, patentee, or his assigns or legal representatives may in like manner grant and convey an exclusive right under his application for patent, or patents, to the whole or any specified part of the United States.
>   A certificate of acknowledgment under the hand and official seal of a person authorized to administer oaths within the United States, or, in a foreign country, of a diplomatic or consular officer of the United States or an officer authorized to administer oaths whose authority is proved by a certificate of a diplomatic or consular officer of the United States, or apostille of an official designated by a foreign country which, by treaty or convention, accords like effect to apostilles of designated officials in the United States, shall be prima facie evidence of the execution of an assignment, grant or conveyance of a patent or application for patent.
>   *An assignment, grant or conveyance shall be void as against any subsequent purchaser or mortgagee for a valuable consideration, without notice, unless it is recorded in the Patent and Trademark Office* within three months from its date or prior to the date of such subsequent purchase or mortgage. (Emphasis added.)

If the Trustee's reading of the relevant portion of § 261 is correct, then to the extent that Article 9 allows a different method of perfection, it would be preempted under either a "field" or "conflict" preemption theory. That is because recording systems increase a patent's marketability and thus play an integral role in the incentive scheme created by Congress. Recording systems provide notice and certainty to present and future parties to a transaction; they work "by virtue of the fact that interested parties have a specific place to look in order to discover with certainty whether a particular interest has been transferred." If, as the Trustee argues, the Patent Act expressly delineates the place where a party must go to acquire notice and certainty about liens on patents, then a state law that requires the public to look elsewhere unquestionably would undercut the value of the Patent Act's recording scheme. If, on the other hand, § 261 does not cover liens on patents, then Article 9's filing requirements do not conflict with any policies inherent in the Patent Act's recording scheme. Article 9 itself recognizes the existence of preemption principles. California Commercial Code § 9104(a) [the precursor to present § 9-109(c)(1)] expressly subordinates Article 9's requirements to those of federal law.

2. The Patent Act Requires Parties to Record with the PTO Only Ownership Interest in Patents

As noted, the Patent Act's recording provision provides that an "assignment, grant or conveyance shall be void as against any subsequent purchaser or mortgagee for a valuable consideration, without notice, unless it is recorded in the [PTO]." 35 U.S.C. § 261. In order to determine whether Congress intended for parties to record with the PTO the type of interest that is at issue in this case, we must give the words of the statute the meaning that they had in 1870, the year in which the current version of § 261 was enacted. Our task is not an easy one because security interests, and the words used to describe them, have changed significantly since the 19th Century. *See generally* 4 James J. White & Robert S. Summers, *Uniform Commercial Code* § 30-1, at 2 (4th ed. 1995) (noting that, before the advent of Article 9, "the lawyer had to work with a variety of security devices, each governed by its own law"). For example, before Article 9, a party could secure property using a pledge, an assignment, a chattel mortgage, a chattel trust, a trust deed, a factor's lien, or a conditional sale. Grant Gilmore, *Security Interests in Personal Property* § 10.1, at 296 (1965). Each type of device carried with it elaborate rules that controlled its use, and each conferred different rights and liabilities upon the contracting parties. *See id.* § 11.1, at 333 (noting that a "considerable amount of pre-Code case law was devoted to the invalidation of security transactions on the ground that one of the specialized devices had been used outside its 'proper' field"). Article 9, which was first enacted in 1962, brought the "long history of the proliferation of independent security devices . . . to an end." *Id.* § 10.1, at 296. It did so in part by introducing a body of law that would govern a "single, 'unitary' security device": the Article 9 security interest. 4 White & Summers § 30-1, at 2.

With that history in mind, we must determine whether Congress intended to include the kind of transaction at issue in this case within the scope of 35 U.S.C. § 261. The first phrase in § 261's recording provision — "assignment, grant or conveyance" — refers to different types of transactions. The neighboring clause — "shall be void as against any subsequent purchaser or mortgagee" — refers to the status of the party that receives an interest in the patent. Therefore, for the Trustee to prevail in this case, (1) Petitioners' transaction with Debtor must have been the type of "assignment, grant or conveyance" referred to in § 261, and (2) the Trustee, who has the status of a hypothetical lien creditor, must be a "subsequent purchaser or mortgagee." We hold that neither condition is met.

As we will discuss next, our conclusion finds support in the text of § 261, keeping in view the historical definitions of the terms used in the recording provision; the context, structure, and policy behind § 261; Supreme Court precedent; and PTO regulations. We will begin by analyzing the statute's text and context, as interpreted by the Supreme Court. For the sake of clarity, we will discuss the two relevant phrases in the recording provision of § 261 separately.

a. The Phrase "Assignment, Grant or Conveyance" Concerns Transfers of Ownership Interests Only.

The historical meanings of the terms "assignment, grant or conveyance" all involved the transfer of an ownership interest. A patent "assignment" referred to a transaction that transferred specific rights in the patent, all involving the patent's title. A "grant," historically, also referred to a transfer of an ownership interest in a patent, but only as to a specific geographic area. Although older cases defining the term "conveyance" in the context of intangible property are sparse, and its historic meaning tended to vary, the common contemporaneous definition was "to transfer the legal title . . . from the present owner to another." That Congress intended to incorporate the common, contemporaneous meanings of the words "assignment," "grant," and "conveyance" into the Patent Act's recording provision can be seen when § 261 is examined in its entirety. By using the unambiguous words "ownership; assignment," Congress must have intended to introduce the subject that was to follow: the ownership of patents and the assignment thereof.

Continuing through § 261, the second paragraph states that patents shall be assignable by an instrument in writing. That paragraph goes on to provide that the patentee or the patentee's assigns "may in like manner *grant and convey an exclusive right* under his application for patent . . . to the whole or any specified part of the United States." (Emphasis added.) The types of transactions referred to in § 261's second paragraph — (1) the assignment of a patent, and (2) the grant or conveyance of an exclusive right in a patent in the whole or part of the United States — track the historical definitions of assignment, grant, and conveyance that we just discussed — transactions that all involve the transfer of an ownership interest in a patent.

Moreover, we presume that words used more than once in the same statute have the same meaning throughout. Here, the second paragraph of § 261 uses the words "grant and convey" to signify the transfer of an "exclusive right [in a patent] . . . to the whole or any specified part of the United States." We presume, then, that when Congress used the words "grant or conveyance" two paragraphs later in the same statute, Congress still intended to refer to ownership interests only.

Supreme Court precedent supports our view that the terms "assignment, grant or conveyance" refer to ownership interests only. [The court discusses the cases of *Waterman v. MacKenzie*, 138 U.S. 252, 255, 34 L. Ed. 923, 11 S. Ct. 334 (1891) and *Littlefield v. Perry*, 88 U.S. 205, 221, 22 L. Ed. 577 (1874).]

In summary, the statute's text, context, and structure, when read in the light of Supreme Court precedent, compel the conclusion that a security interest in a patent that does not involve a transfer of the rights of ownership is a "mere license" and is not an "assignment, grant or conveyance" within the meaning of 35 U.S.C. § 261. And because § 261 provides that only an "assignment, grant or conveyance shall be void" as against subsequent purchasers and mortgagees, only transfers of ownership interests need to be recorded with the PTO. In the present case, the parties do not dispute that the transaction that gave Petitioners their interest in the patent did not involve a transfer of an ownership interest in the patent. Petitioners held a "mere license," which did not have to be recorded with the PTO.

b. The Phrase "Subsequent Purchaser or Mortgagee" Does Not Include Subsequent Lien Creditors.

The Trustee's argument fails not only because a security interest that does not transfer ownership is not an "assignment, grant or conveyance," but also because he is not a subsequent "purchaser or mortgagee." Congress intended for parties to record their ownership interests in a patent so as to provide constructive notice only to subsequent holders of an ownership interest. Again, we derive our conclusion from the historical definitions of the words, from the context and structure of § 261, and from Supreme Court precedent.

The historical meaning of "purchaser or mortgagee" proves that Congress intended for the recording provision to give constructive notice only to subsequent holders of an ownership interest. For the sake of convenience, we begin with the definition of "mortgagee." Historically, a "mortgagee" was someone who obtained title to property used to secure a debt. *See* James Schouler, Personal Property § 416, at 622 (5th ed. 1918) (noting that "mortgages of chattels, then, are to be distinguished at common law from liens and pledges in this sort of out-and-out transfer of the title conditionally which is carried by the original transaction"). A "mortgage" must be differentiated from a "pledge," a term that is absent from the Patent Act. Professor Gilmore, in his treatise, Security Interests in Personal Property § 1.1, at 8, notes that the historical distinction between a pledge and a mortgage was that "the mortgagee got title or an estate whereas the pledgee got merely possession with a right to foreclose on default." Similarly, Judge Learned Hand wrote, in 1922, that it "is everywhere agreed that the significant distinction between a pledge and a mortgage is that in the first the creditor gets no title, . . . while in the second he does." *Ex parte Crombie & La Mothe, Inc. (In re German Publ'n Soc'y)*, 289 F. 509, 509 (S.D.N.Y. 1922).

That the Patent Act refers to securing a patent through a "mortgage" but not through a "pledge" is significant, for both were common methods of using a patent as collateral. Generally, the inclusion of certain terms in a statute implies the exclusion of others. It seems then, that by using the term "mortgagee," but not "lien" or "pledge," Congress intended in 1870 for the Patent Act's recording provision to protect only those who obtained title to a patent.

The term "purchaser" does not detract from this conclusion. Section 261 instructs that an unrecorded "assignment, grant or conveyance" shall be void as against a subsequent "purchaser . . . for a valuable consideration, without notice." The historical definition of a "purchaser for value and without notice" was a "*bona fide* purchaser. A purchaser . . . who takes a conveyance purporting to pass the entire title, legal and equitable," who pays value and does not have notice of the rights of others to the property. Bouvier's Law Dictionary 1005 (Baldwin's Century ed. 1926). The Supreme Court seems to have accepted this definition as well. *See Littlefield*, 88 U.S. at 221 (noting that "*bona fide* purchasers look to [the Patent Act's recording provision] for their protection").

Congress, by stating that certain transactions shall be void as against a subsequent "purchaser or mortgagee" intended for the words to be read together: A "purchaser" is one who buys an ownership interest in the patent, while a "mortgagee" is one who obtains an ownership interest in a patent as collateral for a debt.

Our previous comments about the context and structure of §261 support our conclusion that Congress intended to protect only subsequent holders of an ownership interest. As noted, the title of §261 is "Ownership; assignment," which suggests that the recording provision is concerned only with ownership interests. Similarly, the second paragraph delineates the types of transactions that §261 covers — (1) the assignment of a patent, and (2) the grant or conveyance of an exclusive right in the patent to the whole or any specified part of the United States — each involving the transfer of an ownership interest in a patent. It follows that, when Congress referred to a "subsequent purchaser or mortgagee," it was simply describing the future recipients of those transactions. In one case the recipient bought the interest (purchaser), while in the other the recipient loaned money and received the interest as collateral (mortgagee). In either case, an ownership interest was transferred. Precedent confirms our reading of the statute. The Supreme Court has endorsed the view that Congress intended to provide constructive notice only to subsequent recipients of an ownership interest in a patent. In *Waterman*, the Court observed, as we do, that the Patent Act refers to a "mortgage" but not to a "pledge." Moreover, with title or possession of the property came certain rights in the mortgagee. But a patent right "is incorporeal property, not susceptible of actual delivery or possession." Therefore, when "it is provided by statute that a mortgage of personal property shall not be valid against third persons, unless the mortgage is recorded, *a recording of the mortgage is a substitute for, and . . . equivalent to, a delivery of possession, and makes the title and the possession of the mortgagee good against all the world.*"

In summary, the historical definitions of the terms "purchaser or mortgagee," taken in context and read in the light of Supreme Court precedent, establish that Congress was concerned only with providing constructive notice to subsequent parties who take an ownership interest in the patent in question. The Trustee is not a subsequent "mortgagee," as that term is used in 35 U.S.C. §261, because the holder of a patent mortgage holds title to the patent itself. *Waterman*, 138 U.S. at 258. Instead, the Trustee is a hypothetical lien creditor. The Patent Act does not require parties to record documents in order to provide constructive notice to subsequent lien creditors who do not hold title to the patent.

3. Public Policies that Underlie Recording Provisions Cannot Override the Text of the Patent Act

The Trustee argues that requiring lien creditors to record their interests with the PTO is in line with the general policy behind recording statutes. It

may be, as the Trustee argues, that a national system of filing security interests is more efficient and effective than a state-by-state system. However,
there is no statutory hook upon which to hang the Trustee's policy arguments. Moreover, we are not concerned with the policy behind recording
statutes generally but, rather, with the policy behind 35 U.S.C. § 261
specifically.

Title 35 U.S.C. § 261, as we have demonstrated and as its label suggests, is
concerned with patent ownership. In that provision Congress gave patent
holders the right to transfer their ownership interests, but only in specific
ways. The congressional policy behind that decision was to protect the
patent holder and the public for, as the Supreme Court put it,

> it was obviously not the intention of the legislature to permit several monopolies
> to be made out of one, and divided among different persons within the same
> limits. Such a division would inevitably lead to fraudulent impositions upon per-
> sons who desired to purchase the use of the improvement, and would subject a
> party who, under a mistake as to his rights, used the invention without authority,
> to be harassed by a multiplicity of suits instead of one, and to successive recoveries
> of damages by different persons holding different portions of the patent right in
> the same place.

Gayler v. Wilder, 51 U.S. (10 How.) 477, 494, 13 L. Ed. 504, 10 How. 477
(1850) The recording provision, if read to include ownership interests only,
is perfectly aligned with that policy. By contrast, a security interest in a
patent does not make "several monopolies . . . out of one, . . . divided
among different persons within the same limits." *Gayler*, 51 U.S. at 494.

We must interpret § 261 in the light of the purposes that Congress was
seeking to serve. Congress simply was not concerned with nonownership
interests in patents, and this limitation was well understood at the time. As
explained in a venerable treatise on the law of patents:

> A license is not such a conveyance of an interest in the patented invention as to
> affect its ownership, and hence is not required to be recorded. . . . The value of
> the patented invention to the vendee may be impaired by such outstanding
> licenses, but of this he must inform himself at his own risk as best he may. The
> record of a license, not being legally required, is not constructive notice to any
> person for any purpose.

2 Robinson § 817, at 602-03 (footnotes omitted).

The Patent Act was written long before the advent of the "unitary"
Article 9 security interest. But we must interpret 35 U.S.C. § 261 as Congress
wrote it. The Constitution entrusts to Congress, not to the courts, the role of
ensuring that statutes keep up with changes in financing practices. It is
notable that Congress has revised the Patent Act numerous times since
its enactment, most recently in 1999, but it has not updated the Act's recording provision. We decline the Trustee's invitation to do so in Congress'
place.

4. Cases Interpreting the Copyright Act Do Not Control

The Trustee's final argument is that this court should follow *Nat'l Peregrine, Inc. v. Capitol Fed. Savs. & Loan Ass'n (In re Peregrine Entm't, Ltd.)*, 116 B.R. 194, 200 (C.D. Cal. 1990), in which a bankruptcy court held that the Copyright Act preempts state methods of perfecting security interests in copyrights. The court in *Peregrine* observed that the "federal copyright laws ensure predictability and certainty of copyright ownership, promote national uniformity and avoid the practical difficulties of determining and enforcing an author's rights under the differing laws and in the separate courts of the various States." The court reasoned that allowing state methods to stand would conflict with those goals. *But see* 4 White & Summers § 30-12, at 86 (referring to *Peregrine* as "misguided").

Of course, *Peregrine* is not binding on this court although, in the present case, we have no occasion to pass on its correctness as an interpretation of the Copyright Act. We note, however, that the Copyright Act, by its terms, governs security interests. The Copyright Act governs any "transfer" of ownership, which is defined by statute to include any "hypothecation." 17 U.S.C. § § 101, 201(d)(1). A "hypothecation" is the "pledging of something as security without delivery of title or possession." Black's Law Dictionary 747 (7th ed. 1999).

By contrast, the Patent Act does not refer to a "hypothecation" and, as we have demonstrated, does not refer to security interests at all. The fact that one federal intellectual property statute with a recording provision expressly refers to security interests (the Copyright Act), while another does not (the Patent Act), is more evidence that security interests are *outside* the scope of 35 U.S.C. § 261.

5. PTO Regulations Require Only the Recording of Documents that Transfer Ownership in a Patent

It is worthy of mention that the applicable PTO regulations parallel our interpretation of 35 U.S.C. § 261. Title 37 C.F.R. § 3.11(a) provides that "assignments" must be recorded in the PTO. That regulation also states that "other documents *affecting title* to applications, patents, or registrations, will be recorded at the discretion of the Commissioner" of Patents and Trademarks. (Emphasis added.) Section 313 of the Manual of Patent Examining Procedure (7th ed. 1998) explains that "other documents" that may be filed include "agreements which convey a security interest. Such documents are recorded in the public interest in order to give third parties notification of equitable interests. . . ."

Title 37 C.F.R. § 3.11 is illuminating because it shows that the PTO does not consider security interests to be "assignments, grants or conveyances." Under 35 U.S.C. § 261, certain conveyances — those that transfer an ownership interest — *must* be recorded to be effective as against a subsequent purchaser or mortgagee. If security interests *were* "assignments, grants or conveyances," then they would *have* to be filed to provide constructive notice to a subsequent purchaser or mortgagee, consistent with the Patent

Act. As a matter of law and logic, the Commissioner would not have the "discretion" to reject federal filing.

The PTO consistently has interpreted 35 U.S.C. § 261 in this way. An earlier version of the regulation, 37 C.F.R. § 1.331, which was originally enacted in 1959, allowed for the federal filing of "other instruments affecting title to a patent . . . *even though the recording thereof may not serve as constructive notice under 35 U.S.C. 261.*"(emphasis added). Similarly, 37 C.F.R. § 7, also originally enacted in 1959, distinguished between "assignments" and "licenses," much as *Waterman* had. "Assignment[ ]" meant any "instrument which conveys to the Government only the title to a patent." 37 C.F.R. § 7.2 (removed and reserved Oct. 10, 1997). "Licenses" were any instruments other than assignments. 37 C.F.R. § 7.3 (removed and reserved Oct. 10, 1997).

We acknowledge that the issue in this case "is a pure question of statutory construction for the courts to decide" and that the PTO's interpretation is not entitled to any particular deference. Although the statute is ambiguous now, it seems not to have been in 1870. Moreover, we do not believe that 35 U.S.C. § 261 contains within it a delegation of authority, either explicit or implicit, that would enable the PTO to broaden or narrow the reach of the Patent Act's recording provision. However, when we must interpret an archaic statute, the historic practice of the agency that was created to help implement that statute can shed light on its meaning. Under 37 C.F.R. § 3.11, Petitioners were not required to record with the PTO their security interest in order to perfect as to the Trustee.

6. There is no Conflict Between the Patent Act and Article 9 in this Case

Because the Patent Act does not cover security interests or lien creditors at all, there is no conflict between 35 U.S.C. § 261 and Article 9. Petitioners did not have to file with the PTO to perfect their security interest as to a subsequent lien creditor. . . .

C. CONCLUSION

Because 35 U.S.C. § 261 concerns only transactions that effect a transfer of an ownership interest in a patent, the Patent Act does not preempt Article 9, and neither California Commercial Code § 9104(a) nor § 9302(3) applies. Consequently, Petitioners perfected their security interest in Debtor's patent by recording it with the California Secretary of State. They have priority over the Trustee's claim because they recorded their interest before the filing of the bankruptcy petition.

AFFIRMED.

PERFECTING ON INTELLECTUAL PROPERTY

The Supreme Court denied a petition for a writ of certiorari filed in connection with the *Cybernetics* case, 534 U.S. 1130 (2002). While the

Ninth Circuit's decision was rendered under the prerevision version of Article 9, there seems little reason to expect that it would be handled any differently today under the present version of Article 9. In addition, several cases decided after *Cybernetics* have come to the same conclusion — the way to perfect on a patent is to file a UCC1 in whichever jurisdiction Article 9 would have you file given the location of the debtor.

A natural follow-up question is whether the same result holds true for other types of intellectual property, which is in some sense a creature of federal law given the possible exclusion from the coverage of Article 9 set out in §9-109(1)(c). As the court in *Cybernetics* points out, the case of *In re Peregrine Entertainment, Ltd.*, 116 Bankr. 194, 11 U.C.C.2d 1025 (C.D. Cal. 1990) held that the appropriate place for filing in order to perfect on a registered copyright is with the federal Copyright Office. While this result has been criticized by commentators — as you may have noted in the *Cybernetics* case — the United States Court of Appeals for the Ninth Circuit adopted its basic conclusion in the case of *In re World Auxiliary Power Co.*, 303 F.3d 1120 (9th Cir. 2002). In the *World Auxiliary Power* case itself, however, the court determined that *Peregrine* held true only for a registered copyright. When the collateral is an *unregistered* copyright, the court ruled, perfection should be by filing in the Article 9 filing system. The Supreme Court once again passed on the opportunity to weigh in on the matter by denying a petition for certiorari. 537 U.S. 1146 (2003). Earlier a judge of the District Court for the Central District of California declared in *In re 199Z, Inc.*, 137 Bankr. 778, 17 U.C.C.2d 598 (C.D. Cal. 1992), that the *Peregrine* decision was distinguishable when the collateral at issue was a federally registered *trademark* and that the correct method of perfection on such a mark was via the Article 9 filing system.

THE FEDERAL TAX LIEN

There is a good deal that could be written about federal tax liens, and it will not surprise you that you would find it a fairly heady experience if you chose to read in its entirety the Federal Tax Lien Act of 1966 as set out in §§6321 through 6323 of the Internal Revenue Code. Here we will look at just the highlights, and even then in somewhat abbreviated form. We start with the fact that Congress has written into the Internal Revenue Code the possibility of a lien in favor of the federal government to aid it in the collection of taxes.

§6321. Lien for taxes

If any person liable to pay any tax neglects or refuses to pay the same after demand, the amount (including any interest, additional amount, addition to tax, or assessable penalty, together with any costs that may accrue in addition thereto) shall be a lien in favor of the United States upon all property and rights to property, whether real or personal, belonging to such person.

Fair enough. The problem comes in — at least as we and not the hapless taxpayers are concerned — when we look to how any federal tax lien authorized under this section stacks up against security interests created under and governed by Article 9. Obvious the federal law will have the decisive say on the matter. We start by checking out the first subsection of § 6323:

> **§ 6323. Validity and priority against certain persons**
> (a) Purchasers, holders of security interests, mechanic's lienors, and judgment lien creditors. The lien imposed by section 6321 shall not be valid as against any purchaser, holder of a security interest, mechanic's lienor, or judgment lien creditor until notice thereof which meets the requirements of subsection (f) has been filed by the Secretary.

The effect of this provision is straightforward enough. A party holding an Article 9 security interest in the taxpayer's property will have priority over the federal government claiming a tax lien in the same property, but *only* before the IRS files a notice of its lien. You can appreciate the difficulty this causes for any lender considering taking an Article 9 security interest in any of the borrower's property as collateral. Under this provision, should the debtor ever fail to pay its federal taxes and the IRS then *file* with respect to its lien on the debtor's property — and you can be sure the Internal Revenue Service is quite willing to and capable of doing just this — the secured party's interest has lost its priority in the subject property. The Federal Tax Lien jumps to the head of the line. In recognition of this problem, which would obviously deter secured lending of the type we have been considering throughout this entire course, § 6323 steps back from this position of absolute priority for the federal tax lien in certain well-defined situations. That in which we are interested is found in subsections (c) and (d).

> (c) Protection for certain commercial transactions financing agreements, etc.
>   (1) In general. To the extent provided in this subsection, even though notice of a lien imposed by section 6321 has been filed, such lien shall not be valid with respect to a security interest which came into existence after tax lien filing but which —
>   (A) is in qualified property covered by the terms of a written agreement entered into before tax lien filing and constituting —
>   (i) a commercial transactions financing agreement,
>   (ii) a real property construction or improvement financing agreement, or
>   (iii) an obligatory disbursement agreement, and
>   (B) is protected under local law against a judgment lien arising, as of the time of tax lien filing, out of an unsecured obligation.
>   (2) Commercial transactions financing agreement. For purposes of this subsection —
>   (A) Definition. The term "commercial transactions financing agreement" means an agreement (entered into by a person in the course of his trade or business) —
>   (i) to make loans to the taxpayer to be secured by commercial financing security acquired by the taxpayer in the ordinary course of his trade or business, or

(ii) to purchase commercial financing security (other than inventory) acquired by the taxpayer in the ordinary course of his trade or business; but such an agreement shall be treated as coming within the term only to the extent that such loan or purchase is made before the 46th day after the date of tax lien filing or (if earlier) before the lender or purchaser had actual notice or knowledge of such tax lien filing.

(B) Limitation on Qualified Property. The term "qualified property," when used with respect to a commercial transactions financing agreement, includes only commercial financing security acquired by the taxpayer before the 46th day after the date of tax lien filing.

(C) Commercial Financing Security Defined. The term "commercial financing security" means (i) paper of a kind ordinarily arising in commercial transactions, (ii) accounts receivable, (iii) mortgages on real property, and (iv) inventory.

(d) 45-day period for making disbursements. Even though notice of a lien imposed by section 6321 has been filed, such lien shall not be valid with respect to a security interest which came into existence after tax lien filing by reason of disbursements made before the 46th day after the date of tax lien filing, or (if earlier) before the person making such disbursements had actual notice or knowledge of tax lien filing, but only if such security interest—

(1) is in property (A) subject, at the time of tax lien filing, to the lien imposed by section 6321, and (B) covered by the terms of a written agreement entered into before tax lien filing, and

(2) is protected under local law against a judgment lien arising, as of the time of tax lien filing, out of an unsecured obligation.

That would seem to offer sufficient protection to a secured party, at least if it knew not only Article 9 law but this part of the federal tax law as well. The secured party would know what to search for, and even how often to search if it was making future advances as part of some kind of continuing financing arrangement. The problem comes up, however, at least since the advent of the most recent version of Article 9, because of the manner in which and the place where the IRS files on the liens it assesses. Section 6323 concludes with the following provision, to which you will notice subsection (a) refers:

(f) Place for filing notice; form.

(1) Place for filing. The notice referred to in subsection (a) shall be filed—

(A) Under state laws.

(i) Real property. . . .

(ii) Personal property. In the case of personal property, whether tangible or intangible, in one office within the State (or the county, or other governmental subdivision), as designated by the laws of such State, in which the property subject to the lien is situated, except that State law merely conforming to or reenacting Federal law establishing a national filing system does not constitute a second office for filing as designated by the laws of such State; or

(B) With clerk of district court. In the office of the clerk of the United States district court for the judicial district in which the property subject to the lien is situated, whenever the State has not by law designated one office which meets the requirements of subparagraph (A); or

(C) With recorder of deeds of the District of Columbia. In the office of the Recorder of Deeds of the District of Columbia, if the property subject to the lien is situated in the District of Columbia.

(2) Situs of property subject to lien. For purposes of paragraphs (1) and (4), property shall be deemed to be situated—

(A) Real property. In the case of real property, at its physical location; or

(B) Personal property. In the case of personal property, whether tangible or intangible, at the residence of the taxpayer at the time the notice of lien is filed. For purposes of paragraph (2)(B), the residence of a corporation or partnership shall be deemed to be the place at which the principal executive office of the business is located, and the residence of a taxpayer whose residence is without the United States shall be deemed to be in the District of Columbia.

(3) Form. The form and content of the notice referred to in subsection (a) shall be prescribed by the Secretary. Such notice shall be valid notwithstanding any other provision of law regarding the form or content of a notice of lien.

All of which sets you up to read the following famous—or should I say infamous?—recent case.

IN RE SPEARING TOOL AND MANUFACTURING CO., INC.

United States Court of Appeals for the Sixth Circuit, 2005
412 F.3d 653. 56 U.C.C. Rep. Serv. 2d 807

COOK, Circuit Judge: In this case arising out of bankruptcy proceedings, the government appeals the district court's reversal of the bankruptcy court's grant of summary judgment for the government. For the following reasons, we reverse the district court, and affirm the bankruptcy court.

I. BACKGROUND AND PROCEDURAL HISTORY

In April 1998, Spearing Tool and Manufacturing Co. and appellee Crestmark entered into a lending agreement, which granted Crestmark a security interest in all of Spearing's assets. The bank perfected its security interest by filing a financing statement under the Uniform Commercial Code, identifying Spearing as "Spearing Tool and Manufacturing Co.," its precise name registered with the Michigan Secretary of State.

In April 2001, Spearing entered into a secured financing arrangement with Crestmark, under which Crestmark agreed to purchase accounts receivable from Spearing, and Spearing granted Crestmark a security interest in all its assets. Crestmark perfected its security interest by filing a UCC financing statement, again using Spearing's precise name registered with the Michigan Secretary of State.

Meanwhile, Spearing fell behind in its federal employment-tax payments. On October 15, 2001, the IRS filed two notices of federal tax lien against Spearing with the Michigan Secretary of State. Each lien identified Spearing as "SPEARING TOOL & MFG. COMPANY INC.," which varied from Spearing's precise Michigan-registered name, because it used an ampersand in place of "and," abbreviated "Manufacturing" as "Mfg.," and spelled out "Company" rather than use the abbreviation "Co." But the name on the IRS lien notices was the precise name Spearing gave on its quarterly federal tax return for the third quarter of 2001, as well as its return for fourth-quarter 1994, the first quarter for which it was delinquent. For most of the relevant tax periods, however, Spearing filed returns as "Spearing Tool & Manufacturing"—neither its precise Michigan-registered name, nor the name on the IRS tax liens.

Crestmark periodically submitted lien search requests to the Michigan Secretary of State, using Spearing's exact registered name. Because Michigan has limited electronic-search technology, searches disclose only liens matching the precise name searched—not liens such as the IRS's, filed under slightly different or abbreviated names. [In a note, the Court explains that Michigan's search engine ignores various "noise words" and their abbreviations, including "Incorporated" and "Company," but *not* "Manufacturing" or "and."] Crestmark's February 2002 search results came back from the Secretary of State's office with a handwritten note stating: "You may wish to search using Spearing Tool & Mfg. Company Inc." But Crestmark did not search for that name at the time, and its exact-registered-name searches thus did not reveal the IRS liens. So Crestmark, unaware of the tax liens, advanced more funds to Spearing between October 2001 and April 2002.

On April 16, 2002, Spearing filed a Chapter-11 bankruptcy petition. Only afterward did Crestmark finally search for "Spearing Tool & Mfg. Company Inc." and discover the tax-lien notices. Crestmark then filed the complaint in this case to determine lien priority. The bankruptcy court determined the government had priority; the district court reversed. The questions now before us are whether state or federal law determines the sufficiency of the IRS's tax-lien notices, and whether the IRS notices sufficed to give the IRS liens priority.

II. FEDERAL LAW CONTROLS WHETHER THE IRS's LIEN NOTICE SUFFICED

Crestmark argues Michigan law should control the form and content of the IRS's tax lien with respect to taxpayer identification. The district court, though it decided in favor of Crestmark on other grounds, rightly disagreed.

When the IRS files a lien against a taxpayer's property, it must do so "in one office within the State . . . as designated by the laws of such State, in which the property subject to the lien is situated." 26 U.S.C. § 6323(f)(1)(A). The Internal Revenue Code provides that the form and content "shall be prescribed by the [U.S. Treasury] Secretary" and "be valid *notwithstanding any other provision of law regarding the form or content of a notice of lien.*" 26 U.S.C. §6323(f)(3) (emphasis added). Regulations provide that the IRS must file tax-lien notices using IRS Form 668, which must "identify the taxpayer, the tax liability giving rise to the lien, and the date the assessment arose." 26 C.F.R. §301.6323(f)-1(d)(2). Form-668 notice "is valid notwithstanding any other provision of law regarding the form or content of a notice of lien. For example, omission from the notice of lien of a description of the property subject to the lien does not affect the validity thereof even though State law may require that the notice contain a description of property subject to the lien." §301.6323(f)-1(d)(1); *see also United States v. Union Cent. Life Ins. Co.*, 368 U.S. 291, 296, 7 L. Ed. 2d 294, 82 S. Ct. 349, 1962-1 C.B. 328 (1961) (Michigan's requirement that tax liens describe relevant property "placed obstacles to the enforcement of federal tax liens that Congress had not permitted.").

The plain text of the statute and regulations indicates Form-668 notice suffices, regardless of state law. We therefore need only consider how much specificity federal law requires for taxpayer identification on tax liens.

III. THE NOTICE HERE SUFFICED

An IRS tax lien need not perfectly identify the taxpayer. *See, e.g., Hudgins v. IRS (In re Hudgins)*, 967 F.2d 973, 976 (4th Cir. 1992); *Tony Thornton Auction Serv., Inc. v. United States*, 791 F.2d 635, 639 (8th Cir. 1986); *Reid v. IRS (In re Reid)*, 182 B.R. 443, 446 (Bankr. E.D. Va. 1995). The question before us is whether the IRS's identification of Spearing was sufficient. We conclude it was.

The critical issue in determining whether an abbreviated or erroneous name sufficiently identifies a taxpayer is whether a "reasonable and diligent search would have revealed the existence of the notices of the federal tax liens under these names." *Tony Thornton*, 791 F.2d at 639. In *Tony Thornton*, for example, liens identifying the taxpayer as "Davis's Restaurant" and "Daviss (sic) Restaurant" sufficed to identify a business correctly known as "Davis Family Restaurant." In *Hudgins*, the IRS lien identified the taxpayer as "Hudgins Masonry, Inc." instead of by the taxpayer's personal name, Michael Steven Hudgins. This notice nonetheless sufficed, given that both names would be listed on the same page of the state's lien index.

Crestmark argues, and we agree, that those cases mean little here because in each, creditors could search a physical index and were likely to notice similar entries listed next to or near one another—an option which no longer exists under Michigan's electronic-search system. So the question for this case becomes whether Crestmark conducted a reasonable and diligent electronic search. It did not.

Crestmark should have searched here for "Spearing Tool & Mfg." as well as "Spearing Tool and Manufacturing." "Mfg." and the ampersand are, of course, most common abbreviations—so common that, for example, we use them as a rule in our case citations. Crestmark had notice that Spearing sometimes used these abbreviations, and the Michigan Secretary of State's office *recommended* a search using the abbreviations. Combined, these factors indicate that a reasonable, diligent search by Crestmark of the Michigan lien filings for this business would have disclosed Spearing's IRS tax liens.

Crestmark argues for the unreasonableness of requiring multiple searches by offering the extreme example of a name it claims could be abbreviated 288 different ways ("ABCD Christian Brothers Construction and Development Company of Michigan, Inc."). Here, however, only two relevant words could be, and commonly are, abbreviated: "Manufacturing" and "and" — and the Secretary of State specifically recommended searching for those abbreviations. We express no opinion about whether creditors have a general obligation to search name variations. Our holding is limited to these facts.

Finally, we note that policy considerations also support the IRS's position. A requirement that tax liens identify a taxpayer with absolute precision would be unduly burdensome to the government's tax-collection efforts. Indeed, such a requirement might burden the government at least as much as Crestmark claims it would be burdened by having to perform multiple lien searches. "The overriding purpose of the tax lien statute obviously is to ensure prompt revenue collection." *United States v. Kimbell Foods, Inc.*, 440 U.S. 715, 734-35, 59 L. Ed. 2d 711, 99 S. Ct. 1448 (1979). "To attribute to Congress a purpose so to weaken the tax liens it has created would require very clear language," which we lack here. *Union Central,* 368 U.S. at 294. Further, to subject the federal government to different identification requirements — varying with each state's electronic-search technology — "would run counter to the principle of uniformity which has long been the accepted practice in the field of federal taxation." *Id.*

Crestmark urges us to require IRS liens to meet the same precise-identification requirement other lien notices now must meet under Uniform Commercial Code Article 9. *See* Mich. Comp. Laws § 440.9503(1) ("A financing statement sufficiently provides the name of [a] debtor [that is] a registered organization, only if the financing statement provides the name of the debtor indicated on the public record of the debtor's jurisdiction of organization which shows the debtor to have been organized."). We decline to do so. The UCC applies to transactions "that create[ ] a security interest in personal property or fixtures *by contract.*" Mich. Comp. Laws § 440.9109(1)(a) (emphasis added). Thus, the IRS would be exempt from UCC requirements even without the strong federal policy favoring unfettered tax collection.

More importantly, the Supreme Court has noted that the United States, as an involuntary creditor of delinquent taxpayers, is entitled to special priority over voluntary creditors. *See, e.g., Kimbell Foods,* 440 U.S. at 734-35, 737-38. Thus, while we understand that a requirement that the IRS comply with UCC Article 9 would spare banks considerable inconvenience, we conclude from Supreme-Court precedent that the federal government's interest in prompt, effective tax collection trumps the banks' convenience in loan collection.

IV. Conclusion

We reverse the district court and affirm the bankruptcy court's grant of summary judgment for the government.

ON THE SPEARING TOOL DECISION

Following this decision a petition for a rehearing en banc was denied in *United States v. Crestmark Bank (In re Spearing Tool & Mfg. Co.)*, 2005 U.S. App. LEXIS 29219 (6th Cir., Dec. 30, 2005). The Supreme Court denied a petition for certiorari in *Crestmark Bank v. United States*, 127 S. Ct. 41, 166 L. Ed. 2d 18, 2006 U.S. LEXIS 5700 (U.S., Oct. 2, 2006).

The result of the case, and the reasoning used by the panel of the Sixth Circuit to come to its decision caused considerable commentary, most if not all of it unfavorable. Typical is a column in the American Bankruptcy Institute Journal, which concluded:

> While the holding of *Spearing Tool* is limited to its facts and therefore of questionable precedent, from a policy perspective the ruling is troubling for at least two reasons. This case presented an excellent opportunity for the court to address the modern electronic filing environment and keep tax-collection practices in pace with the evolving changes in state law and private commerce. As it stands, the ruling only serves to increase the disconnect between state and federal law as the former struggles to adapt to technical evolution and the latter appears intransigent and unmoved by the resulting dilemma to secured creditors.
>
> To shield this anachronism within the bulwark of federal policy only serves to question the limits of such doctrines. It is not, quite frankly, too much to ask that the government get the name right. Such judicial paternalism seems to go too far if it essentially says, "we have to do everything in our power to save the government from itself just to keep the lights on around this place." The district court should be applauded for its efforts to reconcile these recurring tensions, however ephemeral and unrewarded they might have been.

Edmund S. Whitson, III, *"Spearing" the Secured Creditor: Sixth Circuit Applies "Bluebook" Rule to Lien Notice Requirements*, 24 Am. Bankr. Inst. J. 7 (Sept. 2005).

IN RE ALSTON

United States Bankruptcy Court for the District of New Jersey, 2005
322 Bankr. 265, 2005 Bankr. LEXIS 462

Raymond T. Lyons, United States Bankruptcy Judge: The issues in this adversary proceeding are:

1. Does an insurance adjuster have an equitable lien on the proceeds of a fire insurance policy?

2. If so, does the adjuster's equitable lien have priority over the claim to
    the insurance proceeds by secured creditors with a mortgage on the
    damaged real property?

Because (a) the adjuster's efforts created the fund, (b) the insured agreed
to compensate the adjuster from the fund, and (c) the secured creditor's
rights to the fund are derivative of the insured's, the court holds that the
insurance adjuster has an equitable lien on the fire insurance proceeds with
priority over the secured creditors.

FACTS AND PROCEDURAL HISTORY

Anthony and Lorraine Alston (the "Debtors") owned a commercial property in Irvington, New Jersey that they leased to tenants. Mr. & Mrs. Alston
had purchased the property from Hilton and Elizabeth Rose who took back
a purchase money mortgage to secure payment of the balance of the
purchase price. The mortgage required the Alstons to insure the property,
which they did, and to name the Roses on the policy, which they did not.
Fire severely damaged the building on December 29, 1999. The Alstons
retained plaintiff, Stuart Kramer, a licensed insurance adjuster, to assist
in the settlement of their claim under their insurance policies. The adjuster's compensation was agreed at 5% of the amounts recovered by the
Alstons from their insurance companies; and Alston assigned the insurance
proceeds to Kramer to secure his fee. Kramer assembled the information to
present the insurance claim, prepared the sworn statements and proof of
loss, submitted the same to the insurance companies and communicated
with the independent adjuster hired by the insurance companies to settle
the lose [sic].

About a year after the fire, but before the claim was settled, the Alstons
filed a voluntary petition under chapter 13 of the Bankruptcy Code. Mr. &
Mrs. Rose were listed as secured creditors holding a mortgage on the
commercial property. The insurance adjuster was not listed as a creditor
and did not receive notice of the bankruptcy filing.

After filing their bankruptcy petition, the Debtors' insurance claim
remained unresolved. The Debtors hired special counsel to commence a
lawsuit against the insurance carrier in state court. The lawsuit settled for
$160,000.00. After payment of the 1/3 contingency fee to special counsel,
approximately $106,000.00 was available as a net settlement. Mr. & Mrs.
Rose, the mortgagees, claimed that they were entitled to the net proceeds
of the settlement. The note and mortgage given by the Alstons to the Roses
required the Alstons to insure their property against fire loss for the benefit
of the Roses. The Alstons had obtained fire insurance but neglected to have
the Roses' interest as mortgagee noted on the policy. The court previously
ruled that when a mortgage requires the mortgagor to carry insurance, the
mortgagee has an equitable lien on the insurance proceeds. *In re Moore,*

54 B.R. 781 (Bankr. E.D.N.C. 1985); In re Natalie, 174 B.R. 362 (Bankr. D.R.I. 1994).

Kramer first learned of the settlement of the insurance litigation through communication from the insurance carrier. Kramer then initiated this adversary proceeding asserting an equitable lien on the proceeds of the fire insurance litigation and priority over the secured creditors.

Discussion

New Jersey state law governs whether the adjuster has a lien on the insurance proceeds. No statute gives a public adjuster a lien; therefore, the adjuster claims an equitable lien. Neither the New Jersey Supreme Court nor any other New Jersey state court has addressed the issue of a public adjuster's equitable lien. Likewise, there are few decisions from other states on this subject. Cozen, *Insuring Real Property* § 26.02 (2004). Therefore, in the absence of a decision on point, it is the task of this court to predict how the New Jersey Supreme Court would rule if presented with the same issues.

I.   EQUITABLE LIEN OF THE INSURANCE ADJUSTER

In bankruptcy, the validity and extent of liens is ruled by state law, unless a federal policy would be frustrated by its application. [The court then discusses the law pertinent to the creation of equitable liens under the law of New Jersey.] In reviewing the facts of this case, equitable principles lead to a finding of an equitable lien on the insurance proceeds for the insurance adjuster. To begin with, while there was no written agreement between the adjuster and the secured creditors, there was a written agreement signed by the adjuster and the Debtors on December 29, 1999. This brief, one-page document recites the services the adjuster agreed to render and states that the signatories "hereby agree to pay and assign to [the adjuster] for services rendered 5% when adjusted, paid or otherwise recovered from the insurance companies." Thus, the adjuster expended effort and resources under the belief that he would be paid out of the insurance proceeds. The secured creditors concede that the adjuster did in fact render services—including reviewing the insurance coverage, preparing and submitting necessary documentation to the insurance company—which resulted in a settlement of insurance claims.

Accordingly, this court finds an equitable lien upon the insurance settlement proceeds in favor of the adjuster.

II.   PRIORITY OF THE FIRE ADJUSTER'S LIEN

The priority of the adjuster's equitable lien is the next question. Once again no New Jersey case is directly on point. "One case has held that if a public adjuster is retained by a named insured, and therefore has a contractual right to payment from that insured, he is probably not entitled to *quantum meruit* recovery from other insureds, such as a loss payee or mortgagee insured pursuant to a standard union mortgage clause." Cozen, *Insuring Real Property* § 26.02[3] (2004) citing *Public Adjustment Bureau, Inc. v. Bankers Federal Sav. & Loan Asso.*, 83 Misc. 2d 317, 371 N.Y.S.2d 347 (Civil Ct. 1975), *aff'd*, 61 A.D.2d 930, 403 N.Y.S.2d 19 (App. Div. 1978).

Most analogous is a case cited by plaintiffs, *First Federal Sav. & Loan Assn. v. Nieder*, 163 N.J. Super. 308, 394 A.2d 896 (App. Div. 1978). In *First Federal*, a mortgagor suffered fire damage and eventually obtained a judgment against the insurance carrier and its agents. The trial court ruled that the mortgagee was entitled to the proceeds of the judgment by reason of a provision in the mortgage requiring the mortgagor to insure the property. However, the court also ruled that the lien of the attorney for the mortgagor had to be paid prior to the mortgagee. The Appellate Division upheld the trial court's decision, stating that while the mortgagee was subrogated to the mortgagor's right to insurance proceeds, "it [also] stands in her shoes as well with respect to the lien of her attorney." *Id. at 313.* The court concluded that "it would be unconscionable to allow [the mortgagee] to take the fund without bearing the legal expense incurred in creating it."

There is also the treatment of the common-law artisan's lien by New Jersey courts. The common-law artisan's lien has long been recognized in New Jersey. See *White v. Smith*, 44 N.J.L. 105 (Supreme Court 1882). When an artisan improves property, and therefore enhances the value of the property by his skill, labor, or materials, he acquires the right to a specific lien on the property. *Ferrante Equipment Company v. Foley Machinery Co.*, 49 NJ. 432, 437, 231 A.2d 208 (1967); *White*, at 109 (artisan's lien attaches when a bailee "has expended his skill and labor in the improvement of the chattel and thereby conferred an additional value on it). This right is not extinguished until the lienholder is paid. *Ferrante*, 49 N.J. at 437. The priority of the artisan's lien was examined by the New Jersey Supreme Court in *Ferrante*.

In *Ferrante*, an equipment company sold a bulldozer to buyer and promptly filed a financing statement under the Uniform Commercial Code. After defaulting on payments, the buyer brought the bulldozer to a mechanic to get it repaired, then subsequently failed to pay the bill for such repairs. The secured creditor sued for possession of the bulldozer. The mechanic refused to surrender possession, arguing that it had a lien on the amount of work and materials it provided. The court reviewed the statute governing U.C.C. priorities, which states that a possessory lien "has priority over a security interest in the goods unless the lien is created by a statute that expressly provides otherwise." The court then ruled that "the holder of an artisan's lien takes priority over the holder of a perfected security interest under the Uniform Commercial Code." The court's reasoning was that the mechanic's efforts had enhanced the value of the bulldozer, creating a common-law artisan's lien superior to that of the equipment company that had recorded its lien. *Ferrante* illustrates the importance New Jersey courts place on compensating those whose efforts enhance the value of property.

Examination of statutory liens might shed light on the public policy recognized by the legislature. *See* N.J.S.A. 2A:44-125 et seq. (Municipal Mechanics' Lien Law); N.J.S.A. 2A:42-1 (Landlord's Lien); N.J.S.A. 12A:7-209 (Warehouseman's Lien); N.J.S.A. 2A:44-20 (Garage Keeper's Lien); N.J.S.A. 2A:13-5 (Attorney's Lien); N.J.S.A. 2A:44A-1 et. seq. (Construction Lien Law). These straightforward priority schemes illustrate the legislature's preference for giving priority to those who goods or services bring value, or increase value to the collateral on which others claim. See *Craft v. Stevenson Lumber Yard, Inc.* 179 N.J. 56, 68, 843 A.2d 1076 (2004) (main purpose of Construction Lien Law and Mechanic's Lien law is to help secure those contractors and suppliers who furnish goods and services pursuant to a written contract).

The court is particularly persuaded, however, by the ruling and reasoning of *First Federal.* In *First Federal,* as in this case, a secured creditor had rights to proceeds of an insurance policy by stepping into the shoes of the named insured, the mortgagor. In both First Federal and this case, there is a third-party whose efforts created the fund. To permit the secured creditor to reap the benefits of the insurance settlement without assuring full payment to the insurance adjusters whose efforts lead to that settlement would be inequitable. Therefore, the court finds that the adjuster's equitable lien on the insurance settlement proceeds must be paid in full before release of that fund to the secured creditors.

QUESTION ON ALSTON

The court ruled in this case that the equitable lien of the insurance adjuster would prevail over another party's security interest in real property, that is, its rights under a real estate mortgage. Do you see any reason to doubt that it would have ruled in the same way if the property that had been destroyed had been personal property and the party contesting the priority of the adjuster had been an Article 9 secured party with a perfected interest in the stuff that had been destroyed by the fire?

PROBLEM

30.3 Matteo buys an auto on credit from Sheldon's Motors of Secaucus, New Jersey, with the dealership retaining a security interest in the auto to secure Matteo's regular payment of the monthly payments called for under his loan agreement. Prior to his having made the last payment to the dealership, Matteo takes the auto into a McGeehan's garage to have some repair work done on it. When Matteo comes back to the garage, he finds the work has been done, but McGeehan insists that she is not obligated to let him have the car back until he, Matteo, pays her for the work she has done on it. She says she is asserting her rights under a mechanic's lien statute in effect in New Jersey. Before he can get the car back, Matteo files a petition in bankruptcy. As the bankruptcy proceedings play out, will the dealership's or McGeehan's interest in the vehicle have priority? See § 9-333.

PART VII

DEFAULT AND ENFORCEMENT

CHAPTER
31

Default

A. INTRODUCTION

1. *"Events of Default"*

As we know from § 9-203(a), the very essence of a security interest that has attached to some particular collateral is that it is then "enforceable against the debtor with respect to the collateral." In this and the chapters to follow we consider exactly when, how, and following what rules the secured party may enforce its security interest under the provisions of Article 9. We begin with what is, at least initially, a very simple statement. The rights of the secured party to enforce in accordance with Article 9 (and that's the way it will have to be done, obviously, the secured party's right to enforce arising out of the article) are all predicated upon the debtor's being in *default* in some way.

Article 9 does not set out what kind of acts or omissions by the debtor will cause the debtor to be in default. Other than the failure to pay the obligation being secured when and as due, which all seem to agree is by its very nature a default even if it is never explicitly charactered as such anywhere, it is left to the parties to specify by their agreement what events or circumstances will constitute what we tend to call "events of default" by the debtor, triggering enforcement rights in the secured party with respect to the particular transaction. A written security agreement will typically include (it certainly should include) a distinct section setting forth, either rather briefly or in elaborate detail as the individual transaction warrants, what happenings will constitute a default. The sort of events or circumstances which you will regularly see among the listing of events of default in even fairly simple written security agreements would include:

- The making of any false or misleading statements or the provision of any false information by the debtor in connection with its obtaining the loan or the making of the security agreement.
- The collateral being lost, stolen, damaged, or destroyed.

- The failure of the debtor to keep the collateral insured and in good repair.
- A grant by the debtor of a security interest in the same collateral to any other party.
- Any levy upon or seizure of the collateral or subjection of it to any judicial process.
- Failure of the debtor to notify the secured party as required by other provisions of the agreement of any change of name, change in location of the debtor, and so on.
- A disposition of any or all of the collateral other than in a manner specifically authorized in the agreement.
- Failure of the debtor to properly inform the secured party or account for any proceeds of an authorized disposition of the collateral as it has agreed to elsewhere in the security agreement.
- Death, dissolution, termination of existence, reorganization, insolvency, or business failure of the debtor.

And this can be just the beginning. In a large, highly complex financing, the debtor may have made many other promises in the security agreement — as to how it will run its business, maintain its financial structure, etc. — and its breach of any of these promises will typically be set out as an event of default. So too will the debtor's resistance to any inspection — of the collateral or of the debtor's books — which the secured party was given the right to carry out under the agreement.

2.   General Insecurity and Acceleration Clauses

Just in case the secured party, in drafting up the listing of specified events of default for inclusion in the written security agreement, may have failed to anticipate some event which would later cause it anxiety, the security agreement will often contain what is referred to as a "general insecurity clause." The exact wording varies, but such a provision will usually read something like this, tacked on at the end of the detailed listing of the type given above:

- Any other change in the condition or affairs, financial or otherwise, of the Debtor or any guarantor or surety of the liability secured by this agreement which in the sole opinion of the Secured Party impairs the value of the collateral or imperils the prospect of the Debtor's full performance or satisfaction of the obligation secured by this agreement.

Such a provision is often teamed up with what is termed an "acceleration clause." Such a clause is found in language of the agreement of the parties which provides that upon either some specified, or perhaps any, default by the debtor the *entire amount* the debtor owes to the secured party, and not just an upcoming installment, becomes due.

Your initial reaction upon hearing of such provisions might understandably be to wonder whether they are too vague or one-sided to be enforceable as a general matter. As you will see, however, the Uniform Commercial Code explicitly recognizes and indeed validates both general insecurity and acceleration provisions, limiting their use only in that the secured party must be acting in good faith in relying upon them. This brings to center stage, as you will see in material to follow, what the measure of "good faith" is for these purposes.

B. PREPARATION

In preparation for discussion of the problems and the cases in this chapter, read the following parts of the Code:

* Section 9-601 along with Comments 2 and 3 to this section
* If you are studying from the Original Version of Article 1, look at § 1-208, its Official Comment, and the definitions of "good faith" in both § 1-201(19) and § 9-102(a)(43)
* If you are studying from the Revised Version of Article 1, look at § 1R-309, its Official Comment, and the definitions of "good faith" in § 1R-201(b)(20) and § 9-102(a)(43)

C. PROBLEMS AND CASES

PROBLEM

31.1 Carlos buys a new automobile with the help of an auto loan which he obtains from the Smallville State Bank. His dealings with the bank are all carried out with one particular loan officer, Jennie, who works for the bank. As part of this loan transaction Carlos grants a purchase-money security interest in the auto to the bank, which duly perfects its interest. The security agreement signed by Carlos contains a clause providing that among the listed instances of default by Carlos would be

> Any change in the condition or affairs, financial or otherwise, of the Debtor which in the sole opinion of the Secured Party impairs the value of the collateral or imperils the prospect of the Debtor's full performance or satisfaction of the obligation secured by this agreement.

One month after Carlos has obtained this loan from the bank and bought the car, a supervisor in the loan department of the bank, in the course of her review of Jennie's performance as a loan officer, notices that Jennie had granted the loan to Carlos even though the information he had given to Jennie (all true) should have led to a rejection of his loan application under the standards that had been adopted by the bank's lending committee and which Jennie had been instructed to apply.

(a) Can the bank now rightfully consider Carlos in default on his loan based on the general insecurity clause included in the security agreement as quoted above?

(b) Suppose instead that the loan to Carlos had originally fell, if just barely, within the guidelines set by the bank's lending committee. A few months later the country's economy goes into a deep recession. The bank's lending committee, noting a steady rise in defaults by borrowers very much like Carlos, decides to tighten up its lending policy. Under the new policy, Carlos would no longer qualify for the auto loan he had earlier received. Would the bank be within its rights to consider Carlos in default, invoking the general insecurity clause he had agreed to?

(c) Continuing on from the prior part of this problem, suppose further than because of the general country-wide recession there is considerable speculation that the largest employer in town, a major manufacturer which as it happens is where Carlos works, may have to close its plant or at least lay off a significant number of workers. Could the bank call a default given this situation?

(d) What if Carlos's employer does decide to lay off a number of workers and Carlos is among them. He informs the bank of this fact, but also gives his assurances that he will be keeping up with his auto payments, thanks to some savings he has in reserve, and that he will be "most aggressively" seeking other employment. Would the bank be justified in invoking its rights under the general insecurity clause now?

(e) Finally, suppose that the situation is as in (d) above. Within a few months, Carlos is late in making his monthly payment to the bank. An officer of the bank has also heard rumors from a usually reliable source in the community to the effect that Carlos has not been paying his rent for the past couple of months but has worked out an arrangement with his landlord under which he will be given some leeway in paying his rent for at least a few months until he is able to land a new job. May the bank regard Carlos as in default under the general insecurity clause in light of this further information?

STAR BANK, KENTON COUNTY, INC. v. PARNELL

Court of Appeals of Kentucky, 1998
992 S.W.2d 189, 39 U.C.C. Rep. Serv. 2d 972

JOHNSON, Judge: Star Bank, Kenton Co., Inc. (the Bank) appeals from a judgment entered following a jury verdict that denied the Bank the right to enforce personal guaranties given by Ralph Parnell (Parnell) and Arvind Karnik (Karnik) to secure promissory notes for ARRA Enterprises, Inc. (ARRA), Parnell's and Karnik's recreational vehicle dealership corporation which had declared bankruptcy. Having concluded that there is insufficient evidence to support the jury's verdict, we reverse and remand.

Parnell and Karnik incorporated ARRA in 1983 to purchase the assets of a recreational vehicle (R.V.) and camper sales and rental dealership located in West Chester, Ohio. The Bank loaned Parnell and Karnik each $12,500 and ARRA $25,000 to purchase the dealership. The Bank's vice-president of commercial lending, Clint Carmack (Carmack), assisted in making the loans. Over the next several years, ARRA sought additional funds from the Bank, and on each occasion, Carmack assisted Parnell and Karnik in obtaining the loans. Parnell testified that with the assistance of Carmack, ARRA never had any trouble obtaining financing from the Bank. The assets and the debts of the corporation grew and in December 1985, the Bank approved a $750,000 line of credit for ARRA.

Carmack left the Bank in late December 1985, for a reason not indicated in the record. In early 1986, Dan Baker (Baker) replaced Carmack as vice-president of commercial lending. Baker testified that he reviewed ARRA's file and did not find any documents concerning the financial status of ARRA. In February 1986, Baker estimated ARRA's assets to be valued at $427,000 and determined that ARRA had drawn approximately $635,000 against its line of credit. The difference of over $200,000 between ARRA's assets and ARRA's liabilities caused Baker to be concerned about the Bank's security. Baker then requested financial statements from ARRA for 1984 and 1985. These statements, which Baker received in April 1986, revealed losses for these two years and a negative net worth of approximately $127,000. Baker expressed concern to Parnell and Karnik that the Bank's note was undersecured. He told them that there were two options: to move the line of credit to another bank or to restructure the notes to secure the Bank's position. When ARRA was unable to obtain financing from another bank, Baker asked that Parnell and Karnik provide additional collateral for the loan. This request was based on the following provisions in the note:

> Should the holder deem itself insecure, the Obligors shall deliver to the holder such additional Collateral as the holder requests.
>
> . . . .
>
> At the holder's option, all Obligations shall become immediately due and payable without notice or demand upon the occurrence of any of the following events of Default:
>
> . . . (vi) if the holder for any good faith reason deems itself insecure. . . .

Parnell and Karnik refused to provide additional collateral. Baker then told them that unless additional collateral was given as security, the Bank would accelerate the note and call it due. On July 15, 1986, Parnell and Karnik personally guaranteed the note and executed second mortgages on their homes.

For the next three years, ARRA had difficulty paying the Bank as well as other creditors. On July 1, 1989, the Bank declared the loans in default for non payment. On March 22, 1990, the Bank brought suit against ARRA, Parnell and Karnik to enforce the personal guaranties on the ARRA notes. It is unclear from the record, but near the same time, ARRA filed for bankruptcy relief.

In June 1996, a jury trial was held. At the close of the evidence, the Bank moved for a directed verdict, which the trial court denied. The jury was instructed as follows:

> You shall find in favor of the plaintiff and against the defendants, unless you are satisfied from the evidence that plaintiff did not act in good faith when it made the determination that its loans were insecure and in requesting additional collateral from defendants to secure the loans to ARRA Enterprises, Inc. "Good faith" for purposes of this instruction means honesty in fact in the conduct or the transaction concerned.

The jury was charged under this instruction at approximately 10:30 A.M. Sometime shortly thereafter, the jury sent a note to the trial court with three questions. One question concerned Instruction No. 2, and read as follows: "In instruction no. II, what does 'honesty in fact' mean? Moral or legal?" The trial court responded that it could not answer the jury's questions. At approximately 2:00 P.M., the jury sent another note to the trial court which stated as follows: "We cannot come to agreement to question A. (unanimous verdict instruction) 4-8 What should we do? Where's lunch?" The trial court gave the jury a "modified Allen" charge similar to Kentucky Rules of Criminal Procedure 9.57. At 2:37 P.M. the jury returned a verdict against the Bank. The Bank moved the trial court for a judgment notwithstanding the verdict based on the lack of evidence that the Bank had acted "dishonestly or in bad faith." The trial court denied the motion. This appeal followed.

Since this case involves a secured transaction, a review of the relevant provisions of the Uniform Commercial Code (UCC) is required. UCC Section 1-208 provides as follows: [The court quotes that section.] "Good faith" is defined in UCC Section 1-201(19) as "honesty in fact in the conduct or transaction concerned." [Note the court is quoting the definition found in the prerevision version of Article 1. See the note that follows this case.]

Kentucky courts have adopted the majority position that "good faith" is a subjective determination. In *Fort Knox National Bank v. Gustafson*, Ky., 385 S.W.2d 196 (1964), one of only two Kentucky cases to discuss the "good faith" requirement of Section 1-201(19), the former Court of Appeals addressed the "good faith" needed to accelerate a bank note when the bank felt insecure. Gustafson had borrowed money to purchase a trailer to operate a diner and entered into a lease for property on which to place the trailer/diner. Within the next two years, the restaurant's checking account was overdrawn thirteen of twenty-five months and the lease payments were eight months in arrears. Gustafson had made 22 of 23 payments on the note, but he had been allowed to remain almost two months behind on the final payment because of the bank's "indulgence." However, the bank argued that this "indulgence" was contingent upon an earlier agreement that Gustafson obtain the consent of all creditors to likewise "indulge" her and that such agreements had not been obtained. The Court stated as follows:

> It has been mentioned that the note contained the acceleration clause upon the bank's feeling insecure. The Uniform Commercial Code deals with this basis for acceleration in *KRS 355.1-208*, as hereinbefore quoted.
>
> It will be observed that the statute places the burden of establishing the lack of good faith upon the party against whom the acceleration power has been exercised. "Good faith" is a golden thread woven into the entire fabric of the Uniform Commercial Code. See *KRS 355.1-203*. "Good faith," as defined in the Uniform Commercial Code, "means honesty in fact in the conduct or transaction concerned." *KRS 355.1-201(19)*.
>
> By the terms of *KRS 355.1-201(8)* the "burden of establishing" any fact is said to mean "the burden of persuading the triers of fact that the existence of the fact is more probable than its non-existence." We construe the latter provision as requiring the submission to the jury of the issue of good faith unless the evidence relating to it is no more than a scintilla, or lacks probative value having fitness to induce conviction in the minds of reasonable men. It is our view that the evidence on that score is so conclusive as to warrant a directed verdict for the bank on this issue. It must be remembered that here we are dealing with the "good faith" *belief* of the bank — that is, its state of mind.

385 S.W.2d at 200 (citation omitted) (emphasis in original).

Since one of the purposes of the UCC is "to make uniform the law among the various jurisdictions," foreign cases which discuss UCC Section 1-208 and the subjective standard of "good faith" are persuasive. In *Fulton v. Anchor Savings Bank, FSB*, 215 Ga. App. 456, 452 S.E.2d 208, 218 (Ga. Ct. App. 1994), the Court of Appeals discussed Section 1-201(19) and stated that "the material issue . . . 'is not whether the loan was in fact insecure, but whether, in determining the loan insecure, [the bank] acted honestly, in good faith, and not arbitrarily or capriciously. . . . ' "

In *United States National Bank of Oregon v. Boge*, 311 Ore. 550, 814 P.2d 1082 (Or. 1991) quoting *Community Bank v. Ell*, 278 Ore. 417, 564 P.2d 685 (Or. 1977), the Supreme Court described the appropriate standard to be used in determining good faith under UCC Section 1-201(19) as

> a subjective one, looking to the intent or state of mind of the party concerned. The question is generally one for the jury unless only one inference from the evidence is possible. Although mere negligence of failure to make the inquiries which a reasonably prudent person would make does not of itself amount to bad faith, if a party fails to make an inquiry for the purpose of remaining ignorant of facts which he believes or fears would disclose a defect in the transaction, he may be found to have acted in bad faith. As one commentator has phrased it: "[The UCC's definition of good faith] sets forth a 'subjective' standard. In other words, good faith does not require the absence of negligence or the following of the standards of the 'reasonable and prudent' person. All that is necessary is 'a pure heart and empty head.' "

814 P.2d at 1090.

Parnell and Karnik argue that the Bank's negligence in administering the loan should be considered in determining its good faith. However, Kentucky courts have rejected this argument and determined that the definition of "good faith" does not include negligence. KRS 355.1-201(19) defines good faith as "honesty in fact in the conduct or transaction concerned." This definition simply does not include negligence. We can envision circumstances whereby a lending institution's contrivance to remain ignorant of someone acting without authority would amount to bad faith under the statute. However, if that situation were to arise then the intent would negate negligence by the most elemental definition of the word.

As our Supreme Court stated in *Crest Coal Company, Inc. v. Bailey*, Ky., 602 S.W.2d 425, 426-427 (1980):

> We are acutely aware that an appellate court must give great weight . . . to the verdict of a jury. However, where the record shows, as it does here, that only one fair and reasonable conclusion can be drawn from the evidence, the case should not be submitted to the jury.

See also *Wittmer v. Jones*, Ky., 864 S.W.2d 885 (1993).

Baker's determination of the Bank's insecurity was based in part on his review of past financial statements and in part on the financial condition of Parnell and Karnik during the first quarter of 1986. In early February, Baker, by memorandum to another Bank employee in the collections department, stated that the Bank, with regard to ARRA, was "undercollateralized." His determination was based on an evaluation of ARRA's assets and liabilities. At this point in time, Baker had not received financial statements from ARRA's accountant. In April, when Baker received those statements which revealed a negative net worth and substantial losses, he deemed the Bank insecure and insisted on further collateral. There was no evidence that Baker's determination to accelerate, in and of itself, was not made in "good faith." Parnell and Karnik state in their brief that there was ample proof of other motives of the Bank to accelerate the note; however, this allegation is simply not supported by the record. Again, any negligence by the Bank in not acquiring knowledge of ARRA's financial condition when the loan was initially approved, does not go to the question of good faith.

Accordingly, we hold that Parnell and Karnik failed to meet their burden of proving that the Bank did not act in good faith in deeming itself insecure. Thus, the trial court erred in denying the Bank's motion for a directed verdict. The judgment of the Kenton Circuit Court is reversed and this matter is remanded for entry of a judgment in favor of the Bank.

NOTE ON STAR BANK AND THE STANDARD FOR GOOD FAITH

As the court correctly noted, at the time of its decision the definition of "good faith" which was to be applied was to be found in § 1-201(19). The prerevision version of Article 1 featured this so-called subjective standard of good faith. The prerevision version of Article 9 did not have a distinct definition of the term at all. As you will have seen, the current Article 9 defines good faith for the purposes of that article in a different way. In § 9-102(a)(43) good faith is defined to mean, "honesty in fact and the observance of reasonable commercial standards of faith dealing." This recites what is conventionally referred to as the objective standard of good faith, although as you can read it contains *both* a subjective and objective component. Both must be met by an actor if his, her, or its behavior is to be characterized as having met the standard of good faith. This much is clear, at least when the term "good faith" appears in Article 9, since all states have adopted this definition as part of their overall adoption of the revised Article 9, effective in 2001.

A question remains, however, and it's a trickier one. The general provision governing contractual terms like the general insecurity clause we have been considering appears not in Article 9, but in Article 1. See § 1R-309 or § 1-208, depending on which version of Article 1 to which you are referring in your studies. Can't an argument be made that, this being so, the application of this section should make use of the *Article 1* definition of good faith and not that found in Article 9? This would not seem to be more than a minor, and indeed terribly finicky, point, except for one important consideration. As of this writing some of the states have adopted the revised version of Article 1 and some have not. Those that have not would still presumably be working with an Article 1 definition of good faith of the purely subjective variety. Those states which have adopted without variation the Official Version of Revised Article 1 will have, in so doing, adopted a general definition of good faith of the objective sort. Just to make things that much more interesting, however, a handful of states which have adopted for the most part Revised Article 1 have done so with at least one significant variation — they have chosen to *retain* the purely subjective test of good faith as found in the original Article 1. In a state that has gone this route, what standard of good faith should be applied to a party claiming to have made proper use of a general insecurity clause in a security agreement?

As a practical matter, I believe you would be justified in wondering how much difference the particular definition of good faith would make in actual fact. How likely is it, do you think, that either the jury or the appellate court in the *Star Bank* case would have come to a different conclusion if it had been considering the question before it under the objective, rather than the subjective, definition of good faith? Would your answer to any of the parts of Problem 31.1 be different depending on which concept of good faith you applied to the situation?

PROBLEM

31.2   Benny buys a new car from the Audrey's Autos, a dealership in new and used cars. He signs a note under which he will make 48 monthly payments to Audrey, each payment due "no later than the first day of the month beginning with June 1, 2009." Benny also signs a security agreement granting Audrey an interest in the car he is buying to secure his obligation to make the installment payments over the next four years. Since Benny does not receive his last paycheck for any given month until the first working day of the following month, he quickly falls into the habit of sending off a check to Audrey as soon as he gets this paycheck. From October of 2009 through April of 2010, Audrey receives Benny's check for the correct amount sometime during the first week or so, but never by the first day, of the month. Audrey simply deposits these checks as she would any other amount due her. She makes no comment to Benny about the timing of his payments. When Benny's check for the month of May 2010 does not arrive until May 15, Audrey decides she has had enough and, without giving any notice to Benny, has Benny's car repossessed.

(a) Did Audrey have the right to declare a default based on Benny's late payment in May 2010? What argument can Benny make that the repossession was wrongful as he was not in default?

(b) Would it make any difference to your analysis of the situation if among all the fine print in the security agreement Benny signed was to be found the following language: "Waiver or condonation of any breach or default by Secured Party shall not constitute a waiver of any other or subsequent breach or default by Debtor?"

MOE v. JOHN DEERE COMPANY

Supreme Court of South Dakota, 1994
516 N.W.2d 332, 25 U.C.C. Rep. Serv. 2d 997

Moses, Circuit Judge: This is an appeal by Ted Moe (Moe) from a summary judgment granted by Third Judicial Circuit Court in favor of John Deere Company (Deere) and Day County Implement Company (Implement). We reverse.

FACTS

On September 29, 1983, Moe bought a farm tractor from Day County Equipment in Watertown, South Dakota. He purchased a John Deere D8850 for a cash price of $121,268.00. In financing the transaction, Moe traded in two old tractors for the amount of $77,543.00 and agreed to pay the $59,802.40 difference in five equal installments of $11,960.48 each due on October 1st for the years 1984, 1985, 1986, 1987 and 1988. After the contract was completed it was assigned to Deere on September 30, 1983.

Moe was two months late in paying his first installment. Rather than paying $11,960.48 on October 1, 1984, Moe paid $12,212.87 on

December 3, 1984. On October 1, 1985, Moe was again unable to timely pay his second installment. Deere waived full payment and extended the time in which Moe was to make this payment. On January 13, 1986, Moe made a partial payment in the amount of $6,200.00, over three months late. Moe and Deere agreed that Moe was to pay a second amount on March 1, 1986 in the amount of $6,350.17 to complete the second install-ment. On March 10, 1986, Deere sent a notice to Moe indicating that Moe's second installment was past due and that he had until March 20, 1986 to pay $6,389.48 to bring his account current. Again Moe missed this payment deadline.

Deere did not follow up on the delinquent payment until a representative from Deere contacted Moe sometime in May or the first part of June 1986, over seven months after the second installment was originally due. Deere's representative and Moe agreed that Moe would pay $2,000.00 of the $6,389.48 plus interest owing to Deere and Deere would allow Moe to pay the balance when he started to harvest. Deere's representative and Moe failed to specify the due date for either the $2,000.00 payment or when the balance was due. Moe had no further conversations with the representative from Deere about the $2,000.00 until after Deere repossessed the tractor on July 30, 1986.

Moe, who was in Oklahoma at the time of repossession, did not receive any notice from Deere's representative that the tractor was going to be repossessed because his payments were delinquent. Deere reassigned Moe's contract to Implement following the repossession. On August 1, 1986, Deere mailed from Minneapolis, Minnesota a certified letter dated July 31, 1986 to Moe which indicated that Deere "[found] it necessary to gain possession of the equipment involved." This letter apparently was returned to Deere undelivered to Moe. Thus, Deere hand-addressed a new letter and sent it to Moe who picked it up on August 18, 1986. The letter indicated:

> We intend to reassign your contract to the above named dealer. Once we reassign it, two weeks from the date of this letter, you will contact them on all matters concerning the disposition of the equipment or the amount owed under the contract. They intend to dispose of said collateral by public or private sale. If you wish to redeem this equipment, you must pay to John Deere Company $37,591.20 plus any expenses incurred from this repossession, in cash certified funds, before we reassign the contract.
>
> We hope you will be able to pay this amount within the prescribed period. If you have any questions regarding this matter please contact us. M.K. Mehus, Manager Financial Services.

Implement sold the tractor on August 19, 1986 for $44,000.00. Implement paid Deere in full on the contract and applied the proceeds to the debt and turned over the excess proceeds to Moe's lender by mailing two (2) checks totalling $2,616.77 to the Farmers and Merchants Bank on December 1, 1986.

Moe sued Deere and Implement on the following causes of action: (1) wrongful repossession; (2) fraudulent repossession; (3) commercially unreasonable sale; and (4) failure to account for the surplus.

Deere moved for partial summary judgment on the third and fourth issues of commercially unreasonable sale and failure to account for surplus. The trial court granted Deere's motion. Then, Deere moved for summary judgment on the first and second issues of wrongful repossession and fraudulent repossession. On February 5, 1993, the trial court issued an order granting Deere's summary judgment motion on both issues. Moe appeals.

ISSUE

DO GENUINE ISSUES OF MATERIAL FACT AS TO WHETHER MOE WAS IN "DEFAULT" PRECLUDE THE GRANTING OF SUMMARY JUDGMENT?

We recognized in *First Nat. Bank of Black Hills v. Beug*, 400 N.W.2d 893, 896 (S.D. 1987), that "the term 'default' is not defined in the Uniform Commercial Code, thus we must look to other sources for a definition." Then, we turned to hornbook law for a definition of default:

> Default' triggers the secured creditor's rights under Part Five of Article Nine [Ed.: Now Part Six of the Revised Article 9]. But what is "default?" Article Nine does not define the word; instead it leaves this to the parties and to any scraps of common law lying around. Apart from the modest limitations imposed by the unconscionability doctrine and the requirement of good faith, default is "whatever the security agreement says it is." (quoting J. White & R. Summers, Uniform Commercial Code § 26-22 at 1085-86 (2d ed. 1980)).

Several jurisdictions recognize that the determination of default is not a matter of law for the court to decide. [Citations omitted]

Here, the promissory note provided a definition of default:

> The borrower shall be in default upon the occurrence of any one or more of the following events: (1) the Borrower shall fail to pay, when due, any amount required hereunder, or any other indebtedness of the borrower to the Lender of any third parties; (2) the Borrower shall be in default in the performance of any covenant or obligation under the line of credit or equivalent agreement for future advances (if applicable) or any document or agreement related thereto; (3) any warranty or representation made by the Borrower shall prove false or misleading in any respect; (4) the Borrower or any Guarantor of this promissory note shall liquidate, merge dissolve, terminate its existence, suspend business operations, die (if individual), have a receiver appointed for all or any part of its property, make an assignment for the benefit of creditors, or file or have filed against it any petition under any existing or future bankruptcy or insolvency law; (5) any change that occurs in the condition or affairs (financial or otherwise) of the Borrower or any Guarantor of this promissory note which, in the opinion of the lender, impairs, the Lender's security or increases its risk with respect to this promissory note or (6) an event of default shall occur under any agreements intended to secure the repayment of this promissory note. Unless prohibited by law, the Lender may, at its option, declare the entire unpaid balance of principal and

interest immediately due and payable without notice or demand at any time after default as such term is defined in this paragraph.

Technically, there was a breach of the security agreement and the promissory note when Moe did not make his payment on October 1, 1984, but instead paid it on December 3, 1984. One could find Moe in default, and under SDCL 57A-9-503 [now § 9-609], Deere would have had a right to repossess the tractor. However, Deere's right to a default or remedies under breach of contract can be modified or waived by the conduct of the parties.

The trial court's memorandum opinion indicated that "The terms of the written contract should control. Further the 'course of dealing' between the parties is not persuasive." However, here there is a question of fact. Did the oral statements and conduct of the parties modify the written agreement? In *Alaska Statebank v. Fairco Fin.*, 674 P.2d 288 (Alaska 1983), the issue was if the parties' oral statements and conduct between September 15, 1978 and November 6, 1978 modified the written agreement so that pre-possession notice was required. The court held:

> Modification of a written contract may be effected either through subsequent conduct or oral agreements. Whether a modification has occurred is a question of fact. The superior court found that the parties had agreed to such modification, "given the course of dealings between the parties. . . ."

See also South Dakota Pattern Jury Instruction No. 47-16 for Modification of a Written Contract by Subsequent Oral Agreement.

The record reveals through affidavits and depositions that the oral statements and conduct of the parties herein between October 1, 1984 and July 30, 1986 appear to modify the written agreement. Deere sent notice to Moe that he had until March 20, 1986 to pay $6,389.48 including late charges. Moe admits that in May or the first week of June 1986 he agreed to pay the March installment in two parts. He agreed to pay $2,000.00 with the balance due in August 1986 when he commenced his wheat harvest. There was no date certain by which Moe was to pay the $2,000.00. In determining if there was a default on the part of Moe in complying with this contract, all statements and conduct of the parties are essential in determining whether there was an oral modification or waiver of the promissory note or security agreement by John Deere.

WHETHER A NON-WAIVER CLAUSE IN THIS CONTRACT IS ENFORCEABLE?

The second issue that needs to be addressed is whether the "non-waiver clause" is enforceable in this contract. Deere's brief refers to this clause as an "anti-waiver" clause but we will refer to it as a "non-waiver" clause. The security agreement between Moe and Deere contained the following provisions:

> In the event of default (as defined on the reverse side hereof), holder may take possession of the Goods and exercise any other remedies provided by law.

> This contract shall be in default if I (we) shall fail to pay any installment when due. . . .
>
> In any such event (default) the holder may immediately and without notice declare the entire balance of this contract due and payable together with reasonable expenses incurred in realizing on the security interest granted hereunder, including reasonable attorney's fees.
>
> Waiver or condonation of any breach or default shall not constitute a waiver of any other or subsequent breach or default.

We now turn to other jurisdictions' interpretations of the "non-waiver" clause. Courts have adopted two basic rules for interpreting situations where repeated late payments have been accepted by a creditor who has the contractual (i.e., "non-waiver" clauses) and the statutory right to repossess the collateral without notice. Some courts have held that the acceptance of late payments does not waive or otherwise affect the right of a creditor to repossess without notice after subsequent late payment defaults. *Westinghouse Credit Corp. v. Shelton*, 645 F.2d 869 (10th Cir. 1981); *Tillquist v. Ford Motor Credit Co.*, 714 F. Supp. 607 (D. Conn. 1989); *Wade v. Ford Motor Credit Co.*, 455 F. Supp. 147 (E.D. Mo. 1978); *Hale v. Ford Motor Credit Co.*, 374 So. 2d 849 (Ala. 1979); *Van Bibber v. Norris*, 275 Ind. 555, 419 N.E.2d 115 (Ind. 1981). Other courts have imposed a duty on the creditor to notify the debtor that strict compliance with the time for payment will be required in the future or else the contract remedies may be invoked. See, e.g., *Cobb v. Midwest Recovery Bureau Co.*, 295 N.W.2d 232 (Minn. 1980); *Ford Motor Credit Co. v. Washington*, 573 S.W.2d 616 (Tex Civ. App. 1978); *Lee v. Wood Products Credit Union*, 275 Ore. 445, 551 P.2d 446 (Or. 1976); *Nevada Nat. Bank v. Huff*, 94 Nev. 506, 582 P.2d 364, 369 (Nev. 1978); *Pierce v. Leasing Intern., Inc.*, 142 Ga. App. 371, 235 S.E.2d 752 (Ga. 1977); *Ford Motor Credit Company v. Waters*, 273 So. 2d 96 (Fla. App. 1973); See also 2 J. White & R. Summers, Uniform Commercial Code, §27-2 at 563-65 (3d ed. 1988).

Deere urges us to adopt the position that the acceptance of late payments does not waive or otherwise affect the right of a creditor to repossess without notice after subsequent late payment defaults stating to do so would mean that the "non-waiver" clause is a nullity.

A majority of states who have considered the issue adhere to the general rule that "a secured party who has not insisted upon strict compliance in the past, who has accepted late payments as a matter of course, must, before he may validly rely upon such a clause to declare a default and effect repossession, give notice to the debtor . . . that strict compliance with the terms of the contract will be demanded henceforth if repossession is to be avoided." *Nevada Nat. Bank v. Huff*, 94 Nev. 506, 582 P.2d 364, 369 (Nev. 1978).

The basis for imposing this duty on the secured party is that the secured party is estopped from asserting his contract rights because his conduct has induced the debtor's justified reliance in believing that late payments were acceptable. SDCL 57A-1-103 preserves the law of estoppel. The acts which induced reliance are the repeated acceptance of late payments. The reliance is evidenced by the continual pattern of irregular and late payments.

The debtor has the right to rely on the continuation of the course of performance and that right to rely is sufficient to satisfy the reliance element. This right to rely is supported by the policy of the Uniform Commercial Code which encourages the continual development of "commercial practices through, custom, usage, and agreement between the parties." See U.C.C. § 1-102(2) [or § 1R-102(a)(2)]. South Dakota's adaptation of the Uniform Commercial Code is found in Title 57A of the South Dakota Code. The Uniform Commercial Code should be liberally construed and applied to promote its underlying purposes and policies. *First Nat. Bank v. John Deere Co.*, 409 N.W.2d 664 (S.D. 1987).

Adopting the rule that a creditor must give pre-possession notice upon modification of a contract results in both the debtor and the creditor being protected. The debtor would be protected from surprise and from a damaging repossession by being forewarned that late payments would no longer be acceptable. Likewise, the creditor would be protected utilizing the device of "one letter." The creditor can totally preserve his remedies so that if the account continues in default, repossession could be pursued as provided in the contract without further demand or notice. It is recognized that this rule does place the creditor in a slightly worse position because if a creditor sends out a letter to preserve his rights and then once again accepts late payments another notice would be required. The second notice would be required because the acceptance of the late payment after the initial letter could again act as a waiver of the rights asserted in the letter.

We hold that the repeated acceptance of late payments by a creditor who has the contractual right to repossess the property imposes a duty on the creditor to notify the debtor that strict compliance with the contract terms will be required before the creditor can lawfully repossess the collateral.

The dispositive issue is if the plaintiff was in default. Whether a default exists is a factual question not properly resolved on a motion for summary judgment. Defendant's right to repossess turns on this default. We reverse this order and the judgment of the circuit court and remand for trial.

CHAPTER

32

Repossession

A. INTRODUCTION

1. The Secured Party's Options upon Default

It is important to recognize that, while under § 9-601 a secured party gains upon the debtor's default *the right* to enforce its interest in the collateral in the manner we will be looking at in this and the following chapters, it is never under *the obligation* to do so. The secured party has to evaluate the options open to it under the circumstances, and it is probably the rare situation where its first thoughts will be of repossession, disposition of the collateral as considered in the following chapter, and so forth. This full measure of enforcement may, of course, eventually be seen as unavoidable by the secured party if it is to salvage what it can out of a bad situation. It would be a pretty unusual secured party, however, which looks on this type of ultimate action as anything other than an unattractive, even if necessary, road to start on down. The full set of remedies provided the secured party under Part Six are, it is undoubtedly fair to say, at best a considerable headache to carry out properly. Beyond that the secured party may find itself falling into any number of traps for the unwary which will result in *it*, the secured party, being branded the wrongdoer and suffering one of a number of unpleasant consequences. Repossession of tangible collateral and the process that follows thereafter are not contemplated by a thoughtful secured party with anything even bordering on relish. This course of action is more properly seen as the last resort available to a secured party in the event of a default, or a series of defaults, when it has concluded that all other possible actions would be even more frustrating and no more likely to produce any positive results.

This being so, one option which a secured party will seriously consider if an event of default has occurred is to do nothing or at least not much. If the debtor has for a long period of time been diligent in making its payments punctually and otherwise living up to all the other obligations it has taken on under the security agreement, upon the occurrence of a single default that is not particularly egregious or threatening to the long-term debtor-creditor relationship, the secured party may simply chalk it up to the debtor's making a bit of a slip-up and leave it at that. Of course, as we saw in the last chapter, if the secured party repeatedly becomes aware of instances of default and makes no protest or disapproving comment to the debtor, it may be held to have "waived" its right to future performance on exactly the terms of the agreement, at least until it takes some positive action to reinstate its right to the debtor's carrying out its duties with a more rigid regard to the details of the agreement. It may make sense, therefore, for the secured party to comment on even the minor default even if it has decided to take no remedial action based on that single default. The secured party, of course, may add on a "friendly reminder" to the debtor of the exact nature of its obligations along with a statement of its "confidence that such a problem will not be repeated in the future."

In other instances, the secured party may reasonably decide that the best course is to work with the debtor who is experiencing some difficulties, for instances, in making payments as due—fashioning some adjustment that can work to the mutual advantage of both the debtor and the secured party under the circumstances. It is all too easy for the secured party's repossession of collateral vital to the debtor's ongoing business to "bring down the debtor's entire house of cards," as the saying goes, which may hurt the lender as much as the borrower as it effectively prevents the borrower from carrying on its business, itself receiving payment for the goods it makes or the services it renders, and thus ever paying back any further portion of what is now due the lender. If the lender and borrower work together, it is possible that they can come up with a plan — perhaps allowing the borrower to skip a payment or two for the present or having the borrower refinance its debt with the goal of lowering its monthly payments to a manageable level — that shows prospects for the lender's getting back on a sound financial footing. If so, then a little "give" by the lender at this crucial moment may result in its getting all, or at least a much greater portion, of what it is due in the long run than it would stand to recover if it were immediately to repossess the collateral and start down that long and winding path.

2.   *Collecting on Receivables*

When all is said and done, of of course, there may be no other tack for the secured party to take than to invoke its full measure of remedies under Part Six of Article 9. While in this chapter we will soon move on to the repossession of collateral, it should be obvious that repossession is not a viable option in all situations. For one thing, in some cases the collateral is what we have termed intangible personal property, in particular accounts or general intangibles. It stands to reason that when there is nothing tangible at play there is no way for the secured party to get possession of it, however hard it might try. In other situations, the collateral may be what I have termed for want of a better phrase some type of quasi-intangible, such as an instrument or a piece of tangible chattel paper. True, the secured party could take possession of the piece or pieces of paper involved, but the paper is valuable not necessarily in its own right — although there will be a market in such things just as there is a market in just about everything — but because of the right to payment that it represents. Note, first of all, the definition of "account debtor" in § 9-102(a)(3). Then take a look at § 9-607, along with its Comment 2, followed by § 9-608. While we will not go though either of these sections in detail, you should be able to appreciate how they allow a secured party whose interest is in receivables as collateral to, upon a default, collect on those receivables without disrupting the ongoing operation of the debtor. Note as well that if it has been careful to insist that the debtor regularly deposit all cash it receives on account of the collateral into a special proceeds account — and if it has been careful to obtain an interest in that account perfected by control — then it may exercise its control under § 9-607(a)(4) or (5) to get money out of that deposit account without needing the debtor's cooperation. That is, as we know, what lies behind the whole notion of perfection by control of a deposit account, and exactly why it comes in so very handy in just the right circumstances.

3.   Self-Help Repossession

There isn't much that will need to be said in introduction to the subject of repossession. In some instances the collateral will already be in the hands of the secured party in the event of a default, because the interest had been perfected in that way for instance. In other situations the collateral is not any tangible stuff (for example, accounts) so there is no way for the secured party to repossess.

When the collateral is tangible stuff and there has been a default, the secured party may decide that the only sensible thing at this point is to repossess the collateral, but it is not a decision to be taken lightly. The secured party may be facing a lot of grief if it repossesses when it has no right to, if the repossession isn't carried out properly, or if it doesn't deal with the repossessed collateral in the proper way once it has been picked up. (The final two chapters will deal with this last part of the problem.)

This chapter deals with the basic question of what the secured party — or an agent employed by it for this purpose — may do to effectuate a repossession. And what it may not do as well. Article 9, as you will see, says very little on this. There are, however, a slew of cases, almost all of which involve the repossession of automobiles or trucks, which set up some rough (and that's exactly the right word here) guidelines.

This chapter will eventually have a couple or three problems for discussion, but the real action is in the cases, a few of which I've picked out and set forth below.

B. PREPARATION

- Read § 9-609 and its Official Comments

C. PROBLEMS AND CASES

CALLAWAY v. WHITTENTON

Supreme Court of Alabama, 2003
892 So. 2d 852, 52 U.C.C. Rep. Serv. 2d 525

SEE, Justice: Christopher Callaway and Joy Callaway appeal from a judgment as a matter of law entered in favor of Michael Whittenton. They argue that their claims alleging wrongful repossession and trespass should have been submitted to the jury. We affirm the trial court's judgment as a matter of law as to the trespass claim, reverse it as to the wrongful-repossession claim, and remand the case.

On May 10, 2000, Christopher Callaway purchased a 1993 Geo Tracker sport utility vehicle from Summerdale Budget Auto & Truck, Inc. ("Budget"). Baldwin Finance, Inc., which financed the Callaways' purchase of the Tracker, held a lien on the Tracker; the sales agreement entered into by the Callaways and Budget gave Budget and Baldwin Finance the right to repossess the vehicle in the event of a default. [The Callaways did not make the payment due in August and Budget repossessed the vehicle without incident, using the services of Whittenton, who repossessed cars as an unincorporated independent contractor. Mr. Callaway then paid the past-due amount and the repossession fee, and the Tracker was returned to him. The Callaways then did not make the October payment when due — claiming, but having no evidence supporting their claim — that the time for this payment had been extended by Budget. Whittenton repossessed the Tracker again on November 6, 2000, at approximately 11:00 A.M. The second repossession is the subject of this action.]

The parties disagree as to what happened on November 6, 2000. What follows is the not altogether consistent account of events according to the Callaways. Joy heard noises outside their residence, and when she went outside to see what was happening, she saw Whittenton, who was repossessing the Tracker. Joy asked Whittenton to leave the property, but Whittenton continued with the repossession. Joy went back inside the house and told Christopher that Whittenton was taking the Tracker. Christopher told Whittenton to stop and told Whittenton that he needed to get some things out of the Tracker before Whittenton took it. Joy telephoned Budget to make sure that the due date for the October payment had been extended and, while she was on the telephone with Budget, she heard Christopher talking to Whittenton. Then, she heard her husband scream. The following events apparently preceded his scream. Whittenton had secured the Tracker to his truck, and Christopher saw Whittenton walk around to the driver's side of his truck and get in. Whittenton was not looking in Christopher's direction when Christopher walked outside. Christopher grabbed the roll bar on the Tracker as Whittenton began to drive away. Christopher banged on Whittenton's truck and yelled to get Whittenton's attention. Then, as Whittenton was driving down the driveway, the Tracker hit a pothole, and Christopher lost his balance. While he was trying to regain his balance, the rear tire on the driver's side of the Tracker ran over Christopher's foot. Christopher then grabbed the roll bar on the Tracker again so that it would not run over him. Whittenton continued driving, dragging Christopher down the driveway and 60-100 feet down Highway 10. One of the vehicles ran over the family's cat.

Whittenton's testimony differs markedly from that of the Callaways. He says that he did not have a conversation with Joy as he was hooking up the Tracker in order to tow it, and that he saw Christopher run through a ditch, run beside the Tracker, and jump onto the vehicle. Whittenton testified that he stopped his truck after turning onto Highway 10 because he saw Christopher jump between the truck towing the Tracker and the Tracker. Another witness, Ronnie Black, testified that he saw Christopher run through a ditch and jump onto the Tracker while it was on Highway 10.

The Callaways sued Whittenton, Budget, and Baldwin Finance, alleging assault and battery, negligence, wantonness, trespass, civil conspiracy, and wrongful repossession (a violation of § 7-9-503, Ala. Code 1975 (secured party's right to take possession after default; replaced by § 7-9A-609)); Joy alleged loss of consortium. Budget and Baldwin Finance separately moved to compel arbitration, and on October 30, 2001, the trial court granted their motions. The Callaways' claims against Whittenton were tried. The arbitration proceeding remains pending; there is some confusion regarding which claims are foreclosed by the trial court's disposition of the claims against Whittenton.

On December 12, 2002, at the close of the Callaways' case, the trial court granted Whittenton's motion for a judgment as a matter of law as to the wrongful-repossession, trespass, and civil-conspiracy claims. The remaining claims — negligence, wantonness, assault and battery, and loss of consortium — were submitted to the jury. The jury found in favor of Whittenton on all claims. The Callaways appeal the trial court's judgment as a matter of law as to their claims of wrongful repossession and trespass.

[The court considered the appeal under the prerevision version of what now is found in § 9-609, which for all intents and purposes was the same as the current version. As the court noted, neither version gives a definition of "breach of the peace."]

This Court, in *Madden v. Deere Credit Services, Inc.*, 598 So. 2d 860 (1992), describes the right of self-help repossession as a "limited privilege":

Under Alabama law, the secured creditor, in exercising the privilege to enter upon the premises of another to repossess collateral, may not perpetrate "any act or action manifesting force or violence, or naturally calculated to provide a breach of the peace." Neither may a creditor resort to constructive force, such as "threats or intimidation," or to "fraud, trickery, chicanery, and subterfuge."

The phrase "breach of the peace" has been further defined as any "situation tending to disturb the public order." It is "a disturbance of the public tranquility, by any act or conduct inciting to violence or tending to provoke or excite others to break the peace, or, as is sometimes said, it includes any violation of any law enacted to preserve the peace and good order." Consequently, actual "confrontation or violence is not necessary to finding a breach of the peace."

This Court in *General Finance Corp. v. Smith*, 505 So. 2d 1045, 1048 (Ala. 1987), stated that § 7-9-503 (now § 7-9A-609) "allows the secured party to proceed without judicial process only if that can be done peacefully (i.e., without risk of injury to the secured party, the debtor, or any innocent bystanders)."

In *W.J. Speigle v. Chrysler Credit Corp.*, 56 Ala. App. 469, 323 So. 2d 360 (Ala. Civ. App. 1975), the Court of Civil Appeals held that there was no breach of the peace when the secured creditor parked behind the debtor's car in order to prevent the debtor from leaving the secured creditor's parking lot. The Court of Civil Appeals stated:

> The record presented no evidence of any threats or rude language spoken by the defendants or their agents during the repossession. . . . Since there is no evidence that any actual physical force or constructive force was exercised by defendants in carrying out the repossession of the vehicle or that a breach of the peace occurred during that time, the trial court's finding [that there was no breach of the peace] is not erroneous.

4 James J. White & Robert S. Summers, *Uniform Commercial Code* § 34-7 (4th ed. 1995), states:

> The great majority of courts find unauthorized entries into the debtor's residence to be breaches of the peace, and may find entry into his garage to be such a breach. As one moves away from the residential threshold to the yard, the driveway, and finally the public street, however, the debtor's argument becomes progressively more tenuous. We have found no case which holds that the repossession of an automobile from a driveway or a public street (absent other circumstances, such as the debtor's objection) itself constitutes a breach of the peace, and many cases uphold such a repossession. (Footnotes omitted.)

In *Chrysler Credit Corp. v. Koontz*, 277 Ill. App. 3d 1078, 661 N.E.2d 1171, 214 Ill. Dec. 726 (1996), the Appellate Court of Illinois found that there was no breach of the peace when the debtor ran outside while the creditor was repossessing the car and yelled, "Don't take it," and the creditor continued the repossession of the car. In *Clark v. Auto Recovery Bureau Conn., Inc.*, 889 F. Supp. 543 (D. Conn. 1994), the repossessing team had hooked the plaintiff's car to the tow truck and had started driving away when the plaintiff voiced an objection to the repossession and started moving toward the car. A third person restrained the plaintiff, and the car was successfully repossessed. The court stated: " 'Once a repossession agent has gained sufficient dominion over collateral to control it, the repossession has been completed.'" (quoting *James v. Ford Motor Credit Co.*, 842 F. Supp. 1202, 1209 (D. Minn. 1994)). In Clark, the car had already been moved from its parking spot when the plaintiff began objecting to the repossession.

On the other hand, in *Burgin v. Universal Credit Co.*, 2 Wn. 2d 364, 98 P.2d 291 (1940), and *Sanchez v. Mbank of El Paso*, 792 S.W.2d 530 (Tex. Ct. App. 1990), the courts held that the creditor was liable for the debtor's injuries when the debtor offered passive physical resistance, such as refusing to leave the car. In *DeMary v. Rieker*, 302 N.J. Super. 208, 695 A.2d 294 (1997), the court held that a breach of the peace occurred when the debtor, who had positioned herself on the passenger side of the truck towing the collateral before it pulled away, was thrown from the truck.

The parties before us dispute the events that took place on November 6, but the testimony of the Callaways, though somewhat contradictory, is substantial evidence that the repossession was not accomplished "peacefully (i.e., without risk of injury to the secured party, the debtor, or any innocent bystanders)." *Smith*, 505 So. 2d at 1048. Christopher's testimony, if it is to be believed, is that while the Tracker was still in the driveway, he was beating on the side of Whittenton's truck and yelling loudly enough to get Whittenton's attention as Whittenton began to drive away. Christopher testified that the Tracker ran over his foot, that he grabbed the roll bar on the Tracker, and that Whittenton continued to drive the truck towing the Tracker, dragging Christopher down the driveway.

Viewing the evidence in the light most favorable to the Callaways as the nonmovants, as we must, we conclude that the Callaways presented sufficient evidence from which a jury could conclude that a breach of the peace occurred during the repossession because Whittenton used physical force to overcome Christopher's efforts to prevent the removal of the Tracker from the Callaways' front yard. Because we find that the Callaways' wrongful-repossession claim should have been submitted to the jury on the question whether there had been a breach of the peace before the Tracker was removed from the Callaways' property, we reverse the judgment as a matter of law as to this issue and remand the case for further proceedings consistent with this opinion.

The Callaways also argue that the trial court erred in granting Whittenton's motion for a judgment as a matter of law as to their trespass claim. Restatement (Second) of Torts § 158 (1965) states:

> One is subject to liability to another for trespass, irrespective of whether he thereby causes harm to any legally protected interest of the other, if he intentionally
>
>   (a) enters land in the possession of the other, or causes a thing or a third person to do so, or
>   (b) remains on the land, or
>   (c) fails to remove from the land a thing which he is under a duty to remove.

The Court of Civil Appeals in *Garrison v. Alabama Power Co.*, 807 So. 2d 567, 570 (Ala. Civ. App. 2001), stated: "We note that 'trespass has been defined as any entry on the land of another without express or implied authority. . . . ' " Also, "trespass is the unlawful or wrongful interference with another's possession of property. . . ." Michael L. Roberts & Gregory S. Cusimano, Alabama Tort Law § 30.0 (3d ed. 2000).

Whittenton does not deny that he entered the Callaways' property; however, § 7-9A-609 gives a secured creditor the right to enter a debtor's land for the purpose of repossession. See § 7-9A-609, Ala. Code 1975, and *Madden*, 598 So. 2d at 865 ("Under Alabama law, the secured creditor, in exercising the privilege to enter upon the premises of another to repossess collateral, may not perpetrate 'any act or action manifesting force or vio-lence, or naturally calculated to provide a breach of the peace. . . . ' "). Because Whittenton entered onto the Callaways' property for the purpose of repossessing the Tracker, Whittenton had a legal right to be on the premises, and we affirm the trial court's judgment as a matter of law on this issue.

Because Whittenton had a legal right to be on the Callaways' premises, he did not trespass on their property; therefore, we affirm the trial court's judgment as a matter of law as to the trespass claim. However, viewing the evidence in the light most favorable to the nonmovant Callaways, as we must, we conclude that they presented sufficient evidence from which a jury could conclude that in repossessing the Tracker Whittenton breached the peace; therefore, the claim alleging wrongful repossession should have been submitted to a jury. We reverse the judgment as a matter of law as to the wrongful-repossession claim and remand the case for further proceed-ings consistent with this opinion.

Affirmed in part; reversed in part; and remanded.

EXCERPTS FROM TWO CASES CITED BY THE COURT IN CALLAWAY

CHRYSLER CREDIT CORPORATION v. KOONTZ

Appellate Court of Illinois, 1996
277 Ill. App. 3d 1078, 661 N.E.2d 1171, 29 U.C.C. Rep. Serv. 2d 1

[As the *Callaway* court noted, in this case "the Appellate Court of Illinois found that there was no breach of the peace when the debtor ran outside while the creditor was repossessing the car and yelled, "Don't take it," and the creditor continued the repossession of the car." Here's a bit more detail.]

After a thorough examination of the record, we find no abuse of discre-tion on the part of the trial court in ruling that Chrysler's repossession did not breach the peace. Whether a given act provokes a breach of the peace depends upon the accompanying circumstances of each particular case. In this case, Koontz testified that he only yelled, "Don't take it," and that the repossessor made no verbal or physical response. He also testified that although he was close enough to the repossessor to run over and get into a fight, he elected not to because he was in his underwear. Furthermore, there was no evidence in the record that Koontz implied violence at the time of or immediately prior to the repossession by holding a weapon, clenching a fist, or even vehemently arguing toe-to-toe with the repossessor so that a reasonable repossessor would understand that violence was likely to ensue if he continued with the vehicle repossession. We think that the evidence, viewed as a whole, could lead a reasonable fact finder to determine that the circumstances of the repossession did not amount to a breach of the peace.

We note that to rule otherwise would be to invite the ridiculous situation whereby a debtor could avoid a deficiency judgment by merely stepping out of his house and yelling once at a nonresponsive repossessor. Such a narrow definition of the conduct necessary to breach the peace would, we think, render the self-help repossession statute useless. Therefore, we reject Koontz's invitation to define "an unequivocal oral protest," without more, as a breach of the peace.

JAMES v. FORD MOTOR CREDIT COMPANY

United States District Court for the District of Minnesota, 1994
842 F. Supp. 1202, 24 U.C.C. Rep. Serv. 2d 363

[The *Callaway* court cites this case for the proposition that, "Once a repossession agent has gained sufficient dominion over collateral to control it, the repossession has been completed." True enough. This except will give you some understanding of what was done by, and to, the repossession agent.]

On June 24, 1992, . . . Ford contacted James regarding the late payments. Ford informed her that the car would be repossessed if payment was not made. It is undisputed that James specifically told Ford that she did not want the car repossessed and that Ford could not take the car. On June 29, 1992, defendant Robert Klave ("Klave"), an employee of defendant Special Agents Consultants ("Special Agents"), acting on behalf of Ford, removed plaintiffs' car from a parking lot. Klave reported by telephone to Ford that he had repossessed the car and received instructions to deliver it to Minneapolis AutoAuction. Approximately one hour later and several miles away from the parking lot, James saw Klave driving the car. She entered the car and an altercation ensued. Klave drove the car into a parking lot where the struggle continued inside the car, then outside the car and finally inside the car again. James gained control of the car and drove it home. Klave reported the incident to the police, accusing James of assault, theft and damage to property. Klave reported the car as stolen. Defendants contend that because

Klave was in possession of the car for approximately one hour on June 29, 1992, that date serves as the date on which the car was repossessed.

On July 8, 1992, police officers observed the car being driven in Minneapolis. The car was stopped and the officers identified James as a passenger in the car. James was arrested on a complaint made by a Minneapolis Police Sergeant. Klave then repossessed the car. During discovery Special Agents produced at least three documents which specifically list July 8, 1992, as alternately "repo date," "date of repossession," or "date repossessed." Plaintiffs contend that this is the date of repossession.

PROBLEMS

32.1 Irving's Autos of Irvine, California sells a new Aspen Supreme auto to one Matteo, providing him with a loan with which to buy the auto and retaining a purchase-money security interest in the auto. Matteo is to pay off this loan in 36 monthly installments. Within a year, Matteo has repeatedly fallen seriously behind in his payments. The dealership determines it has no option but to repossess this auto. It sends one of its employees, Lincoln "Linc" Cornhusker, out on a mission to carry out the repossession. Linc finds the car parked on the street in front of Matteo's home. He is able to quickly hitch the auto up to the pick-up truck he is driving and tow it away.

(a) Is the legality of this repossession rendered questionable because the security agreement signed by Matteo nowhere explicitly gave the dealership the right to repossess the auto upon default?

(b) Suppose the dealership had received a letter from Matteo some time before Linc went on his mission stating that, "I, Matteo, hereby object to any attempt you may make to repossess the automobile in which you have a security interest. In the event you believe me to be in default, I expect that you will first contact me and give me a reasonable opportunity to settle any dispute you may wish to assert against me. This letter is intended as a formal letter of objection to repossession." Does this call into question the legality of the repossession by Linc?

(c) Suppose instead that, just as Linc was getting ready to tow the auto off, Matteo comes to a second-story window of his house shouting, "Stop it this instant! I fully object as is my right under the law!" Does this change your evaluation?

(d) Suppose that the situation is as in part (c) above except that Matteo is also brandishing a gun of some kind and the sound of a shot rings out into the air. Linc is still able to speed away in his truck with the auto in tow. How do you evaluated the situation, given this scenario? Would it matter that you were later to find out that Matteo's gun was only a starting pistol and shot nothing but blanks?

(e) Would your answer to any of the previous parts of this question be changed if Linc had taken the auto not from the public street in front of Matteo's home, but from where it was parked in his driveway? What if it had been in the garage attached to Matteo's home, but the door to the garage had been open when Linc arrived on the scene? If the garage door had been closed and locked, but Linc had easily been able to break the lock? If the garage door had been closed but not locked?

32.2   In the prior problem we were told that Linc Cornhusker was an employee of the auto dealership. You may well have concluded that, at least under certain of the parts of that problem, the repossession was not conducted properly. If so, as you doubt noted, both Linc as an individual and the dealership as his employer would suffer the consequences. What if instead, Linc operated a business, Lincoln Cornhusker's Property Restoration Service, Inc., as a truly independent entity. His business contracts with various auto dealerships in the area to repossess autos or trucks on a case-by-case basis and is paid for his successful efforts. Would this isolate Irving's auto dealership from responsibility if it contracts with Linc's corporation to repossess Matteo's Aspen Supreme and for one reason or another the repossession is found to be faulty, either because Matteo was not in default at the time or, even if he was, the repossession was improperly carried out?

32.3   What if, after it had been determined that Matteo was clearly in default, the service manager of the dealership had called Matteo telling him that, "I'm concerned that when we delivered your car we might not have properly aligned the turbo gaskets. Why don't you drop it off so I can check on this?" Matteo does drop his auto off at the dealership early one day the following week. When he comes to pick it up, he is told that this is not in the cards. His auto has been repossessed and has been taken to some undisclosed location, "waiting our decision on how to proceed." Can Matteo object (successfully, that is) to the manner in which he auto was repossessed?

32.4   Oliver has also purchased an Aspen Supreme from Irving's Autos on terms essential identical to those agreed to by Matteo. When Oliver falls terribly behind in his payments, the dealership arranges for Linc to repossess this auto. Linc is able to quickly determine that Oliver has parked the Supreme in his garage, has locked the garage with a good sound lock, and does not appear to be taking the auto out on the road (or even onto his driveway) at any time. Oliver is apparently driving another car entirely on a routine basis. Nor does Oliver appear to be the kind of person who will fall for any cheap tricks. Is the dealership effectively barred from ever repossessing the Supreme auto? If not, what will it have to do to get possession of the vehicle?

32.5   Return to the situation of Problem 32.1 as initially presented. Linc has quickly and efficiently repossessed Matteo's auto, when Matteo was indisputably in default, with not even a hint of anything that could be characterized as a breach of the peace. Linc takes the auto back to Irving's dealership, where it is parked in the rear of the lot. Neither Linc nor anyone else at the dealership contacts Matteo to let him know what has happened or where his auto now is, nor does anyone look into either the glove compartment or the trunk of the car. It turns out that the trunk contains a collapsible child's playpen and a whole host of elaborate children's playthings. Matteo, as it happens, is out of town. By the time his wife, who has been driving the car in his absence, is able to determine where the car is, she has been driven to near madness by her son's crying and screaming because all of his favorite toys have disappeared. She can think of nothing to do but to take a taxi to the nearest toy store and buy replacements to appease, to the extent it is possible, the child. When Matteo returns home and all becomes clear, can you think of any argument he could make against the auto dealership for the harm it has done to him and his loved ones? See the case that follows.

ELEY v. MID/EAST ACCEPTANCE CORP. OF N.C., INC.

Court of Appeals of North Carolina, 2005
171 N.C. App. 368, 614 S.E.2d 555

GEER, Judge: Defendant Mid/East Acceptance Corporation of N.C., Inc. appeals from an order entered in favor of plaintiff Jackie L. Eley following a bench trial in Hertford County District Court. Plaintiff's claims for conversion and unfair and deceptive trade practices were based on defendant's otherwise lawful repossession of plaintiff's truck, which contained a load of watermelons belonging to plaintiff. After defendant caused plaintiff's truck to be repossessed, the melons, which were still in the truck bed, quickly spoiled in the summer heat, rendering them valueless. On appeal, defendant argues that it is not liable for conversion because it did not engage in the unauthorized assumption and exercise of the right of ownership over plaintiff's watermelons to the exclusion of plaintiff's rights. It also argues that it did not commit an unfair and deceptive trade practice under N.C. Gen. Stat. § 75-1.1 (2003). Because we find that competent evidence exists to support the trial court's findings of fact and those findings are sufficient to establish conversion and unfair and deceptive trade practices, we affirm.

FACTS

Plaintiff's evidence tended to show the following. Plaintiff was the owner of a 1995 Ford F150 pick-up truck that she had purchased through a loan from defendant, using the truck as collateral. In the summer of 2002, plaintiff missed two consecutive payments on the loan, and defendant made repossession arrangements with Carolina Repossessions. At approximately

4:00 A.M. on 29 July 2002, employees of Carolina Repossessions, Roger Pinkham and his brother, arrived at plaintiff's residence and began to hitch plaintiff's pick-up truck to their tow truck. Plaintiff heard them and went outside to investigate. When she requested to see the paperwork related to the repossession, one of the men briefly showed it to her.

Plaintiff explained to Pinkham that she was not contesting the repossession of the truck, but that she was concerned about the 130 watermelons in the truck bed. She had purchased and loaded them into the truck on the previous day and had planned to drive them to Maryland for re-sale. In addition to the watermelons, the truck also contained some other personal items belonging to plaintiff, including a coat, an ice chest, and some children's toys. Plaintiff asked Pinkham if she could unload her melons and other personal property before he towed the truck. Pinkham refused, telling her he was in a hurry because he had to get to his regular job. Pinkham also refused to allow plaintiff to deliver the truck herself later that morning after she had had time to unload the melons.

Plaintiff called defendant's office at about 8:00 A.M. the same morning and spoke to defendant's employee, Joyce White. When plaintiff asked White if she could retrieve her watermelons out of the repossessed truck, White replied, "What truck?" Fearing that the melons would quickly spoil in the summer heat, plaintiff, on the same day, filed a complaint alleging conversion in the Hertford County Small Claims Court.

Defendant's evidence tended to show that on Wednesday, 31 July 2002, two days after the repossession, one of defendant's employees called plaintiff and asked her to bring her truck key to defendant's office, but plaintiff refused. White testified that it was not defendant's practice to allow public access to the lot where repossessed items were kept; rather, defendant usually sent an employee to the lot to gather up personal property left in repossessed vehicles and bring it to defendant's office for the owners to collect. White noted that plaintiff's load of watermelons created an unusual situation, and defendant had asked plaintiff to furnish her truck keys so that defendant could drive the truck to its office and allow plaintiff to unload it there.

Defendant then mailed plaintiff a letter, stating, "The watermelons are rotting and the smell is polluting the storage lot. If something is not done with them by 12:00 P.M., Friday, August 2, 2002, we will have to hire someone to dispose of them for us and the fee will be charged to your account." Although the post office attempted to deliver this letter to plaintiff, she never received it, and it was later returned to defendant's office.

On Thursday, 1 August 2002, the day after defendant mailed the letter, defendant called plaintiff again and asked her to come retrieve her watermelons from the repossessed truck because they were spoiling and creating a mess. Plaintiff informed defendant that since the melons were rotten, she no longer wanted them.

The small claims court dismissed plaintiff's conversion claim in a judgment dated 19 August 2002. Plaintiff filed a timely appeal to the Hertford

County District Court. Following a bench trial, the district court entered an order on 12 November 2003, concluding that defendant had converted plaintiff's property and committed an unfair and deceptive trade practice under N.C. Gen. Stat. § 75-1.1. The order awarded damages in the amount of $455.00, the value of the watermelons. These damages were then trebled in accordance with North Carolina's unfair and deceptive trade practice statute, N.C. Gen. Stat. § 75-16 (2003), for a total liability of $1,365.00. The court also awarded plaintiff $1,562.50 in attorneys' fees, under N.C. Gen. Stat. § 75-16.1 (2003). Defendant has appealed to this Court.

I

" 'Conversion is defined as: (1) the unauthorized assumption and exercise of the right of ownership; (2) over the goods or personal property; (3) of another; (4) to the exclusion of the rights of the true owner.' " *Estate of Graham v. Morrison,* 168 N.C. App. 63, 72, 607 S.E.2d 295, 302 (2005) (quoting *Di Frega v. Pugliese,* 164 N.C. App. 499, 509, 596 S.E.2d 456, 463 (2004)). "Conversion may occur when a valid repossession of collateral results in an incidental taking of other property, *unless* the loan agreement includes the debtor's consent to the incidental taking." *Clark v. Auto Recovery Bureau Conn., Inc.,* 889 F. Supp. 543, 548 (D. Conn. 1994); *see also Rea v. Universal C. I. T. Credit Corp.,* 257 N.C. 639, 642, 127 S.E.2d 225, 228 (1962) (holding that plaintiff was entitled to a new trial on his conversion claim when the trial court failed to submit to the jury the question whether, at the time of repossession, plaintiff's car contained tools belonging to plaintiff); *Kitchen v. Wachovia Bank & Trust Co., N.A.,* 44 N.C. App. 332, 334, 260 S.E.2d 772, 773 (1979) (denying a lender's motion for summary judgment on the issue of conversion when the lender repossessed plaintiff's mobile home containing some of her personal property in which the lender did not have a security interest).

Defendant in this case contends that there was no unauthorized assumption and exercise of the right of ownership over the watermelons to the exclusion of the rights of the true owner. In support of this contention, defendant asserts (1) that plaintiff had an opportunity to remove the watermelons before the repossession and (2) that the loss of the watermelons was due to plaintiff's subsequent failure to supply defendant with her truck key.

With regard to the first assertion, defendant argues that there is no competent evidence to support the trial court's finding that defendant's agent, Carolina Repossessions, failed to give plaintiff "a reasonable amount of time to unload her watermelons during the repossession." We disagree. Plaintiff testified specifically that she requested an opportunity to remove her melons from the truck at the time of repossession and that her request was refused. Even Mr. Pinkham, one of the repossessors, testified that "when I got the truck turned around to leave, [plaintiff] did say that she wanted to get her belongings out of the truck, and I told her that if she wanted to get her belongings she needed to go ahead and get them because I did have to get back to Washington, and after about 15 minutes of being there, I figured that had been enough time for her to get the belongings, so I left. I did have other things to do, and so I pulled out."

The record thus contains competent evidence allowing the trial court to find that plaintiff was not allowed a reasonable time to unload her 130 watermelons. Although it is arguable that the record might also support a finding that plaintiff did have time to unload her melons, but failed to do so, the trial court's finding of fact otherwise is supported by ample evidence and is, therefore, binding on appeal.

With regard to defendant's second assertion regarding plaintiff's failure to give defendant her truck keys, the trial court made the following pertinent findings of fact:

> 9. Ms. Eley contacted Ms. White, of Mid-East Acceptance, on the morning of July 29, 2003 to inquire as to the location of her truck so she could retrieve her watermelons. Ms. White's reply was "What truck?"
> 10. Mid-East Acceptance was the bailee of Ms. Eley's personal property and had an obligation to protect this collateral from harm.
> 11. When Mid-East Acceptance contacted Ms. Eley on July (sic) 31st to tell her where her truck was located the watermelons were already decomposing.
> 12. Mid-East Acceptance placed a condition on the return of Ms. Eley's property by requiring her to bring them the vehicle ignition key prior to that return.

Since defendant has not assigned error to these findings of fact, they are binding on this Court. These findings of fact establish that the loss was not due to plaintiff's failure to deliver the truck key because the request for the key came too late to preserve the watermelons.

Taken together, all of these facts combine to support the inference that defendant assumed and exercised the right of ownership over plaintiff's watermelons without her permission, to the exclusion of her own rightful ownership interest. More colloquially, as plaintiff put it, "It was too hot. The melons was already there a week. The melons were spoiled. They wouldn't do me any good. They were their melons. They took the truck, they took the melons. They were their melons then." The trial court, therefore, did not err in entering judgment in favor of plaintiff on her claim for conversion.

II

[The defendant also argued that the trial court had erred in its conclusion that its actions amounted to an unfair and deceptive trade practice under N.C. Gen. Stat. § 75-1.1. The court, after a review of cases interpreting this statute under similar situations and the facts as determined by the trial court, affirmed the trial court's determination that the defendant could be held liable — and hence responsible for treble damages — under the statute.]

III

The trial court awarded damages to plaintiff in the amount of $455.00 on her conversion claim, an amount that reflects the trial court's finding that plaintiff's truck bed contained approximately 130 watermelons valued at

$3.50 each. Defendant challenges this award on the ground that there was insufficient evidence of the value of the watermelons. Specifically, defendant contends that plaintiff's oral testimony as to the value of the watermelons is "not even adequate in the most basic business setting, and is woefully inadequate in a court of law." To the contrary, it is well-settled in this state that "the opinion of a property owner is *competent evidence* as to the value of such property." *Compton v. Kirby*, 157 N.C. App. 1, 18, 577 S.E.2d 905, 916 (2003) (emphasis added) (finding that competent evidence supported a finding that plaintiff's allegedly converted partnership interest was worth over $ 50,000.00 when plaintiff sent defendant a letter to that effect).

Here, when asked how much she had paid for the watermelons, plaintiff opined, "About $3.50 apiece." In accordance with *Compton,* this testimony is sufficient to support the trial court's calculation of plaintiff's damages. Moreover, since we have upheld the trial court's conclusion that defendant committed an unfair and deceptive trade practice under Chapter 75, we also affirm the trebling of the $455.00 to $1,365.00 in accordance with N.C. Gen. Stat. § 75-16.

Defendant also challenges the trial court's award of attorneys' fees under N.C. Gen. Stat. § 75-16.1. Defendant offers no argument as to why the award in this case is improper apart from its contention that plaintiff was not entitled to recover under N.C. Gen. Stat. § 75-1.1. We, therefore, affirm the trial court's attorneys' fee award.

Plaintiff has filed a motion for attorneys' fees incurred during this appeal. This Court has previously held that: "Upon a finding that [appellees] were entitled to attorney's fees in obtaining their judgment [under N.C. Gen. Stat. § 75-16.1], any effort by [appellees] to protect that judgment should likewise entitle them to attorney's fees." *City Fin. Co. of Goldsboro, Inc. v. Boykin,* 86 N.C. App. 446, 449, 358 S.E.2d 83, 85 (1987). Accordingly, because plaintiff was entitled to attorneys' fees for hours expended at the trial level, we hold plaintiff is entitled to attorneys' fees on appeal, especially in light of the limited amount of money at issue in the litigation. Id. at 450, 358 S.E.2d at 85 (noting that because the damages amounted to only $500.00, defense of the judgment would not be "economically feasible" in the absence of an award of attorneys' fees). We remand to the trial court for a determination of the hours spent on appeal and a reasonable hourly rate and for the entry of an appropriate attorneys' fee award.

Affirmed and remanded.

NOTE ON THE DUTIES OF THE SECURED PARTY WITH RESPECT TO REPOSSESSED COLLATERAL

Section 9-207 places certain duties upon a secured party that is in possession of collateral. These duties were considered at the end of Chapter 13.

Note now the language in Comment 4 to that section: "This section applies where the secured party has possession of collateral either before or after default. (See Sections 9-106(b), 9-609)." So the secured party which finds itself in possession of the goods, or any tangible collateral for that matter, following a repossession has the obligations set out in §9-207, in particular the duty to use reasonable care "in the custody and preservation" of that collateral. What *rights* the secured party has with respect to the collateral now in its possession is the subject to be taken up in the following chapters.

CHAPTER
33

The Foreclosure Sale

A. INTRODUCTION

1. *The Secured Party's Right to Dispose of the Collateral*

Upon a default by the debtor, the secured party having possession of the collateral, either because it had possession from an earlier date, or because it had exercised its right to repossess as dealt with in the previous chapter, is in a position to dispose of the collateral. The object of such a disposition is, of course, not simply for the secured party to get the stuff off of its hands and out from underfoot. The secured party's purpose in disposing of the collateral will be to generate cash proceeds of the disposition out of which it will hope to recover all, or at least as much as it is able, of the amount due it on the underlying obligation which was being secured by that very collateral. The secured party is given broad discretion in § 9-610(a) in determining how it will dispose of the collateral. Key to understanding how the default provisions of Article 6 operate is to appreciate that the secured party is given the power — even if as we will soon see that power is hedged in by a number of provisions which will give the debtor the opportunity to later hold the secured party responsible if that power is abused in one way or another — to dispose of the collateral as it sees fit. The secured party in disposing of the collateral is not operating under the watchful eye of any court. It certainly does not need to obtain any approval or other cooperation from the debtor for how it carries out a § 9-610 disposition, or as it is often referred to a "foreclosure sale" of the collateral.

Note, in addition, that a secured party which does not have possession of the collateral but which is in "control" of it as that term is used to define a type of perfection possible on certain specified types of collateral — such as investment property or deposit accounts — will be upon default prepared to exercise that control to dispose of the collateral without either the consent or cooperation of the debtor. The essence of control, as that word is used in Article 9, is that the secured party with control is in the position to have the investment property sold or funds in the deposit account disbursed as it, the secured party, directs, without further action or consent by the owner of the securities or the deposit account. That's in the very nature of control over the collateral.

2. Dividing Up the Proceeds of Disposition

Section 9-615 sets out the manner in which the secured party is to parcel out whatever cash proceeds are realized on the disposition of the collateral. The money taken in is first to be applied to the reasonable expenses which the secured party has incurred in retaking and then arranging for the disposition of the collateral. This includes any attorneys fees and legal expenses incurred by the secured party "to the extent provided for by agreement and not prohibited by law." It will not surprise you to learn that most security agreements do in fact provide for the secured party getting its legal fees and expenses in such a situation.

The proceeds of the foreclosure sale are next applied to satisfaction of the obligation secured by the security interest under which the disposition has been carried out. That is, the secured party gets paid off what it is then owed on the underlying obligation which created the need for the security interest in the first place. Whether this obligation is fully paid off or only partially satisfied depends, of course, on how much has been realized from the foreclosure sale. If the proceeds of that sale were enough to pay for the reasonable expenses of repossession and disposition as well as the full amount the foreclosing secured party is owed, admittedly not a terribly likely situation, any amount left over is then applied to satisfaction of what is owed to any party claiming a subordinate security interest in the collateral. If after any such party or parties are paid off fully, there is still some cash left in the pot — by now truly exceptional scenario — this residual amount is referred to as a *surplus* and, under § 9-615(d)(1), "the secured party shall account to and pay a debtor" the amount of the surplus. In the much more likely event that the amount realized upon disposition are not even sufficient to fully paid what is owed the foreclosing secured party we refer to the amount still owed as a *deficiency.* Under § 9-615(d)(2), "the obligor is liable for any deficiency." (You should be able to appreciate why Article 9 provides that any surplus is owed to the *debtor* while a deficiency is owed by the *obligor.* As we saw from the very first chapter, these titles usually, but not invariably, refer to the exact same party. If they do not, however, § 9-615(d)'s allocation of who is owed a surplus and who is left owing a deficiency should make sense to you when you think about it.)

Following the flow of the money in § 9-615 leads to two very important practical conclusions. First, there is no inherent incentive for the secured party conducting the disposition of the collateral to realize from that disposition any amount greater than what would cover the expenses it has already or will incur plus what it is owed. If the foreclosing secured party puts in any extra expense or effort resulting in proceeds which exceed this amount, this will not redound to its benefit but will have to be paid over to some other party. The second point to note is that the *debtor* (assuming as we usually do that he, she, or it is the obligor as well) does indeed have a very strong interest in the greatest possible amount being received for the collateral being disposed of. The greater the amount taken in from the foreclosure sale the greater the surplus — in the unlikely event there is a surplus even in the best case scenario — it will recover when all is said and done. In the much more typical situation in which the debtor is going to be left owing a deficiency, the size of the deficiency depends on how much the collateral went for in the foreclosure sale. The drafters of Article 9 were perfectly well aware of the possibility that the secured party may not do all that it reasonably could or should be expected to do to bring in as much as possible from the disposition. Which leads to the next topic.

3. Protections for the Debtor

When it comes to disposition of the collateral following a debtor's default, it is the secured party that runs the show. The debtor, who is after all sometimes in a better position to know what manner of disposition will be best suited to disposition of the particular type of collateral involved, or who may even know of some specific parties most likely to value the stuff most highly, may of course make suggestions to the secured party about how to proceed and whom to contact. The secured party may be well advised to take such suggestions or advice seriously, but it is not under any obligation to follow them. The debtor is, in effect, relegated to a place on the sidelines, observing the disposition but in no position to control it. Article 9 does, however, include a number of provisions which assure the debtor that its view from the sidelines will not be obscured and furthermore that what it gets to watch is carried out according to the rules of the game. Should the secured creditor fail to meet the criteria set forth in Article 9 which place constraints on what it may or must do in carrying out a foreclosure sale, the debtor will later be able to use the secured party's failure to either collect damages or, as is more likely, lessen or perhaps even eliminate any deficiency which it is later asked to make up.

The first constraint placed on the secured party's right to dispose of the collateral as it sees fit is that found in §9-610(b): "*Every aspect* of a disposition of collateral, including the method, manner, time, place, and other terms, must be *commercially reasonable.*" This requirement of a commercially reasonable disposition is set forth in one simple sentence, but as you can see (especially with the help of the emphasis I have added) its scope is broad, and the consequences for a secured party that the debtor is able to show has failed to come up to the standard can be severe indeed.

In addition to the comprehensive requirement of commercial reasonableness, Article 9 also requires that the debtor (along with other specified parties who have a stake in the outcome of the disposition) be given *notification* prior to the event. This notification must give specified information as to the type of disposition, when it is to occur, and so on. The original version of Article 9 was very sparing, allocating only three sentences (albeit long and tangled ones), in what it said about this notification requirement. The result was a consistent stream of litigation where the central issue was whether or not proper notification had been given. The drafters of the present revised version of Article 9 took it as one of their major tasks to elaborate significantly on the notification requirement. The result is an entire series of sections, §§9-611 through 9-614, each rendered in generous detail. The sections also provide certain so-called "safe harbor" provisions which are intended to give the secured party greater assurance that its notification, if it meets certain criteria, cannot later be attacked as failing to meet the statutory requirement.

In addition to greatly fleshing out what is called for by the notification requirement relating to a successful disposition of the collateral by the secured party, the revision of Article 9 added two new provisions of which you should be aware. Section 9-616 requires that when the initial transaction had been a consumer-goods transaction the secured party is to provide the debtor an "explanation" of how any surplus or claimed deficiency has been calculated. A new subsection (f) to §9-615 provides a special method for calculating any surplus or deficiency when the disposition has been one of what Comment 6 to that section refers to as "Certain 'Low-Price' Dispositions." The caption to this comment should, if nothing else, pique your interest. What exactly is meant by this, and how the situation is to be treated, will be dealt with in Problem 33.4(b) below.

4. Debtor's Remedies for the Secured Party's Noncompliance

Article 9 provides, in §9-625(b), that a secured party can be held liable for a damages "in the amount of any loss caused by a failure to comply with this article." As a practical matter, however, it is often difficult if not impossible for a debtor to specify with any certainty how much it has been harmed by a secured party's failure to comply with one or another of its obligations under Part 6 of the article in its disposition of collateral. Even if, say, the "manner" of the disposition was commercially unreasonable, how does one calculate that greater amount which would have been realized if things had been otherwise? If the debtor was not furnished with proper notification of the disposition, how if at all did that affect the proceeds generated? The debtor in a consumer-goods transaction is given some help by a measure of minimal statutory damages under §9-625(c). These two provisions are as far as the prior version of Article 9 went in stipulation of what the consequences of a secured party's noncompliance could be.

Under that prior version of Article 9 the courts were often presented with the argument that the article as then written left open the question of how a secured party's failure to meet its statutory obligations of commercially reasonable disposition and proper notification should be treated when the secured party brought an action for any claimed deficiency. This being so, the argument went, it was for the court to determine under other law how to handle the secured party's dereliction of its duty in the context of a deficiency action brought by that very secured party. Some courts adopted what became known as the "absolute bar" rule, under which the secured party was absolutely barred from recovery of *any* deficiency if it could be shown it had disposed of the collateral other than as Article 9 required. This rule was, needless to say, greatly favored by debtors and those who represented them, especially consumer rights advocates litigating on behalf of consumer debtors who saw themselves as not only losing their property by its repossession but then being "hit" with an action for a deficiency as well. Lenders and their advocates, of course, did not see it this way. The absolute bar rule, they would contend, could result in their being penalized to the full degree of what they were rightfully owed for what might have been only a "minor" or a "technical" transgression. Most courts faced with this problem did not, in fact, adopt the absolute bar rule but ruled instead that in the context of a deficiency action, if it was determined that the secured party's disposition was not up to the Article 9 standards, the consequence would be a rebuttable presumption that the collateral was worth at the time of the sale, and thus had sold for, the amount owed by the debtor to the secured party at the time of the default. Under this "rebuttable presumption" rule, the burden thus rested on the secured party to prove that the collateral had been worth less than the amount of the outstanding debt and by how much, that is, to prove the measure of its deficiency. A third approach to the issue adopted in a handful of jurisdictions was the so-called "set-off" rule. Under this rule the secured party was entitled to the deficiency measured in terms of what it actually had received on disposition reduced only to the extent that the debtor could prove some measure of statutory damages as allowed for in Article 9 itself.

One of the most controversial, if not the most controversial, problems confronted by the drafters of the latest revision of Article 9 was whether to address this issue at all and, if so, what to say about it. The result is set forth in a new section, §9-626. The compromise hammered out there—what it does say in subsection (a) as to the rule when the deficiency action arises in the context of a transaction other than a consumer transaction, and what it defiantly refuses to say or even speculate about in (b) when a consumer transaction is involved—makes for interesting reading. How this all plays out, at least in the consumer transaction situation, is explored (along with a number of other issues) in the *Coxall* case which concludes this chapter.

B. PREPARATION

A common criticism of the prior version of Article 9 was that, given all that is at stake in the secured party's disposition of collateral, those sections dealing with such a disposition and its consequences seemed particularly sketchy and failed to address many issues that regularly were to come up and lead to litigation. The drafter of the present version took this critique to heart. The result is a much more complete, and complex, set of sections each with its own detailed commentary. In looking over the statutory material before you proceed into the problems and cases, I am suggesting only the highlights. As you work through the later material, you may find yourself wanting to return in search of further enlightenment to (or your instructor may point you to) the exact detailed language of some particular section or to a exceptionally helpful comment.

- On the right of the secured party to carry out the disposition, see §9-610(a) and (c)
- On the need for the disposition to be carried out in all respects in a "commercially reasonable" manner, see §9-610(b) and §9-627
- On the notification requirement, read §9-611(b); then skim over the rest of this section along with §§9-612 through §9-614
- On the consequences of a secured party's noncompliance, see §9-625(a) through (c) and §9-626; see also §9-615(f)

C. PROBLEMS AND CASES

PROBLEM

33.1 In 2008 Heavy Lifting Lenders, makes a loan of $50,000 to the Crusty Construction Company. The loan is to be repaid, with interest, at the end of two years. As part of the loan agreement, Crusty grants Heavy Lifting a security interest in a particular piece of its equipment, an 80-foot boomlift, to secure its payment obligation. In 2010 Crusty began to experience financial difficulties and is unable to pay off the loan. Heavy Lifting is able to repossess the boomlift from Crusty with no difficulty. The President of Heavy Lifting is now considering disposing of the repossessed boomlift and comes to you for advice.

(a) The President is concerned that upon inspection she finds that the boomlift has not been kept in good condition by Crusty. She is considering having a firm of mechanics which specializes in working on such equipment come in and give it a "good clean up and repair to get it in top-notch condition" before she even attempts to dispose of it.

Do you foresee any problem for her if she does so? Will she be able to recover the cost of doing the refurbishment from Crusty?

(b) The President tells you that she is already aware of one possible buyer for the boomlift, whom she believes would be willing to pay a decent price for it once it is in better condition. She is thinking of entering into negotiations with this buyer and then selling it to him at the best price she can get him to agree to. Does she face any problems if she simply proceeds in this fashion?

(c) What procedures do you suggest she follow if her plan is to sell the boomlift and apply what money she gets to the debt owed her firm?

FEDERAL EXPRESS CREDIT UNION v. LANIER

Court of Appeals of Tennessee, 2005
2005 Tenn. App. LEXIS 674, 60 U.C.C. Rep. Serv. 2d 518

ALAN E. HIGHERS, Judge: In this appeal, we are called upon to evaluate the propriety of the trial court's decision to award a creditor a deficiency judgment against the debtor following the sale of the collateral after the debtor defaulted on the loan. The debtor filed an appeal to this Court arguing that the creditor failed to provide him with reasonable notice of the sale of the collateral and that the creditor did not conduct the sale in a commercially reasonable manner. We hold that the creditor did not provide the debtor with reasonable notice. Accordingly, we reverse the decision of the trial court and remand this case to the trial court for further proceedings.

FACTUAL BACKGROUND AND PROCEDURAL HISTORY

For purposes of this appeal, the facts have been set forth in a "Joint Statement of the Evidence" entered into between the parties pursuant to Rule 24(c) of the Tennessee Rules of Appellate Procedure. On August 23, 1995, Barry Lanier ("Mr. Lanier" or "Appellant") signed a promissory note and security agreement in favor of Federal Express Credit Union (the "Credit Union" or "Appellee") to secure funds to purchase a 1995 Lexus automobile. The promissory note called for Mr. Lanier to make payments in the amount of $199.01 for fifty-nine (59) consecutive months followed by a balloon payment in the amount of $26,327.55 on July 31, 2000. Mr. Lanier made the required fifty-nine (59) consecutive monthly payments. However, when it came time to pay the final balloon payment, he was unable to tender the amount owed. The parties subsequently entered into negotiations in an effort to refinance the balloon payment, but the negotiations proved unsuccessful.

At the time of the events giving rise to the instant litigation, Mr. Lanier was employed by Federal Express Corporation ("Federal Express"). On the promissory note, Mr. Lanier listed his address as 1214 Central Avenue,

Memphis, Tennessee, which remained his home address at the time the loan matured. After Mr. Lanier defaulted on the loan, the Credit Union repossessed the 1995 Lexus automobile from Mr. Lanier's home address. On November 29, 2000, the Credit Union sent a letter by certified mail to Mr. Lanier at his home address advising him that it intended to sell the vehicle at a private sale on December 15, 2000. The certified mail return receipt was never signed for or returned. At trial, Mr. Lanier testified that, at the time the Credit Union sent the notice, it knew he had been in Saudi Arabia for the past several years conducting business for his employer. In support of this assertion, Mr. Lanier testified to the following: the Credit Union had access to the computer files of Federal Express which enabled it to learn of Mr. Lanier's location (*i.e.*, Saudi Arabia) at the time the notice was sent; the Credit Union and Mr. Lanier spoke several times by phone and e-mail while he was in Saudi Arabia to negotiate the re-financing of the outstanding balance; and the Credit Union even contacted him in Saudi Arabia to discuss the indebtedness. Conversely, Larry Stevenson, the collection manager for the Credit Union, testified that the Credit Union is a separate and distinct entity from Federal Express, and it did not have direct access to any of the computer records maintained by Federal Express.

As promised in the letter sent to Mr. Lanier, the Credit Union conducted a private sale of the 1995 Lexus automobile on December 15, 2000. A deficiency remained after the Credit Union applied the proceeds of the sale to the outstanding loan amount. On May 31, 2001, the Credit Union filed a "Civil Warrant" in the General Sessions Court of Shelby County against Mr. Lanier to recoup $10,645.04 remaining on the promissory note and $3,547.99 in attorney's fees, for a total requested judgment in the amount of $14,193.03. Ultimately, the case came to be heard by the Circuit Court of Shelby County. The circuit court entered an order on January 3, 2005 finding "that [the Credit Union] should be awarded judgment against [Mr. Lanier] for the sum of $14,193.03." No additional findings of fact or conclusions of law are contained in the order.

[One of the arguments Lanier made on appeal was that the trial court had erred in finding that the Credit Union's notice of the sale of the collateral was reasonable.]

DISCUSSION

We begin with an examination of whether the notice of the private sale provided to Mr. Lanier by the Credit Union was reasonable. Implicit in the trial court's ruling in this case is a finding that, as a matter of law, the notice provided by the Credit Union was sufficient.

The official comment to section 47-9-611(b) provides as follows: "The notification must be *reasonable* as to the manner in which it is sent, its timeliness (i.e., a reasonable time before the disposition is to take place), and its content." Tenn. Code Ann. § 47-9-611 cmt. 2 (2003) (emphasis added).

This Court has previously addressed the policy justification for requiring the creditor to send the debtor reasonable notice of the sale of the collateral:

> We think the provision for notice in connection with a sale is intended to afford the debtor a reasonable opportunity (1) to avoid a sale altogether by discharging the debt and redeeming the collateral or (2) in case of sale, to see that the collateral brings a fair price.

Int'l Harvester Credit Corp. v. Ingram, 619 S.W.2d 134, 137 (Tenn. Ct. App. 1981) (citing *Mallicoat v. Volunteer Fin. Loan Corp.*, 57 Tenn. App. 106, 415 S.W.2d 347, 350 (Tenn. Ct. App. 1966)).

On appeal, Mr. Lanier argues that the trial court erred in finding that the notice of the sale of the collateral provided by the Credit Union was reasonable and adequate under the circumstances present in this case. Mr. Lanier does not contest the timeliness or content of the notice. Instead, he contests the reasonableness of the manner in which it was sent. "The reasonableness of the notice also encompasses a consideration of where the notice was sent." *R & J of Tenn., Inc. v. Blankenship-Melton Real Estate, Inc.*, 166 S.W.3d 195, 203 (Tenn. Ct. App. 2004) (citing *Commercial Credit Corp. v. Cutshall*, 28 U.C.C. Rep. Serv. (Callaghan) 277 (Tenn. Ct. App. 1979)). He urges this Court to find that the notice sent by the Credit Union does not amount to reasonable notice where (1) the record establishes that the Credit Union knew he was not at his home address but in a foreign country at the time it sent the notice, and (2) the certified mail return receipt was never signed for by Mr. Lanier or returned to the Credit Union. Conversely, the Credit Union urges this Court to find that the notice provided was reasonable because (1) Mr. Lanier maintained his home address in Memphis while he worked in Saudi Arabia, (2) he could have his mail forwarded to him by Federal Express at no charge since he worked in Saudi Arabia, (3) his wife remained in Memphis while he was in Saudi Arabia, and (4) it must be assumed that Mr. Lanier received the letter since the letter was not returned to the Credit Union.

At the outset, we must ascertain those facts which can be supported by the limited record in this case. After reading the "Joint Statement of the Evidence" filed by the parties, it appears that the question of whether the Credit Union knew that Mr. Lanier was in Saudi Arabia when it sent the notice of the sale of the collateral was a disputed issue of fact at trial. In the "Joint Statement of the Evidence," the parties stipulate that Mr. Lanier testified that the Credit Union knew he was in Saudi Arabia when it sent the notice of the sale of the collateral. The Credit Union concedes in its brief that it had knowledge that Mr. Lanier was in Saudi Arabia when it sent the notice, stating as follows: "Granted, he was working in Saudi Arabia for Federal Express, but he was still maintaining his residence in Memphis"; "he most assuredly had set up some method to have his mail forwarded to him"; "Appellant's wife was still in Memphis." Thus, we must conclude that the Credit Union knew that Mr. Lanier was living in Saudi Arabia at the time it sent the notice of the sale of the collateral to his home address in Memphis.

The Credit Union states that, since the letter was not returned to the Credit Union, this Court is to assume that it reached Mr. Lanier. The "Joint Statement of the Evidence" merely provides as follows: "The certified mail return receipt was never signed for or returned." This Court is not permitted to make the assumption urged upon it by the Credit Union. We must simply take the following stipulated fact to be true: the Credit Union never received any certified mail return receipt indicating that Mr. Lanier received the notice. There are additional statements of fact made by the Credit Union on appeal which have no support in the record. The Credit Union asserts as fact that Mr. Lanier was capable of having his mail forwarded to him in Saudi Arabia free of charge by Federal Express. This fact is nowhere in the "Joint Statement of the Evidence" presented to this Court on appeal. Therefore, this unproven fact has no bearing on our decision on appeal. Moreover, the Credit Union asserts that Mr. Lanier's wife remained in Memphis while he was in Saudi Arabia, presumably at the same address where it sent the notice. However, the "Joint Statement of the Evidence" merely provides as follows: "The Appellant was married, with his wife living at said residence." From this terse statement we cannot assume as true the fact the Credit Union urges upon this Court. There is nothing in the limited record to indicate that Mr. Lanier's wife lived at the residence when the notice was delivered or that she received the notice sent by the Credit Union.

Thus, we are only concerned with whether the notice of the sale of the collateral was proper based on the following facts: (1) the Credit Union knew that Mr. Lanier was in Saudi Arabia when it mailed the notice to his residence in Memphis, and (2) the Credit Union proceeded with a sale of the collateral when it had yet to receive a certified mail return receipt indicating that Mr. Lanier had or had not received the notice it sent to his residence in Memphis. Both parties have cited this Court to cases supporting their respective position on appeal. However, our decision in *R & J of Tennessee, Inc. v. Blankenship-Melton Real Estate, Inc.*, 166 S.W.3d 195 (Tenn. Ct. App. 2004), which discusses the cases relied on by the parties, controls our resolution of this case and requires that we find that the Credit Union did not provide Mr. Lanier with reasonable notice of the sale of the collateral at issue in this case.

In *R & J of Tennessee, Inc.*, the debtor executed a guaranty agreement promising to remain personally liable on a promissory note entered into by his business, in which he provided his home address. However, the debtor moved after entering into the personal guaranty, and he never notified the bank of his new address. When the company defaulted on the loan, the creditor sent, by certified mail, a notice to the debtor at the address listed on the personal guaranty indicating that the collateral would be sold at a public sale. Even though the creditor had yet to receive any indication that the notice had reached the debtor, it went ahead and conducted a sale of the collateral. On appeal, the debtor argued that the notice given by the creditor was not reasonable. We agreed with the debtor and reversed the trial court's decision that the notice of the sale of the collateral was reasonable.

In finding that the creditor in *R & J of Tennessee, Inc.* did not provide reasonable notice of the sale of the collateral to the debtor, we stated:

> The definition section applicable to Tennessee's version of Article 9 does not define "notice," but we find guidance in the general definition section of the Code, which provides:
>
> A person "notifies" or "gives" a notice or notification to another by taking such steps as may be reasonably required to inform the other in ordinary course *whether or not such other actually comes to know of it.* A person "receives" a notice or notification when:
>
> (A) It comes to his attention; or
>
> (B) It is duly delivered at the place of business *through which the contract was made or at any other place held out by him* as the place for receipt of such communications[.]

Tenn. Code Ann. § 47-1-201(26) (2003) (emphasis added).

In support of his argument that the notice given was not reasonable, [the debtor] relies on our decision in *Mallicoat v. Volunteer Finance & Loan Corp.*, 57 Tenn. App. 106, 415 S.W.2d 347 (Tenn. Ct. App. 1966). In *Mallicoat*, the secured party sent a notice of sale to the debtor by certified mail, but the notice was returned to the secured party undelivered. After receiving the returned notice, the secured party continued to conduct a sale of the collateral and sued the debtor for a deficiency judgment. In finding the notice in that case insufficient under the predecessor statute to section 47-9-611, we stated:

> In view of the undisputed proof in this case that the debtor did not receive the notice and that the secured creditor was aware that he had not received it, it is our opinion the creditor not only failed to show a compliance with the Act but that the record affirmatively shows a lack of compliance and a conscious disregard of the debtor's right to notice. The property was not perishable. The debtor lived in Knoxville where the creditor had its place of business and sold the property. In addition, the creditor had information as to where the debtor was employed and where his parents lived. Yet, the sale was allowed to proceed without any further effort to comply with the notice requirement.

Courts throughout the country vary as to whether the secured party has the burden of proving that the debtor or a secondary obligor received actual notice of a pending sale. *See* Richard C. Tinney, Annotation, *Sufficiency of Secured Party's Notification of Sale or Other Intended Disposition of Collateral Under UCC § 9-504(3)*, 11 A.L.R. 4th 241, §§ 14-16 (2003). Many of our sister states interpret the notice provision to require only that the creditor send notice. Our decision in *Mallicoat*, however, demonstrates that Tennessee requires more than a mere "sending" in order for a secured party to be in compliance with the statute. James J. White & Robert S. Summers, *Uniform Commercial Code* § 26-10, at 987 (1972).

At the other end of the notice spectrum, we have held that the notice requirement is satisfied when the following occurs:

> The sending of notice, certified, return receipt requested, is commercially reasonable. When a plaintiff forwards notice to the debtor's proper address, certified, return receipt requested, and the notice is received at that address and returned signed by someone at the address, it is reasonable for plaintiff to assume that the defendant received the notice.

Caterpillar Fin. Services Corp. v. Woods, No. 89-326-II, 1990 Tenn. App. LEXIS 117, at *7-8 (Tenn. Ct. App. Feb. 22, 1990). Our case law makes clear that "the creditor will not be forced to take responsibility for lost mail or the debtor's refusal to accept properly delivered mail." *Nationsbank v. Clegg*, No. 01-A-01-9510-CH-00469, 1996 Tenn. App. LEXIS 214, at *14 (Tenn. Ct. App. Apr. 10, 1996). Yet, we have also made clear that:

> While absolute proof of receipt of notice may not be required in every instance, a creditor, who only makes one attempt to contact the debtor, and is left uncertain of receipt of the notice, has not fulfilled its obligation to the debtor when it proceeds with a disposition less than two weeks from mailing its first notice.

1996 Tenn. App. LEXIS 214 at *15-16.

We disagree with (the debtor's) assertion that section 47-9-611(b) requires the secured party to prove that the secondary obligor actually received the notice. *See Commercial Credit Corp. v. Cutshall*, 28 U.C.C. Rep. Serv. (Callaghan) 277 (Tenn. Ct. App. 1979). Based on the facts presented to the trial court below, however, we find the trial court's holding that notice in this case was sufficient under the statute to be erroneous as a matter of law. We are mindful that (the debtor) bears some responsibility for not receiving notice in this case. However, (the creditor) sent the notice to (the debtor) on June 11, 2002, and conducted a sale ten days later on June 21, 2002, without receiving any indication as to whether the notice actually reached (the debtor). We find, therefore, that this amounts to unreasonable notice under the statute and reverse the trial court's holding on this issue.

The facts in the instant case fit squarely within our holding in *R & J of Tennessee, Inc.* Like the creditor in *R & J of Tennessee, Inc.*, the Credit Union, on November 29, 2000, sent the notice of the sale of the collateral to the address Mr. Lanier provided on the promissory note. On December 15, 2000, approximately seventeen (17) days later, the Credit Union, as did the creditor in *R & J of Tennessee, Inc.*, proceeded to conduct a sale of the collateral without having received any indication as to whether the notice reached the debtor. As we stated in *R & J of Tennessee, Inc.*, this amounts to unreasonable notice. Moreover, the facts present in this case more forcefully support a finding that the Credit Union did not provide Mr. Lanier with reasonable notice. Unlike the creditor in *R & J of Tennessee, Inc.*, the Credit Union, as it readily concedes in its brief filed with this Court, had actual knowledge that Mr. Lanier was in Saudi Arabia and not at the address where it sent the notice.

Despite knowing the exact whereabouts of Mr. Lanier, nothing in the record indicates that the Credit Union did anything to ensure that Mr. Lanier received the notice while in Saudi Arabia.

"The requirement of notice is for the benefit and protection of the debtor." *Mallicoat*, 415 S.W.2d at 350. "The requirement of notice is not a mere formality. . . ." *Gen. Motors Acceptance Corp. v. Middleton*, No. 02A01-9103-CH-00033, 1991 Tenn. App. LEXIS 820, at *5 (Tenn. Ct. App. Oct. 16, 1991) (no perm. app. filed). This Court has previously expressed its disfavor with the practice of providing perfunctory notice as a matter of form, stating: "Notice which is a mere gesture is not notice. The means employed must be such as one desirous of actually informing the absent party might reasonably adopt. *Mullane v. Central Hanover Bank & Trust Co.*, 339 U.S. 306, 70 S. Ct. 652, 94 L. Ed. 865." *Mallicoat, 415 S.W.2d at 351.* Accordingly, we conclude that the Credit Union did not provide Mr. Lanier with reasonable notice of the sale of the collateral as required by section 47-9-611 of the Tennessee Code.

A BRIEF EXCERPT ON THE NOTIFICATION REQUIREMENT

PANORA STATE BANK v. DICKINSON

Court of Appeals of Iowa, 2006
2006 Iowa App. LEXIS 93, 58 U.C.C. Rep. Serv. 2d 727

When a secured party learns the notice was not received by the debtor, the question of whether reasonable notification requires a "second try" is a matter left "to judicial resolution, based upon the facts of each case. . . ." § 554.9611 U.C.C. cmt. 6.

We agree with the district court, that under the particular facts of this case, a "second try," although perhaps advisable, was not required. Janet [the debtor] testified she was aware the post office was attempting to deliver a certified letter from the bank, but declined to pick it up as she was "communicating with Mr. Marso [a bank employee] on a daily basis [and] if he had anything to say to me, he could say it to my face or deliver it in person." Like the district court, which specifically found Janet less credible than the bank's witnesses, we determine Janet refused to accept the letter. We also conclude that, because any lack of notice was due to Janet's own actions, the notice sent by the bank was sufficient.

PROBLEMS

33.2 In order to borrow some money from the Lone Star Bank, Lance Cashmore grants the bank a security interest in a securities account (#13131313) he has with the brokerage firm of Shakes and Rattles. The Bank perfects on this interest by the preparation of a Control Agreement which is signed by both a representative of the bank, an authorized representative of the brokerage firm, and Lance. When Lance defaults on his loan, a representative of the bank issues an entitlement order to Shakes and Rattles directing it to sell all shares of the corporation, Green Organic Hyperwidgets, Incorporated — a corporation whose shares are traded on the New York Stock Exchange — and to pay it, the bank, the amount Lance owes it out of the proceeds of this sale.

(a) Is the brokerage firm obligated to follow this instruction from the bank regarding account #13131313?
(b) If the brokerage does execute the trade as called for by the bank and then disperses to the bank out of the proceeds of the sale the amount the bank is owed by Lance, will Lance have any way of challenging either the brokerage or the bank on the basis of what has transpired?

33.3   Colonial Car Loans makes an auto loan to Kailey of Waltham, Massachusetts with which she buys a new Aspen automobile from a local dealership. Kailey is to pay off this loan in 36 monthly installments. Within a year, Kailey has repeatedly fallen seriously behind in her payments. Colonial Car Loans is able to repossess the auto without incident. It plans to take this auto, along with those others that it has had repossessed during the past month to a dealers-only auction which is held regularly in Manard, Massachusetts. The Manard Auto Auction is well known to those looking to buy numbers of used cars which the (successful high-bidding) buyers then take away to stock the lots at their used-car sales establishments.

(a) If Colonial does proceed in this fashion, will the resultant sale of the car repossessed from Kailey be considered a public or a private disposition for the purposes of Article 9?
(b) What procedures should Colonial be sure to follow to ensure that no argument can later be raised that in disposing of the car in this manner it has acted in accordance with its obligations as set forth in Article 9?

33.4   Earl's Autos of Upstate, New York sells a new Aspen Supreme auto to one Brady, of the neighboring town of North Upstate, providing him with a loan with which to buy the auto and retaining a purchase-money security interest in the auto. Brady is to pay off this loan in 36 monthly installments. Within a year, Brady has repeatedly fallen seriously behind in his payments. The dealership is able to repossess car with no difficulty. Earl decides that the easiest way to deal with the situation is first to evaluate the car based on what he would pay for a similar used car if it was presented to him for sale by its owner. Once he has transferred title to himself he would then notify Brady of what he has done and also of either what surplus Brady is owed or what deficiency Brady will be expected to now pay.

(a) Do you see any problems for Earl if he does proceed in this fashion?
(b) What if instead, Earl sell the repossessed auto to his brother-in-law, one Isaac, for the amount he has calculated based on prior sales of similar vehicles. Earl does send Brady a proper notice of his intention to enter

into this private sale. After the sale to Isaac is completed, Earl sends Brady a second notice, informing him of the deficiency he is obligated to make up. Brady becomes aware that the buyer of the auto was Earl's brother-in-law. Does Brady have an argument that he is not obligated to pay the deficiency as calculated by Earl?

COXALL v. CLOVER COMMERCIAL CORP.

Civil Court of the City of New York, 2004
4 Misc. 3d 654, 781 N.Y.S.2d 567, 54 U.C.C. Rep. Serv. 2d 5

JACK M. BATTAGLIA, J.: On October 21, 2002, Jason Coxall and Utho Coxall purchased a 1991 model Lexus automobile, executing a Security Agreement/Retail Installment Contract. The "cash price" on the contract was $8,100, against which the Coxalls made a "cash down payment" of $3,798.25 and financed the balance of $4,970. Apparently simultaneously with the sale, the contract was assigned to Clover Commercial Corp., whose name was printed on the top and at other places. Although Majestic Capital Inc. is designated as the "Seller" and "Dealer" in the assignment, at trial the parties referred to the seller of the automobile as Jafas Auto Sales. Title to the vehicle was put in Jason Coxall's name.

The Coxalls were required by the contract to make monthly payments of $333.68 each, beginning November 21, 2002. No payments were made, however, because Jason Coxall experienced mechanical difficulties with the vehicle soon after purchase. On February 19, 2003, Clover Commercial took possession of the vehicle, and on the next day mailed two letters to Jason Coxall; in one, Clover told Mr. Coxall that he could redeem the vehicle with a payment of $5,969.28, exclusive of storage charges and a redemption fee; in the other, Clover gave Mr. Coxall notice that the vehicle would be offered for private sale after 12:00 noon on March 3, 2003.

On March 3, 2003, the Lexus was sold back to Jafas Auto Sales for $1,500. On April 22, 2003, Clover Commercial wrote to Jason Coxall demanding that he pay a "remaining balance" of $4,998.09.

Jason Coxall commenced action No. 1 with a summons with endorsed complaint dated April 29, 2003 that states the nature and substance of the cause of action as "automobile illegally repossed (sic)," and seeks damages of $8,000 with interest from February 19, 2003.

Meanwhile, with a summons and verified complaint dated June 16, 2003 and filed on June 25, Clover Commercial commenced action No. 2 against Jason Coxall and Utho Coxall, seeking $4,630.62 with interest from October 21, 2002 plus reasonable attorney fees. The verified complaint alleges that "(p)laintiff is the holder for value of a promissory instrument dated 10/21/02 duly executed and delivered and/or guaranteed by the defendant(s)."

Trial was held on March 18. Clover Commercial was represented by Alan Levin, Esq., and Adam Greenberg and Lynval Wittaker testified on its behalf. Jason Coxall appeared and testified, but Utho Coxall did not.

The enforcement of Clover Commercial's security interest in Mr. Coxall's Lexus is governed by article 9 of the Uniform Commercial Code. An extensively revised article 9 became effective in New York on July 4, 2001 [actually July 1, 2001] and applies to these actions. Revised article 9 makes significant changes in the law as it applies to the respective rights and obligations of the Coxalls and Clover Commercial. Under both former and revised article 9, however, if the Coxalls defaulted under the contract, Clover was entitled to take possession of its collateral, the Lexus, and it could proceed without judicial process, if it could obtain possession without breach of the peace. There was no evidence at trial that Clover breached the peace in taking possession of the vehicle.

DEFAULT

[The court first determined that the Coxalls were not relieved of their obligation to make payments on the car as they had taken no action which, under Article 2 of the U.C.C., demonstrated any desire on their part to reject or revoke acceptance of the vehicle. "Indeed," as the court noted Jason Coxall's action against Clover "is based upon his claim of ownership and right to possession of the vehicle." The Coxalls were, therefore, in default at the time of the repossession.]

After Clover Commercial took possession of the Lexus, it was obligated to deal with the vehicle in accordance with the requirements of article 9. Under former article 9, those requirements were contained in a single section (*see* former UCC 9-504), and there was much uncertainty about the consequences of the creditor's failure to comply. Revised article 9 expands greatly upon the statutory requirements, and clears some, but not all, of the uncertainty.

For the secured party who chooses to sell the collateral, article 9 imposes two overriding requirements: the secured party must send "a reasonable authenticated notification of disposition" to the debtor; and the sale must be "commercially reasonable." The court has determined that Clover Commercial failed to comply with these requirements.

REASONABLE NOTIFICATION

"The purpose of the notice requirement is 'to give the debtor an opportunity to protect his interest in the collateral by exercising any right of redemption or by bidding at the sale, to challenge any aspect of the disposition before it is made, or to interest potential purchasers in the sale, all to the end that the merchandise not be sacrificed by sale at less than the true value.' "

"(W)hether a notification is sent within a reasonable time is a question of fact." (UCC 9-612(a).) "A notification that is sent so near to the disposition date that a notified person could not be expected to act on or take account of the notification would be unreasonable." (UCC 9-612, Comment 2.) For secured transactions other than consumer transactions, "a notification . . . sent . . . 10 days or more before the earliest time of disposition . . . is sent within a reasonable time before the disposition." (UCC 9-612(b).) The 10-day period for nonconsumer transactions "is intended to be a 'safe-harbor' and not a minimum requirement." (UCC 9-612, Comment 3.) The terms "consumer goods," "consumer-goods transaction" and "consumer transaction" are defined. (*See* UCC 9-102(a)(23), (24), (26).)

The contents and form of the notification are prescribed generally for all transactions (*see* UCC 9-613(a)) and for consumer-goods transactions (*see* UCC 9-614(a)). A notification in a nonconsumer transaction that does not include all of the prescribed information may still be found sufficient as a matter of fact. (*See* UCC 9-613(b).) But in a consumer transaction, "(a) notification that lacks any of the (prescribed) information . . . is insufficient as a matter of law." (UCC 9-614, Comment 2.)

Here, Clover Commercial mailed two letters to Jason Coxall on February 20, 2003: one advised primarily as to the time after which the sale would be made, i.e., "12 noon on 3/03/03"; the other advised primarily as to Mr. Coxall's right to redeem the automobile. Although each of these letters shows a "(c)opy to: Utho Coxall," there is no evidence of any mailing to him. As to Utho Coxall, therefore, it appears that he may not have been sent any notification; at the least, we do not know when any notification was sent.

The court will assume, for purposes of these actions only, that separate writings that in combination provide to the debtor all of the prescribed information may be found to comply sufficiently with the "reasonable notification" requirement. Even so, and read generously, Clover Commercial's two letters did not provide Jason Coxall with all of the information it was required to provide. Neither letter stated that Mr. Coxall was "entitled to an accounting of the unpaid indebtedness" nor stated "the charge, if any, for an accounting." (*See* UCC 9-613(a)(4); UCC 9-614(a)(1).)

COMMERCIALLY REASONABLE SALE

"Every aspect of a disposition of collateral, including the method, manner, time, place, and other terms, must be commercially reasonable." (UCC 9-610(b)) Private dispositions, as compared to public auction, are encouraged "on the assumption that they frequently will result in higher realization on collateral for the benefit of all concerned." (UCC 9-610, Comment 2.) "A disposition of collateral is made in a commercially reasonable manner if the disposition is made . . . in conformity with reasonable commercial practices among dealers in the type of property that was the subject of the disposition." (UCC 9-627(b)(3).)

New York courts have determined commercial reasonableness by whether the secured party "acted in good faith and to the parties' mutual best advantage." When a secured party is seeking a deficiency from the debtor, the secured party bears the burden of proving the sale was commercially reasonable. "Whether a sale was commercially reasonable is, like other questions about 'reasonableness,' a fact-intensive inquiry; no magic set of procedures will immunize a sale from scrutiny."

Here, Clover Commercial sold Mr. Coxall's Lexus in a private sale to the dealer from whom Mr. Coxall had purchased it. Clover Commercial provided no evidence on its procedure for the sale, its identification of prospective buyers, or any other details of the sale, except for the price. There was no showing that dealers sell their trade-ins in the same manner or that dealers or secured parties sell repossessed automobiles in the same manner. On the other hand, one court has noted that "the sale of (a) repossessed vehicle by private auto auction is in conformity with the reasonable commercial practices of lenders disposing of motor vehicles." (*Charter One Auto Fin. Corp. v. Vaglio*, 2003 N.Y. Slip Op. 50638(U), *5, 2003 N.Y. Misc. LEXIS 253 (Sup. Ct., Nassau County).) This case is different, however, in that the vehicle was sold back to the dealer who sold it to the debtor.

All we have, therefore, as evidence of commercial reasonableness is the price. Clover Commercial received $1,500 on the sale of a Lexus that had been purchased by the Coxalls approximately four months earlier for $8,100; that is a sales price of 18.5% of the purchase price.

"The fact that a greater amount could have been obtained by a . . . disposition . . . at a different time or in a different method from that selected by the secured party is not of itself sufficient to preclude the secured party from establishing that the . . . disposition . . . was made in a commercially reasonable manner." (UCC 9-627(a),) But "(w)hile not itself sufficient to establish a violation of (code requirements), a low price suggests that a court should scrutinize carefully all aspects of a disposition to ensure that each aspect was commercially reasonable." (UCC 9-627, Comment 2.)

New York courts have, indeed, scrutinized "low price" sales. A low price, of course, "might simply reflect a greatly depreciated piece of collateral." But, here, Clover Commercial acknowledged that Mr. Coxall's Lexus had not sustained any physical damage while in his possession. Clover's suggestion that the low price may have been due to the mechanical difficulties experienced by Mr. Coxall was contradicted by its own testimony that the car was running fine when repossessed, and would, in any event, be specious.

As previously indicated, Clover Commercial provided no evidence as to the commercial reasonableness of the sale; it provided no evidence that any prospective buyer was contacted, other than the original seller; and provided no evidence of the fair market value of the Lexus on the date of sale, or any other evidence that would justify a sale price of $1,500. In short, Clover Commercial failed to sustain its burden of showing that the sale of Mr. Coxall's Lexus was commercially reasonable.

When the secured party has disposed of the collateral in a commercially reasonable manner after sending reasonable notification to the debtor, the debtor will be liable for any deficiency if the proceeds of the disposition are not sufficient to satisfy the debt and allowed expenses. (*See* UCC 9-615(d).) Former article 9 was silent, however, on whether the secured party that had failed to send reasonable notification or had not disposed of the collateral in a commercially reasonable manner — or both, as here — could obtain a deficiency judgment against the debtor. "Three general approaches emerged. Some courts have held that a noncomplying secured party may not recover a deficiency (the 'absolute bar' rule). A few courts held that the debtor can offset against a claim to a deficiency all damages recoverable under former Section 9-507 resulting from the secured party's noncompliance (the 'offset' rule). A plurality of courts considering the issue held that the noncomplying secured party is barred from recovering a deficiency unless it overcomes a rebuttable presumption that compliance with former Part 5 would have yielded an amount sufficient to satisfy the secured debt." (UCC 9-626, Comment 4.)

In New York, the departments of the Appellate Division were not in agreement as to which of the approaches to follow, with the Second Department alone adopting the "absolute bar" rule. Revised article 9 resolves the conflict and uncertainty for transactions other than consumer transactions by adopting the "rebuttable presumption" rule. (*See* UCC 9-626(a)(3).) The limitation of the "rebuttable presumption" rule to nonconsumer transactions "is intended to leave to the court the determination of the proper rules in consumer transactions," and the court "may continue to apply established approaches." (UCC 9-626(b).)

It is clear, therefore, that the "rebuttable presumption" rule is now the law in the Second Department for nonconsumer transactions. The question remains, however, whether the "absolute bar" rule is to be applied in these actions, involving, as they do, a consumer transaction. A review of the legislative history provides no guidance. The report of the New York Law Revision Commission that accompanied revised article 9 through enactment states only that, "(w)ith respect to consumer defaults, Revised article 9 makes no recommendation whatsoever, leaving the courts free to shape a remedy as is appropriate in each case." (2001 Report of NY Law Rev. Comm'n on Proposed Revised UCC art. 9, at 158.)

Up to now, New York courts have not distinguished between consumer and nonconsumer transactions in fashioning rules where the enforcement provisions of article 9 were silent, suggesting that the "rebuttable presumption" rule will be adopted for all transactions. But at this time, for a court sitting in the Second Department, there is an "absolute bar" rule that has not been legislatively displaced by revised article 9.

Having found, therefore, that Clover Commercial failed to comply with both the reasonable notification and commercially reasonable disposition requirements of article 9, the "absolute bar" rule precludes it from recovering a deficiency from the Coxalls. Even if, however, the "rebuttable presumption" rule were to be applied, the result would be the same. Clover introduced no evidence of "the amount of proceeds that would have been realized had (it) proceeded in accordance with the provisions of" the code relating to disposition of the collateral. (*See* UCC 9-626(a)(3)(B).)

Specifically, Clover Commercial provided no evidence as to the fair market value of the Lexus on the date of the sale, either by reference to "blue book" value, appraisal, sales of similar vehicles or other measure. Moreover, Clover's witness, Adam Greenberg, acknowledged that Clover considered the Lexus to be of sufficient value to serve as collateral for the secured debt, which, at the least, was the amount financed, $4,970.

Although Clover Commercial cannot recover for any deficiency, it may recover "the sums owed to it prior to the repossession as well as the repossession charges." (*See Avis Rent-A-Car Sys. v. Franklin*, 82 Misc. 2d at 67.) Clover's failure to comply with the enforcement provisions of article 9 "would not discharge the (Coxalls) from all liability under the contract." At the time of repossession, three monthly payments of $333.68 were unpaid for a total due of $1,001.04, and the contract provided for a 10% late charge for each payment not made when due, for an additional charge of $100.11. Clover is entitled, therefore, to $1,101.15 for payments in default and related late charges.

The contract also provides that the debtor must pay the "cost of repossession, storage and preparation for sale" and "an attorney's fee of up to 15% of the amount due . . . unless the court sets a smaller fee." Clover Commercial includes $325 in its computation of the deficiency, which apparently is intended as a charge for repossession, storage, and preparation charges, but, unlike the late charge, the amount is not specified in the contract, and no evidence was submitted to explain or support it. Similarly, there was no evidence to support an award of attorney's fees.

COXALL'S CLAIM AGAINST CLOVER

Jason Coxall no longer has his Lexus. His down payment was $3,798.25, and he owes $1,101.15 for overdue payments. In effect, approximately four months' use of the vehicle has cost him approximately $5,000, not including alleged repair and towing expenses. Of course, "the debtor who precipitated the sale by defaulting on a debt is certainly not to be freed lightly from fault." Nonetheless, does Mr. Coxall have a remedy for Clover Commercial's failure to comply with article 9, beyond being relieved of any liability for a deficiency?

Under article 9, "a person is liable for damages in the amount of any loss caused by a failure to comply" with the statute. (UCC 9-625 (b).) "Damages for violation of the requirements of (the statute) . . . are those reasonably calculated to put an eligible claimant in the position that it would have occupied had no violation occurred." (UCC 9-625, Comment 3.) There are, however, both supplements to and limitations on this general liability principle.

"(A) debtor . . . whose deficiency is eliminated or reduced under Section 9-626 may not otherwise recover . . . for noncompliance with the provisions . . . relating to . . . enforcement." (UCC 9-625(d).) This provision "eliminates the possibility of double recovery or other over-compensation," but "(b)ecause Section 9-626 does not apply to consumer transactions, the statute is silent as to whether a double recovery or other over-compensation is possible in a consumer transaction." (UCC 9-625, Comment 3.) Respected commentators "argue that 'double recoveries' should be denied in consumer cases too." (*See* White and Summers, *Uniform Commercial Code*, § 25-13, at 919 (5th ed. 2000).)

The law in New York under former article 9 allowed a debtor to recover any loss resulting from the secured party's noncompliance, even though the secured party was deprived of recovery for a deficiency because of noncompliance. Here again, since revised article 9 does not displace existing law for consumer transactions, this court must apply the prerevision law. At the least, denial of a deficiency to the noncomplying secured party should not preclude the debtor's recovery of the statutorily-prescribed minimum damages.

Revised article 9, like its predecessor, "provides a minimum, statutory, damage recovery for a debtor . . . in a consumer-goods transaction" that "is designed to ensure that every noncompliance . . . in a consumer-goods transaction results in liability." (*See* UCC 9-625, Comment 4; UCC 9-625(c).) The debtor may recover "an amount not less than the credit service charge plus 10 percent of the principal amount of the obligation or the time-price differential plus 10 percent of the cash price." (UCC 9-625(c)(2).) The statute "does not include a definition or explanation of the terms" used in the damage formula, but "leaves their construction and application to the court, taking into account the . . . purpose of providing a minimum recovery." (UCC 9-625, Comment 4.)

Here, according to the contract, the time-price differential is $1,036.24 and 10% of the cash price is $810, for a total statutory damage recovery of $1,846.24. Mr. Coxall is entitled to this recovery even if he sustained no actual loss from Clover Commercial's failure to comply with article 9. But, although Clover Commercial failed to comply with both the requirement for reasonable notification and the requirement for a commercially reasonable disposition, it is obligated for only one statutory damage remedy. Mr. Coxall would also be entitled to the value of the personal property that, he says, was contained in the vehicle when it was repossessed, but which has not been returned to him. But Mr. Coxall introduced no admissible evidence of that value.

Finally, under the contract, Mr. Coxall could assert against Clover Commercial any claim he might have against Jafas Auto Sales, the seller of the Lexus, for breach of any contractual or statutory warranty of the vehicle. It cannot be said, however, that such a claim is fairly included within the cause of action asserted in his endorsed complaint for "automobile illegally repossed (sic) $8000." Mr. Coxall did not present any of the type of expert testimony that would be required to support such a claim, nor did he present documentary evidence that would obviate the need for such testimony. The court offers no opinion on whether such a claim might be asserted against Clover or Jafas, or both, in a separate action.

DISPOSITION

In action No. 1, judgment is rendered in favor of Jason Coxall against Clover Commercial for $745.09, representing the difference between Mr. Coxall's statutory damages of $1,846.24 and Clover Commercial's damages for breach of the contract of $1,101.15, with interest from March 3, 2003, plus costs.

In action No. 2, judgment is rendered in favor of Jason Coxall, dismissing the verified complaint as to him. Any amount due Clover under the contract has been offset against the amount that would otherwise be due to Mr. Coxall in action No. 1.

In action No. 2, judgment is rendered in favor of Clover Commercial against Utho Coxall for $1,101.15, with interest from December 21, 2002, plus costs. Utho Coxall is not a plaintiff in action No. 1, did not answer Clover's verified complaint, and did not appear for trial. The court offers no opinion on whether Utho Coxall may seek statutory damages or other damages against Clover in a separate action.

NOTE ON COXALL

As you can see, prior to the revision of Article 9, the Code had offered no guidance on the question of whether a debtor could escape entirely from a deficiency judgment by establishing the secured party's failure to proceed in accordance with its obligations under the remedies portion of Article 9 in disposing of the collateral. The rule varied from state to state, and in the case of New York from county to county. As Judge Battaglia notes in his opinion, the various departments of that state's Appellate Division were not in agreement prior to 2001 as to which of the approaches was the correct one to follow. The Second Department, of the four Judicial Departments in the New York appellate system, was alone in adopting the "absolute bar" rule. The Second Department includes just over 8 percent of New York's land area and contains slightly more than one-half of the State's population. It is comprised of the 10 downstate counties of Kings (that's Brooklyn to you), Richmond (Staten Island), Queens, Nassau, Suffolk, Westchester, Dutchess, Orange, Rockland, and Putnam.

Now with the adoption of Revised Article 9, the "rebuttable presumption" rule is mandated for non-consumer transactions in § 9-626(a), but consumer advocates argued for and got § 9-626(b) into the final version of the new Article 9, leaving the question of what rule to apply in consumer goods transactions "to the courts." So the question is far from settled. In *ESL Federal Credit Union v. Bovee*, 9 Misc. 3d 256, 801 N.Y.S.2d 482, 56 U.C.C. Rep. Serv. 2d 517 (2005), Judge Kenneth R. Fisher, presiding over a case brought in Monroe County (definitely upstate and not part of the Second Department), noted that New York courts outside of the Second Department had not previously picked up the "absolute bar" rule. Judge Fisher concluded: "There is, to be sure, no guidance on the issue from the Court of Appeals. The available cases from other New York courts on the subject generally do not distinguish between consumer and nonconsumer contexts, as Judge Battaglia in *Coxall* has demonstrated. Presumably, the struggle New York courts have had with this issue predicts an impending struggle to find the correct rule to be applied in the consumer context."

CHAPTER

34

Strict Foreclosure and the Right of Redemption

A. INTRODUCTION

Having considered the possible repossession by the secured party of the collateral and the mechanisms under which the secured party may dispose of the stuff repossessed under § 9-610, there remain only two more pieces of the "enforcement" part of Article 9 for us to consider. These are the possibilities for what are termed *strict foreclosure* on or the debtor's possible *redemption* of the collateral. There is not much that need be said in introduction to these two topics other than what you will be able to pick up from the Code provisions you will read in preparation.

B. PREPARATION

In preparation for discussion of the problems and the cases in this chapter, read:

- Section 9-620 and the Commentary to this section
- Sections 9-621(a) and 9-622(a)
- Sections 9-623 and 9-624 and the Comments to these two sections

C. PROBLEMS AND CASES

PROBLEMS

34.1 In 2007, Flora, a florist, purchases a panel truck for use in her business from Irving's Auto's of Irvine California. Flora buys the truck by making a small down payment and in addition agreeing, by her signing a note, to pay Irving the remainder of the price in equal installments over the next 48 months. Flora grants Irving a security interest in the truck to secure her payment of these monthly payments. In 2010, after having made 36 payments, Flora realizes that her business is not a success and that she will have to close up shop. She stops making payments to Irving and does not object when Irving has one of his employees come to repossess the truck. Flora comes into Irvine's office and the two of them agree that Irvine will accept the truck in full satisfaction of the debt owed to him. That is, she will transfer the title in the truck, which he intends to have cleaned up and then put on the lot where he displays the used trucks he has for sale, over to him. In exchange, Irvine will release Flora from any obligation on her part to make the twelve remaining payments. They shake hands on the deal.

(a) Is this 2010 agreement binding on each?
(b) Suppose instead that Flora does not venture into Irving's place of business following the repossession of the truck. If Irving unilaterally decides he would like take back ownership of the truck in exchange for his forgoing his right to the remaining twelve payments due on the note, how should he proceed in an effort to get Flora's agreement, expressly or implicitly, to this resolution of the situation? Does Irving have the right to *force* Flora's acceptance of this proposal?

34.2   Assume that, one way or another, Irving and Flora do agree to his taking back title to the truck in exchange for his releasing her from any further obligation on the note. Very soon after putting the truck on his lot, Irving is able to sell it to one Dora for a particularly handsome price. Flora finds out what price the truck went for and is able to easily calculate that, had she not agreed to Irving's proposal but had rather insisted that he dispose of the truck as called for in § 9-610, the sale to Dora or to someone else at roughly the same price would have resulted in her, Flora, receiving a sizeable surplus, even after all of the costs of repossession and resale were taken into account. Flora protests to Irving that she has the right to the "surplus" generated by the sale of her truck to Dora. Flora has every right to make her displeasure known, of course, but does she have a legal right to any money from Irving?

34.3   Change the facts of the initial problem so that Flora stops making payments about one year after her purchase of the panel truck, in 2008. Irving proposes to Flora that he take back title to the truck in exchange for which he will agree to reduce the amount she must continue to pay on the note each month by one-half. If Flora agrees to this deal, and it is then set out in a writing signed by both, are Irving and Flora both then bound to this agreement under Article 9?

34.4   Irving has also sold an auto to one Carlos on a 48 month payment plan. Carlos both plans to and does use this car for his personal use only.

After having made 36 of the payments, Carlos is laid off from his job because of an economic downturn. He defaults on his car loan payments and Irving is able to repossess the vehicle without incident. Irving the sends a letter to Carlos proposing the he, Irvine, will retain the car, "in full and final satisfaction of all you owe me." Carlos receives this letter, and, glad to be offered the chance to be released from any further obligation to make monthly payments on a car he no longer has possession of, does not object to this proposal. Is Irving then able to claim that he has successfully retaken the auto under the strict foreclosure mechanism and, when he resells the auto, keep all the proceeds for himself?

34.5 In 2008, Heavy Lifting Lenders makes a loan to the Crusty Construction Company. The loan is to be repaid, with interest, in 24 monthly installments. As part of the loan agreement, Crusty grants Heavy Lifting a security interest in a particular piece of its equipment, an 80-foot boomlift, to secure its payment obligation. In 2009 Crusty began to experience financial difficulties and is unable to continue paying off the loan. Heavy Lifting is able to repossess the boomlift from Crusty with no difficulty. Mr. Krustofsky, the President of Crusty Construction awaits a notice from the lender indicating how it plans to dispose of the repossessed piece of equipment. Several months pass, but no notice is forthcoming. Krustofsky goes to the offices of Heavy Lifting and asks the loan officer there what is to be done with the boomlift. The loan officer responds, "As you probably know, the construction industry is in a real slum at the moment. We figure this isn't a good time to try to sell off a lift like that, so we've put it in a storage facility we have for just such situations and plan to wait until things pick up considerably before we try to dispose of it." Krustofsky says that as far as he can tell the construction slow-down could last for several years. The loan officer agrees. "We're all just going to have to be patient and wait this one out if we want to get a decent price for that piece." Krustofsky comes to you for advice. Is there any way he can force the lender to dispose of the property sooner rather than later, if for no other reason so that he will know for certain then how much surplus or deficiency his company will receive or be expected to pay, in order to better make plans for the future? See the case that follows.

TEE VEE TOONS INC. v. PRUDENTIAL SECURITIES CREDITS CORP., LLC

Supreme Court of New York, New York County, 2005
2005 N.Y. Misc. LEXIS 3474, 234 N.Y.L.J. 58

Justice CAHN: Defendant secured creditor moves to dismiss the first cause of action of the amended complaint, for violation of UCC 9-610 (commercial reasonable disposition of collateral), and for breach of its Loan Agreement with plaintiffs debtors, dated February 19, 1999. Defendants further moves to dismiss the punitive damages claims asserted in both causes of action in the amended complaint.

BACKGROUND

This action was commenced shortly after Prudential's commencement of the companion case, *Prudential Securities Credit Corp., LLC v. Teevee Toons, Inc.,* 2003 N.Y. Misc. LEXIS 90, 2003 NY Slip Op. 50560U, which sought foreclosure of its security interest in collateralized assets of the TVT entities due to an outstanding indebtedness of more than $16,000,000.00. By decision and order in the companion case, dated September 23, 2003, the court granted Prudential's motion for summary judgment and directed a turnover of the collateralized assets (aff'd 5 A.D.3d 226, 772 N.Y.S.2d 821 (1st Dep't 2004)). The assets, consisting of copyrighted and trademarked musical works, have remained in Prudential's possession, and under its supervision and control, since that time. No public or private sale of the assets has occurred.

The TVT entities served an amended complaint . . . adding a first cause of action which essentially asserts that Prudential has no right to retain the collateral indefinitely without any foreseeable plan to dispose of it, in a commercially reasonable manner, and thereby, extinguish the debt to the extent of the proceeds on such disposition. The claim is succinctly put in paragraph 10 of the amended complaint: the UCC "duty to act in a commercially reasonable manner requires Prudential to proceed with the required disposition without undue delay."

The essence of Prudential's contrary position, forming the basis of this motion to dismiss, is summed up in its counsel's letter to plaintiffs' counsel, dated November 19, 2003: "Prudential may dispose of the Collateral at any time and in any way it sees fit." The court disagrees, for the reasons that follow.

DISCUSSION

The statutory motif of the UCC is imbued with the recognition that both the creditor and the debtor possess rights vis-a-vis collateral, even after default and lawful seizure by the creditor. The creditor's duty to employ commercially reasonable liquidation measures is a prime example. Section 9-610 provides, in pertinent part:

> Disposition after default. After default, a secured party may sell, lease, license, or otherwise dispose of any or all to the collateral in its present condition or following any commercially reasonable preparation or processing.
>
> Commercially reasonable disposition. Every aspect of a disposition of collateral, including the method, manner, time, place, and other terms, must be commercially reasonable. . . .

Sections 9-625 and 626 provide specific remedies for a secured creditor's failure to comply with its post-seizure responsibilities, vis-a-vis the collateral, such as liability for "loss resulting from the debtor's inability to obtain, or increased costs of, alternative financing." A secured creditor's right to pursue a deficiency judgment against the debtor may be impaired if it cannot demonstrate that its liquidation efforts were sufficient.

The debtor's protections under the UCC, vis-a-vis the collateral, exist regardless of whether the loan or security agreement vests the creditor with title to the collateral, post seizure (UCC 9-202, -619(c)). A debtor is without capacity to waive various UCC protections, including those "which deal with disposition of collateral" (id., 9-602(g)). Section 8.2 of the parties Security Agreement acknowledges that Prudential's disposition of the assets must be "in compliance with any mandatory requirements of Applicable Law. . . ."

The upshot of the foregoing is plain. Prudential may not dispose of the Collateral at any time and in any way it sees fit. Modern commercial law places certain responsibilities on the creditor and vests the debtor with certain rights vis-a-vis the collateral, even post-default and seizure. Prudential has been in possession of the collateral for nearly two years. During this time, it has been exploiting those assets, lawfully, as permitted by the court's decision and order in the companion case, dated June 7, 2004 (affd 16 A.D.3d 192, 791 N.Y.S.2d 95 (1st Dept 2005)).

Prudential is not restricted to selling the assets to a third party. UCC 9-610(c) recognizes a secured creditor's right to acquire ownership of the assets itself, through public or private disposition. It is also possible that the proper disposition of the assets is to retain a manager to manage them under reasonable terms. However, Prudential has not yet done so; nor has it furnished notification of proposal to accept collateral in full or partial satisfaction pursuant to UCC 9-621. Rather, it continues to hold the assets without conceding satisfaction of any portion of the $16,000,000.00 debt.

Indeed, the Official Comment to UCC 9-610 expressly cautions that a secured party's right to remain in seizure of collateral, without disposition, is not indefinite:

> *Time of Disposition.* This Article does not specify a time period within which secured party must dispose of collateral. This is consistent with this Article's Policy to encourage private dispositions through regular commercial channels. It may, for example, be prudent not to dispose of goods when the market has collapsed. Or, it might be more appropriate to sell a large inventory in parcels over a period of time instead of in bulk. Of course, under subsection (b) every aspect of a disposition of collateral must be commercially reasonable. This requirement explicitly includes the "method, manner, time, place and other terms." For example, if a secured party does not proceed under Section 9-620 and holds collateral for a long period of time without disposing of it, and if there is no good reason for not making a prompt disposition, the secured party may be determined not to have acted in a "Commercially reasonable" manner. See also Section 1-203 (general obligation of good faith).

(Official Comment 3, McKinney's Cons Laws of NY, Book 62 1/2, UCC 9-610, at 194 (2002) (emphasis added).)

To be sure, Prudential, as secured creditor in possession, enjoys discretion with regard to commercial reasonableness. For example, UCC 9-610(a) recognizes that seized assets might require "preparation or processing" before they can be deemed ready for liquidation, *see also, Bankers Trust Co. v. J.V. Dowler & Co., Inc.,* 47 N.Y.2d 128, 390 N.E.2d 766, 417 N.Y.S.2d 47 (a secured creditor is not required to consult the debtor as to its preferences for asset disposition), rearg denied 46 N.Y.2d 771 (1979); UCC 9-627(a) (the fact that a greater return might have been achieved is not, standing alone, evidence that the creditor proceeded unreasonably). Prudential may be able to show that its delay is necessary to maximize asset value for final disposition. Further, if the TVT entities by their own actions, failures to cooperate, threats of litigation or otherwise, prevent Prudential from acting in a way that would be otherwise reasonable, Prudential's failure to act more quickly may be excused.

However, at this pleading stage, the issue raised in the first cause of action, relating to the commercial reasonableness of the delay, is one of fact which cannot be disposed of on motion Consequently, the motion to dismiss the first cause of action of the amended complaint is denied.

———————————

PROBLEM

34.6 In January of 2008, Irving's Autos of Irvine, California sells a new Aspen Finale auto to one Matteo, providing him with a 36-month loan with which to buy the auto and retaining a purchase-money security interest in the auto. After making 24 payments, Matteo finds himself temporarily short of funds due to a slowdown in his line of work, and fails to make several payments in a row. Irving's Auto repossesses the auto without incident. It then sends Matteo a notice following the form set out in §9-614(3) informing Matteo that it intends to sell the auto "at private sale sometime after May 1, 2010." Matteo receives this notice on April 15. He immediately calls Irving at the telephone number given in the notice and says that he wants to retake possession of the auto and that he would be able, by scraping together all the cash he has available, to come up with the total of the three payments he has missed. He would then, he promises keep up with the remaining payments as provided for in the initial loan agreement. Is Irving obligated to accept Matteo's proposal and return the car to him on these terms?

AUTOMOTIVE FINANCE CORP. v. SMART AUTO CENTER, INC.

United States Court of Appeals for the Seventh Circuit, 2003
334 F.3d 685, 51 U.C.C. Rep. Serv. 2d 297

EVANS, Circuit Judge. This case arises out of the efforts of Automotive Finance Corporation (AFC) to collect on loans it made to Carl Schwibinger, a used car dealer, and Smart Auto Center, Inc., his dealership. Before filing suit, AFC tried a little self-help — repossessing a number of Smart Auto cars and attempting to take others that Schwibinger purchased individually. Smart Auto and Schwibinger (whom we'll refer to together as Schwibinger) filed counterclaims based on these previous collection efforts and, after a bench trial, won about $12,000 in damages. AFC may have lost a couple of battles to Schwibinger, but it won the war when the district court awarded it roughly $165,000 for the balance of the loans and costs associated with the collection action. Schwibinger appeals.

The agreement between the parties was fairly simple. AFC issued Schwibinger a line of credit to purchase used cars at auto auctions. Each car purchase was treated as a separate loan for the purposes of calculating payment due dates. Schwibinger had to either pay the balance of each loan within 45 days or pay a "curtailment" to extend the loan another 45 days. Once Schwibinger sold a vehicle, he had to repay the loan within 48 hours. If he failed to do so, the vehicle was considered to be "out of trust."

Apparently the used car business was not going well for Schwibinger and, around November 1999, he was behind in his payments and some of his vehicles were out of trust. In December 1999, two representatives from AFC paid him a visit to discuss getting his account current. AFC arranged a "swap out," taking the titles to 11 vehicles that Schwibinger owned outright in exchange for a new loan. The new loan was used to pay off the out-of-trust vehicles and put a second curtailment on the past-due vehicles. AFC did not otherwise alter the payment terms of the note. During the meeting, Schwibinger told AFC that he was selling his dealership and inventory to another car dealer in mid-January.

By the end of December, Schwibinger was again in default and AFC believed that more vehicles were out of trust. Schwibinger attempted to put off AFC's collection efforts. He sent AFC a check that bounced (although he later made good on it), and he made promises (which he didn't keep) that he would wire AFC payments, deliver cashier's checks, send confirmation of the sale of the dealership, and fax copies of payment checks. AFC's regional manager, Chad Hopkins, told Schwibinger to relinquish possession of the vehicles that served as collateral for the loans. Although Schwibinger initially agreed, he later changed his mind.

At this point, AFC decided to take matters into its own hands. On January 18, 2000, it sent America Auto Recovery (AAR) to Schwibinger's lot to repossess vehicles. Schwibinger arrived on the scene after AAR had taken 16 vehicles. While his wife called the police, Schwibinger pursued a more confrontational strategy. He blocked the driveway with his car and confronted the AAR tow truck drivers. An altercation ensued and, once the sheriff's department arrived, Schwibinger was arrested for disorderly conduct. AAR repossessed 4 more vehicles for a total of 20. Because the repossessed vehicles didn't cover the outstanding loan balance, AFC also attempted to take four vehicles in North Dakota that Schwibinger owned individually.

In March 2000, Schwibinger tried to settle his differences with AFC, offering it roughly $265,000 to cover the amount owed on the vehicles and fees for the repossession. The money was to come from the sale of Smart Auto, and Schwibinger wanted AFC to give his attorney the vehicles under a bailment agreement until the deal closed. AFC requested a hold harmless clause in the agreement for any claims based on the repossession, but Schwibinger refused. Ultimately, the deal fell through.

AFC sold nine of the repossessed vehicles at auto auctions. As it turns out, the 11 other vehicles had odometer or title problems because they were from Canada. These vehicles would not have fetched a good price at an auction because they would have had to be sold "mileage unknown." Therefore, AFC sold these cars to a dealer (with whom it had a lending relationship) who knew how to handle Canadian vehicles with unknown mileage. AFC received $160,000 for all of the vehicles, leaving a loan balance due of $117,000.

AFC brought suit to recover the remaining balance on the loans plus costs and fees associated with collection. Schwibinger responded that he had not defaulted on the loans and AFC failed to mitigate its damages by refusing to allow him to redeem his vehicles and then selling them for too low a price. He also counterclaimed that AFC had repossessed the vehicles over his objection and interfered with his ownership of other vehicles. Following a bench trial, the district court found that AFC was entitled to repossess the vehicles because Schwibinger had been in default on the loans and that it had properly handled the vehicles after repossessing them. Schwibinger was entitled to damages, however, for the four cars that AAR had taken over his objection and for AFC's attempt to take the North Dakota cars that Schwibinger had purchased individually. Schwibinger appeals both the court's holding as to AFC's claim and its determination of the amount of damages to award him on his claims.

We review the district court's findings of fact for clear error and its legal conclusions *de novo*. To set aside a finding of fact, we must have "a definite and firm conviction that a mistake has been committed." *Cohen Dev. Co. v. JMJ Props.*, 317 F.3d 729, 735 (7th Cir. 2003) (citations omitted). In a case arising under our diversity jurisdiction, we apply the law of the forum state, and here that's Indiana.

We'll start with Schwibinger's arguments relating to AFC's claim. Schwibinger says that he didn't default on the loans and, even if he did, AFC did not properly handle the vehicles that it repossessed. We can quickly put

Schwibinger's first contention, that he was not in default on the loans, to rest. [After a review of the evidence offered by Schwibinger, the court determines that they don't add up to equitable estoppel and that the dealer was in fact in default.]

Schwibinger next argues that, even if he was in default on the loans, he is entitled to a new trial on damages because AFC mishandled the repossessed vehicles. First, Schwibinger contends that AFC wrongly rejected his offer to buy the cars back because he refused to add a hold harmless clause to the agreement for any claims arising from the repossession. Under the Indiana Uniform Commercial Code, a debtor can redeem collateral by tendering the full amount due. See Ind. Code § 26-1-9.1-623. While the Indiana Supreme Court, in an opinion that is a little less than clear, seems to indicate that a creditor may not defeat a debtor's right to redeem his collateral by insisting that redemption be contingent upon signing a release, see *Star Bank, N.A. v. Laker*, 637 N.E.2d 805, 807 (Ind. 1994), a debtor must nevertheless *tender* the full amount due. Schwibinger never did that as his offer was contingent on the sale of his dealership, Smart Auto. He essentially only offered to enter into a new agreement extending his payment time on the loans. What he did falls short of "tendering payment" which requires more than a new promise to perform an existing promise. "Tendering payment" means offering "payment in full of all monetary obligations then due and performance in full of all other obligations then matured," Ind. Code § 26-1-9.1-623, comment 2. Since Schwibinger never tendered payment, AFC was not required to release the vehicles.

[The court also finds against Schwibinger on his arguments that AFC mishandled the repossessed vehicles by failing to dispose of them in a commercially reasonable manner and that the district court had improperly assessed damages.]

For all these reasons, the judgment of the district court is AFFIRMED. One final matter remains: AFC is entitled to appellate attorney fees under its contract with Schwibinger. Within 15 days, AFC should submit a statement of the attorney fees it incurred in connection with this appeal. Schwibinger may, if desired, file an opposing brief within 10 days thereafter.

PROBLEM

34.7   Returning to the situation of Problem 34.6, suppose that a group of Matteo's friends, hearing of his financial difficulties, tell him that they come up with a significant sum of money they would like to loan him on a personal basis for him to repay when he is able. ("It's the least we could do for a wonderful guy like you," they explain, "especially considering how you've always been there for us in the past.") The amount is more than enough to allow Matteo, after getting the notice on April 15 of Irving's intent to resell the car "sometime after May 1, 2010," to contact the auto dealer and offer to make one lump sum payment which would cover all past due and future payments called for by his original loan agreement as well as any reasonable expenses which Irving has incurred in the course of his repossession and preparation for resale of the vehicle. Irving says that he is not willing to accept this offer. He points to language in the loan and security agreement which Matteo had signed in 2008 under which, "Buyer hereby waives without reservation any right of redemption which he may otherwise have by reason of any statute, regulation, or treaty in connection with the vehicle in which he has granted Seller a security interest hereby." Does this provision stand in the way of Matteo's getting back his beloved Aspen Finale? See § 9-602(11).

APPENDIX

Sample Forms

The following two forms are reprinted from *Debtor-Creditor Law* with permission. Copyright © 2007 by Matthew Bender & Company, Inc., a member of the LexisNexis Group. All Rights Reserved.

PROMISSORY NOTE

[City, State]

$_____   [Date]

FOR VALUE RECEIVED, the undersigned promises to pay to _____
or order, at _____ or at such other place as the holder hereof may
from time to time in writing designate, in lawful money of the United States
of America, the principal sum of _____ Dollars ($_____)
together with interest on the unpaid principal balance outstanding under
this Note from time to time at a rate of _____ per cent per annum.
Payments shall be in _____ monthly installments due on the first day
of each month beginning _____, [date], with a final installment
_____ on _____. Interest shall be computed on the basis of
a 365 day (or 366 day, as applicable) year and actual days elapsed.

All payments shall be applied first to interest and then to principal. Interest
not paid when due shall, at the option of the holder hereof, be added to
principal and shall bear interest as principal. This Note may be prepaid at
any time, provided, however, that the minimum amount of principal to be
prepaid under this Note at any time shall be $_____.

This note is secured by a security agreement of even date herewith.

Time is of the essence hereof. The occurrence of any of the following events
("events of default") shall, at the option of the holder hereof, make all sums
of principal and interest on this Note immediately due and payable without
notice of default, presentment, demand for payment, protest, notice of protest, notice of nonpayment or dishonor, or other notices or demands of any
kind whatsoever, all of which are hereby expressly waived by the undersigned:
(a) default in the payment when due of any installment of principal or
interest on this Note; (b) default or breach of representation, warranty or
covenant under any agreement or other writing securing or executed in favor
of the holder hereof in connection with this Note; (c) filing by or against any
of the undersigned or any guarantor of this Note of a petition in bankruptcy
or for relief under any bankruptcy or similar laws or for a receiver for such
person or any property of such person; (d) default in any obligation secured
by a lien on any property securing this Note; (e) death, insolvency, cessation
of business, or assignment for benefit of creditors, of any of the undersigned
or any guarantor of this Note; or (f) attachment, seizure, foreclosure or
sequestration of or with respect to any property of any of the undersigned
or any guarantor of this Note. Acceptance of payment in arrears shall not
waive or affect the right to accelerate this Note.

The undersigned agrees to pay all costs and expenses of collection, including without limitation reasonable attorneys' fees, whether or not suit is filed

hereon. Any married person signing this Note agrees that recourse may be had to both community property and his or her separate property in the enforcement hereof. Where the context permits, the plural term shall include the singular, and vice versa. This Note shall be governed by the law of the State of _____. Where more than one person signs this Note, their obligations hereunder shall be joint and several.

DEBTOR:

_____

By: _____
                                                              President

Attest:

By: _____
             Secretary

SECURITY AGREEMENT

This Security Agreement ("Agreement") is made as of the date set forth below by the undersigned ("Debtor") in favor of _____ ("Secured Party").

1. For valuable consideration, and to secure the payment and performance of the obligations hereinafter described, Debtor hereby grants to Secured Party, pursuant to the Uniform Commercial Code of the state of _____, a security interest in the items described in Exhibit "A" attached hereto and incorporated herein by this reference, together with all present and future accessories, additions, attachments, proceeds, products, replacements and substitutions of or to all of the foregoing (all of which shall be collectively referred to here as "the Collateral").

2. This Agreement and the security interest created hereby are given for the purpose of securing: (a) payment of the indebtedness evidenced by that certain Promissory Note dated the date hereof executed by Debtor in favor of Secured Party in the principal sum of $_____; (b) performance of each agreement of Debtor herein contained; (c) payment and performance of all existing and future obligations of Debtor to Secured Party; and (d) any and all amendments, modifications, renewals and/or extensions of any of the foregoing, including, but not limited to, amendments, modifications, renewals or extensions which are evidenced by new or additional instruments, documents or agreements or which change the rate of interest on any obligations secured hereby. It is the express purpose of Debtor and Secured Party that all obligations of Debtor to Secured Party shall be subject to Secured Party's security interest in the Collateral, regardless of whether such obligations shall be of the same class as the obligations initially contemplated at the time this transaction was entered into.

3. Debtor represents, warrants and agrees that: (a) Debtor has full title to the Collateral, free from any liens, leases, encumbrances, defenses or other claims; the security interest in the Collateral constitutes a first, prior and indefeasible security interest; and no financing statement covering the Collateral, or any part thereof, is on file in any public office; (b) Debtor will execute all documents (including financing statements) and take such other action as Secured Party deems necessary to create and perfect a security interest in the Collateral; (c) Debtor will, at its sole cost and expense, defend any claims that may be made against the Collateral; (d) except as otherwise provided herein, the Collateral shall be kept at Debtor's address set forth herein and Debtor will not, without Secured Party's prior written consent, part with possession of, transfer, sell, lease, encumber, conceal or otherwise dispose of the Collateral or any interest therein; (e) the Collateral will be maintained in good condition and repair, and will not be used in

violation of any applicable laws, rules or regulations; (f) Debtor will pay and discharge all taxes and liens on the Collateral prior to delinquency; (g) Debtor will maintain insurance on the Collateral covering such risks and in such form and amount as may be required by Secured Party from time to time, with insurers satisfactory to Secured Party and with loss payable to Secured Party as its interest may appear, and upon request Debtor will deliver the original of such policy or policies to Secured Party; (h) Debtor will permit Secured Party to inspect the Collateral and Debtor's books and records (including computer files) pertaining thereto at any time; and (i) the Collateral will at all times remain personal property.

4. In the event that Debtor shall fail to perform any obligation hereunder, Secured Party may, but shall not be obligated to, perform the same, and the cost thereof shall be payable by Debtor to Secured Party immediately and without demand, shall bear interest at the rate set forth in the note or other obligation described in Paragraph 2(a) above, or 10% per annum, whichever is greater, and shall be secured by this Agreement.

5. If this Security Agreement is given to secure obligations of any person or entity other than Debtor (such person or entity being hereinafter referred to as "Principal"), Debtor waives notice of default, presentment, demand for payment, protest, notice of protest, notice of nonpayment or dishonor, and all other notices and demands of any kind whatsoever; and Debtor consents and agrees that Secured Party may, from time to time, without notice or demand and without affecting the enforceability or security hereof: (a) take, alter, enforce or release any additional security for the obligations secured hereby; (b) renew, extend, modify, amend, accelerate, accept partial payments on, release, settle, compromise, compound, collect or otherwise liquidate the obligations secured hereby or any security therefor, and bid and purchase at any sale; or (c) release or substitute Principal or any guarantors of the obligations secured hereby. If any default should be made in the payment or performance of any obligations secured hereby or in the terms and conditions of any security held therefor, Secured Party may enforce this Agreement independently of any other remedy or security Secured Party may at any time hold in connection with the obligations secured hereby, and it shall not be necessary for Secured Party to proceed upon or against, and/or exhaust, any other security or remedy before proceeding to enforce this Security Agreement. Until all obligations secured hereby are paid in full, Debtor waives all right of subrogation.

6. There shall be a "default" or an "event of default" hereunder upon the occurrence of any of the following events: (a) default in the payment or performance of any obligations secured hereby or contained herein; or (b) occurrence of any "default" or "event of default" under any note or other obligation secured hereby or any security therefor.

7. Upon the occurrence of any event of default, all obligations secured hereby shall, at Secured Party's option, immediately become due and payable without notice or demand, and Secured Party shall have in any jurisdiction where enforcement hereof is sought, in addition to all other rights and remedies which Secured Party may have under law, all rights and remedies of a secured party under the Uniform Commercial Code and in addition the following rights and remedies, all of which may be exercised with or without further notice to Debtor: (a) to settle, compromise or release on terms acceptable to Secured Party, in whole or in part, any amounts owing on the Collateral; (b) to enforce payment and prosecute any action or proceeding with respect to any and all of the Collateral; (c) to extend the time of payment, make allowances and adjustments and issue credits in Secured Party's name or in the name of Debtor; (d) to foreclose the liens and security interests created under this Agreement or under any other agreement relating to the Collateral by any available judicial procedure or without judicial process; (e) to enter any premises where any Collateral may be located for the purpose of taking possession of or removing the same; (f) to remove from any premises where the same may be located the collateral and any and all documents instruments, files and records, and any receptacles and cabinets containing the same, relating to the Collateral, and Secured Party may, at Debtor's cost and expense, use the supplies and space of Debtor at any or all of its places of business as may be necessary or appropriate to properly administer and control the Collateral or the handling of collections and realizations thereon; (g) to receive, open and dispose of all mail addressed to Debtor and notify postal authorities to change the address for delivery thereof to such address as Secured Party may designate; (h) to sell, assign, lease, or otherwise dispose of the Collateral or any part thereof, either at public or private sale, in lots or in bulk, for cash, on credit or otherwise, with or without representations or warranties, and upon such terms as shall be acceptable to Secured Party, all at Secured Party's sole option and as Secured Party in its sole discretion may deem advisable. The net cash proceeds resulting from the collection, liquidation, sale, lease or other disposition of the Collateral shall be applied, first, to the expenses (including all attorneys' fees) of retaking, holding, storing, processing and preparing for sale, selling, collecting, liquidating and the like, and then to the satisfaction of all obligations and indebtedness or against principal or interest to be in Secured Party's absolute discretion. Debtor will, at Secured Party's request, assemble all Collateral and make it available to Secured Party at such place or places as Secured Party may designate which are reasonably convenient to both parties, whether at the premises of Debtor or elsewhere, and will make available to Secured Party all premises and facilities of Debtor for the purpose of Secured Party's taking possession of the Collateral or removing or putting the Collateral in saleable form. Debtor agrees to pay all costs and expenses incurred by Secured Party in the enforcement of this Agreement, including without limitation reasonable attorneys' fees, whether or not suit is filed hereon.

8. This Agreement expresses the entire understanding of the parties hereto and may not be altered or amended except with the written consent of each of the parties. This Agreement shall be binding upon and inure to the benefit of the respective heirs, executors, administrators, assigns and successors of the parties hereto. All of Secured Party's rights and remedies hereunder are cumulative and not exclusive, and are in addition to all rights and remedies provided by law or under any other agreement between Debtor and Secured Party, or otherwise. Where the context permits, the plural term shall include the singular, and vice versa. This Security Agreement shall be governed by the law of the State of _____. Where more than one person signs this Security Agreement, their obligations hereunder shall be joint and several.

DATED: _____

DEBTOR: _____

By: _____
                              President

Attest:
By: _____
              Secretary

Debtor's
    Address: _____
                _____

TABLE OF CASES

All cases are principal cases unless otherwise indicated.

TABLE OF STATUTES

INDEX